Stephen Chambers

1990

GALLIA NARBONENSIS

A.L.F. RIVET

GALLIA NARBONENSIS

with a chapter on ALPES MARITIMAE

Southern France in Roman Times

B.T. Batsford Ltd · London

Typeset by Progress Print
Printed and bound in Great Britain by
Mackays of Chatham PLC,
Chatham, Kent
for the Publishers
B.T. Batsford Ltd
4 Fitzhardinge St.
London W1H 0AH

British Library Cataloguing in Publication Data

Rivet, A.L.F.
    Gallia Narbonensis: southern France in
    Roman times. —— (The provinces of the
    Roman Empire).
    1. France——History——To 987
    I. Title   II. Series
    936.4'02   DC61

    ISBN 0-7134-5860-7

To Audrey
in celebration of our ruby wedding anniversary

οὐ μὲν γὰρ τοῦ γε κρεῖσσον καὶ ἄρειον
ἢ ὅθ' ὁμοφρονέοντε νοήμασιν οἶκον ἔχητον
ἀνὴρ ἠδὲ γυνὴ· πόλλ'ἄλγεα δυσμενέεσσιν
χάρματα δ'εὐμενέτῃσι· μάλιστα δέ τ' ἔκλυον αὐτοί.

Contents

Contents

PART III: **ALPES MARITIMAE**

Preface

The primary aim of this book is to draw to the attention of British students of the Roman Empire the present state of knowledge regarding southern Gaul. I originally undertook to produce it in the 1960s, but when the series for which it was meant had to be suspended I turned my thoughts to other things until retirement. I now realise that if I had written it then I could have completed it in a half of the time—and at least a quarter of it would have been wrong.

As may be seen from the bibliography and the notes, archaeological research in this area has developed enormously in the last quarter of a century and its presentation has been very greatly improved, especially with the emergence in 1968 of the annual journal *Revue Archéologique de Narbonnaise* and, more recently, with the establishment of the biennial Congrès Archéologique de la Gaule Méridionale—the meetings of which have so far been attended by too few British archaeologists. *Gallia Narbonensis* (and *Alpes Maritimae*) should be visited much more, not just to view the well-known monuments in places like Arles, Nîmes and Orange, but to take in all the other cities and the countryside; it is for this reason that, rather than flooding the plates with reproductions of the great photographs of theatres and amphitheatres, I have used most of them for my own small snapshots of minor features that should be sought out and further examined.

I am grateful to Frank Walbank for kindly looking over Chapter 2, to John Percival for some additions to the villas shown on figure 7, and to Guy Barruol, Raymond Boyer, Pierre Broise, Raymond Chevallier, Henri Desaye, Paul-Albert Février, Christian Goudineau, Gabrielle Laguerre, André Nickels, George Rogers and others for points of detail regarding individual sites: any errors in the text and in the maps and plans (which I have drawn and redrawn several times) are my own.

I am also most grateful to the Leverhulme Trust for granting me a two-year Emeritus Fellowship, which made it possible to make additional and more extensive tours and to attend the meetings of the Congrès Archéologique in Antibes and Lyon: but, above all, to my wife, who accompanied me on very many tours and typed up all my drafted text. It is to her that the book is dedicated—and indeed Odysseus, as quoted in the dedication, knew the truth!

Keele, May 1987   A.L.F. RIVET

Figures in the text

The Plates

PART I

THE PROVINCE

I

The Background

GEOGRAPHY

The area that became the Roman province of *Gallia Narbonensis* includes not only Provence itself but also Languedoc, Roussillon and Foix to the west and the Dauphiné and Savoie to the north. That this area should form one province was not merely an accident of history, for it is remarkably well defined physically—by the Mediterranean to the south, by the Alps on the east, by the Cévennes and the Massif Central in the north and by the Pyrenees to the south-west. Of these mountain ranges the Alps and the Pyrenees are, of course, the highest, but the northern barrier is in some ways the most important, because it shuts the province off from the Great European Plain. It is true that in ancient times the area was counted as a part of Gaul, as it is now a part of France, but these conventions tend to obscure the essential fact that *Gallia Narbonensis* is quite different from the country to the north of it. If one crosses the mountains from Auvergne the break is obvious, but it is scarcely less noticeable if one takes one of the easier routes. Around Toulouse in the west or, if one travels down the Rhône valley in the east, between Lyon and Vienne, one becomes aware of a change of atmosphere—a change of climate and vegetation and even a change in the attitude of the people. Unlike northern France this area looks out on the Mediterranean, and it is in all ways a Mediterranean land. The rainfall and temperature are closely comparable with those of Italy and Greece and even the soil is largely of the type loosely described as *terra rossa*, which is also common in those countries (fig 1a). As a corollary, the vegetation is also of Mediterranean type and most of the province lies within the olive belt (fig 1b). This is especially important for our study because it means that the area was attractive to Greeks and Italians not merely for commercial exploitation but also for settlement; it also means that the earlier inhabitants, before the irruption of any Greeks and Italians, were already conditioned to a Mediterranean way of life.

3

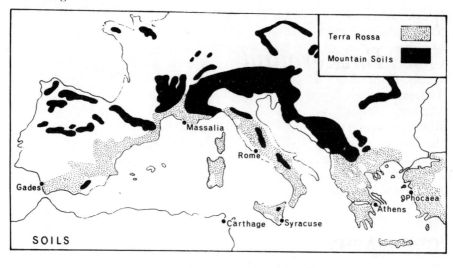

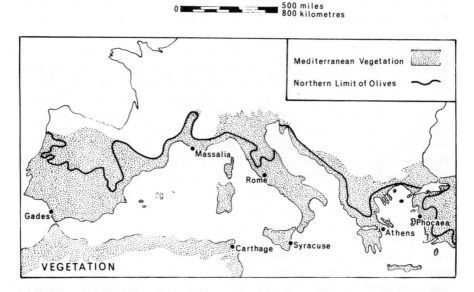

1 The Mediterranean setting of *Gallia Narbonensis*

Within these limits there is a great deal of variation in the terrain and the uses to which it can be put (fig 2). The central feature is the valley of the river Rhône (*Rhodanus*), from Lake Geneva (*Lacus Lemanus*) to the sea, and this formed the core of the province. After emerging from the lake, which has cleansed it of alpine sediment, the river is first reinforced by the Arve and then has to negotiate the fold-ridges of the southern Jura, so that deep gorges (notably the Défilé de l'Ecluse and the Défilé de Pierre Chatel) alternate with slow and sometimes marshy meanders. Near Lagnieu it reaches the southern part of the Plaine de

4

Bresse, where it is joined first by the Ain and then by the much greater Saône (*Arar*). This plain, with the curious waterlogged plateau of La Dombes, lies just outside our province, which the river re-enters near Givors at the mouth of the Gier, a stream whose valley gives easy access from the Rhône to the upper water of the Loire (*Liger*). Thereafter come a series of basins linked by gorges: the little plain of Vienne; a small basin around St-Rambert, at the confluence with the Rival; the much larger basin of Valence, where both the Isère (*Isara*) and the Drôme (*Druma*) flow in; the Cruas Gorge; the Montélimar Basin, where the Roubion flows in; the Donzère Gorge; the plain of Pierrelatte; the Mondragon couloir; the plain of Orange, accommodating both the Aygues and the Ouvèze (*Ovidis*); the Défilé de Roquemaure; and the plain of Avignon with the mouth of the Durance (*Druentia*). The influence of this series on the pattern of settlement and communication is easy to see, but one aspect of it is often overlooked—the fact that the Rhône itself is, as Strabo noted,[1] not entirely an ideal river for navigation; as a result, early traffic seems to have passed not up the stream itself but higher up the valley to the east.

The plain of Avignon is bounded on the south by the Chaine des Alpilles and the Rhône passes west of it to Arles, which stands at the apex of the delta. The actual number of mouths to be attributed to the river was a matter for debate among the ancients,[2] but only two are of real significance, those of the Great Rhône to the east and the Little Rhône to the west. As its name implies, the former is the more important and it was to improve navigation on it that Marius cut his celebrated canal. Between these two branches lies the marshy plain of the Camargue, a maze of canals and étangs, thinly populated in ancient as in modern times. To the east of the Great Rhône is the plain of la Crau, known to the Greeks as Λιθῶδες ('stony') and this too attracted speculation—whether it was, as Aristotle maintained, due to volcanic action, or, as Poseidonius had it, a solidified lake, or even, with Aeschylus and Mela, the scene of Zeus' timely aid to Heracles in his fight with the Ligurians;[3] the more prosaic explanation is that it represents an old delta of the Durance. While it does provide some winter grazing, it is poor and unattractive land, and in due course this fact affected the political geography of the province so far as the territory of Arles was concerned.

On the west side of the Rhône its valley is closely constricted by the Cévennes (*Mons Cebenna*), which formed the natural boundary of the province, and it is not until the Ardèche is reached that the country really begins to open out, to be extended still further by the valley of the Gard. On the east, however, the Alpine summits, though much higher, are also more distant, and the tributaries on this side include several rivers notable in their own right. Especially important are the Arve, the Isère, on which stands Grenoble, the Drôme, with Die, the Aygues, with Nyon, the Ouvèze, with Vaison, and the Durance. The

5

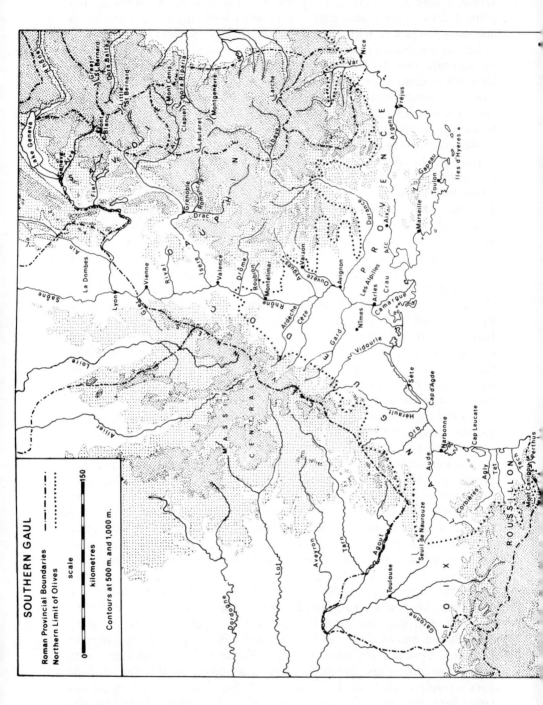

2 The geography of *Gallia Narbonensis*

Durance has a special significance because in early times its valley provided the usual line of communication between the lower Rhône and Italy, by way of the passes in the Cottian Alps.

Before we leave it, one other peculiarity of the Rhône valley needs to be mentioned—the Mistral. This tempestuous wind, known to the Romans as *Circius*,[4] is produced by the difference in pressure of the air over the Massif Central and that over the Mediterranean, and in late spring, from Valence southwards, it can assume alarming strength (for three, six or nine days, it is alleged), overturning trucks and blowing soil from unprotected land.

Between the Durance and the sea is Provence proper. The geology of this region is very complex, including, from east to west, the limestone Maritime Alps, la Basse-Provence cristalline (the Esterel and Maures Massifs, with some mineral resources) and la Basse-Provence calcaire (the hinterland of Marseille), but the overall impression is of a dry and hilly country with a rocky coast indented by deep bays. There are few rivers of any size and only four are worthy of mention—the Var (*Varus*), which traditionally formed the boundary between Gaul and Italy, the Argens (*Argenteus*), at whose mouth Fréjus was founded, the Gapeau, which flows out near Hyères, and the Arc, which feeds the Etang de Berre. Present appearances, however, are partly deceptive. Like much of the Mediterranean littoral, Provence was once more heavily wooded and it has suffered deforestation both naturally, through the forest fires that still afflict it, and by human agency: the naval shipyards of Toulon, for example, date back to the time of Richelieu. And while olives and figs were always a favoured crop, and sheep and goats were always kept, even on the Côte d'Azur cattle were pastured and some wheat grown until comparatively recent times.

To the west of the Rhône delta the coasts of Languedoc and Roussillon present a complete contrast. Here are no rocky bays but a great sweep of sand dunes backed by long shallow lagoons and punctuated only by occasional hills—the Cap de Sète (*Mons Setius*), the Cap d'Agde, the Montagne de la Clape (between Narbonne and the sea) and Cap Leucate (*Candidum Promontorium*). These hills were islands in the mid-Pliocene, but by classical times the coast had, with a few exceptions (as at Narbonne), already assumed its present general aspect, though its actual line is still being slowly modified by the silt brought down by the rivers. Of these the most notable in Languedoc are the Vidourle, the Hérault (*Arauris*), the Orb (*Orobis*) and the Aude (*Atax*), and in Roussillon the Agly (*Sordus*), the Tet (*Tetis*) and the Tech (*Ticis*). The Plaine de Roussillon itself, dominated by Mont Canigou and separated from Languedoc by the uplands of Corbières, is largely covered with sheets of Pliocene gravel and is not a rich area agriculturally, so that it is not surprising that neither of the ancient cities here, *Ruscino* (Château Roussillon) and *Illiberis* (Elne), flourished for long, while the modern centre, Perpignan, is the only town of any importance in the whole province that is not of Roman or earlier origin. Languedoc, on the other hand, is rich and fertile, at least in the undulating lowlands which stretch between the sands of the coast and the foothills of the Cévennes, and this was especially true in Roman times, when the region produced enough grain not only to meet local needs but also to supplement the *annona* of Rome itself. Even the garrigue country which lies behind it was probably in better case then than now, for it too had suffered from deforestation and the overgrazing of sheep and goats before modern schemes of regeneration were put in hand. Both Languedoc and Roussillon were also a minor source of some minerals.

West of Languedoc lies the one part of our province that appears anomalous—the basin of the upper Garonne, centred on Toulouse. Geographically this might form part of *Aquitania* rather than *Narbonensis*, but the reasons for its incorporation go back beyond the Roman occupation, for the *Volcae Tectosages* had already spread into it from the south-east. How this should occur is not difficult to see. The country, though not especially rich, is attractive enough and the passage from the Aude to the Garonne, through the so-called Gate of Carcassonne, is easy. The highest point on this route, the Seuil de Naurouze, is at no more than 194m and the absence of an obstacle here is vividly confirmed by the view from the nearby hilltop village of Montferrand which, while revealing the barrier of the mountains to the east, gives the impression of rolling country to the south-west stretching as far as the snow-capped Pyrenees—a magnificent panorama that echoes the words of Ausonius.[5] There was, then, nothing serious in the way of a migrating tribe[6] and this may serve to make the point that while the province is, with this one exception, clearly defined physically, there were ways into it and out of it and through it.

This particular passage, using the valleys of the Aude and the Garonne, was not the most important, since it led only to *Aquitania* and the Atlantic coast. Though it acquired some commercial significance by the movement southward of British tin and northward of Mediterranean wine, it was not the main migration route. The Rhône valley, on the other hand, provided the chief connection between *Narbonensis* and the Great European Plain, including not only northern France but also Germany. Up it passed trade goods, again especially wine, from the Mediterranean lands, and down it came not only tin but also the invading Celts.

The east to west route is much more difficult. There was such a route from early times—the ancients associated it with Heracles on his way back from his tenth labour—but the passage from Italy to Provence is not easy. The coastal route, though occasionally used (as by Opimius in 154 BC), did not become fully operative until Augustus engineered the so-called *Via Julia Augusta*, and the Alpine passes, used alike by the Celts and the Carthaginians when they invaded Italy, are steep and often blocked by snow. Of these passes[7] the most useful, and those which ultimately accommodated Roman roads,[8] are the two related to the upper valley of the Durance—the Col de Larche (or de la Madeleine) at 1,994m and the Col de Mont-Genèvre (*Alpis Cottiae*) at 1,854m—and, further to the north and related to the Isère, the Col du Petit-St-Bernard (*Alpis Graiae*) at 2,188m, though there are others, most notably the passes of Clapier and Mont-Cenis (2,084m, related to the Arc), which may possibly have been used by Hannibal. The Pyrenean end is rather better, since the Col de Perthus, at only 290m, provides a good alternative to the rocky coast road, lies not far inland and is never blocked.[9] One effect of this difference was that while there was some community between the coastal people of north-west Italy and those of Provence (they all spoke the same Ligurian language), there was a much stronger link between the Iberians on both sides of the Pyrenees. This prevails even today, and Catalan is almost as much spoken in some parts of Roussillon as French.

But the best and the easiest route into and out of the province was by sea. It is, as we saw at the beginning, essentially a Mediterranean land, both geographically and ecologically, and attractive to Mediterranean peoples both for trade and for settlement. It seems therefore, appropriate that we should commence our study with the beginning of Greek settlement here, with the foundation of *Massalia*.

PROTOHISTORY

The prehistory of the area has been extensively researched,[10] but it is not proposed to discuss this here, nor even the earliest phase of Etruscan, Phoenician and Greek trade. Protohistory might be said to begin with the chance visit of the Samian Colaeus to *Tartessos* in the middle of the seventh century BC[11], for although Gaul is not mentioned in this connection both Colaeus on his way home and other Greek merchants, especially Rhodians, on their way to and from Spain must surely have sought watering-places along its coasts; and this may well be the origin not only of *Rhode* (Rosas, in Spain) but also of the elusive *Rhodanusia* mentioned below. But from the point of view of our study the first important historical event is the foundation of the Phocaean colony of *Massalia* (Marseille) in or about 600 BC.

This date is remarkably well attested by a number of sources. Timaeus put it 120 years before the battle of Salamis (that is, in 600 or 599 BC.)[12] Livy, followed by Pompeius Trogus, in the reign of Tarquinius Priscus (that is, by Varro's reckoning, between 616 and 579 BC)[13] and Solinus in the 45th Olympiad (600–596 BC)[14]; and the approximate date is fully confirmed by the archaeological evidence[15]—against a later time, associated with the fall of *Phocaea* to the Persians, which seems to be implied by Thucydides and Pausanias.[16]

The fullest account of the actual foundation—the 'foundation myth'—is that given by Pompeius Trogus who, since he was a Gaul from the nearby tribe of the *Vocontii*,[17] presumably repeats the version that was current in the city in the first century. Unfortunately his statement is preserved only in the epitome of his work made by Justin in the third century, but since no English version of it is readily available it is worth quoting in full:

> In the time of King Tarquin a party of young Phocaean warriors, sailing to the mouth of the Tiber, entered into an alliance with the Romans. From there, sailing into the distant bays of Gaul, they founded *Massilia* among the Ligurians and the fierce tribes of the Gauls; and they did mighty deeds, whether in protecting themselves against the savagery of the Gauls or in provoking them to fight—having themselves first been provoked. For the Phocaeans were forced by the meanness and poverty of their soil to pay more attention to the sea than to the land: they eked out an existence by fishing, by trading, and largely by piracy, which in those days was reckoned honourable. So they dared to sail to the furthest shore of the ocean and came to the Gallic gulf, by the mouth of the Rhône. Taken by the pleasantness of the place, they returned home to report what they had seen and enlisted the support of more people. The commanders of the fleet were Simos and Protis. So they came and sought the friendship of the king of the *Segobrigii*, by name Nannus, in whose territory they desired to found a city. It so happened that on that day the king was engaged in arranging the marriage of his daughter Gyptis: in accordance with the custom of the tribe, he was preparing to give her to be married to a son-in-law chosen at a banquet. So since all the suitors had been invited to the wedding, the Greek guests too were asked to the feast. Then the girl was brought in, and when she was asked by her father to offer water to the man she chose as her husband, she passed them all over and, turning to the Greeks, gave the water to Protis; and he, thus changed from a guest into a son-in-law, was given the site for founding the city by his father-in-law. So *Massilia* was founded near the mouths of the river Rhône, in a deep inlet, as it were in a corner of the sea.[18]

A very similar, though shorter, version, extracted from Aristotle's lost *Constitution of Massalia*, is given by Athenaeus:[19] the founder here is Euxenos who marries the girl (here called first Petta, later Aristoxene), by whom he has a son called Protis, but the king's name is still Nannos ('dwarf'), and the tale has interesting implications. First, while no one would now accept that the alliance between Rome and *Massalia* was quite so old as this, its antiquity was of great importance to their later relations—including the remarkable indulgence shown to the city by Caesar after he had had to besiege it. Secondly, it raises the question of why *Massalia* was founded where it was. As has already been remarked, Greeks were already trading with the west, but it was only after its foundation that Greek trade began to develop up the Rhône valley, and even if this could have been foreseen Marseille is not the ideal site for it: *pace* Trogus, it is almost 50km (a day's sailing) from the nearest mouth of the river. The most likely explanation is that its sheltered harbour was picked as an ideal staging-post on the way to the silver of *Tartessos*—along a route that lost much of its importance when the Carthaginians took *Maenaca*, after which the Phocaeans had to turn their attention to Gaul. Thirdly, and perhaps more importantly, it illustrated the contast between Greek and Roman expansion: here the intention was not to dominate but to establish friendly relations with the locals and to trade.

Such a relationship, of course, was not very easy to maintain, and Trogus (or Justin) continues as follows:

> But the Ligurians, envious of the city's growth, harassed the Greeks with perpetual wars; but they were so successful in repelling these dangers that, having conquered their enemies, they founded many colonies in the lands they had captured. From these people, then, the Gauls, putting aside and restraining their barbarity, learned a more cultured way of life and how to till their fields and wall their cities. Then too they became accustomed to living by law rather than by force and also to tend the vine and plant the olive. And so great an elegance came over the people and their possessions that it appeared not that Greece had colonised Gaul but that Gaul had been transported to Greece (*Gallia in Graeciam translata*).
>
> On the death of Nannus, the king of the *Segobrigii* from whom the site for founding the city had been obtained, when his son Comanus had succeeded to the kingdom, a certain Ligurian made this affirmation: that one day *Massilia* would be the ruin of the neighbouring peoples, and that it ought to be destroyed while it was young, lest, becoming stronger, it should overwhelm the king himself. And he added this fable: once upon a time a bitch who was pregnant begged from a shepherd a place where she might have her litter; when this was granted, she asked that she might be allowed to rear her puppies in the same place; finally, when the puppies were fully grown, supported by her family forces she took over the ownership of the place. Just so the Massilians, who then appeared as mere lodgers, would one day be lords of the land.[20]

Spurred on by this, the king tried to use the festival of the *Floralia* (the same as Beltane: was it his intention to make a bone-fire of the city?) to infiltrate *Massalia*, but fortunately his plot was betrayed by yet another local woman who was in love with a Greek and so it failed. Nevertheless great wars with the Ligurians and great wars with the Gauls continued—and the Greeks also defeated the Carthaginians several times. And another unsuccessful attempt was made to capture the city, this time by a prince called Catumandus, just before *Massalia* allegedly collected money to ransom Rome from the Gauls (that is, again by Varronian dating, in 390 BC) and thereby gained special privileges in Rome and an equal-rights treaty with her (*foedus aequo iure percussum*).[21]

Apart from a reference to Massaliote intervention on behalf of the mother-city of Phocaea in 130 BC,[22] this is all that Trogus has to say of the history of the city. Yet it is by far the fullest account that we have, and although Justin has evidently garbled it a little in making his

11

epitome (so that the order of events is sometimes a little confusing), it again raises matters that require discussion. We may conveniently deal first with the question of the date of *Massalia's* pregnancy. Strabo, writing at much the same time as Trogus, though relying on different sources, says of the Massaliotes:

> They own a country which is planted with olives and vines but is rather poor in grain because of its ruggedness so that, trusting in the sea more than the land, they turned rather to their native seamanship. But later by their bravery they were able to take in some part of the surrounding plains, by the same strength as that with which they founded their cities, strongholds (ἐπιτειχίσματα)—those in Iberia against the Iberians . . .; *Rhoe Agathe* against the barbarians living around the river Rhône; and *Tauroentium* and *Olbia* and *Antipolis* and *Nicaea* against the tribe of the *Sallyes* and the Ligurians who live in the Alps . . . Sextius, having defeated the *Sallyes*, founded not far from *Massalia* a city that bears his name . . . and he both settled a garrison of Romans there and drove the barbarians from the sea-coast that stretches from *Massalia* to Italy, the Massaliotes not being able to keep them back completely. But not even he could achieve more than this, that the barbarians retired twelve *stadia* from the sea in the parts with good harbours and eight *stadia* in the rougher parts.[23]

Recent archaeological research has greatly helped towards a solution of the problem—though it must always be borne in mind that the mere discovery of pottery or other artefacts without contemporary Greek buildings may indicate trade rather than settlement. As things stand, however, of all the places listed by Strabo only *Agathe* (Agde) and *Antipolis* (Antibes) can fairly claim to have been founded as early as the sixth century[24]—and both of them would, like *Massalia* itself, have been ideal staging points on the route to the west. Of the others, *Tauroentium* (also known as *Taurois*, now le Brusc) is difficult to interpret because the site has been built over, but there is nothing to support the claim of Stephanus that it was founded by the crew of one of the ships in the *Massalia* expedition and took its name from a bull depicted on its sail;[25] *Olbia* (Almanarre, near Hyères) has been most fully excavated, and while its walls fully support the description of it as a 'fortress' their first phase has been dated to the fourth century;[26] as for *Nicaea*, although very limited excavations have produced finds that indicate early trade, the date of its establishment remains in doubt and the old claim that it must be as old as Antibes because *Antipolis* means 'the city opposite (Nice)' has been undermined by the persuasive argument that both *Nicaea* and *Antipolis* are merely hellenisations of Ligurian names that meant something quite different.[27]

There is, however, one other place that might claim to be an early foundation, one that is not mentioned by Strabo, presumably because in his day it had changed both its name and its nature. This is *Theline*, mentioned in the *Ora Maritima* of Avienius as the early name of Arles and there stated to be inhabited by Greeks. Here early pottery has long been found, and, more recently, some early structures, and it is highly likely that as soon as trade up the Rhône valley began to develop the Massaliotes found it necessary to establish a base better situated than their own city.[28] By contrast, excavation has shown the establishment of two other Greek colonies in this area to be later. Although trade certainly preceded it, the Greek occupation of the hill-fort of St-Blaise has been dated to the end of the fourth or early in the third century: this is probably the *Mastrabala* of Avienius, still a native *oppidum* in the sixth century but evidently Greek by the time of Artemidorus (who calls it *Mastramele*) and its walls, possibly designed by a Sicilian architect, constitute the finest surviving Greek monument in all Gaul (pl 1).[29] The Greek occupation of *Glanum* (south of St-Rémy), a town which is discussed more fully in its Roman setting (pp 198–200), was of a later date still, beginning in the second century, and may be related to the landward extension mentioned by Strabo.

The date of the other Greek places shown on the map (fig 3) is largely a matter for speculation—they may have been ports of call from a very early date, but only *Citharista* (la Ciotat) and *Athenopolis* (St-Tropez) are actually mentioned in the sources as towns.[30] *Portus Aemines* (probably Bandol) and *Heraclea Caccabaria* (Cavalaire) both appear in the Maritime Itinerary as ports of call (though the former, despite its full name, is there listed merely as a *positio*),[31] but *Pergantium* (Brégançon) is found only in Stephanus and *Agathonis Portus* (Agay?) in an eighth-century hagiography,[32] and they are included here because they have Greek names and because the evidence of wrecks indicates constant Greek trading along the coast. West of the Rhône, although *Agathe* is the only identifiable place that was certainly a Greek colony, two other names are mentioned: these are another *Heraclea*, described by Pliny as sited 'by some authors' *in ostio Rhodani*,[33] and *Rhodanusia*, also near the river, which is first mentioned by Timaeus (quoted by Pseudo-Scymnus) and may be the *Rhode* which Strabo joins to *Agathe*, but which by the time of Pliny (assuming that it is indeed his *Rhode Rhodiorum*) had already ceased to exist.[34] Neither of these can be located with certainty (though *Heraclea* was very probably near St-Gilles) but both the intimate knowledge of this coast displayed in the *Ora Maritima*[35] and the frequent finds of Greek pottery a little way inland suggest that others may have existed. When threatened by Carthaginians or local pirates, traders on the long haul from Marseille to Agde, or on the longer voyage from Agde to Rosas or Ampurias, would surely have been glad of intermediate ports of refuge; but once again, the mere discovery of Greek pottery cannot prove a Greek settlement.

What is clear—and this needs to be stressed—is that this expansion did not lead to the creation of a continuous Massaliote empire on Roman lines. No doubt each of the more important foundations, such as those mentioned by Strabo, acquired some local territory to supply them with food, and it was presumably this that led to the Segobrigian

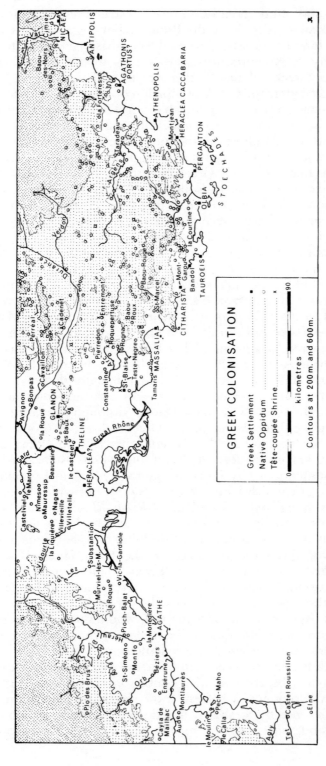

3 Iron Age hill-forts and Greek colonisation in southern Gaul. For further details of the hill-forts see the Appendix (pp 20–6)

GREEK COLONISATION

Greek Settlement ■

Native Oppidum o

Tête-coupée Shrine ×

Contours at 200 m. and 600 m.

0   kilometres   90

hostility to *Massalia* described by Trogus and, in 154 BC, to the reaction of the *Oxybii* and *Deciates* against *Antipolis* and *Nicaea* (a matter that is dealt with below, pp 32–5). But it was not until the advent of the Romans that, under Roman influence and with Roman support, tribes were actually subjected and a substantial territory was attributed to *Massalia*.[36] In the meantime what existed was a series of trading posts and ports which was of great use to the Greeks in transit along the coast—and also to the Romans for nearly a century after the second Punic war (though it should, perhaps, be noted that the relatively early construction of the *Via Domitia*, which ran only from the Rhône to Spain, suggests that the western coast was less well organised than the eastern).

What we need to discuss now is the effect that this Greek colonisation had on the natives—how far Trogus' *Gallia in Graeciam translata* is an exaggeration—and for this we must first consider the native background. The vexed question of the earlier division between Iberians in the west and Ligurians in the east is largely irrelevant to our study: the source of Avienius seems to put it at the mouth of the river *Oranus* (perhaps then the name of the Lez and in any case east of Sète), but this has been disputed[37] and Pseudo-Scylax, writing in the fourth century BC, has a mixture of the two stretching apparently from the Pyrenees to the Rhône.[38] East of the Rhône, Strabo remarks that while earlier writers called the *Sallyes* Ligurians, the more recent ones called them Celto-Ligurians.[39] The date at which Celts first appeared in the coastal area is also a matter of some dispute,[40] but in seeking a conclusion on this one should always bear in mind that the question is primarily a linguistic one: if they were simply a dominant minority they could introduce their rule and their language without noticeably altering the way of life, or the artefacts, of the local population, so that their arrival would not at once be recognisable archaeologically. As we have seen, Trogus believed both Ligurians and Gauls (that is, Celts) to be in occupation at the time of the foundation of *Massalia*, and the personal names Comanus and Catumandus would both appear to be Celtic rather than Ligurian. Beyond this, Livy[41] says that Gauls (certainly Celts), who were then in the process of invading Italy, actually overcame the opposition of the (Ligurian) *Sallyes* and helped the Phocaeans to found their city. And the way of life that prevailed was determined less by racial origins than by the ecology of the country that was, as we have also seen, essentially Mediterranean.

This is relevant too to the influence of the Greeks. Whether they really improved the methods of ploughing is somewhat questionable, since, in Roman times at least, the more northerly Celts were more responsible than the Mediterranean peoples for advances in agricultural machinery.[42] The planting of olives was indeed a new introduction, and although wild vines grew throughout the Mediterranean area their cultivation and their use for the production of wine certainly does seem to have been an innovation—though to judge from the constant references to Celtic drunkenness[43] its contribution to the restraint of barbarity is more doubtful: and even here the methods, noted by Pliny,[44] that were necessary to defend vines from the onslaught of the Mistral must have been due to local rather than imported experience. Some improvement in sculpture must also be attributed to Greek influence, though this affected the presentation of religion rather than its content, as is illustrated by the têtes-coupées and the interesting statues associated with them.[45]

The most important element of all is the hill-forts. These are extraordinarily numerous in our area (fig 3)—much more so than in northern Gaul or even in our own Welsh Marches—and while almost all of those excavated have yielded Greek imports it is certain that the natives did not have to learn the basic principles of walling them from the invaders. Some modifications can, however, be attributed to them. These include the introduction of stone columns with capitals at Ensérune,[46] some elements of town-planning at Entremont[47] and, most relevant to Trogus's claim, the application of bastions to forts like Nages, Constantine and, again, Entremont.[48]

These forts are referred to by Trogus as 'cities', and while the use of the word *urbes* in this context may be due simply to redrafting by Justin in the third century (when Latin was already becoming less precise), it is not altogether inappropriate because many of them do represent in embryo form the nucleated organisations that were typical of the whole Mediterranean world and in other areas developed into recognisable city-states. And this brings us to the most important consideration of all—its supreme importance resting on the fact that when Rome expanded she did not take over mere areas of land but rather states, whether they were city-states of Mediterranean type or tribal states of the kind that were common elsewhere in Europe. The tribes, too, are remarkably numerous in our area, especially in Provence proper (fig 4) and most of them, though often they had by then lost their full political identity, were still recognisable by Pliny. The identification and location of these tribes has been excellently discussed by Barruol, who argues convincingly that by Roman times they had, while not losing their identity, come together to form federations.[49] The most obvious case is that of the *Sallyes* (or *Salluvii*), who are frequently referred to in contexts that imply that they included numerous smaller tribes (according to Barruol the *Libii*, *Nearchi*, *Avatici*, *Anatilii*, *Dexivates*, *Segobrigii*, *Comani*, *Tricores*, *Tritolli*, *Camactulici*, *Suelteri*, *Oxybii*, *Ligauni*, *Deciates* and *Reii*); and he argues also for a confederation of *Cavares* (to include the *Memini*, *Tricastini* and *Segovellauni*) and another of the *Vocontii* (to include the *Sogiontii*, *Avantici*, *Sebaginni*, and *Vertamocorii*). What minor tribes the *Allobroges*, whose territory was so vast and so fragmented, had also assimilated is uncertain, and the peculiar case of the *Albici* and the *Vulgientes* will be discussed below (pp

16

66, 256). West of the Rhône there had certainly been some Iberian and also Ligurian peoples before the advent of the Celts, but by Roman times most of these were dominated by the *Helvii*, the *Volcae Arecomici* and the *Volcae Tectosages*, although in the extreme south-west the Iberian *Sordi* and *Elisyces* seem to have preserved some at least of their independence.[50]

To summarise, then, the land to which the Romans came was not unlike the Italy that they had already conquered. It was a Mediterranean land, with a climate and a soil similar to their own, inhabited by peoples who, though more primitive than themselves, were not opposed to their general way of life and who had already been influenced, even if only in limited ways, by a string of Greek settlements along the coast. *Massalia*, the mother-city and controller of these settlements, was already an ally of Rome, and in fact it was this alliance that led ultimately to the absorption of the area within the Roman Empire. Trade was already of some importance, at least from the end of the fourth century, for it is at about the time that Rome took over Naples (in 326 BC) that Campanian pottery first appears in Marseille, and this may also be when she began to develop the overland route for tin from the north-west;[51] but the overriding consideration, as we shall see, was that the two allies were united in their opposition to Carthage.

REFERENCES AND NOTES

1 Strabo IV,1,14, *cf* IV,1,2, where he also stresses the similarity of *Narbonensis* to Italy.
2 Strabo IV,1,8 (citing Polybius, Timaeus and Artemidorus).
3 Strabo IV,1,7 (citing Aristotle, Poseidonius and Aeschylus); Mela II,5,78; Pliny, *HN* III,34 (*Campi Lapidei, Herculis proeliorum memoria*).
4 Pliny, *HN* II,121; here Pliny mentions only its use for shipping, but later (XIV,14) he notes its effect on vines. Diodorus Siculus V,26 (based on Poseidonius) appears to be speaking of the Mistral but applies it, in error, to 'most of Gaul' (κατὰ τὴν πλείστην τῆς Γαλατίας).
5 Ausonius, *Ordo Urbium Nobilium*, Tolosa, 4–5; *confinia . . . ninguida Pyrenes et pinea Cebennarum.*
6 Nor, of course, to the Canal du Midi, thanks to the brilliance of Pierre-Paul Riquet, the 17th-cent. self-styled 'Moyse du Languedoc', whose work is commemorated by an obelisk at the Seuil de Naurouze. The nearest analogy in Britain is the Watford Gap, which likewise accommodates a Roman road, a modern road, a railway and a canal.
7 For an excellent discussion of the passes see Barruol 1969, 58–71.
8 In fact many of the roads were constructed by the client king Cottius— Ammianus XV,10,8; Cicero, *de Prov. Cons.* 13,33, refers to the route by Mont-Genèvre as no more than a *semita*.

9 The summit can easily be reached in top gear even along the N.9, let alone the more recent motorway.

10 See, for example, S. Piggott, G. Daniel and C. McBurney (edd): *France before the Romans*, London, 1973, chaps 1–5, with references, and Guilaine 1976.

11 Herodotus IV, 152.

12 Timaeus, quoted by Pseudo-Scymnus 211–14.

13 Livy, v, 34.

14 Solinus, *Collectanea Memorabilia* II, 52.

15 Villard 1960; Benoit 1965; Clavel-Lévêque 1977.

16 Thucydides I, 13; Pausanias, *Periegesis* x, 8, 6. For a good discussion of this discrepancy see Villard 1960, 76–81.

17 Justin, *Historiae Philippicae ex Trogo Pompeio* XLIII, 4, 11–12: his grandfather had been granted Roman citizenship by Pompey for service in the Sertorian War, his uncle had led cavalry for Pompey in the Mithridatic War, and his father had been a secretary of Caesar. A Loeb edition is advertised as in preparation.

18 Justin XLIII, 3, 4–12; Protis was also the founder according to Plutarch, *Solon* 2, 4, where he is described as a merchant.

19 Athenaeus, *Deipnosophistae* XLIII, 5 (576).

20 Justin XLIII, 3, 13–4, 6.

21 Justin XLIII, 4, 7–5, 10. Even this date for the alliance is somewhat early.

22 Justin XXXVII, 1, 1.

23 Strabo IV, 1, 5. For useful discussion of the extension of Massaliote territory see Barruol 1969, 221–30 and Clavel-Lévêque 1977, 79–87.

24 On Agde see Clavel 1970, 103–14, with references; on Antibes, J. Clergues: *La recherche archéologique à Antibes*, Antibes, 1966.

25 Stephanus of Byzantium *sv*, calling it Ταυρόεις, as does also Pseudo-Scymnus 215; it is *Tauroenta* (acc.) in Caesar, *BC* II, 4, Ταυροέντιον in Strabo, *Tauroin* (acc.) in Mela II, 5, 77, and Ταυροέντιον in Ptolemy, *Geog.* II, 10, 5 (who curiously lists it between *Massalia* and *Citharista*). On the probable Ligurian origin of the name, Benoit 1965, 104, and on the difficulties of research here Fr. Brien in *Hist. Arch.* No 57 (Oct 1981), 31.

26 J. Coupry, *ibid.*, 29–32, for the most recent summary, but for reports *Gallia* VI (1948)—XXXI (1973), *passim* (for details, n 61 on p 209).

27 Benoit 1965, 108, 110.

28 Avienius, *Ora Maritima*, 689–91: *Arelatus illic civitas attollitur/Theline vocata sub priore saeculo/Graio incolente*; for early pottery, *Gallia* XVIII (1960), 101, early (6th cent) buildings XXXV (1977), 515.

29 H. Rolland: *Fouilles de Saint-Blaise* I (1951), II (1956) and III (1970) (supplements to *Gallia*); Avienius, *Ora Maritima*, 701; Artemidorus, cited by Stephanus *sv* Μαστραμέλη from the Epitome of Marcian.

30 *Citharista*, *Itin. Mar.* 506, 3–4, Mela II, 5, 77, Pliny, *HN* III, 35, Ptolemy, *Geog.*, II, 10, 5; *Athenopolis*, Mela, *ibid*, Pliny, *ibid*, Stephanus *sv* ’Αθηναι, citing Philo.

31 *Itin. Mar.* 506, 4–6.

32 *Pergantium*, Stephanus, *sv*; *Agathonis Portus*, hagiography of St-Porcaire, cited by Benoit 1965, 107, and, pointing out that the antiquity of the port is quite uncertain, Février 1977, 169.

33 Pliny, *HN* III, 34.

34 Pseudo-Scymnus 207–209; Pliny, *HN* III, 33.

35 Avienius, *Ora Maritima*, 554–627. For *Heraclea* v p 175, below.

36 For good discussions of this, with references to sources and other theories, see Barruol 1969, 221–30, Clavel-Lévêque 1977, 79–87, and Ebel 1976, 26–40.

37 Avienius, *Ora Maritima*, 612–13 (after *Setius Mons*, 608–09); but see N. Lamboglia, 'Prata Liguriae', *REL* xxv (1959), 5–22, and 'Le Regnum des Liguri Elisyci' in *Narbonne: archéologie et histoire: Montlaurès et les origines de Narbonne*, Montpellier, 1973, 65–9.

38 Pseudo-Scylax 3: ἀπὸ δὲ Ἰβήρων ἔχονται Λίγυες καὶ Ἴβηρες μιγάδες μέχρι ποταμοῦ Ῥοδανοῦ.

39 Strabo IV, 6, 3.

40 Benoit, for example (Benoit 1965, 97, 133), put it as late as the 4th century, but for a full discussion see Barruol 1969, 157–61.

41 Livy v, 34.

42 *Eg* Pliny, *HN* XVIII, 296, on the *vallus*.

43 *Eg* Diodorus Siculus v, 26 (based on Poseidonius) and Ammianus XV, 12, 4 (quoting a lost piece of Cicero, *Pro Fonteio*).

44 Pliny, *HN* XIV, 14.

45 See F. Benoit: *L'art primitif mediterranéen de la vallée de la Rhône*, Aix, 1955, and, for a convenient English summary, his paper 'The Celtic *Oppidum* of Entremont' in R. Bruce-Mitford (ed), *Recent Archaeological Excavations in Europe*, London 1975.

46 J. Jannoray: *Ensérune*, Paris, 1955.

47 F. Benoit: *Entremont*, Aix, 1957, and the English summary cited in n 45.

48 For Nages, M. Aliger, *Ogam* XIX (1967), 1–64; for Constantine, J. Gourvest, *Ogam* XVIII (1965); for Entremont, see notes 45 and 47. For sites in Languedoc, G. Barruol, 'Les civilisations de l'Age du Fer en Languedoc' in Guilaine 1976, Pt III, 676–86, and for an extensive bibliography of hill-forts up to 1974, R. Chevallier in *ANRW* II, iii, 1975, 783–9.

49 Barruol 1969, *Salluvii* and their associates, 187–221; *Cavares*, 231–72; *Vocontii*, 278–84; the location of the *Sebaginni* (or *Sebagnini*) who are mentioned only in Cicero, *Pro Quinctio* 25 (80), is a little doubtful, but their stated distance of 700 miles from Rome fits Barruol's location much better than those suggested by Hirschfeld (*CIL* XII, i, p 221), who relates them to the Cevennes, and by Ebel (Ebel 1976, 92), who also prefers one nearer to Narbonne.

50 N. Lamboglia (*opp citt*, note 37) argues that the *Elisyces* were Ligurian rather than Iberian and this is also accepted by Benoit 1965, *passim*. For an excellent summary of Iron Age sites in the west see Barruol. 'Les civilisations de L'Age du Fer en Languedoc' in Guilaine, 1976, Pt III 676–86.

51 Villard, 1960, on the earliest Campanian pottery, 32, 34; on the development of the tin trade, 143–61 (a very good discussion of sources and theories.)

APPENDIX: BIBLIOGRAPHY OF HILL-FORT EXCAVATIONS (excluding Savoie & Dauphiné)

(Sites marked with an asterisk are named on the map, fig 3)

Alpes-Maritimes

Baou-des-Noirs (Vence). Octobon 1962, 122; *Gallia* XXVII(1969), 458, XXIX(1971), 465, XXXIII(1975), 570, XXXV(1977), 510

Cimiez (Nice). P.-M. Duval: 'Rapport préliminaire sur les fouilles de Cemenelum, 1943', *Gallia* IV(1946), 77–136. See also p 341 for the Roman city of *Cemenelum*

Encourdoules (Vallauris). *FOR* I, no 70; Octobon 1962, 122; *Gallia* XII(1954), 440–1

Escragnolles (le Camp de Colette). *FOR* I, no 199; Octobon 1962, 108–09

Mont Bastide (Eze). Octobon 1962, 109–12; *Gallia* VIII(1950), 130, XI(1953), 116, XII(1954), 442

Rouret (le Camp du Bois). *FOR* I, no 140; Octobon 1962, 107–08

Ardèche

Lussas (Jastres-Nord). *FOR* XV, no 59; Y. Burnand; 'Documents sur l'oppidum de Jastres-Nord à Lussas', *Gallia* XXXV(1977), 271–8; *Gallia* XXXIII(1975), 533–4, XXXVIII(1980), 506, XL(1982), 395–6, XLIII(1985), 539–40; *Antiquity* XLIII(1969), 268; *Hist. Arch.* 78(1983), 15–17

Lussas (Jastres-Sud). *Gallia* XL(1982), 395–6; *Hist. Arch.* 78(1983), 15–17

St-Marcel-d'Ardèche (St-Etienne-de-Dions). *FOR* XV, no 3; *Gallia* XXIX(1971), 442, XXXIII(1975), 534, XXXVIII(1980), 508, XLIII(1985), 540–1

Soyons (Malpas). *FOR* XV, no 94; *Gallia* XIV(1956), 260, XVIII(1960), 376

Ariège

Belesta (le Mayné). *Gallia* XXXIV(1976), 463

St-Jean-de-Verges (Tour d'Opio). *Gallia* XXII(1964), 427, XXIV(1966), 411, XXVI(1968), 515, XXVIII(1970), 397, XXX(1972), 469

Aude

le Calla (Durban). *Gallia* XXII(1964), 477, XXIV(1966), 453, XXVII(1969), 382–3

Carcassonne. *FOR* XII, no 71. *Gallia* XXXI(1973) 476–7. See also p 137 for the Roman town

le Cayla de Mailhac. *FOR* XII, no 29; J. Martin-Granel, 'Les Fouilles de l'oppidum du Cayla', *Gallia* II(1944), 1–24; O. and J. Taffanel, 'Le Cayla de Mailhac', *Bull. de la Soc. d'Etudes Scient. de l'Aude* XLII(1938), 110–47 and 'Les civilisations préromaines dans la région de Mailhac', *Et. Roussillonaises* V(1956), 7–29, 103–30; O. and J. Taffanel and J.-C. Richard, 'Les monnaies de Mailhac', *Gallia* XXXVI(1979), 1–53; *Gallia* V(1947), 143–6, VI(1948), 200–01, VIII(1950), 110–11, XI(1953), 93–4, XII(1954), 412–13, XIV(1956),

205–06, XVII(1959), 451–2, XVIII(1960), 1–37, XX(1962), 3–32, 614–15, XXII(1964), 478, XXIV(1966), 454–5, XXVII(1969), 383–4, XXIX(1971), 373–4, XXXI(1973), 479, XXXIII(1975), 497

★*Montlaurès. FOR* XII, no 1 *Bull. Arch. de Narbonne* XXV(1961), 159–73. XXVI(1962), 76–88; *Gallia* XX(1962), 616, XXII(1964), 479–80, XXXI(1973), 480, XXXVII(1979), 525, XXXIX(1981), 504

★*le Moulin* (Peyriac-de-Mer). *Gallia* XX(1962), 618–19, XXII(1964), 480, XXIV(1966), 458–9, XXVII(1969), 387, XXIX(1971), 375–6, XXXI(1973), 483

★*Pech-Maho* (Sigean). *FOR* XII, no 8; *Gallia* XI(1953), 94–5, XII(1954) 414–15, XVII(1959), 452–4, XX(1962), 620–2, XXII(1964), 484–5, XXIV(1966), 460–1, XXVII(1969), 388–91, XXIX(1971), 377–9, XXXI(1973), 484–6, XXXIII(1975), 500–01, XXXVI(1978), 438

Pomas-et-Rouffiac (Camp de Ker and Oppidum of Lagaste). *FOR* XII, no 83; *Gallia* XXVII(1969), 388, XXIX(1971), 376, XXXI(1973), 483–4

Bouches-du-Rhône

★*Baou-Rouge* (Auriol). *FOR* V, no 38; M. Honoré: 'L'oppidum préromain du Baou-Rouge', *Cahiers Ligures de Préhistoire* XVII(1968), 102–30; *Gallia* XVIII(1960), 291, XXV(1967), 402, XXVII(1969), 422, XXX(1972), 517

★*Baou-Roux* (Bouc-Bel-Air). *FOR* V, no 114; J.P. Tennevin; *Le Baou-Roux, oppidum celto-ligure*, Aix, 1974; *Gallia* XXII(1964), 576–7, XXV(1967), 402, XXVII(1969), 423, XXX(1972), 517, XXXV(1977), 517

★*les Baux. FOR* V, no 521; *Gallia* XXXV:(1977), 518

★*le Castelet* (Fontvieille). *FOR* V, no 487; *Gallia* XI(1953), 112, XII(1954), 430–1, XVIII(1960), 305–07, XXV(1967), 403, XXVII(1969), 423, XXX(1972), 518, XXXII(1974), 509, XXXV(1977), 517

le Castellan d'Istres (Istres). *FOR* V, no 297; *Gallia* XII(1954), 433

la Cloche (les Pennes-Mirabeau) *FOR* V, no 135; *Gallia* XXVII(1969), 432, XXX(1972), 519–20, XXXII(1974), 511–12, XXXV(1977), 519–20

★*Constantine. FOR* V, no 313; J. Gourvest, 'A Propos de la civilisation des oppida en Provence occidentale; l'oppidum de Constantine', *Ogam* VIII(1954), 51–62, *Gallia* VI(1948), 214, XVI(1958), 427–8

★*Entremont. FOR* V, no 245; F. Benoit, 'Les fouilles d'Entremont en 1946', *Gallia* V(1947), 81–97, 'Les fouilles d'Entremont en 1953–1954', *Gallia* XII(1954), 285–94, *Entremont*, Aix, 1957, 'Résultats historiques des fouilles d'Entremont (1946–67)', *Gallia* XXVI(1968), 1–31; *Gallia* VI(1948), 213, VIII(1950), 117–19, XI(1953), 106–07, XIV(1956), 218–22, XVI(1958), 412–15, XVIII(1960), 291–4, XX(1962), 690–2, XXII(1964), 573–5, XXV(1967), 397, XXVII(1969), 419, XXX(1972), 511–14, XXXII(1974), 501–05, XXXV(1977), 511

Jouques (Oppidum of Nôtre-Dame-de-Consolation). *FOR* V, no 333, *Gallia* XXII(1964), 578

★*Pierredon* (Eguilles). *FOR* V, no 258; *Gallia* XII(1954), 431–2, XXII(1964), 578, XXV(1967), 403, XXX(1972), 518

★*Rognac* (le Castellas). *FOR* V, no 270; *Gallia* XXV(1967), 405, XXVII(1969), 432–3, XXX(1972), 525–6, XXXII(1974), 520

★*la Roque* (Graveson), *FOR* V, no 558; *Gallia* XXII(1964), 578

★*St-Blaise* (St-Mitre). *FOR* V, no 292; Rolland 1951 and 1956; F. Bouloumié, 'Saint-Blaise: notes sommaires sur cinq années de fouilles et de recherches'

(1974–1978)', *Gallia* XXXVII(1979), 229–35; *Gallia* VI(1948), 212–13,
XVI(1958), 430–2, XXII(1964), 569–72, XXV(1967), 410–17, XXVII(1969),
433–5, XXX(1972), 526–7, XXXII(1974), 520–1, XXXV(1977), 526–7

★*St-Marcel* (Marseille), *FOR* V, no 78; *Gallia* XXV(1967), 404–05, XXVII(1969),
430, XXX(1972), 527, XXXII(1974), 512, XXXV(1977), 524

St-Martin de Castillon (Paradou). *FOR* V, no 515; *Gallia* XXV(1977), 518

★*Tamaris* (Martigues). *FOR* V, no 155; *Gallia* XVIII(1960), 290–1

★*la Teste-Nègre* (Pennes-Mirabeau). *FOR* V, no 132; *Gallia* XI(1953), 113,
XII(1954), 431, XXXV(1977), 520

★*Roquepertuse* (Velaux). (Shrine, not a hill-fort). *FOR* V, no 275; *Gallia*
XVIII(1960), 295–6, XX(1962), 693–4, XXVII(1969), 446; H.-P. Eydoux;
Révélations de l'archéologie, Paris, 1963, 41–61

Drôme

le Pègue. *FOR* XI, no 45; Hatt 1976–7; *Gallia* XVI(1958), 384–6, XXII(1964),
526–31, XXIII(1965), 237–9, XXIV(1966), 512–4, XXVI(1968), 589–91,
XXIX(1971), 431–3, XXXI(1973), 535–6, XXXV(1977), 476–7, XXXVIII(1980),
510, XL(1982), 398, XLIII(1985), 543

Gard

Alès (l'Hermitage). *FOR* VIII, no 366; *Gallia* XXIX(1971), 389–90, XXXIII(1975),
512, XXXIX(1981), 514, XLI(1983), 509, XLIII(1985), 394–5

★*Beaucaire* (*Ugernum*, la Redoute). *FOR* VIII, no 3; *Gallia* XXXVI(1978), 446

Bouquet (Gauto-Fracho). *FOR* VIII, no 321; *Gallia* XXXIII(1975), 513; *RAN*
VIII(1975), 1–32

Brignon (le Sierre de Brienne). *Gallia* XXIX(1971), 390, XXXI(1973), 500,
XXXIII(1975), 513–14, XXXVII(1979), 537

Calvisson (le Font de Coucou). *Gallia* XXIX(1971), 391–2, XXXI(1973), 501;
RAN VIII(1975), 33–65

Calvisson (le Roc de Gachonne). *Gallia* XXXVII(1979), 537(all B.A.)

Collias (Castres). *Gallia* XXII(1964), 500, XXXI(1973), 501–02

Comps (la Roche de Comps). *FOR* VIII, no 125; *Gallia* XXXIX(1981), 515–16,
XLI(1983), 509

Gailhan (Plan de la Tour). *Gallia* XXXIII(1975), 514, XXXVI(1978), 447,
XXXVII(1979), 538, XXXIX(1981), 516–17, XLI(1983), 510–11, XLIII(1985),
395–6

Laudun (Camp de César). *FOR* VIII, no 170; *Gallia* XXXI(1973), 503,
XXXIII(1975), 515

★*la Liquière* (Calvisson). *FOR* VIII, no 62; *Gallia* XXVII(1969), 403, XXIX(1971),
390–1, XXXI(1973), 500–01

Lombren (Vénéjan). *Gallia* XX(1962), 637–8, XXII(1964), 506–07, XXIV(1966),
481–2, XXVII(1969), 413

★*Mauressip* (St-Côme-et-Maruéjols). *FOR* VIII, no 137; *Gallia* XXII(1964), 504,
XXIV(1966), 479–81, XXVII(1969), 408, XXIX(1971), 397–8, XXXI(1973), 510,
XXXV(1975), 524

Montfaucon (St-Maur). *Gallia* XXIX(1971), 393

★*Nages* (les Castels, Nages-et-Solorgues). *FOR* VIII, no 67; Py 1978; *Gallia* xx(1962), 631–2, xxII(1964), 500–02, xxIV(1966), 477–8, xxVII(1969), 406, xxIX(1971), 393–4, xxXI(1973), 503–06, xxxIII(1975), 517–21, xxxVI(1978), 452–4, xxxVII(1979), 540–3, xxxIX(1981), 518–21 (and on Roque-de-Viou, *RAN* vII(1974), 1–24)

★*Nîmes* (*Nemausus, oppidum* of Mont Cavalier). *FOR* vIII, no 85; Py 1981; *Gallia* xxII(1964), 500–02, xxxIII(1975), 521–2, xxxVII(1979), 545; xLI(1983), 513–15. See also Chapter 12 for the Roman city

Roquecourbe (Marguerittes). *Gallia* xxVII(1969), 405, xxxVI(1978), 448

★*Ste-Anastasie* (Castelviel). *FOR* vIII, no 275; *Gallia* xxxIII(1975), 526–7, xxxVI(1978), 458

★*St-Bonnet-du-Gard* (le Marduel). *FOR* vIII, no 117; *Gallia* xxxVI(1978), 455–6, xxxVII(1979), 547–8, xxxIX(1981), 522–4, xLIII(1985), 398–401

St-Dionisy (Roque de Viou). *FOR* vIII, no 69; *Gallia* xxIX(1971), 399–400, xxXI(1973), 510–11, xxxIII(1975), 524–6

St-Laurent-de-Carnols. *Gallia* xx(1962), 636, xxVII(1969), 409, xLI(1983), 517, xLIII(1985), 401

St-Vincent (Gaujac). *FOR* vIII, no 217; *Gallia* xxIV(1966), 475–6, xxVII(1969), 404–05, xxIX(1971), 392, xxXI(1973), 502, xxxIII(1975), 514–15, xxxVI(1978), 447–8, xxxVII(1979), 538–9, xxxIX(1981), 517–18

San-Peyre (Suzon, Bouquet). *FOR* vIII, no 323; *Gallia* xxxIII(1975), 513

Tornac (la Madeleine). *FOR* vIII, no 377; *Gallia* xxxVII(1979), 549, xxxIX(1981), 525

Vié-Cioutat (Mons-et-Monteils). *FOR* vIII, no 314; B. Dedet, 'Les niveaux protohistoriques de l'oppidum de Vié-Cioutat à Mons-Monteils, Gard (fouilles 1966–1968)', *RAN* vI(1973), 1–72; *Gallia* xII(1954), 424–5, xxVII(1969), 405, xxIX(1971), 393, xxXI(1973), 503, xxxIII(1975), 517, xxxVI(1978), 449–52, xxxVII(1979), 539, xxxIX(1981), 519

★*Villevieille* (Sommières). *FOR* vIII, no 55; M. Py, 'L'oppidum préromain de Villevieille (Gard)', *RAN* IV(1971), 217–32; *Gallia* xxXI(1973), 512–13

Haute Garonne

Vieille-Toulouse. *Pallas* IX(1960), 177–217, x(1961), 69–90; *Gallia* xv(1957), 256–8, xvI(1958), 115–17, xvII(1959), 433–5, xx(1962), 576–8, xxII(1964), 450–1, xxIV(1966), 429–30, xxVI(1968), 537–8, xxVIII(1970), 410–13, xxx(1972), 491–5, xxxII(1974), 474–6, xxxIV(1976), 482–4, xxxVI(1978), 409–11, xxxVIII(1980), 483–7, xLI(1983), 485

Hérault

Aigues-Vives (St-Vincent). *FOR* x, no 144; *Gallia* xxII(1964), 487

★*Béziers* (Besara). *FOR* x, no 99; Clavel 1970, 41–4, 51, 61–65, 71–3, 99–101. See also Chapter 10 for the Roman city, *Baeterrae*.

★*Ensérune* (Nissan). *FOR* x, no 106; Jannoray 1965; Gallet de Santerre 1980; Clavel 1970, 67–8, 93–4; *Gallia* vI(1948), 112–15, vIII(1950), 112–15, xI(1953), 96–9, xII(1954), 417–22, xIV(1956), 210–15, xxII(1964), 495, xxIV(1966), 470, xxVII(1969), 397, xxXI(1973), 496, xxxIII(1975), 508, xxxVII(1979), 532

★*la Monedière* (Bessan). *FOR* x, no 81; J. Coulouma and l'Abbé Thomas,

'L'oppidum ibéro-grecque de Bessan', *Cahiers d'Histoire et d'Archéologie* XI(1936), 690–712; Clavel 1970, 69–70, 98–9,129–30; A. Nickels, 'Les maisons à abside d'époque grecque archaïque de la Monedière, à Bessan', *Gallia* XXXIV(1976), 95–128; *Gallia* VI(1948), 175–9, XII(1954), 416, XIV(1956), 207, XX(1962), 623, XXXI(1973), 489, XXXIII(1975), 502–03

*Montfo (Magalas). *FOR* x, no 119; Clavel 1970, 94–8; *Gallia* I(1942), 225–6, II(1943), 18, VI(1948), 175–9, XXII(1964), 493, XXIV(1966), 468, XXVII(1969), 396, XXIX(1971), 384, XXXI(1973), 495, XXXIII(1975), 506–07, XXXVI(1978), 442–3, XXXVII(1979), 531, XXXIX(1981), 510–11

*Murviel-lès-Montpellier. *FOR* x, no 29; *Gallia* XII(1954), 423, XVII(1959), 466–7, XX(1962), 625–6, XXII(1964), 494, XXIV(1966), 468–70, XXVII(1969), 397, XXXVI(1978), 443, XXXVII(1979), 532, XXXIX(1981), 511, XLI(1983), 523, XLIII(1985), 410

Olanzac (Bassanel, or Mourrel Forrat). *Gallia* XXXI(1973), 496, XXXVI(1978), 443–4, XXXVII(1979), 532

Pignan (les Barres). *FOR* x, no 28; *Gallia* XXXVI(1978), 444, XXXIX(1981), 511

*Pioch-Balat (Aumes). *FOR* x, no 83; Clavel 1970, 103; *Gallia* VIII(1950), 112

Pioch-du-Télégraphe (Aumes). *FOR* x, no 84; Clavel 1970, 73, 102; *Gallia* XXI(1973), 488–9

*Plo-des-Brus (Castanet-le-Haut). *FOR* x, no 134; *Gallia* XXVII(1969), 399, XXXIII(1975), 509, XXXVII(1979), 533

*la Roque (Fabrègues). *FOR* x, no 27; P. Larderet, 'L'oppidum préromain de la Roque, Commune de Fabrègues', *Gallia* XV(1957), 1–40; *Gallia* XII(1954), 422–3, XIV(1956), 215–16, XVII(1959), 462–4, XX(1962), 623–4, XXII(1964), 491, XXIV(1966), 466

*St-Siméon (Pézenas, *Piscenae*). Clavel 1970, 66; *Gallia* XXIV(1966), 470–1, XXVII(1969), 397–8

St-Thibéry (*Cessero*). *FOR* x, no 89; *Gallia* II(1943), 8–18, VI(1947), 175–9, XXXIII(1975), 510, XLIII(1985), 411. See also p 153 for the Roman town

Siran (le Pic St-Martin). *FOR* x, no 157; *Gallia* XXII(1964), 497

*Substantion (Castelnau-le-Lez, *Sextantio*). *FOR* x, no 19; F. Daumas and R. Majurel, 'Rapport préliminaire sur les fouilles de Substantion', *Gallia* XIX(1961), 5–30; *Gallia* XVII(1959), 237–41, XX(1962), 623, XXII(1964), 490, XXIV(1966), 464–6, XXVII(1969), 392, XXIX(1971), 380, XXXI(1973), 490. See also p 170 for the Roman town

*Vic-le-Gardiole (Combe de Bestiou, ? *Naustalo*) *FOR* x, no 34; Benoit 1965, 123 (for name); *Gallia* XXXVII(1979), 534–5

Vic-la-Gardiole (la Roubine) *Gallia* XX(1962), 628, XXVII(1969), 400–01

*Villetelle (*Ambrussum*). *FOR* x, no 4; J.L. Fiches and M. Fenouillet, 'L'oppidum d'Ambrussum, relais sur la voie domitienne', *Arch.* 51(1972), 15–20; J.L. Fiches, M. Fenouillet and C. Wujek: 'Sept ans de recherches à Ambrussum, oppidum relais de la voie domitienne (1968–1974)', *Cahier No 4 de l'Association pour la recherche archéologique en Languedoc oriental*, Caveirac, 1976; *Gallia* XXVII(1969), 401, XXIX(1971), 388–9, XXXI(1973), 498, XXXIII(1975), 510–12, XXXVI(1978), 445, XXXVII(1979), 535–6, XXXIX(1981), 511–13, XLI(1983), 524–6, XLIII(1985), 411–13. See also p 172 for the Roman town

Pyrénées-orientales

*Castel Roussillon (now Château Roussillon, Ruscino) Espérandieu 1936, 21–26;
  Gallia* VIII(1950), 108–10, XI(1953), 90–93, XII(1954), 411–12, XIV(1956),
  203–05, XVII(1959), 449–50, XX(1962), 611–12, XXII(1964), 473–4,
  XXIV(1966), 449–50, XXVII(1969), 381–2, XXXVI(1978), 431–3, XXXVII(1979).
  521–2, XXXIX(1981), 501–03. See also p 136 for the Roman town
Elne (Illiberis). Espérandieu 1936, 28–9; *Gallia* XX(1962), 611, XXII(1964), 473,
  XXIX(1971), 369, XXXI(1963), 475, XLIII(1985), 414. See also p 141 for the
  Roman town
Llo (Llo Ladre). *Gallia* XXXIII(1975), 491, XXXVI(1978), 431–2, XXXVII(1979),
  521, XXXIX(1981), 501, XLI(1983), 527

Tarn

Berniquaut (Sorèze). *Gallia* XXVI(1968), 555, XXVIII(1970), 436, XXX(1972), 508,
  XXXII(1974), 495–6, XXXIV(1976), 499, XXXVI(1968), 425, XXXVIII(1980),
  502

Var

Bousque Boulène (la Verdière/Varages). *Gallia* XXXI(1973), 564
Costebelle (Hyères). *FOR* II, no 35; *Gallia* XXVII(1969), 452
la Courtine-d'Ollioules. FOR II no 74; J. Layet; *Le livre de la Courtine,* Toulon,
  1950; *Gallia* VI(1948), 215, VIII(1950), 126
Evenos (St-Estève). *Gallia* XIV(1956), 231, XVI(1958), 432, XXXV(1977), 497
la Forteresse (Bagnols-en-Foret). Gallia XXVII(1969), 447, XXXI(1973), 551–2,
  XXXIII(1975), 558, XXXV(1977), 495, XXXIX(1981), 531; *Hist. Arch.* 57(1981),
  531
la Fouirette (le Luc). *Gallia* XXV(1967), 421–2, XXVII(1969), 453–4
Lorgues (St-Ferréol). *Gallia* XXXVII(1979), 559, XXXIX(1981), 538
Maravieille (la Môle). *FOR* II, no 21; *Gallia* XXV(1967), 423, XXXIX(1981), 538;
  Hist. Arch. 57(1981), 21
Mont-Garou (Sanary). *Gallia* VIII(1950), 128, XVIII(1960), 308–10, XXXI(1973),
  561–2, XXXIII(1975), 565; *Hist. Arch.* 57(1981), 16–18
Montjean (la Mole). D. Wallon, 'L'oppidum de Montjean', *Hommages à
  Fernand Benoit* II(1972), 212–36; *Gallia* XXII(1964), 593, XXV(1967), 423,
  XXXI(1973), 560–1, XXXV(1977), 501, XXXVIII(1979), 559, XXXIX(1981), 538;
  Hist. Arch. 57(1981), 21
le Muy (Fréjus). *Gallia* XXII(1964), 595
Nans-les-Pins. Gallia XVIII(1960), 313
Piégu (Rougiers). *Gallia* XXV(1967), 424–5
St-Hubert (Solliés-Toucas). *Gallia* XVI(1958), 437, XXVII(1969), 455
Solliés-Toucas/Solliés-Pont (le Castellas). *Gallia* XXII(1964), 597, XXXI(1973),
  563, XXXIII(1975), 565, XXXV(1977), 505
Taradeau (le Fort), *Gallia* XXVII(1969), 455, XXIX(1971), 460–1, XXXI(1973),
  563, XXXIII(1975), 565, XXXV(1977), 505; *Hist. Arch.* 57(1981), 22–6
Tourtour (Calamantrau). *Gallia* XXXVII(1979), 564

Vaucluse

*Avignon (Rocher des Doms, *Avennio*). FOR VII, no 64; Gagnière 1970, 62–84;
Gallia XX(1962), 672. See also Chapter 24 for the Roman city

*Bonpas (Caumont). FOR VII, no 63; *Gallia* XVI(1958), 400–01, XVIII(1960),
265–7, XX(1962), 670

*Cadenet (le Castellas). FOR VII, no 8; *Gallia* XVI(1958), 401

*Cavaillon (Colline St-Jacques, *Cabellio*). FOR VII, no 60; A. Dumoulin, 'Les
puits et fosses de la Colline St-Jacques à Cavaillon', *Gallia* XXIII(1965), 1–86;
Gallia VI(1948), 224, VIII(1952), 138, XIV(1956), 249–50, XX(1962), 670,
XXV(1967), 374–5, XLII(1984), 414. See also Chapter 23 for the Roman city

Mourre-de-Sève (Sorgues, *Vindalium*). P. de Brun and S. Gagnière: 'La station
hallstattienne de Mourre-de-Sève', *BSPF* 1934, 68ff, Barruol 1969, 242;
Gallia XVIII(1960), 263–5

*Pérréal (St-Saturnin-d'Apt). FOR VII, no 25; *Gallia* XIV(1956), 251–2,
XVI(1958), 402–05, XVIII(1960), 267–8, XX(1962), 676–9

2
Early Roman Involvement
219–153 BC

The first official Roman involvement in transalpine Gaul arose from the Carthaginian threat. Livy[1] (though not Polybius) tells us that after visiting Carthage in 218 BC the embassy consisting of Q. Fabius, M. Livius, L. Aemilius, C. Licinius and Q. Baebius tried to establish alliances with various tribes, first in Spain and then in Gaul, but met with no success in either country. Unfortunately he does not record which tribes they tried to influence, merely describing the roars of contemptuous laughter that met their appeal, nor indeed does he mention any of the Greek cities like Ampurias and Agde, but the implications of his account are that the journey was made by land from Spain to Marseille. At Marseille the Massaliotes, having, as loyal allies, made detailed enquiries, told them that Hannibal had already seduced the Gauls, though even he would still need to bribe them with gold if he wished to contain their barbarity. The envoys therefore returned to Rome 'not long after the consuls had set out for their *provinciae*'.

The timing of this useless expedition is of some interest.[2] M. Livius Salvinator and L. Aemilius Paullus were the consuls of 219 BC and so cannot have left Rome on the embassy to Carthage before the expiry of their office on 15 March 218 and it has even been suggested (though this does not accord well with Livy) that they may not have done so before the news of Hannibal's crossing of the Ebro reached the city (that is, in June). The despatch of the new consuls to their appointed spheres of action (for that is the meaning of *provinciae* in this context)—of P. Cornelius Scipio to Spain and Ti. Sempronius Longus to Africa—did not take place until late August, and both because of the length of the embassy's journey and because Livy states that when they returned rumours of the Ebro crossing were already circulating it is evident that, little as they knew it, Hannibal must have been almost on their heels.

A further and more serious effect of this ignorance was, of course, to follow shortly. No sooner had envoys from *Massalia* confirmed the crossing of the Ebro than the Cisalpine Gauls staged a revolt, and this meant that one of the legions intended for Scipio's expedition had to be replaced by the enrolment of another. When this was completed, he set sail with two legions and 60 ships, reached *Massalia* in five days and, believing that Hannibal had got no further than the Pyrenees, established a camp at the mouth of the Rhône mainly, it seems, to enable his troops to recover from sea-sickness. A report soon came, however, that Hannibal was already crossing the river so, while still doubting it, Scipio sent out a force of 300 cavalry, guided by Gauls who were serving in *Massalia* as mercenaries.[3] A furious battle took place with some of Hannibal's Numidian scouts and although the Romans claimed the victory it served no useful purpose. When they reached the main Carthaginian camp it was already deserted, and although, according to Livy, Scipio took his main army to it, pursuit would obviously be pointless. According he re-embarked his army, sent it on towards Spain under the command of his brother Cnaeus, and himself returned to Italy.[4]

Hannibal had entered Gaul through the Pyrenees—no doubt by the Col du Perthus[5]—but on his experiences from there to the Rhône Polybius is curiously uninformative, contenting himself with stating distances and saying only that some Gauls had to be bribed and others forced to let him through.[6] Livy is a little more helpful. According to him, a number of unnamed Gaulish tribes, worried by the Carthaginian subjugation of peoples in Spain, had assembled under arms at *Ruscino* (Château Roussillon) to bar his way. Hannibal, however, having pitched camp at *Illiberis* (Elne), sent ambassadors to them and had little difficulty in persuading the Gaulish leaders with gifts to let him pass through their territory without interference. Since *Ruscino* lay on the south bank of the river Tet, an obvious choice for a battle-line, this can hardly be used to prove its especial importance in this period, and even the fact that Livy twice uses the word *reguli* (rather than *principes*) for the Gaulish leaders, interesting though it is, cannot be taken as firm evidence for the current nature of tribal government.[7]

We come now to a group of three issues which have been as widely debated as any points in ancient history—the location of Hannibal's crossing-point, the identity of 'the Island', and the question of which pass he used to cross the Alps. The last of these is largely irrelevant here, since the pass certainly lay outside our territory, and it will suffice to express a personal preference for the Col du Lautaret followed by Mont Genèvre.[8] The other two, however, require some discussion because they have a bearing on the condition of some of the tribes in this period. The problems that arise regarding them are due mainly to differences between the accounts of Polybius and Livy, but also to the fact that the width, the depth, the islands and even the precise course of a powerful river like the Rhône do not remain unchanged through the centuries.

In their description of the crossing itself Polybius and Livy are substantially in agreement.[9] When Hannibal arrived at the river he bought up a large number of boats from the locals and had others constructed. Since, however, a large body of Gauls (*Volcae*, says Livy) had assembled on the opposite bank to prevent his landing, he sent a force under Hanno, son of Bomilcar, higher up the river (200 stades, says Polybius, 25 Roman miles, says Livy)[10] to a place where it was divided into two by an island. Having crossed here, Hanno's troops were able to take the enemy in the rear and so frustrate their attempt to prevent the crossing of Hannibal and his elephants. But Livy offers no direct indication of the location of these crossings, and although Polybius does state that the main one was at a point where the river was single and about four days' march from the sea, this is far from definitive; and the large number of suggestions that have been made depend as much on its distance from 'the Island' (not Hanno's, but Hannibal's next staging-post) as on its distance from the Mediterranean.

These suggestions include Fourques, Beaucaire, Avignon, Roquemaure, Montfaucon, St-Etienne-des-Sorts, Pont-St-Esprit and Bourg-St-Andéol.[11] Of these the first is unlikely, because Fourques is virtually a suburb of Arles, so that it would almost certainly have invited Massaliote intervention and a mention of *Arelate* (or *Theline*) would surely have survived in our sources; and the last two can also be dismissed because, apart from the complications of distances, they were almost certainly already in Helvian, not Volcan territory. As for the rest, preference for one of the more northerly four (Avignon, Roquemaure, Montfaucon, St-Etienne) has largely depended on the belief that the Durance, which joins the Rhône just below Avignon, would have provided some protection from assault from the south and would have been an obstacle to the Carthaginians themselves, first to Hanno and then to Hannibal. This is not, however, a very strong argument since, as Jullian pointed out (though even he called the question 'grave'), the Durance is not a mighty river in August—to which might be added the suggestion that trade up and down the Rhône valley is likely by then to have resulted in the establishment of a regular ford. The strength of the case for Beaucaire rests mainly on the fact that this was the starting-point chosen a century later for the *Via Domitia*, which suggests that it was already in general use and so would have been the most likely place to which Hannibal's guides would lead him.[12]

The matter that most concerns us is the surprising statement of Livy, which needs to be quoted in full:

> Having pacified the rest by fear or by presents, Hannibal had come to the land of the *Volcae*, a powerful people. Moreover they dwell around both banks of the Rhône (*Colunt autem circa utramque ripam Rhodani*). But, unsure whether they could keep the Carthaginians out of the land on the nearer side, having moved almost all their people over the Rhône so that they could use the river as a defence, they were holding the further bank with arms.

29

Hannibal bribed the rest of the people who dwelt by the river (*ceteros accolas fluminis*) and such of their own people as had clung to their homes to collect boats from all directions and to build others, while they themselves were eager that the army should be taken across and that their area should be relieved of the pressure of so great a horde of men.[13]

Two related problems arise from this passage: did the *Volcae Arecomici* really hold land on the east side of the Rhône, and who were the *ceteri accolae fluminis*? To take the second question first, the only other tribe known to us who would fit into this context are the *Helvii* and if, as is argued later (p 184), their boundary with the *Volcae* ran along the ridge between the rivers Ardèche and Cèze, this would strengthen the case for a crossing at Montfaucon or St-Etienne-des-Sorts; this is weakened, however, by the possibility that the *Volcae*, who were indeed a *gens valida*, did, like the larger tribes east of the river which we have already discussed (p 16), progressively incorporate smaller peoples (whose names are unknown to us) into a sort of federation. So far as the first question is concerned, no stress can be laid on the fact that Livy uses the present tense for *colunt*, since Strabo specifically states that the boundary between the *Volcae Arecomici* and the *Sallyes* and *Cavares* was the river Rhône,[14] and Livy must here be simply repeating his source (probably Coelius Antipater, who wrote around 100 BC).[15] Livy is the only surviving ancient author to make this assertion and the only other possible support for it is the discovery in Avignon of a later dedication by a *praetor Volcarum*.[16] This, as we shall see (pp 167, 265), is relevant not only to the history of the *Volcae* and of Avignon, but also to the addition of land to the Massaliotes by Pompey and Caesar.

The day after crossing the river Hannibal resumed his march towards Italy. Although he may have hesitated over which way to take, his decision was determined by two factors—not merely by a wish to avoid involvement with Scipio's forces (which, as Jullian argued,[17] he might well have faced), but also by the arrival of a deputation from the *Boii*, who told him that the Celtic tribes of northern Italy would support him. He therefore went not east, up the valley of the Durance, but northwards, and in four days' time reached a place called 'the Island', where a fertile region resembling the Nile delta was formed by the confluence with the Rhône of one of its tributaries; there a conflict over sovereignty was going on between two brothers, which Hannibal was able to settle.[18]

Thus far Polybius and Livy are in general agreement, but at this point difficulties begin to arise. The first problem concerns the identity of the tributary river, whose name is probably corrupt (and may well have been so in the common source which Polybius was using directly and Livy at one remove)[19]: in Polybius it appears as Σκάρας (*Skaras*) and in Livy as *Sarar*, and this has led to argument between those who prefer the Isère (*Isara*) and those who favour the Aygues (or Eygues—ancient name uncertain). Simple haplography, however, would explain the conversion of *Isarar* to *Sarar* (the preceding word in Livy is *ibi*) and the loss of an iota in the text of Polybius is not difficult to accept. Secondly, while Polybius does not define the nationality of the two brothers, Livy specifically states that they were *Allobroges*. Thirdly, while both authors say that the march took four days, the figures given by Polybius indicate a distance of some 600 stades.[20] All these factors point to the Isère, and this agrees well with the rest of Polybius' account, in which Hannibal is further involved with the *Allobroges* while marching up 'the river' (probably the Isère) to cross an Alpine pass into the Po valley.

Livy's account, however, is somewhat different.[21] Having left 'the Island', near which the *Allobroges* dwelt (*incolunt prope Allobroges*), Hannibal 'turned to the left, to the *Tricastini*, and then passed through the outer border of the *Vocontii* to the *Tricorii*, by a route that was nowhere any trouble (*haud usquam impedita via*) until he came to the Durance (*Druentia*)'. This he describes as a violent and difficult river, but when Hannibal left it it was mostly by a level route (*campestri maxime itinere*) that he came to the Alps and was astonished by the near view of the lofty mountains. This alternative version, which is largely repeated by Silius Italicus and Ammianus,[22] has been used by some to justify an equation of 'the Island' with the confluence of the Aygues with the Rhône, but even this, while it would explain the turn to the left towards the *Tricastini*, does not make the route very easy to understand. A passage along the Drôme, while it would justify the expression *per extremam oram Vocontiorum agri*, would involve a crossing of the ridge between the basins of the Drôme and the Durance (by the Col de Cremone, suggests de Beer, but that is at 1,318m)[23] and this does not accord very well with the description of the *via* as *haud usquam impedita*; and it would leave the *Tricorii* out of the picture.

In fact, as Livy himself makes clear,[24] dispute over which precise route Hannibal took was already raging in his time, and a firm conclusion is unlikely ever to be reached. Polybius deliberately omits names that seemed irrelevant to him, but he had carried out some research in person and it may be that Livy (or perhaps Coelius Antipater before him) took those of the various tribes from a generalised (and perhaps inaccurate) map and inserted them in an attempt to clarify what he thought to be Hannibal's route.[25] If the names are to be accepted, however, the best explanation is surely that Livy has simply got the turn to the left out of order and that it should be placed not after 'the Island' but immediately after the crossing of the Rhône. This would indeed have led Hannibal along the (western) border of the *Vocontii* and through the territory of the *Tricastini* to the confluence of the Isère with the Rhône (that is, to 'the Island'). If from there he followed the valley of the Isère (through Allobrogian territory) as far as Grenoble and then turned into that of the Drac (so touching the land of the *Tricorii*) and finally that of the Romanche (inhabited by the

Icorii, who were probably subordinate to the *Allobroges*), he could, by the Col du Lautaret, have reached the upper water of the Durance near Briançon and finally entered Italy by way of the Col de Montgenèvre; and this route is all the more acceptable because the *Boii* were evidently well-informed on the most suitable routes and the Romanche valley was later used for a Roman road. The subsequent march of Hasdrubal throws no light on the matter since, although Silius Italicus states that he occupied Hannibal's camp on the summit of the Alps, his own account is poetically confused; Livy does not specifically describe it, and the relevant passage of Polybius is lost.[26]

In the meantime, and throughout the Second Punic War, the Massaliotes acted as loyal allies of Rome, not only supplying vital information but also providing naval assistance when it was needed. Because of this, when the Romans took over part of Spain they surely did not feel it necessary to occupy any of the land that separated their new province from Italy but left control of the route to *Massalia*.[27] This could not, of course, ensure absolute security: in 189 BC the praetor L. Baebius was attacked by Ligurians when on his way to Spain and although he (but not his lictors) succeeded in reaching Marseille he died there three days later;[28] in 182, when there seemed to be a threat of an invasion of Italy by transalpine Gauls, both Romans and Massaliotes were troubled by Ligurian piracy and a *duumvir* with ten ships was appointed to patrol the coast as far as *Massalia*;[29] and in 173, though in unstated circumstances, another praetor, N. Fabius, died at Marseille.[30] Positive Roman intervention on land, however, does not seem to have been required until 154 BC, and although even this was a relatively minor affair it demands some detailed attention because it has a bearing on the political geography of part of our province.

Since Livy's books covering this period are lost, we have no more than a brief reference from him,[31] merely confirming the names Opimius, *Antipolis* and *Nicaea*, but by good luck (since the complete book has not survived) we have the particular passage of Polybius that deals with it.[32] In this year news arrived from the Massaliotes that they were hemmed in by the Ligurians and that the cities of *Antipolis* and *Nicaea* were under siege. Accordingly the Romans sent Flaminius, Popilius Laenas and L. Pupius as envoys who, accompanied by some Massaliotes, sailed to the land of the *Oxybii* and landed at the city *Aegitna* (or at 'a sea-coast city': the text has αἰγιαλόν, first emended to Αἰγίτναν by Ursinus in 1581). The Ligurians tried to prevent them from landing and, finding that Flaminius had already done so, they wounded him, killed two of his servants and drove the rest back into the sea. Flaminius was nursed back to health in *Massalia*, but when the Roman senate heard of all this they decided to send the consul Q. Opimius to make war on the *Oxybii* and *Deciates*. Polybius then continues as follows:

Having collected his forces at *Placentia* (Piacenza) and made a march through the Apennine mountains, Quintus came to the *Oxybii*. Having pitched camp beside the river *Apro* (παρὰ τὸν Ἄπρωνα ποταμόν), he waited for the enemy, having learnt that they had assembled and were eager to face the dangers of battle. And leading his army to *Aegitna* [Αἰγίτναν in the MS], in which the envoys had met treachery, he took the city, reduced it to slavery and sent the originators of the insult in chains to Rome. Having achieved this, he went to meet the enemy. The *Oxybii*, thinking that their sin against the envoys was inexpiable, showed astonishing spirit and, making a desperate attack before they were joined by the *Deciates*, collected about 4,000 men and threw them against their enemies. Quintus, seeing the rash attack of the barbarians, was astonished by their desperate courage, but considering that they had no good grounds for it he was very confident, as he had much experience and was by nature a very shrewd commander. So, leading out his army and exhorting them as was appropriate to the occasion, he moved slowly towards the enemy. Vigorously pressing home his attack, he rapidly overcame the men arrayed against him, killed many of them and drove the rest to headlong flight. The *Deciates* then appeared in force, as though to share their dangers with the *Oxybii*, but arriving after the battle they took in the fugitives and after a short time attacked the Romans with great spirit and determination; but when defeated in battle they at once surrendered themselves and their *polis* ['city' or 'state'?] to the Romans. Having become master of these peoples, Quintus handed over as much of their territory as he thought fit to the Massaliotes and compelled the Ligurians in future to give the Massaliotes hostages for certain periods. Then, having disarmed his opponents and distributed his forces to the *poleis*, he went into winter quarters there. This campaign had a rapid beginning and end.

In considering this account one point in particular needs to be borne in mind—something that distinguishes it from the same author's version of Hannibal's march. This campaign took place in his own lifetime, and not only was he in close touch with leading Romans, such as Scipio Aemilianus, but it is almost certain that he visited *Massalia*, on his way back from Spain, only four years after it.[33] It is, therefore, extremely unlikely that such a writer as Polybius, who boasts so frequently of his own historical accuracy, has got his facts wrong. Unfortunately, however, there are only two geographical elements in it that are beyond dispute: first, the reference to *Placentia* and the Apennines makes it clear that Opimius entered Gaul by the coastal route, not by an Alpine pass,[34] and second, the battle with the *Oxybii* obviously took place before that with the *Deciates*. The things that need to be established are the identity of the river *Apro*, the location of *Aegitna* and, above all, the territories of the two tribes.

Ursinus answered the first question by changing τὸν Ἄπρωνα to τὸν Οὐάρον, but although the Var is the most important river in the area (and so was favoured by Jullian),[35] it is difficult to see why Polybius should have named it wrongly or how such a gross textual corruption could have arisen in the excerpts. Accordingly a number of other suggestions have been made—to take them from east to west, the Gabre (a tributary of the Paillon), the Cagne, the Loup, the Siagne and the Reyran. Apart from that of the Gabre (which was based on an unsubstantiated etymological link), these choices depended mainly on the relationship of the river to the site suggested for *Aegitna*, which has also been a matter for speculation: to take them in similar order, the places put forward have been Cagnes, Villeneuve-Loubet, Biot, Golfe-Juan, Cannes, la Napoule, Théoule, Agay and Fréjus. Of these the last, although it (along with the river Reyran) was favoured by Benoit, can safely be dismissed on two grounds: extensive excavation at Fréjus has failed to produce evidence for its occupation in this period, and if *Forum Iulii* had really been founded on the site of *Aegitna* this would surely have been mentioned by Strabo or Pliny. Agay is also unsupported because, as mentioned above (p 13), its later name was *Agathonis Portus* and despite the Greek manipulation of some Ligurian names this could hardly have been derived from *Aegitna* (and that would have been the only reason for the identification). Of the rest, those most worthy of consideration are Cagnes (with the river of the same name) and Théoule (with the river Siagne), and it is the arguments of Dugand[36] in favour of the former and of Barruol[37] for the latter that best expose the underlying problems.

These problems arise from references to this part of the coast in later authors, but only three indisputable facts can be derived from them: first, that the *Oxybii* and the *Deciates* were both Ligurian tribes, second, that they both occupied coastal territory, and third, that *Antipolis* lay in the land of the *Deciates*.[38] This last fact is important because it leads to the conclusion that the land of the *Deciates* was what became in Roman times the territory of *Antipolis* (and, later still, that of the medieval diocese of Antibes), but it does not solve the question of whether the *Oxybii* (and *Aegitna*) lay to the east of them or to the west.

A first reading of Polybius certainly suggests an easterly location, but we must also consider the evidence that has been used to support a westerly one. In describing this part of Gaul, Pliny writes as follows: *In ora autem Athenopolis Massiliensium, Forum Iulii octavanorum colonia quae Pacensis appellatur et Classica, amnis nomine Argenteus, regio Oxubiorum Ligaunorumque, super quos Suebri, Quariates, Adunicates, et in ora oppidum Latinum Antipolis, regio Deciatium, amnis Varus ex Alpium monte Caenia* [or *Cema*] *profusus*, and this does at first sight seem to confirm a westerly position, but it should be noted that he puts the river Argens after Fréjus, although it flows out just west of it. Further, when looking back to this area in his section on Italy he writes: *Ligurum celeberrimi ultra Alpes Sallui, Deciates, Oxubi*,[39] which can only be interpreted in the same way if it is assumed that he is here referring to the *Sallui* as a confederation that includes the other two tribes; and this, though it would be acceptable in another context, is both stylistically and historically improbable here. Beyond this, in Mela's statement that

Nicaea tangit Alpes, tangit oppidum Deciatium, tangit Antipolis,[40] which has also been used to support the argument, it is by no means impossible that *oppidum Deciatium* represents not a separate place between Nice and Antibes but simply a definition of *Antipolis* itself. The only other evidence that might be relevant is the confused account of this coast in the Ravenna Cosmography, but this too seems simply to misdefine *Antipolis* as a *colonia* of the *Deciates*.[41]

While the siting of the *Oxybii* in the hilly country of the Massif d'Esterel (which includes half a dozen hill-forts) would simplify the tribal map, it is surely likely that *Nicaea*, like *Antipolis*, claimed suzerainty over a Ligurian tribe and the disappearance of such a link could be attributed to their different attitudes at the time of Caesar's siege of *Massalia* (see p 68 below). On the whole, then, it seems best to take Polybius's account at its face value and to suppose that the territory of the *Oxybii*, which Opimius entered first, lay to the east rather than to the west of that of the *Deciates*—but at the same time to support the statement of Walbank: 'The information available does not, however, seem adequate to give certainty to any proposed identification of the places mentioned.'[43]

As may be seen from the last few sentences of the account, the Romans still did not feel it necessary to establish a permanent base in Gaul, and it was their Massaliote allies that benefited from the campaign. It is, however, highly probable that another step was taken that is not mentioned by Polybius and may have been of some value to Rome as well as her allies. In the *De Republica* Cicero mentioned a ban on the cultivation of vines and olives being imposed on transalpine peoples,[44] and since the historical setting of this work is 129 BC—earlier, that is, than the establishment of the *Provincia*—this, as Tenney Frank and others have suggested, is the most likely context for it.[45] From Cicero's implied condemnation of it, it appears to have gone out of use by the time he was writing (c 52 BC), but in any case it must surely have applied only to these two tribes.

One other curious fact may be noted. According to Cassiodorus Senator[46] it was in 153 BC, the year after this campaign, that the date at which Roman magistrates assumed office was shifted from March to January. The reason given for the change is a sudden Celtiberian war in Spain, but it is not impossible that it was the experience of the campaign of 154 that led the Romans to realise the advantage of having generals available at the beginning rather than the middle of the campaigning season.

REFERENCES AND NOTES

1 Livy XXI,18,1,1 and 19,6–20,9. Livy's 'Q. Fabius' should almost certainly be replaced by M. Fabius (Buteo), *cos* 245 BC, as this accords well with his description of the ambassadors as *legatos maiores natu* and the name is given as Marcus in Cassius Dio fr. 55,10 and Zonaras 8,22.

2 For the most useful discussion, with references, see Walbank 1970, 333–4, 337, 374, 396 and 1979, 766.

3 Polybius III, 40–1, Livy, XXI, 26. Polybius states that the nearest mouth of the Rhône was called τὸ Μασσαλιωτικόν.

4 Polybius III, 45 and 49, Livy XXI, 29 and 32.

5 Both Polybius (III, 40) and Livy (XXI,33,4) make it clear that he went through the mountains, not along the coast, and no reasonable case can be made for any other pass.

6 Polybius III, 39, where the insertion by many editors of a reference to *Narbo* is without justification (see Walbank 1970, 387–8). The statement in III, 41, that he marched δεξιὸν ἔχων τὸ Σαρδόνιον πέλαγος does not necessarily imply a route along the seashore.

7 Livy XXI, 24.

8 For discussions see Walbank 1970, 382–7, Barruol 1969, 326–8.

9 Polybius II, 42–3, Livy XXI, 26, 6–27, 4 (in both cases followed by details of how the elephants were transported). This account was followed also by Cassius Dio, though Zonaras 8,23, in summarising him, curiously replaces Hanno by Mago.

10 But he was slightly wrong, since Strabo VII, 7,4 states that Polybius used not 8 but 8⅓ stades to make up the Roman mile.

11 The best summary remains the long note 4 attached to Jullian I, 1914, 464–5. To the theories there discussed must now be added that of G. de Beer in *Hannibal's March* (London, 1967), 50–1, where the argument for Fourques is based on a strange coastal route taking in Aigues-Mortes (see n 6, above) and, it would seem, on a misreading of the Vicarello Goblets (*CIL* XI, 3281–4, referred to by de Beer as 'the Gaditanian Vases'): all four of them put the river crossing at Beaucaire and two omit Arles altogether.

12 The fact that the figures given by Polybius III,39 for the journey from Ampurias to the Rhône agree (allowing for the length of the Polybian stade, on which see n 10, above) with those given in later Roman itineraries for Ampurias to Beaucaire is of no significance, since Hannibal had no Roman roads to follow: see Walbank 1970, 371.

13 Livy XXI, 26, 6–7. Variations in the MSS allow for an alternative translation of the last part, such as '. . . that their large area should win relief, a crowd of all of them pressing for this', but this does not affect the main issue here.

14 Strabo IV,1,12.

15 See, for example, P.G. Walsh, *Livy, his Historical Aims and Methods* Cambridge, 1961, 124–5.

16 *CIL* XII, 1028.

17 Jullian I 1908, 470–2.

18 Polybius III, 44, 5–13 (*Boii*), 49, 5–13; Livy XXI, 29, 6–7 (*Boii*), 31, 1–8.

19 Silenus, used by Polybius direct and by Livy via Coelius Antipater. See, for example, Walsh, *op cit*, chapter v, and F.W. Walbank, 'Some reflections on Hannibal's Pass', *JRS* XLVI (1956), 44.

20 Walbank 1970, 371, 387, on Polybius III, 39 and 47–8.

21 Livy XXI, 31 and 32, 6–9.

22 Silius Italicus, *Punica* III, 466–78, Ammianus XV,10–11. What survives of
   Cassius Dio is too slight to indicate his choice and Appian in VI (*Iberica*)
   13–14, and VII (*Hannibal*), 4, does not concern himself with the matter,
   while his IV (*Celtica*) is again too fragmentary to suggest anything.

23 De Beer's suggestion, however, (*op cit*, 66–8) that the Col de Cremone
   represents the *Cremonis iugum* of Coelius which is mentioned (and
   condemned) by Livy XXI,38,6–7, is worthy of some attention.

24 Livy, *ibid*. For fuller discussions see Walbank, *JRS* XLVI(1956), 37–45, and
   Barruol 1969, 326–9.

25 Since Cassius Dio LV, 8,4, tells us that the building that housed it had not
   been completed in 7 BC, Agrippa's Map was not yet on display when Livy
   was writing his third decade, but in view of his friendship with Augustus
   he may well have had access to its earlier drafts. In any case, this was not
   the first map to be made—*cf* Livy XLI,28,8, for the map of Sardinia set up in
   174 BC and Varro, *De Re Rustica* I,2,1, for the map of Italy in the temple of
   Tellus. No really high degree of accuracy could be expected of any of
   these.

26 Silius Italicus, *Punica* XV, 493–515. The *Bebryces* were evidently a Pyrenean
   tribe, probably on the Spanish side (Avienius, *Ora Maritima*, 485, Zonaras
   (summarising Dio), 8,21) and a link with *Illiberis* (Jullian I, 1914, 496, n 4)
   is not readily acceptable. Silius's *Arar* should, from its description, be the
   Saône, but although this chimes with Livy's mention of the *Arverni*
   (XXVII,39,6) it would be rash to accept such a northerly route; here again,
   the *Arverni* may be a later addition, based on their extensive federation in
   the time of Coelius Antipater, and the one relevant fragment of Polybius
   that survives (XI,1) tells us that Hasdrubal's passage was easier and swifter
   than Hannibal's.

27 See, for example, Polybius III,95,6–7, and Livy XXII,19,5, XXVI,19,13,
   XXXVII,36,1–3, and 54,21. The argument in Ebel 1976, 41–63, that Rome
   itself took control of Languedoc just after the Second Punic War is not at all
   convincing.

28 Livy XXXVII,57,1–4.

29 Livy XL,17,8 and 18,4–8.

30 Livy XLII,4,1.

31 Livy, *Periocha* XLVII.

32 Polybius XXXIII, 8–10, preserved in two Constantinian excerpts, the first in
   De Legationibus Gentium, the second in *De Legationibus Romanorum*; on these
   see J.M. Moore, *The Manuscript Tradition of Polybius*, Cambridge, 1965,
   127–67.

33 Walbank 1970, 4. Polybius re-entered Italy by way of the Alps (which
   accounts for some of his conviction regarding Hannibal's route), but he
   must surely have called at *Massalia* on his way from Spain.

34 An approach by sea, which has sometimes been suggested, would surely
   have been mentioned.

35 Jullian, I 1908, 521.

36 J.-E. Dugand, *De l'Aegitna de Polybe au Trophée de la Brague*, Nice, 1970
   (including a postscript in answer to Barruol).

37 Barruol 1969, 212–17, largely following the arguments of N. Lamboglia in

'Questioni di topografia . . .', *REL* x(1944), 45–58, but preferring Théoule to its near neighbour la Napoule (the 12th-cent. name of which, Epulia, could not, as he shows, be derived from *Neapolis*).

38 Ligurian, Strabo IV,1,10 (*Oxybii*), Pliny *HN* III,47 and Florus I,19 (both); coastal, Strabo, ibid., a small harbour called ὁ Ὀξύβιος λιμήν (which may refer to *Aegitna*) and location of the port of *Antipolis* in the land of the *Deciates*, Pliny *HN* III,35, Ptolemy II,10,5.

39 Pliny *HN* III,35.

40 Pliny *HN* III,47.

41 Mela II,5,76–97.

42 *Rav. Cos.* IV,28(243,11–13) and V,3(339,17–19): *Nicea Micalo colonia Diceorum Antipolis* (where 'Micalo' may represent no more than dittography in both directions). The listing by Stephanus of a πόλις Ἰταλίας called Δεκιήτον adds nothing, though the 'Italian' (or rather Italiote) description suggests that either Stephanus or his intermediate source has evidently modified Artemidorus, who is here quoted.

43 Walbank 1979, 549.

44 Cicero, *De Republica* 3,16: *Nos vero iustissimi homines, qui transalpinas gentis oleam et vitem serere non sinimus, quo pluris sint nostra oliveta nostraeque vineae; quod cum faciamus, prudenter facere dicimur, iuste non dicimur, ut intellegatis discrepare ab aequitate sapientiam.* There is no doubt that the Massaliotes benefited most, but the area involved was close enough to have supplied some products to Italy and the passage certainly implies a Roman advantage.

45 T. Frank, *Roman Imperialism* (1925), 280–1 and *An Economic Survey of Ancient Rome* I (1933), 172–4, Badian 1967, 19–20. Goudineau 1978, 686–7 suggests that the ban may have been imposed on Languedoc, but, as stated in n 27 above, we have rejected the idea that that area was already under Roman control.

46 T. Mommsen (ed), *Chronica Minora* II,130. I am grateful to Dr W. Williams for drawing my attention to this reference.

3
Towards the Formation of the Province 153–100 BC

For a generation after the victory of Opimius peace seems to have reigned in southern Gaul and we have no mention of any interference with Romans in transit. This was of considerable advantage to Rome since, besides fierce internal disputes, the period saw not only constant wars in Spain but also the final defeat of Carthage in the Third Punic War and the establishment of Roman control in Greece and Asia Minor. Further north, however, a potential threat was developing in the form of a rare concentration of Celtic power. Under their proud and wealthy king Luerius, the *Arverni* (centred on Auvergne) were extending their influence over a vast area which stretched, according to Strabo, to the Pyrenees and the Atlantic in the west, to the Rhine in the east, and to Narbonne and the boundaries of the lands of *Massalia* in the south.[1] While this account, probably based on Poseidonius, may include an element of exaggeration, the involvement of the *Arverni* with other tribes in the events that followed was not without significance; and the Massaliotes, with their trading relations, cannot have been unaware of its possible effects.

In 125 BC the *Salluvii* attacked *Massalia* and once again a Roman force under a consul was sent to her assistance. The consul chosen was M. Fulvius Flaccus, a strong supporter of the Gracchi, and, much to the satisfaction of the Optimates in the Senate, his duties removed him from Rome for the rest of his consulship. Appian[2] actually states that this was why he was sent, but it was surely not for internal political reasons that the campaign as such was mounted—nor, as Jullian suggested,[3] because the Gracchan party wanted land in which to establish colonies: rather, as in the case of Opimius, it was to support Rome's ally and above all to ensure safe passage to Spain, and it was probably expected to take no longer than the earlier expedition. The slender sources that survive give no details of the battles that Flaccus fought, but the record of his triumph (celebrated in 123 BC) shows that he defeated not only the *Salluvii* but also some other *Ligures* and the *Vocontii*.[4] These other *Ligures* were presumably part of the federation controlled by the *Salluvii* (p 16 above), but the mention of the *Vocontii* raises another question. To judge from the wording of Livy's account (though it unfortunately survives only in summary form)[5] it seems that Flaccus may have travelled not by the coast road but across the Alps (presumably by Mont-Genèvre and the Durance valley), and it may be that it was no more than a chance encounter, but it is also possible that it reflects an already existing alliance of the *Vocontii* with the *Salluvii*, or even the influence of the *Arverni*.

In any case the victories of Flaccus were not decisive and in the following year his place was taken by another consul, C. Sextius Calvinus. He too was involved with the *Vocontii* as well as the *Salluvii*[6] and he not only took the city (πόλις) of the latter[7], but also succeeded in forcing them to withdraw from the coast—to a distance of 12 stades where possible, but only eight in the more rugged areas—handing this strip over to the Massaliotes; and he established a Roman garrison (φρουρά) at Aix, thereafter to be known as *Aquae Sextiae*.[8]

The 'city' of the *Salluvii*, though no source names it, is usually identified with the hill-fort of Entremont. This is almost certainly correct, for it is by far the most likely site for the tribal capital, both because of its high degree of development and because of its proximity to Aix, but it was not the only place to be attacked, as is shown by finds[1] of Roman missiles not only there but also at Baou-Roux, at Roquepertuse and at la Courtine d'Ollioulles.[9] No such archaeological evidence has so far been forthcoming from the territory of the *Vocontii*, but whether or not the main war already extended further north it was shortly to do so. While the victories of Sextius (coupled perhaps with the 'philanthropy' shown towards Craton and his friends who, after capture, claimed to be pro-Roman)[10] do seem to have settled matters in the south, a domino effect developed when the leaders of the *Salluvii*, including their king Toutomotulos (or Teutomalius), fled to the *Allobroges*.[11] And it was at this stage that Rome became inextricably involved in transalpine Gaul.

A demand for the return of these fugitives having been refused, a further and larger force (including elephants) was sent, initially under the command of Cn. Domitius Ahenobarbus. A brief reference in Suetonius suggests that he may have been despatched during his consulship (122 BC), but other sources show that it was in the following year that he began his campaign.[12] Appian[13] tells us that while still in Salluvian territory he was met by an ambassador from Bituitus, the son of Luerius, who asked for pardon for the Salluvian leaders but evidently did not offer their return. Appian here refers to Bituitus as 'king of the *Allobroges*', and while this may be a simple error (perhaps a slip by his excerptor), it may also reflect the fact that the *Allobroges* had already come under the control and had accepted the suzerainty of the *Arverni*—something which helps to explain the confusion in our sources over which general conquered which tribe.[14] It may also help to explain why it is the *Allobroges* who are said by Livy to have attacked the *Aedui*, though the circumstances in which the latter first became *socii populi Romani* remain obscure.[15]

It is in any case clear that the *Arverni* and their allies were intent on preventing any northward movement by the Romans, for the first recorded battle took place at *Vindalium*. Strabo defined this place as being near the confluence of the river *Sulga* (Sorgue) with the Rhône[16] and this has enabled it to be identified with some certainty as Mourre-de-Sève, a hill-fort just 10 km north-east of Avignon, whose occupation has been shown to extend from the sixth century BC to just about this date.[17] Here the Romans soundly defeated the enemy, but this single victory (in which, according to Orosius, 20,000 *Allobroges* were killed and 3,000 taken prisoner)[18] was not enough, and the war was continued further north. In the meantime, while Domitius remained in Gaul as proconsul, the supreme command was taken over by a new consul, Q. Fabius Maximus. Since Fabius triumphed over the *Allobroges* (and so acquired the title of Allobrogicus), while Domitius triumphed over the *Arverni*,[19] it may be that Fabius was already present at the time of the battle of *Vindalium*; certainly both of them were in Gaul at the time of the second major battle.[20]

The precise date of this second battle (8 August 121 BC) is curiously preserved in Pliny's account of the illness of Fabius[21] and its site, though unnamed, is uniformly described by both Strabo and Florus as near the confluence of the *Isar* (Isère) and the Rhône[22]—which, despite the arguments of Jullian for a place lower downstream,[23] agrees well enough with Strabo's complementary description of it as 'where the Cevennes come near the river'. The fullest account of the battle is preserved in Orosius. Bituitus, he says, was scornful of the relatively small size of the Roman force (they were barely enough, he boasted, to feed his dogs), but his own army was so large (180,000 men) that one bridge over the river was not enough for them and he therefore built a second bridge of boats. When the Romans put them to flight, however, this collapsed and as a result some three quarters of the fugitives were slain or drowned.[24] Bituitus himself escaped, but Domitius, having lured him to what he said would be a parley, treacherously had him bound and sent to Rome. There the Senate, while it could not approve this shocking breach of *hospitium*, decided that it could not let him return to Gaul and so kept him in custody at Alba; according to Livy they also arranged for the capture of his son Congonnetiacus.[25]

Each of these two victories was commemorated by the erection of a stone tower on the site of the battle—neither of which, regrettably, has so far been found.[26] They also marked the firm establishment of Roman power in Gaul, as Caesar was to state when talking to Ariovistus some 63 years later.[27] Not unnaturally, in view of his antipathy to the family, he did not mention Domitius, but he claimed that it was Fabius's defeat of the *Arverni* that gave Rome the right to assume sovereignty over the whole country. Since he was here speaking of peoples who until his time had been left to their own devices he did not name the *Allobroges*, but he did, interestingly, couple the name of the *Ruteni* with that of the *Arverni*, presumably because they had contributed a force to the army of Bituitus, and this goes some way towards confirming Strabo's description of the Arvernian empire. Caesar's claim, however, does not necessarily imply that a formal province was established immediately after the war, and this is a question to which we shall return.

Jullian heads the next section of his work 'La ruine commence pour Marseille'[28], but both the literary and the archaeological evidence indicate that this is far from the truth. We have reviewed the earlier extension of Greek settlement along the coast in the previous chapter (pp 12–13) and this was now consolidated by the handing over of the continuous strip by Sextius Calvinus. Inland from *Massalia*, St-Blaise had been taken over by the Greeks about 400 BC and a Greek town was established at *Glanum* at some time in the second century; whether this was before or after the war is a little uncertain (its foundation may even have been a cause for the Salluvian attack), but it certainly flourished in the succeeding period. Further north still, Stephanus[29] defines both *Cabellio* (Cavaillon) and *Avennio* (Avignon) as Massaliote cities, and since he gives Artemidorus as his source for the former it is likely that it was at about this time that Greek control over these Cavaran towns was formally established—even though, as the absence of any mention of the *Cavares* in the records of the Roman victories suggests, friendly relations with them may already have existed.[30] We must also look forward to what was to happen later, to Marius' handing over of his canal to the Massaliotes,[31] to Plutarch's story that the corpses of the men slain at the battle of Aix fertilised Massaliote vineyards,[32] and to the fact that, later still, both Pompey and Caesar were to increase Massaliote resources.[33] All the indications are, therefore, that although they may have maintained a garrison at Aix the Romans were still content to leave control of an area east of the Rhône to the Massaliotes, whom they still regarded as useful and reliable allies.

This offers an adequate explanation for the south-éastern sector, but how the area to the north of it was initially controlled remains obscure. If the Vocontian federation really included the *Avantici*, *Sogiontii* and *Sebaginni*, something must surely have been done to protect the route down the Durance valley against a possible recrudescence of hostility, but there is neither literary nor archaeological evidence to explain what it was. Further north still, the territory of the *Allobroges* was not yet of great interest to Rome, and it may be that the imposition of a severe treaty after their capitulation was considered adequate, with their behaviour being watched over not only by the Fabii in Rome, who became their patrons, but also by the *Aedui*, who were now firmly established as *socii populi Romani*.

Domitius may have included some of these areas in his celebrated tour on an elephant,[34] but it was the region to the west of the Rhône that required more positive action. As we also noted in the previous chapter, while Greek trade had flourished in Languedoc, Greek settlement there is ill-attested and may have been confined to the one port at Agde, so that *Massalia* could not be relied on adequately to protect the route to Spain. While none of the western tribes, apart from the inland *Ruteni*, is mentioned in our sources for the war, it is likely enough that some at least had been in alliance with Bituitus, and while the *Helvii* lay far enough to the north to be dealt with by treaty alone, the lands of the *Volcae Arecomici* demanded sterner measures. So the immediate problem was solved by the construction of the *Via Domitia*. This, the first Roman road to be made in Gaul, ran from the Rhône, probably at *Ugernum* (Beaucaire) to the Col du Perthus in the Pyrenees, following approximately the line of the prehistoric route known as the *Via Heraclea*, and, as Polybius recorded,[35] it was at once equipped with milestones. Fortunately one of these milestones has been found, in the bed of the Rieu de Treilles,[36] and three aspects of it deserve notice. First, it stood to the south, not to the north of Narbonne, which confirms that the purpose of the road was indeed to establish a link with Spain and not merely with the *colonia* that was shortly to be founded; second, the 20 Roman miles that it records represent exactly its distance from Narbonne and not that from Narbonne's native predecessor, the hill-fort of Montlaurès (the *Naro* of Avienius)[37] which lies off the line of the road and some 4km (about 3½ Roman miles) too far to the north, and this shows that a Roman post of some kind preceded the *colonia*; and third, it bears the name of Domitius and was evidently erected while he was still in control.

The first of these points confirms the fact that this was not simply a commercial road, linking established towns, but a *limes* in the traditional sense and as such needed to be protected by military posts. The location of such posts is not stated in any of our literary sources nor has it yet been established by archaeology, but several suggestions have been made.[38] The first is that indicated by the second point, Narbonne itself, and the second is Montbazin, which also lies on the road and was given the name of *Forum Domitii*. Both of these lie in the west, but the eastern half of the road would also have needed protection and here the most likely sites seem to be *Ugernum* (Beaucaire), because that was apparently the road's starting point, and secondly *Nemausus* (Nîmes) not only because of its native importance but also because it is here that the road changes direction, with the intersection of the alignments falling not within the later city (whose street plan is not related to them), but precisely on the site of the later *Porta Augusta*. A final confirmation of the existence of such military posts is provided by the fact that a military garrison certainly was established further inland, in the lands of the *Volcae Tectosages*, at *Tolosa* (Toulouse).[39] As Badian has pointed out,[40] this helps towards a solution of the problem of how long Domitius actually remained in Gaul: while the construction of the road, with its military posts and milestones, must have taken some time, so that the placing of his triumph in 120 BC[41] may still be a year too early, the appearance of his name on the milestone does not necessarily mean that he was still in command when the *colonia* of *Narbo Martius* was founded. It also, of course, allows us to deduct a year or two from the supposed life of Polybius.[42]

The date of the foundation of the *colonia* itself is firmly stated only by Velleius Paterculus, who places it in the consulship of Porcius and Marcius, that is, in 118 BC.[43] It has been argued that this should be moved onward a few years on both numismatic and historical grounds—the former involving the issue of coins that commemorated the foundation and the latter derived from Cicero's reference to L. Licinius Crassus, one of the founders of the *colonia*.[44] Both these arguments, however, have been well contested[45] and there seem now to be no sound grounds for doubting Velleius. In any case, while the Senate's opposition to the project is of interest to us, the precise date is of more importance to central Roman politics than to our study, since it certainly lies before the next major local event, the invasion by the *Cimbri* and *Teutones*. More significant to us is the possibility, put forward by Lamboglia,[46] that by sequestering a part of the territory of the *Volcae Tectosages*, and perhaps reestablishing the independence from them of the *Elisyces*, the foundation provided some new grounds for hostility when the invasion took place.

Owing to the thinness of our sources, the earlier stages of this invasion are a little obscure, but it seems that it was around 120 BC that large numbers of *Cimbri* and *Teutones* (of whom the *Ambrones* may have been a sub-tribe) had left their homeland of Jutland. The fact that their women and children accompanied them and their repeated requests for land show that this was a real migration, not merely a military expedition, and Strabo was probably wrong to follow Poseidonius in discounting the widely held belief that it was mainly due to the inundation of part of their territory by the sea.[47] Having failed to overcome the *Boii* and *Scordisci*, by 113 they had reached the kingdom of Noricum, which was already in alliance with Rome,[48] and accordingly the Romans, fearing that they would next invade Italy, sent an army under the consul Cn. Papirius Carbo. A battle was fought near *Noreia*,[49] in which the Roman force was thoroughly defeated (though it was saved from utter annihilation by the onset of a thunderstorm); but it was only the ambition of Carbo that had led to its taking place at all, for the Germans had offered to withdraw and he had misled their ambassadors.[50]

The Germans then moved west to the land of the *Helvetii*, where they were joined by a *pagus* of that tribe, the *Tigurini*,[51] and from there into Gaul proper. Their precise route thereafter, whether or not they split into groups, is uncertain, but while the Tayac coin-hoard can no longer safely be associated with them[52] they certainly encountered, either now or later, some *Belgae* (the only people, according to Caesar, who managed to prevent an incursion into their territory)[53] and some *Arverni* (who, again according to Caesar, were driven to cannibalism when defending a hill-fort).[54] Florus suggests that in 109 they did enter Italy and that it was from there that they sent envoys *in castra Silani, inde ad senatum*, to ask for land in exchange for employment by the Romans,[55] but this is improbable. While they may well have appealed to Silanus while he was still consul (in 109), the battle that followed the refusal of their request evidently took place in Gaul and it was almost certainly in 108, when he was proconsul, that he established his *castra*—and was thoroughly defeated; and it was for his mistreatment of a transalpine Gaulish noble, Aegritomarus, that he was subsequently prosecuted by the tribune Cn. Domitius.[56]

Further disasters followed. Encouraged by the invaders, the *Volcae Tectosages* broke their treaty with Rome and put the garrison of *Tolosa* in chains,[57] and in 107 BC a further Roman army was sent out under the consul L. Cassius Longinus. According to Orosius[58] he pursued the *Tigurini* 'as far as the Ocean', but was then ambushed and killed, along with his legate, the former consul L. Calpurnius Piso. Another legate, C. Popilius Laenas, saved the lives of the survivors by handing over hostages and half the army's property to the *Tigurini*—an offence for which he was exiled on his return to Rome and an event of which the leader of the tribe, Divico, was to remind Caesar some 49 years later.[59] The site of this battle is uncertain: the text of Livy puts it *in finibus Allobrogum*, but in view of the circumstances surrounding it Mommsen's amendment to *in finibus Nitiobrigum* is generally accepted and this would put it not far from *Aginnum* (Agen), their later capital.[60]

In the following year another consul, Q. Servilius Caepio, was sent to retake *Tolosa*. Having already won a triumph in Lusitania, he was a more experienced general, but he was also unduly proud and covetous. Having retaken the town, he removed much of the treasure stored in its pools and sacred places and when it was mysteriously lost in transit, near *Massalia*, it was believed that he had been responsible for the killing of the men in charge of it.[61] He remained in Gaul, however, for his procunsular year, at first in the western area, and it was then that the greatest catastrophe of all occurred. His successor as supreme commander was the new consul, Cn. Mallius Maximus, who was sent to Gaul (evidently to the eastern area) because of a new threat from the *Cimbri*, and it was in the first action of part of his army that his legate M. Aurelius Scaurus (who had been suffect consul in 108) was captured and, when he tried to persuade the *Cimbri* not to try to cross the Alps, was killed by Boiorix.[62] Mallius then sent for Caepio, who at first refused to join him, saying that each should look after his own section, but then, fearing that Mallius might gain the greater glory, moved towards him. He did not, however, join him, but pitched camp nearer to the *Cimbri* and was incensed—almost to the point of killing their envoys—when he found that it was with Mallius and not with him that they were attempting to negotiate. His troops insisted that he should work out a plan with Mallius, but this had little effect and they were still bitterly divided when the *Cimbri* finally attacked. In the battle, which took place near *Arausio* (Orange), though both generals survived it was said that 80,000 Roman troops and 40,000 camp-followers were slain[63]—the greatest Roman defeat since *Cannae*, so that its date (6 October) became a black day in the Roman calendar.[64]

Caepio was later severely punished for his misbehaviour, but that did nothing to reduce Roman anxiety, and relief came from two remarkable circumstances. For one thing, C. Marius had just triumphed over Jugurtha and, already elected to his second consulship, was available for Gaul from the beginning of 104 BC. More surprisingly, the Germans did not follow up their success by invading Italy. Instead, they split into groups, and while the *Teutones* and *Ambrones* (and perhaps the *Tigurini*) seem to have stayed in Gaul, the *Cimbri* plundered their way into Spain (where, after doing much damage, they were defeated by the *Celtiberi*)[65] and it was not until two years later that the real threat reasserted itself. Marius was, therefore, allowed ample time in which to improve the training of his men and to make the necessary preparations.

In all of this he was outstandingly successful, both making long-standing improvements in the Roman army as a whole and completely restoring morale. This was done by constantly exercising his troops, but these exercises were not entirely training manoeuvres, since Plutarch tells us that it was in 104 BC that Sulla, then a legate of Marius, captured Copillus, a chieftain of the *Tectosages*.[66] This shows that even in the absence of the German invaders the local tribes were not fully pacified, but it was still possible for Marius to visit Rome to ensure his third election as consul, leaving M'. Aquilius in charge in Gaul. When, in his fourth consulate (102 BC), it finally became clear that the invaders were about to attempt an invasion of Italy, he built a fortified camp beside the Rhône (near its confluence with the Isère according to Orosius[67]) and it was the difficulty of stocking this that led to the construction of the *Fossae Marianae*, a canal that facilitated the passage of ships up the river. In the event the invaders split into two groups, the *Cimbri* to cross the eastern Alps and enter Italy by way of Noricum, the *Teutones* and *Ambrones* to approach it from the west,[68] and it was presumably at this stage that Sertorius boldly disguised himself as a Gaul and obtained valuable information for Marius about their intentions.[69]

Marius played his hand very cautiously. Having refused the first challenge to a battle—allegedly on the advice of the Syrian prophetess Martha—he simply defended his camp and, when the enemy scornfully marched past it (which took six days, according to Plutarch's source), he merely followed them, building a series of camps on the way. It was not until they were near Aix that he was prepared to fight, and even here the first encounter occurred almost by chance. He had pitched his camp on a strong but waterless site and when his camp-followers went down to a stream (probably the ruisseau Torse, which runs east of Aix down to the Arc and is fed by hot springs) they found some of the enemy bathing in the warm waters. A mêlée developed, in which the *Ambrones* attacked and were met first by Ligurian auxiliaries and then by Roman legionaries, who thoroughly defeated them—and their remarkably savage women. The Romans then withdrew and spent the night on the alert, but it was not until the next day that the final battle took place. Having sent Cl. Marcellus with 3,000 men (including some camp-followers, to give the impression of a large force)[70] to lie in ambush in the wooded hills, Marius led his main army out and this provoked an immediate response from the *Teutones* and those *Ambrones* that had survived, who foolishly launched an uphill attack. The result was an overwhelming Roman victory, in which over 100,000 of the enemy were slain, either then or when fleeing.[71] Those who fled included Teutobudus, a leader of the *Teutones*, but whether he was then killed or taken with other Teutonic leaders to Italy is disputed; some were eventually captured in the Alps by the *Sequani* and by them handed over to the Romans.[72]

As a result of this spectacular victory[73] Roman security was restored and Marius, now elected to his fifth consulship, went back to Italy to join Q. Lutatius Catulus in defeating the *Cimbri* at *Campi Raudi*. Who was now left in charge of transalpine Gaul is not stated in our sources, but, as will be seen from the next chapter, it is from about this time that normal provincial government becomes evident. It is, therefore, at this stage that we must turn to the vexed question of when our area was converted into a normal Roman province. The traditional view, still widely held, is that the province was established by Domitius when he remained in Gaul after the defeat of the *Arverni* and *Allobroges*—that is, about 120 BC. This has, however, been strongly challenged by Badian,[74] and his objections to it are certainly worthy of consideration. As a preliminary to this, we must first recall that the word *provincia*, which has in fact appeared in a few of the sources already cited, does not necessarily imply a fully-organised 'province' in the imperial Roman and modern sense, but can also mean simply a sphere of action that might be allotted to a consul (for example, the defeat of a specific enemy); and in any case the use of the word in our sources could always imply mere anachronism.

Badian's four objections may be summarised as follows. First, the formation of a new province elsewhere involved the framing of a *lex provinciae*, which was formulated by the commander on the spot with the advice of a commission of ten senators; but none of our sources, not even Cicero, ever mentions a *lex Domitia*. Second, no governor is named as such before the invasion of the *Cimbri* and *Teutones* and all the generals who tried to oppose them were either consuls or proconsuls. Third, if it had not already been a province, that might well have fuelled the known opposition of Roman nobles to the foundation of the *colonia* of *Narbo Martius*. And fourth, the building of the *Via Domitia* offers no support to the idea of a province, since its function was simply to improve communications with Spain. Badian therefore suggests that it was only after the defeat of the Germans that full provincial organisation became inevitable.

The importance of these four arguments varies considerably. With regard to the first, there is indeed no reference to a *lex Domitia*, but neither is there to any other appropriate *lex provinciae*, so this leaves the question hanging in the air. The third point is attractive, but simple political reasons seem adequate to explain opposition to the founding of the *colonia*. It is the second point that most merits discussion and we may in fact link this with the fourth. As may be seen, we have already accepted the Spanish importance of the *Via Domitia*, but in doing so we suggested that it was reliance on the ability of *Massalia* (already strengthened by Sextius Calvinus) to exercise adequate control over the eastern part of our area that led Domitius to concentrate on the west. As to the commanders who opposed the Germans, the use of consuls was surely due to the fact that they were seen as a threat not merely to Gaul but to Rome itself, but the proconsuls raise another matter. We do not know precisely where Silanus was defeated (Sallust does appear to allot him a *provincia*[75]) but, as we have argued, all the evidence suggests that Caepio, in his proconsular year, was operating in the west until he reluctantly obeyed the order of Mallius to move to the Rhône. We therefore have two proconsuls, possibly three, concentrating on the western area, where also the *colonia* was founded, and this suggests at least a possibility that a province of a smaller size had originally been created and that it was only expanded eastward after the experience of Marius. There is nothing anomalous about a gap between it and Italy, since this had long been the case with Spain and an unconquered area in the Alps survived until the time of Augustus; and it might even help to explain the absence of references to a normal *lex provinciae*, since the one that later prevailed would have had to include substantial amendments to the original law. On the other hand, if the western section required administration, this might sometimes, as Ebel suggests,[76] have been made the responsibility of the governor of *Hispania Citerior*—a combination that, as we shall see, was repeated later when the whole province had certainly come into being.

In summary, then, it is impossible to reach a definite conclusion as to the specific date at which our province was formed, and we must now move forward to the first century BC and consider both its political organisation and its economic significance for Rome.

REFERENCES AND NOTES

1 Strabo IV,2,3, probably based on Poseidonius, gives the king's name as *Luerius* (Λουέριος), while Athenaeus IV,37, specifically based on Poseidonius, gives it as *Luernius* (Λουερνίου, gen.); but since Strabo probably had more reliable manuscripts of Poseidonius than Athenaeus the interesting suggest of J. Whatmough: *The Dialects of Ancient Gaul*, Princeton, 1970, 377(151), that it might merely be a corruption of *Arvernus* (Ἀρουερνος) seems unlikely.

2 Appian, *Civil Wars*, 1,34. On other views relating to his appointment see Badian 1958, 178.

3 Julian III, 1909, 9.

4 Degrassi, 105 (*de Liguribus Vocontieis Salluveisque*, the order of words showing that *Liguribus* is not simply adjectival).

5 Livy, *Periocha* LX, *M. Fulvius Flaccus primus transalpinos Ligures domuit bello*; *cf* Florus I, 37 (III,2), *Prima trans Alpes arma nostra sensere Saluvii*. But the campaign of Opimius could be forgotten (or misunderstood geographically), as in Ammianus XV,12,5: *Hae regiones (sc Galliae), praecipueque confines Italicis, paulatim levi sudore sub imperium venere Romanum, primo temptatae per Fulvium, deinde proeliis parvis quassatae per Sextium, ad ultimum per Fabium Maximum domitae.* But for the danger involved in basing much on the words of the *Periochae* see n 8.

6 Degrassi, 106.

7 Diodorus Siculus XXXIV,23.

8 Strabo IV,1,5, and IV,6,3; Livy, *Periocha* LXI, states that *Sextius . . . coloniam Aquas Sextias condidit*, but this is presumably an error of his summariser. The suggestion of Ebel 1976,69, that the base was not *intended* to be permanent is probably correct, and it may well have been expected to last little longer than the winter quarters of Opimius, but, contrary to his statement, its name is mentioned in all the accounts of Marius's battle with the *Ambrones* and there is no evidence for its abandonment.

9 For Entremont, F. Benoit, 'Entremont, capitale celto-ligure de la Provence', *Rhodania* 1947, 58–60 and *Entremont*, Aix, 1957 (finds in Aix Museum); Baou-Roux, J-P. Tennevin, *Gallia* XXIII (1964), 576–7; Roquepertuse (a tête-coupée shrine, not a hill-fort), H. de Gérin-Richard: *Le sanctuaire préromain de Roquepertuse à Velaux*, Marseille, 1927, 40–1 (finds in Musée Borély); La Courtine d'Ollioulles. J. Layet: *Le livre de la Courtine*, Toulon, 1950, II,3 (finds in Toulon Museum). Probably some of these attacks had already been carried out by Flaccus and Entremont may have had to be attacked twice (Benoit, *op cit*); les Baux and Pierredon may also have suffered.

10 Diodorus Siculus XXXIV, 23.

11 Livy, *Periocha* LXI, Appian, *Celtica*, 12. The king's name appears only in Livy and editors differ in the form they prefer: while Rossbach (Teubner, 1910, followed by Schlesinger, Loeb, 1959) takes Toutomotulos as the best reading, Teutomalius (which first appears in the editio princeps of 1469) is favoured by many Celticists.

12 Suetonius, *Nero* 2: *At in consulatu Allobrogibus Arvernisque superatis elephanto per provinciam vectus est*; the tour of the *provincia* was, however, certainly made after his consulship. Livy, *Periocha* LXI: *Cn. Domitius pro cons. adversus*

Allobrogas ad oppidum Vindalium feliciter pugnavit. Orosius v,13,2 (with the date wrong): *Cnaeus quoque Domitius proconsule Allobrogas iuxta oppidum Vindalium gravissimo bello vicit, maxime cum elephantorum nova forma equi hostium hostesque conterriti diffugissent.* Florus I, 37(III,2): *Maximus barbaris terror elephanti fuere.* Strabo IV,2,3.

13 Appian, *Celtica* 12.

14 Even the *Fasti* (Degrassi, 106), in their record of the two triumphs, fuse the two tribes—*Fabius de Allobrogibus at rege Arvernorum Betulto* (sic) and Domitius *de Galleis Arverneis.*

15 Livy, *Periocha* LXI: *Allobrogas . . . quibus bellum inferendi causa fuit quod Toutomotulum Salluviorum regem recepissent et omni ope iuvissent quodque Aeduorum agros [sociorum] populi Romani vastassent*; a word has clearly been omitted before *populi Romani*, and *sociorum* was added in the editio princeps of 1469, while Boendermaker's alternative suggestion of *amicorum* hardly clarifies matters. Florus I,37(III,2) also mentions *Haeduorum querellae* in this context, though he does not define their relationship, and it may be that it was precisely their complaints that led to the alliance.

16 Strabo IV,2,3, though Strabo uniquely lists this battle after the one near the *Arar*; contrast Livy and Orosius, *locc citt.* Florus, *loc cit*, curiously calls the river itself *Vindelicus.*

17 P. de Brun and S. Gagnière, 'La station halstattienne de Mourre-de-Sève', BSPF, 1934, 68ff; *Gallia* XVIII(1960), 263–5; Benoit 1965, 177; Barruol 1969, 242. For earlier suggestions, now weakened by this archaeological evidence, see Jullian III, 1909, 16 n2.

18 Orosius v,13,2.

19 See note 14, above and *cf* Velleius Paterculus II,10,2 (only omitting Bituitus).

20 Valerius Maximus VIII,6,3, seems to imply that Domitius also took part in this battle, but against this see Jullian III,18, n4.

21 Pliny, HN, VII,166; *Q. Fabius Maximus consul apud flumen Isaram proelio commisso adversus Allobrogum Arvernorumque gentes A.D. vi Id. Augustas, CXXX perduellium caesis, febri quartana liberatus est in acie*; according to Appian, *Celtica*, 1,2, he had to be carried in a litter or lean on others while conducting the battle.

22 Strabo IV,2,3; Florus I,37(III,2); Orosius v,14.

23 Jullian, III,1909,17 n4 and 20 n3. As we have already observed (p28), rivers like the Rhône do not remain unchanged and where bridges (especially boat-bridges) might have been built is purely a matter for speculation.

24 Orosius v,14, giving the casualties as 180,000; Livy puts them at 120,000, Pliny at 130,000 and Appian at 120,000 (as against only 15 Romans!)

25 For the disgraceful behaviour of Domitius, Valerius Maximus VIII,6,3; Livy, *Periocha* LXI implies that Bituitus went to Rome voluntarily *ad satisfaciendum senatui*, but this may be due to the summarising of his text. *Pace* Schlesinger (Loeb Livy Vol. XIV, p 73 n5), there is no sound evidence for identifying Livy's Congonnetiacus with the Contoniatus described by Diodorus Siculus XXXIV 36 as φίλος καὶ σύμμαχος Ῥωμαίων.

26 Florus I,37(III,2), claiming that they were the first such trophies to be erected. Jullian's suggestion (III,20, n3) that they might have been at la Sarrasinière and Désaignes is without foundation, not only because of their location (seen by him as on the boundaries of conquered tribes) but also

because of their date: The former (well-preserved) is a funerary monument of much later date (*FOR* xv, no123, with illustrations), and the latter (*ibid* no105) is a supposed temple.

27 Caesar, *BG* I,45.

28 Julian III,33 ff.

29 Stephanus of Byzantium *svv*. Artemidorus wrote at the very end of the 2nd cent.

30 For various discussions of this see Barruol 1969, 233–4, Ebel 1976, 32–3 and Clavel-Lévêque 1977, 85–6. The reference in Aristodemus, *Erotica* 8 (citing Parthenios of Nicaea) to a Gaul called Cavaras adds little.

31 Strabo IV,1,8.

32 Plutarch, *Marius* 21,3.

33 Caesar, *BC* I,35.

34 Suetonius, *Nero* 2.

35 Polybius III,39. For a discussion of the traditional association of Heracles with this area and the prehistoric trackway see Benoit 1965,93–9. The stretches of the Roman road are too straight to be following precisely the line of the trackway and the suggestion of Ebel 1976, 62–3, that a Roman road, with milestones, had already been made before the activity of Domitius is fundamentally improbable.

36 Inscribed CN DOMITIVS CN F/AHENOBARBVS/IMPERATOR/XX. *Gallia* VII,ii (1951), 205–31, *FOR* XII (Aude) (1959), p 233 and pl VIII, König 1970, no256. The Rieu forms the boundary between the communes of Lapalme and Caves-de-Treilles and the stone was found approx. 20m above the Pont-de-Treilles, so very near the line of the Roman road.

37 Avienius, *Ora Maritima* 587, describing it as a capital of the *regnum* of the *Elisyces*: for further discussion see below, p 130.

38 Badian 1958, 244, and 1966, 903–04; he is wrong, however, to describe Narbonne as an 'important (probably walled) Celtic centre' and Nîmes as already 'a walled Celtic town', and for the reasons here indicated Beaucaire seems more likely than his suggestion of Avignon (which did include a hill-fort on the Rocher des Doms).

39 Cassius Dio XXVII, fr 90.

40 Badian, *locc citt* (n38) and 1958, 313—as against Duval 1949.

41 As by Degrassi, 106, and Broughton I,524.

42 Walbank 1970, 1 and 373, accepting the mention of milestones as a late addition by Polybius himself.

43 Velleius Paterculus I,14,5 (Loeb I,15,5), evidently the source for the similar statement of Eutropius IV,10; the repetition of this statement in Velleius II,8,1 (Loeb II,7,8) is clearly a later interpolation.

44 H.B. Mattingly, 'The Foundation of Narbo Martius' in M. Renard (ed): *Hommages à Albert Grenier* (*Latomus* LVIII), Brussels, 1962, 1159–71, and a subsequent paper, 'The Numismatic Evidence and the Founding of Narbo Martius', *RAN* v (1972),1–19; Cicero, *Brutus* 43, 159–61.

45 M.H. Crawford, first in *Roman Republican Coin Hoards* (R. Numismatic Soc. Special Pubn No. 4), London, 1969,5, then more fully in *Roman Republican Coinage*, Cambridge, 1974,71–3; Barbara Levick, 'Cicero, *Brutus* 43,159ff, and the Foundation of Narbo Martius', *Classical Quarterly* LXV (N.S. XXI) (1971), 170–9; for a full discussion, *v* Gayraud 1981, 120–7.

46 N. Lamboglia in 'Le *regnum* des Liguri Elisyci' in *Narbonne: archéologie et*

histoire: *Montlaurès et les origines de Narbonne*, CNRS, Montpellier, 1973,67–8; other aspects of this conference report and the early stages of the *colonia* will be discussed below (pp 130–2).

47 Strabo VII,2,1–3; Florus 1,37(III,3) repeats the inundation theory. Plutarch (*Marius* 11,2), who puts the number of armed men at 300,000, says specifically that they were looking for land in which to settle. The origin of the *Ambrones* is uncertain, as Plutarch, *Marius* 19,4, states that the Ligurians claimed that they were descended from them.

48 See G. Alföldy, *Noricum*, London, 1974, chap 3 for the Norican background to this and pp 47–51 for the identification of *Noreia* as the Magdalensberg.

49 Strabo V,1,8 (the only source that actually sites the battle).

50 Appian, *Celtica*, 13 (though calling them simply *Teutones*, while Livy, *Periocha* LXIII and other sources call them *Cimbri*. For convenience we shall hereafter refer to the combined force as 'Germans').

51 Or two parts—according to Strabo VII,2,2, and IV,1,8, not only the *Tigurini* but also the *Tugeni*, both excited by the wealth that the Germans had acquired.

52 A large hoard found in 1893 some 45km NE of Bordeaux, which included many coins from E and NE Gaul. Robert Forrer and others attributed this remarkable collection to the *Cimbri* and *Teutones*, but for an authoritative discussion, with references, see J.-B. Colbert de Beaulieu, *Traité de numismatique celtique* I, Paris, 1973, 269–70 (n502); as a result of this Forrer's map of the invaders' route (reproduced on p 42 of Hatt, 1966) is highly questionable.

53 Caesar, *BG* II,4, Strabo IV,4,3.

54 Caesar, *BG* VII,77 (the speech of Critognatus during the siege of *Alesia*).

55 Florus 1,37 (III,3).

56 Livy, *Periocha* LXV, Velleius Paterculus II, 12,2, Asconius, *In Corneliam* 60 and 71; only Eutropius, IV, 27, specifically sites the battle in Gaul—and he, again uniquely, says that Silvanus won it! On Aegritomarus, Cicero, *Div. in Caecilium* 20 (67), *In Verrem* II,ii,47 (118). Though Livy too indicated that Silanus was still consul when defeated, so long a gap before the despatch of Longinus (certainly in 107) is surely unacceptable.

57 Cassius Dio XXVII, fr 90.

58 Orosius V,15,23–4.

59 Caesar, *BG* 1,14,7.

60 Livy, *Periocha* LXV.

61 The accounts of this are very confused—how much gold and silver was recovered, where it originally came from (Delphi or local sources?) where it was stored (in temples, enclosures or sacred lakes?), how it was lost and how much was left for subsequent recovery: Strabo IV,1,13 (citing Poseidonius), Trogus (summarised by Justin) XXXIII,3,Dio XXVII, fr 90, Orosius V,15,25; for the proverbial expression *aurum Tolosanum*, Aulus Gellius III,9,7.

62 Livy, *Periocha* LXVII, Dio XXVII, fr 91 and Granius Licinianus p 11F make it clear that it was in a disaster before the battle of *Arausio* that this took place, against Orosius V,16,2 (where the legate is wrongly named as M. Aemilius). Although Livy calls Boiorix a *ferox iuvenis*, he was presumably the Cimbric king later referred to in Plutarch, *Marius* 25,2, and Florus 1,38

(III,2), 18 ('Boleris') and Orosius v,16,20—compare the evident youthfulness at this time of Divico, leader of the Tigurini (n59).

63 Livy, *Periocha* LXVII (citing Valerius Antias for casualties), Dio XXVII, fr 91 (the fullest account of the argument), Orosius v,16,1–7. Sertorius, too, was wounded here, but swam the Rhône to safety (Plutarch, *Sertorius* 3).

64 Plutarch, *Lucullus* 27,7, *Camillus* 19,7.

65 Livy, Periocha LXVII, Plutarch, *Marius* 14,1. Quite where the *Cimbri* and *Teutones* ultimately regrouped is uncertain: the text of Livy reads *inbellicosis et (se) Teutonis coniunxerunt* and most editors accept the emendation *in Veliocassis se Teutonis coniunxerunt*, but since the *Velliocasses* lived around Rouen this seems unlikely: even if it had to be so far north, Tongres (*Aduatuca*) would be more probable, since Caesar, *BG* II,29,4–5, says that the *Aduatuci* were descended from the *Cimbri* and *Teutones*. Elsewhere Livy (XXXII,13,14) uses *imbellis turba* to mean non-combatants, and while the adjective *imbellicosus* is otherwise unknown in classical Latin, might it not here refer to women and children left behind during the Spanish expedition?

66 Plutarch, *Sulla* 4,1. For the rest of this and succeeding paragraphs the basic evidence is supplied by Plutarch, *Marius*, 14–22.

67 Orosius v,16,9.

68 There is some obscurity regarding the division of forces. According to Strabo IV,1,8, it was the *Ambrones* and *Tugeni* (the latter not mentioned by Plutarch) that Marius had to deal with, while Orosius v,16,9, brings not only the *Teutones* and *Ambrones* but also the *Cimbri* and the *Tigurini* to the Rhône, and then (v 16,13–14) has *Teutones* as well as *Cimbri* in the later battle of *Campi Raudi*; Florus 1,38(III,3), on the other hand, sees the *Tigurini* as a separate third force, intended as a reserve for the *Cimbri*, and not actually involved in either of the battles; Livy, *Periocha* LXVIII has only *Teutones* and *Ambrones* at the battle of Aix and only *Cimbri* at *Campi Raudi*.

69 Plutarch, *Sertorius* 3,2.

70 Frontinus, *Strategemata* II,4,6.

71 Livy, *Periocha* LXVIII, has 200,000 killed, 60,000 captured; Velleius Paterculus, 11,12, over 100,000 captured or killed; Plutarch, *Marius* 21,2, over 100,000 killed or captured (in the second battle); Orosius, v,16,12, 200,000 killed, 80,000 captured; Eutropius, v,5,2, 140,000 killed, 60,000 captured.

72 Orosius, *loc cit*, Teutobodus killed; Florus 1,38(III,3) sees him as a notable figure in the triumph. The *Teutones* captured in the Alps were taken to confound the *Cimbri* at *Campi Raudi* (Plutarch, *Marius* 24, 3–4).

73 The Croix de Provence on the neighbouring Mont-Ste-Victoire, with inscriptions in Latin, Provençal and French, was erected (for evident reasons) in 1875. When the widespread local practice of giving boys the Christian name of Marius developed is not quite clear.

74 First in Badian 1958, 264 n3, also in Badian 1967, 23–4,29,98 n30, but most fully in Badian 1966, 901–07.

75 Sallust, *Jugurtha* 43,1, referring to the year 110: *Metellus et Silanus consules designati provincias inter se partiverant*; unfortunately it was only with Metellus that Sallust was concerned and he makes no further mention of Silanus.

76 Ebel 1976, 93.

4
The Republican Period
100–48 BC

Many of the obscurities relating to administration referred to in the last chapter persist as we move into the first century BC, because the ancient historians were unlikely to name the governor of an outlying province unless he was involved in a war, while in our other sources he only finds mention when he is notorious for either vice or virtue. The first possible governor to be considered is L. Licinius Crassus (consul in 95 BC) who, we are told by Valerius Maximus, obtained *Gallia* as his province at the end of his consulship.[1] It is widely held, by Broughton and others,[2] that this was simply *Gallia Cisalpina*, but Badian has argued that he may have governed *Gallia Transalpina*, our province, at the same time.[3] Though it was in cisalpine Gaul that he had, while still consul, vainly sought grounds for a triumph,[4] Crassus had earlier been one of the *duoviri coloniae deducendae* who had founded *Narbo Martius* and many Licinii, possibly descended from men on whom he had conferred Roman citizenship, certainly appear later in *Narbonensis*.[5] But communication between the two areas was not easy at this early date, for while armies could use either the pass of Mont-Genèvre or the difficult coastal route, in both cases it was not until the time of Augustus that proper roads were established and none of the Alpine tribes had yet been subdued. It follows that if a governor were himself operating in one of the areas, any legate in charge of the other area would have to be given a very free hand indeed; and while the combination of the two provinces certainly occurred sometimes, it is not one that should be accepted without convincing evidence for it.

The second candidate for consideration is M. Porcius Cato (a grandson of Cato the Censor), who had been a curule aedile probably in 94 BC and was an ex-praetor when he died in transalpine Gaul, perhaps in 91.[6] Both his dates and his status at the time of his death, however, are so ill-supported that Broughton's suggestion that he may have been governor of the province[7] demands no more than a passing notice. Much more secure is the position of the next man who, as we know from Livy,[8] repressed a revolt of the *Salluvii* in 90 BC. His name appears in the MSS as either Caelius or Coelius (unjustifiably emended to Caecilius by Rossbach, followed by Schlesinger) and Badian has here produced convincing arguments[9] that he should be identified with the consul of 94, C. Coelius Caldus. Precisely when he was appointed, however, how long he remained in charge of the province, and what elements of the *Salluvii* had actually revolted, remains uncertain. His successor may well have been C. Valerius Flaccus, whose first achievement after his consulship (which fell in 93, the year after that of Coelius) was the suppression of a revolt in Spain, in which he slew 20,000 Celtiberians,[10] but when he ultimately celebrated a triumph, in 81, it was not only over Celtiberians but over Gauls too;[11] and although, once again, we have no knowledge of what Gaulish tribes were involved, we do know that he was in Gaul in 83[12] and had probably been there two years earlier, in 85,[13] and he also exercised patronage there, specifically granting Roman citizenship to the grandfather of a Helvian whom Caesar was to use as an envoy when dealing with Ariovistus.[14] Badian therefore suggests[15] that for part of this period he may, while governor of *Hispania Citerior*, have also been responsible for transalpine Gaul. This combination of two provinces is much more readily acceptable than that of the two Gauls, since the Col du Perthus provided easy communication between Gaul and the part of Spain then controlled by the Romans and was already improved by the *Via Domitia*.

We come now to the period following Sulla's dictatorship, and while it might be hoped that his reforms would clarify the way in which our province was administered, this is not so. Things are also complicated by the revolt of Sertorius in Spain, since our next known governor, L. Manlius (or Mallius) not only lost a battle in Aquitania (probably in 79 BC; his legate L. Valerius Praeconinus was killed) but, when sent to assist Q. Caecilius Metellus in Spain, was also defeated by L. Hirtuleius.[16] What tribes were involved in the first action is nowhere stated, but the context of Caesar's reference to it makes it clear that it was outside the area that was recognised as the *provincia* proper in his day. The successor to Manlius should have been M. Aemilius Lepidus (consul in 78) who was allotted the province but instead staged an unsuccessful insurrection in Italy that led to his flight to, and ultimate death in, Sardinia.[17] Instead, his place was effectively taken by the young Pompey who, having defeated him and M. Brutus, succeeded in having himself sent to Spain, as a proconsul, to join Metellus in fighting Sertorius. The route that he took from Italy is curiously described in Sallust's version of a letter he wrote to the senate and, with more perplexing detail, by Appian: the former says that he 'took a different route through the Alps from Hannibal's and opened up a more convenient one for us', while the latter describes it as crossing the Alps 'around the sources of the Po and the Rhône'.[18] Both of these rivers, of course, have many tributaries, and the valley of the Dora Riparia could have taken him up to the Col de Mont-Genèvre or to those of Clapier or Mont-Cenis, while the Dora Baltea could have led him to either the Little St Bernard or the Great St Bernard—this last being the only one that gives access to the upper waters of the Rhône proper. Regardless of which pass Hannibal had actually used (on which see p 31–2 above), the trouble is that, apart from Mont-Genèvre (which other armies had surely used), all those mentioned here would have involved a passage through the territory of the *Allobroges*, and since they were about the most feared tribe in Gaul Pompey would surely have mentioned them (unless, of course, he was concealing his stupidity in going that way when his official commitment was to fight Sertorius). Probably the best explanation is that Appian's geography (and perhaps Pompey's boasting) was a little confused and that either the Col de Larche, leading from the valley of the Stura di Demonte to that of the Ubaye and then the Durance, was the route followed, or that he simply found the better way past Mont-Genèvre itself. But the important point made here is that, as we have argued above, communication between cisalpine and transalpine Gaul was not easy—and that this fact was recognised by the senate.

Pompey's letter continues: 'I recovered (*recepi*) Gaul, the Pyrenees, Lacetania and the Indigetes; with soldiers who were newly enlisted and much fewer in numbers I withstood the first attack of the victorious Sertorius and I spent the winter in camp among most savage foes (*inter saevissumos hostis*), not self-indulgently in towns.'[19] In fact he lost his first battle with Sertorius, at *Lauro*, and even in the following year was not very successful,[20] but the war in Spain does not directly concern us. What is relevant is the possible meaning of the 'retaking' or 'recovery' of Gaul and the location of the *saevissumi hostes* among whom Pompey wintered. When one considers the evident purpose of the letter, to convince the senate of his worth, one sees that not too much should be made of the first point: we simply do not know what parts of it had slipped from Roman control, for none of our sources records any specific battles,[21] although, as we shall see, the *Volcae Arecomici* and the *Helvii*, especially the latter, seem likely to have been involved. So far as the second question is concerned, Appian merely tells us that it was in the Pyrenean mountains that he and Metellus had wintered,[22] and while the Gaulish side of them is likely enough the local tribes, the *Sordi* and the *Elisyces*, were not notoriously fierce. On the other hand, Gaul was certainly involved, since a later passage in the letter says that 'in the previous year it had supplied the army of Metellus with pay and provisions and now scarcely kept itself going with poor crops'.[23] Beyond this, it was no doubt now that Pompey began to recruit troops in Gaul, such as the grandfather of Pompeius Trogus, on whom he conferred Roman citizenship (p 18 above)—just as his legate, L. Afranius, presumably did the same for the ancestor of Nero's praetorian prefect, Sex. Afranius Burrus—and the number of Pompeii who appear later in the province[24] shows that his patronage was extensive; and it must also have been about this time that he handed over additional territory to *Massalia*.[25] Much of this patronage, however, may have been exercised in the following year, when M. Fonteius, who also supported him in his Spanish war, was the official governor.

The contribution to our knowledge of the province supplied by the *Pro Fonteio*,[26] the speech that Cicero made in defence of Fonteius when he had been accused of corrupt practices during his governorship, is of unique importance, but before we consider its content we must first reflect on its nature. In many ways the *Pro Fonteio* of Cicero stands to this province as the *Agricola* of Tacitus does to Britain: neither was primarily concerned with history but rather with the character and actions of an individual—Cicero defending his client, Tacitus extolling his father-in-law—and it follows from this that some matters that are of vital interest to us are either omitted or distorted. Further omissions may be expected from the fact that not only is the text that survives incomplete but also this was not the only speech that Cicero made on the subject.[27] And finally, while it includes some splendid rhetoric, it is not the best of Cicero's speeches, and the weakness of some of his arguments may be deduced from the extraordinary plea that concludes it—that Fonteius should not be condemned, because his sister was a Vestal Virgin! On all these grounds the text must be treated with some caution.

The evidence it provides may conveniently be considered under three headings: first, the extent of the province at this time, second, its administration, including the development of communications, and third, the state of its economy. So far as the first is concerned, the witnesses against Fonteius included not only the *Volcae* and the *Allobroges* (the latter led by Indutiomarus and supported, of course, by a M. Fabius,[28] the former certainly including the *Tectosages* around Toulouse[29]), but also, it seems, the *Ruteni*[30] who, as we saw above (p 42) had collaborated with the *Arverni*; those here mentioned are presumably the people later referred to by Caesar as *Ruteni provinciales*, though how far the tribe was ever fully incorporated into the *provincia* is a question to which we shall return.[31] Besides these the only other tribe to be mentioned is that of the *Vocontii*, against which Fonteius fought a war,[32] and the claim that he had to relieve the *colonia* of *Narbo* from a siege[33], even if this is not a mere exaggeration, really does no more than confirm the involvement of the *Volcae*.

Superficially this gives a picture of a province that generally corresponds with the later *Narbonensis*, but two areas require further consideration. The first is that of the *Helvii*, who occupied territory to the west of the Rhône and to the north of the *Volcae Arecomici*. As we have observed (p 43 above), they could hardly have interfered with the initiation of the *Via Domitia* and so may originally have been controlled only by a treaty, and the grant of Roman citizenship to one of them by C. Valerius Flaccus (p 55 above) does not necessarily imply their total subjugation. Recent excavations at Lussas, however (some 15km north-west of their later capital at *Alba*), have produced some remarkable evidence. Here a long-standing hill-fort of primitive type (Jastres-Sud) was replaced at some in the first half of the first century BC by a new fort (Jastres-Nord) defended by a wall with towers of a very developed style.[34] The *Helvii* are nowhere mentioned in the *Pro Fonteio*, but since it must have been about now that Pompey handed over some of their land to *Massalia*[35] it might be against a full Roman takeover that they tried to defend themselves; alternatively, of course, Jastres-Nord might represent an earlier revolt whose suppression was included in Pompey's 'recovery' of the province on his way to Spain. Secondly, there is the question of how much land was still controlled by *Massalia*. Throughout the speech the Massaliotes are presented as brave and loyal allies,[36] and as supporters of Fonteius (on whom, perhaps wisely, they had conferred their highest honours),[37] but, more significantly, it is also said that, while Fonteius had preserved them, they realised that their geographical situation required that they should prevent the barbarians from harming Romans.[38] When one couples this with Pompey's transfer to them of land of the *Volcae* and the *Helvii* (perhaps small areas that they had held on the east side of the Rhône), it becomes clear that the territory under the control of *Massalia* (and so technically outside the province) had not been reduced—territory that included not only specifically Greek towns like *Nicaea*, *Antipolis*, *Olbia* and *Tauroentium* but also the continuous coastal strip given her by Sextius Calvinus and a substantial area east of the lower Rhône.

To turn now to administration, the text usefully confirms the fact that Fonteius held his governorship for a period of three years, though its precise dates (probably 74–2 BC) remain a little uncertain.[39] Secondly, it provides the names of his two legates, C. Annius Bellienus and C.Fonteius—the latter hardly surprising, although his precise family relationship to the governor is not stated.[40] Their names are cited in connection with road-building, the superintendence of which Fonteius handed over to them when he himself was 'hindered by more important affairs of state', and two aspects of this activity are worthy of note. First, the actual work was done by local contractors who were paid for it, provided that a detailed check showed that it was satisfactory; but second, the only such work that is actually mentioned is the repair or reconstruction of the *Via Domitia*, and the fact that Cicero was answering a general charge (that Fonteius had made a profit out of road-building either by selling exemption from it to some people or by accepting work of inferior quality from others) strongly suggests that no new roads were being made at this time.

This last point is of some significance when we consider the details of the next passage,[41] which deals with the charge that Fonteius had also made money out of excess taxes on imported Italian wine: while all the places now mentioned for the first time—*Crodunum, Vulchalo, Cobiomagus, Elesiodunum*(?)—can no doubt be related to Narbonne and Toulouse (something that is discussed below, pp 122, 139), if trade still followed native tracks not all of them need have been on the precise lines of the Roman roads that later connected the two cities. Apart from the possibility (which depends on a very doubtful emendation of the text)[42] that it was C. Annius who imposed six denarii on each amphora sold to the (unspecified) enemy, the men immediately concerned in this—Titurius, Porcius, Munius and Servaeus—were evidently *publicani*, and the prosecutors claimed that Fonteius had worked out the scheme before leaving Rome. Naturally, the *publicani* supported him in his defence.[43]

This leads us to our third class of evidence, that relating to the economy, in which the importation of Italian wine, and other goods, played a significant part—a fact attested by many finds of amphorae in hill-forts and other native settlements and in wrecks.[44] Here again it is necessary to consider the role of *Massalia*. While the Massaliotes, as Trogus said, produced their own vines and olives, and their own pottery too, their chief activity had always been trade, which involved the import and distribution of goods from other parts of the Mediterranean world—initially from Greece and Sicily and then, increasingly, from all parts of Italy, especially Campania. Their ability in this sphere had been of great benefit to Rome—and that, presumably, is why Marius had seen it fit to hand over his canal to them—but after the formation of the province more and more Italian merchants had moved in, leading to what is probably the best-known passage in the *Pro Fonteio: Referta Gallia negotiatorum est, plena civium Romanorum. Nemo Gallorum sine cive Romano quicquid negotii gerit, nummus in Gallia nullus sine civium Romanorum tabulis commovetur.*[45]

This claim no doubt includes some rhetorical exaggeration, but the most important part of it is stressed by the list of people who, Cicero states, offered no evidence against Fonteius—*negotiatores, coloni, publicani, aratores, pecuarii*.[46] These friendly *aratores* and *pecuarii* did not, of course, include Gauls who had been evicted from their farms by Pompey[47], but the point is that whereas the Greeks had been content to sell and buy and to confine the extension of their settlement to the establishment of what were essentially trading-posts, the Romans had already begun to take over estates. Precisely where these estates lay it is impossible, in the present state of the archaeological evidence, to determine, but an even earlier speech of Cicero, the *Pro Quinctio*, shows that this invasion had been going on for some time and does name one tribe whose territory was involved. As early as 83 BC Publius Quinctius' brother Gaius had 'already for several years'[48] held estates (apparently pastoral ones) in Transalpine Gaul in partnership with Sextius Naevius, and after the death of Gaius (in Gaul) Publius was involved in a dispute with Naevius over the disposal of the property and the debts that its administration had incurred. The location of the estates (including, presumably, that inherited by Publius)[49] is placed in the territory of the *Sebaginni* (variants *Sebaquini*, *Sabaquini*, *Sabaginnes*, *Sebagudii*) and said to be 700 Roman miles from Rome.[50] This figure is obviously approximate, but since Cicero is mocking the suggestion that the distance could be covered in under three days it cannot be increased and the best solution so far seems to be that of Barruol which puts the tribe (which is not mentioned in any other source) near Sisteron and makes them a part of the Vocontian federation.[51] The workers on these estates were slaves.[52]

Another matter bears on both the administration and the economy, the extent to which the province was required to support Pompey in his continuing war with Sertorius. As before, Pompey's army wintered in Gaul and Fonteius was responsible for arranging its winter-quarters[53] and for supplying it with recruits, both infantry and cavalry.[54] While the demand for food, as we have seen, evidently placed heavy demands on the economy, the recruitment could ultimately be beneficial to those Gauls who, like the grandfather of Pompeius Trogus, were granted Roman citizenship on discharge. In any case, enlistment in foreign armies was no new thing to the Celts—Celtic mercenaries had long before this served under the Carthaginians, under Greeks in Sicily, and even as far away as Egypt—and in this instance the later appearance of families of Pompeii in Périgueux suggests that Pompey's net may have extended as far north as the *Petrucorii*.[55] The army of Sertorius, too, · probably included men from Gaul as well as Spain, perhaps some of those who later assisted the *Vocates* and *Tarusates* against Caesar's legate P. Crassus, but also, more significantly for us, some of those whom Pompey ultimately settled in and around St-Bertrand-de-Comminges (*Lugdunum Convenarum*), thus forming the community of the *Convenae*: these people then formed part of our province until Augustus transferred them to *Aquitania*.

The establishment of the *Convenae* must have taken place in 71 BC, since in the previous year Perperna had organised the assassination of Sertorius and it was in 71 that Pompey, having defeated and executed Perperna, was able to return to Rome and to secure the consulship for 70. On his way home he also organised the erection of trophies in the Pyrenees,[57] but these have not been discovered, not do we know who was the immediate successor of Fonteius. The next known governor is C. Calpurnius Piso who, during his consulship of 67 BC, obtained a proconsulate over both Cisalpine and Transalpine Gaul—the first man for whose tenure of this joint governorship there is positive evidence.[58] Little is known, however, of what went on in our province during his term of office, beyond the fact that, despite his initial objections, he had to allow Pompey's legates to recruit men there for the war against the pirates[59] and that he had to pacify the *Allobroges*.[60] Like Fonteius and so many other provincial governors, he was charged with extortion after completion of his governorship, but of this too we have no details.[61]

Piso's successor was L. Licinius Murena, who assumed office in 64 BC.[62] He did not, however, stay in his province for long, since in the following year, having left his brother and legate, C. Murena, in charge, he returned to Rome to campaign for his election to the consulate in 62;[63] and while we are told a good deal about him in the speech that Cicero made to defend him against a charge of bribery—including the fact that he levied his troops in Umbria and the claim that he enabled people in Gaul to reclaim difficult debts[64]—it is the writings of Cicero and Sallust on the Catilinarian conspiracy that yield the most interesting information regarding our province. In this year (63 BC, the consulship of Cicero) there were two envoys (*legati*) of the *Allobroges* in Rome and Catiline tried to enlist their support by raising a revolt in Gaul.[65] Clodius, who had received money from Catiline, had already visited Gaul with Murena (and, of course, had acted criminally there),[66] and now P. Cornelius Lentulus Sura, acting for Catiline, told P. Umbrenus (a *negotiator* who operated in Gaul) to approach the two envoys. They told their patron, Q. Fabius Sanga, who told Cicero,[67] and so, having handed themselves over to the praetors L. Valerius Flaccus and C. Pomptinus, they helped in thwarting the plot;[68] they also gave truthful evidence against P. Autronius Paetus, another associate of Catiline,[69] and as a result of all this they were voted substantial awards.[70]

Seeing that the *Allobroges* were, in Cicero's own words, the one tribe in Gaul *quae bellum populo Romano facere posse et non nolle videatur*,[71] one might have expected that the action of their envoys on behalf of the established government would have led to a period of peace and tranquillity in the province, but in fact the reverse was the case. In 62 BC C. Pomptinus, one of the praetors to whom the envoys had gone, became governor, and within a year he had to deal with a war begun by the *Allobroges*.[72] The reasons for this revolt are nowhere stated, but Dio's account of it raises some interesting geographical questions, most notably the identity of two places mentioned, and his brief text may best be quoted in full:

'The *Allobroges* were plundering Gallia Narbonensis and the governor, C. Pomptinus, sent his legates against the enemy but established himself in a place convenient for observing what went on, so that he was able to give them useful advice and aid, as might from time to time be helpful to them. Manlius Lentinus attacked the city of *Ventia* [Οὐεντίαν, acc] and so frightened the people that most of them fled and the rest sent ambassadors for peace. Then, the rural people having come to their aid, he was driven back from the wall [presumably that of *Ventia*] but fearlessly ravaged the land until Catugnatus, the leader of the whole tribe, and some of the others of those who dwelt along the Isère [καί τινες καὶ ἄλλοι τῶν παρὰ τὸν Ἴσαρα οἰκούντων] came to their aid. Then he did not dare to prevent their crossing, because of the number of their boats, lest they might assemble in a body on seeing the Romans massed against them. But as the land was wooded right down to the river, he set up ambushes there and captured and slew the men as fast as they crossed. While following some of the fugitives he came up against Catugnatus himself and would have been utterly destroyed if a violent storm had not arisen and prevented the barbarians from pursuing. After this, when Catugnatus had retired to a distance, he overran the country again and destroyed the wall at which he had been repulsed.

Marius and Ser. Galba crossed the Rhône and, having ravaged the possessions of the *Allobroges*, finally came to the city of *Solonium* [Σολώνιον, acc], took a certain strong point above it and set fire to parts of the town, which was partly built of wood. They did not, however, take it, being prevented by the arrival of Catugnatus. Learning of this, Pomptinus marched against it with his whole army and having besieged it captured the people, except Catugnatus. Then he more easily subjugated the rest.

It is unfortunate that Dio does not name Pomptinus' own base, nor that of Marius and Galba, since that might have led to the discovery of some early Roman encampments, but both were presumably somewhere in the Rhône valley south of its confluence with the Isère. What is clear, however, is that two separate campaigns were required, and it is highly probable that they took place in different years, with Marius and Galba replacing Lentinus; and this, combined with the statement that the *Allobroges* 'began' the war (which implies that it was not necessarily confined to their territory) means that the two places, *Ventia* and *Solonium*, need not be closely related. Neither of them is mentioned in any other context (and even here Livy's *Periocha* includes only the latter, in the accusative *Solonem*) and a very large number of suggestions have in the past been made for both of them—for *Ventia* le Rocher de Cornillon (near St-Egrève), St-Donat, St-Nazaire-en-Royans, St-Paul-les-Romans, Vence (north of Grenoble), Vinay, and for *Solonium* Saillans, St-Marcellin (or the neighbouring Montmiral), Salagnon, Scillonaz, Solaie, la Sône.[73] For *Ventia*, however, much the most plausible explanation is that the text is slightly corrupt and that it should be either *Vienna* (Vienne) or *Valentia* (Valence). Of these Vienne appears to be too far north of the Isère, but Valence fits the context very well and has been widely accepted[74]—with the implication that as well as the *Allobroges* the *Segovellauni* too were, at least initially, involved in the war. Attempts have also been made to identify *Solonium* with Vienne, especially because it became the tribal capital, but while this would fit well with the completion of the campaign, archaeological research into the Iron Age background of the city has rendered it most improbable.[75] A particular difficulty is that while we know that Marius and Galba crossed the Rhône, we do not know in which direction they did so, and the more recent suggestion of Soyons (in Segovellaunian territory),[76] though attractive in that it offers a site of suitable form, does not provide a really suitable place for a satisfactory completion to the war.

For, whatever happened to Catugnatus, the completion of the war certainly was satisfactory to the Romans, and although Pomptinus met with some opposition to his claim for a triumph (eventually celebrated in 54 BC),[77] this was the last serious revolt to occur in our province. In the last year of Pomptinus's governorship (59 BC) Q. Caecilius Metellus Celer, one of the consuls of 60, had been appointed to succeed him, but before he could do so he died, in somewhat suspicious circumstances, and the cowed senate added this province to the two of Cisalpine Gaul and Illyricum that had already been allocated to C. Iulius Caesar. His tenure of all three was later extended for a further five years, but he was so preoccupied with the conquest of *Gallia Comata* (and, of course, with the maintenance of his status in Rome) that the records of this decade add relatively little to our knowledge of the *provincia* proper— almost as little, indeed, as they do to that of the less important Illyricum.[78] While now for the first time we have the names of two men who served here as quaestors (M. Licinius Crassus in 54 and, more significantly, M. Antonius in 52/51) and also those of a score of his legates,[79] they are always named for their activities in the wars and only L. Iulius Caesar (an uncle of M. Antonius but a very distant relation of the governor) is mentioned as operating actually within our province.[80] And it is of *Gallia Comata* and *Germania*, not of the *provincia*, that Caesar writes his detailed account in Book VI of the *De Bello Gallico*.

Nevertheless some interesting facts do emerge, and perhaps the most important is the apparently unwavering support that Caesar received from the province while conducting his wars. As we have seen, there were already many immigrant Italians there, including the long-established colonists of *Narbo*, and a number of leading Gauls had already had Roman citizenship conferred on them, but it is still a little surprising that the constant involvement of the Roman armies in northern Gaul, and sometimes in Britain and Germany, did not (so far as we know) tempt some successor to Catugnatus to start a revolt. Although the *Allobroges*, despite the hopes of the *Helvetii*, were no doubt glad that Caesar should prevent the invaders from passing through their land, and grateful enough when he destroyed their bridge over the Rhône at *Genava* (now mentioned for the first time as being in their territory);[81] and although the *Tolosates* may have been persuaded that they too were threatened (even though the *Santones*, at whose land the *Helvetii* were aiming, lived not, as Caesar claimed, near them but some 700km away);[82] and although Ariovistus may have been portrayed as someone likely to repeat the behaviour of the *Cimbri* and *Teutones*[83]—all this relates only to the first year of Caesar's campaigns. What is much more remarkable is the general failure of Vercingetorix, at a time when the Roman forces were really in danger, to obtain support from tribes within the province. Instead, he had to send *Aedui* against the *Allobroges*, *Gabali* and *Arverni* against the *Helvii*, and *Ruteni* and *Cadurci* against the *Volcae Arecomici*. But the *Allobroges* (presumably then ruled by Adbucillus),[84] even though they were also tempted by bribes and a promise that they might control the whole province, built fortifications against them along the Rhône, the *Helvii*, though at first defeated, stood out against them, and no progress seems to have been made against the *Volcae*.[85] The only tribe in this area that seems to have been divided in its attitude is that of the *Ruteni*, since besides those who supported Vercingetorix we also have mention of some *Ruteni provinciales*. The wording of the chapter that includes them (*Lucterius Cadurcus in Rutenos missus eam civitatem Arvernis conciliat*, then *Caesar . . . praesidia in Rutenis provincialibus, Volcis Arecomicis, Tolosatibus, circumque Narbonem, quae loca hostibus erant finitima, constituit*)[86] makes it clear that they were not merely individuals but occupied a recognisable area, presumably a *pagus* of the tribe that had accepted Roman suzerainty, and geography and history combine to indicate their location: while the capital of the *civitas* lay, at least in later times, at Rodez (*Segodunum Rutenorum*), the Romanised *pagus* may have been that centred on *Albiga* (Albi, up the Tarn from the territory of the *Tolosates*) which, although it was evidently reunited with the *civitas* under Augustus and so included in *Aquitania*, had reasserted its independence from Rodez by the 5th century.[87] Even here, then, there was no provincial revolt, and throughout his Gallic wars and after Caesar was always able to raise Gaulish recruits in the *provincia* and even formed a legion, the *Legio V Alaudae*, from them;[88] also, by various means including the extensive granting of Roman citizenship, he greatly extended his patronage in the *provincia*.

This stood him in especially good stead during the civil wars that followed, and here too some important things, both stated and implied, must be noted. In Book VIII of the *De Bello Gallico* Hirtius, coming to the end of 50 BC, places four legions under C.Trebonius in winter-quarters *in Belgio* and another four under C.Fabius among the *Aedui*,[89] but when we move to Book I of the *De Bello Civili* the situation has changed and we find Fabius in charge of three legions that have in fact wintered *Narbone circumque ea loca*.[90] With the prospect of confronting Pompeian forces in Spain, the old-established *colonia* of *Narbo* was an obvious choice, but since *Baeterrae* (Béziers, only 25km from Narbonne) was also to become a *colonia* it is probable that this place too was now chosen for a camp—and it is even possible that it was occupied by *Legio VII*, whose veterans were later to provide the colonists.[91] The same sort of thing may have happened in the eastern part of the province. Caesar had already transferred *Legio XIII* to Cisalpine Gaul,[92] but he also required the support of *Legio XII* and *Legio VIII*.[93] Although, owing to the confused state of the Roman calendar (soon to be corrected by Caesar himself), the January in which he crossed the Rubicon corresponded with the solar October-November, he must have realised that if they used the Alpine passes they might be delayed and a coastal route for them is highly probable. So these legions too will have been moved south and here again places that were later to become veteran colonies may well have been selected for their camps—Fréjus for *Legio VIII* and perhaps Aix for *Legio XII*. Fréjus is especially attractive for several reasons: not only was it the place where veterans of the eighth legion were ultimately settled, but it also offered the possibilities of transport to Italy by sea as well as by land, and thirdly, its establishment now would explain the appearance of the name *Forum Iulii* before the Augustan *colonia* was founded.[94] Besides this, the useful ports that already existed along this coast belonged not to Rome but to *Massalia*, and although Fréjus lay within their 8-stade coastal territory the establishment of a new one here might even, at this stage, have appeared attractive to the Greeks; Aix, on the other hand, was already a Roman base.

The senate had, to Caesar's chagrin, appointed L. Domitius to succeed him as governor of Gaul, and Domitius played a considerable part in the attempt to block Caesar's invasion of Italy. Caesar defeated him at *Corfinium* and, in the hope of winning him over, not only released him and his associates but also returned his money to him.[95] This did not, however, have the required effect, and by the time Caesar, having won over Italy, was on his way to Spain, Domitius was sailing to *Massalia*—to which Pompey had already sent back some Massaliote envoys with instructions that they should close their gates to Caesar.[96] Caesar accordingly summoned the Massaliote ruling committee of 15 to meet him (where is not stated) and argued that they should follow the example of Italy rather than obey Pompey. His advice was duly reported back to the city, presumably to the 600 *timuchi*, and the 15 then returned with their answer. This was that, while they understood that the Romans were split into two factions, and that both the leaders had been their benefactors, it was not for them to decide between them.[97] It was while this meeting was going on that Domitius arrived in *Massalia* and the Massaliotes, who had already called in the *Albici* to assist them, received him, put him in command, and closed their gates to Caesar—at least, that is how Caesar relates it: but even if we disregard the poetical flourishes of Lucan, the brief accounts of Velleius Paterculus and Cassius Dio present the actions of the Greeks in a much more honest light.[98]

Two geographical questions arise from the account. In the first place, for the benefactions conferred on the Massaliotes it is said that *alter agros Volcarum Arecomicorum et Helviorum eis concesserit, alter bello victas Gallias attribuerit vectigaliaque auxerit*. Which *patronus* had conferred which benefits is not stated, but it is virtually certain that some lands of the *Volcae* and the *Helvii* had been handed over to *Massalia* by Pompey, and it is in this belief that we have referred to them above (pp 56, 58) and shall discuss them below (pp 162, 182). For the second item, however, Glandorp's emendation of *victas Gallias* to *victos Sallyas* has been so widely accepted that it has found its way (without warning comment) into too many translations. But if Caesar had had to fight a war in the *provincia* (whether against the *Sallyes*—who are usually referred to in Latin as *Salluvii*—or, for that matter, against the *Volcae* and the *Helvii*) we would surely have heard of it, and the plural *Gallias* could well represent the 'three parts' into which Caesar saw *Gallia Comata* as divisible. A reasonable explanation would seem to be that what he had given *Massalia* was some of the tribute from tribes he had conquered— and had increased her *vectigalia* by deliberately channelling increased trade through her ports.[99] The second question concerns the location of the *Albici*. For a long time they were taken to be associated with Riez (*Alebaece Reiorum*), but this disagrees with the description of them as people *qui in eorum fide erant montisque supra Massiliam incolebant*, and Barruol has made an excellent case for identifying them with the *Albieis* and *Albioeci* of Strabo and placing them just north of Apt, perhaps centred on the hill-fort of Perréal (figs 3 and 4). Here they would not only be in a position that accords reasonably well with the description but would be near neighbours of (if not actually in) the territory that was still under Massaliote control.[100]

Most of this territory was now occupied by Caesar's troops and he had 12 warships built at Arles (which now appears for the first time under the name of *Arelate*) in the remarkably short time of 30 days, but whether this was, as he implies, the limit of his stay in the neighbourhood is open to question. Both Dio and Lucan seem to indicate that the delay was considerably longer, the latter including his memorable account of how Caesar himself swung the first axe at a sacred grove, but eventually he departed to fight Afranius and Petreius in Spain, leaving his legates D. Brutus in charge of the fleet and C. Trebonius in command of the troops.[101] The details of the siege and the naval battles that followed, which are set out in remarkably full detail in view of the fact that Caesar was not present (supplemented by the gory particulars offered by Lucan) do not much concern us, but some points must be noted. First, when Caesar had won his first victory in Spain, he sent the captives back past *Massalia* and had them released at the river Var—a clear indication that at this time that was considered the boundary between Gaul and Italy.[102] Second, when L. Nasidius came to help them, the Massaliotes were able to use *Tauroentum* (le Brusc) as a supplementary base, which shows that at least some of the city's dependencies were still under her control.[103] It was not until Caesar himself returned from his final victory in Spain, where Varro had submitted to him, that *Massalia* finally collapsed, and even then L. Domitius escaped by sea to fight another day.[104]

Allegedly because of the reputation and age of the city, but no doubt also to discourage a further revolt while he was engaged in more important operations elsewhere, Caesar treated *Massalia* with some moderation. While leaving two legions there, he did not formally take

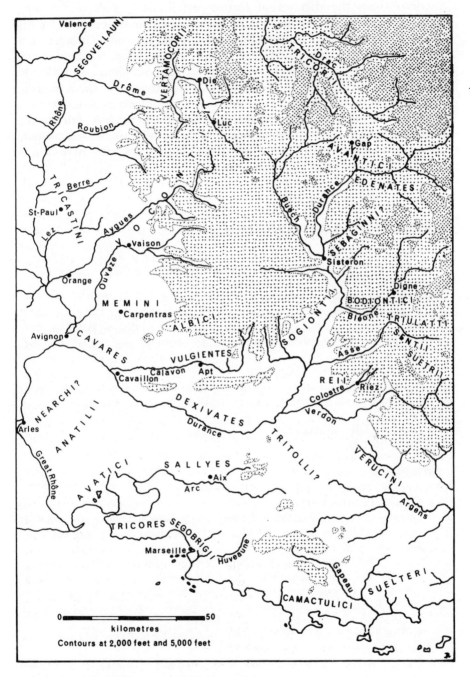

4 Iron Age tribes in Provence (after Barruol)

it over and in due course it became a *civitas foederata*, with a little freedom from the dictates of future provincial governors.[105] What happened to most of its dependent Greek towns is obscure, but while *Nicaea* (Nice), though technically within Italy, remained subject to it, *Antipolis* (Antibes) detached itself from it and chose to become an Italiote Greek city.[106] But the Gaulish territory hitherto controlled by *Massalia* was now reduced to a very small area around it, the remainder being attributed to other cities, especially to the *colonia* of Arles that was founded in 46 BC, probably the year in which the praetor A. Hirtius was appointed governor of the province.[107] The foundation of new *coloniae*, however, and the effects that this had on Gaul as a whole, may best be considered together in the next chapter.

REFERENCES AND NOTES

1 Valerius Maximus III,7,6: *cum ex consulatu provinciam Galliam obtineret*, to which C. Carbo (whose father he had condemned) made a *peregrinatio* to see how Crassus conducted affairs.

2 Broughton II,13.

3 Badian 1966, 907; for reasons given below, his statement (approved by Ebel, 94) that 'nothing was easier or more obvious than to throw them (sc *Cisalpina* and *Transalpina*) together under one *imperium*' is not geographically acceptable.

4 Cicero, *De Inventione* II,37(111).

5 Badian 1958,309, lists 102, possibly 103; for the founders being *duoviri* and not *triumviri* (as sometimes stated by Broughton), v. Gayraud 1981, 124 and 141.

6 Aulus Gellius XIII,20,12.

7 Broughton II,22.

8 Livy, *Periocha* LXXIII.

9 Badian 1964, 90–1.

10 Appian, *Iberica* 100,(6).

11 Granius Licinianus 39B.

12 Cicero, *Pro Quinctio* 24(6) and 28(7), the former passage giving the date (the consulship of Scipio and Norbanus), the latter describing Flaccus as *imperator*.

13 Cicero, *Pro Flacco* 63(26) recording the presence there of his nephew.

14 Caesar, *BG* I,47,4. Opinion differs on whether the name of Caesar's envoy was Procillus or Troucillus; for a full discussion see Ellis Evans, 380–2. For his Helvian ancestry see BG VII,65, on his brother C. Valerius Donnotaurus, then *princeps civitatis Helviorum*.

15 Badian 1964,88–90; cf Badian 1966, 908 and Ebel, 94–5, and for further particulars Broughton II,14–78.

16 Caesar, *BG* III,20,1; Livy *Periocha* XC; Plutarch, *Sertorius* 12,4; Orosius V,23,4; while Caesar, Livy and Orosius all describe him as *proconsul*, he had not held a consulship but may have been *praetor* in 79 BC (Broughton II,83,87).

17 Appian, *BC,* 1,107(13) specifically defines the province as τὴν 'ὑπὲϱ ''Άλπεις Γαλατίαν that is, *Transalpina.* Badian 1958,275, and 1966,910, argues that the passage in Plutarch, *Pompey* 16,2 (Λέπιδον'ήδη πολλὰ τῆς 'Ιταλίας κεκινηκότα καὶ τὴν ἐντὸς 'Άλπεων Γαλατίαν διὰ Βϱούτου στϱατεύματι) shows that he was allotted *Cisalpina* too. But he had not certainly taken over his province when he raised his insurrection and even if Brutus was his legate (which is uncertain, Broughton II,91) he may only, at least officially, have been in the process of taking his army to *Transalpina.*

18 Sallust, *Hist.* II 98: *Per eas* (sc *Alpes*) *iter aliud atque Hannibal nobis opportunius patefeci*; Appian, *BC* 1,109(13): 'Ο δὲ 'ες τὰ 'Άλπεια'όϱη μετὰ φϱονήματος 'ανήει, οὐ κατὰ τὴν Αννίβου μεγαλουϱγίαν, ἑτέϱαν δ'εχάϱασσεν ἀμφὶ ταῖς πηγαῖς τοῦ τε'Ροδανοῦ καὶ'Ηϱιδανοῦ.

19 Sallust, *ibid*; on the point of his not being self-indulgent (the apparent meaning of *ambitio* here) cf Plutarch, *Pompey* 18, on the contrast with the behaviour of Metellus.

20 Appian, *ibid*; Plutarch, *Sertorius* 18, *Pompey* 18; Frontinus, *Strategemata* II,5,31 (with the clear definition *hoc primum proelium inter Sertorium et Pompeium fuit*); Orosius V,23,6. On the next year, Livy, *Periocha* XCII &c.

21 According to Pliny, *HN* III,18, Pompey claimed on his trophies in the Pyrenees that he had subdued 876 *oppida ab Alpibus ad fines Hispaniae ulterioris*, and Cicero, *Pro Lege Manilia* 11(30) cites *testis Gallia per quam legionibus nostris iter in Hispaniam Gallorum internicione patefactum est.* Jullian III,111, note 1, suggested the *Vocontii*, which is very acceptable geographically, but any fight with them by Pompey would be too early to be fused with the Vocontian war of Fonteius mentioned below.

22 Appian, *BC* 1,110(13): in the spring Μέτελλος καὶ Πομπήιος ἀπὸ τῶν Πυϱηναίων ὀϱῶν, ἔνθα διεχείμαζον. This and the letter in Sallust are the only sources cited by Broughton II,90, for its being in Gaul.

23 Sallust, *ibid*: *Gallia superiore anno Metelli exercitum stipendio frumentoque aluit et nunc malis fructibus ipsa vix agitat.*

24 Badian 1958, 310, lists 223, possibly 225.

25 Caesar, *BC* 1,35,4; for a discussion of this see p 65.

26 The best edition of this speech, with exhaustive references, is contained in Clemente 1974.

27 Cicero, *Pro Fonteio* 16(37), possibly indicating that there had been an earlier adjournment of the case.

28 *Ibid* 12(26,27), 13(29), 16(36), 21(46), the last referring to Indutiomarus as *dux Allobrogum ceterorumque Gallorum.*

29 *Ibid* 9(19).

30 *Ibid* 3(4).

31 Caesar, *BG* 1,45 and VII,7. For further discussion see p 64.

32 *Pro Fonteio* 9(20); unforunately no details of this war are provided – see note 21 above.

33 *Ibid* 20(46).

34 Y. Burnand, 'Documents sur l'oppidum de Jastres-Nord à Lussas', *Gallia* XXXV(1977), 271–8, and C. Lefebvre, 'Romanisation d'un oppidum celtique', *Hist. Arch.* no 78 (Nov 1983), 15–17 (and for other refs, p 20); Lefebvre's 'romanisation' is apparently derived largely from the fact that although the towers (like those of Entremont etc.) could be derived from Greek models, they incorporate mortar.

35 Caesar, *BC* 1,35.
36 *Pro Fonteio* 5(13), 15(34).
37 *Ibid* 5(14).
38 *Ibid* 20(45): *Venit huic subsidio misero atque innocenti* (sc *Fonteio*) *Massilien-sium cuncta civitas, quae non solum ob eam causam laborat ut huic, a quo ipsa servata est, parem gratiam referre videatur, sed etiam quod ea condicione atque eo fato se in iis terris collacatam esse arbitratur ne quid nostris hominibus istae gentes nocere possint;* the *noxia*, of course, might be juridical as well as military, but *iis terris* implies the possibility of the latter.
39 *Ibid* 14(32): . . . *omnes legati nostri qui illo triennio in Galliam venerunt* . . . For a full discussion of the date see Clemente 1974, 111.
40 *Ibid* 8(17–19).
41 *Ibid* 9(19–20), Clemente 1974, 131–8.
42 The MS reading (*ibid* 9(19)) is *elesioduluscantum senos denarios ab eis qui ad hostem portarent exegissent*, emended to *Elesiodulis C. Annium senos denarios . . . exegisse*. While the place-name should doubtless be related to the *Elusio* (Alzonne) of the Bordeaux Itinerary (551.5) and, as *Elesiodunum*, fits well the hill-fort (now village) of Montferrand above the later *mansio*, the introduction of the name C. Annius, though accepted by Clark (OCT, 1910) and Boulanger (Budé, 1929) and, in discussion of the passage, by Grenier 1937, 432, de Laet 1949, 81, and Clemente 1974, 137, is highly questionable and is understandingly rejected by Mueller (Teubner, 1903) and Watts (Loeb, 1931). He cannot be the legate C.Annius Bellienus who, it has been claimed in the preceding section, would be recognised by the jury as a *primarius vir*, and it would be very surprising, especially in these circumstances, if he were to be the only *publicanus* to have a *praenomen* mentioned by Cicero. A reading such as *Elesioduno autem senos denarios* . . . seems much preferable, with the implication that it was the *publicani* already named who levied this high tax on wine exported to 'the enemy'. The identity of 'the enemy' is also doubtful: A. Soutou (*Ogam* XII, 1960, 12ff) has suggested Sertorius, which would at least explain the singular *hostem*, but both de Laet and Clemente assume that it refers simply to people outside the province.
43 *Ibid* 5(12). For a discussion of the taxes see de Laet 1949, 79–84, and, for the background, Badian 1972, 101–08, with footnote 117 (p 153) comparing Fonteius with Verres.
44 For an excellent detailed discussion of this, Clemente 1974, 21–91; see also F. Benoit, 'La romanisation de la Narbonnaise à la fin de l'époque republicaine', *Rivista di Studi Liguri* XXXII(1966), 287–303.
46 *Ibid* 5(12).
47 *Ibid* 6(14).
48 *Pro Quinctio* 6(24) for the date (consulship of Scipio and Norbanus) and 4(14), *complures iam annos*.
49 *Ibid* 29(90), his *praedia privata*.
50 *Ibid* 25(79–80).
51 *Ibid* 25(80): *Adminstri et satellites Sex. Naevi Roma trans Alpis Sebaginnos biduo veniunt. O hominem fortunatum qui eius modi nuntios seu potius Pegasos habeat!* Barruol 1969, 291–3, which is the more acceptable because the normal route *trans Alpis* led down the Durance valley. Baiter's emenda-tion to *Segusiavos* (followed by Freese, Loeb, 1930) can be dismissed

because they lay outside the province (around Lyon and Feurs), while those of Hirschfeld (*CIL* XII, p 221, *ad Cebennas*) and Clark (OCT, 1909, *Samnagenses*, shown to be a western tribe by Pliny, *HN* III,37) are unlikely because, besides the distance, the normal way that an individual would have travelled to the western half of the province was by sea. This fact also weakens the argument of Ebel 1976, 92, that the estate should be near *Narbo* because the auction (4(15)) was held there; and as *Narbo* was the administrative centre of the province, with the most likely customers, this was the obvious place to hold it.

52 *Ibid* 29(90).

53 *Pro Fonteio* 9(20); unfortunately the details *de dispositione hibernorum* are omitted.

54 *Ibid* 3(8) (a fragment preserved by Aquila Romanus).

55 *Eg CIL* XIII, 950–4, 1004–08 (all from Périgueux) and 1704 (from Lyon): for a possible family tree see P. Barrière, *Vesunna Petrucoriorum*, Périgueux, 1930,71–3. *Cf* also *CIL* XIII,1686, for a Cadurcan Pompeius.

56 For the skilful opponents of Crassus, Caesar, *BG* III, 23; for the *Convenae*, Jerome, *Adversus Vigilantium* (comparing his wickedness with that of his ancestors), Pliny, *HN* IV,108 (*in oppidum contributi Convenae*) Strabo IV,2,1 (τὴν (sc γῆν) τῶν Κωνουενῶν, ὅ ἐστι συγκλύδων), both confirming the idea that they were an artificially-created tribe, and Strabo IV,2,2 (stating that by his time they had been granted *ius Latii*), *cf* also Caesar *BC* III,19,2. As is often suggested, the area may previously have belonged to the *Volcae Tectosages*, but there is no direct evidence for this. For a study of the tribe, R. Lizop, *Les Convenae et les Consoranni*, Toulouse, 1931, and for an idiosyncratic study of their capital, B. Sapène, *Saint-Bertrand-de-Comminges: Lugdunum Convenarum: Centre Touristique d'art et d'histoire*, Toulouse, 1961.

57 Pliny, *HN* III,18, and VII,96; their places are not stated, but since more than one is implied they should perhaps be sought not only near the Col du Perthus but also in the Cerdagne, since it was presumably by a more westerly route that the men were transported.

58 Cassius Dio XXXVI,37, puts him specifically in *Transalpina* (ἐν τῇ Γαλατίᾳ Ναρβωνησίᾳ) and Sallust, *Cat* xlix,1, says that he tried to persuade Cicero to use the *Allobroges* as witnesses against Caesar, which confirms the identification of the *pacificator Allobrogum* in Cicero, *Ad Att.* I,13,2, as Piso. The fact that Cicero (*Ad Att.* I,1,2) intended to visit Piso's staff to secure support for his own election to the consulship points to *Cisalpina*, and this is confirmed by Caesar's charge against Piso that he had unjustly treated a Transpadane (Sallust, *Cat* xlix,2).

59 Dio, *loc cit*.

60 See n 58. His evident later influence on the *Allobroges* suggests that this was not a very serious war.

61 Cicero, *Pro Flacco* 39(98).

62 Cicero, *Pro Murena* 41(89) Cicero's specific reference here to *Gallia Transalpina*, combined with the evidence in the notes that follow, indicate that Sallust, *Cat* 42,3, is in error in calling his province *Citerior Gallia*.

63 Cicero, *Pro Murena* 26(53), 33(68–9), 41(89); Sallust, *Cat* 42,3 (emended as in n 62).

64 *Pro Murena* 20(42). The raising of troops in Umbria reminds us that it was

71

not yet the general practice that men should be stationed permanently in a province.

65 Cicero, *In Catilinam* iii, 2(4); that there were only two of them is shown by Plutarch, *Cicero* 28,3.

66 Cicero, *De Haruspicum Responso* 20(42).

67 Sallust, *Cat* 40–1; *cf* Cicero, *In Catilinam* iii,2(6).

68 Sallust, *ibid* 40–5.

69 Cicero, *Pro Sulla* 5(17), 13(38); but, according to Cicero, the evidence they gave against his client was false!

70 Cicero, *In Catilinam* iv,3(5); Sallust, *Cat* 50.

71 Cicero, *In Catilinam* iii,9(22).

72 Cicero, *De Prov. Cons.* 13(32); Livy, *Periocha* ciii; Cassius Dio XXXVII, 47–8.

73 For a list of the advocates of these see Jullian III,122 n8 and 123 n5. It is regrettable that some of them have been adopted in standard works—*eg* Salagnon for *Solonium* in Holder II,1611, and St-Nazaire-en-Royans for *Ventia* and St-Marcellin for *Solonium*, both without queries attached, in *TIR* L.31.

74 *Eg* Hirschfeld, *CIL* XII, p 207, Jullian III,122–3, Barruol 1969, 304. Pelletier 1982, 26 n4, prefers the idea of somewhere on the right bank of the Rhône near Tournon.

75 Jullian III,123, n5, was inclined to favour it, but see now G. Chapotat, *Vienne Gauloise: le matériel de la Tène III trouvé sur la colline de Ste-Blandine*, 1970, 150, and Pelletier, *op cit*, 26–7.

76 A. Blanc, *Valence des origines aux Carolingiens*, 1964, 38, and *FOR* XV,18–19.

77 *CIL* I, pp 460,464; Cicero, *Ad Att.* IV,16,3, *Ad Quint. Fr.* III,4,6; Cassius Dio XXXIX, 65.

78 For a summary of this see J.J. Wilkes, *Dalmatia*, 1969,37–40.

79 For their names, with references, see Broughton II,204–53.

80 In 52 BC, when he raised 22 cohorts *ex ipsa coacta provincia* to oppose the intended attacks of Vercingetorix; Caesar, *BG* VII,65.

81 Caesar, *BG*, 1,6–7.

82 *BG* 1,10; in Roman times the capital of the *Santones* was Saintes (*Mediolanum Santonum*).

83 As is suggested in Plutarch, *Caesar*, 19, where Ariovistus and his Germans are described as ἀφόρητοι τοῖς ὑπηκόοις αὐτοῦ γείτονες and Caesar claims that they are no better than the *Cimbri* and he himself is as good as Marius.

84 *BC* III,59, where it is stated that the Allobrogan Abducillus *principatum in civitate multis annis habuerat*.

85 *BG* VII,64–5.

86 *BG* VII,7.

87 And so it appears in the *Notitia Galliarum* XII,4, as *Civitas Albigensium*. For an argument that the *provinciales* occupied a more limited area, between the river Thoré and the Montagne Noire (so excluding Albi), see Canon Griffe, *Bull. Philologique et Historique du Comité des Travaux historiques* 1953–4, 45–50, summarised in *Gallia* XVII(1959), 440–1.

88 For *Legio V Alaudae*, Suetonius, *Divus Iulius* xxiv,2; on the possible raising of a second legion, H.M.D. Parker, *The Roman Legions*, 1928,

57–8. Of the non-legionary recruits the most interesting are the Allobrogian cavalry led by Roucillus and Egus (sons of Abducillus), the two men who defected to Pompey at Dyrrachium, Caesar, *BC* III, 59–84; Caesar also used Rutenian archers and Gallic cavalry in Spain (*BC* I.51).

89 *BG*, VIII, 54.

90 *BC*, I, 37.

91 Béziers became *Colonia Baeterrae Septimanorum* (Pliny, *HN* III, 36, Mela II, 5, 75): for a discussion of this see Clavel 1970, 163–7.

92 *BG*, VIII, 54, *BC* I, 7.

93 *Legio XII*, *BC* I, 15; *Legio VIII*, *BC* I, 18.

94 For a discussion of this possibility see C.F.C. Hawkes in 'Britain and Julius Caesar', *Procs. British Academy* LXIII(1977), 180–3 (the suggestion of Fréjus was first put to him by the present author). The first mention of *Forum Iulii* is in 43 BC (Cicero, *Ad Fam.* X, 15, 3).

95 *BC*, I, 16–23. It should be noted that *Corfinium* (mod Corfinio, formerly Pentina) lies east of Rome, so that Domitius was not then heading for his province.

96 *BC*, I, 34. Caesar's statement that Domitius was going *ad occupandam Massiliam* is, of course, an exaggeration; the bias of Caesar's writings needs to be especially borne in mind when trying to interpret the account of the siege and the events leading up to it.

97 *BC*, I, 35. For the constitution of *Massalia* see Strabo IV, 5; it is regrettable that some English translations of the *BC* (*eg* Warner, Mentor, 1960, and, more surprisingly, M'Devitte, Bohn, 1851) misrepresent the *xv primos* as merely 'leading citizens'.

98 *BC*, I, 34–6; Lucan, *Pharsalia* III, 300–74; Velleius Paterculus II, 50; Cassius Dio XLI, 19. Curiously, there is no reference to the siege in Plutarch, *Caesar*, and Livy, *Periocha* CX, merely says that they closed their gates to Caesar, as also do Suetonius, *Divus Iulius* XXXIV, 2 and Florus II, 13, 22, while Orosius VI, 15, 6, does not go into details. For a defence of Caesar's account see Jullian III, 125 n6.

99 Jullian's suggestion (*loc cit*) that the reference might be to one of the earlier wars against the *Salluvii* and that their domains were handed over to Marseille much later seems a somewhat far-fetched justification for a textual emendation. For other suggestions, Goudineau in *RAN* IX(1976), 108–11.

100 G. Barruol, 'Le Territoire des Albiques', *REL* XXIV(1958), 228–56, conveniently summarised in Barruol 1969, 273–4; Strabo IV, 6, 4.

101 *BC*, I, 36; Cassius Dio XLI, 19; Lucan, *Pharsalia* III, 388–452 (allowing for the style of Lucan, it is tempting to identify the sacred grove with Roquepertuse). The fact that the ships were built so quickly, of green timber, later proved a disadvantage (*BC*, I, 58)!

102 *BC*, I, 86; Appian, *BC*, II, 43 (evidently in error in saying that Caesar himself accompanied them to the river); *cf* Strabo IV, 1, 9.

103 *BC*, II, 4.

104 *BC*, II, 22.

105 Pliny, *HN* III, 34.

106 Strabo IV, 1, 9.

107 Broughton II, 309, based on Cicero, *Ad Att.* XIV, 9, 3.

5
From Caesar to Augustus
48BC—AD 14

Caesar did not, of course, linger in Gaul, having much more important things to deal with in the east (where, so Dio tells us, Pompey countered the capture of *Massalia* by granting freedom to her mother city of *Phocaea*)[1] and his only other passage through our area was on his rapid journey to Spain, to suppress the rising of Pompey's sons, in 45 BC.[2] He did, however, control the organisation of our province and in this connection it is worth noting that it was immediately after the surrender of *Massalia* that some of his men mutinied at *Placentia* in Italy,[3] on the grounds that they were not given adequate rewards for their service, for it was surely this tendency, which recurred elsewhere during the civil wars, that partly led to the promise of land, especially in the form of military *coloniae*, when discharge became possible.

Because of its minor significance during these wars the literary sources offer only chance references to the administration of our province while they were in progress. D. Iunius Brutus Albinus certainly operated in Gaul for the next few years, as a *legatus pro praetore*, but whether he was responsible for the southern part as well as for the northern is quite uncertain: Appian initially refers to his area simply as νεόληπτος Γαλατία ('newly-taken Gaul') and in 46 BC he had to deal with a revolt of the *Bellovaci*, in *Gallia Comata*, not *Narbonensis*.[4] Again, it was in 46 BC that Ti. Claudius Nero, the father of the emperor Tiberius, was sent to Gaul (whether as *legatus* or as *praefectus* is not known) to found *coloniae*, but unfortunately Suetonius, who alone relates this fact, describes them as *colonias in quis Narbo et Arelate erant*[5] and this raises a difficult question. We do know that both of those he names were military foundations—veterans of the tenth legion being added to the colonists who already occupied Narbonne, which became *Colonia Iulia Paterna Narbo Martius Decumanorum*, and some of the sixth legion being settled at Arles, Caesar's former shipyard, which became *Colonia Iulia Paterna Arelate Sextanorum*[6]—and since the adjective *paterna* (no doubt added by Octavian to distinguish the most important foundations of his adopted father) is not known to be applied to any others, it is often concluded that these were the only fully Roman *coloniae* founded here at Caesar's instigation. But what of the other *coloniae* implied by the *in quis* in the text of Suetonius?

It has sometimes been suggested that they include a colony in what later became *Germania Superior*, namely *Colonia Iulia Equestris* (Nyon), where cavalry, not legionary, veterans were installed,[7] but there are several possibilities in *Narbonensis* itself though conclusive evidence is lacking in every case, as may be seen from the references cited in the chapters below that deal with individual *civitates*. On the legionary side there are a few that should be mentioned—*Vienna* (Vienne, though we prefer the view that it was from the beginning a *colonia Latina*), *Valentia* (Valence, though even its full title has not yet been revealed by inscriptions) and *Baeterrae* (Béziers, though we prefer the date 36–35 BC)—but several *coloniae Latinae* seem more likely: among these are *Luteva* (Lodève, whose people are referred to by Pliny as *Lutevani qui et Foroneronienses*), *Carpentorate* (Carpentras, though the only slight evidence for this is Ptolemy's attribution of a *Forum Neronis* to the *Memini*) and *Apta Iulia* (Apt, a city apparently created to control the *Albici*, who had fought on the side of Marseille). It is very probable that many minor communities (not only the 24 *ignobilia oppida* that became subject to *Nemausus*, but also most of the others in Pliny's long list) were granted *ius Latii* by Caesar, most likely as a reward for their loyalty when he was campaigning further north, but whether *Nemausus* (Nîmes) itself or *Cabellio* (Cavaillon), each of which minted pre-Augustan coins inscribed COL.NEM. and COL.CAB. respectively, was made a *colonia Latina* by him or by the Triumvirate that succeeded him is still a little uncertain. In any case, although *Narbonensis* is unique in its number of *coloniae Latinae*, they were not a new invention, since some had been created in Cisalpine Gaul by Pompeius Strabo 40 years earlier, and Caesar was always very ready to grant not only Latin but even Roman citizenship to those who supported him: indeed, it is even possible that some of the *semibarbari Galli* that he admitted to the Senate came from Transalpine as well as Cisalpine Gaul.[8]

In 45 BC A. Hirtius became *proconsul* of *Gallia Transalpina* (possibly, though not certainly, the whole of it) and he was still there at the time of Caesar's assassination,[9] but for 44 the dictator had decided to allot *Gallia Comata* to L. Munatius Plancus, while M. Aemilius Lepidus was to become *proconsul* of both *Gallia Narbonensis* and *Hispania Citerior*.[10] The main achievement of Lepidus about this time was to make an agreement in Spain with Sex. Pompeius (who, surprisingly, was able to spend part of 43 refurbishing his fleet at *Massilia*)[11] but while the fight between Antony and Brutus was in progress he moved back into Gaul and was encamped first near the Rhône and then at *Forum Voconii* (les Blaïs).[12]

This last fact is known from the correspondence of Cicero and it is the letters between him and Munatius Plancus that tell us more about our province. Late in 44 or early in 43 Plancus had been operating fully within his own area, founding colonies at Augst and Lyon (the latter with men from Vienne)[13] but in the spring of 43, requested by the Senate to bring military aid to Italy, he began to move his army south and having sent 1,000 cavalry ahead to Vienne he took his main force across the Rhône on April 26th.[14] Then, sending his brother ahead with 3,000 cavalry and himself advancing 'along the road towards *Mutina* (Modena)', he heard of the raising of the siege there and so halted in the territory of the *Allobroges*.[15] Soon afterwards, however, having made (as he thought) an agreement with Lepidus, he built a bridge over the Isère, took his army over it on 9 May and two days later, having heard that L. Antonius (the brother of Mark Antony) had reached *Forum Iulii* (Fréjus), he sent his brother ahead with 4,000 cavalry to oppose him.[16] The Senate heartily approved of his action,[17] but in the meantime Plancus despaired of the support of Lepidus and so decided to remain where he was, to protect his own province. On 18 May he changed his mind again and began to move south, leaving the bridge over the Isère intact, with manned fortlets at each end of it.[19] On 6 June he wrote to Cicero from *Cularo* (Grenoble), describing what had finally happened. He had advanced to within 40 miles of Antony (who was now at Fréjus) and Lepidus and had chosen a position with a river in front of it that could not be crossed rapidly, near the *Vocontii*, through whose territory he could pass with confidence. Lepidus had tried to persuade him to proceed further, but when he refused to do this Lepidus had joined forces with Antony on 29 May and together they had advanced towards him. Having learnt this when they were only 20 miles away, Plancus had retreated rapidly and on 4 June he had re-crossed the Isère and destroyed the bridge and its fortlets.[20]

Two aspects of this campaign deserve notice. First, it is in this remarkably detailed account of it that the names of three places appear for the first time—*Forum Iulii*, *Forum Voconii* and *Cularo*. The mention of *Forum Iulii* proves beyond doubt that it was founded, if only as a base, before the *colonia* of *Legio VIII* was established there and a reason for this has been suggested above (p 65). So far as *Forum Voconii* is concerned, it is useful that Plancus describes it as 24 Roman miles from *Forum Iulii*, since this enables us to improve the figures of the Antonine Itinerary and the Peutinger Table, which give the distance as *xii* and *xvii mp* respectively[21]—both, presumably, corruptions of *xxii*, which became the measured Roman mileage when (after Cicero's time) the main road between the two places had been properly built. The name itself, however, raises another question. The best MS of Cicero's text (though not those of the Itineraries) gives it in the form *Forum Vocontium* and this has led some people, most notably Barruol,[22] to suggest a connection with the *Vocontii*, a tribe that Plancus also mentions in his letter. Against this, it must be remembered that the Voconii were a well-established Roman family, at least five of whom held offices, and one of them—perhaps the man who was *praetor* in 54 or 50 BC.[23]—might well have founded the place while acting as a legate for Caesar (who very seldom indicates who was responsible for affairs in the south when describing his Gallic Wars). As for *Cularo*, the bridge over the Isère has not been identified, but it must surely have been at or near Grenoble (*qv*) and such limited Iron Age finds as have been made there indicate that there was already a settlement on the south bank of the river.

Secondly, the course taken by Plancus throws an interesting light on what routes armies could reasonably follow in this period. Where he started from is not stated, but since his first stop was at Vienne it was presumably either there or near Lyon that he crossed the Rhône. Thereafter, heading specifically for Modena, he evidently intended to march up the valleys of the Isère and the Romanche, to cross the Alps by way of the Col du Lautaret and the Col de Mont-Genèvre, and although, as far as we know, no formal Roman roads had yet been built in this area, this was already a well-established and reasonable route. But all the evidence suggests that it was at Grenoble that he changed his mind and his march southwards from there is more surprising. The river on the bank of which he finally halted—one wide enough to prevent a rapid crossing—must surely have been the Verdon, which runs just about 40 Roman miles from Fréjus and the most likely place would be St-Croix-de-Verdon, where the later Roman road south-east from Riez crossed it and where a Roman bridge has now been identified.[24] Allowing for the difficulties of the heights along the present N75, he must approximately followed the well-known Route Napoléon, through Gap to Sisteron, thereafter skirting the eastern frontier on the *Vocontii* and probably branching off through Riez to reach the Verdon. The exact course of the later Roman road linking Grenoble and Gap is still a little uncertain, but however one interprets it the length of the march was some 220km in each direction, so that the retreat along this largely unbeaten track, with fords to cross and hills to surmount, in six or seven days was something of an achievement.[25]

Plancus finally joined Antony and Lepidus, when they had made peace with one another,[26] in the late summer and thereafter pursued a successful career elsewhere under both Antony and Octavian (indeed it was he who in 27 BC proposed the title of Augustus for the latter), but when the triumvirate was formed Antony took over his province, using L. Varius Cotyla as his legate, and in 42 BC, after the battle of Philippi, assumed command of *Narbonensis* too.[27] He continued to control it even when he was in the east, with Q. Fufius Calenus as his agent, but when Calenus died in 40 BC Octavian seized all of Transalpine Gaul. The man he appointed to represent him, however, Q. Salvidienus Rufus, plotted to desert to Antony and, having been accused of treachery (remarkably, through information supplied by

Antony himself), committed suicide,[28] and it was probably then that M. Vipsanius Agrippa was first sent to the province. He was certainly *proconsul* in Gaul in 39, when Octavian himself paid a brief visit,[29] and was not recalled until 38 (after he had both crossed the Rhine and crushed a revolt in *Aquitania*), first to build a new fleet against Sex. Pompeius and then to become consul in 37.[30]

This new fleet was used to drive Pompeius from Sicily and although the triumvirate continued, more or less, until 32 BC (Antony held a consulship again in 34), Octavian was now in effective control of all the western half of the empire—something that ultimately assured his victory over Antony.[31] What most concerns us in this period, however, is an event that happened in Sicily. A considerable part of his army mutinied and to calm them Octavian made substantial promises not only of money but also of land, especially in their own cities,[32] and Dio tells us that in the following year he sent a few of the oldest of them to be colonists in Gaul.[33] Dio's text seems to imply that these 'few' came from the new legion that Octavian had formed from still-discontented veterans, but he was writing some two centuries after the event and may well have confused his sources and in view of the current size of the army a considerable number, from many legions, may have been settled. It is, therefore, to this time—that is, between 36 and 33 BC—that we can attentively ascribe the foundation of two of those legionary *coloniae* that we have not attributed to Caesar, namely *Colonia Urbs Iulia Baeterrae Septimanorum* (Béziers, *qv*) and *Colonia Firma Secundanorum Arausio* (Orange, *qv*),[34] and possibly a third, Fréjus (*qv*) which at this stage would be merely *Colonia Forum Iulii Octavanorum*. As Tacitus tells us, the fleet was not installed there until after the battle of Actium in 31 BC and the addition of *Pacensis* as well as *Classica* in its final title suggests that it was a year or two later,[35] just as it seems likely that some veterans from the capture of Alexandria were added to the *colonia Latina* of *Nemausus* which, in or about 28 BC, began to mint coins showing a crocodile chained to a palm-tree and for whom its centuriation may have been laid out.[36]

To revert to chronology, Octavian was again briefly in Gaul in 34 BC, apparently with the intention of leading an expedition to Britain, but he gave this up[37] and so little is said about it that we do not know who was governing our province in the next few years. In 35 and 34 BC it may have been C. Antistius Vetus, who attacked the *Salassi*, since they controlled the Col du Petit-St-Bernard and his assault on them may have been launched from the valley of the Isère.[38] Thereafter C. Carrinas and Nonius Gallus certainly conducted successful campaigns in the north, the former against the *Morini* and the latter against the *Treveri*,[39] and then, more closely, and probably in 28 BC, M. Valerius Corvinus won a victory in *Aquitania*.[40] In any case, in 27 BC, when Octavian had just acquired the title of Augustus, all Gaul, including *Narbonensis*, was placed under his imperial control.[41] In this same year he again visited Gaul (in the expectation, so Dio says, that the Britons would come to terms with him), held a *conventus* at Narbonne and took a census of the three northern provinces and organised their administration, before passing on to Spain to subdue the *Cantabri* and *Astures*.[42]

In 22 BC *Narbonensis*, along with Cyprus, was officially returned to senatorial control,[43] but unforunately only two proconsular governors of it are known in the Augustan period, Cn. Pullius Pollio, who probably ruled it between 18 and 16 BC, and Titedius Labeo, some time between AD 12 and 15,[44] and more significant are the visits of Agrippa and Augustus himself, both of them primarily involved in activities in northern Gaul. So far as Agrippa is concerned, it was evidently during his presence there in 20–19 BC that the main road down the left bank of the Rhône, from Lyon to Arles, was properly laid out (along with the others in northern Gaul), though the earliest recorded milestone on it dates from 3 BC, nine years after his death,[45] but his supposed other activities in our province are highly questionable: as is pointed out under Nîmes (*qv*), the inclusion of his name in the first inscription on the Maison Carrée can no longer be accepted and while he evidently made some gift to that city, whether it was really the aqueduct is by no means certain. When Augustus was next in Gaul, however, in 16–13 BC, among other things he authorised the building of the walls and the gates of Nîmes and Vienne at his expense[46] and it was probably then that he arranged the improvement of both the roads to Italy, the one along the coast (?*Via Iulia Augusta*, but later *Via Aurelia*) and the other over the Alps through the Col de Mont-Genèvre, where Cottius provided assistance.[47]

The last visit of Augustus to Gaul was in 10 BC, when he spent some time in Lyon, largely overlooking the work of Tiberius in the north,[48] so that this does not much concern us, and only a few other events are recorded in *Narbonensis* before the end of Augustus's reign. One is the story of Suetonius that when Tiberius was in exile the *Nemausenses* threw down any local statues of him and, at a party, someone told the visiting Gaius that he was prepared to go to Rhodes to assassinate him, and then the death of Gaius's brother Lucius at *Massilia* in AD 2:[49] and while it is doubtful whether these two sons of Agrippa are really recorded on the monument at *Glanum* (*qv* in the chapter on Arles), their names evidently were added to the temple inscription in Nîmes (*qv*) in AD 4–5. Since the organisation of the province was now complete, however, it seems proper here to list the names and the status of the *civitates* included in it at the end of the Augustan period; all the cities marked with an asterisk are known to have had centuriation in the are they controlled.

Coloniae Romanae

★Arles: *Colonia Iulia Paterna Sextanorum Arelate*
★Béziers: *Colonia Urbs Iulia Baeterrae Septimanorum*
★Fréjus: *Colonia Octavanorum Pacensis Classica Forum Iulii*
★Narbonne: *Colonia Iulia Paterna Narbo Martius Decumanorum*
★Orange: *Colonia Firma Iulia Arausio Secundanorum*
★?Valence: *Colonia Valentia* (possibly only with Latin Rights)

Coloniae Latinae

Aix: *Colonia Iulia Augusta Aquae Sextiae* (later a *colonia Romana*)
Apt: *Colonia Iulia Apta*
Avignon: *Colonia Iulia Avennio* (later to be *Iulia Hadriana*)
Carcassonne: *Colonia Iulia Carcaso*
Carpentras: *Colonia Iulia Meminorum* (*Carpentorate*)
Cavaillon: *Colonia Cabellio*
★Château Roussillon: *Colonia Iulia Ruscino*
Lodève: *Colonia Claudia Luteva* (also *Forum Neronis*)
★Nimes: *Colonia Augusta Nemausus*
Riez: *Colonia Iulia Augusta Apollinaris Reiorum* (also *Alebaece*)
?Toulouse: *Colonia Tolosa* (but called *colonia* only by Ptolemy)
Vienne: *Colonia Iulia Augusta Florentia Vienna* (later a *colonia Romana*)

Other cities with Latin Rights

Alba: *Alba Helviorum* (possibly a *colonia*)
Antibes: *Antipolis*
St-Paul-Trois-Châteaux: *Augusta Tricastinorum* (later to become *Colonia Flavia*)

Civitates Foederatae

Marseille: *Massilia* (controlling *Nicaea*, Nice, the *Stoechades Insulae,* the Iles d'Hyères, and probably *Athenopolis*, St-Tropez)
The *Vocontii*, (with centres as *Vasio*, Vaison, and *Lucus*, Luc-en-Diois)

All of these are dealt with in later pages under their own names, but three further points should be added here: first, the cities of Digne (*Dinia*) and Gap (*Vapincum*) had not yet been transferred to this province; second, while *Narbo* later took over control of *Carcaso* and *Ruscino*, Grenoble (*Cularo*) and Geneva (*Genava*) were made independent of Vienne; and third, as Pliny's account makes clear, a very large number of *vici* and *pagi* which were subject to the cities listed above had themselves been granted Latin rights.

REFERENCES AND NOTES

1 Cassius Dio XLI, 25.
2 He travelled from Rome to *Obulco* (near Cordoba) in only 27 days: Strabo III,4,9, Appian, *BC* II,5. How he returned after his victory at *Munda*, whether by sea or by land, is not recorded, but he had every reason to do so rapidly.
3 Appian, *BC* II,47, Cassius Dio XLI,26–36 (including a long and curious speech attributed to Caesar), Suetonius, *Divus Iulius* lxix-lxx; *cf* Tacitus, *Ann.* I,42.
4 Appian, *BC* II,48 and III; Livy, *Periocha* 114.
5 Suetonius, *Tiberius* iv, I.
6 For Narbonne, *CIL* XII, p 521 and the inscriptions there cited; for Arles, ibid, p 83 (and especially no 738).
7 K. Kraft, *Jahrbüch des Römisch-Germanischen Zentralmuseums* IV(1957), 81–107.
8 On the general question see, for example, Vittinghof 1942, *passim* (with the suggestion, here rejected, that *Baeterrae* was also a Caesarian legionary colony on p 268, n 149); Sherwin White 1973, 111, 159, 364–9; Goudineau 1979, 249–306. For Pompeius Strabo, Asconius, *Comm. on Cicero's Ad Pisonem*, 3; for *semibarbari*, Suetonius, *Divus Iulius* lxxvi, 3 (not the same as the *orcivi* enrolled *post necem Caesaris* cited in *Divus Augustus* xxxv, 1).
9 Cicero, *Ad. Att.* XIV,9,3, mentioning also his legate Aurelius, to whom some German tribes had sent friendly envoys.
10 Cassius Dio XLIII,51,8.
11 Appian, *BC* IV,84.
12 Cicero, *Ad Fam.* X,17 and 34.
13 Cassius Dio XLVI,50.
14 Cicero, *Ad Fam.* X,9.
15 *Ibid* X,11.
16 *Ibid* X,15.
17 *Ibid* X,16 and 19.
18 *Ibid* X,21
19 *Ibid* X,18: *pontem tamen, quem in Isara feceram, castellis duobus ad capita positis, reliqui, praesidiaque ibi firma posui, ut venienti Bruto exercituique eius sine mora transitus esset paratus.* Since the bridge had been built in only one day (*ibid* X,21), it must have been merely of timber, but it might be hoped that the presence of fortifications at each end could eventually lead to its identification.
20 *Ibid* X,23.
21 *Ibid* X,21; *It. Ant.* 298.1. On its location at or near les Blaïs, R. Boyer and P.-A. Février, 'Stations routières de Provence', *REL* XXV(1959), 168–78.
22 Barruol 1969, 280–1.
23 Broughton II(1952), 222, 635 and Additions p 70.
24 *Gallia* XXVIII(1970), 452–3, with good illustrations. The remains of the bridge are now submerged by the Barrage de Ste-Croix.
25 *Cf* Vegetius, *Epitoma Rei Militaris* I,9, where four Roman miles a Roman hour is the basic training rate.
26 Plutarch, *Antony* xviii. The river that Antony crossed to approach Lepidus was presumably the Aille, a tributary of the Argens, rather than the Argens itself.

27 Plutarch, *ibid*; Appian, *BC*. v,51; Cassius Dio xlviii,10 (which also mentions P. Ventidius Bassus, but he is more likely to have been in command in Cisalpine Gaul).

28 Livy, *Periocha* 127; Appian, *BC*. v,51 and 56 (which says that Salvidienus was executed); Vell. Pat. ii,76,4; Cassius Dio xlviii,20,3.

29 Appian, *BC* v,75.

30 Cassius Dio xlviii,49,2–4.

31 So that in 32 BC not only Italy but also Gaul, Spain, Africa, Sicily and Sardinia swore oaths of allegiance to him (*Res Gestae* xxv,2).

32 Appian, *BC* v,127–9 (saying that 2,000 were sent out of Sicily at once); Cassius Dio xlix,13–14; Vell. Pat. ii,81; Orosius vi,18,33 (putting the total of legions under Octavian's command at 44 and stating that it was specifically for land that they mutinied).

33 Cassius Dio xlix,34,4.

34 J. Kromayer, 'Die Militärcolonien Octavians und Caesars in Gallia Narbonensis', *Hermes* xxi(1896),1–18, followed by Ritterling, *P-W* xii,1614–15, suggested 36 BC for Béziers (*cf* Appian in n 32, above) and 35–33 BC for Orange; Piganiol 1962, 83, followed by Clavel 1970, 166–7, prefers 35 BC for both. The inclusion of both Béziers and Fréjus by Hatt 1966, 80, in his list of Caesarean colonies seems rather improbable, though Wittinghoff 1942, 268, argues for the former and Février (*JRS* lxiii(1973) 20–4) still considers this a faint possibility for the latter. In any case, as stated in *Res Gestae* 28, Augustus founded *some colonias militum* in *Gallia Narbonensis*.

35 On this see Février, *loc cit*. One of the difficulties here is Tacitus's loose use of terms: in *Agr.* 4,1, he rightly describes his father-in-law as *vetere et inlustri Foroiuliensium colonia ortus*, but in *Ann.* iv,5, he says that *Augustus* (a name that should imply 27 BC or later) sent ships captured in his victory at Actium *in oppidum Foroiuliense* (*cf* his vexed attribution of the word *municipium* to *Verulamium* in *Ann*, xiv,33).

36 For a useful discussion of the date of these coins, reviewing a number of theories, C.M. Wells, *The German Policy of Augustus*, 1972, Appx ii (pp 266–88); for the centuriation *v* Nîmes, p. 167.

37 Cassius Dio xlix,38.

38 Appian, *Illyr.* iv(17); for a general account of the *Salassi* (though with no mention of Antistius Vetus), Strabo iv,6,7.

39 For Carrinas, Cassius Dio li,21,6 (recording his triumph, which was held in 28 BC); for Nonius, Dio li,20,5 (dating his campaign to 29 BC).

40 Appian, *BC* iv,38 (putting it after the battle of Actium); Tibullus i,vii,3–9,ii,i,33; *Panegyricus Messallae* 138–39.

41 Cassius Dio liii,12,5.

42 Cassius Dio liii,22,5; Livy, *Periocha* cxxxiv.

43 Cassius Dio liv,4,4.

44 Pflaum 1978, 3–4.

45 Strabo iv,11 (and for their primarily military use *cf Panegyrici Latini* v(viii),7,2; only Augustan milestone, found near Vienne, *CIL* xii,5510 (König no 114): for comment on date, Grenier 1934, 33–4.

46 *Res Gestae* xii,2, Cassius Dio liv,25,1 (mentioning his gifts to special districts in Gaul and Spain): inscriptions of walls and gates, Nîmes, *CIL* xii,3151, Vienne, *ILGN*, 263, both here discussed under those cities.

47 Earliest milestones on southern route, *CIL* XII, 5454, 5455 (König nos 35, 36, both near Fréjus and both 12 BC), on Alpine route, *CIL* XII, 5497, 5500 (König nos 82, 86, on either side of Apt, both 3 BC). On the names of the southern road, Grenier 1934, 32: on the work of Cottius in the Alps, Strabo IV, 1, 3, and especially Ammianus XV, 10, 3, where he says that he did it *in amicitiam principis Octaviani* (not *Augusti*) *receptus*, which might imply an earlier date.

48 Cassius Dio LIV, 36, 3–4; about this time Tiberius did settle some dissent among the *Viennenses* (Velleius Paterculus II, 121, 1)

49 Suetonius, *Tiberius* xiii, 1; Cassius Dio LV, 10a, 9, *CIL* XI, 1420.

50 Pliny, *HN* III, 36–7.

6
From Tiberius to Carus AD 14–283

The prosperity of *Narbonensis* in the early imperial period is already implied by Pomponius Mela, who lists as its *urbes opulentissimae* Vaison, Vienne, Avignon, Nîmes, Toulouse, Orange, Arles and Béziers,[1] but much more informative is Pliny the Elder who, some 35 years later, says of it *agrorum cultu, virorum morumque dignatione, amplitudine opum, nulli provinciarum postferenda breviterque Italia verius quam provincia*[2] and later refers to its wheat, to several of its wines, to fishing and to one kind of wool.[3] Columella, Martial and Plutarch also mention its wines (and Martial its cheese and fish-sauce too)[4] and it is evident that Domitian's attempt to restrict the cultivation of vines was not successful, at least in this province, for exports to the north continued and, in the second century, some of its wine was sold to Rome.[5] Moreover, while the more northerly provinces and probably Italy imported oil from *Narbonensis*, it also contributed wheat to the *annona* and it must have benefited from the fact that any that came from *Aquitania* would have been channelled through Narbonne.[6] Our knowledge of the production of both wine and oil has been greatly increased by recent excavations, as may be seen from the references to oil-presses in our sections on Aix, Antibes and Fréjus and especially the remarkable wine-producing site at Donzère (under St-Paul-Trois-Châteaux) with its 200 jars storing some 2,500 hectolitres.

Agriculture, however, was not the only source of wealth. As may also be seen in the *civitas* chapters, extensive mining of iron, copper, lead and silver took place in a number of districts, especially those under Narbonne, Béziers, Nîmes and Fréjus, but also a little in the territories of Apt and Valence, and while the source of the gold stolen by Caepio from the *Tectosages* in 106 BC was probably la Montagne Noire, which now yielded some for Carcassonne and Narbonne, even Toulouse may still have gained a little brought down by rivers. Pottery production also flourished: not only could most of our *civitates* make their own necessary wares, including amphorae, but *terra sigillata* was produced at an early date at Bram, in the territory of Carcassonne, and later at Chatière and Portout, in that of the *Viennenses*. As for trade, customs duties (the *quadragesima Galliarum*), which were reorganised either in late Augustan or early Tiberian days, did not affect movements to or from the other Gallic provinces, but they were imposed on traffic with Italy and Spain and, as will be seen, offices are referred to in both the Alpine and the Pyrenean areas.[7]

In any case, the richness of the province is well illustrated by buildings. While only Vienne acquired an odeon, theatres were built in so many towns, not just the still-visible ones at Alba, Arles, Orange, Vaison and Vienne, along with the little hellenistic one at Marseille, but also at Narbonne, Nîmes, Toulouse, Antibes, Valence, Apt, Annecy and Bram and probably at Avignon, Béziers, St-Paul-Trois-Châteaux and Carcassonne. Similarly, there were amphitheatres at Arles, Nîmes, Fréjus, Narbonne, Béziers, Toulouse, and possibly at Orange and Die, and circuses at Arles, Nîmes and Vienne. Almost all cities and many *vici* built their own aqueducts, about a dozen spas were developed and while the dating of many villas still requires clarification some of them (like that at Chiragan) were highly productive, while others (like the coastal one at la Madrague-de-St-Cyr) were very luxurious.

To turn now to the *dignatio virorum*, this province was already providing senators and in the first century AD at least a dozen achieved the consulship. Whether P. Memmius Regulus (a patron of *Ruscino* who first became suffect consul in 31) was of Narbonnese origin remains uncertain, but D. Valerius Asiaticus (*cos* 35) certainly came from Vienne, Cn. Domitius Afer (*praetor* in 25 and *cos* 39) from Nîmes, Pompeius Paullinus (a nephew of Seneca, *cos c* 53) from Arles, L. Duvius Avitus (*cos* 56) from Vaison, P. Marius Celsus (*cos* 62 and 69) probably from Nîmes, M. Vestinus Atticus (*cos* 65) and L. Pompeius Vopiscus (*cos* 69) from Vienne and, of course, the great Cn. Iulius Agricola (*cos* 77) from Fréjus, while T. Aurelius Fulvus (the grandfather of the emperor Antoninus Pius) who came from Nîmes, was probably suffect consul in 70 before becoming full consul in 85.[8] Many others followed in later years and it should be noted that most of them were not from the original *coloniae Romanae* but from the *coloniae Latinae*. With regard to Pliny's phrase *Italia verius quam provincia*, in AD 49 Claudius had granted to senators from *Narbonensis* the right to visit their estates without imperial permission, a privilege hitherto shared only by Sicilians.[9]

Of the senators who did not fully achieve the consulship the most famous is M. Antonius Primus (nicknamed 'the Beak'), who led a rascally life according to Tacitus but greatly helped Vespasian (from whom he received consular *insignia* for his military activity against Vitellius) and ultimately retired in peace to his home city of Toulouse.[10] Among the numerous *equites* recorded in inscriptions the best known is L. Afranius Burrus, the equestrian procurator of Livia, Tiberius and Claudius and the tutor and adviser of Nero, who came from Vaison, and another possibility, as we shall see, is Cornelius Fuscus, son of a senatorial family, who preferred an equestrian career and may well have come from one of our *coloniae*.[11]

On the educational side Marseille continued to prosper, not only offering a sound training to people like Agricola and the notable philosophical rhetor Favorinus but also harbouring other famous rhetoricians, duly recorded by Seneca, such as Agroitas, Pacatus and the exiled Volcacius Moschus, along with the doctors Crinas (who also dabbled in astrology) and Charmis. Orators also flourished in Toulouse (L.Statius Ursulus) and Narbonne (Votienus Montanus) and whether or not Tacitus really came from Vaison, that city certainly produced a notable historian in Pompeius Trogus. Poetry and philosophy, however, seem to have declined: of the poets, P.Terentius Varro Atacinus of Narbonne and C.Cornelius Gallus had both flourished in the republican period (the latter having to commit suicide in 27 BC after boasting too much as Prefect of Egypt) and the Stoic philosopher of Narbonne, Fabius Maximus, is recorded only by Horace.

Since this was a prosperous and usually peaceful province, with the rest of Gaul to the north of it now effectively tamed, the names of its governors very seldom appear in literary sources and it therefore seems best to list those that have been identified (mainly from inscriptions) before proceeding with the fragmentary history. The first two known proconsuls, Cn.Pullius Pollio and Titedius Labeo, have already been mentioned in the last chapter and while Titedius' period may have extended after the death of Augustus we shall now begin with those who certainly ruled in the Julio-Claudian period. All the lists that follow are derived mainly from H.-G.Pflaum's great work *Les Fastes de la province de Narbonnaise*, but, as will be observed, doubts still persist regarding many of the dates.

Proconsuls[12]

Approx. Dates	Name	Country of Origin
15–17	M'.Vibius Balbinus	Italy
30–34	Torquatus Novellius Atticus (a great drinker who died at Fréjus aged 44)	Italy
34–37	T.Mussidius Pollianus	Italy
54–60	T.Vinius Rufus (the best known)	?
77	L.V..dius Bassus (on Orange Cadastre A)	?
pre-78	C.Iulius Cornutus Tertullus	?
103–109[13]	A.Larcius Priscus	Italy
118–120	M.Acilius Priscus Egrilius Plarianus	Italy
124	L.Aninius Sextius Florentinus	?
124–127	L.Aurelius Gallus	?
144–145	L.Novius Crispinus Martialis Saturninus	?
pre-150	C.Seius Calpurnius Quadratus Sittianus	?
165–183	L.Cestius Gallus Cerrinius Iustus Lutatius Natalis	?
138–192	Cn.Cornelius Aquilius Niger	?
180–192	L.Fabius Cilo Septiminus Catinius Lepidus Acilianus Fulcinianus (earlier a *legatus*)	Spain
2nd cent	? . .dius Titii filius	?
197–214	L.Ranius Optatus Novatus	?
210	Anon, allegedly killed for supporting Geta[15]	?
210–230	. . . .us	?
216–217	Tib.Claudius Paulinus	Asia?
222–235	C.Aemilius Berenicianus Maximus	?
222–235	Iulianus	?

A few other possibilities are also suggested by Pflaum (M'.Acilius Aviola and four others recorded without names), but the claim by the author of *Scriptores Historiae Augustae* that M.Clodius Pupienus Maximus (briefly emperor March–June 238) was a proconsul here is probably false.[16]

Though they were doubtless more numerous, it is not surprising that fewer names are known of the legates who assisted the proconsuls and these too are taken from Pflaum's analysis:

Legates[17]

Approx. Dates	Name	Country of Origin
pre 30–34	Torquatus Novellius Atticus	Italy
pre 69	Proculus	Italy
78	P.Baebius Italicus	Italy
103–105	T.Calestrius Tiro	?
115	Q.Caecilius Marcellus	Africa
128–132	M.Vettius Valens	Italy
135–137	M.Gavius Appalius Maximus	Italy
168–170	P.Cornelius Anullinus	Italy
177–183	L.Fabius Cilo Septiminus Catinius Lepidus Acilianus Fulcinianus	Italy
200	Q.Iulius Maximus	Spain
235–260	Ti.Claudius Memmius Priscus	Italy

Again, four others are recorded without names.

Too few are also known of the quaestors, but here there is a possibility that two of them may have originated in the province:

Quaestors[18]

Approx. Dates	Name	Country of Origin
35–50	Q.Trebellius Catulus	Arles ?
95–114	Q.Caecilius Marcellus	Africa
123	M.Pontius Laelianus Larcius Sabinus	Béziers ?[19]
125	C.Herennius Caecilianus	Italy
180	C.Caesonius Macer Rufinianus	Italy
98–192	T.Didius Priscus	Italy
98–192	Q.Gavius Fulvius Tranquillus	Italy
98–192	L.Vettius Statura	Italy
98–152	Q.Petronius Melior	Italy

Here too one other unnamed is also recorded and, as may be seen from the list, the dates of most of their offices are very uncertain indeed.

The last table worth recording in full is that of the procurators who were officially in charge of the emperor's properties but sometimes were involved in playing a wider role:

Procurators[20]

Approx. Dates	Name	Country of Origin
14–37	Vitrasius Pollio (also responsible for *Aquitania*)	Italy
27–30	M.Hordeonius	?
69	Valerius Paulinus	Fréjus
(?70	C.Plinius Secundus	Italy)[21]
78	Cassius Marianus	?
81–96	C.Terentius Iunior	Italy ?
1st cent	Gemellus	?
140	T.Pontius Sabinus	Italy
172	Marius Pudens	?
174–176	Q.Domitius Marsianus	Africa
178–180	T.Petronius Sabinus	Italy
198–208	Septimius Honoratus	?

On the whole the finances of this province were well run and only occasionally, it seems, had *curatores* to be appointed to oversee those of individual cities—of senatorial ones L.Burbuleius Optatus Ligarianus working at *Narbo* in the Antonine period (probably after the serious fire there), M.Pontius Laelianus (already noted as a *quaestor*) overseeing *Arausio c* 130 and someone whose name is not recorded at *Avennio*; and of equestrians M.Cominius Aemilianus at *Aquae Sextiae* under Trajan and, in the second century, Q.Soillius Valerianus at *Cabellio, Avennio* and *Forum Iulii*.[22] As we have already noted, a few *procuratores* of the *annona* and the *quadragesima Galliarum* are known, but there were also *procuratores Augusti ferrariarum Galliarum* (first established by Trajan), *procuratores Augusti xx hereditatum* (all three of them being responsible for *Aquitania* as well as *Narbonensis*) and *praefecti vehiculorum per Gallias* (all third century, after Septimius Severus had reorganised the *cursus publicus*), but the work of these was not, of course, confined to our province—neither was that of the curious L.Didius Marinus, who had been *procurator familiarium gladiatoriarum* in the Gauls, Britain, Spain, Germany and Raetia.[23] On the imperial religious side, eight *flamines* and one *flaminica* of the province are recorded, in the time of Vespasian one called Mercator at Fréjus, in the late first century Q.Trebellius Rufus at Toulouse, in the second century M.Cominius Aemilianus, Q.Solonius Severinus, L.Sammius Aemilianus and Q.Soillius Valerianus, all at Nîmes, Sex.Atticus and the *flaminica* Iullina at Vienne, and in Severan times C.Batonius Primus, who was involved in a *taurobolium* at Narbonne.[24]

Peaceful and fully organised, *Narbonensis* played little part in the recorded history of the first two centuries. Whether or not any of its leading men should be included among the *principes Galliarum* whose property, according to Suetonius, was confiscated by Tiberius,[25] they certainly did not join in the revolt of Florus and Sacrovir in AD 21 and this event is here reflected only in the arch of Orange (*qv*) and possibly in that of Carpentras (*qv*).[26] As for Caligula, we do not know by what routes he travelled to and from northern Gaul, nor whether any of our people were involved in the games he held at Lyon, but the change from *quattuorviri* to *duoviri* in Vienne at about this time suggests that it may have been he who raised that city from a *colonia Latina* to a *colonia Romana* in about AD 40. Claudius, however, certainly did pass through this province on his way to Britain, sailing from Ostia and, because of the gales that attacked his ship, disembarking at Marseille to take to the roads, and it is possible that the evidently early maritime itinerary along this coast may originally have been designed for his passage.[27]

While Claudius had, characteristically, granted additional land and the title of king to M.Iulius Cottius in the Cottian Alps,[28] Nero duly abolished that kingdom, but in AD 63 he did grant *ius Latii* to all the people of *Alpes Maritimae*.[30] How far *Narbonensis* suffered from his impositions in his more savage later years[31] is not known, but some implications emerge. In the first place, Vienne (as usual, in opposition to Lyon) was very ready to side with C.Iulius Vindex when he began his revolt in 68 and later recruited legionaries for Galba,[32] then, when Galba himself was on his way from his province of *Tarraconensis* to Italy, he was enthusiastically greeted by senators at Narbonne,[33] and it is even possible that the *colonia* where Cornelius Fuscus welcomed him was in our province.[34] Nevertheless, Galba's decision to transfer the *civitates* of the *Avantici* and *Bodiontici* to *Narbonensis* or perhaps simply to grant them *ius Latii*, may have been due to the influence of the former provincial governor, T.Vinius Rufus, who effectively controlled Galba and joined him in the consulship in 69.[35]

In the chaotic year of the four emperors our province was affected in several ways. In the first place, since Vitellius was as much opposed to Galba as to Otho, Vienne was badly threatened when Fabius Valens, with troops largely drawn from Lyon, first approached it: the *Viennenses* had to offer a most humble and expensive surrender to him, the acceptance of which may have been influenced not only by money but also by the fact that although this Fabius came from a mere equestrian family he might have claimed the great Fabius Allobrogicus as a remote ancestor: money, however, was all that could save the town of Luc from destruction as Valens marched up the valley of the Drome.[36] Secondly, Galba had appointed a man called Q.Pomponius Rufus as *praefectus orae maritimae Hispaniae Citerioris (et) Galliae Narbonensis*[37] and Otho accordingly tried to invade this province with naval help. Both *Narbonensis* and *Alpes Maritimae* it seems, had now sworn loyalty to Vitellius, and while the governor of the latter, Marius Maturus, failed to defeat the Othonian troops, Fabius Valens sent forces (partly under Iulius Classicus) to Fréjus and after a bloody battle in this area the Vitellians had to withdraw to Antibes and the Othonians to Albenga.[38] Thereafter all the more significant events took place in Italy and the east and when the star of Vespasian had risen (largely with the help of the Tolosan Antonius Primus) Fabius Valens sailed back along our coast and, having called on Marius Maturus (still faithful to Vitellius, but about to move over to Vespasian), was forced to land on the *Stoechades Insulae*, where he was arrested by Vespasian's supporter Valerius Paulinus, who had already taken over Fréjus.[39]

After that our province was loyal to Vespasian and while troubles continued in northern Gaul a long period of peace began here. Under Vespasian himself, the two most notable events to mention are the erection of the inscription of Cadastre A at Orange—to be followed, certainly in the Flavian period, by the elevation of St-Paul-Trois-Châteaux to *Colonia Flavia Tricastinorum*—and the careful definition of the boundary between the *Viennenses* and the *Ceutrones* by two boundary stones.[40] The emperor Titus is distinguished from our point of view only by the dedication to him of Pliny's invaluable *Historiae Naturales* and Domitian by his unsuccessful attempt, already mentioned, to limit the production of vines—though some of our more notable figures doubtless suffered execution in his later years. Nerva's brief reign yields nothing.

While Trajan's personal activity was concentrated mainly on the eastern half of the empire, this western province can still offer some indications of the effectiveness of his general government, not only the erection of Cadastre B at Orange but also the suppression of a *gymnicus agon* at Vienne, curiously described by Pliny the Younger (who also refers to the vices of that city!),[41] while, if the author of the *Scriptores Historiae Augustae* is telling the truth, though the emperor himself was of Spanish origin, the Plotina to whom he was married must have come from Nîmes and it was there that Hadrian erected a basilica in her memory.[42] In any case, Hadrian himself certainly visited this province, renaming Avignon *Colonia Iulia Hadriana* and erecting a monument to his famous horse Borysthenes when it died near Apt.[43] Antoninus Pius, though he belonged to a family of Nemausensian origin, did not come here in person, but his generosity to all provinces is well reflected in his contribution to the restoration of Narbonne after a serious fire,[44] while the first appearance of milestones along roads in the territory of *Alba Helviorum* suggests that serious steps were now taken to improve communications on routes other than the main arteries.[45] Besides this, it was in this period that the goddess Cybele came into her own, with the introduction of *taurobolia*—something that becomes most notable in the Isère valley, where she seems to have been identified with Andarta, the local Dea Augusta.[46] Since many soldiers retired here, Mithras was also widely revered, but too little is known about when the most important religion of oriental origin, Christianity, spread into this province. We shall return to its development in the final chapter, but here it must be noted that the main event in the otherwise considerate reign of Marcus Aurelius was the slaughter of Christians in Lyon and at least one of the martyrs, called Sanctus, came from the city of Vienne, where he was said to be a deacon.[47]

Marcus Aurelius was widely honoured in the province, most notably by a building erected in his honour at Aôste after the defeat of Avidius Cassius in the east,[48] and although a law was passed in 176 forbidding people to become governors of the provinces from which they had come[49] *Narbonensis* continued to produce notable figures, such as Martius Verus, from Toulouse, who, when governor of Cappadocia, assisted in suppressing Avidius Cassius and was consul in 166 and 179.[50] Nevertheless, it was only marginally involved in the struggle of the five would-be emperors that followed the deplorable reign of Commodus. Severus was able to defeat Clodius Albinus at Lyon, just outside our province,[51] and whether or not the curious schoolmaster and would-be senator Numerianus had raised some of his troops and money in *Alpes Maritimae*, it was surely in *Alpes Cottiae* that C.Iulius Pacatianus (an *eques* from Vienne, later to become *comes imperatoris*) played his useful part.[52]

Nothing is recorded of what went on here in the reign of Severus himself, apart from standard dedications in his honour,[53] but under his savage son Caracalla several relevant things occurred. In the first place, the *Scriptores Historiae Augustae* claim that as soon as entering Gaul he killed an unnamed governor of *Narbonensis*, despite which he too was officially honoured in cities like Narbonne and Vienne,[54] but, not surprisingly, it was Iulius Honoratus, the equestrian governor of *Alpes Maritimae*, who, under Caracalla's instruction, restored the road between Vence and Digne.[55] Secondly, both *Narbonensis* and *Alpes Maritimae*, like the rest of the empire, were subject in 212 to the *Constitutio Antoniniana*, granting Roman citizenship to all free people— and thereby increasing the taxes drawn from them, especially for the payment of soldiers[56]—but much more accurate archaeological dating is, of course, required before the effect of this, or that of the debased *antoninianus* coinage (introduced in 215) can be established.

In any case, while inscriptions recording respect for emperors continue to appear, literary sources become even more fragmentary and very little is said specifically about this province in the third century. As may be seen from the list already shown, despite the fact that the emperor Macrinus, the immediate successor to Caracalla, was merely an *eques, Narbonensis* still had a proconsular governor in the 230s, thus reflecting the attempt of Severus Alexander (Emperor 222–35) to restore the constitution after Elagabalus had been disposed of, but only a few other matters deserve attention in this tortuous period. The first is the statement of Gregory of Tours that out of seven bishops sent to Gaul during the persecution by the Emperor Decius (249–51) three came here—Trophimus to Arles, Paulus to Narbonne and Saturninus to Toulouse—and while Saturninus was martyred the other two 'passed their lives in great holiness'. While the dates of their arrival are clearly confused, this seems to be the first evidence for a fully-established Christian church in our area.[57]

Secondly, the involvement of this province in the *Imperium Galliarum* of Postumus, Victorinus and Tetricus. It is not directly mentioned in any of the fragmentary documents that cover this period and while in 269 the legitimate Emperor Claudius Gothicus was able to send troops under Iulius Placidianus at least as far as Grenoble[58] (probably in the hope of assisting Autun, which had then revolted against Victorinus), the only inscriptions recording a Gallic emperor are those on three milestones of Tetricus, one found near Béziers, one near Carcassonne and one south-east of Toulouse, so it is tempting to believe that they really controlled only the western area.[59] Nevertheless, Aurelian is duly recorded as *Restitutor Galliarum*, not only at Alba but also at Fréjus (the latter on one of several milestones that regularly name him as such).[60]

Closely related to this is the question of how much the province was really affected by the barbarian invasions that took place *c* 259–60 and 270–80. While one unreliable source, the *Scriptores Historiae Augustae*, claims that Probus recovered and restored sixty of the notable cities of Gaul, not only is this rather improbable but, while some damage was certainly done in northern Italy, most of the plundering in Gaul must have happened in the other Gallic provinces. There is some evidence that trouble took place here (whether due to invaders or to local insurgents), such as fires (*eg* the well-dated one in the Maison au Dauphin in Vaison, *qv*), the temporary occupation (especially in the 270s) of some caves and the reoccupation of some hill-forts,[61] but quite why the notable town of *Glanum*, even if pillaged, should have been totally abandoned in this period is very perplexing.

Aurelian and Probus had done their best to restore the security of the empire, in both the east and the west, but its major reorganisation took place under Diocletian and the effect of this will be considered in our next chapter, so only one other thing needs to be mentioned here. While authors such as Eutropius and Orosius firmly state that Carus, who succeeded Probus and sent his son Carinus to oversee Gaul, was of Narbonensian origin, it seems that, for once, the *Scriptores Historiae Augustae* are correct in doubting this and it is more probable that, like Probus and Diocletian, he came from *Illyria*, perhaps from *Narona* (Vid).[62]

REFERENCES AND NOTES

1 Mela II, 5, 75.
2 Pliny, *HN* III, 31

3 Pliny, *HN* xviii, 85 (wheat from Vienne), xiv, 18, 26, 27, 43, 68 (wine from Vienne, Alba, Marseille, Béziers), ix, 29–32 (fishing near Lattes), xxxi, 94–7 (fish-sauces from Fréjus and Antibes), viii, 191 (wool from Pézenas).

4 Columella xii, 23 (wine of Vienne); Martial x, 36 (wine of Marseille), xiii, 107 (wine of Vienne), xii, 32 (cheese of Toulouse); Plutarch, *Quaestiones Conviviales* v, 31 (Vienne); *cf* also Strabo iv, 1, 8, (oysters and fish).

5 For Domitian's restriction, Suetonius, *Domitian* 7, 2 and 14, 2; for exports to Rome, *CIL* xv, 4542–3 (Béziers wine-jars at Monte Testaccio); for northern exports, such as barrels at Neumagen and Langres, E. Wightman, *Gallia Belgica* (1985), 148–9; Grenier 1937, 578–91.

6 Oil exports, *eg CIL* vi, 9717 (an *olearius* from Aix who died at Rome); for *procuratores annonae*, *CIL* xii, 672 (Cominius Claudius, *procurator Augustorum ad annonam provinciae Narbonensis*, at Arles) and C. Attius Alcimus Felicianus, recorded elsewhere (Pflaum 1978, 167–72).

7 On the customs, de Laet 1949, 76–84 (republican period), 144–73 (imperial period), 364–5 (date of reorganisation); summary, Grenier 1959, 500–03; for eight *procuratores quadragesimae Galliarum* in the 2nd and 3rd centuries, Pflaum 1978, 145–52.

8 For Memmius as patron of *Ruscino*, *ILGN*, 633; for references of other consuls see notes on chapters below (Arles, n 8, Fréjus, nn 11–12, Nîmes, nn 7–8, *Vocontii*, n 9) and for a general discussion Syme 1958, 786–8 (including the possibility that Corbulo also came from this province).

9 Tacitus, *Ann* xii, 23, 1.

10 Antonius Primus, Tacitus, *Ann* xiv, 40 (exiled for forgery), *Hist* ii, 86 (restored by Galba and given command of *Leg* vii), iii, *passim* (mainly military support for Vespasian against Vitellius), iv, 4 (consular *insignia*), &c; Suetonius, *Vitellius* 18 (*Becco*, 'Beak'); Martial ix, 99, x, 23 (retirement to Toulouse).

11 Syme 1958, 683–4, with references.

12 Pflaum 1978, 4–57.

13 Pflaum 1978, 48, suggests 103–04, but A. Birley, *The Fasti of Roman Britain* (1981), 235–7, prefers 109 as more likely.

14 Pflaum 1978, 26–30; Birley, *op cit*, 258–9, again with doubts on date.

15 *SHA, Caracalla,* 5, 1.

16 *SHA, Maximus et Balbinus,* 5, 7.

17 Pflaum 1978, 59–78.

18 Pflaum 1978, 79–85.

19 Pflaum suggests *Narbonensis* but, as pointed out by Birley, *op cit*, 274, Béziers is the only city in this province whose citizens were enrolled in his voting-tribe *Pupinia*. The man became consul in 144.

20 Pflaum 1978, 109–33.

21 Pflaum follows the suggestion of Münzer in *Bonner Jahrbücher* civ(1899), 103–11, that Pliny's procuratorship here is proved by his extensive knowledge of our province, but this has been seriously questioned by R. Syme, 'Pliny the Procurator', *Harvard Studies in Classical Philology* lxxiii(1969), 201–36 (reprinted in E. Badian (ed), *Ronald Syme: Roman Papers*, 1979, 742–3) and this is why it is here placed in brackets.

22 Pflaum 1978, 97–101.

23 Pflaum 1978, 135–43 (*procuratores ferrariarum*), 159–65 (*procuratores heredita-*

tum), 153–7 (*praefecti vehiculorum*), 173–6 (Didius Marinus, on whom see also Birley, *op cit*, 300).

24 Pflaum 1978, 103–08; as indicated in our chapter on Nîmes, the suggestion of Grenier on p xi of his preface to Pflaum that the number of *flamines* recorded there indicates that it replaced Narbonne as the provincial capital requires more proof.

25 Suetonius, *Tiberius* xlix, 2; contrast Velleius Paterculus II, 129, where the suppression of Florus and Sacrovir is included in a chapter that praises Tiberius for his generosity!

26 It is surprising that the revolt, so vividly described in Tacitus, *Ann* III, 40–7, is not mentioned by Cassius Dio nor (unless the passage cited in n 25 is partly relevant) by Suetonius.

27 Suetonius, *Claudius* xvii, 1–2; Cassius Dio LX, 21, 3. On the early date of *Itin.Marit.* 497.9–508.1, which lists *Centumcellae*, which was converted into a splendid port by Trajan in AD 107 (Pliny, *Epp* VI, 31), merely as a *positio, v* R.Lugand, 'Note sur l'Itinéraire Maritime de Rome à Arles', *Mélanges de l'Ecole Francaise à Rome* 1926, 124–39. Interestingly, two milestones on the *Via Agrippina* were erected in AD 43 (*CIL* XII, 5542 + p 858 and 5546, König Nos 110 and 118), either to ensure that the land route was in good shape for the emperor's passage or simply to greet him.

28 Cassius Dio LX, 24, 4.

29 Suetonius, *Nero* xviii.

30 Tacitus, *Ann* XV, 32.

31 *Eg* Tacitus, *Ann* XV, 45, 1: *Interea conferendis pecuniis pervastata Italia, provinciae eversae sociique populi et quae liberae vocantur; cf* Zonaras XI, 13 and Suetonius, *Nero* xliii, 1 (with his intention to murder all people of Gallic origin after learning of the revolt of Vindex).

32 Tacitus, *Hist* I, 65.

33 Plutarch, *Galba* xi, 1.

34 As suggested by Syme 1958, 683–4, citing, among other things, the inscription of a Cornelius Fuscus at Béziers (*CIL* XII, 4267, though it is regrettably fragmentary), but also the possibility of Fréjus (*ibid* 677).

35 Pliny, *HN* III, 37; on the influence of Vinius over Galba, Suetonius, *Galba* xiv, 2, Plutarch, *Galba* xi–xii, and for a summary of his career, Tacitus, *Hist* I, 48.

36 Tacitus, *Hist* I, 66; Suetonius, *Vitellius* ix (on Vienne only).

37 *AE* 1948, 3.

38 Tacitus, *Hist* II, 12–14.

39 Tacitus, *Hist* III, 42–4.

40 For the Orange Cadastres, Piganiol 1962; boundary stones, *CIL* XII, 113 (Forclaz), *AE* 1966, 243 (Jaillet)

41 Pliny, *Epp* IV, xxii.

42 *SHA, Hadrian* xii; *cf* Cassius Dio LXIX, 10, 3, for the basilica, but without the name of the place.

43 *CIL* XII, 1122, also mentioned in Cassius Dio LXIX, 10, 2.

44 *CIL* XII, 4342.

45 For these milestones, *CIL* XII, 5573–83 (König, nos 153–64); interestingly, these are datable to AD 144–5, a few years before Alba produced its first recorded consul (M.Iallius Bassus Gabius Valerianus, *cos* 158 or 160), but perhaps he had persuaded the emperor.

95

46 The first recorded *taurobolium* in AD 160, was held at Lyon, just outside our province (*CIL* XIII, 1751), but, as mentioned under several *civitas* chapters, they became widespread in the following years. On Andarta *v* the chapter on the *Vocontii*.

47 Eusebius, *Hist Eccl*, v, 17.

48 *CIL* XII, 2391, 2392.

49 Cassius Dio LXXII, 31, 1.

50 For his career, P–W XIV, 2024–5, and G. Alföldy in *Bonner Jahrbücher* CLXVIII (1968), 147.

51 Cassius Dio LXXVI, 6–7, Herodian III, 7, 2–6.

52 Numerianus, Cassius Dio LXXVI, 6–7; for the career of Iulius Patianus, Pflaum 1960, no 229.

53 *Eg CIL* XII, 4323 (a *taurobolium*) and 4347 at Narbonne, 2183 at Vienne.

54 *SHA, Antoninus Caracalla* v, 1; honours to Caracalla, *CIL* XII, 1851 (Vienne), 4347 (Narbonne).

55 Milestones (all with M. Aurelius Antoninus in the nominative) *CIL* XII, 5430–2, 5438 and ?5439 (König nos 6–8, 13, 17); this is of some significance because extensive similar work was carried out in northern Gaul (where also the *leuga* measurement was introduced), but no more in our province.

56 Cassius Dio LXXVIII, 9, 5.

57 Gregory, *Hist Franc* I, 30; for a discussion, Griffe 1964, 91–115, 395–402.

58 *CIL* XII, 2228 (from Grenoble; *cf* also 1551, from Vif).

59 Milestones, *ILGN* 655 (König no 249, near Béziers), *ILGN* 656 (König no 261, from Barbaira), *AE* 1960, no 175 (König no 264, from Montgaillard-Lauragais); for a general discussion of the Gallic Empire, Hatt 1966, 222–6 and, from our point of view, König, p 19.

60 Alba, *CIL* XII, 2673, Fréjus, *CIL* XII, 5553 (König no 31).

61 S. Gagniere and J. Granier, 'L'occupation des grottes du IIIe au Ve siècle et les invasions germaniques dans la basse vallée du Rhône', *Provence Historique* 1963; G. Barruol, 'Oppida pré-romains et romains en Haute-Provence', *CR* VIII (1961); for a summary of these, Clébert 1970, 74–5.

62 Eutropius IX, 18, 1; Orosius VII, 24, 4; PIR^2 I, p 299, no 1475.

7
The late Roman period AD *285–475*

The sons of Carus, the last emperor mentioned in Chapter VI, survived him by one and two years respectively, Numerian dying in curious circumstances in the east in 284 and Carinus being murdered when nearly winning the battle of Verona in 285, and they were at once succeeded by Diocletian. In his first year he put Maximian in charge of the western half of the empire, first as a Caesar and then as an Augustus, and in 292/3 he completed the tetrarchy, with Constantius Chlorus as the Caesar of the west and Galerius as the Caesar of the east. His reorganisation, however, was not confined to the central government and what must first concern us is the rearrangement of the provinces. To enable their rulers to act more efficiently, he divided many of the old provinces into several parts, but also grouped several of these fractions into dioceses with each group under a *vicarius*. The first evidence for the effect of this is the Verona List (*Laterculus Veronensis*), evidently compiled *c*312, in which our area is covered as follows:[1]

Diocensis Biennensis habet provincias numero VII

Biennensis
Narbonensis Prima
Narbonensis Secunda
Novem Populi
Aquitanica Prima
Aquitanica Secunda
Alpes Maritimae

As may have been noticed (p 89), some officers, such as the *procuratores Augusti* xx *hereditatum*, had been responsible for both *Gallia Narbonensis* and *Aquitania* in the past and their combination here is reasonable, because it was not this area, but the more northerly part of Gaul (now grouped together under the *Dioecesis Galliarum*), that was directly threatened by barbarian invasions: similarly, the inclusion of

97

Alpes Maritimae in our diocese, while the *Alpes Cottiae* were put in that of the *Dioececis Italiciana*, makes good sense, but some problems arise.

In the first place, while the same number of provinces appear in both the *Notitia Galliarum* (originally compiled *c*400, though much revised later) and the *Notitia Dignitatum* (*c*408, but partly revised down to 423, with all the provinces of Gaul in one group, under a single *Vicarius Septem Provinciarum*), a number of anomalies appear elsewhere, especially in the books of Ammianus Marcellinus (published in the 390s, but obviously using some slightly earlier sources). In his history *provincia Narbonensis* is referred to only in the singular—on two occasions when he mentions a *rector* of *Narbonensis*—and in his general description of Gaul *Elusa* (Eauze, formerly in *Aquitania*) is said, along with Narbonne and Toulouse, to be one of the leading cities of *Narbonensis*, while *Aquae Sextiae* (which should be the capital of *Narbonensis Secunda*), seems to be in *Provincia Viennensis* and is included in a list of relatively unimportant places.[2]

This has led to the conclusion that *Narbonensis Secunda* did not maintain its separate identity throughout the fourth century, being sometimes incorporated in *Provincia Viennensis*, while the boundaries of all the provinces may well have shifted,[3] but it still seems best here to list the cities incorporated in each of our provinces in the *Notitia Galliarum*:

ITEM IN PROVINCIIS NUMERO VII

In Provincia Viennensi civitates numero xiii

Metropolis Civitas Viennensium (capital, Vienne)
Civitas Genavensium (Geneva)
Civitas Gratianopolitana (Grenoble)
Civitas Albensium (Alba)
Civitas Deensium (Die)
Civitas Valentinorum (Valence)
Civitas Tricastinorum (St-Paul-Trois-Châteaux)
Civitas Vasiensium (Vaison)
Civitas Arausicorum (Orange)
Civitas Cabellicorum (Cavaillon)
Civitas Avennicorum (Avignon)
Civitas Arelatensium (Arles)
Civitas Massiliensium (Marseille)
(with *Civitas Carpentoratensium* (Carpentras) listed between Orange and Cavaillon only in a revised edition)

In Provincia Aquitanica Prima civitates numero viii

(duly listed, with *Civitas Biturigum* (Bourges) as *metropolis*)

In Provincia Aquitanica Secunda civitates numero vi

(duly listed, with *Civitas Burdegalensium* (Bordeaux) as *metropolis*)

In Provincia Novempopulana civitates numero xii

(duly listed, with *Civitas Elusatium* (Eauze) as *metropolis*)

In Provincia Narbonensi Prima civitates numero v

Metropolis Civitas Narbonensium (Narbonne)
Civitas Tolosatium (Toulouse)
Civitas Beterrensium (Béziers)
Civitas Nemausensium (Nîmes)
Civitas Lutevensium (Lodève)
Castrum Uceciense (Uzès)
(with *Civitas Agatensium* (Agde) and *Civitas Magalonensium* (Maguelone) added, between Béziers and Nîmes, in a later edition)

In Provincia Narbonensi Secunda civitates numero vii

Metropolis Civitas Aquensium (Aix-en-Provence)
Civitas Aptensium (Apt)
Civitas Reiensium (Riez)
Civitas Foroiuliensium (Fréjus)
Civitas Vappencensium (Gap)
Civitas Segestericorum (Sisteron)
Civitas Antipolitana (Antibes)

In Provincia Alpium Maritimarum civitates numero viii

Metropolis Civitas Ebrodunensium (Embrun)
Civitas Diniensium (Digne)
Civitas Rigomagensium (Barcelonnette)
Civitas Soliniensium (Castellane)
Civitas Sanisiensium (Senez)
Civitas Glannatena (Glandève)
Civitas Cemelensium (Cimiez)
Civitas Vintiensium (Vence)

While the revised versions of the *Notitia Galliarum* were certainly ecclesiastical, the question of whether the earliest text was truly secular is still not fully resolved,[4] but since Christianity was already well established in this province in the fourth century it still reflects the political geography and the various anomalies in it can thus be considered from either point of view. In *Provincia Viennensis* the first is the omission of *Carpentorate*: as may be seen, this is reintroduced in the revised texts in the form *Civitas Carpentoratensium, nunc Vindasca* and while the seat of the bishop was evidently then moved to Vénasque, the city of Carpentras must surely still have existed in the fourth and early fifth centuries, so this should be regarded simply as an error. Secondly, the division of the *Civitas Viennensium* into three parts, with *Genava* and *Gratianopolis* as separate cities: this must have taken place before *Cularo* was renamed *Gratianopolis* under the emperor Gratian, most likely when Diocletian and Maximian gave that city walls, and this is slightly supported by the fact that an apparently Constantinian milestone found at Veyrier-du-Lac (though a little misplaced) gives a mileage figure from Geneva.[5]

In *Provincia Narbonensis Prima*, on the other hand, the main change is not the division of an earlier *civitas* but the grouping of three into one, specifically the incorporation of *Ruscino* (Château Roussillon) and *Carcaso* (Carcassonne) in that of *Narbo*. As may be seen from Chapter 9, the investigation of *Ruscino* has greatly improved in recent years, but the date of its downgrading is still uncertain, as is that of *Carcaso*, though since a milestone of Tetricus seems to have had its mileage marked from *Civitas* (or *Colonia*) *Iulia Carcaso*,[6] a relatively late date seems probable and this too may have been the work of Diocletian and Maximian, or perhaps Constantine. A similar date also seems likely for the original building of the walls of *Carcaso*, which is given the unique title of *castellum* in the Bordeaux Itinerary, but quite why this provincial list should include *Castrum Uceciense* remains obscure, though Uzès did have its own bishop in 442.[7] While Agde and Maguelone are added only in the later, and certainly ecclesiastical, versions, it seems probable that, as noted in Chapter 12, the latter may have replaced the hitherto important port of Lattes in late imperial times.

As for *Provincia Narbonensis Secunda*, the most notable thing there is the inclusion of *Segestero*, for Sisteron earlier lay within the *Civitas Foederata Vocontiorum*, the two other cities of which (Vaison and Die) are both in the *Provincia Viennensis*, while *Provincia Alpium Maritimarum* has now been both increased in size and substantially reorganised: not only has it taken in Digne (though not Gap) from *Narbonensis*, but, having also absorbed two *civitates* from *Alpes Cottiae* (Embrun and Barcelonnette), one of them has replaced Cimiez as the provincial capital.

All these provinces are also listed (though without the names of the cities within them) in the *Notitia Dignitatum* and it is there made clear that while the governor of *Provincia Viennensis* was of consular rank, all the others were merely *praesides*.[8] Regrettably, very few of them are recorded in this later period and even of those included in the following list three are rather doubtful, since they are mentioned only in somewhat dubious accounts of martyrdoms imposed under Maximian:

Approx date	Name	Province
c300	Annius Rufus[9]	*Alpes Maritimae*
c303	? Euticius[10]	*Viennensis?*
c303	? Asterius[11]	*Viennensis?*
c304	? Crispinus[12]	*Viennensis*
c312–37	M. Alfius Apronianus[13]	*Viennensis*
c358–9	Numerius[14]	*Narbonensis*
c361–3	Aprunculus[15]	*Narbonensis*
pre-407	Cl. Postumus Dardanus[16]	*Viennensis*
pre-407	Eventius[17]	*Viennensis*
mid-5th cent	Fl. Lacanius[18]	*Viennensis?*

The *Notitia Dignitatum* also tells us the location of a number of important offices within our area and while the text is of early fifth-century date not only was the coin mint at Arles opened under Constantine I but *fabricae* are also mentioned in his Constitution in 326, so that all of them (with the possible exception of the woollen mills at Arles) were probably of early fourth-century origin. Listing (though not naming) the officers in charge, the *Notitia* includes the *Praepositus thesaurorum Arelatensium* (in charge of the store of gold and other goods at Arles)[19] and the *Procurator monetae Arelatensis* (the coin mint)[20] and then the *Procurator gynaecii Arelatensis* (woollen mills),[21] *Procurator linyfii Viennensis* (linen works at Vienne),[22] *Procurator bafii Telonensis* and *Procurator bafii Narbonensis* (dye works at Toulon and Narbonne)[23] and *Praepositus barbaricariorum sive argentariorum Arelatensis* (silversmiths and makers of officers' armour at Arles).[24] All of these factories, of course, were producing things for the imperial armies, but in passing we may note the curious fact that no commercial products, not even wines, are related specifically to our area in the Edict of Diocletian.

One other entry in the *Notitia Dignitatum* that concerns us is the following:[25]

In Provincia (Gallia) Riparensi

Praefectus classis fluminis Rhodani, Viennae sive Arelati
Praefectus classis barcariorum Ebruduni Sapaudiae
Praefectus militum musculariorum Massiliae Graecorum
Tribunus Cohortis Primae Flaviae Sapaudicae Calaronae

Since three of the units here listed are those of sailors (the *barcarii*, of course, were some sort of bargees and the word *musculus* was by now applied to a small sailing boat)[26] this underlines the importance of official water transport and the need to protect it against local more

101

than invading barbarians, but neither the dates of their installation nor their sites are very clear. *Sapaudia* (Savoie) first appears elsewhere in Ammianus' general description of Gaul[27] but two of the place-names raise questions. *Ebruduni* is generally taken to represent *Ebrodunum* (Yverdon, at the south end of Lake Neuchâtel, where a late Roman fort has been excavated), but this is well outside *Sapaudia* and while some people have tried (unsuccessfully) to locate a suitable base at Yvoire (on the south bank of Lake Geneva),[28] it seems not quite impossible that some things may have been floated down the upper waters of the Durance from Embrun. *Calaronae* is usually assumed to be a corruption of *Cularo* (though some have tried to find this too beside Lake Geneva), but if this is correct the form of the name indicates that the unit should have been installed there before the reign of Gratian—rather an early date for a *Cohors Sapaudica*. Finally, the heading of the entry: some have suggested that it implies the temporary existence of a *Provincia Riparensis*,[29] but it seems better to interpret it adjectivally as 'in a province of Gaul along the banks of rivers and the sea'.

In trying to sort out the history of our area in this period some difficulties arise not only from the documents we have already discussed but also from the literary sources and from archaeology. The first half of the fourth century is, of course, treated to some extent by things like the *Panegyrici Latini* and the works of authors such as Aurelius Victor and Eutropius, the whole of the fourth century by those of Orosius and Zosimus and the fifth century by the Byzantine Zonaras, but none of these is fully informative and the surviving books of the best historical author, Ammianus Marcellinus, cover in detail only the period 351–78: in fact, as may be seen from references in our *civitas* chapters, the best information regarding our individual cities can be gathered from the writings of the poets Ausonius (of Bordeaux) and Sidonius (of Lyon) and occasionally from inscriptions. As for archaeology, the main outstanding question is the dating of city walls. In the early empire, in places like Nîmes and Vienne, these represented status rather than security and some cities, such as Toulouse and Valence, may well have acquired them for the same reason in the second century, but in this later period they were of much greater practical use—once again, for defence against local brigands as well as invaders—and it would be better if we could draw historical information from them rather than guess their dates. As we have already mentioned, two inscriptions certainly prove that the walls of Grenoble were built under Diocletian and Maximian, while the siege of Maximian at Marseille points convincingly to AD 310 for the recently discovered reconstructions there, but at other towns major questions remain: in particular, when were the smaller, inner walls of Vienne, Arles and Nîmes built, when were Narbonne, Béziers and Geneva first walled, when were such places as Antibes, Apt, Avignon, Die and Gap, and when was the river wall added at Toulouse? Sadly, in most of these cases the answer can at present only be "at some time in the late empire".

In any case, until the beginning of the fifth century the main events in Gaul (that is, the military ones, which were always of most interest to the ancient historians) were concentrated on the Rhine frontier. How much Gaul really suffered from Diocletian's anti-Christian policy is very doubtful,[30] but it was, of course, subject to all his legal and financial reforms and besides the walling of Grenoble (probably to secure it against local brigands)[31] the appearance of many milestones makes it clear that considerable improvements were made to the roads—something that went still further under Constantine I and it is from this period that the very first ones along the road from Vienne to Geneva come to light.[32] Much more significant, however, is the increase of the importance of Arles under Constantine. It was there that in 310 the old Maximian, trying to suppress the new emperor (who was by now his son-in-law), first established himself, until Constantine drove him off to Marseille, where he committed suicide,[33] and it was there too that the impressive ecclesiastical Council of 314 was held (attended by, among many others, the bishops of Arles, Vienne, Marseille and Vaison, priests from Orange and Apt, and a deacon from Nice),[34] but beyond this, while the effective capital of all Gaul was Trier and while the local province was governed from Vienne, Arles evidently became the most important southern city. As we have already mentioned, Constantine established both a mint and a treasury there and substantial remains clearly indicate its added splendour—the development of the north side of the forum (coupled with further additions under Constantine II), the great Constantinian baths, the splendid tombstones in les Alyscamps and probably the building of the huge flour mills on the aqueduct at Barbégal. Vienne, too, was further developed, with a *palatium* for the governor and probably a castrum on the Pipet hill, while the finds of coins indicate that its circus remained in use until the 5th century, but much more still needs to be discovered at places like Narbonne, Nîmes and Toulouse, especially since they are all praised by Ausonius and referred to (Narbonne still with much praise) by Sidonius.[35]

Rather surprisingly, after the time of Constantine I, and apart from that recording the erection of the monument in the Place du Forum in Arles under Constantine II,[36] imperial inscriptions appear only on milestones, the last of which, on the road from Arles to Marseille, was set up as late as 435,[37] but some important events did occur. In the first place, Constans, who, along with Constantine II, had become an Augustus after their father's death in 337, spent some time in Gaul (and Britain) after defeating and killing his brother at Aquileia in 340 and it was at Elne, on the road to Spain, that his new rival Magnentius had him assassinated in 350.[38] Secondly, it was at *Mons Seleucus* (la Batie Mont-Saléon) that Magnentius himself, already beaten in the battle of Mursa in the Danube valley, was finally defeated in the summer of 353,[39] after which Constantius II, the third son of Constantine and now the sole emperor, spent the winter at Arles, with great celebrations in the theatre and the circus.[40] Thereafter, having among other things tortured and exiled Gerontius, who had supported Magnentius, he moved north by way of Valence to attack the *Alamanni*, who had once again been raiding the Rhine frontier,[41] but in the meantime he had arranged for an ecclesiastical Council to be held at Arles. While the one held here in 314 had been partly concerned with Donatism, this one was intended to support Arianism, to which Constantius himself was attached, but as it was not decisive on this another had to be held, more strongly controlled, at Milan two years later;[42] nevertheless, Paulinus, the bishop of Trier who opposed it, was exiled, as was Hilarius, bishop of Poitiers, after yet another Council at Béziers in 356,[43] and Arianism evidently had some strength until, in 360-1, the Council of Paris excommunicated Saturninus, the bishop of Arles, for his heresy.[44]

The Christian Church suffered less from the next emperor, even though he openly professed his paganism as soon as he became Augustus, since Julian was evidently a much more humane man. Constantius had made him a Caesar in 355, sending him to Gaul from Turin, and on his arrival at Vienne he was received with great public enthusiasm.[45] He did not, however, stay there at this time, having heard with horror that Cologne had been stormed, and in the following years he carried out highly successful campaigns against the Franks and the *Alamanni* until he was forced to move to the eastern empire. He reduced the taxation in Gaul[46] and, besides the event just mentioned, Ammianus gives other evidence of the importance of Vienne in this period—as the place to collect supplies for the army (and also, from the point of view of the *praefectus* Florentius, to avoid troubles)[47] and the place to which Julian himself went to spend the winter in 360, celebrating quinquennial games there but also attending the Epiphany festival (posing for a time as a Christian) and, so he claimed, hearing in a dream the Greek verses that foretold the welcome death of Constantius.[48]

Julian's immediate successor, Jovian, spent his one remaining year in the east (where he gave up much to the Persians), but Valentinian I, who succeeded him, operated in the west, handing over the east to his brother Valens, and in 367 he also elevated his son Gratian to the rank of Augustus. As usual, the main events took place in northern Gaul, but besides the conferment of the name *Gratianopolis* on Grenoble a few other matters emerge regarding our area. For one thing, Gratian was an earnest Christian (influenced by St Ambrose) and in 374 an ecclesiastical Council was held at Valence, supervised by Florentius, bishop of Vienne, to combat such things as sexual crimes and sacrifices to demons.[49] On the other hand Ausonius (by no means so keen a Christian) had been tutor to Gratian before achieving his consulship and while he was not an historian it is the content of his works that tells us most about southern Gaul in this period. Besides the descriptions of Arles, Toulouse and Narbonne (along with a complimentary reference to Nîmes in his praise of Bordeaux) in his *Ordo Urbium Nobilium*,[50] his *Commemoratio Professorum Burdigalium* brings out the dignity of our area with accounts of his uncle Aemilius Magnus Arborius of Toulouse, Exuperius of Toulouse, Marcellus of Narbonne and Sedatus of Toulouse,[51] while he also mentions such things as the tasty oysters of Marseille.[52] On the military side, Ammianus tells us that it was from Arles that Count Theodosius, who had previously restored the situation in Britain, sailed in 373 to suppress Firmus in *Mauretania*— something that shows that the canal was still in effective operation.[53]

Valentinian I died at *Brigetio*, on the Danube, in 375 and Valens in the battle of Adrianople in 378 (the year at which the History of Ammianus ends), but it seems that in the last four years of Gratian's rule Gaul saw peace. In 388, however, Magnus Maximus, having taken over Britain, crossed the Channel and successfully captured Gaul, having Gratian assassinated at or near Lyon. The direct concern of Maximus with southern Gaul is obscure, though it must have suffered from his raised taxes and his fierce attack on Priscillianist Christians, which was successfully modified by the influence of St Martin of Tours, and while it was his march into Italy that finally led to his defeat and execution by Theodosius I in 388, the precise route he followed is not recorded. His end did, however, lead to the despatch to Gaul of Valentinian II, then only 17 years old, and after he had spent some time in Trier it was at Vienne that he was strangled to death in 392, apparently on the angry orders of Arbogast, under whose tutelage he had been but whom he had intended to dismiss. Arbogast then proclaimed Eugenius as Augustus,[54] but they were both defeated in 394 by Theodosius, who died only the next year, to be succeeded by his two sons, Arcadius in the east and Honorius in the west.

It was about this time that the military and administrative capital of the Gauls was moved from Trier to Arles although, as we have noted, this city still lay within the *Provincia Viennensis*. In 394 or 396 (the precise date is uncertain) an ecclesiastical Council was held at Nîmes, its main point of interest for us being the appearance there of Genialis, the first recorded bishop of Cavaillon,[55] and in 398 a more important one took place, actually at Turin but specifically at the request of the clergy of Gaul, in which, among other things, Proculus, then bishop of Marseille, argued that he (and so not the bishop of Aix) should be the metropolitan of all churches in *Narbonensis Secunda*, and an argument also took place over the relative importance of Arles and Vienne.[56] In the meantime Stilicho, currently the main general of the whole empire and operating with some success against both Visigoths and Ostrogoths in the east, withdrew troops from Gaul as well as from Britain and, partly as a result of this, on the last day of AD 406 a large body of Vandals, Alans and Suevians crossed the frozen river Rhine near Mainz.

These invaders ravaged much of Gaul, but how far our area was affected is uncertain: while Jerome includes *Narbonensis* in his list of areas plundered, the only one of our cities that had to defend itself seems to have been Toulouse, and although they did make some invasions of northern Italy it is evident that their main movement was through the northern provinces towards *Aquitania*.[57] In any case, the usurper Constantine III brought troops from Britain, very quickly installing himself at Arles. Some officials opposed him (including our Postumus Dardanus, who was to become Praetorian Prefect of the Gauls by 412, when a Constitution was addressed to him),[58] but the Gallic legions sided with him and while he fought successfully against some of the invaders he also seems to have made agreements with them.[59] The first imperial attempt to dislodge him took place as early as 408, but while the army led by Sarus (a Goth who did not agree with Alaric) won a battle, it failed to take Valence after besieging it for seven days and so had to return to Italy.[60] Constantine then made his son Constans (originally a monk) Caesar and sent him, along with Gerontius and Apollinaris, to take over Spain.[61] Constans then came back to Gaul, to be made an Augustus by his father, while Constantine himself got temporary acknowledgement of his title from Honorius. In the autumn of 409 most of the invading barbarians passed through the Pyrenees into Spain and Constans went back there to supersede Gerontius, who was evidently blamed for this. Gerontius, however, was the stronger man and, having raised Maximus (probably his son) to the rank of Augustus, he pursued Constans back into Gaul and defeated and killed him at Vienne.[62] Nevertheless Gerontius himself withdrew in fear when the official imperial army, led by Constantius (the successor to Stilicho as the empire's leading general) and Ulfila, came from Italy to suppress Constantine. The siege of Arles lasted three months, but despite the ultimate arrival of his general Edobich with reinforcements from the Franks and *Alamanni* Constantine was finally defeated and, having in vain had himself ordained as a priest, was killed under the orders of Honorius when he was taken into Italy.[63]

Constantius and Ulfila returned to Italy, but further troubles developed here almost at once. In 412 yet another emperor, Jovinus, had been proclaimed at Mainz by the Burgundians and Alans and in the same year Athaulf, the new leader of the Visigoths, led his people into southern Gaul, taking with him both the deposed usurper Attalus and Gallia Placidia, the sister of Honorius. In opposition to Jovinus, Athaulf communicated with Postumus Dardanus and some envoys sent to Ravenna won the support of Honorius, so they besieged and captured Jovinus at Valence, to which he had moved, and carried him off to Narbonne where, by the order of Dardanus, he was executed in 413.[64]

Athaulf had promised Honorius that he would give up Placidia, but since vital food supplies from Africa were prevented from arriving he now refused to do so and, after an unsuccessful attack on Marseille, he captured Narbonne, Toulouse and Bordeaux, marrying her at Narbonne in 414.[65] Constantius then returned to Arles and prevented all ships from reaching any part of the Mediterranean coast of Gaul, so, leaving Attalus behind (who was eventually taken back to Rome and maimed), Athaulf moved into Spain, where he was killed in 415.[66] Then, when the Goths, now led by Wallia, had done valuable work in Spain against the Silings and Alans, they were granted permanent settlement in *Aquitania* and parts of *Narbonensis Prima*, including Toulouse but not Narbonne or the Mediterranean coast. So they permanently took over part of our territory, though for the time being Roman citizens in their area remained under imperial control and were allowed to retain one third of their land.[67] In the meantime Placidia had been returned to Italy and at the beginning of 417 she married Constantius.

In 418 Honorius laid it down that an annual meeting of provincial governors and other leading people should take place every autumn at Arles—something that a Praetorian Prefect had earlier tried to arrange—but while Constantius evidently did further work in Gaul before his one year as an Augustus in 421, how far it affected the south is obscure. The death of Honorius in 423 led to a year or two of Roman chaos and although Valentinian III was technically ruler of the west from 425 to 455 he was only seven years old when he became Augustus and the effective rule fell into the hands of Placidia and Aetius. While some Goths—such as the one to whom Paulinus of Pella sold his farm near Marseille[69]—were evidently acceptable residents, in 427 Aetius had to relieve Arles from a siege by Theoderic's people and in 430 succeeded in confining them to their proper territory in the west, apparently now granting them full rule over it.[70] But the Goths again attacked Arles in 436 and this time it was saved by Litorius, who drove them back to Toulouse, where he died, after which Avitius, then Praetorian Prefect, made peace with them.[71] In the meantime Aetius had used Huns to defeat the Burgundians, who had invaded *Belgica Prima*, but about 443 the surviving Burgundians were installed in *Sapaudia* (the modern Savoie)[72] and about this time Alans were settled in land, apparently now unoccupied, near Valence.[73]

Placidia died in 450 and Aetius was killed by Petronius Maximus, the man that tried to succeed Valentinian III when he died in 455. Maximus, however, was not successful, being thrown out by Gaiseric and the Vandals who plundered Rome, and the real successor turned out to be Avitus, currently a leader in Gaul. He was in Toulouse when he learned that Maximus was dead and, supported by Theoderic II, then king of the Visigoths, he was first proclaimed emperor there. His progress, along with his earlier career, is recorded in the Panegyric that Sidonius (his son-in-law) compiled for him:[74] he moved to Arles where, after a meeting of notables held, it seems, in the *atria* of *Ugernum* (Beaucaire), he was fully installed and thereafter went on to Rome, where he assumed the consulship in 456. His reign lasted only a year, however, for he was captured by Ricimer and Majorian, who became his successor, when trying to return to Gaul. Majorian, who ruled from 457 to 461, spent a year in Gaul and fortunately Sidonius made a Panegyric for him too,[75] besides mentioning things about him in letters. He first relieved Lyon, which was then occupied by Burgundians, and then his general Aegidius drove Theoderic II from the walls of Arles and Majorian himself visited it more than once: the letter of Sidonius to Montius gives a fair account both of the good state of the city at this time and of the celebratory events, such as circus games, that took place there.[76] Majorian's successor, Libius Severus, was not at all outstanding, though Aegidius tried to defend Roman Gaul against the Visigoths until his death in 463, and while Sidonius produced yet another Panegyric for the next emperor, Anthemius,[77] and was rewarded for it by being made Prefect of Rome for a time, the final troubles developed with the accession of Euric to the kingship of the Visigoths. Chilperic, the king of the Burgundians who ruled at Vienne as well as Lyon, assisted the Romans for a time, but Euric, after victories in the north, succeeded in taking Arles and then seems to have inflicted fire on many cities and adjoining lands in a move to the north. By 475 he held everything west of the Rhône and after he had mastered Marseille as well as Arles, thus able to control the coast, Zeno, who now made the decisions regarding all the surviving Roman empire from Constantinople, conceded our whole area to him.[78]

So we come to the end of the Roman period. It was not, however, so much of a change as that in Britain. For one thing, Christianity continued to flourish and while the Burgundians and Visigoths were merely Arians at this time they were later converted to Catholicism (in 516 and 589 respectively) and the Catholic churches duly survived, as did the notable monastery of Lérins, founded about 410.[79] Secondly, as is shown by the works of several writers, including Sidonius, who, though imprisoned for a short time at *Liviana* (le Viala) in 476, survived until 480, good Latinity remained in use[80]—much better than that of Britain's Gildas. As for the economy, as later periods show, the coast was still worth plundering by other barbarians, such as the Saracens and Moors. But all this is for consideration elsewhere and here we must turn to a more detailed account of the individual *civitates*.

REFERENCES AND NOTES

1 For the texts, not only of the *Laterculus Veronensis*, but also of the *Notitia Galliarum* and the *Laterculus Polemii Silvii* (compiled AD 448, but using some outdated material) *v* Seeck 1876.

2 Ammianus XVIII, i, 4 (Numerius, recently *rector Narbonensis*, examined by Julian, then Caesar, so *c* 358), XXII, i, 4 (Aprunculus, later to be *rector Narbonensis*, advising Julian, now Augustus in *Illyricum*, in 361), XV, xi, 14–15 (in a general description of *Gallia* as a whole and so of uncertain date); for further references, *v* n 3.

3 For fuller discussions, J.B.Bury, *JRS* XIII (1923), 127–151, A.H.M.Jones *JRS* XLIV (1954), 21–9 (reprinted in Jones, *The Roman Economy*, 1974).

4 For ecclesiastical, Mommsen, *Chronica Minora* I, 552–612, Rivet 1976; for secular, Jones 1964 II, 712, III, 225 n 2, Harries 1978.

5 Walls of Grenoble, *CIL* XII, 2229; milestone, König no 102, Broise 1984, 290–1.

6 *ILGN* 656 (König no 261).

7 Carcassonne, *It Burd* 551.9 (the only place called a *castellum* in the *whole* itinerary, so perhaps a surprise to the pilgrim); for the bishop of Uzès (Constantius), Munier 1963, 94–104, 107–10; on the meaning of *castrum* in this period, Rivet 1976, 134–5, Harries 1978, 35–6.

8 *Not Dig Occ* XXII, 21, 28–36.

9 *CIL* XII 78 (+p 804); *PLRE* I, 775.

10 *Passio Sanctorum Victoris et al.*; *PLRE* I, 316. On these martyrdoms, Griffe 1964 I, 154–7, 161–2.

11 *Passio Sanctorum Victoris et al.*; *PLRE* I, 118.

12 *Passio Sancti Ferreoli* (at Vienne); *PLRE* I, 232.

13 *CIL* XII, 1852; *PLRE* I, 86.

14 Ammianus XVIII, i, 4; *PLRE* I, 634.

15 Ammianus XXII, i, 4.

16 Much the best known: *CIL* XII, 1524 (the Pierre Ecrite); Jerome, *Epp* 129 (in his favour); Sidonius, *Epp* v, 9, 1 (against him); *PLRE* II, 346–7. He was *Praefectus Praetorio Galliarum* in 412.

17 *AE* 1953, 200; *PLRE* II, 652.

18 Possibly outside our period: *PLRE* II, 652.

19 *Not Dig Occ* XI, 33; Jones 1964, 428–9.

20 *Not Dig Occ* XI, 43; Jones 1964, 437.

21 *Not Dig Occ* XI, 54; Jones 1964, 66. For a possible change here *cf* XII, 27: *Procurator gynaecii Vivarensis rei privatae Metti translate Anhelat* (the last word taken by some to be a corruption implying that it had been moved to *Arelate*).

22 *Not Dig Occ* XI, 62; Jones 1964, 66, 836–7.

23 *Not Dig Occ* XI, 72–73; Jones 1964, 66, 836–7.

24 *Not Dig Occ* XI, 75; Jones 1964, 370.

25 *Not Dig Occ* XLII, 13–17.

26 In contrast to the meaning of this word used by Caesar and Vegetius, *v* Isidorus, *Origenes* 19, 1: *musculus, curtum navigium*.

27 Ammianus XV, xi, 17, where he also describes the Rhône as flowing between *Sapaudia* and the *Sequani* (*Provincia Sequania* being the name already applied in the Verona list to the southern half of what had been *Germania Prima*).

28 For some references, Grenier 1931, 393–4, with notes; the *Not Dig* reference is still applied to Yverdon in *TIR* L32 (1966).

29 *Eg* Hatt 1966, 248, following Nesselhauf; contrast Jones 1964, 99, suggesting that the *legiones pseudocomitatenses* may have 'belonged to a

military district obsolete by the time of the Notitia called Gallia Riparensis, which included the Rhône valley and the adjacent Alpine provinces, and have been intended to secure the important lines of communication through this area against the local Bacaudae'.

30 On this subject, Griffe 1964, I, Chapter iv, 'Martyrs et confesseurs de la Gaule'.

31 For the walls, *CIL* XII, 2229. Brigandage no doubt continued in our area as well as northern Gaul, but unfortunately the inscription recording *praefecti arcendis latrociniis* referred to in Hatt 1966, 240, as '*CIL* XII, 510' is actually *CIL* XIII, 5010, and was found at Nyon, on the northern shore of Lake Geneva and outside our province.

32 For a useful summary of the 47 milestones dating from 286 to 337, König pp 94–104.

33 *Panegyrici* VI (VII), 18–19 (by an orator who, from his statement on *Massilia*, had never visited the place); *cf* Zonaras XII, 33, Lactantius, *De Mortibus Persecutorum*, 29–30.

34 For details, Munier 1963, 9–25, Griffe 1964, I, 191–200.

35 Narbonne, Ausonius, *Ordo Urbium Nobilium* xix, Sidonius, *Carmina* xxiii, 37–68; Nîmes, Ausonius, *op cit* xx, 34 (comparing it with his own Bordeaux), Sidonius, *Epp* II, ix (when he visited it and stayed on a fine estate, probably at Alès); Toulouse, Ausonius, *op cit* xviii, Sidonius, *Epp* III, *passim*.

36 *CIL* XII, 667, 668 (improved as *AE* 1952, 37).

37 *CIL* XII, 5494, König no 53.

38 Eutropius X, 9, 4, Orosius VII, 29, 7, *Epitome de Caesaribus* 41, 23, Zosimus II, xlii, 5, Zonaras XIII, 6. For an argument against the claim of Zonaras that the name *Helena* was derived from that of the empress, *Ruscino* I (*RAN* Suppl 7, 1976), 346–50.

39 Sozomenos IV, vii, 3; Socrates, *Hist Eccles* II, 326. Curiously, Julian (who must have known the area) in *Oratio* ii, 71c does not name the place but says the battle took place in the Cottian Alps; does this indicate yet another temporary rearrangement of the provincial frontiers?

40 Ammianus XIV, v, 1.

41 Ammianus XIV, x, 1.

42 Munier 1963, 30, Griffe 1964 I, 215–18 (both with references).

43 Munier 1963, 31, Griffe 1964 I, 224–48.

44 Munier 1963, 32–4, Griffe 1964 I, 262, 331, 343.

45 Ammianus XV, viii, 21.

46 Ammianus XVII, iii.

47 Ammianus XX, IV, 6, viii, 20.

48 Ammianus XX, x, 3, XXI, i, 1, ii, 2; for verses, also Zonaras XIII, xic, Zosimus III, ix.

49 Munier 1963, 35–45, Griffe 1964 I, 304–05, 312, 314, 343, 371.

50 Ausonius, *Ordo Urbium Nobilium* x, xviii, xix, and xx, 34–35 (Nîmes).

51 Ausonius, *Commemoratio Professorum Burdigalensium* xvi (Aemilius, who had tutored Constantius II, and with a reference, otherwise unconfirmed, that brothers of a Constantine had been exiled in Toulouse), xvii (Exuperius), xviii (Marcellus), xix (Sedatus).

52 Ausonius, *Epp* v, 27–8. The *Hebromagus*, where Paulinus had an estate, referred to in *Epp* xxv and xxvi, cannot have been our Bram, since (in the

absence of the 17th cent canal of Paul-Pierre Riquet!) barges could not have brought wheat from there to Bordeaux and there must have been another place of this name somewhere on a tributary of the Tarn or the Garonne.

53 Ammianus XXIX, v, 5.
54 Orosius VII, XXXV, 10–11; Zosimus IV, 53–4; Sozomenos *Hist Eccl* VII, 22; Socrates, *Hist Eccl* v, 25.
55 Munier 1963, 49–51, Griffe 1964 I, 183.
56 Munier 1963, 52–60, Griffe 1964 I, 336–40.
57 Jerome, *Epp* cxxiii, 15; Zosimus VI, iii; Salvian VII, 12, 2.
58 *Codex Theodosianus* XII, i, 171.
59 Orosius VII, xl, 4.
60 Zosimus VI, ii, 3.
61 Orosius VII, xl, 7; Zosimus VI, iv. This Apollinaris was the grandfather of Sidonius (Sidonius, *Epp* III, xii, &c). For the best organised account of this confused period, *v* Bury 1923, chapter VI.
62 Orosius VII, xlii, 4; Sozomenos IX, xiii.
63 Orosius VII, xlii; Sozomenos IX, xiv–xv; Olympiodorus, frag. 16.
64 Orosius VII, xlii, 6; Olympiodorus, *frag* 16.
65 Rutilius Namatianus I, 496; Paulinus of Pella, *Eucharisticus*, 312; *Chronica Gallica*, 654. On the strange dependence of Goths on some imported food, E.A.Thompson, *The Visigoths in the Time of Ulfila*, 19–20.
66 Orosius VII, xlii, 9–12; Olympiodorus, *frag* 27; *Chronicon Paschale*, sub a.
67 Orosius VII, xliii; *Chronica Minora* I, 469.
68 Bury 1923, VI, 4, referring to the Edict addressed to Agrippa, then the Praetorian Prefect of Gaul, and citing especially E.Carette, *Les assemblées provinciales de la Gaule romaine*, 1895.
69 Paulinus, *Eucharisticus*, 572–81.
70 Prosper, *Chronica*, 1290; *Chronica Gallica*, 658; *cf* Bury 1923, VIII, 1.
71 Sidonius, *Carmina* vii (Panegyric of Avitus); Prosper, *Chron* I 324; Hydatius, *chron* 116, 117; Isidore, *Historia de Regibus Gothorum, Vandalorum, Suevorum*, 24.
72 *Chronica Gallica*, 660; Prosper, *Chron*, 1322.
73 *Chronica Minora* I, 660 § 440: *Deserta Valentinae urbis rura Alanis, quibus Sambida praeerat, partienda traduntur.*
74 Sidonius, *Carm* vii; for Theoderic's help, Isidore, *Hist Vand*, 31.
75 Sidonius, *Carm* v, and *cf Carm* xiii.
76 Sidonius, *Epp* I, xi: the date of this visit was probably 461.
77 Sidonius, *Carm* ii.
78 Sidonius, *Epp* VI, xii, addressed to Patiens, archbishop of Lyon, who had sent supplies to the peoples of Arles, Riez, Avignon, Orange, Viviers (the successor to Alba), Valence and St-Paul-Trois-Châteaux; *cf* VII, i, addressed to Mamertus, bishop of Vienne and other letters; capture of Arles and Marseille, Isidore, *Hist Vand*, 34, and on the ultimate death of Euric at Arles, 35.
79 See Munier 1963, *passim*, for Councils and Griffe 1964, *passim*, for general accounts.
80 On Sidonius, see not only Stevens 1933 but also the excellent discussion by W.B.Anderson in the preface to Vol. I of the Loeb edition (published 1936, reprinted 1956).

PART II

THE CIVITATES

8

Tolosa (Toulouse)

As with most Celtic migrations, the date at which the *Volcae Tectosages* established themselves in this region remains somewhat uncertain.[1] No doubt their invasion of southern Gaul was combined with that of the *Volcae Arecomici* (which would mean that they entered the area not from the north but from the south, by way of the Seuil de Naurouze), but this does not really clarify matters: as we have seen, in dealing with Hannibal's march in 218 BC Livy[2] does not mention any *Volcae* until he had reached the Rhône and does not add either of the qualifying second names. The *Tectosages* surely dominated the area around Toulouse a century later, but even then the general situation remains obscure. Since Strabo states that the empire of the *Arverni* extended to the neighbourhood of Narbonne,[3] the *Tectosages* must for a time have been allies, if not actually subjects, of Luerius and Bituitus, and it is generally assumed that it was they who until then dominated the *Elisyces*,[4] and when the Romans had defeated Bituitus and established the *colonia* of *Narbo Martius* the *Tectosages* were forced to sign a treaty—evidently a *foedus* very *iniquum*, since a Roman garrison was installed at Toulouse;[5] and it was the breach of this treaty, with the support of the *Cimbri* and the *Tigurini*, that led to their first fully-attested war with Rome.

The campaigns of L.Cassius Longinus and Q.Servilius Caepio have already been dealt with (p 45), but two matters need to be briefly discussed here, the origin of the treasure that Caepio stole and the place where he found it—that is, to what site the name *Tolosa* was then applied. On the first point there was, as we have seen, some dispute among the classical authors, some claiming that it had come from Delphi, which in 279 BC had been sacked by Celts, including the *Tectosages* who finally settled in Galatia. But while the two tribes of *Tectosages* may have been distantly related, perhaps sharing the same ancestry in the remote past, their later connections are unlikely to have been any closer than those between the *Brigantes* in Britain, Spain and Switzerland, and Strabo[6] is very sensible in following Poseidonius in dismissing this as phantasy, pointing out that this area of Gaul was sufficiently rich in gold and silver to accumulate such wealth from its own resources.

On the second point dispute is somewhat more recent, having originated, it seems, in the early sixteenth century, when Vieille Toulouse was first put forward as the likely place.[7] Although *Vetus Tolosa* does already appear in a charter of 1279, the name itself may have no more relevance than others such as Vieux-Poitiers (the site of an interesting small Roman town some 24km NNE of Poitiers itself); and while Vieille Toulouse is indeed an impressive elevated site (albeit without any identified defences) and has yielded much Iron Age material,[8] so also have a number of other sites to the north of it, especially la Butte de Cluzel and St-Roch[9] (fig 6). It is evident, therefore, that pre-Roman occupation extended along a considerable stretch of the right bank of the Garonne and *Tolosa* was probably already approximately in its later position. The most likely situation for the temple and its pools is taken to be la Daurade (on which see below) and, as Strabo tells us, the latter were effectively cleared of their remaining riches after Caepio had made his haul.

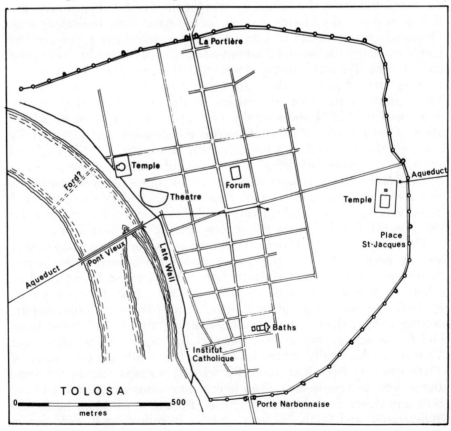

5 Plan of Toulouse (after Baccrabère)

In the Republican period the *Tectosages* evidently created some trouble and they were probably the *Volcae* who had to be subdued by either Pompey or Fonteius (p 57 above) but, as finds of pottery and coins show, they also enjoyed considerable prosperity—largely, no doubt, through the notable increase of trade up and down the Aude and the Garonne; and while some of their land, as well as some of their trade, was taken over by Italian immigrants (for, so Cicero claims, the province was full of them), they still continued to mint their own silver coins, the so-called monnaies-à-la-croix.[10] During Caesar's campaigns they, like the other peoples of the province, appear to have remained loyal to the Romans: men were enlisted here to reinforce the troops of P.Crassus in *Aquitania*[11] and when, in the last major rising of the northern Gauls, Lucterius was aiming at Narbonne, the places where Caesar established garrisons to block his way included the territory of the *Tolosates* (from now on the usual name for the area)—though in what precise part of it is not stated:[12] and after Caesar's death Octavian succeeded in enlisting the support of the whole province.

Like so many cities and tribes *Tolosa* acquired *ius Latii*,[13] but whether she was also elevated, like *Nemausus*, to the rank of *colonia* is not absolutely certain, since the title appears only in Ptolemy and there is no epigraphic evidence to support him. Certainly *Tolosa*, unlike *Nemausus* and *Vienna* (which Ptolemy does not call a *colonia*!), was not given a dignified town wall by Augustus, but those of her inhabitants who acquired Roman citizenship were, as usual, enrolled in the voting-tribe *Voltinia*, as is shown by one of the few inscriptions found here—that of a *quaestor* whose name is not known.[15] She also had a *praefectus fabrum* (Sex. Iulius),[16] but for more information on her standing in the early Empire we have to rely on evidence from elsewhere. Inscriptions from distant places reveal two *equites*—Cornelius Taurus, who died in *Umbria*[17] and Q.Trebellius Rufus, who was accorded statues in Athens in the Flavian period.[18] The most notable figure of all, however, is M.Antonius Primus, the senator who played a major part in Vespasian's takeover of the Empire. He carried the nickname of *Becco* ('Beak'), but finally retired to a quiet old age in his city of origin, and whether the characteristics ascribed to him by Tacitus were typical of Tolosans is questionable, except perhaps that of being *sermone promptus*.[19] Martial gave Toulouse the epithet *Palladia*,[20] and while the context suggests that this was due to his respect for Antonius, the city had already produced another notable rhetor in L.Statius Ursulus;[21] and it is on rhetoricians, partly his own relations, that Ausonius pours his praise in the fourth century—Aemilius Magnus Arborius (his uncle), Exuperius and Sedatus: it probably had a bishop (Saturninus) already in the mid-third century.[22]

In a large and busy modern city like Toulouse it is hard to establish either the full extent of the Roman settlement or the stages by which it grew, and this is made even more difficult by the remarkable shortage of inscriptions and the fact that the city walls were not built until the second century. The general course of these walls (fig 5), which enclose an area of some 90 hectares, has long been known and recent excavations have yielded much information:[23] in particular, the plan of the north gate (la Porterie) has been established[24] and one of the circular towers, that in the Place St-Jacques, has been conserved and left open to view (pl 2). The south gate remains uninvestigated, but it is probable, though not absolutely certain, that it was preceded by a monumental arch that was later incorporated in the long-vanished Château Narbonnais.[25] As in London, the riverside wall was added in the fourth century and impressive remains of the southern part of it, including a postern, can still be seen in the Institut Catholique: the main part of it is built of brick, but it also incorporates columns and fragments of sculpture from earlier tombs.[26]

Of the buildings inside the walls, some remains of the theatre were found as long ago as 1869, but none, of course, are visible to-day: it may date back to the first century.[27] The baths in the Rue du Languedoc were discovered as recently as 1975: they were built in the second century and reconstructed in the fourth, and since they occupied an entire insula they were evidently public.[28] The temples shown on the plan are deduced from finds made near, in and under Christian churches: that under the church of Nôtre-Dame la Daurade (the one beside the bank of the Garonne) is believed to have been the successor to the shrine plundered by Caepio, while the other is on the site of the former church of St-Jacques (demolished in 1811–12), beside the cathedral of St-Etienne.[29] The site of the forum and capitol is largely deduced from the street plan, which is reconstructed from the modern street alignments and from several discoveries of Roman drains.[30]

Outside the walls two aqueducts have been identified, each of them evidently drawing on two sources of water. The more notable is that of Lardenne, probably of second century date and traditionally called 'l'aqueduc de la Reine Pédauque', which, coming from the west, involved a crossing of the river over le Pont Vieux, while that of Guilheméry simply used minor sources from the slight hills to the east (now well within the modern city limits).[31] The amphitheatre is the largest surviving monument in the area and it raises an important question. As may be seen from the map (fig 6), it stands over 4km from the city walls, on the wrong side of the river, and is very much more closely associated with the notable sanctuary of St-Michel-du-Touch, which has been the subject of much excavation in recent years.[32] Since the amphitheatre appears to have remained in use for a very long period, with some rebuilding with Pyrenean marble in the second century, this connection may well be significant for part of its life, but limited excavations in 1961 suggested a much earlier origin, most probably, as with the amphitheatre of Cimiez (*qv*, p 341), for military purposes.[33] No early fort has, however, yet been found and although

the amphitheatre was officially classified as a monument historique in
1974 its remains were still in a sorry state in 1982 (pl 3). Fuller
excavation is clearly required, both to confirm its date and to allow it to
be consolidated.

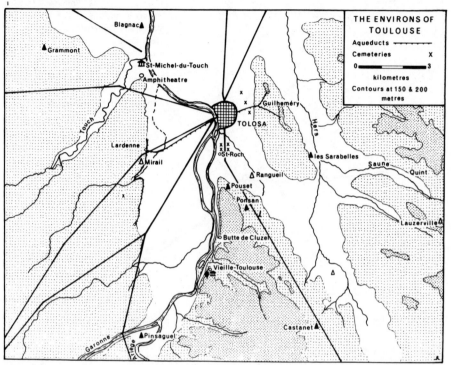

6 The environs of Toulouse

To turn now to the *civitas* as a whole, the definition of its boundaries
(fig 7) has some importance, because three quarters of them also
constitute the boundaries of our province, at least from the time of the
Augustan reorganisation. As we have noted (p 60), it is probable that
the *Convenae*, and likewise the *Consoranni*, lay within the province in
the Republican period, but under Augustus they were transferred to
Aquitania. Again, it is sometimes argued, on the evidence of Pliny's
description of it as *Carcasum Volcarum Tectosagum*, that Carcassonne
was still subject to Toulouse in the first century AD, but he is
presumably referring only to its origin and in any case the Peutinger
Table locates *Fines* at a place between *Badera* (Baziège) and *Eburomagus*
(Bram).[35] The natural eastern boundary between the *civitates* of *Narbo*
and *Tolosa* can best be understood, southwards from the Montagne
Noire, as the watershed between the tributaries of the Aude and those
of the Ariège. The southern boundary, that between the provinces of
Narbonensis and *Hispania Tarraconensis*, was undoubtedly the summit of
the Pyrenees. The southern part of the western boundary with

119

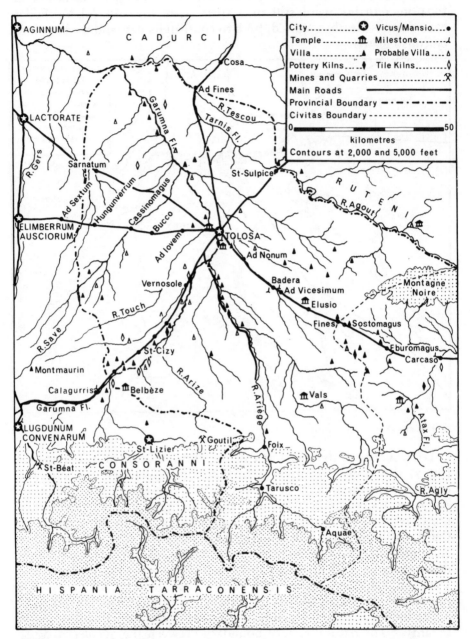

7 The territory of the *Tolosates*

Aquitania is again defined first by the basin of the Ariège and then by the chain of les Petites Pyrénées (shown on fig 8), but north of this one has to depend almost entirely on the limits of the medieval dioceses of Auch, Lectoure and Lombez.[36] In the north Pliny, though with somewhat confused wording,[37] sets some of the boundary between *Narbonensis* and *Aquitania* at the river Tarn and fortunately this is confirmed by another *Fines* on the Peutinger Table, this one at xxviii *mp* from *Tolosa*. The Tarn, however, could hardly provide more than a few miles of the boundary with the *Ruteni*, and here we have followed Labrousse in assuming that the former *Ruteni Provinciales* were now absorbed into their Aquitanian *civitas* and that the later diocese of Albi provides a reasonable limit, along the river Agout.[38]

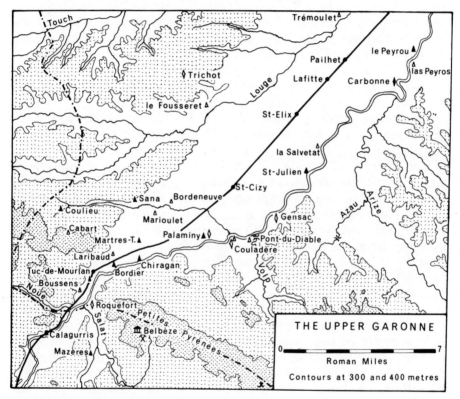

8 The upper valley of the river Garonne

For the main Roman roads north of Toulouse we have to rely mainly on the course of suitable modern roads and boundaries, and for the names of stations on them upon the evidence of the Peutinger Table and the Bordeaux Itinerary. From this it is probable the *Ad Sextum* (defined by the Itinerary as six *leugae*, not miles, from Auch) lay near Marsan, *Hungunverrum* a little north of Cimont, *Bucco* near Isle-Jourdain (not far from the still-existing Fôret de Bouconne) and *Ad*

Iovem just east of Léguevin (at the junction of the modern D24 with N124); *Casinomagus*, which appears not in the Itinerary but only on the Peutinger Table, should (assuming that this too was using *leugae*) be somewhere near Garbic.[39] The direct road from *Lactorate* (Lectoure) to *Tolosa* is recorded only on the Peutinger Table and the only *mansio* that it shows between the two cities, *Sarnati* (or a similar name—the lettering is unclear) is probably near Sarrant; an interesting point here is that as it approaches the Garonne, along the line of the modern D1, the road is aligned very accurately on the northern gate of the city, but presumably it was diverted southwards to cross the river by the same means (a ford or a bridge) as the road from Auch.[40] The Peutinger Table also provides the evidence for the road from Cahors, with stations named only at *Cosa* (probably Albias, in Cadurcan territory) and *Fines* (near Montauban)—though there must have been at least one other within our *civitas*.[41] The last of the northern roads, that linking Toulouse with Albi and Rodez, does not appear in any ancient source, but it has been reasonably well established archaeologically, while the settlement at St-Sulpice-la-Pointe, near the confluence of the Agout with the Tarn, provides an obviously required *mansio*.[42]

The roads running south from the city are somewhat more interesting for a variety of reasons. That leading to Carcassonne and Narbonne has yielded seven milestones, ranging in date from Tetricus to Theodosius and Arcadius,[43] which indicate the constant importance attached to it. Besides this, we are here involved in the question of the identity of at least one of the places named by Cicero in the *Pro Fonteio*. As we have suggested (p 70, n 42), his *Elesiodunum* must surely be related to the *mansio Elusione* of the Bordeaux Itinerary,[44] which sets it as ix mp from the *mutatio ad Vicesimum* (somewhere near the border between Villenouvelle and Montgaillard)[45] and ix mp from *Sostomagus* (certainly Castelnaudary), and presumably it was the name of the hill-fort of Montferrand. The *mansio* itself, however, still invites further investigation, since the most important remains so far excavated (now conserved and open to public view), near the church of St-Pierre-d'Alzone, are of late, palaeochristian date, and the outlines of other buildings have been observed on air photographs.[46] Of the other places named on this road, Labrousse satisfactorily locates the *Ad Nonum* of the Bordeaux Itinerary at l'Espitalet, on the modern N113 near Pompertuzat, and the *Fines* of the Peutinger Table about 2km sw of the village of Ricaud—that is, 3km wnw of Castelnaudary.[47]

The course of the road running up the valley of the Ariège is largely speculative—it may well have continued as far south as Tarascon (*Tarusco*) or even to Ax-les-Thermes (*Aquae*)—but at least its existence has recently been confirmed by the discovery of its junction with the other main road, that towards *Lugdunum Convenarum* (St-Bertrand-de-Comminges),[48] which in turn requires more discussion. It is not included in the Peutinger Table—perhaps because of the loss of the western section before the existing version was produced—but it is the one route in this *civitas* that is covered by the Antonine Itinerary. Its course is well established and it has been excavated in several places,[49] but the identity of one of the stations named on it has been widely questioned. For the background to the argument it is necessary to quote the figures in the Itinerary, which read as follows:[50]

Calagorris		
Aquis Siccis	xvi	mp
Vernosole	xii	mp
Tolosa	xv	mp

To take them in reverse order, the Roman settlement at Ox is some 16 Roman miles from Toulouse and so can very reasonably be identified with *Vernosole*, and St-Martory, which is generally accepted as the site of *Calagurris*, is 30 Roman miles from Ox (close enough to the sum of 28 in the Itinerary). The identification (by Labrousse and Manière)[51] of *Aquae Siccae* with St-Cizy (19 Roman miles from Ox and only 11.7 from St-Martory), however, implies that the two mileage figures, though not the names, have been transposed. As Joulin long ago demonstrated, the settlement at St-Cizy is a very large one (much larger, for example, than that at Tuc-de-Mourlan, which he also excavated and planned), but a number of others have been found along this road—notably at Pailhet, Lafitte-Vigordanne and near St-Elix—and the Itinerary does not always select its stopping-places by size.[52] It is for this reason that the name of *Aquae Siccae* does not appear on the maps (figs 7, 8).

The main purpose of including the more detailed map of the Upper Garonne, however, is to draw attention to the discoveries made here since the brilliant work of Joulin at the turn of the century.[53] So far as the Chiragan villa itself is concerned (fig 9) the only significant addition has been some trace of an aqueduct leading to it,[54] but additional villas have been excavated at le Peyrou, Palaminy and Martres-Tolosanes, more buildings at Boussens and one at le Fousseret, pottery kilns at Carbonne, and early tile kilns at Palaminy and late ones at Trichot.[55] Especially since Fouet's investigation of Montmaurin (which, though it was in *Aquitania*, lay only 30km to the west, fig 7) it has been widely suggested that the huge Chiragan villa dominated a huge estate (perhaps the *Massa Aconiana* comparable to the *Massa Nepotiana*, though unfortunately no medieval name analogous to the Pays Nébouzan has been noted) and that their histories were broadly comparable, perhaps with the owner moving in the fourth century to the new residence at Martres-Tolosanes.[56] This is highly probable, but in comparing the supposed subsidiary villas one must note the difference in size and complexity between the smaller ones, like Coulieu and Bordier, and Sana, which evidently extended further than Joulin's plan and underwent much reconstruction (fig 10)—and so might be the centre of a separate estate.

123

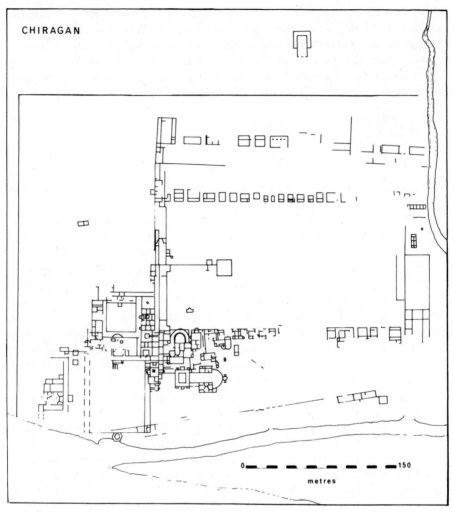

9 The villa of Chiragan (after Joulin)

Intensive Roman development on this side of the Garonne is not surprising, but when, some 20 years ago, one looked·across the river from the site of Chiragan, one formed the impression that the area on the right bank would have been suitable only for hunting. More recent discoveries, however, have altered the picture. Substantial finds of buildings and tile kilns have been made around Couladère and Gensac[57] and the idea that the ancient Pont-du-Diable, over the river Volp, is in fact of Roman origin[58] suggests that a road existed also on this bank of the Garonne. Whether this ran directly towards Toulouse (past the building recently found near Marquefave at las Peyros)[59] is, however, still questionable, since another bridge of very similar type has also been observed over the river Azau, 4km west of Montesquieu-

Volvestre:[60] a course up the river Arize seems a possibility, perhaps to copper mines that may have succeeded the first-century one at Goutil.[61] The temple on the hill of Pédégas-d'en-Haut, north-west of Belbèze, seems to stand just outside our province.[62]

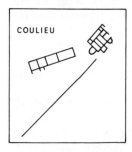 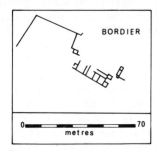 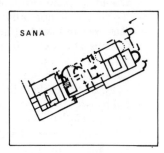

10 The villas of Coulieu, Bordier and Sana, all at the same scale (after Joulin)

As may be seen from the general map (fig 7), a number of villas or other settlements have also been found in the valley of the Ariège since Joulin's general survey in 1907—to take them in order southwards from the confluence with the Garonne, at Pinsaguel, Clermont, Venergue, Grépiac, Auterive, Cintegabelle (very large and luxurious and compared with Montmaurin) and St-Jean-de-Verges (where one building, on the site of the Tour d'Opio, may be a temple)[63]. Further to the south, only small finds are recorded from Foix, Tarascon (*Tarusco*) and Ax-les-Thermes (presumably *Aquae*), but surely they were occupied, because this must have been an area that contributed to the wealth of Toulouse—a source not only of iron but also of gold brought down by the river, and something of added importance because most of the mines of the Montagne Noire, from which the *Volcae Tectosages* had derived much in earlier times, were now under the control of Narbonne or Béziers.

Metals, however, were only one of the sources of wealth, and in conclusion we must reflect on the agricultural and pastoral excellence of the country.[64] Although it lay beyond the olive belt, so that oil had to be imported, it could produce its own wine[65], both Caesar and Strabo appear to refer to its fertility[66] and Martial to its cheese.[67] As the map shows, a considerable number of villas have now been located and, to judge from the large number of -ac place names, especially in the northern half of the *civitas*, many more still remain to be found.

REFERENCES AND NOTES

1 For a full discussion see Labrousse 1968, 85–90.
2 Livy XXI, 26.

Tolosa (Toulouse)

3 Strabo IV, 2, 3; against this, in IV, I, 12 he has called *Narbo* the ἐπίνειον (seaport) of the *Volcae Arecomici* but, as Labrousse 1968, 91–2, points out, the situation could be changeable.

4 For the implications of this, see *Narbo* (p 130). Among other things, it would explain Ptolemy's characteristically archaic attribution to the *Tectosages* of not only *Tolosa* but also *Illiberis, Ruscino, Cessero, Carcaso, Baeterrae* and *Narbo* (*Geog* II, x, 6).

5 Cassius Dio XXVII, fr 90.

6 Strabo IV, I, 13.

7 Labrousse 1968, 92–105, citing Nicolas Bertrand: *De Tholosanorum gestis,* 1515, as the earliest literary presentation of the argument.

8 Labrousse 1968, 93, nos 66, 67, 68; *Pallas* IX(1960), 177–217, X(1961), 69–90; *Gallia* XV(1957), 256–8, XVI(1958), 115–17, XVII(1959), 433–5, XX(1962), 576–8, XXII(1964), 449–51, XXIV(1966), 429–30, XXVI(1968), 537–8, XXVIII(1970), 410–13, XXX(1972), 491–5, XXXII(1974), 474–6, XXXIV(1976), 482–4, XXXVI(1978), 409–11, XXXVIII(1980), 480–7.

9 Labrousse 1968, 99–100; *Gallia* XVII(1959), 427–8, XXII(1964), 447–8, XXIV(1966), 424, XXXVI(1978), 405–08, XXXVIII(1980), 481.

10 A type based, curiously, on the coinage of *Rhode* (Rosas, just across the border in Spain). On this coinage, and especially the vexed question of when it began, see D.F.Allen, 'Monnaies à la Croix', *Num Chron*[7] IX(1969), 33–78; Allen 1980, 54–9, 169, 171; Colbert de Beaulieu 1973, 278–95.

11 Caesar, *BG* III, 20.

12 Caesar, *BG* VII, 7.

13 Pliny, *HN* III, 37: *Oppida Latina . . . Samnagenses Tolosani Tectosagum Aquitaniae contermini Tasgoduni Tarusconienses Umbranici Vocontiorum civitatis duo capita . . . .* This is deliberately written here without commas and it may well be that the words *Aquitaniae contermini* refer to the *Tasgoduni* rather than the *Tolosani,* which would support the view of Labrousse 1968, 488 (citing other authors) that the former dwelt near the river Tescou in the northern part of the *civitas.* The claim that the *Tarusconienses* were the people of Tarascon-sur-Ariège, however, though widely held (*eg* Weiss in P–W, *sv*), is quite unconvincing, since Pliny's list (as the quotation shows) is roughly alphabetical and Tarascon-sur-Rhône is a much more likely candidate

14 Ptolemy, *Geog* II, 10, 6.

15 *CIL* XII, 5387.

16 *CIL* XII, 5386.

17 *CIL* XI, 6366.

18 *ILG,*[2] 4193, says he was born ἐν τῇ πατρίδι Τολώσῃ.

19 Suetonius, *Vitellius* 18 (for Becco); Martial IX, 99; Tacitus *Hist* II, 86 (*strenuus manu, sermone promptus, serendae in alios invidiae artifex, discordiis et seditionibus potens, raptor, largitor, pace pessimus, bello non spernendus*).

20 Martial IX, 99, 3.

21 Suetonius, fr 90; Cassiodorus Senator 673 (after *coss* Marcellinus and Aviola); Jerome, *Chron* 2073 (calling him Statius Surculus)

22 Ausonius, *Parentalia* iii, *Professores* xvi (Aemilius); *Professores* xvi (Exuperius); *Professores* xix (Sedatus): for a detailed discussion of them, with other references, Labrousse 1968, 511–16. Bishop, Gregory, *Hist Franc* I, 30.

23 Labrousse 1968, 237–76; G.Baccrabère, 'Etude de Toulouse romaine', *Chronique* no 3, Institut Catholique de Toulouse, 1977; *Gallia* VII(1949), 132–3, XIII(1955), 211–13, XXII(1964), 444–6 (St-Jacques), XXIV(1966), 424–5, XXXII(1974), 470–3 (St-Jacques), XXXIV(1976), 476, XXVI(1978) 404, XXXVIII(1980), 479. The small portion of wall formerly visible in the Square Charles de Gaulle has now been turfed over.

24 *Gallia* XXX(1972) 486–8, with plan.

25 Labrousse 1968, 281–90; Baccrabère, *op cit*, 62–3.

26 Labrousse 1968, 276–81; G.Baccrabère, 'Le rampart antique de l'Institut Catholique de Toulouse', *Chronique* no 4, Institut Catholique de Toulouse, 1974.

27 Labrousse 1968, 437–45, with a tentative plan: Baccrabère, *Chronique* no 3 (1977), 64–6, with a modified plan resulting from later observations.

28 Baccrabère, *op cit*, 71–5; *Gallia* XXXIV(1976), 476.

29 On la Daurade, Labrousse 1968, 412–17; Baccrabère, *op cit*, 69–70. On St-Etienne, Labrousse 1968, 433–4; Baccrabère, *op cit*, 70–1.

30 Labrousse 1968, 293–302; Baccrabère, *op cit*, 21–41, including an important section on the streets following the walls. What is clear is that the rigid lay-out suggested by P.Pinon and reproduced in Chevallier 1982, fig XXXII did not apply.

31 On the Lardenne aqueduct, Baccrabère, *Méms de la Soc Arch du Midi de la France* XXX(1964), 59–116; Labrousse 1968, 389–401 (there was no 'Queen Pedauque'; as Dumiège, quoted by Labrousse, explained, she was 'la reine aux pieds d'oie' or 'Regina pé d'auca'!) On Guilheméry, Labrousse 1968, 401–07.

32 Labrousse 1968, 435, but also, since the refs there cited, *Gallia* XXIV(1966), 425–7, XXVI(1968), 534, XXVIII(1970), 410–13, XXXIV(1976), 477.

33 Labrousse 1968, 445–55; excavation report, *Gallia* XX(1962), 571–2.

34 Pliny, *HN* III, 36; *Oppida Latina . . . Cabellio, Carcasum Volcarum Tectosagum, Cessero . . .*

35 On the probable location of this *Fines*, Labrousse 1968, 323–6.

36 Labrousse 1968, 329; for the river Noue as the boundary just north of the Garonne, *Gallia* XXII(1964), 439–40.

37 Pliny, *HN* IV, 109 (writing on Aquitania): *Rursus Narbonensi provinciae contermini Ruteni, Cadurci, Nitiobriges, Tarneque amne discreti a Tolosanis Petrocori* (though the *Petrucorii* were, of course, far from the Tarn.)

38 Labrousse 1968, 328, with important footnotes; the *Ruteni*, however, were still partly in the province when Pliny (*HN* III, 37) compiled his list of *oppida Latina*.

39 For a detailed discussion of this road and its stations, Labrousse 1968, 353–8.

40 *Ibid*, 360–2.

41 *Ibid*, 363–8.

42 *Ibid*, 368–71.

43 One of Decentius Caesar from Pouvourville, *iii mp* from *Tolosa* (*CIL* XII, 5677; *ILS* 764; König no 267; see fig 6); one from Baziège, *xv mp* from *Tolosa*, inscribed three times, to Galerius, to Delmatius Caesar and to another uncertain emperor (*CIL* XII, 5676; König no 265); one from Ayguevives, at *xv* or *xvi mp*, also with three inscriptions, to Constantine I, to Magnus Maximus and Flavius Victor, and to Theodosius and Arcadius

127

Tolosa (Toulouse)

(*CIL* xii, 5675; König no 266); one from Montgaillard-Lauragais, again marking *xv mp* and inscribed to Tetricus (*Pallas* vi(1958), 55–78; *Gallia* xvii(1959), 422–3; *REA* lxi(1959), 379; König no 264); and two stones from Villenouvelle, *19 mp* from *Tolosa*, one with two inscriptions, to Constantine i and perhaps Decentius, the other inscribed to Constantine ii (*CIL* xii, 5673–4; König nos 262–3).

44 Bordeaux Itinerary 551.5.
45 Labrousse 1968, 339.
46 *FOR* xii(1959), no 94a; Labrousse 1968, 340–1; *Gallia* xxxi(1973), 479.
47 Labrousse 1968, 338 and 341.
48 Labrousse 1968, 352; road junction, *Gallia* xxxi(1973), 541.
49 Labrousse 1968, 349–51; *Gallia* xxxvi(1978), 401.
50 *It. Ant.* 457.9–458.3.
51 Labrousse 1968, 346–8, with many references.
52 For St-Cizy and Tuc-de-Mourlan, Joulin 1901; for Pailhet, Lafitte and St-Elix (Amourés), *Gallia* xxxvi(1978), 401.
53 Joulin 1901.
54 *Gallia* xvii(1959), 422.
55 The villa shown at St-Julien is deduced from the mosaic recorded there in Joulin 1907. For the large villa and cemetery at le Peyrou (across the river from Marquefave, under which name it is often listed), *Gallia* xx(1962), 561–2, xxii(1964), 440, xxvi(1968), 526, xxviii(1970), 406; for Palaminy villa (at les Boulbènes), *Gallia* xxvi(1958), 528, xxviii(1970), 408, xxxii(1974), 469; for Martres-Tolosanes villa (under church), *Pallas* iii(1955), 89–115, *Gallia* ix(1951), 128–9, xii(1954), 214–15, xiii(1955), 203–04, xv(1957), 259, xxvi(1968), 526; for buildings near Boussens, *Gallia* xii(1954), 215, xvii(1959), 421, xxvi(1968), 524, xxviii(1970), 405–06, xxxiv(1976), 472–3; at Fousseret, *Gallia* xxx(1972), 484; for pottery kilns at Carbonne, *Gallia* xxx(1972), 481; for tile kilns at Palaminy and Trichot, G.Manière, 'Fours à tuiles gallo-romains de Trichot', *Gallia* xxxiii(1975), 207–12 (with useful discussion of others).
56 For general discussions see, besides Joulin 1901, Grenier 1934, 888–97, Percival 1976, 129–30.
57 G.Manière, 'Une officine de tuilier gallo-romain de Haut-Empire à Couladère par Cazères', *Gallia* xxix(1979), 191–9, and *Gallia* xxx(1972), 483–4; on Gensac, *Gallia* xxxiii(1975), 211 n 10.
58 Manière, *op cit*, 199 (and *Gallia* xxvi(1963), 530).
59 *Gallia* xxxvi(1978), 402.
60 *Gallia* xxvi(1968), 402–03.
61 J.-E.Guilbaut, 'La mine de cuivre gallo-romaine du Goutil, à la Bastide-de-Sérou (Ariège)', *Gallia* xxxix(1981), 171–80.
62 *Gallia* xxiv(1966) 418–19 (also covering the stone quarries), xxvi(1968), 524.
63 Pinsaguel, *Gallia* xxxvi(1978), 403; Clermont, *Gallia* xv(1957), 258, xvii(1959), 421, xxxvi(1978), 399–400, xxxviii(1980), 482; Venergue, Joulin 1907 (coins only), *Gallia* xxxviii(1980), 482; Grépiac, *Gallia* xxiv(1966), 420; Auterive, Joulin 1907, *Gallia* xxii(1964), 435–7, xxiv(1966), 418, xxvi(1968), 523–4, xxviii(1970), 403–04 (workshop buildings), xxx(1972), 479, xxxii(1974), 465–6, xxxiv(1976), 471 (pottery kilns); Cintegabelle, *Gallia* xxvi(1968), 525, xxviii(1970), 406, xxx(1972),

482 (bath house); XXXII(1974), 468, XXXIV(1976), 475, XXXVI(1978), 399; St-Jean-de-Verges, *Gallia* XXVIII(1970), 397.

64 For a brief survey, Labrousse 1968, 501–05.

65 In *Gallia* XXVI(1968), 524, it is suggested that one of the buildings at Boussens was a wine entrepôt.

66 Caesar, *BG* I, 10—assuming that the words *locis patentibus maximeque frumentariis* apply to the *Tolosani* to whom he has just referred and not simply to the *provincia* as a whole (*cf* Strabo IV, 1, 14).

67 Martial, *Epig* XII, 32, 18; *nec quadra deerat casei Tolosani.*

9

Narbo Martius (Narbonne), with *Ruscino* (Château Roussillon) and *Carcaso* (Carcassonne)

The choice of Narbonne as the site for the first Roman *colonia* in Gaul owed much to its geographical position, and for an understanding of this some facts must be borne in mind. For example, while the watercourse called la Robine that now passes through the city is merely a canal, the Pont Vieux across it certainly began as a Roman bridge (pl 4). It follows that, although its course is slightly different, this canal, dug in the seventeenth century and in the eighteenth century linked to Riquet's great Canal du Midi, is actually a reconstruction of one of the branches of the river Aude (the *Atax* of the ancients)—one that then flowed into the *Lacus Rubrensis* (approximately the modern Etang de Bages et de Sigean)[1]. More important still is the fact that in both pre-Roman and Roman times a series of climatic changes progressively modified both the habitability of parts of the delta of the Aude and the navigability of its branches, so that the modern map does not adequately explain the background to its history.[2]

The native predecessor of *Narbo* was the hill-fort of Montlaurès, which stands 4km to the NE of the city, was occupied from the seventh century BC onwards and is certainly the place referred to by Avienius as *Naro*, the capital of the *Elisyces*[3]. These people, probably Ligurian in origin but perhaps with some Iberian elements, appear to have extended over a considerable area, to include, among the hill-forts named on fig 3 (p 14 above), Pech-Maho, Cayla de Mailhac, Ensérune, Béziers, Montfo and St-Siméon,[4] while their prosperity benefited from trade not only along the *Via Herculea* but also from a harbour which may have lain on the then wider river Aude near Montlaurès itself.[5] At some time in the third century BC, however, the *Elisyces* were overrun by the *Volcae*, to whom they became in effect a client tribe. Whether the *Volcae* had already split into their two parts of the *Arecomici* and the *Tectosages* remains a vexed question,[6] but it seems evident that the *Elisyces*, while retaining some limited individuality, were themselves fragmented, for it was only after this event that they began to produce their own coins—those centred on Montlaurès minting issues with the

Iberian inscription NERONCEN, while others, now to be known as the *Longostaletes* (apparently a Celtic name) used Béziers as their base.[7] Further, by 125 BC the western *Volcae* themselves had become clients of the *Arverni*—at least, Strabo tells us that the Arvernian empire then extended as far as Narbonne.[8] All these political changes, however, did not destroy the importance of Montlaurès as a trading centre. Though it suffered from fires in the 5th and 3rd centuries (the latter, perhaps, when the *Volcae* conquered it), it has yielded imports of all periods, while even the transport of British tin up the valley of the Garonne and down the Aude may have begun earlier than is sometimes supposed.[9]

As we have seen above (p 43), it was in the aftermath of the wars with the *Arverni* and their allies that the Romans became officially interested in this area, laying out the *Via Domitia* and in 118 BC settling here their first colony. Arguments regarding this date have also been dealt with above, but the precise choice of location still demands a little more explanation. There is no doubt that the continuous drying out of the area meant that Montlaurès had needed to develop a port or ports nearer the coastline,[10] and it has sometimes been suggested that the colony simply took over the site of one of them, but there is very little to support this. Narbonne has yielded remarkably little pre-Roman evidence and even the latest suggestion—that of a settlement slightly wsw of the *colonia*, in the area of the Place Barra (the possible settlement shown on fig 11)—is not wholly convincing.[11] In any case, the milestone of Domitius records the distance from *Narbo* with remarkable accuracy and such measurements are unlikely to have been made from a mere collection of native huts. Much more probable, it seems to us, is a Roman fort, set up to control the area and to serve as a base for the builders of the road: any material that is supposed to relate to the earliest phase of the *colonia* could equally well derive from such an establishment and there is, indeed, some evidence—though still very little—for early earthwork defences.[12]

The *duoviri* who founded the *colonia* were L. Licinius Crassus and Cn. Domitius Ahenobarbus (son of the *imperator* of that name)[13] and the majority of the colonists appear to have come from *Umbria*, *Picenum*, *Latium* and *Campania* and were enrolled in the voting tribe *Pollia*.[14] How many of them were settled here in the first place is, of course, uncertain, but recent evidence has indicated that extensive centuriation was imposed at an early date, as may be deduced from its orientation, clearly related to the earlier course of the *Via Domitia*. Owing, once again, to the change in climate, it has been proved that this road (as indicated by the pecked line on fig 12) originally passed north of the Etang de Capestang and it was not until the time of Augustus that the more direct route between Béziers and Narbonne, using the now-lost bridge at Ponserme on the southern edge of the étang, could be established.[15] The application of the name *Narbo* to the new site raises some problems, but in general it may be accepted that it probably

11 A tentative plan of Narbonne

described the area rather than only the actual hill-fort of Montlaurès; as to the addition to it of the adjective *Martius*, the name of one of the consuls in the year of its foundation, Q.Marcius Rex, has been widely taken to be its source but the alternative suggestion, that it reflects rather the war-god Mars, becomes all the more attractive if, as has been suggested above, a military fort preceded the establishment of the *colonia*.[16]

As soon as the formal *provincia* was created, *Narbo* naturally became its effective capital and there is an indication that it was here that Pompey held a *concilium Gallorum* when on his way to Spain in 76 BC.[17] There is also ample evidence that the official Roman presence led to a considerable development of trade, most notably that of wine up the valley of the Aude, so well illustrated both by the references to it in Cicero's *Pro Fonteio* and by extensive finds of amphorae,[18] while the full romanity of the place is attested by the origin here of people like the poet P.Terentius Varro Atacinus, the stoic philosopher Fabius Max-

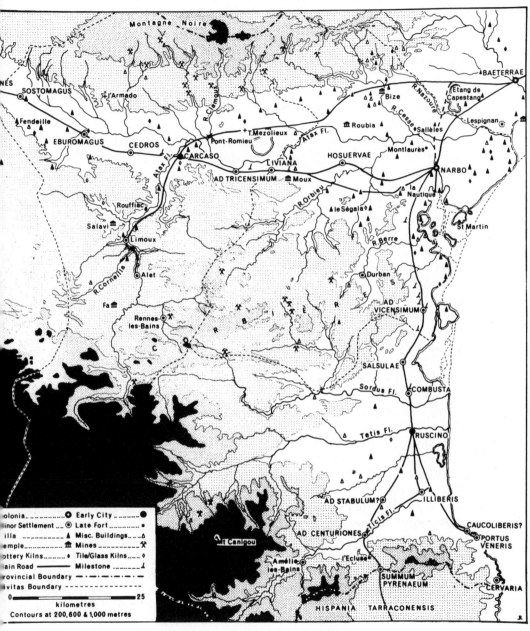

12 The territory of *Narbo Martius,* including *Carcaso* and *Ruscino*

imus and, a man who was to become an outstanding orator in the imperial period, Votienus Montanus.[19] Archaeological evidence for the development of the city during the republican period, on the other hand, remains distressingly slight and it is not until Augustan times that a picture begins to emerge. In the meantime, of course, Julius Caesar had, through Ti.Claudius Nero, refounded the colony with veterans of *Legio X*, so that its full title was expanded to *Colonia Iulia Paterna Narbo Martius Decumanorum*—with the additional word *Claudia* to be inserted a century later by the emperor Claudius—and its official voting tribe became *Papiria*.

Narbonne is unusual in that, while it has an unrivalled collection of Roman inscriptions, it is remarkably lacking in visible Roman monuments. Until recently all the inscriptions, along with impressive reliefs,[20] had been presented in cemented rows in the deconsecrated church of Nôtre-Dame-de-Lamourgier, but a progressive number of them have now been detached and moved to a better display, along with other finds, in the museum in the old Palais des Archévêques. A high proportion of the inscriptions and reliefs were recovered at various times from the dismantling of the Roman town wall, and while this means that their precise original locations are uncertain, the periods to which they belong allow a reasonably firm date to be attributed to the wall itself; all the evidence indicates that, like many others in Gaul, it was not built before the late third or early fourth century,[21] and it was presumably this, rather than specific wars, that led to the demolitions in *Narbo* to which Sidonius refers in his praise of the city.[22]

Sadly, very few of the monuments named by Sidonius have been firmly identified. Apart from the bridge over la Robine, the only one visible and open to the public is a large part of the underground *Horrea*. These were identified in 1838 and excavated first in 1842–3, then, much more thoroughly, in 1938–44 and 1967–8. Analysis of the structure and of the finds within it has indicated a date in the first century BC, probably related to the Caesarean refoundation of the *colonia*, and it is likely that the earlier forum also lay in this area.[23] If this is so, it must be near here that there stood the altar bearing the best-known of all Narbonne's inscriptions, a dedication to the *numen Augusti* in AD 11.[24]

The later forum certainly lay a little further to the north-east, related to the capitol. Some remains of the capitol were noted in 1869 and excavations in 1877–89 enabled a plan to be established, but thereafter it was built over, so that relatively little investigation has been possible since and only its plan and a few fragments of it are now displayed in public. From the various pieces of evidence, especially reliefs and inscriptions, Grenier dated it to Antoninus Pius, but Gayraud, after re-examining the material, argues strongly for Hadrian.[25] The date and precise site of the monumental arch, whose existence nearby is attested by numerous fragments, is still uncertain.[26]

The only other major buildings of which plans have been obtained

Narbo (Narbonne), *Ruscino* (Château Roussillon), *Carcaso* (Carcassonne)

stood to the east, well outside the town walls. The amphitheatre—the largest in the province—was mentioned as early as 1604, but it was not examined until 1838, when its plan was worked out, and although slight excavations in 1963 and 1964 enabled minor corrections to be made to the plan none of it is now visible.[27] A small distance to the north-west of it, a temple with a large stylobate and a *piscina* was found in the nineteenth century and since it was in this *piscina*, in 1888, that a fragment of a bronze tablet recording the *Lex de flamonio provinciae Narbonensis* was discovered, it is highly probable that this was the provincial temple and that the baths related to it were those whose restoration by Antoninus Pius after a fire is also recorded in an inscription.[28]

Other shrines certainly existed. While Sidonius cites the deities Lenaeus (that is, Bacchus), Ceres, Pales and Minerva, a temple of Cybele is attested by no less than nine taurobolic altars and since all of them were found in the stretch of wall between the bastion of St-François and that of St-Cosme, this too must have been in the eastern part of the city.[29] Again, there was certainly a theatre—not only does Sidonius mention it, but, unlike the amphitheatre, it is recorded in an inscription.[30] Finally, aqueducts must also have existed—here again, we have epigraphic evidence—but none has so far been certainly traced.[31] Thus, while various rescue excavations have located houses, some with very fine mosaics,[32] and also cemeteries,[33] which do at least provide some evidence for the extent of the city in its prime, a very great deal still remains to be found.

As for sea communications, in the early imperial period the lower part of the Aude was still navigable to some extent—Strabo tells us that in his day traffic still went up the river for some distance beyond Narbonne—but this was doubtless for barges rather than for sea-going ships, for Pliny (who stresses that the city was then 12 Roman miles from the coast), Mela and Lucan all point to the difficulties of navigation.[24] Inevitably, then, ports were developed on the shores of the Etang de Bages et de Sigean and the most important of these—the true port of the city—was at la Nautique, a site that has yielded much pottery.[35] Minor ports, such as that on the Ile St-Martin (which was still an island in Roman times) have also been located.

While inscriptions give us the names of very many people born or resident here, regrettably few are mentioned in literature. In the first century Martial tells us of Arcanus, and in the fourth Ausonius of the grammarian Marcellus,[36] but, despite the claims of several authors, the emperor Carus may have been of Illyrian rather than Narbonnese origin.[37] The earliest bishop to be mentioned is Paulus, one of the seven whose appointment Gregory of Tours places in the reign of Decius.[38]

By the fourth century, or perhaps earlier, *Narbo* controlled the whole territory from the Montagne Noire to the Pyrenees as a single unit, but since in the earlier period this was divided into three separate *civitates*

135

Narbo (Narbonne), *Ruscino* (Château Roussillon), *Carcaso* (Carcassonne)

(see fig 12 for their approximate boundaries), it is best that, before discussing the economy as a whole, we should first consider the two other cities—*Ruscino* and *Carcaso*.

Ruscino (Château Roussillon) was a hill-fort long before the Roman invasion, lying in the territory of the *Sordi* or *Sordones*.[39] Although Avienius does not mention the place, he does refer to the river *Rhoscynus* and this, or *Ruscino*, still appears as the name of the Tet in Polybius (as quoted by Athenaeus), in Strabo and in Ptolemy;[40] in Mela it has become the *Tetis*[41]. The hill-fort evidently flourished in prehistoric times, having yielded many finds not only of Attic and Campanian pottery but also of Punic ware,[42] and, as we have seen (p 28, above), it was here that in 218 BC some unidentified tribes assembled to bar the passage of Hannibal, but it was not until the construction of the *Via Domitia* that the Romans became interested in the place. Whether the *Sordi* had come under the control of the *Volcae Tectosages*, as Ptolemy's text indicates,[43] is uncertain, but no early Roman fort or posting station either on the hill or on the lower ground nearby has been identified.

Though excavations first began in 1816 and in 1909–14 Thiers recovered a number of vital inscriptions, for many years the only recognised archaeological feature was the forum,[44] which is situated surprisingly near the edge of a bluff. Ever since the last war, however, a great deal of work has taken place here. Not only has the forum been tidied up (the site was taken over by the city of Perpignan in 1972; pl 5), but excavations elsewhere on the hill have revealed both Iron Age structures, including silos, and Republican and early imperial buildings, with at least one mosaic, and centuriation has also been observed.[45] The results of much of this work were admirably discussed in a colloque held at Perpignan in 1975.[46]

That *Ruscino* became a *colonia Latina* in Augustan times is hardly in doubt. Mela specifically calls it *colonia Ruscino* and Pliny *Ruscino Latinorum*,[47] and one inscription with the letters *CIR* indicates that its full name was *Colonia Iulia Ruscino*[48]. The idea that it was a *colonia Romana*, with *duoviri* rather than *quattuorviri*, can now be dismissed, since this derived from no more than a guess by Thiers when trying to restore an inscription.[49] In the first half of the first century AD it was evidently flourishing, brandishing its prosperity with dedications around the forum to Tiberius, Drusus, Germanicus, Agrippina, Agrippina Junior and Drusilla, but this did not last for long. The archaeological evidence points to a steady decline in the second century and while some structures of the late Empire have been found—so that it certainly continued to be occupied—it could have been as early as the third century that its territory was incorporated by *Narbo*,[51] but for reasons given above (p 100) a later date is more probable.

Carcaso (Carcassonne) presents some problems similar to those of *Ruscino*, but others as well. It too began as a hill-fort, but the density of medieval and modern buildings, with numerous tourist shops, gravely limits the possibility of excavation. In the early 1970s, however, the construction of an open-air theatre just south of the Basilique St-Nazaire enabled some work to be done, which yielded finds back to the sixth century BC, including Etruscan, Phocaean, Attic and Massaliote imports[52]—a good indication of the early development of Greek trade up the Aude, which is further confirmed by finds from Carsac during the construction of the A61 motorway.[53]

Despite its evident prosperity, *Carcaso* is not mentioned in Cicero's *Pro Fonteio*, and its name is even omitted from half the manuscripts of Caesar's *De Bello Gallico*,[54] so that the first reliable source is Pliny, who includes it in his list of *oppida Latina*, calling it *Carcasum Volcarum Tectosagum*.[55] Ptolemy also attributes it to the *Tectosages* and while it is not there called a *colonia*,[56] evidence that it could claim that title is provided by two inscriptions, one from Rieux-Minervois, 20km to the north-east, which records a *praitor CIC* (which should stand for *Coloniae Iuliae Carcasonis*),[57] and the other a milestone from Barbaira, 8km to the east, inscribed XICIK (? XI (*mp/a*) *Colonia Iulia Karkasone*).[58]

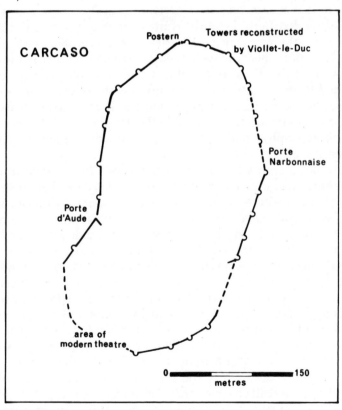

13 A tentative plan of Carcassone

Narbo (Narbonne), *Ruscino* (Château Roussillon), *Carcaso* (Carcassonne)

The only visible remains are parts of the Roman town walls and the appreciation of these is confused by a number of factors, especially the medieval rebuilding and extension of the defences. The addition of the outer defences began in the eighth century, but it was in the thirteenth century that the inner defences were also slightly extended, on the one hand near the Porte Narbonnaise (which was itself constructed in this period) and on the other to take in the slightly lower area to the south, where the open-air theatre now stands; further, a few of the bastions were reconstructed by Viollet-le-Duc in the nineteenth century.

Like most of his contemporaries—and too many of his successors—Viollet-le-Duc seems to have believed that these bastions and the wall as a whole, though Roman in style, had been built not by Romans but by the Visigoths in the fifth century. One of the reasons for this belief may have been that below the main structure one can in some places see larger stonework (pl 6), but this does not represent earlier work but simply the foundation, which must have been revealed when the outer walls were built and the ditch between the two elements (les Lices) was deepened. Beyond this there is no evidence that the Visigoths undertook any such work in this area, and in any case Carcassonne is referred to as a *castellum* in the Bordeaux Itinerary, so that the probability is that here, as with so many towns in Gaul, the defences were built in the late third or early fourth century.[59] More recent research has confirmed this belief. Some small-scale excavations were carried out near the Tour du Moulin, where a postern and the base of a demolished Roman bastion were found, the line of the Roman wall has been identified both in the area behind the Porte Narbonnaise and in that of the open-air theatre, a possible Roman theatre has been observed on air photographs, and traces of an aqueduct coming from the north-east have been noted.[60]

While *Carcaso* seems to have been a *Colonia Iulia Latina* in the first century and a mere *castellum* in the fourth (and is described as such in an itinerary that elsewhere carefully calls a city a *civitas*), the date at which its status was reduced remains uncertain. In the absence of inscriptions from the town itself, the best evidence is provided by the Barbaira milestone already mentioned: this dates from the consulship of Tetricus II (AD 274) and if the interpretation of its last line is correct the change must surely have taken place in the late third or early fourth century.[61] This probability points to a similar date for the incorporation by *Narbo* of *Ruscino*. Certainly both towns had lost their independence by AD 417, since neither is listed in the *Notitia Galliarum* by that date, and in this context it may be noted that *Ruscino* never acquired a bishop and even *Carcaso* does not appear in the texts of the *Notitia* until the twelfth century. Beyond this, while the loss of Latin status had little legal meaning after Caracalla's *Constitutio Antoniniana*, the dignity of the title of *colonia* still survived and only a reorganisation imposed by a dictatorial emperor like Diocletian could have brought about the change. It would be strange indeed if two such reductions, in neighbouring areas, were brought about at different times yet neither found its way into any historic records.

The prosperity for which *Narbo* was noted derived mainly from the northern part of its territory, and since this prosperity still survived in the days of Sidonius we may best consider this area (roughly the modern département of Aude) as a whole. As may be seen from the map (fig 12), a large number of villas have been located and while many of them seem to have decayed in the third century, some survived until the fifth; many were extremely rich, with fine mosaics, and a few, most notably that at Fendeille, have also yielded bronze inscriptions.[62] Funerary monuments are also common and two mausolea have been located, both of them resembling the 'piles' that are more common in *Aquitania*.[63]

But Narbonne's wealth did not come entirely from agriculture. For one thing, there were ample metal resources, both on the slopes of the Montagne Noire and, further south, in the Corbières. Most of the mines yielded iron or copper, but a few in the north-west of the area also produced gold and silver.[64] Secondly, some important potteries developed in the first century BC; while that at Sallèles-d'Aude made amphorae and that at Rouffiac imitated Campanian ware, the most notable of all is the factory discovered just north-east of *Eburomagus* (Bram), one of the first in Gaul to produce terra sigillata.[65]

As is often the case, the identification of towns and villages depends largely on the evidence of itineraries. The roads from Narbonne to Carcassonne, and onwards to Toulouse, are not covered by the Antonine Itinerary and here we have to depend on the mileages supplied by the Peutinger Table and the Bordeaux Itinerary. Reading them from west to east, the former lists *Badera* (Baziège) – *xviiii* – Fines – (?) – *Eburomagi* – *xvii* – *Carcassione* – *xii* – *Liviana* – xi – *Usuerva* – *xvi* – *Narbone*, and the latter can be tabulated as follows;[66]

mutatio Sostamagus	*mil viiii* (from *Elusione*/St-Pierre-d'Alzonne)
vicus Hebromago	*mil x*
mutatio Cedros	*mil vi*
castellum Carcassone	*mil viii*
mutatio Tricensimum	*mil viii*
mutatio Hosuervas	*mil xv*
civitas Narbone	*mil xv*

The location of *Fines*, between Castelnaudary and Ricaud, is best discussed in the section on *Tolosa* (p 122). Castelnaudary itself is presumably the location of *Sostomagus*, but the precise site of the *mutatio* has still to be established.[67] *Eburomagus* is certainly Bram, and suggestions have been made that this was also the *Cobiomachus* referred to by Cicero in the *Pro Fonteio*.[68] Besides the potteries already noted above, an important inscription has been found here recording the dedication of a theatre to the *numen Augusti* and Apollo by three *magistri Vici Eburomagi*, which, among other things, confirms the most acceptable form of the name.[69] The mileages given in the Itinerary and the course of the road (here roughly represented by the modern D 33) indicate that *Cedros* must have stood just north of Caux, though little has so far been found here. On similar grounds, *Tricensimum* must have been near Floure, and since it is from *Narbo* that the 30 miles are measured it seems probable that this *mutatio* was established only after the incorporation of *Carcaso*. *Liviana* is surely the place now called le Viala, just NE of Douzens, where substantial finds have been made, including remains of a temple, houses and even a small aqueduct fed by the Aude just north of Capendu.[70] *Hosuervae* should be located somewhere between Lézignan-Corbières and Fontcouvert, on the more northerly of the two alternative routes, but although many remains have been found in this area (including an oil-press) its precise site remains uncertain.[71]

No such itineraries cover the direct road from *Baeterrae* to *Carcaso*, so that it is not surprising that no *vici* or *mansiones*, let alone *mutationes*, have so far been identified along it. That it was a fully-made road, however, not merely a track, is confirmed by several stretches of it that have been examined, by antique names such as le Chemin Romieu, and not least by the evident solidarity of the Pont Romieu over the river Clamoux, of which some remains are still visible (pl 7). Much the same applies to the road running up the valley of the Aude southwards from *Carcaso*, whose solidarity is also confirmed by the remains of a bridge crossing a stream just south of Limoux.[73] Limoux itself has provided enough material to justify its presentation as a settlement (perhaps a *vicus*) and the same applies to Alet, where the finds include an altar dedicated to the *mater Deum* by Cn.Pompeius Probus, *curator templi*.[74] This road presumably ran much further south and a branch from it must also have led to Rennes-les-Bains, certainly a spa, where remains of large Roman baths are known and notable inscriptions have also been found.[75] As for Durban, SW of Narbonne, the main evidence is the incorporation of substantial Roman remains in the château, but a minor road may also have led to it too.[76]

Of the isolated temples shown on the map, the only two that are absolutely certain are Salavi (in the commune of Gaja-et-Villedieu, observed on air photographs) and Moux, a small sanctuary dedicated to the god Larraso (for whom four *magistri pagi* had constructed some *cellae*).[77] Of the others, Roubia appears to have been a shrine, with mosaics, related to a spring, Bize a small structure with antefixes of women and fighters, and Fa, whose name is taken to derive from the Latin *fanum*, still requires investigation.[78]

When we move south to what was originally the territory of *Ruscino* (and is now le Roussillon) the evidence is much thinner, for not only was this area less prosperous but, apart from *Ruscino* itself, less research

Narbo (Narbonne), *Ruscino* (Château Roussillon), *Carcaso* (Carcassonne) has been carried out in it. As may be seen, a few villas have been identified (and several more are assumed)[79] and some iron mines at Taurinya (and also at Llo, some 30km to the wsw and so not included on the map),[80] but most of the interest lies in the roads and the settlements related to them. This part of the *Via Domitia* is, of course, listed not only in the Antonine Itinerary but also on the Vicarello Goblets and the Peutinger Table. The only places that appear on the goblets, however, are *Combusta* (*xxxii mp* from *Narbo* on two of them, but *xxxiiii mp* on the other two), *Ruscino* (*vi mp* beyond *Combusta*) and *in Pyreneum* (or *Summo Pyrenae*) *xxv mp* from *Ruscino*; while Peutinger has *Narbo* – *vi* – *Ruscione* – *vii* – *Illibere* – *xii* – *ad Centenarium* – *v* – *In Summo Pyreneo*. The two routes in the Antonine Itinerary appear as follows:

389.6 *Narbone*			397.2 *Narbone*		
			3 *Ad Vicensimum*	*mp xx*	
7 *Salsulis*	*mp xxx*				
			4 *Combusta*	*mp xiiii*	
			5 *Ruscione*	*mp vi*	
390.1 *Ad Stabulum*	*mp xlviii*				
			6 *Ad Centuriones*	*mp xx*	
2 *Ad Pireneum*	*mp xvi*		7 *Summo Pyreneo*	*mp v*	

The change in the spelling of the Pyrenees (*Summo Pyreneo* being the earlier) suggests that, as is often the case, the two Antonine routes apply to different periods, and certainly the travellers on the one were in more of a hurry than those on the other, but the most interesting thing here is that neither mentions *Illiberis* (Elne). This is included by the Peutinger Table (no doubt repeating an earlier route, with some of the mileages wildly wrong) and although it is omitted from the Vicarello Goblets, the distance that they give between *Ruscino* and *in Pyreneum* indicate a passage that is likely to have included the place. There is, therefore, little doubt that the original *Via Domitia* did take in Elne (which in any case was still an important hill-fort when the road was first built) and this would also account for the total of 25 Roman miles from *Ruscino* to the Pyrenees given by the earlier of the Antonine routes. The later one, however, raises severe problems. No reasonable route could account for 94 Roman miles between Narbonne and the Col du Perthus and the simplest explanation is that *Ad Stabulum* xlviii should read *Ad Stabulum* xviii, which would reduce the total to 64, probably following the more direct route that can be traced past Villeneuve-de-la-Raho, Bages and St-Jean-Lasseille; and this is why the elusive *Ad Stabulum* has been tentatively marked at this last place, just 16 Roman miles from Perthus.[81] Besides this, another Roman road is known, running more directly from *Ruscino* to *Portus Veneris* (Port-Vendres) and this was connected to Elne by a short spur road (later known as the Cami du Carlos Magnos), which left it near the villa at Palol.[82]

Narbo (Narbonne), *Ruscino* (Château Roussillon), *Carcaso* (Carcassonne)

All this indicates that, as happened north of Narbonne (p 131 above), the course of the *Via Domitia* underwent some modification, and bearing this in mind we may briefly consider the location of the other stations. *Ad Vicensimum* roughly reflects the positioning of the milestones of Domitius, but its precise site, presumably between Treilles and Caves-de-Treilles, has yet to be established.[83] *Salsulae* was surely at Salses (which retains its name), though little has been found there, and *Combusta* at the Mas Guiter, near Claira.[84] Mela records a saline well at *Salsulae* and both he and Strabo report the curious way in which mullets could be dug up on the shore of *Leucata* near here.[85] For *Ad Centuriones* the mileages point clearly to le Boulou, at the crossing of the river Tech (*Ticis flumen*), while *Summum Pyrenaeum* is obviously at the Col-du-Perthus, where not only pottery and coins but also Roman foundations have been noted.[86] It is at the approach to this important pass, at l'Ecluse, that a late Roman fort (the Castel dels Moros) has been investigated.[87]

It remains to consider the three most important places in this southern area—*Illiberis*, *Portus Veneris* and Amélie-les-Bains. As both Mela and Pliny inform us, *Illiberis* (Elne) was once a flourishing place but by the first century AD had fallen into insignificance.[88] Its power as a hill-fort is easy to understand from its magnificent command of all the surrounding country and some excavations have revealed not only parts of its defences and silos but also many pre-Roman imports.[89] It was not wholly deserted in Roman times—marble columns and mosaic fragments have been found at the Castel de Reina Helena and also some extramural buildings[90]—but it next comes into prominence in AD 350, when the emperor Constans was murdered here by supporters of Magnentius, by which time its name had been changed to *Helena*.[91] *Portus Veneris* (Port-Vendres) is recorded in Strabo, Mela, Pliny, Ptolemy and perhaps Stephanus of Byzantium (though not in Avienius)[92] and evidently became a useful port in Roman times— though the most important find here has been the wreck of a ship carrying Spanish tin.[93] The neighbouring harbour of Collioure has produced many coins and amphorae and so may have been the *Caucoliberis* listed in the Ravenna Cosmography,[94] while Cerbère is surely the *Cervaria* described by Mela as *Galliae finis*.[95] Whether Amélie-les-Bains should be identified with the *Aquae Calidae* of the Ravenna Cosmography is questionable because of the randomness of the cartographer's listing (Rennes-les-Bains is another possibility), but its prosperity as a spa in Roman times, as now, is certain, and substantial remains of the baths can still be seen in the cellars of the modern 'Thermes Romains'.

Finally, since we are here dealing with the boundary between Gaul and Spain, an office of the *quadragesima Galliarum*, to impose a 2½ per cent tax on imports and exports, is to be expected in this area and this is confirmed by the discovery of an inscription, but it does not reveal the

Narbo (Narbonne), *Ruscino* (Château Roussillon), *Carcaso* (Carcassonne) precise site of the office. In the first place, before being moved to Théza it is known to have stood in another chapel at Villeneuve-la-Raho, near which a probable villa has been found, and secondly, it is not an official inscription but merely a dedication to Mercury by an employee of the office and so could have been set up at some distance from where he worked. On both these grounds it is surely reasonable to suppose that it was either at the Col-du-Perthus or at Port-Vendres, each of them just 20km from Villeneuve, that the taxes were imposed.[97]

REFERENCES AND NOTES

1 The Aude is *Atax* in Strabo, Pliny, Mela etc, but *Attagus* (perhaps reflecting an earlier form) in Avienius, *Ora Maritima* 589; the étang is *Lacus Rubrensis* in Pliny, *HN* III, 4, but *Rubresus* in Mela II, 5, 6, while Strabo IV, 1, 6, calls it simply ἡ λίμνη Ναρβωνίτις. For further evidence of how the canal replaces the Aude, a river bank has been identified between the Rue Turgot and the canal (*Gallia* XXXI(1973), 482).

2 See especially M.Guy, 'Le cadre géographique et géologique de Mont-laurès', *Narbonne: Archéologie et Histoire* (CNRS, Montpellier, 1973), 27–43 and Gayraud 1981, 35–67.

3 Avienius, *Ora Maritima* 586–8: *gens Elisycum prius/loca haec tenebat atque Naro civitas/erat ferocis maximum regni caput.* Stephanus of Byzantium, *sv* Νάρβων states, Ἑκαταῖος καὶ Ναρβαίους αὐτοὺς φησί but this is no sound evidence for the early inclusion of the –β–.

4 P.Barruol, 'Les Elisyques et leur capitale NARO/NARBO', *Narbonne: Archéolo-gie et Histoire* (1973), 49–63, where the hill-forts of Bassenel (near Olonzac) and Cessero and le Plan de Céresson (Fontès) are also included; Gayraud 1981, 102–05.

5 M.Guy, *op cit*.

6 Livy XXI, 26, in dealing with Hannibal's march uses only the general name *Volcae* as does Cicero, *Pro Fonteio* 12 (26), while even the later authors seem confused: Strabo IV, 1, 12, calls *Narbo* the seaport of the *Arecomici*, while Ptolemy, *Geog* II, 10, 6 (surely based on an outdated source) attributes not only *Narbo* and places to the south and west to the *Tectosages* but also *Baeterrae* and *Cessero*. For a discussion, Gayraud 1981, 106–08; an early division is most likely, since *Tectosages* also appear in Galatia and the name must have been of ancient origin.

7 For a discussion of the coinage see especially J.-C.-M.Richard, 'Les monnayages indigènes de Narbonne et sa région', *Narbonne: Archéologie et Histoire* (1973) 135–43, and Gayraud 1981, 108–18.

8 Strabo IV, 2, 3.

9 As Gayraud 1981, 98, points out, despite the arguments of Villard 1960, 157, and others, Poseidonius's story (quoted in Strabo IV, 2, 1) that Scipio Aemilianus, on his way to or from Spain, questioned people from '*Narbo*' about Britain must surely put the tin trade here back at least to the middle of the 2nd cent BC. On evidence for all kinds of pre-Roman trade, see Gayraud 1981, 75–6 and 87–102.

Narbo (Narbonne), *Ruscino* (Château Roussillon), *Carcaso* (Carcassonne)

10 For a good summary of the history of Montlaurès, Gayraud 1981, 70–6.

11 Gayraud 1981, 81–5.

12 For evidence of earthwork defences, Gayraud 1981, 281–2.

13 Gayraud 1981, 120–7.

14 Gayraud 1981, 149–53, confirming this from the number of inscriptions recording members of *Pollia*, compared with those of other tribes, including *Papiria*, that of the Caesarean veterans later settled here.

15 On the centuriation and its relation to the *Via Domitia*, Gayraud 1981, 204–40, largely based on the fundamental work of M.Guy (*Gallia* XIII(1955), 103–08 and *Etudes Roussillonnaises* IV(1955), 217–38). So far as its date is concerned, Gayraud (p 211) argues for 118 BC, but while it may have begun then it should be noted that Cicero, *Pro Fonteio* 6(14) refers to people *qui ex agris ex Cn.Pompeii decreto decedere sunt coacti* so that an extension at least seems probable in or about 76 BC.

16 For a discussion of the two elements, Gayraud 1981, 79–80 and 146–8—though he does not consider the possibility of a fort.

17 B.Maurenbrecher, *C.Sallustii Crispi Historiarum Reliquiae* (Teubner, 1891), frag II, 22.

18 On the *Pro Fonteio* see p 59 above; on the wine trade in general, R.Etienne, 'Les importations de vin campanien en Aquitaine', in *Vignobles et vins d'Aquitaine* (Bordeaux, 1970), 13–25, and other refs cited by P.Gailliou, 'Days of Wine and Roses' in S.Macready and F.H.Thompson (edd), *Cross-Channel Trade between Gaul and Britain in the pre-Roman Iron Age* (Soc of Ants, London, 1984), 24–36.

19 For Varro Atacinus, Propertius II, xxxiv, 85–6, Horace, *Sat* I, x, 46–7, Ovid, *Amores* I, xv, 21, Quintilian x, i, 87; for Fabius, Horace, *Sat* I, i, 13–14, as commented on by Porphyrius; on Votienus, Seneca, *Controversiae* IX. *praef* i and vi, 18, Tacitus, *Ann* IV, 42; Martial VIII, lxxii, 5; on all three, including a discussion of the significance of the word *Atacinus*, Gayraud 1981, 153–8.

20 *CIL* XII, 4314–6037; *ILGN* nos 571–613; reliefs, Espérandieu 1907, nos 556–819.

21 Gayraud 1981, 281–90.

22 Sidonius, *Carmina* xxiii, 37–68. *Cf* Ausonius, *Ordo Urbium Nobilium* xix.

23 Gayraud 1981, 247–58. Though the *horrea* were evidently used not only throughout the Roman period but also in the middle ages, their opening up is not yet so complete as that of the *cryptoporticus* of Arles, but a visit is most rewarding.

24 *CIL* XII 4333, found in the 16th cent near Porte Royale and evidently built into the town wall.

25 A.Grenier, *Latomus* XXVIII(1957) 245–8; *FOR* XII, pp 94–6; Gayraud 1981, 258–72.

26 Espérandieu 1907, nos 688–9, 691–702, 706, 708, 711–13, 717–20, 722–23, 725–8, 731–8, 745, 748–9; Gayraud 1981, 282–4.

27 Gayraud 1981, 274–8.

28 *Lex de flamonio*, *CIL* XII, 6038; temple, Gayraud 1981, 384–90; baths constructed by two 1st-cent *praetores duoviri*, *CIL* XII, 4338, restored by Pius, *CIL* XII, 4342, Gayraud 1981, 279–80.

29 *CIL* XII, 4321–9; Gayraud 1981, 272–3.

30 *CIL* XII, 4445.

Narbo (Narbonne), *Ruscino* (Château Roussillon), *Carcaso* (Carcassonne)

31 *CIL* xii, 4388, serving a bath built for 1st-cent *sevir* Chrysanthus and his wife Clodia Agathe; for its relation to a house rather than public baths, Gayraud 1981, 279–80. For parts of an aqueduct possibly serving Narbonne and located near Sallèles-d'Aude, *Gallia* xxxvii(1979) 525–6, xxxix(1981), 505–06.

32 Gayraud 1981, 293–306.

33 Gayraud 1981, 306–18; for later finds, including a palaeo-Christian cemetery, *Gallia* xxxvii(1979), 523–4, xxxix(1981), 503–04.

34 Strabo iv, 1, 14; Pliny, *HN* iii, 32; Mela ii, 5, 81; Lucan, *Pharsalia* i, 403.

35 M.Guy, *REL* xxi(1955), 213–40; A.Grenier, *FOR* xii(1959), 105–16; Gayraud 1981, 526–7; *Gallia* xxiv(1966), 456, xxxi(1973), 483.

36 Martial viii, lxxii, 3–5; Ausonius, *Comm.Professorum Burdigalensium* xviii.

37 Aurelius Victor, *De Caesaribus* 39, 12; Eutropius ix, 12, 1; Jerome, 256th Olympiad; Jordanes, *Romana* 294; Zonaras xii, 30; *SHA*, *Vitae Cari et Carini et Numeriani* iv, 6-v, 3. For discussion of the people, including the rather doubtful Sex. Pompeius Festus, Gayraud 1981, 413–14.

38 Gregory, *Hist Francorum* i, 30.

39 The *Sordi* appear in Avienius, *Ora Maritima* 553–70, in Mela ii, 5, 84 and in Pliny, *HN* iii, 32, but no great role is anywhere attributed to them. They were presumably Iberian in origin.

40 Avienius, *Ora Maritima* 567; Athenaeus viii, 332a; Strabo iv, 1, 6; Ptolemy, *Geog* ii, 10, 2.

41 Mela ii, 5, 84 (with variant *Telis*).

42 *Gallia* viii(1950), 108–10, xiv(1956), 203–05, xvii(1959), 449–50, xxiv(1966), 449–50.

43 Ptolemy, *Geog* ii, 10, 6, which, whether inaccurate or merely anachronistic, lists *Ruscino* under the *Tectosages*.

44 For a summary of pre-war accounts, Espérandieu 1936, 21–6; for inscriptions, *ILGN* nos 614–41.

45 In addition to the refs in note 42 above, *Gallia* xi(1953), 90–3 (a probable temple), xx(1962), 473–4 (including a mosaic), xxxiii(1975) 491–3, and xxxvi(1978) 431–3 (re-excavation and consolidation of forum), xxxvii(1979) 521–2 (evidence of Augustan re-organisation), xxxix(1981), 501–03 (evidence for decline in 2nd cent), xli(1983), 527–8; on centuriation, extending well to the north of the river Agly, see also M.Guy, *Etudes Roussillonnaises* iv(1954–5) 220–7.

46 G.Barruol (ed), *Ruscino I* (Suppl 7 to *RAN*), Perpignan 1976.

47 Mela ii, 5, 84; Pliny, *HN* iii, 32.

48 *ILGN* 637; it may also be noted that this inscription gives us a member of the voting tribe *Voltinia*, normal in Latin colonies.

49 *ILGN* 630; on this subject see especially M.Gayraud in *Ruscino I*, 67–98.

50 *Eg Gallia* xxxvi(1978), 431–3.

51 As Gayraud 1981, 330, points out, at least one Narbonne inscription, from St. André-de-Sorène, south of Elne (*CIL* xii, 5366), belongs to the time of Gordian iii.

52 *Gallia* xxxi(1973), 476–7; see also *Gallia* xxxiii(1975), 495, and xxxix(1981), 503.

53 *Gallia* xxxvii(1979), 522.

54 Caesar, *BG* iii, 20, 2.

55 Pliny, *HN* iii, 36.

Narbo (Narbonne), *Ruscino* (Château Roussillon), *Carcaso* (Carcassonne)

56 Ptolemy, *Geog* II, 10, 6.

57 *CIL* XII, 5371; another early inscription (*CIL* XIII, 7234, found at Mainz) records the death of a soldier of Legio II from here, and both he and C.Comminius, the *praetor* (also seen to be early from the spelling *praitor*) were enrolled in the *Voltinia* voting tribe.

58 *ILGN* 656, König no 261.

59 *It Burd* 551.9. For a sensible discussion of the evidence, see the notes contributed by A.Blanchet to *FOR* XII, pp 166–7.

60 Walls, *Gallia* XXIX(1971), 371, XXXI(1973), 476–7, XXXIII(1975), 495; theatre, M.Guy, *Revue de photo-interprétation* 1962, 4, no 12; aqueduct, *FOR* XII, p 168.

61 See n59, above. For discussion, Gayraud 1981, 323, where another possibility, the milestone of Numerian found at Villesquelade (*CIL* XII, 5672) is also considered. The *CIL* reading of the last line of this (repeated by Grenier in *FOR* XII, nos 81 and 89 and pp 131–2) has, however, been questioned by Duval (*Gallia* XXII(1964), 336 n38) and by König (no 259), who prefer *(A) N(arbone) M P I*. This would imply that it had been carried a very long way from its original site, but in any case Villeséquelade is *vii mp*, not one, from *Carcaso* (just as Barbaira is some *viii mp* from the town, not *xi*).

62 *Gallia* XXIX(1971), 372–3. The inscription reads VERBA CICERO/NIS QVOSQ/TANDEM ABUTE/RE CATELINA PA/TIENTIA NOS/TRA (with QVIS/PRIMUS on another sheet.) This rich villa was destroyed in the 3rd century, but farming continued there.

63 Tour de Mezolieux, south of Laure-Minervois and beside the Roman road, *FOR* XII, no 61; l'Armado, near Villelongue, *Gallia* XXII(1964), 485–6.

64 For a summary account, Gayraud 1981, 479–82, with map on p 95; silver and gold from Cuxac-Cabardès, Fournes and la Combe.

65 Sallèles-d'Aude, *FOR* XII, no 31, *Gallia* XXIX(1971), 377, XXXVI(1978), 437–8, XXXVII(1979), 525, XLI(1983), 507–08; Rouffiac, *FOR* XII, no 83, *Gallia* XXIV(1966), 459, XXVII(1969), 388; Bram, *Gallia* XXXIII(1975), 494–5, XXXIX(1981), 503; other kilns also stood south of this *vicus*, *Gallia* XXIX(1971), 371. A glass kiln at le Ségala, St-André-de-Roquelongue, may also be noted—*Gallia* XXIV(1966), 460.

66 *It Burd* 551.6–552.2; for a general discussion of this route, 'la Voie d'Aquitaine', *FOR* XII, pp 128–32.

67 *FOR* XII, no 91; for some allegedly Roman (but probably medieval) vaults, *Gallia* XVII(1959), 459.

68 Cicero, *Pro Fonteio* 20(9). For a discussion of the names, not only *Cobiomachus* but also the elusive *Crodunum* and *Vulchalo*, see Gayraud 1981, 196–7 and *RAN* III(1970), 103–14.

69 *Gallia* XXIX(1971), 370–1, *RAN* III(1970), 71–101, *AE* 1969, 70.

70 *FOR* XII, no 104 and p 130. Unfortunately le Viala is not marked on standard 1: 50,000.

71 For a general discussion, *FOR* XII, pp 121–2, 128–32; for finds, *ibid*, nos 38, 47.

72 On the road, *FOR* XII, p 133, the bridge, no 67.

73 *FOR* XII, pp 132–3; the bridge here referred to is not the supposed Roman one over the Aude cited by Grenier in *FOR* XII, no 111, but one over the tributary Corneilla, now in the land of the Auberge de la Corneilla, just

1 *top left* The Greek walls of St-Blaise

2 *top right* The remains of the bastion in Place St-Jacques, Toulouse

3 Remains of the amphitheatre, 4km from Toulouse

4 The Pont Vieux, Narbonne

5 The basilica of the forum of *Ruscino; curia* in the foreground

6 The Tour St-Sernin, Carcassonne, showing large-stone
fragments of the Roman foundations, later under-pinned.
This bastion was later used for a chapel

7 The remains of the Pont Romieu over the river Clamoux

8 The Pont Vieux over the river Orb, overlooked by the Belvedere of Béziers

9 The St-Thibéry bridge over the river Hérault, long taken to be Roman but more probably medieval

10 *top left* A circular tower attached to the walls of Nîmes just outside the amphitheatre

11 *top right* The Porte d'Auguste of Nîmes

12 *left* The Porte de France of Nîmes

13 *right* The Tour Magne of Nîmes

14 *top left* The Maison Carrée of Nîmes *Copyright A. F. Kersting*

15 *top right* The Sacred Waters of Nîmes, with the so-called Temple de Diane on the right

16 *left* The *castellum divisorium* of Nîmes

17 *right* The Pont du Gard, carrying the aqueduct of Nîmes *Copyright Mansell Collection*

18 *top left* Traces of the Nîmes aqueduct near St-Maximin, upstream from the Pont du Gard

19 *top right* The Pont Ambroix over the river Vidourle, at Ambrussum

20 *left* The bridge of Sommières, originally Roman

21 *right* The remains of a Roman bridge, Moulin de Boisseron

22 The bridge over the river Escoutay, just north of Viviers, with probable Roman foundations

Narbo (Narbonne), *Ruscino* (Château Roussillon), *Carcaso* (Carcassonne) upstream from the modern bridge of the D118 (visited 1982).

74 Limoux, *FOR* XII, no 111; Alet, no 112, inscription *CIL* XII, 5374.

75 *FOR* XII, no 120 and p 226; Rennes is not, however, so prosperous as Amélie-les-Bains and the remains are not so readily visible as Grenier's note suggests. The inscriptions include one by a C.Pompeius Quartus and one (possibly two) of people enrolled in the tribe *Voltinia* (*CIL* XII, 5377, 5378, *Bull de la Soc Arch du Midi de la France*[3] IV(1942), 374–5), which confirms the inclusion of this area in the territory of *Carcaso*.

76 *FOR* XII, no 147; apart from the tower, the main remains noted are early Christian. For the road, *ibid*, pp 127–8.

77 Salavi, *Gallia* XXXIX(1981), 503; Moux, *FOR* XII, no 103, with inscriptions *CIL* XII, 5369, 5370, and a possible third.

78 Roubia, *FOR* XII, no 37; Bize, no 28; Fa, no 126.

79 Those shown are at Palau-de-Vidre (*Gallia* XXXI(1973), 475), Palol (*Gallia* XXIX(1971), 369), Peyresortes (Espérandieu 1936, 35), la Vallaurie (Espérandieu 1936, 34) and Villeneuve-de-la-Raho (Espérandieu 1936, 45); for supposed additions, see, for example, the map opposite p 64 in J.Pascot, *Le Roussillon dans l'histoire* (Privat, Toulouse, 1967).

80 Taurinya (south of Prades), *Gallia* XXII(1964), 476; Llo, *Gallia* XX(1962), 611, XXXIII(1975), 491.

81 No reliable finds from here, but at Villa Vella, in the commune of Banyuls-dels-Aspres, immediately to the south, a cemetery, buildings and coins are recorded; Espérandieu 1936, 20.

82 *Gallia* XXIX(1971), 369.

83 Treilles and Caves-de-Treilles, *FOR* XII, nos 16, 17; see also *ibid*, pp 126–8, where Grenier effectively argues against the suggestion of Campardou (in *Gallia* V (1947), 195–205) that the winding 'Route des Collines' replaced the original *Via Domitia* in Augustan times.

84 *Salsulae*, Espérandieu 1936, 42; *Combusta*, H.Guiter, *Bull de la Soc Agr Scient et Litt des Pyrenées-Orientales* LXVIII(1953), 29–37, supported by Gayraud 1981, 500, n 152.

85 Strabo IV, 1, 6; Mela II, 5, 82.

86 Le Boulou, Espérandieu 1936, 21 (with a curious suggestion for *Ad Stabulum*); le Perthus, *ibid*, 34.

87 *Gallia* XX(1962), 473, XXII(1964), 473, XXIV(1966), 449–50, XXVII(1969), 381.

88 Mela II, 5, 84, Pliny, *HN* III, 32; even this place is attributed to the *Tectosages* by Ptolemy (*Geog* II, 10, 6).

89 *Gallia* XX(1962), 611, XXII(1964), 473, XXIX(1971), 369, XXXI(1973), 475.

90 Castel de la Reina Helena, *Gallia* XX(1962), 611; extramural buildings, XXIV(1966), 449.

91 Eutropius X, 9, 4, Orosius VII, 29, 7, *Epitome de Caesaribus* 41, 23, Zosimus II, 42, 5, Zonaras XIII, 6 (PII, 14B). The identity of the place is not in question, since Eutropius, Orosius and the *Epitome* all indicate its geographical position and its modern name is certainly derived from Helena, but the only author who relates the name to the empress is Zonaras (ἐν γὰρ πολίχνῃ Ἑλένῃ, καλουμένῃ εἰς ὄνομα τῆς βασιλίσσης ἐκείνης, ὃ Κώνστας ἀνῃρῇτο) and it has been strongly argued that he (or his source) was merely guessing and that the name was of Celtic origin, to replace the Iberian *Illiberis* (see M.Chalou in *Ruscino* I (*RAN* Suppl 7, 1976), 346–50).

Narbo (Narbonne), *Ruscino* (Château Roussillon), *Carcaso* (Carcassonne)

92 Strabo IV, I, 3 (μέχρι τοῦ ἱεροῦ τῆς Πυρηναίας ᾿Αφροδίτης), Mela II, 5, 84, Pliny, *HN* III, 22 (*Pyrenaea Venus*), Ptolemy, *Geog* II, 10, I and 2 (τὸ ᾿Αφροδισίον), Stephanus *sv* ᾿Αφροδισιας πόλις. Its omission by Avienius might suggest the possibility that it was developed late, but against this see Jannoray in *Gallia* XII(1954), 410.

93 D.Colls, C.Domergue, F.Laubenheimer and B.Liou, 'Les lingots d'étain de l'épave Port-Vendres II', *Gallia* XXXIII(1975), 61–94 and XLIII(1985), 547–53; for earlier underwater finds, *Gallia* XII(1954), 410, XVII(1959), 450–1, XX(1960), 612–13, XXIV(1966), 450–2.

94 *Rav Cos* IV, 28 (245, 3); Espérandieu 1936, 27.

95 Mela II, 5, 84.

96 *Rav Cos* IV, 28 (245, 14), where it is placed immediately after *Rusino*, but its name was *Arulae* in the 9th cent. Espérandieu 1936, 13–19 (including reference to a pottery kiln and to lead inscriptions—*CIL* XII, 5367); *Etudes Roussillonnaises* IV(1954–5), 83–90; Grenier 1960, 409–10; *Gallia* XXXIII(1975), 491.

97 *CIL* XII, 5362, EVHANGELVS/SOC XXXX SER/MERCVRIO/VSLM; de Laet 1949, 143, 163. It is regrettable that the name Théza has got into general use and that this, taken together with a minor burial inscription (*CIL* XII, 5363), also now built into a wall of the church there, has led to exaggerated ideas of the place's importance.

10

Baeterrae (Béziers)

As may be seen from the map at fig 3 (p 14), the département de l'Hérault included a considerable number of hill-forts, and anyone interested in the Iron Age would first of all visit the well-excavated and well-conserved example of Ensérune.[1] This, however, is a little misleading, since there is no doubt that in pre-Roman times it was Béziers, not Ensérune, that dominated this region. Though the density of the modern city that covers the hill has limited the amount of excavation possible, enough has been found to show that it was occupied at least from the seventh century BC, when Etruscan and Greek ware was imported, and it, unlike Ensérune, is named in the *Ora Maritima* of Avienius.[2] The form of the name there given to it, *Besara*, may be based on an Iberian term for a rock,[3] and it evidently belonged for a time to the tribe of the *Elisyces*, ruled from Montlaurès, but after the invasion of the *Volcae* it became the head of a distinct territory: it was after this invasion—and in some cases after the arrival of the Romans—that coins of the *Longostaletes* and their rulers, and some actually inscribed BHTAPPATIC in Greek lettering, were minted here.[4] Whether the *Longostaletes* were subject to the *Volcae Arecomici* or to the *Volcae Tectosages* remains a little uncertain, since while Ptolemy attributes Béziers to the latter, Strabo calls Narbonne the seaport of the former.[5]

In the meantime, however, the Greeks had long established their colony of *Agatha* (Agde) near the head of what was then the delta of the river *Arauris* (Hérault). Agde is not mentioned by Avienius (though a *lacuna* in his text may easily account for this), but Stephanus of Byzantium tells us that Scymnus said it was founded by the Phocaeans,[6] and finds from several places in the lower valley of the river indicate that Greek navigators were calling here as early as the seventh century BC.[7] While the precise date of its initial foundation— whether before or after that of *Massalia*—thus remains a little uncertain, there is no doubt that it was taken over by the Massaliotes since Strabo says they founded it and Pliny describes it as *Agatha quondam*

149

Massiliensium.[8] Recent research has shown that it was especially active in the fourth and third centuries BC, and it was then that the Greek town wall, of which small fragments survive, was built,[9] but the investigation of a series of wrecks nearby has shown that trade always flourished.[10] Beyond this, an area eventually extending about as far north as the course of the *Via Domitia*, corresponding closely with what in post-Roman times became the diocese of Agde (and so presumably that of the *pagus* centred on Agde in the Roman period) was covered by Greek cadastration[11]—the only example in Gaul so far that shows what land the Greeks took over to support their colonies.

No doubt Roman fleets on their way to Spain during the second Carthaginian war called at Agde, but it was not until the construction of the *Via Domitia* that the Romans became directly interested in the area. Not unnaturally this road, like the modern railway, passed not over the top but just to the south of the hill-fort of Béziers and no evidence has been found of the installation of a Roman posting-station. Further, as we have seen, the *Longostaletes* retained some degree of individuality, and it was not until 36 or 35 BC that the Roman *Colonia Urbs Iulia Baeterrae Septimanorum* was implanted: the colonists were veterans of *Legio VII* and the voting tribe in which they were enrolled was *Pupinia*.[12] That the *colonia* was fully organised and governed in the normal colonial manner is amply attested by inscriptions,[13] but while one at least of its *flamines* was also a decurion of Narbonne,[14] few of its people appear to have been of great distinction. Perhaps the most notable is L. Aponius, an *eques* on the staff of Drusus, who was sent as a delegate to Tiberius after the Pannonian mutiny in AD 14 and for whom, as the first *flamen* of their city, the people of *Baeterrae* erected a statue.[15] The only other *eques* securely recorded is C. Cassius Primus, sometime commander of the *Cohors I Raetorum* and subsequently the holder of many offices here,[16] while the question of whether this could have been the place of origin of Cornelius Fuscus, who persuaded his unnamed *colonia* to support Galba in AD 68, remains unresolved.[17]

Strabo's reference to Béziers as a πόλις ἀσφαλής, a secure city,[18] led some people to believe that it was walled in his time, but no archaeological evidence supports this and it appears certain that he was referring simply to the dominance of the hill on which it stood (pl 8). Even in the Iron Age the defences of the hill-fort seem not to have been continuous[19] and the only Roman town wall of which limited stretches have been discovered can safely be dated to the late third century AD.[20] As may be seen from the tentative plan (fig 14), this enclosed a limited area, not taking in all of the earlier street plan, and the western part of it, which has been securely identified, stood further back from the bluff overlooking the Orb than the existing ramparts, on which the Belvedere, with its Table d'Orientation, now offers such a splendid view westwards as far as Ensérune.

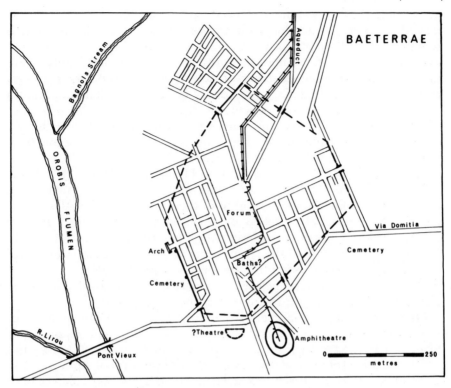

14 A tentative plan of Béziers (mostly after Clavel)

As with so many heavily-occupied sites, the city is lacking in visible Roman monuments and all that can be seen—and that with some difficulty—are some parts of the amphitheatre. This abutted against the small hill of St-Jacques, south of the city, and while the area is now built over its outline can be seen on air photographs. This, combined with studies of it in earlier times (including especially a drawing made by Anne de Rulman in the seventeenth century), enables its size to be estimated (a little smaller than that of Fréjus but considerably larger than that of Cimiez), but its date, probably early, remains uncertain.[21] The possible existence of a theatre, just to the west of it, is deduced from air photographs.[22]

To return to the central area of the city, much of the lay-out of the streets and the location of the forum can also be reproduced from aerial photography, supplemented by the seventeenth-century town-plan drawn by de Rulman,[23] and a further extension to the north is indicated by recent discoveries.[24] The location of the monumental arch is fairly secure, since the fragments of it were found near the line of what must have been the *decumanus maximus*; their style is earlier than that of the arch of Orange, so it may have been of Augustan date.[25] A temple of

151

the imperial cult must have existed, as attested by the inscriptions related to *flamines*, and this should have stood near the forum, but it was in the Rue Riquet (not the grand Allées Paul Riquet, but near the market hall) that nine marble heads of the imperial family were found.[26] The probable existence of other temples round the forum is rather better supported by the discovery beside it of a statue of Apollo and heads of Jupiter and Hercules.[27] Whether the public baths are correctly located remains a little uncertain, but an aqueduct to supply them, and the amphitheatre, has long been recognised (some of it remained in use until the 18th century): it drew water from three northern sources, at Laurens, Gabian and Pouzolles (see fig 15).[28] A few houses have been identified, some with mosaics, and the extent of the city is partly defined by the location of the cemeteries.[29] Finally, while the Orb was probably crossed by fords in the Iron Age, a Roman bridge must surely have been built over it and the alignment of the *Via Domitia* on the far side of the river points directly at the Pont Vieux (pl 8); this has, however, obviously undergone a great deal of reconstruction and, as will be seen below, its similarity to the bridge over the Hérault at St-Thibéry no longer underlines its romanity.[30]

Of the territory attributed to the city (fig 15) the northern limit, which was also the boundary between *Narbonensis* and *Aquitania*, is identified as the crest of the Cevennes, but mere geography does not define the others. Fortunately, besides the cadastration of Agde, already mentioned, two centuriations related to Béziers itself have been identified, the first ('Cadastre B') apparently being the earlier one and probably related to the organised installation of Italian immigrants in the Republican period, while the second ('Cadastre A') overlaps that of Narbonne and evidently indicates the division of land between the two *coloniae* after 35 BC; this enables the drawing of a boundary that roughly follows the old course of the river Nazoure. Bézier's centuriation also extends far enough east to establish an approximate boundary with the territory of Nîmes, but for some of this, and for the boundary with Lodève, some reliance has also been placed on the outlines presented by the medieval dioceses.[31]

Two of the towns within this area are included in Pliny's list of *oppida Latina*, *Cessero* (St-Thibéry) and *Piscenae* (or *Piscinae*, Pézenas),[32] both of them successors to Iron Age hill-forts and in each case more is known about the hill-fort than about the Roman town. *Piscenae* evidently developed on the right bank of the river Peyne, at or near its junction with the Hérault, about 2km ESE of the hill-fort of St-Siméon, and the most notable finds have come from the pre-Roman and Roman cemenery of St-Julien, midway between the two.[33] Famous mending wool was produced in the surrounding area,[34] but the place's prosperity must have derived largely from passing trade: though not named in the Peutinger Table, it clearly lay on the road from Agde northwards to Lodéve and Rodez, and there is good evidence that it was also linked

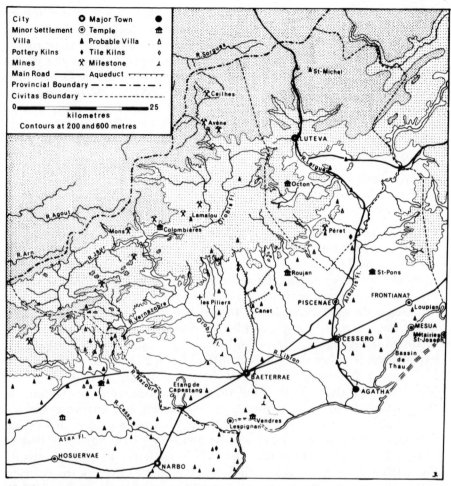

15 The territories of *Baeterrae* and *Luteva*

directly with Béziers itself.[35] *Cessero* too lay on the right bank of the Hérault, just where it was crossed by the *Via Domitia*, and is therefore named in all the itineraries.[36] Slight excavations have been carried out on the hill-fort and a variety of finds have been made around the town, but its lay-out remains uncertain.[37] The most famous monument here, of course, is the bridge over the river (pl 9), but whether it is really a Roman bridge is highly questionable. As a glance at a 1:50,000 scale map will show, the line of the *Via Domitia* (here well preserved) does not point to this crossing (though it may point to the early ford), while its traditional name here, 'Chemin de la Reine Juliette', reminds one that it was used, and maintained, in the middle ages; secondly, immediately upstream there are the substantial remains of a medieval mill which certainly incorporates many Roman stones; and finally, the whole style of the bridge indicates a medieval rather than a Roman

153

origin. It seems more likely, therefore, that while the Romans doubtless built a bridge to replace the prehistoric ford, it was constructed a little further up the river than these notable remains.[38]

Further to the east, *Frontiana*, which is named only on the fourth Vicarello Goblet (at *x mp* from *Cessero* and *viii* from *Forum Domitii*) has not yet been located, but more can be said of Mela's *Mesua* (probably the same place as the *Mansa* of Avienius).[39] Its name points to its identification with Mèze, on the north shore of the Bassin de Thau, but Mela's text is a little surprising and must be cited in full. Working along the coast from east to west, he writes:

> *Ultra stagna Volcarum Ledum flumen* (the river Lez) *castellum Latara* (Lattes)
> *Mesua collis incinctus mari paene undique ac nisi quod angusto aggere continenti*
> *adnectitur insula. Tum ex Cebennis* (the Cévennes) *demissus Arauris . . .*

Limited excavations of the small settlement, mainly pre-Roman, at Mèze[40] have shown that it must have acted as a port (so confirming that the Bassin de Thau was not then cut off from the sea) and it may well be that the little cape on which it stood then projected well into the water, but it is surely unlikely that Mela would have picked out this little place for such a detailed description. Rather the *collis incinctus mari* must be Sète, *Mons Seteius*, the great hill that dominates the area and is duly recorded by Avienius, Strabo and Ptolemy,[41] and the most reasonable explanation is either that the text suffers from a *lacuna* or that Mela (or his source) has simply confused Mèze with the settlement of les Métairies St-Joseph. This, lying on the promontory of le Barrou, on the north side of Sète, is much better known and has now yielded substantial Roman remains, including baths and fish-processing factories:[42] whether it fell within the territory of Béziers or in that of Nîmes, however, remains uncertain. The last settlement site shown on the map, Lespignan, is also included as the result of recent discoveries. Here, on a site called Vivios, near the Etang de Vendres, mosaics and part of an aqueduct were noted in 1839 and a villa then seemed probable, but further excavations have revealed a larger complex, with several *insulae*, apparently occupied from the first to the fourth century AD.[43]

As for temples, while the shrines at Roujan, now being investigated, will no doubt prove important, the only one whose character is firmly established is that at Colombières, which has yielded much material and the plan of which has been largely recovered: it appears to have been in use from the late Iron Age to the fourth century AD, but although it was evidently related to hot springs the main deity to whom it was dedicated remains uncertain.[44] The likelihood that a temple stood at St-Pons-de-Mauchiens derives from the discovery there of an inscription to Mercury so large that it must have formed part of a building.[45] The case of Vendres raises another problem: though long supposed to be a temple of Venus—and conserved as such as a monument—the character of the building has been severely questioned by Mme. Clavel-Lévêque, who suggests that it may have been merely a villa.[46] Against this, the name of Vendres certainly derives from Venus (as she agrees, it was *de Veneris* in 1140) and it may even be this area that is referred to by Ausonius when writing about oysters,[47] and anyone who has made his way to it through the marshes must find it difficult to imagine a villa in such a position; after all, the sea has retreated, rather than advanced, since Roman times. It is just possible that there was a temple near Causses-et-Veyran, but what remains there is a curious line of four towers (shown on the map as les Piliers), two of which still stand to a height of some 5m. In some respects they resemble the 'piles' that one sees in *Aquitania*, but these never appear in groups, while another suggestion, that they supported an aqueduct, can safely be ruled out by their location; the best explanation so far offered is that they are a monument erected either by Pompey or, more probably, by Cn. Domitius after the defeat of the *Ruteni* or the *Volcae*.[48]

Of the villas in the territory of Béziers perhaps the two most outstanding are that at Clavel (in the commune of Puissalicon), occupied from the first to the fourth century,[49] and that at les Près Bas (Loupian, fig 16) also in existence from the first century but above all notable for its fourth-century mosaics, now well preserved.[50] There certainly existed many more than are shown on the map (fig 15), but the majority are still indicated mainly by the names of places and by inscriptions and other odd finds and only those whose certain character

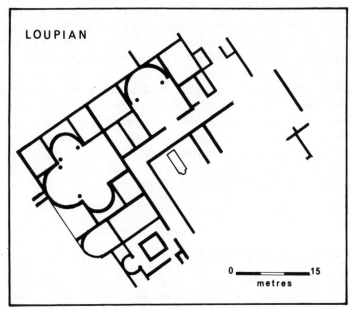

LOUPIAN

0 — 15
metres

16 The Villa of Loupian (after Prudhomme)

and location have been confirmed by excavation are included here.[51] That the land was rich and prosperous is beyond doubt: the notability of some of its wool has already been mentioned and Pliny also singles out this area for praise when discussing the wine produced in the province, the export of which is attested by inscriptions on amphorae found in Italy,[52] while oyster farms have been discovered, especially around the Etang de Vendres and the Bassin de Thau.[53] Besides its own production of the necessities of life—wheat, oil, wine and fish—*Baeterrae* also produced some pottery (including its own *terra sigillata*, at Aspiran)[54] and, above all, benefited from its mineral resources. Like other areas backing on to the Cevennes and the Montagne Noire, such as that of Narbonne (*qv*), it included a number of mines yielding argentiferous lead, copper, iron, and even a little gold.[55]

Finally, there remains the question of roads. The course of the *Via Domitia* is well enough established (though curiously it has allegedly yielded only two milestones in this area, one of Tiberius at les Castans and one of Tetricus Junior in Béziers itself)[56] and the road from Agde northwards is included on the Peutinger Table, while the direct route from Béziers to Pézenas has been mentioned above and that from Béziers to Carcassonne is discussed under Narbonne (*qv*, p 140). Problems are, however, raised by one certain and one possible milestone, neither clearly related to any of these roads. The certain stone, that found at Sauvain (south of Béziers), has by some been taken to indicate a separate route from Béziers to Agde, but its Tiberian inscription, ending REFECIT. (MP) III agrees so closely with that of the Castans stone (which also includes REFECIT) that it must surely originally have stood three miles from Béziers on the *Via Domitia*.[57] The other stone, found at Maraussan (NW of Béziers), with the figure XX on it (approximately the mileage from Narbonne), has to some suggested the existence of a main road running NE from Ponserme (beside the Etang de Capestang) and, after avoiding Béziers, joining the N–S road a little south of Lodève. Against this, it is difficult to appreciate the purpose of this as a main road or, above all, to understand why a milestone (unless it was from the *Via Domitia*) should carry a figure giving the distance from *Narbo*, and this supposed road has therefore been omitted from the map.[58]

REFERENCES AND NOTES

1 The main report on this remains J.Jannoray, *Ensérune, contribution a l'étude des civilisations préromaines de la Gaule Méridionale*, Paris, 1965, but for subsequent work see *Gallia* xxiv(1966), 470, xxvii(1969), 397, xxxi(1973), 496, xxxiii(1975), 508, xxxvii(1979), 532, and H.Gallet de Santerre, *Ensérune, les silos de la terrasse est*, Suppl to *Gallia* xxxix(1980).

2 Avienius, *Ora Maritima* 591 (immediately after *Helice palus*, which is evidently L'Etang de Capestang). On the early history of Béziers, see Clavel 1970, 41–144, and on more recent early finds, including Etruscan pottery, *Gallia* XXXVII(1979), 527.

3 Clavel 1970, 143–4.

4 On the *Elisyces* and the *Longostaletes* and their coins, Clavel 1970, 57–9, 134–5, 180–200, also P.Barruol, 'Les Elisyques et leur capitale NARO/NARBO', *Narbonne: Archéologie et Histoire* (CNRS, Montpellier, 1973), 49–63, and J.-C.-M.Richard, Les monnayages indigènes de Narbonne et sa region', *ibid*, 108–18.

5 Ptolemy, *Geog* II, 10, 6 (evidently using an older source and not giving Βαιτιραί the title of *colonia*) Strabo IV, 1, 12.

6 On the *lacuna* in Avienius, see Schulten's note on lines 596–600; Stephanus, *sv*, not only records Scymnus but also says that Timosthenes called it not just 'Αγάθη, but 'Αγάθη Τύχη.

7 For general discussions, Clavel 1970, 105–14, A.Nickels and G.Marchand, 'Recherches statigraphiques ponctuelles à proximité des ramparts antiques d'Agde', *RAN* IX(1976), 45–62 (with a tentative town plan and suggesting a foundation date *c* 550 BC), and J.J.Jully 'Agde antique', *Bull des Amis de Pézenas*, 1978.

8 Strabo IV, 1, 6; Pliny, *HN* III, 33.

9 Nickels and Marchand, *op cit*; for further excavations of parts of the wall, *Gallia* XXXVI(1978), 438, XXXIX(1981), 507.

10 For underwater investigation, *Gallia* XII(1954) 415, XVII(1959), 467–8, XX(1962), 622, XXII(1964), 486.

11 Clavel-Lévêque 1984, 207–58, where the cadastration is tentatively dated between the 4th and 2nd cent BC.

12 Clavel 1970, 161–7; for a general discussion of the foundation of this and other *coloniae* see also pp 75, 78 above.

13 *CIL* XII, 4230–53, *ILGN* 558–61 *passim*; for a general discussion, Clavel 1970, 167–9.

14 *CIL* XII, 4402 (from Narbonne).

15 Tacitus, *Ann* I, 29, *CIL* XII, 4230, Clavel 1970, 600–03.

16 *CIL* XII, 4232—*duumvir*, *augur*, twice *quaestor* and *flamen*.

17 Tacitus, *Hist* II, 86. As Syme has argued (*Am J Phil* LVIII (1937), 7–18, *Tacitus* (1963) II, App 33, pp 683–4) a place on the road from Spain to Italy is very likely, but Fréjus is more probable; for other refs, Clavel 1970, 171–2.

18 Strabo IV, 1, 6.

19 Clavel 1970, 101; it should be noted, however, that the limited remains of the defences there referred to, probably of the 3rd century BC, stood at the strongest point (near the cathedral of St-Nazaire, overlooking the Orb) and more effective works must surely have covered the northern side of the *oppidum*, where there is no notable drop to a lower level.

20 Clavel 1970, 246–57; for the bastions, see especially the drawings of de Rulman, reproduced on p 250.

21 Grenier 1958, 643–5, Clavel 1970, 278–86, including a print of the de Rulman drawing; this seems to make its identification as an amphitheatre certain, but some claims that it was really a theatre still survive (infm M.J.Aspres, who lives on the site).

Baeterrae (Béziers)

22 M.Guy, *Photo Interprétation* II(1962), Clavel 1970, 286–8.
23 Clavel 1970, 236–46 (with de Rulman plan on p 238 and air photograph on p 239).
24 *Gallia* XXXI(1973), 490, XLIII(1985), 404.
25 Fragments, Espérandieu 1907, nos 531–3; discussion, Amy 1962, 116, Clavel 1970, 261–71.
26 Clavel 1970, 271–5; on the imperial heads, ranging from Augustus to Germanicus and Antonia Junior, and now in Toulouse museum, Espérandieu 1907, no 528, Clavel 1970, 464–93.
27 Espérandieu 1907, nos 552, 6869, 6680; Clavel 1970, 274–6, 518, 538–40.
28 On the baths, Clavel 1970, 288, but see also *Gallia* XXII(1964), 489–90; on the aqueduct, Clavel 1970, 288–93.
29 *FOR* x, no 99, Clavel 1970, 604–05 (houses) and 244 (cemeteries)
30 Clavel 1970, 417–19 (though she still then regarded the St-Thibéry bridge as Roman).
31 For an admirable discussion of the boundaries, Clavel 1970, 201–32, now partly modified by Clavel–Lévêque 1984, 219–58.
32 Pliny, *HN* III, 36 and 37.
33 *FOR* x, no 88; *Gallia* XXII(1964) 495–6, XXIV(1966), 470–1, XXVII(1969) 397–8, XXIX(1971), 386, XXXI(1973), 496–7, XXXVII(1979), 553.
34 Pliny, *HN* VIII, 191; it is described as a chequered fleece, comparable to some produced in Lusitania and Egypt, and used for repairing clothes in such a way as to make them last a very long time, so apparently dark and very strong.
35 Clavel 1970, 425.
36 Vicarello Goblets: *It Ant* 389.4: *It Burd* 552.4 (as a *mansio*): Peutinger Table. Ptolemy also names it (*Geog* II, 10, 6), attributing it, like so many places, to the *Volcae Tectosages*.
37 *FOR* x, no 89 *Gallia* II(1943), 8–18, VI(1948), 175–9, XXVII(1969), 399, XXIX(1971), 387, XXXI(1973), 497, XXXIII(1975), 510.
38 On its medieval date, infm from G.Barruol: see also Y.Solier, Princeton 1976, 214. Clavel 1970, 417, still regarded it as Roman.
39 Mela II, 5: Avienius, *Ora Maritima* 616 (Clavel 1970, 57 n 5, does agree with the identity of the two names, but Schulten, in his textual note on Avienius, does not).
40 Clavel 1970, 74, 103, 192: G.Barruol, Princeton 1976, 574: J.-B.Colbert-de-Beaulieu, *Ogam* VI(1954), 126–7 (on a hoard of coins, including monnaies à la croix): *Gallia* XXVII(1969), 396, XXIX(1971), 384.
41 Avienius, *Ora Maritima* 608, 609: Strabo IV, 1.6: Ptolemy, *Geog* II, 10, 2.
42 *FOR* x, nos 38, 39: G.Barruol, Princeton 1976, 830 (*sv* Sète): *Gallia* XX(1962), 627, XXII(1964), 497, XXIV(1966), 472, XXVII(1969), 400, XXIX(1971), 387, XXXI(1973), 498, XXXIII(1975), 510, XXXVI(1978), 444, XXXVII(1979), 534.
43 *FOR* x, no 98: *Gallia* XXVII(1969), 394–5, XXIX(1971), 383, XXXI(1973), 494, XXXIII(1975), 506, XXXVII(1979), 530.
44 Roujan, *FOR* x, no 112, *Hist Arch* no 99 (Nov 1985), 45: Colombières, *Gallia* XII(1954), 417, XIV(1956), 208–10, Clavel 1970, 554–60.
45 *FOR* x, no 87; Clavel 1970, 228, 523.
46 *FOR* x, no 96; Clavel 1970, 552–4, 610–11.
47 Ausonius, *Epp* v, 27–8: (*ostrea) portum quae Narbo ad Veneris nutrit*: this

Vendres seems more probable than the *Portus Veneris* (Port-Vendres) by the Pyrenees, some 80km from Narbonne.

48 *FOR* x, no 126; Clavel 1970, 149–51 (with good plates): *cf* Florus III, 2, 6 (I, xxxvii, 6): *et Domitius Ahenobarbus et Fabius Maximus ipsis quibus dimicaverant locis saxeas erexere turres, et desuper exornata armis hostilibus tropaea fixerunt, cum hic mos inusitatus fuerit nostris.*

49 Clavel 1970, 606–09: *Gallia* xvii(1959), 465–6, xxiv(1966), 471, xxvii(1969), 399, xxix(1971), 387: for a full report, *RAN* iv(1971), 93–147. For the second villa shown in the commune of Puissalicon (at Peyresegnale), *FOR* x, no 94; *Gallia* xvii(1969), 465–6.

50 H.Lavagne, R.Prudhomme and D.Rouquette, 'La villa gallo-romaine des Près-Bas à Loupian', *Gallia* xxxiv(1976), 215–35, supplemented by *Gallia* xxxvi(1978), 442, xxxvii(1979), 530, xxxix(1981), 540, xli(1983), 521.

51 For maps showing supposed villas, Clavel 1970, 298, 300, 301, and for analysis of place-names, 352–408.

52 Pliny, *HN* xiv, 68; *CIL* xv, 4542–3, (both from Testaccio).

53 Clavel 1970, 326–8; for les Metairies St-Joseph (Sète), see n 42 above.

54 Clavel 1970, 344–7; Aspiran, *Gallia* xxxi(1973), 488, xxxvi(1978), 438–9, xxxvii(1979), 526–7; other recent excavations at les Tuileries (Laurens), *Gallia* xxxi(1973), 493, xxxvi(1978), 441.

55 Clavel 1970, 329–38. More recent excavations, Ceilhes, *Gallia* xxvii(1969), 392–3, xxix(1971), 380, xxxi(1973), 490–1, xxxiii(1975), 504, xxxvi(1978), 440; Péret, *Gallia* xxxvi(1978), 444; Avène, *Gallia* xxxvii(1979), 527, xxxix(1981), 506.

56 Tiberius, *CIL* xii 5665, König no 248; Tetricus, *ILGN* 655, König, no 249.

57 *CIL* xii, 5666, König no 250; for the supposed separate road, Clavel 1970, 420–1, 451.

58 Clavel 1970, 425, 452; not in König. For a Claudian milestone on the *Via Domitia* measuring *lxxxv mp* from Narbonne (found in the territory of *Nemausus*) *CIL* xii, 5634, König, no 215.

II

Luteva (Lodève)

This is the least-investigated of all the *civitates* of *Gallia Narbonensis*. In pre-Roman times it presumably formed part of the territory of the *Volcae Arecomici* and the Roman town, which first appears as either *Luteva* or *Forum Neronis*, was evidently founded about 46 BC by Tiberius Claudius Nero and was accorded Latin rights.[1] It has itself so far yielded no inscriptions, but one found in 1878 at Corneilhan (*c* 9 km NW of Béziers, well outside the *civitas*) records the death of L. Terentius Politus, who, before later promotion in *Baeterrae*, had apparently been a *decurio* of *Colonia Claudia Luteva*.[2] In the late Empire it became a Christian diocese, but the earliest bishop recorded is Maternus, who attended the Council of Agde in AD 506.[3]

Very little archaeological work has been done in the city itself—though more is now in prospect—and apart from small finds little is known of its structure; the main monument to be identified lies on the outskirts, a mausoleum located under the romanesque chapel of St-Martin-de-Combas.[4]

The limits of the territory that was attributed to it (fig 15) are based partly on the watershed between the tributaries of the Lergue and those of the Sorgues—evidently the boundary between *Narbonensis* and *Aquitania*—and partly on those of the later diocese.[5] The temple at Octon is no more than a small shrine with various votive objects, while the two villas marked, at Clermont-l'Hérault and Péret,[7] are not very luxurious, but the distribution of other, unclassified, buildings suggests that more are to be found, and that at St-Michel-d'Alajou (which has silos associated with it)[8] spreads this possibility into the uplands.

A copper mine has been located near Péret[9] and the area was always notable for its wool[10]—as in later times Lodève became 'La ville des draps'—but the city probably depended for prosperity as much on trade as on its local products. The road that passed through it, clearly provided the main route for the southward transport of samian pottery from *Condatomagus* (Millau), as is shown on the Tabula Peutingeriana, and from la Graufesenque, while lead and silver extracted from the mines around Ceilhes and Avène may well have been channelled through it.

REFERENCES AND NOTES

1 Pliny, *HN* III, 37: *Oppida Latina . . . Lutevani qui et Foroneronienses . . .* (which may, perhaps, be the origin of the surprising, and unsubstantiated, statement in the Michelin Guide Vert of les Causses that 'Néron y faisait frapper la monnaie nécessaire à la paye et à l'entretien des légions romains'!). It is off the routes of the Antonine Itinerary and does not appear in Ptolemy nor in the Ravenna Cosmography, but it becomes *Loteva* in the Tabula Peutingeriana and *Civitas Lutevensium* (in the province of *Narbonensis Prima*) in *Notitia Galliarum* xv 5.

2 *CIL* XII 4247: DECVRIONI.C(ol?)/CLAVD.LVTEVA.Q.IIVIR. D(esign.); his quaestorship and designation as a *duovir* presumably apply to Béziers rather than to Lodève.

3 *Concilia Galliarum* I (*Corpus Christianorum* CXLVIII), 1943, 213.

4 For summary accounts see *FOR* x, no 71, and Barruol in Princeton 1976, 535; on the mausoleum, *Gallia* XXII(1964), 491–3, and Burnand 1975, 124–5.

5 On these see Clavel 1970, 201–32, dealing with the matter from the point of view of Béziers.

6 *Gallia* XVII(1959), 464.

7 Clermont-l'Herault, *Gallia* XXXVI(1978), 441 (with little detail); Péret, *Gallia* XXXIX(1981), 511 (a small 2nd-cent villa at Combe de Fignal).

8 *FOR* x, no 72.

9 *Gallia* XXII(1964), 494, XXIV(1966), 470.

10 *Cf* Pliny, *HN* VIII 191, though he here refers specifically to *Piscenae* (Pézenas), which was probably in the *civitas* of *Baeterrae*.

12
Nemausus (Nîmes)

The site of *Nemausus* was inhabited at least from the Bronze Age onwards and the Iron Age settlement on and to the south of Mont Cavalier, its most important hill, began to develop greatly about the end of the sixth century BC, thereafter benefiting from trade with the Massaliotes.[1] Quite when it was taken over by the *Volcae Arecomici* remains obscure and since some of the other hill-forts in this area, such as Nages, were much more strongly defended, the idea that it was their capital in pre-Roman times[2] can be based only on the importance of the sacred spring at the foot of the hill. As we have suggested above (p 43), a Roman station of some kind must have been established here when the *Via Domitia* was built, but while the course of the road points to somewhere near the later *Porta Augusta* this has not yet been identified. Similarly, we still do not know which lands of this people were handed over to the Massaliotes by Pompey, but Caesar's description of them as *agros Volcarum Arecomicorum et Helviorum*[3] surely points to an area in the north adjoining the territory of the *Helvii*, most probably near the river Rhône.

Yet another unsolved question is precisely when *Nemausus* first became a *colonia Latina*. The fact that in several stone inscriptions it is given the title *Augusta* for long led to the belief that it was not founded before 27 BC, but the recognition that some coins inscribed COL NEM are certainly pre-Augustan issues clearly points to an earlier date. It is likely enough that *ius Latii* was granted to a number of places in this area by Caesar, perhaps in recognition of their loyalty during the revolt of Vercingetorix, but whether it was Caesar or the Triumvirate that ruled for a time after his death that first elevated *Nemausus* to a *colonia* and gave it control over the 24 *ignobilia oppida* discussed below remains a little uncertain. In any case, it cannot have been called a *colonia Augusta* until after some new settlers had been introduced from Egypt—something that is reflected by the later coins carrying the heads of Augustus and Agrippa on one side and a crocodile chained to a palm-tree on the other.[4]

Whatever the date of its foundation, *Nemausus* soon became nearly the most distinguished city in the province, not only economically (it has yielded over 80 mosaics, numerous statues and over 2,000 inscriptions, many of them of first-century date),[5] but also socially. While *Narbo* remained the official capital and *Nemausus* a *colonia Latina*, ruled by *quattuorviri* (originally *praetores*) enrolled in the voting-tribe *Voltinia*[6], it was from here that in AD 39 came the second Narbonensian to reach the consulship—the great orator Cn. Domitius Afer.[7] Beyond this, it seems probable that this city was the origin of Trajan's wife Plotina, if the one source is correct in saying that it was here that Hadrian erected a basilica in her memory,[8] and while the next emperor, Antoninus Pius, was born and brought up near Rome he was certainly descended from a family based in Nîmes.[9] On the economic side, besides minting large numbers of coins for the armies operating in Gaul and Germany in the Augustan period,[10] several establishments are recorded, including *collegia centonariorum* and *fabrorum tignuariorum* and, surprisingly, a *collegium utriclariorum Nemausensium*.[11] As for religion, some 70 dedications have been found, the most numerous being to the local deity *Nemausus* and to ancestors (*proxumi*), but the introduction of Christianity cannot be accurately fixed: while a Council was held here in 394 or 396, the first recorded bishop is Sedatus, who attended the Council of Arles in 506.[12]

The course of the city walls, *c* 6 km in length and enclosing about 200 ha (fig 17), has long been known and some stretches of them, with external circular towers, have been excavated and preserved in recent times (pl 10).[13] The most important gate is the Porte d'Auguste (pl 11), which was originally flanked by two towers, had four arcaded passages and carried the bronze-letter inscription stating that *Augustus portas murosque col(oniae) dat* in his 8th year of *tribunicia potestas* (16 BC),[14] but when the other surviving gate, the Porte de France (sometimes called Porte d'Espagne) (pl 12), was built remains obscure. The reason for the erection of the massive octagonal Tour Magne (pl 13) on the summit of Mont Cavalier has now been somewhat clarified by the discovery that it was preceded by an impressive Iron Age tower[15] and the magnificent view from it, including the sacred fountain below, suggests that it may have had some religious significance. While several funerary stones have been found within the walls, this is no doubt due to their widespread re-use in medieval building and, as is shown on fig 17, cemeteries developed in the normal way outside the enceinte, especially beside the outgoing roads.[16] As with several other cities in Gaul that had already been walled at an early date, such as Arles and Vienne (*qq v*), it seems likely that a much smaller fortified area was established in the late Empire, since substantial remains of a massive wall were recently uncovered, and partly conserved in an underground room, when the Palais de Justice (just east of the amphitheatre) was being extended, but its full size has yet to be established.[17]

163

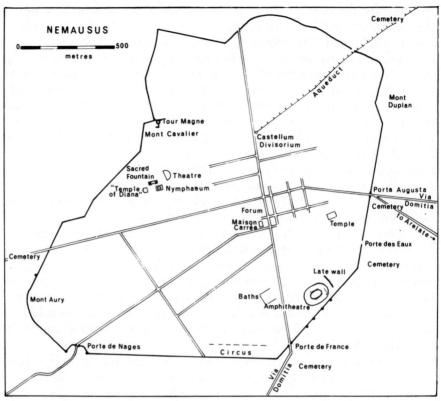

17 A tentative plan of Nîmes

The forum of the city almost certainly lay near the centre,[18] just north of the Maison Carrée. This magnificent temple (pl 14), which owes its survival to an extraordinary series of uses, both civil and religious, throughout the ages, is one of the most outstanding monuments of Gaul, but the precise date of its erection, depending on the reconstruction of bronze-letter inscriptions, has presented problems. The first interpretation, offered by J.-F. Séguier in 1758, placed it in AD 2, but in 1919 Espérandieu put forward the view that the dedication to Caius and Lucius Caesar, recognised by Séguier, was secondary and that the original inscription had recorded a gift by Agrippa in 20–19 BC. While this idea was for long widely accepted, the most recent study, by R. Amy and P. Gros, has convincingly eliminated Agrippa and put the original construction in AD 2–3, allowing that the second line (PRINCIPIBVS·IVVENTVTIS), which is anomalously placed on the architrave, was added in AD 4–5. At the same time, the discovery that the temple was built over the remains of some earlier Roman structure further strengthened this conclusion.[19]

Another substantial building also existed under or near the cathedral

164

that stands some 800m east of the Maison Carrée and this too was probably a temple (rather than the basilica erected by Hadrian in memory of Plotina, as has sometimes been claimed).[20] The so-called 'Temple of Diana', on the other hand, a very complicated building, does not really represent a temple, even though it was used as a church from 991 to 1562—something that involved various modifications—before it was pillaged.[21] Whatever the function of this surviving building, however, this was a very holy area, centred on the spring that was already sacred in the Iron Age. The Romans developed it, at least from 25 BC onwards, in an impressive way, including the construction of a *nymphaeum*, and numerous dedications have been found here, especially to the god Nemausus and to the Nymphs, but unfortunately it was 'modernised' in the eighteenth century, so that the present lay-out, though attractive enough (pl 15), is not fully representative.[22] Even more hidden are the remains of a relatively small theatre that was also observed in the eighteenth century but which for over a century has been buried under steps leading up towards the Tour Magne.[23]

While this, the only known Roman theatre in Nîmes, is now invisible, the amphitheatre is the largest and most impressive monument of all. It is 133.38m long and 101.4m broad, with accommodation for over 20,000 spectators, and while some of it had to be restored (to make it usable for the modern bull-fights), it retains enough of the upper stories to reveal such things as the emplacement of a *velum*. It is closely similar to that of Arles (*qv*) and here too the time of its construction has been much questioned. While it includes in its underground chambers two inscriptions recording an architect (*T.Crispius Reburrus fecit*), he is not otherwise known and dates ranging from the Augustan to the Hadrianic period have been suggested. The uncial lettering of the inscriptions, however, can hardly be pre-Tiberian and recent analysis of the structure points fairly clearly to the time of Domitian or Nerva (AD 75–97).[24] Nîmes also had a circus which, unlike those of Arles and Vienne (*qq v*), was located within the city walls, but while much of it is said to have been visible in the seventeenth century and some remains were identified in 1874, both its precise shape and the date of its construction are still unknown, though some statues found there, including a large white marble head, probably representing an emperor, seem to suggest the first century AD.[25]

Although many other buildings have been located, the only probable public baths so far noted stood partly under the Lycée Alphonse Daudet, where substantial remains were found in 1811.[26] This is the more surprising because within the city there is much evidence for the water supply—not only the remarkably well preserved *castellum divisorium* (pl 16), but also many traces of pipes and drains, and even the 'Water Gate', which was briefly visible in 1892, may also have been of Roman date.[27] As for the aqueduct itself, the course of this remarkable structure, some 50km in length but with a fall of only 17m, can best be

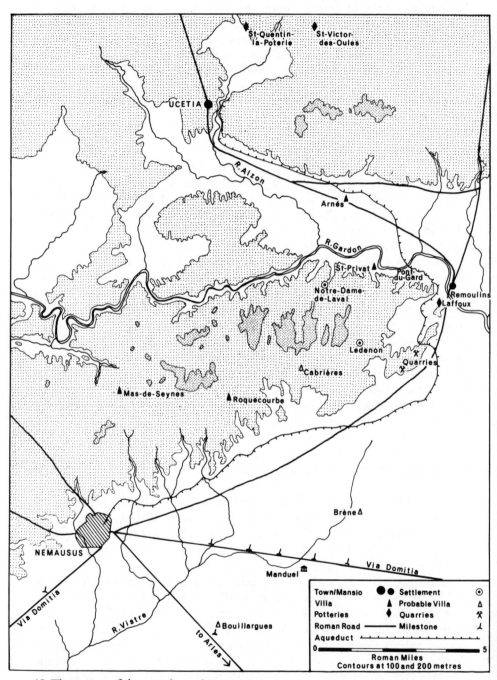

18 The course of the aqueduct of *Nemausus*

shown on a map (fig 18). Besides the magnificent Pont du Gard, which carries the water over the river Gardon (pl 17), many other parts of it have been located, including not only other smaller bridges but also underground stretches, and small pieces of it can still be seen, especially between Uzès and the Pont (*eg*, pl 18). That its main source was the river Ure, near Uzès, is clearly demonstrated by a dedication set up by CVLTORES·URAE·FONTIS (found not near the aqueduct itself but beside the *nymphaeum*),[28] but the widespread attribution of its construction to Agrippa is highly questionable. That Agrippa worked on the aqueducts of Rome itself is well known and that he made some gifts to *Nemausus* is suggested by two inscriptions, though the word *fecit* does not survive on either of them and neither was found near the actual aqueduct—one not far from the *Porta Augusta* and the other near the Jardin de la Fontaine.[29] Beyond this, while on the Pont du Gard, as in the amphitheatre, the inscriptions (here mainly recording architectural instructions) include the name of a man (Veranius), he is otherwise unknown and the possibility that such a structure could have been completed in the Augustan period has recently been questioned.[30] Finally, even leaving aside the intricacy of the work, the building of so large an aqueduct so early in this area seems highly improbable and a date no earlier than the late first century AD (in the time of Frontinus) or a little later seems much more likely.

The extent of the territory controlled by *Nemausus* raises certain problems. Livy tells us that, at least in the time of Hannibal, the *Volcae* lived on both banks of the Rhône[31] and it is sometimes suggested that an inscription recording a gift to *Avennio* by T.Carisius, a *praetor Volcarum*, means that in Caesarian times (or in any case before the title of *praetor* was replaced by that of *quattuorvir*) Avignon was subject to Nîmes,[32] but this is far from certain and it is clear that the Rhône, along the course that it then followed, early became the eastern boundary. The northern boundary, beyond which were the *Helvii*, is often taken to have been the lower reaches of the river Ardèche, but this is partly based on the belief that its ancient name was *Atrica* and that this is reflected in an inscription (found in the amphitheatre of Nîmes) recording a gift of seats to *nautae Atr(icae) et Ovidis*,[33] but the fact that the Antonine milestone found between Barjac and Vagnas clearly gives the distance (*mp xxxiii*) from *Alba* rather than from *Nemausus* makes the ridge between the Ardèche and the Cèze more probable.[34] The north-western boundary is clearly defined by the crest of the Cévennes and between this and the Mediterranean coast the centuriation of *Baeterrae* (Béziers, *qv*) provides some useful evidence: the centuriation of Nîmes so far identified is confined to an area east of the city and to one around St-Gilles.[35]

Both Strabo and Pliny tell us that *Nemausus* had 24 places subject to it, the former calling them κωμαι, the latter *oppida ignobilia* but still including them in his list of *oppida Latina*.[36] The names of eleven of them are clearly provided by an inscription on the base of a column apparently found in 1747 near the sacred fountain in Nîmes, which lists them as follows:[37]

ANDVSIA
BRVGETIA
TEDVSIA
VATRVTE
VGERNI
SEXTANT
BRIGINN
STATVMAE
VIRINN
VCETIAE
SEGVSION

The fact that the names of the two best-known towns in this list, *Ugernum* (Beaucaire) and *Ucetia* (Uzès) are presented in the genitive and in larger letters than the rest suggests at first sight that it is dealing with the *civitas* area by area, but this cannot be maintained if the SEXTANT that it includes is to be identified with the *Sextantio* (Substantion/Castelnau-le-Lez) of the Antonine Itinerary, since this, just outside Montpellier, is 65km from both Beaucaire and Uzès. It seems best, therefore, simply to take them in the order given, bearing in mind that they may well have been given Latin rights in the time of Caesar and may not all have developed into proper Roman towns.

Andusia was certainly Anduze, 40km NW of Nîmes and on a Roman road that probably led over the Cévennes to the territory of the *Gabali*, though its precise course has still to be established: a few finds have been made in the area of the town and in the neighbouring hill-fort of St-Julien a probable Roman temple has been noted.[38] *Brugetia* has usually been identified as Bruyès, a little hamlet north-west of Uzès, again with a nearby hill-fort: here too there have been some discoveries and it has been tentatively marked on our map (fig 19), but Brouzet, 9km to the north of it, has also been suggested as a possibility.[39] The best suggestion for *Tedusia* seems to be Théziers, although only burials and funerary inscriptions have been found there,[40] but Vié Cioutat (near Monteils) as *Vatrute* is rather more convincing: the impressive Iron Age hill-fort here has long been recognised and extensive excavations since the war have revealed not only details of the Iron Age fortifications but also Roman buildings of the first century and even a street.[41]

Ugernum was certainly Beaucaire and besides the correct distance from *Nemausus* given by the Vicarello Goblets and the Peutinger Table it has yielded an inscribed gravestone set up by the *centonarii Ugernenses*.[42] It has sometimes been suggested that for a time this was *Rhodanusia*, the Greek city beside the Rhône mentioned by Pseudo-

Scymnus, but this seems improbable: while excavations, especially on the hill-fort of la Redoute, have revealed Greek imports from the seventh century BC onwards and while here, as at Nîmes, some native inscriptions using Greek lettering have been found, no evidence of actual Greek occupation has come to light.[43] As we have suggested above (p 43), a Roman post of some kind must have been set up here when the *Via Domitia* was first built, but although this has not been located ample material of the main Roman period, including buildings

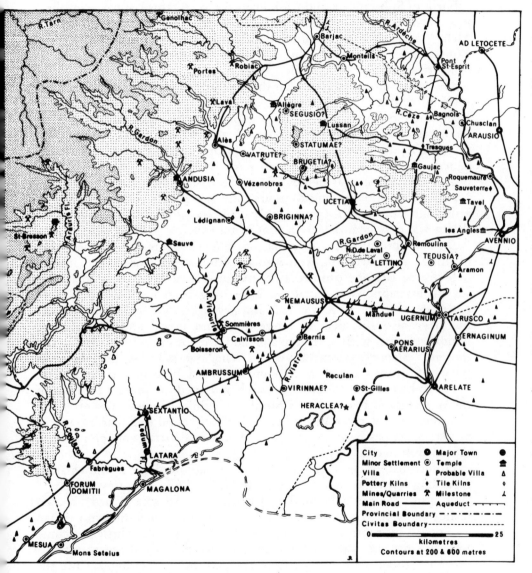

19 The territory of *Nemausus*. Some of the 'probable villas' included here are based on the discovery of groups of funerary inscriptions

with mosaics, statues and inscriptions, has been recovered and there is a good local museum.[44] Despite the fact that the importance of *Arelate* made that, rather than *Ugernum*, the normal place for distinguished travellers to cross the Rhône (as in the Antonine and Bordeaux Itineraries), the continuing prosperity of this town is illustrated by a meeting in the *atria* here of provincial notabilities in the fifth century.[45]

Montpellier is now one of the largest cities in southern France, but *Sextantio* was situated not in the present city centre but in the NE suburbs of Substantion and Castelnau-le-Lez. As this last name implies, it was where the *Via Domitia* crossed the river Lez (the *Ledum flumen* of Mela)[46] and the ancient name of the town was of Gaulish rather than Roman origin—certainly the distance from the next stations in the itineraries was never six miles[47]—it was not a legionary colony and while it was once suggested that the hill-fort (occupied from at least the seventh century BC, with the usual mediterranean imports) was abandoned before the Roman occupation, this now appears to be incorrect. Finds here have included several buildings, some with mosaics, a public monument near the bridge over the river, traces of an aqueduct, statues and a number of inscriptions. These include dedications to several deities (Fortuna, Isis, Minerva, Neptune, the Nymphs and Abianus and Mercury) and also record the presence of an aedile and a *quattuorvir* (presumably of *Nemausus*), so there is no doubt that it was a substantial town, not just a *mansio*.[48]

Briginn (presumably *Briginna* or *Briginnum*) is very reasonably identified with Brignon. Iron Age and Roman remains on and around le Sierre de Brienne (immediately NW of the present town), including several inscriptions and statues, have long been recorded and more recent excavations have not only improved knowledge of the hill-fort but have also revealed an interesting coin hoard and two Roman buildings, one with a colonnade and the other with a geometric mosaic.[49] *Statumae* is generally taken to be Seynes, but while 'numerous traces of Roman occupation' were recorded here in the past, there seems to have been no recent research and even the present location of the one epitaph is obscure.[50] Similarly, while *Virinnae* was probably Védrines, on the river Vistre between Vauvert and le Cailar, no recent investigation has been carried out and only one partial epitaph has been recorded in detail.[51]

Unfortunately we are also short of archaeological information regarding *Ucetia*, which was certainly Uzès. While it figures notably in later history, especially in the early Middle Ages, and had its own bishop as early as 442,[52] and while several finds, including more than two dozen inscriptions, were recorded in the past, very little has come to light since the war. The inscriptions include dedications to Jupiter, Mars and the obscure deity *Segomanna* and, not surprisingly, since the town is just beside the *Urae Fons*, one records the building of a temple of the Nymphs, while the funerary ones include a *sevir* (doubtless of

Nemausus) and veterans of both *Legio II Augusta* and *Legio XV*. It is likely enough that it was walled, both in the Iron Age and in the later Roman period, but the fact that the *Notitia Galliarum*—the earliest literary source that mentions it—calls it *castrum Ucetiense* does not prove this, since by the fifth century *castrum* could mean no more than *vicus*.[53] Finally, *Segusio(n)* was presumably Suzon, where the hill-fort of San-Peyre, midway between Allègre and Bouquet, was also occupied in Roman times: not only suitable pottery but also some altars are recorded here, while a Roman cemetery lay at the foot of the hill.[54]

Despite the shortage of evidence, some tentative conclusions can be drawn from this superficial review of the eleven places listed in the inscription. On the one hand, the Iron Age background of the majority of them suggests that it was at a relatively early date that *ius Latii* was granted to them, but on the other it seems clear that some of these *oppida* remained *ignobilia* throughout the Roman period. Until more convincing inscriptions are found, therefore, it is impossible to guess which of the other known settlements in this area were the 13 that are missing from the inscription and it seems best to begin on the Mediterranean coast, then look at those sited on known Roman roads and beside the river Rhône, ending up with the remainder.

As recent research has shown, *Latara* (Lattes), now an established archaeological centre with its own museum,[55] was certainly one of the most important towns both in the Iron Age and in the earlier half of the Roman period. While it is the *castellum Latara* of Mela, the fact that Pliny does not name it individually is a little surprising because it was hardly an *oppidum ignobile* and it appears that he had actually visited it—at least, the *stagnum Latara appellatum*, no doubt an adjoining lagoon, is the scene of his entertaining account of how dolphins helped fishermen to catch mullets.[56] Various finds were recorded before the war, including buildings (one with a hypocaust and one with columns) and also burials, but since the early 1960s a great deal more has been revealed, especially after the discovery of an inscription that mentions not only *seviri* but also *fabri et utriclarii Lattarenses*, indicating that it was a port for *Sextantio*, to which things were carried up the river Lez (*Ledum flumen*).[57] Its history goes back at least to the sixth century BC, with notable Greek imports, and in Roman times it was greatly developed, with its own temple of Mercury and many other buildings.[58] It seems, however, that its importance declined in the later Empire, owing to a change in the coastline, and it was presumably also this that led to the development of *Magalona* (Maguelone). Relatively little is known of the early history of this place, though it too has yielded a few inscriptions, including not only one on a milestone of Tiberius—that was evidently brought here from the *Via Domitia* simply for use in making the lintel of the cathedral—but also some funerary ones, and it became prosperous in the early Middle Ages: it had its own bishop by the late fifth century and so was duly added to the revised *Notitia Galliarum*.[59]

To turn now to the road, as the Vicarello Goblets, both the Antonine and the Bordeaux Itineraries and the Peutinger Table tell us, *Forum Domitii* was *xv mp* from *Sextantio* and *xviii mp* from *Cessero* (St-Thibéry) and this points unequivocally to Montbazin.[60] Its name implies that it was one of the earliest specifically Roman establishments in the area and its inclusion in the Bordeaux Itinerary (though only as a *mutatio*) indicates that it always remained in use. Several buildings have been noted here, including some with mosaics and colonnades, and a few burial inscriptions, including one of a *sevir*.[61] Another *mansio* or *mutatio* evidently stood some four Roman miles further up the road, at the crossing of the river Coulazou just NE of Fabrègues. Whether the bridge here, still marked on some maps as a 'pont romain', is really Roman is questionable, but remains of buildings and burials have long been recorded and post-war finds have indicated that the main settlement was on the right bank of the river.[62]

Our knowledge of *Ambrussum*, like that of *Latara*, has been greatly increased by recent excavations. Apart from the imposing remains of the Roman bridge (the Pont Ambroix) over the river Vidourle (pl 19), Volume X of the *Forma Orbis Romani*, published in 1946, could record here only a few remains and two inscriptions—a milestone of Julian and a tombstone—but since 1967 very much more has been discovered. The hill-fort on the hill of le Devès was strongly fortified in the middle of the third century BC, but it must have come under Roman control when the road was built and in the first century BC a settlement was certainly developing at its foot. Despite some changes noted in the occupation of parts of it, this surely remained in use throughout the Roman period, since it too was used by the Bordeaux pilgrim as a *mutatio*.[63]

While it is likely enough that the name of the village of Uchaud, exactly 8 Roman miles from the centre of *Nemausus*, was derived from *Ad Octavum*, especially since an Antonine milestone with a probable figure VIII was found here, the only other significant find has been a dedication to Mars by a *sevir*, possibly transported from elsewhere, and it is not therefore included in our map (fig 19).[64] A settlement near Bernis, however, one Roman mile closer to the city, has been recorded in an area called Campferren, including a probable shrine with columns, pottery, and again three or four milestones—one of Claudius that seems to record the distance of *lxxxv mp* from *Narbo*.[65]

To turn now to another road, five milestones, including one of Augustus and two of Claudius, were found in a chapel at Bouillargues, 7km SE of Nîmes, but it is generally agreed that they had all been transported there from the *Via Domitia* between Nîmes and Beaucaire[66] and when this direct road from *Nemausus* to *Arelate* was first built remains obscure. Both of the Vicarello Goblets that take in Arles include *Ugernum* among their stations, but the Antonine and the Bordeaux Itineraries only follow this more direct route. The Bordeaux

Itinerary, however, names a *mutatio* along it, *Ponte Aerarium*, and the stated mileages, *xii mp* from *Nemausus* and *viii mp* from *Arelate*, point clearly to Bellegarde. A few inscriptions have been found here, including a dedication by someone from Riez (*qv*) and traces of an aqueduct (both the date and the purpose of which are unclear) have been reported at Mas Soulier, 2km west of the town, but very much more needs to be known.[67]

No further places are included in the itineraries, so in selecting settlements we must now depend entirely on discoveries. Calvisson, on the rather winding road running south-east from Nîmes, lies in an area especially notable for hill-forts—with Nages 4km to the east of it and la Liquière and Mauressip 3km and 5km to the north—but the small one overlooking the town itself, the Roc de Gachone, seems not to have lasted long after the late Bronze Age and the Roman settlement was probably on an entirely new site. Besides three inscriptions and several buildings, traces of the road have also been observed and it is suggested that the Pont de Bagnols, that carries the modern D37 from Nages to Calvisson over the little river Rhôny, was also of Roman origin.[68]

Further to the west, the road had to cross the much larger river Vidourle and here a problem regarding its precise course arises. It has long been claimed that the bridge at Sommières, rebuilt in the eighteenth century (pl 20), is of Roman origin and this is likely enough, since between it and the hill-fort of Villevieille adequate evidence for a Roman settlement has been recovered, not only epitaphs (including one of a *sevir*) and an altar (though the deity is uncertain) but also buildings with mosaics and a hypocaust. There was, however, another bridge over this river, 3km downstream and 1km SE of Boisseron, and the remains of this, though it was converted into a mill-dam in the Middle Ages and so is now called le Moulin de Boisseron, are still more convincingly Roman (pl 21). The question then arises which was the main river crossing, especially as it appears that it was from quarries in this area that some of the stone used in the building of the amphitheatre of Nîmes was obtained.[69]

On the road towards *Andusia* substantial remains, including buildings with mosaics and tile-kilns, have been recorded at Lédignan, as well as a statue of Apollo, and it is therefore tentatively marked as a *vicus* on the map.[70] On the other road further north, Vézenobres (claimed by some to be the *Virinn* that we have taken to be Védrines) also had several buildings, together with four epitaphs, and a stamp of the oculist T.Claudius Hesychius was also found here,[71] but the remains noted at Alès (which must surely have been called *Alesia*, like the better-known Alise-Ste-Reine in the land of the *Aedui*) are still more significant. They include workshops dealing with silver and lead from the neighbouring mines marked on the map and it has been suggested that near this town were the estates of Tonantius Ferreolus and Apollinaris at which Sidonius was entertained in the middle of the fifth century.[72]

173

To the east of Nîmes, Remoulins must surely have flourished, since it was an important road junction and traces of the Roman bridge over the Gardon have been seen, but while pottery kilns have been found just across the river very little is recorded regarding the town itself, apart from a dedication to Jupiter and Augustus and a few epitaphs.[73] Further east again, Aramon (the ancient name of which must be related to the god *Aramo*, to whom a dedication was found not here but at Nôtre-Dame-de-Laval, on which see below) was evidently a port on the Rhône: a dozen inscriptions found here—some of them of very high quality—include one for the *Lares Augusti* and another set up by an aedile.[74] The inclusion of Roquemaure on the map is due primarily to its position on the road, for only burials and a number of small finds are recorded here,[75] but further up the Rhône rescue excavations in the late 1960s at Chusclan, or rather in the area between this town and the river, now covered by the Centre atomique de Marcoule, exposed substantial buildings, one with a mosaic, a kiln and a funerary inscription to be added to the half dozen already known: this, then, doubtless was a port.[76]

Barjac, near the northern boundary of the *civitas*, was a road junction and not only two inscriptions but also some columns and much pottery have been found there,[77] while substantial finds are also recorded near Monteils, a hamlet in the parish of Montclus, just north of the river Cèze.[78] Somewhat more interesting is the place east of Remoulins, around the Hermitage de Nôtre-Dame-de-Laval, beside a little tributary of the Gardon and in the parish of Collias. This appears to have been a religious centre and it is shown as a settlement rather than just a temple because besides half a dozen epitaphs it has produced a remarkable number of dedications, one to *Mars Budenicus*, one to *Sulvia Idennica Minerva* and one to *Aramo*, along with an altar to *Andoounnabo* inscribed in Celtic with Greek lettering. The probable connection of the god *Aramo* with the settlement at Aramon has already been noted, but while the suggestion that the *Coriossedentes* were the people of the surrounding area called Couveyrac (once *Coriobedum*) seems not too improbable, the idea that the *Budennicenses* lived around Bézuc (now shown on most maps as Bézut, near Baron, some 22km to the NE) demands more proof.[79] That the neighbouring village of Lédenon was called *Lettino* is proved by the discovery there of an inscription recording a gift to it by the *Nemausenses* for good work done—perhaps labour in the local quarries when the city's aqueduct was being built—but no other finds are recorded.[80]

Finally, in the south there was certainly a settlement in Roman times at St-Gilles (now most notable for the magnificent façade of its medieval church), since both mosaics and a very large number of inscriptions have been found in this area, the latter including six religious dedications, one to a *sevir* and one for the *curator* of both the *nautae Atr . . . et Ovidis* (a body also recorded, as we have noted, in the amphitheatre of Nîmes) and of the *utriclarii Arelatenses* (who evidently worked down the Little Rhône).[81] It has often been suggested that St-Gilles was the *Heraclea* mentioned by Pliny, but since his words (*sunt auctores et Heracleam oppidum in ostio Rhodani fuisse*) clearly imply that it no longer existed in his time, the flourishing Roman settlement makes this unlikely and recent research has shown that although a Greek settlement did exist in this commune it was not at St-Gilles itself but at Espeyran, some 4km SE of the town and nearer to the Etang de Scamandre.[82]

Several other *vici* no doubt existed, as is indicated by the extraordinary number of Roman inscriptions recorded in this *civitas*—approximately the same as the total of those so far found in the whole of Britain—but on our map (fig 19) most other sites that have produced three or more epitaphs are tentatively included among the 'probable villas'. One further inscription, however, demands mention, that found just north of *Ugernum* in 1968 when the Barrage de Vallabrègues was being constructed. As the current boundary between the departements of Gard and Bouches-du-Rhône indicates, both the mausolea found in this area, including even the one on the old Ile du Comte, must have been in the territory of *Nemausus*, not that of *Avennio*, and in any case C.Sergius, for whom that on the right bank of the river was built by his freedman, must have been an *agonothetes*, a *quattuorvir, pontifex and praefectus (vigilum) et armorum* of our city, besides being an honorary decurion of (probably) *Cabellio* (Cavaillon).[83]

A number of temples have been identified, besides those in towns and the one already mentioned near *Andusia*. Dedications to Diana as a moon-goddess and possibly one to *Nemausus* have long been known at Manduel,[84] as has the existence of the sacred sulphurous spring at Allègre, with a *piscina* and dedications to the Nymphs.[85] The shrine at Lussan is a little less certain, depending on the supposition that the discovery of mosaics and other remains in a nearby hamlet called Fan implies the former presence of a *fanum*,[86] but knowledge of the temple in the hill-fort at Gaujac, with its own baths (and, curiously, an epitaph for three brothers called Tacitus), has been greatly improved by recent excavations[87] and three new discoveries have been made since the war, at les Angles, Tavel (with notable baths) and Sauve.[88] It is interesting that while that at Sauve flourished from the first to the second century, that at Tavel from the first to the third and the one at les Angles was succeeded by a palaeochristian chapel, the temple at Gaujac seems to have continued in use in the late Empire, despite the probable christianisation of Nîmes.

While relatively few villas have convincingly been identified, modern research is steadily increasing our knowledge—for example, the excavations at Aigues-Vives, just NE of *Ambrussum*, where a luxurious mansion of the late Empire has been examined[89]—and this was certainly a prosperous *civitas*. Besides agriculture and fishing it produced, especially in the later period, many of its own amphorae, lamps and other pottery, as at Bagnols-sur-Cèze, Tresques, Sauveterre and Reculan,[90] and in the higher regions mining also went on: in the land above 600m, as shown on the map, silver, lead, copper and iron were all extracted.[91]

REFERENCES AND NOTES

1 For a full account of the pre-Roman occupation of the site, M.Py, *Recherches sur Nîmes préromaine*, *Gallia* Suppl XLI(1981), with an excellent summary on pp 199–210; for more recent Iron Age finds, *Gallia* XLI(1983), 513–15.

2 Strabo's statement (IV, 1, 12) that it is the μητρόπολις τῶν 'Αρηκομίσκων is, of course, set in the Roman period.

3 Caesar, *BC* I, 35, 4.

4 On coins, C.M.Kraay, 'The chronology of the coinage of Colonia Nemausus', *Num Chron* XV(1955), 75–87; for a general discussion, C.Goudineau, 'Le statut de Nîmes et des Volques Arécomiques', *RAN* IX(1976), 105–14.

5 Mosaics, *FOR* VIII, no 85, *passim*: *Gallia* VIII(1950), 115–16, XI(1953), 249–71 (Bellerophon), XXXIII(1975), 514–15; *Hist Arch* no 99(Nov 1985), 48–59. Statues, *FOR* VIII, no 85; *Gallia* XVII(1959), 469–73, XXXIX(1981), 522. Inscriptions, *CIL* XII 3042–4059, 5890–5944; *ILGN*, 406–79, 481–96; *Gallia* XVII(1959), 469–73; for a larger selection of inscriptions in Greek lettering, E. and F.Germer-Durand and A.Almer, *Inscriptions Antiques de Nîmes* (Toulouse, 1893). Mela II, 5, 75, rightly includes *Nemausus* (but not *Narbo*) in his list of *urbes opulentissimae*. For the city that overtook it in distinction, *v Vienna* (Vienne).

6 Both Strabo IV, 1, 12, and Pliny, *HN* III, 37, make this clear and none of the numerous inscriptions recording its various officials (*v CIL* XII, p 382, for lists) indicates that it was raised to full Roman status before the time of Caracalla. For a recent discussion, C Goudineau, *op cit* in n 4, above.

7 Cassius Dio LIX, 19–20; on his oratory, Tacitus, *Dial de Or*, xiii, 3 and xv, 3, and especially Quintillian, *Inst Or* x. 1.118, and *passim*. Unfortunately only Jerome, *Chron* 179H, reports his Nemausian origin.

8 Cassius Dio LXIX, 10, 3 (not stating where), *SHA*, Hadrian xii, 2 (saying at *Nemausus*).

9 His name before he was adopted by Hadrian was T.Aurelius Fulvius Boionius Arrius Antoninus (*CIL* VIII, 8239) His family's connection with the city is surely an equally good explanation of the inscriptions of his period that have suggested to some that the capital of the province was moved here after a fire in *Narbo* (*cf* Grenier in Pflaum 1978, preface, pp xi–xii, citing two dedications to proconsuls and the inscriptions of four *flamines* of the province in Nîmes).

10 C.M.Kraay, *op cit*, in n 3; for their use in Germany, C.M.Wells, *The German Policy of Augustus* (Oxford, 1972), 266–88. The epitaph of a *nummularius* was found in 1933 among the burials located near l'Eglise Ste-Perpétue (*FOR* VIII, p 46).

11 *Centonarii, CIL* xii, 3232 (partly in Greek); *fabri tignuarii*, 3165; *utriclarii*, 3351 ('surprisingly' because *Nemausus* stood on no navigable river; the inscription was found in the amphitheatre and it may be that *Nemausenses* reflects the whole territory rather than the city itself); *cf* also the inscription found in Lattes, noted below).

12 For pagan inscriptions, *eg CIL* xii, 3042–3141, *ILGN*, 406–416. Council of Nîmes, Munier 1963, 49–51, Sedatus, 189–228.

13 *FOR* viii, no 85, *passim*: more recent excavations, *Gallia* xxii(1964), 500–04, xxiv(1966), 478–9, xxxi(1973), 508–09, xxxiii(1975), 521–4, xxxvii(1979), 543–4, xli(1983), 514; *Hist Arch* no 99 (Nov, 1985), 38–41 (with a photograph of another tower, in the nearby Jardin de la Clinique St-Joseph).

14 *CIL* xii, 3151. The reconstruction of this bronze-letter inscription (unlike that of the Maison Carrée) has never been seriously questioned.

15 *Gallia* xxii(1964), 500–02, xxiv(1966), 478–9, xxxiii(1975), 521–2; M.Py, *op cit* (n 1)

16 *FOR* viii, no 85, *passim*; *Gallia* xxvii(1969) 406–07, xxviii(1970), 91–126, xxxvii(1979), 543, 546, xxxix(1981), 522.

17 *Gallia* xxxvi(1978), 454–5, xxxvii(1979), 543, xxxix(1981), 522; *RAN* xv(1982), 273–318; *Hist Arch* no 99(Nov 1985), 40, for a photograph of the preserved remains. The position of this stretch of wall makes it clear that the area enclosed was much smaller than that defended by the medieval enceinte that still survived in the 16th cent when a full picture of it was drawn.

18 Grenier 1958, 147. While the junction of the *cardo* and *decumanus* of the city probably did lie here, the reconstruction of the streets in the plan on the opposite page is not quite accurate. (*cf* fig 17).

19 Séguier, *Dissertation sur l'ancienne inscription de la Maison Carrée de Nismes* (Paris, 1759), followed by *CIL* xii, 3156; Espérandieu, *CRAI* 1919, 332 ff, followed by *AE* 1920, no 43, *ILGN* 417, Espérandieu, *La Maison-Carrée de Nîmes* (1929), Grenier 1958, 388–92, etc; Amy and Gros, *La Maison Carrée de Nîmes*, Suppl xxxviii to *Gallia* (1979). For the temple as a whole, see also J.C.Balty, *Études sur la Maison Carrée de Nîmes* (Brussels, 1960). For the discovery of a wall under the temple, *Gallia* xxix(1971), 396–7.

20 *FOR* viii, pp 66–8; Grenier 1958, 149–50.

21 *FOR* viii, pp 110–12; Grenier 1960, 502–06 (with plan).

22 *FOR* viii, pp 104–10; Grenier 1960, 493–502 (with plan and photographs); *Hist Arch* no 99 (Nov 1985), 48–9. For dedications, mostly found during the 18th-cent reconstruction, to Nemausus, *CIL* xii, 3070, 3072, 3093–3102, and to Nymphs, 3103–09; located also in 1751, two dedications to Augustus in 25 bc, *CIL* xii, 3148–9—now accompanied by a Latin inscription of 1753 that records their discovery, while others praise the 'new Augustus' (Louis xiv)! P.Gros, *RAN* xvii(1984), 123–34 suggests that the *Augusteum* of *Nemausus* was in the area of the Jardin de la Fontaine.

23 *FOR* viii, p 103; Grenier 1958, 153.

24 E.Espérandieu, *L'amphithéâtre de Nîmes* (Paris, 1933, but slightly revised, with a fuller bibliography, in 2nd ed, 1967); Grenier 1958, 613–39; for the date here adopted, R.Etienne, 'La date de l'amphithéâtre de Nîmes', *Mélanges A.Piganiol* (Paris, 1966) ii, 985–1010; *cf* J.C.Bessac, M.Fincker, P.Garny, J.Pey, 'Recherches sur les fondations de l'amphithéâtre de Nîmes', *RAN* xvii(1984), 223–37.

25 *FOR* VIII, pp 97–8; Grenier 1958, 988–9.

26 *FOR* VIII, p 94; for various recent excavations, *Gallia* XLII(1985), 396–398.

27 *FOR* VIII, no 85, *passim*; Grenier 1960, 97–101.

28 *FOR* VIII, nos 85, 96, 107, 110, 115, 116, 120, 179 (Pont du Gard), 181, 187, 188, 197, 198 (Uzès), 199 (*Ura Fons*); E.Espérandieu, *Le Pont du Gard et l'aqueduc de Nîmes* (Paris, 1936); Grenier, 1960, 88–101; *Gallia* XXXIII (1975), 527 (underground stretches near Sernhac). *Ura Fons* inscription, *CIL* XII, 3076.

29 Frontinus, *De Aquis Urbis Romae*, *passim*. Nîmes inscriptions, *CIL* XII, 3153–4.

30 Inscription of Veranius, *CIL* XII, 2980. On the architectural date, I.S.Nikolaev, *Sovetskaya Archeologija* 1967, ii, 38–54, cited by Chevallier 1975, 748 and 1982, 61. On the probability of a later date, *cf* also P.-A. Février in *JRS* LXII(1973), 26.

31 Livy XXI, 26; his use of the present tense may reflect his source rather than his current knowledge.

32 *CIL* XII, 1028.

33 *CIL* XII, 3316; *cf* 3317, also 4107 (found at St-Gilles, west of the Rhône delta). In any case, the name *Ovidis* is clearly that of the Ouvèze, east of the Rhône, and the other sailors included in the same inscription ploughed the waters of the *Arar* (the Saône), much further north.

34 *CIL* XII, 5583, König no 164.

35 For a suggestion that *Sextantio* was actually on the western boundary, F.Danmas and R.Majurel, *Gallia* XIX(1961), 5–30, but on centuriation, J.Soyer, *RAN* VII(1974), 179–99, and J.L.Fiches and J.Soyer in Clavel-Lévêque 1984, 259–74.

36 Strabo IV, 1.12; Pliny, *HN* III, 37.

37 *CIL* XII, 3362, regularly printed on a postcard in Nîmes. For the possibility that it was found somewhere else, see n40 on Théziers, below.

38 *FOR* VIII, nos 376–7; inscriptions, both dedications, *CIL* XII, 2895, *Gallia* XX(1962), 628.

39 Bruyès, *FOR* VIII, no 212; Brouzet, no 319.

40 *FOR* VIII, no 128. M.Louis (or perhaps A.Blanchet, his editor) there states that it was here, not in Nîmes, that the inscribed list of places was first found and since the authors he cites for this include the 18th cent L.Ménard one supposes that this may be correct.

41 *FOR* VIII, no 314; *Gallia* XII(1954), 424–5, XXVII(1969), 405, XXIX(1971), 393, XXXI(1973), 503, XXXIII(1975), 517, XXXV(1977), 449–52, XXXVII(1979), 539, XXXIX(1981), 519; *Hist Arch* no 99 (Nov 1985), 27, for a good air photo of the hill-fort defences.

42 It appears on all the Goblets and while nos 1 and 3 take the traveller from it to Arles, nos 2 and 4, which omit Arles, clearly point to a direct crossing of the Rhône here. For the *centonari*, *CIL* XII, 2824.

43 Pseudo-Scymnus 208–09. Greek-lettered inscriptions, *CIL* XII, pp 356, 832, *Gallia* XXII(1964), 498. Finds of the pre-Roman period, *Gallia* XX(1962), 628, XXVII(1969), 403, XXXVI(1978), 446 (on la Redoute). Arguments for *Rhodanusia*, *FOR* VIII, nos 3 and 4 (citing sources); against, Benoit 1965, 132, Barruol 1969, 198.

44 *FOR* VIII, no 3; *Gallia* XX(1962), 628–30, XXII(1964), 498–9, XXIV(1966), 174, XXVII(1969), 403.

45 *It Ant* 388.5, *It Burd* 552.10. For the 5th-cent meeting, Sidonius, *Carm* vii, 571 ff; though the MS reads *atria . . . Vierni*, *Ugerni* seems the only reasonable interpretation, since full meetings were normally held at nearby Arles.

46 Mela II, 5, 50; whether this was earlier the *Oranus* river in Avienius, *Ora Maritima*, 612, as suggested by Schulten, seems questionable.

47 Vicarello Goblets (on all four), *It Ant* 389.2, 396.7, *It Burd* 552.6 (*Sostantione*, here used only as a *mutatio*), *Tab Peut* (*Sextatione*), *Rav Cos* IV, 28(245.9) (*Sestantione*)

48 *FOR* x, no 19; post-war excavations, including both Iron Age and Roman finds, *Gallia* XVII(1959), 237–41 (a stone horse's head), XIX(1961) 5–30 (including the monument near the river), XX(1962), 623, XXII(1964), 490, XXIV(1966), 464–6, XXVII(1969), 392, XXIX(1971), 380, XXXI(1973), 490, XXXIII(1975), 503–04; J.-C.M.Richard, 'La région montpellieraine à l'époque préromaine (750–121 BC)', *Latomus* CXXX(1973). Inscriptions, *CIL* XII, 4183–98, 5660–2, *ILGN*, 665–8; the reference to *colonis et incolis* in *CIL* 4189 does not elevate the town to a *colonia*.

49 *FOR* VIII, no 297; inscriptions, *CIL* XII, 2913–24 (and possibly 3323; this is not the epitaph quoted in *FOR*—that is 2923—but records a gladiator and was found *either* at Brignon or in Nîmes); recent excavations, *Gallia* XX(1962), 630 (colonnade), XXIX(1971), 390 (mosaic and hoard, including native and Roman imperial coins), XXXI(1973), 500, XXXIII(1975), 513–14, XXXVII(1979), 537.

50 *FOR* VIII, no 316; *CIL* XII, 2854.

51 *FOR* VIII, no 35; only known inscription, *CIL* XII, 4094. The reader will not find Védrines on Michelin 1:200,000 and even on IGN 1:50,000 no 2843 it is called Virunes and the site of the church of St-Sauveur de Védrines is not there marked. As a possible alternative, see Vézenobres, dealt with below.

52 Constantius, who attended the Council of Vaison in 442 and was also a signatory of the letter to Pope Leo in 451: Munier 1963, 94–104, 107–10.

53 *FOR* VIII, no 198; inscriptions, *CIL* XII, 2925–61, 5886, *ILGN*, 393–5; recent finds, *Gallia* XXII(1964), 506, XXIX(1971), 401–02 (including a further funerary inscription); *Not Gall* xv, 6, but on *castrum*, Rivet 1976, 134–5, Harries 1978, 35–6.

54 *FOR* VIII, no 323; *Gallia* XXXIII(1975), 513.

55 For a recent description, *Hist Arch* no 99(Nov 1985), 74–9.

56 Mela II, 5, 80 (*cf Rav Cos* IV, 28(245, 8) and v, 3(340.15)); Pliny, *HN* IX, 29–32 (*cf* Mela, II, 5, 80, *stagna Volcarum*).

57 *AE* 1966, no 247.

58 *FOR* x, no 23; *Gallia* XXII(1964), 491, XXIV(1966), 467–8, XXV(1967), 185–7, XXVII(1969), 393–4, XXIX(1971), 381–3, XXXI(1973), 491–3, XXXVI(1978), 441, XXXVII(1979), 529, XXXIX(1981), 508–09, XLI(1983), 520–1, XLIII(1985), 406–08; *Archéologia* 31(1969), 69–72; J.Arnal, R.Majurel, H.Prades, *Le port de Lattara* (Lattes, 1974).

59 *FOR* x, no 33; *Gallia* XXVII(1969), 401, XXIX(1971), 388, XXXVI(1978), 445; milestone, *ILGN*, 654, König no 247; other inscriptions, *CIL* XII, 4193, *ILGN*, 547, 552–5; *Not Gall* xv, 8 (*Civitas Magalonensium*)

60 *It Ant* 359.2–4, 396.7–9; *It Burd* 552.4–6. Among the Vicarello Goblets no 4 also includes a place called *Frontiana*, *viii mp* west of *Forum Domitii*, but this

has not been identified and it evidently lay in the territory of *Baeterrae*.

61 *FOR* x, no 41; *Gallia* xxii(1964), 494, xxix(1971), 385.

62 *FOR* x, no 27; *Gallia* xi(1953), 99–100.

63 For its name, Vicarello Goblets (*Ambrussum* in nos 1, 2 and 3, but *Ambrusio* in 4), *It Ant* 389.1, 396.6, *It Burd* 552.7 (*mutatio Ambrosi*) *Tab Peut* (*Ambrusium*). For discoveries, *FOR* x, no 4 (with good photographs of the bridge in its earlier condition, but for refs to it *cf FOR* viii, no 49); milestone, *CIL* xii, 5648, König no 225; *Gallia* xxvii(1969), 401, xxix(1971), 388–9, xxxi(1973), 498, xxxiii(1975), 510–12, xxxvi(1978), 445, xxxvii(1979), 535–6, xxxix(1981), 511–13, xli(1983), 524–6 (with plan of a building); for a good air photograph of the hill-fort, *Hist Arch* no 99(Nov, 1985), 27. Forthcoming, J.-L.Fiches, *Les maisons gallo-romaines d'Ambrussum*, Documents d'Archéologie Française no 5, (Paris).

64 *FOR* viii, no 44; milestones, *CIL* xii, 5639, 5640, König nos 219–20; dedication, *CIL* xii, 4081. *Cf* also the place called Quart, 4 Roman miles e of Nîmes (*FOR* viii, no 100) and Septême and Oytier, near Vienne (*qv*).

65 *FOR* viii, no 43; milestones, *CIL* xii, 5633–6, König nos 214–17.

66 *CIL* xii, 5611–15, König nos 195–8.

67 *FOR* viii, nos 9 and 10; *CIL* xii, 4082–6.

68 *FOR* viii, no 61; *CIL* xii, 4153–4, *ILGN*, 539–40; the bridge, *FOR* viii, no 63. For references to the hill-forts, see the bibliography on p 22, above.

69 *FOR* viii, nos 54–5; recent finds in this area, *Gallia* xvii(1959), 475, xxii(1964), 407, xxiv(1966), 482, xxxi(1973), 513, xxxiii(1975), 527 (hill-fort of Villevieille).

70 *FOR* viii, no 387; for the statue, long called 'the Venus of Nîmes', Espérandieu 1907–, iii, no 2652; tile-kilns, *Gallia* xxiv(1966), 477.

71 *FOR* viii, no 306; oculist's stamp. *CIL* xii, 5691(2).

72 *FOR* viii, no 365; Sidonius, *Epp* ii, ix (written to Donidius, who was an Arvernian, explaining how his return from Nîmes had been delayed, so a site on this road is likely enough). For some reason Alès was called *Alestum* on TIR L 31.

73 *FOR* viii, nos 172–4; for the kilns, no 119.

74 *FOR* viii, no 127 (though evidence for the idea that there was a *collegium* of *utricularii* here is not supplied); inscriptions, *CIL* xii, 2807–17 and perhaps 1023.

75 *FOR* viii, no 159.

76 Earlier finds, *CIL* xii, 2742–6, *ILGN* 511; recent excavations, *Gallia* xxvii(1969), 403–04, xxix (1971), 392.

77 *FOR* viii, no 342

78 *FOR* viii, no 248

79 *FOR* viii, no 184; dedication to Aramo, *CIL* xii, 2971, to Jupiter, 2972, to Mars Budenicus, 2973, to Minerva, 2974, to Andoounnabo, 5887.

80 *FOR* viii, no 114 and for the quarries (shown on our map of the aqueduct, fig 18), no 115; inscription, *CIL* xii, 2990.

81 *FOR* viii, nos 20 and 21; inscriptions, *CIL* xii, 4099–135. *ILGN*, 515–16. For a villa at la Baume, sw of the town, *Gallia* xx(1962), 636.

82 Pliny, *HN* iii, 34; G.Barruol and M.Py, 'Recherches récentes sur la ville antique d'Espeyran à St-Gilles-du-Gard', *RAN* xi(1978), 19–104.

83 *Gallia* xxvii(1969), 411–13 (with photographs); *AE* 1969/70, no 376; *Revue des études latines* xlix(1971), 262–5; Burnand 1975, 124.

84 *FOR* VIII, no 105; dedications, *CIL* XII, 4068–9, and perhaps 3097.

85 *FOR* VIII, no 326; dedications, *CIL* XII, 2845–9.

86 *FOR* VIII, no 261.

87 *FOR* VIII, no 217: Tacitus epitaph, *CIL* XII, 2803; *Gallia* XXVII(1969), 404–05, XXXI(1973), 502, XXXIII(1975), 515, XXXVII(1979), 538–9, XXXIX(1981), 514.

88 Les Angles, *Gallia* XXII(1964), 498, XXIV(1966), 474; Tavel, *Gallia* XXXI(1973), 511–12, *RAN* VI(1973), 233–52; Sauve, *Gallia* XXXVII(1979), 549.

89 *FOR* VIII, no 51; *Gallia* XXIV(1966), 472–4, XXVII(1969), 401–02 (with illustrations).

90 Bagnols-sur-Cèze (at les Eyrieux), *Gallia* XXIX(1971), 390, XXXI(1973), 498, XXXIII(1975), 512; Tresques (at Bouyas), *Gallia* XXXVII(1979), 549, XXXIX(1981), 525; Sauveterre, *Gallia* XXVII(1969), 409; *RAN* XV(1982), 373–80. Reculan (south of Générac), *Gallia* XXVII(1969), 405, *RAN* XV(1981), 325–50.

91 *FOR* VIII, nos 344(Robiac), 345(Portes), 349(Genolhac), 350(Laval), 422, 425, 427, 430(around St-Bresson).

13

Alba Helviorum (Alba, formerly Aps)

Since they dwelt so far from the Mediterranean coast the *Helvii* are not mentioned by any of the earlier Greek writers and it seems that only one of their hill-forts so far examined, that at St-Etienne-de-Dion, has yielded Greek imports.[1] Even after the Romans have become involved we hear very little about these people. They probably came under the control of the *Arverni* around 125 BC, though this is nowhere stated, and both Caepio and Domitius may well have crossed their territory, but the first definite pieces of information we have come from Caesar. For one thing, it is he who tells us that Pompey had handed over some of their land (presumably a small area in the south-east) to *Massalia*, probably after a revolt with which, as we have suggested above (p 58), the remarkable refortification of the hill-fort of Jastres-Nord may have been associated.[2] For another, he tells us that C. Valerius Flaccus (who was governor in the 80s BC) had conferred Roman citizenship on C. Valerius Caburus, of whose sons one, C. Valerius Procillus (or Troucillus), acted as his interpreter when he was talking to Diviciacus and another, C. Valerius Donnotaurus, led the *Helvii* against Vercingetorix (and died in the battle).[3] It was in Helvian territory that Caesar had assembled his newly-enlisted troops in 52 BC and through it that he marched against the *Arverni*; the route that he took, which involved clearing deep snow on the Cevennes, is not defined, but was probably the same as that, up the upper valley of the Ardèche, followed by the Roman road shown on the map in fig 21.[4]

No doubt Caesar returned the land taken by *Massalia* in 49 BC but even in the early imperial period our information is slight. Strabo introduces a problem by apparently attributing the *Helvii* to *Aquitania*, but since he there says that he is listing tribes 'between the Garonne and the Loire' this is doubtless a simple error.[5] Again, Ptolemy does not mention the *Helvii* as such, but when dealing with the other side of the Rhône he includes the '*Elycoci*' (Ἑλύκωκοι) and attributes to them a city that he calls *Albaugusta* (Ἀλβαυγούστα); neither this people nor a city of this name has been located, and while a confusion between two tribes is an obvious possibility there is no other evidence that our Alba ever acquired the title of *Augusta*.[6] Fortunately Pliny brings things into line by including *Alba Helvorum* in his list of Narbonensian *oppida Latina*.[7] This is confirmed by a number of inscriptions giving the voting tribe *Voltinia* and, while it is nowhere as yet called a *colonia Latina*, it had not only *quattuorviri* but also *flamines* and *seviri Augusti*. One of the *quattuorviri*, L. Valerius Optatus (whose name again reminds us of Flaccus), having served as a tribune in *Legio III Gallica*, was an *eques*, and another inscription, found not at *Alba* but at Rosières, some 30km to the sw, suggests that the great M. Iallius Bassus Fabius Valerianus, suffect consul in 158 or 160, may well have been of Helvian origin.[8]

Whether the Roman city was preceded by an important native settlement is uncertain—there may have been a hill-fort on the hill south of the river Escoutay now occupied by the modern village, though no finds are recorded there, and excavations on the Roman site itself have produced only a little Iron Age pottery[9]—but the general plan of the city itself is now emerging, as shown on fig 20. The most notable monument so far is the theatre, where investigations began in 1936 and which is now suitably consolidated. It has been tentatively dated to the second century and is somewhat similar in size to that of Fréjus, and the most curious aspect of it is the way in which the stream (variously called the Ruisseau du Massacre or the Ruisseau de St Martin) has channelled out the space between the *orchestra* and the back of the *proscenium*.[10] The supposed *forum* is a little questionable: though it is suitably positioned, all the buildings related to it that have so far been uncovered appear to be shops and include nothing resembling a capitol or a temple, and in fact not a single temple has so far been identified in the city.[11] While only one set of baths has so far been excavated (at la Planchette), there are indications that others existed, and although its course has not been established there is good evidence for an aqueduct coming from a dam across the stream of le Vernet near St-Pons (some 4km to the nw), while lead pipes to distribute its water, some bearing inscriptions, have also been found.[12] The collection of buildings shown south-east of the theatre (and south of the modern N102) are houses, which have yielded good mosaics of the second–third centuries,[13] but another complex served by the aqueduct was that at St-Pierre. Here there was a large Severan building (partly now visible), with mosaics, an important inscription (discussed below) and a fountain, overlain by palaeo-Christian structures of the fifth–sixth centuries.[14] As it happens, *Alba* had been the seat of a bishop much earlier than this: a fairly reliable list, compiled by Thomas II (a tenth-century bishop of Viviers, to which the episcopate had been transferred between 517 and 535) survives, and while the dates of the first four on it are unknown the fifth, Melanius (or Melanus), attended the council of Nîmes in AD 394 or 396.[15]

Alba Helviorum (Alba, formerly Aps)

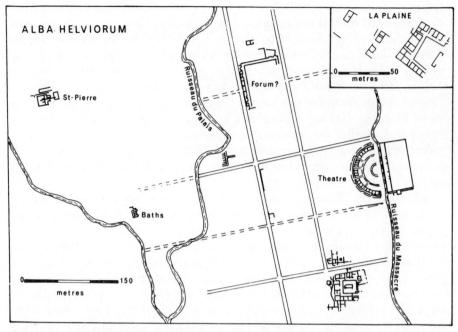

20 A tentative plan of Alba: inset, the villa of la Plaine (after A. Buissen)

The building at la Plaine (shown in the inset on fig 20) is a suburban villa some 800m NE of the theatre. Recently excavated, it was built in the first century on a site that had apparently been occupied in the Iron Age, was greatly modified in the early third century, remained in use until the end of the fourth century and has yielded fine mosaics.[16] This discovery, no less than the many gaps in the lay-out of the city itself (which is not built over), underlines how much remains to be discovered in this area.

Of the territory attributed to the city (fig 21) the western boundary was certainly the crest of the Cevennes, on the other side of which, in the province of *Aquitania*, were the *Gabali* and the *Vellavii*, but the others require some further consideration. To the east, while the Rhône provides the most obvious limit, some problems are raised by the fact that in a few areas, especially that near Viviers, 'cadastre B' of the centuriation of Orange appears to cross the river—a matter still more complicated by the most recent observations.[17] The southern boundary has often been identified with the course of the Ardèche, but a milestone of Antoninus Pius, found between Barjac and Vagnas, clearly gives the mileage (*mp xxxiii*) not from Nîmes but from Alba, so that it seems better to run the division between the *Helvii* and the *Nemausenses* along the ridge between the Ardèche and the Cèze.[18] In the north the neighbours were the *Segovellauni*, who in Roman times had become subject to the *colonia* of *Valentia*. The boundary of the medieval diocese of Valence seems to have been the valley of the Eyrieux, but this does not quite correspond with that of the territory ruled by the Carolingian counts, and once again a ridge, that between the Eyrieux and the Ouvèze, seems more likely.[19]

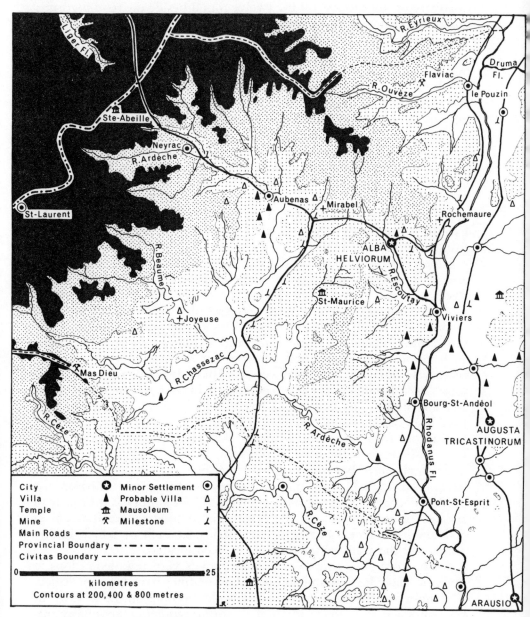

21 The Territory of *Alba Helviorum*

Alba Helviorum (Alba, formerly Aps)

Unfortunately no part of this territory is covered by any of the itineraries, which makes it difficult both to identify the most important roads or to apply names to the more important settlements, but so far as the roads are concerned some useful evidence is provided by the discovery of milestones. Of the twelve found beside the road that runs down the right bank of the Rhône no less than seven can be dated to AD 144–5 (the seventh *trib pot* of Antoninus Pius), while the remainder are all of later date, and this greatly weakens the idea, held by some, that this road, like that to the east of the river, was built by Agrippa.[20] Similarly, of the 13 stones related to the road running west out of *Alba* and then south through the middle of the territory towards Nîmes, all but one are certainly of the same Antonine date, while the only one so far discovered by the road running up the Ardèche and its tributary the Fontaulière to the Cevennes, and so presumably towards *Revessio* (St-Paulien, the capital of the *Vellavii*), is Constantinian.[21] All of this indicates that it was not until the middle of the second century that the *Helvii* began to bring their roads up to the standards that were normal in the Mediterranean area, and it may be then that the bridge over the Escoutay, just north of Viviers, the foundations of which are probably Roman (pl 22) was built.[22]

Other roads no doubt existed,[23] but it is on these routes that *mansiones* or towns are especially to be expected, and one turns first to Viviers, since this succeeded *Alba* as the chief city in the fifth century. Until recently only chance finds were recorded here—including, most surprisingly, some stamped tiles of *Legio VIII Augusta* reused in a late fifth-century cemetery[24]—but excavations near the cathedral in 1978–80 have now provided good evidence for occupation from the first century BC onwards and it may very well have developed as a river-port for *Alba*.[25] Bourg-St-Andéol has long yielded more buildings, finds and inscriptions (including one to Mithras) and its importance may have been due not only to the road but also to the fact that here there was an old ford across the Rhône.[26] The evidence for le Pouzin and Pont-St-Esprit, on the other hand, remains very slight, though there must surely have been *mansiones* in such places[27] *Mansiones* must also have been available on the inland roads, but even Aubenas has produced no real evidence and it is included here simply as the centre of an area so rich in villas.[28] Rather more convincing are the spas at St-Laurent-les-Bains and Neyrac-les-Bains, at each of which both a *piscina* and the walls of buildings have been located.[29]

Away from *Alba* and these possible towns very few dedications to divinities have been found and very few temples have been identified. The most convincing is that at Ste-Abeille, high up on the crest of the Cevennes and so perhaps a boundary shrine, while the possibility that the finds from St-Maurice-d'Ibie come from a temple of Mercury is based on the name of the site, Mercoyras,[30] Pagan epitaphs are much more common[31] and some mausolea are to be expected: of these the most notable is that most recently discovered, at Rochemaure, but two other probabilities are also included on the map, at Mirabel and Joyeuse.[32]

As may be seen, the villas so far discovered are most plentiful in the valley of the Rhône and in the fertile area around Aubenas. While the *Helvii* lived within the olive belt and so were able to produce their own oil as well as wheat, their most notable crop was the grape. Pliny records that just seven years before he was writing a vine had been discovered here whose flowers withered in one day and which was therefore unaffected by bad weather; it was called *carbunica* and was already being planted throughout the province.[33] And this is not the only evidence for the prosperity of Helvian viticulturists: an amphora found as far away as Vechten in the Netherlands bore the inscription *Helviorum* and a most notable *negotiator vinarius* of Lyon, M.Inthatius Vitalis, was honoured by membership of the *ordo splendidissimus civitatis Albensium*.[34]

Minerals seem to have been little exploited and only two probable lead mines can be included—one near Mas Dieu, where metal-working certainly did take place, and the other at Flaviac, where a miner's implement inscribed *Licinius* was found in an abandoned gallery.[35] Again, no pottery kilns or tile kilns have so far been discovered, but other industrial activities are proved by the inscription referred to above that was found on a stone re-used for a medieval sarcophagus at St-Pierre in *Alba*. This, probably of late second-century date, records the distribution of *sportulae* to *collegia* of *dendrophori, fabri, centonarii* and *utricularii*.[36] The first three of these (timber-merchants, builders and drapers) offer no surprise, but the recording of a *collegium* of boatmen at *Alba*, up the small and not easily navigable river of the Escoutay, raises a problem—one similar to that at Cimiez,[37] where *utricularii* appear to have operated up the little stream of the Paillon. Here the most likely explanation is that the *collegia* were spread throughout the *civitas* and that here, as at Soyons a little further north, in the territory of *Valentia*,[38] the reference is to men working on the Rhône, while there is some evidence for navigation (by others) on the lower reaches of the Ardèche.[39]

REFERENCES AND NOTES

1 *FOR* xv, no 3; on pre-Roman imports by the *Helvii* in general, Lauxerois 1983, 34–9.

2 Caesar, *BC* I, 35; on Jastres-Nord see Chapter 4 n 34.

3 Caesar, *BG* I, 19. I, 47, VII, 65; for a discussion of these names, including the vexed question of whether Procillus and Troucillus were the same man, Ellis Evans 1967, 84–5, 380–2, and Lauxerois 1983, 70–6.

4 Caesar, *BG* VII, 7–8; on various suggestions for the route, with full references, Lauxerois 1983, 76–8.
5 Strabo IV, 2, 2.
6 Ptolemy, *Geog* II, 10, 8; for useful discussions of this, with references, Barruol 1969, 272, Lauxerois 1983, 81–2.
7 Pliny, *HN* III, 36.
8 *CIL* XII 2674–6, the last of which records L.Valerius Optatus. Other Helvians who served in the imperial army were T.Carisius and P.Clodius, both in *Legio I Germanica* (*CIL* XIII, 8055–6, both from Bonn), and C Lucretius Suadullus in *Legio XIIII Gemina* and D.Marius Vegetus in *Legio X Gemina* (*AE* 1929, 198 and 190, both from Carnuntum). Iallius Bassus (also recorded in Rome, *CIL* VI, 1119b, and in Dio LXXI, 3, 1) had a very distinguished career, including the command of *Legio XIII Gemina Martia Victrix*, the governorship of Pannonia Inferior, Mysia Inferior and Pannonia Superior and was a *comes Augustorum* in the Parthian expedition of 162–4; on the Rosières inscription (*CIL* XII, 2718) see especially the restorations in *Gallia* XVIII(1960), 375–6 and XXXIII(1975), 241–4 and Lauxerois 1983, 146–7. For inscriptions in general, R.Lauxerois, 'Inscriptions d'Alba', *RAN* VII(1974), 159–78, and Lauxerois 1983, 239–97.
9 R.Lauxerois and M.Vichy, 'A propos les origines d'Alba Helvetiorum', *Gallia* XXXIII(1975), 49–60.
10 Grenier 1958, 830–1; *FOR* XV, no 38, I, 2; *Gallia* VI(1948), 216–18, XII(1954), 452–3, XXIV(1966), 522–3, XXIX(1971), 439–41, XXXI(1973), 537–9, XXXIII(1975), 531; Lauxerois 1983, 146–7.
11 *FOR* XV, no 38, I, 1; *Gallia* VI(1948), 216–18, XXVI(1968), 596–9, XXIX(1971), 439–41, XXXVIII(1980), 507; M.Leglay and S.Tourrenc, 'Le forum d'Alba Augusta Helviorum', *Ogam* CIII(1969), 346–59; Lauxerois 1983, 141–5; for the question of its identity, J.Lasfargues in *A Rh A* 1983–4, 18. On the absence of temples (and the improbability of the 'temple of Jupiter'), *FOR* XV, no 38, I, 5–7, Lauxerois 1983, 163–4.
12 *FOR* XV, no 38, I, 3–4; *Gallia* XXVI(1968), 596; M.Leglay and S.Tourrenc, 'Un curieux ouvrage hydraulique d'Alba Augusta Helviorum', *Hommages à Fernand Benoit* IV, 131–41 (Bordighera, 1972); Lauxerois 1983, 147–50.
13 *FOR* XV, no 38, II; *Gallia* XXVI(1968), 598, XXIX(1971), 440; Lauxerois 1983, 150–1 and, for a summary account of all mosaics from Alba, 152–7 with plates 3–5.
14 *FOR* XV, no 38, II, 12; *Gallia* XXVI(1968), 597, XXIX(1973), 441, XXXI(1973), 540, XXXIII(1975), 532, XXXV(1977), 473; Lauxerois 1983, 147.
15 For Melanius at Council of Nîmes, *Corpus Christianorum, Series Latina* CXLVIII, 49–51; for a full discussion of the list, Lauxerois 1983, 224–34, and compare his long discussions of the alleged destruction of *Alba* by Crocus (190–204) and of the largely mythical history of St Andeolus (205–21).
16 *Gallia* XL(1982), 393–5, XLIII(1985), 538–9; J.-C.Beal, *A Rh-A* 1983–4, 19–21. The excavation was prompted by the uprooting of part of a vineyard and in 1983 the mosaics were being restored at St-Romain-en-Gal.
17 Piganiol 1962, pl XL; Lauxerois 1983, 49–56; for more recent observations, F.Chouquer, 'Localisation et extension géographique des cadastres affichés à Orange', Clavel–Lévêque 1984, 275–97.
18 *CIL* XII, 5583; König no 164; cf Lauxerois 1983, 56–8, with some variations.

19 Lauxerois 1983, 59–60, bringing the boundary to the Rhône opposite the mouth of the Drôme; for a variation, *FOR* xv, fig 1 on p 33.

20 *CIL* xii, 5564–72, *ILGN* 653, König nos 137–50. Some of them, of course, were found in groups or cannot be precisely located, so that not all are marked on the map.

21 For the road towards Nîmes, *CIL* xii, 5573–83, *ILGN* 652, König nos 151, 153–64; the milestone of Pont-de-Labaume, by the Ardèche, *CIL* xii, 5584, König no 152 (which he attributes to the other road.)

22 For discussions of other likely roads, *FOR* xv, pp 25–31, Lauxerois 1983, 117–24.

23 *FOR* xv, no 35; tiles, *CIL* xii, 5679. It is, perhaps, just possible that a veteran brought them home with him after service in the legion at Mirebeau or Mainz.

24 *Gallia* xxiv(1966), 80.

25 Lauxerois 1983, 101, 112–15 (citing Y Esquieu, 'Notes préliminaires sur les fouilles archéologiques de Viviers', *Révue de Vivarais* 1981, 50–6); *Gallia* xl(1982), 396.

26 Mithras inscription, *CIL* xii, 2706; *FOR* xv, no 4; Lauxerois 1983, 51, 112–13 (with a useful plan), followed by a dismissal of the idea that this was *Bergoiate*, 115–17.

27 Le Pouzin, *FOR* xv, no 79, Lauxerois 1983, 112–13; for bridge, *Gallia* xxiv(1966), 86. Pont-St-Esprit, *FOR* viii, no 239, with one inscription (*CIL* xii, 2723).

28 *FOR* xv, no 59 mainly lists the villas in the commune and Lauxerois 1983 offers no evidence.

29 St-Laurent, *FOR* xv, no 68, Lauxerois 1983, 94; Neyrac, *FOR* xv, no 67, Lauxerois 1983, 94.

30 Ste-Abeille (near le Roux), *FOR* xv, no 70, Lauxerois 1983, 162; St-Maurice-d'Ibie, *FOR* xv, no 42, Lauxerois 1983, 160 n6.

31 Lauxerois 1983, 268–89, listing 46 (including Alba and the towns).

32 Rochemaure, found 1982, P.Porte, *A Rh-A* 1983–4, 24–5; Mirabel (at Costerande), *FOR* xv, no 48, *Gallia* xxxi(1973), 540, Burnand 1975, 121; Joyeuse, Burnand 1975, 121, Lauxerois 1983, 179.

33 Pliny, *HN* xiv, 43.

34 Vechten amphora, *CIL* xiii, 1004.8; inscription of statue of Inthatius at Lyon, *CIL* xiii, 1954, *FOR* xv, p 22, Lauxerois 1983, 95–7.

35 Mas Dieu (near Gravières), *FOR* xv, no 25; Flaviac, *ibid*, no 81. For general discussions, *FOR* xv, p 21, Lauxerois 1983, 93.

36 *AE* 1965, 144, *FOR* xv, p 21, Lauxerois 1983, 97–101, 249–50.

37 No 66 in Laguerre 197.

38 *CIL* xii, 3316.

39 *CIL* xii, 3316 (from Nîmes) and 4107 (from St-Gilles) for sailors on the river ATR . . ., taken to be the Ardèche; Y.Burnand, 'Un aspect de la géographie des transports dans la Narbonnaise: les nautes d'Ardèche et de l'Ouvèze', *RAN* iv(1971), 149–58.

14

Arelate (Arles), with *Glanum* (St-Rémy), *Olbia* (Almanarre) etc

The name *Arelate* does not appear in any surviving literature until Caesar's *De Bello Civile* and Avienius tells us that in earlier times the place was called *Theline* and was inhabited by the Greeks.[1] The truth of this used to be questioned by various authors, while some suggested that *Theline* must have been simply Trinquetaille, across the river, but from 1941 onwards various finds of Greek pottery have been made in the main city and in 1976 the evidence was further improved by the discovery, beside the Boulevard des Lices, of a pre-Roman building, occupied from the sixth to the second century BC, with plenty of relevant material.[2] It is, therefore, evident that the Greeks did control the place and the Massaliotes must for this reason have been all the more pleased when Marius handed over his canal to them—and all the more distressed when Caesar chose Arles as the site on which to build the ships that he used against them.

The *colonia* is one of the two that Suetonius specifically states were founded for Caesar by Ti.Claudius Nero in 46 BC, and veterans of *Legio VI* were installed here. This is duly confirmed by the names given to it by Mela and Pliny[4] and its full title, *Colonia Iulia Paterna Sextanorum Arelate*, is shown by several of the 400-odd inscriptions found here,[5] which also show that its voting-tribe was *Teretina* and provide evidence for all the normal officials (except, curiously, any *quaestores*). They also reveal a number of organisations that underline its importance as a shipyard and a port—*Fabri Tignarii* (carpenters), *Fabri Navales* (ship-builders, along with an *Architectus Navalis*, a ship-designer), *Utricularii* (who used river-craft), and *Navicularii Marini* (sea-captains)—and, rather entertainingly, a man whose personal name was Q.Navicularius Victorinus.[6] Similarly, the numerous veterans who later settled here include not only men from seven different legions (among them one from Britain's *II Augusta* and two from her *XX Valeria Victrix*) but also officers from the *Classis Germanica* and the *Classis Britannica*, some of them with distinguished service throughout the empire[7]. More interesting still are the *eques* Pompeius Paullinus (certainly of native

Gaulish descent) who became a *praefectus annonae* in Rome, to whom Seneca, having married his sister, dedicated his *De Brevitate Vitae* and whose son became consul *c* AD 53 and governed Upper Germany in 58,[8] and, later, the family of Mettii, descended from one of the original colonists, who held many offices and also reached the consulship, and the great Greek-speaking eunuch Favorinus, certainly of Arlesian origin but spending most of his life in Rome and the east.[9] The growing importance of the city itself, however, especially under Constantine and in the early fifth century, is best dealt with in the historical chapters.

Known religious inscriptions from Arles are relatively few, but finds of statues and reliefs add a lot, and besides those normally to be expected the deities include Bona Dea, Isis, Mithras and, inevitably, Neptune.[10] Also, Christianity was introduced here at a relatively early date. Though the splendid Christian sarcophagi preserved in the museum belong to a much later period, it is not altogether unreasonable to accept the suggestion of Gregory of Tours that Trophimus was sent here as a bishop when the Emperor Decius was consul (250/1) and it was certainly at Arles that the first Christian Council in Gaul, ordered by Constantine, who had already spent much time here, was held in 314.[11]

Arles has many fine Roman monuments, but a number of questions still remain to be answered, especially concerning its city walls. The only parts of the earlier defences that can be seen (though even they are much overlaid by medieval additions) are on the east side, overlooking the deceptively deepened Boulevard Emile Combes. The studies of these, published by August Véran in 1876 and by Constans in 1921, were considerably improved by the paper of Mortimer Wheeler in 1926, which made it clear that the actual gate ('La Redoute'), the SE tower (Tour des Mourgues) and the adjoining short stretch of the southern wall were secondary additions to the original half-moon structure—conclusions that were readily accepted by Grenier in 1931 and Benoit in 1936.[12] What Wheeler was unable to check was precisely where the wall went when it turned towards the NW at the NE angle (his 'Tower G'). Véran had stated that a stretch of the early wall underlay the northern part of the amphitheatre, but Constans had argued that this was merely something to support the amphitheatre itself[13] and accordingly the plans published by Wheeler, Grenier and Benoit all showed a wall heading straight towards the convent of Ste-Claire and the garden of St-Julien, where portions of it (the one said to be certain, the other probable) had earlier been reported. Investigation in 1946 under the NE edge of the amphitheatre, however, revealed not only remains of a real wall but also the base of a tower resembling that of the Tour des Mourgues, and this indicates a direction from the north-east tower along a line some 8° south of that towards Ste-Claire.[14] While the surviving remains of the NE tower are purely medieval or later, the fact that it was precisely here that the Roman wall turned in a NW direction is amply proved not only by the short cut-off of the medieval wall but also by Roman remains noted in the Rue de la Roque,[15] and three possibilities therefore arise: first, that the Roman wall followed a sinuous line, second, that the walls recorded at Ste-Claire and St-Julien indicate a reconstruction when the amphitheatre was built, and third, that the Ste-Claire and St-Julien fragments represent not the early but the late wall. The first two of these seem highly improbable—there is little geographical reason for sinuosity and by the time the amphitheatre was built (see below) fresh walling was unlikely to be demanded—so the third is surely the most likely.[16]

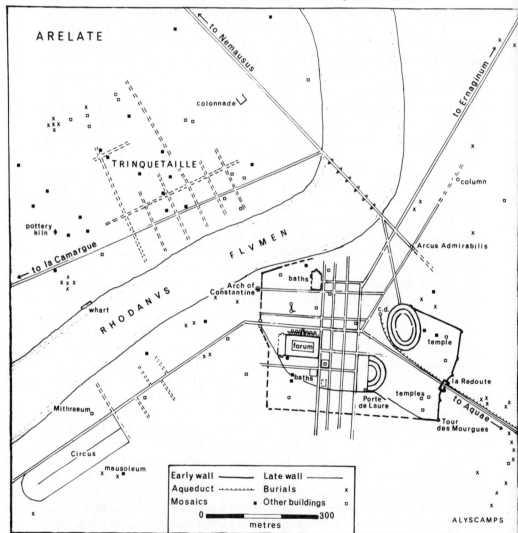

22 A tentative plan of Arles

Apart from the short stretch in the SE already referred to and some finds along the river,[17] very little more is known of the course of the early walls. They cannot have extended west of the so-called 'Arch of Constantine' which, despite its debatable name, was originally no later than Augustan in date and stood near the junction of the Rue de Dr Fanton and the Rue de l'Arc-Constantin, for this, like the Arcus Admirabilis which stood in the east of the Place Voltaire, seems to have marked the original *pomerium* of the city,[18] so on our tentative plan (fig 22) we have followed the approximate line shown by several authors,[19] bringing it together with the late wall at the western gate. Much more is recorded about this late wall, at least in the south and west and, besides the western gate, an early version of the Porte de Laure, between the Tour des Mourgues and the theatre, may have existed then too;[20] and, as suggested above, this late enciente may also have extended to St-Julien in the NE.

As for the precise dates of these walls, Wheeler's hypothesis regarding the earlier one, putting his 'Period II' (including the gate and the Tour des Mourgues) after the building of the theatre and amphitheatre, cannot now be accepted, but he was surely right in attributing the main building to the Augustan age and his Period II must now fall in that too: while some sort of defence may have been required in the early days of the *colonia*, they could have been just earthern ramparts and the structures that survive clearly reflect *dignitas* rather than mere defence and are typically Augustan. He was also surely right to correct the suggestion of Constans that the later walls dated from the eighth or ninth century: the fourth century, in truly Roman times, is much more probable.[21]

While the original course of streets in the eastern part of the city is largely a matter for conjecture, since the amphitheatre evidently covered some of them and the levelling of its site involved extensive excavation (pl 23), the pattern of the central area can be reconstructed with confidence both from various discoveries and from the modern street-plan.[22] The early forum[23] lay sw of the junction of the two streets that are reasonably taken to be the *cardo* and *decumanus* and the massive cryptoporticos underlying three sides of it, with their southern galleries lit by vents and the northern ones open to the *decumanus*, provided a level base: some Augustan monuments on it are attested by the discovery in 1950, at the east end of the northern cryptoportico, of a bust of Octavian, a marble buckler copying the golden shield set up in Rome's *Curia Iulia* in 27 BC and several fragments of inscriptions.[24] To the west of it are the remains of a large paved courtyard, bounded on the south by substantial remains of an *exedra* with a gate cut into it (preserved in the courtyard of the Museon Arleten) and with colonnades leading north that suggest the previous existence of a similar *exedra* at the other end, the whole probably the *peribolos* of a temple of Trajanic or Hadrianic date. North of the early forum additions were made to the cryptoportico in the Constantinian period, perhaps marking the southern limit of a new forum, and these were in turn cut into by a new monument (of which two columns and part of the architrave still survive in the Place du Forum, behind the statue of Frédéric Mistral, pl 24), the bronze inscription on which, now convincingly revised, indicates the time of Constantine II.[25] Whether this secondary forum extended to the southern limit of the Constantinian baths, the northern part of which are still impressively preserved, (pls 25, 26) seems questionable, since parts of Formigé's plan of the building, long accepted as correct, were proved wrong by excavations carried out in the early 1970s, nor is enough known about the tower and wall west of the presumed forum (in the Rue du Dr Fanton), though this too is evidently of fourth-century date.[26]

Whether or not the Constantinian baths replaced some earlier ones, others have long been known to have existed south of the original forum and these were presumably the original central baths of the city, but while hypocausts, mosaics and water pipes are duly recorded their plan cannot be reconstructed.[27] A basilica may have existed between them and the theatre,[28] but this too requires further investigation and so too do the supposed remains of a number of temples. The largest of these, traditionally called 'le Temple de Diane' and which may have been replaced by the earliest Christian cathedral, stood in the SE corner of the walled city (approximately on the site of the Asile St-Cesaire), where substantial remains, including walls, columns and fragments of marble statues, have been found,[29] while that of Bona Dea apparently stood in the area of the church of Nôtre-Dame-de-la-Major, just inside the north-east corner of the walls, where a marble altar dedicated to her was found in 1758.[30] The main evidence for the *mithraeum*, north of the circus (a headless statue of Kronos) was found still earlier, in 1598,[31] and that for the other supposed temples—of Mars and Isis, both across the river near the churches of St-Pierre and St-Genest-de-la-Colonne in Trinquetaille respectively—is too unconvincing for them to be included on our plan.[32]

The best-known upstanding monuments of Arles are, of course, the theatre and amphitheatre, but in fact a very substantial part of the theatre has had to be reconstructed. While it is based on a slope downwards from east to west, this was much too slight to provide a base for the *cavea* (as was possible, for example, at Orange and Vienne), so that a great deal is missing and the main contributor to Formigé's impressive restoration was the survival of structures at the south end, by the square Tour de Roland that was incorporated in the late city wall. In general, however, it bears a considerable resemblance to the theatre of Orange (overall diameter here 102m, at Orange 103m) and its approximate date is well indicated by the discovery in it of a statue of Augustus.[33] The massive remains of the amphitheatre—two stories of 60 arcades, to disregard the modern additions—owe their survival to the fact that it was used as a fortress in the middle ages, when four towers (three of which are still visible) were built on to it. It has a good deal in common with the amphitheatre of Nîmes (*qv*), including its size (Arles 136.2 X 106.75 m, Nîmes 133.38 X 104.4 m) and though the date of its construction is still debated the Flavian period is the most probable;[34] as noted above, it was certainly considerably later than the early city walls and, as may be seen from pl 23, apparently earlier than the laying out of the aqueduct (on which see below). Not at all upstanding is the circus. Its site, some 500m sw of the central city, was long indicated by an obelisk, which in 1675 was removed to the present Place de la Republique, where it still stands, and various parts of it were discovered from the eighteenth century onwards, especially when the Arles-Bouc canal was built in 1831, but much more has been investigated since then, especially in the 1970s.[35] An early date seems to be indicated by a Flavian inscription recording the gift of money by Annius Camars to finance *ludi athletarum aut circensium* but, as Grenier suggests, the first structure may well have been of timber and the more recent excavations indicate that the stone circus was built in the early second century.[36] In any case, it evidently remained in use at least until the middle of the fifth century: in his entertaining letter to Montius, Sidonius tells us that when he visited Arles in 461 (when the Emperor Majorian was also there) some *ludi circenses* took place.[37]

As with all other cities, burials were made beside the roads leading out of Arles, but an extensive cemetery also developed over a large area to the west of the main road to the SE and while numerous fine sargophagi have been removed from here to the museum, it must be borne in mind that the beautiful and moving Allée des Alyscamps is not itself a Roman road.[38] Further, at least two cemeteries existed on the other side of the river, one beside the main road towards Nîmes and the other to the west of Trinquetaille, which have yielded relatively early pagan as well as Christian epitaphs[39] and this reflects the early development of the suburb, to which we must now turn.

Though Arles is first called an *urbs duplex* by Ausonius,[40] Trinquetaille had clearly been a prosperous suburb of the city long before his time. It has yielded many mosaics as well as inscriptions (including one of an *architectus navalis* and one of the *utricularii*, already mentioned above) and it also included docks.[41] More recently, an impressive colonnade, built in the first century, modified in the second and abandoned in the fourth or fifth, has been excavated just west of the road running north from the bridge.[42] The reasons for the development of this area make an interesting comparison with that of St-Romain-en-Gal, opposite Vienne (*qv*): while the citizens of Vienne could hardly spread up the steep hills behind the main city, those of Arles were evidently encouraged to settle across the river by the marshiness of the land to the south. In any case, every possible step was taken to unite Trinquetaille with Arles. Not only were they linked by a pontoon bridge, recorded by Ausonius and pictured on the well-known mosaic in Ostia, the position of which is well established (pl 27),[43] but even the waters of the Arles aqueduct were pumped across by a syphon system under the river.[44]

A great deal is known about the distribution of water in the main city—the entry of the aqueduct under the early gate is exposed to view (pl 28), the *castellum divisorium* was identified in the seventeenth century,[45] and many pipes have been located [46]—but while the main routes of the aqueduct towards the city, though largely underground, have been traced,[47] the date of its installation remains questionable. The tunnel under the gate presents no problems (it could have been made at any time), but the deviation round the amphitheatre suggests a date no earlier than the Flavian period—unless, of course, the stone amphitheatre replaced a timber one or the original line of the aqueduct was more direct. Beyond this, it can hardly be believed that all the many sources of waters were drawn on at once, rather a progressive development must be envisaged, and the main question here is which was the earliest to be used. As may be seen from the map (fig 23), water was brought from both the north and the south of the chain of les Alpilles, 5–20 km NE of Arles, but while both the main courses were presumably expanded over the years, one of them does not reach the city but terminates at Barbégal. The true nature of the remarkable monument to be seen there (pl 29) was not understood until the careful investigation of it by Benoit in 1937–8 (after his compilation of *FOR* v), which proved it to be a huge flour mill, with 16 wheels driven by water, probably of Constantinian date.[48] While remains of the pair of aqueducts running parallel to each other just north of the mill can still be seen (as can the channel that here turns east towards Arles) it seems highly probable that this was a modification—in effect a cutting-off of what may well have been the earlier of the two.

After the foundation of the *colonia* a very large area (fig 26) became subject to Arles, not only to govern the *Salluvii* but also, more importantly, to take over much of their land that had previously been controlled by *Massalia*. This produced a situation that was not fully maintained in the post-Roman period, so that the earliest known boundaries of the Christian dioceses offer relatively little help towards its definition and other evidence has to be given priority.[49] That the city owned the whole of the Rhône delta—or so much of it as then existed—is beyond doubt, but problems begin with the northern frontier. That *Ernaginum* (St-Gabriel) and *Glanum* (nr St-Rémy) were within the territory is indicated by the course of the northern part of the Arles aqueduct, but Constans also included *Tarusco* (Tarascon). The basis of his argument, however, is merely the fact that Ptolemy attributes it to the *Salluvii* and since, as Barruol has convincingly suggested, the boundary between the Salluvian and the Cavaran federations must have run just near here it seems equally fair to follow

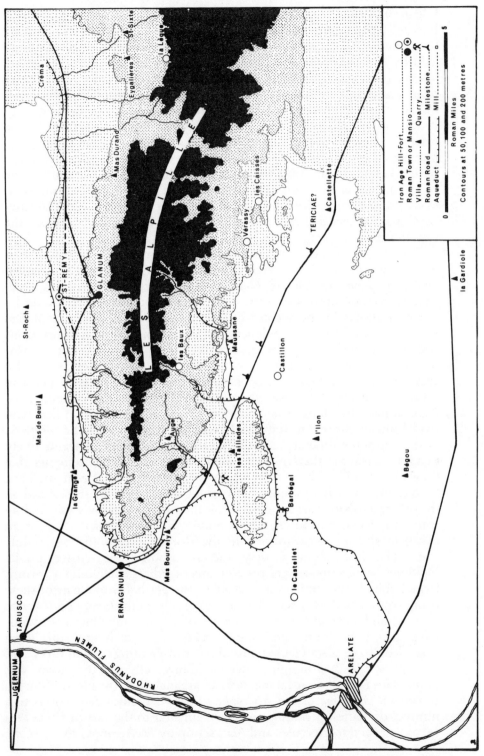

Arelate (Arles), with *Glanum* (St-Rémy) and *Olbia* (Almanarre)

23 The course of the aqueducts of *Arelate* and the location of the Barlegal flour mill

Jullian and include it under *Avennio* (Avignon, *qv*)[50] Similarly, Barruol's boundary, together with the mileage given on a milestone found near Orgon, suggests that a small area south of the Durance was held by *Cabellio* (Cavaillon, *qv*).[51] Further to the east a little evidence has been produced by the observation of some centuriation, apparently related to Arles, that takes in Pélissanne, and so probably the station of *Pisavis*,[52] but the boundary between *Arelate* and *Aquae Sextiae* is mostly defined by the discovery of a dozen inscribed boundary stones.[53] The extreme eastern frontier, facing the territory of *Forum Iulii* (Fréjus, *qv*), remains a little uncertain, but the course of the Réal Martin, a tributary of the Gapeau, seems most likely. Some indication of the amount of the coast taken over from *Massilia* is provided in the east by the indication in a letter of Pope Zosimus, dated 417, that *Citharista* and *Gargarius* were then subject to Arles and in the west by the division between the two dioceses.[54]

This extent of territory involved the control of several towns that had earlier been Greek, including, besides *Citharista* and *Glanum*, probably *Olbia* and *Taurois*. *Glanum*, at the north end of a gorge, had already been occupied for a very long time before it was taken over by the Massaliotes in the second century BC and even after that it had retained some degree of independence—minting its own silver coins and preserving an interesting native shrine (pl 30)—but it was thoroughly Romanised in the Augustan period and remained so until it was rendered uninhabitable perhaps by one of the bands of German invaders *c* AD 270. This disaster had two effects: on the one hand, while *Glanum* itself had long been an important stopping-place on the main road from the Rhône to Italy (duly recorded on the Vicarello Goblets, in the Antonine Itinerary and on the Peutinger Table), it seems likely that the *mansio* was then re-established in the village of St-Rémy itself, a little over 1km north of the early town, where several remains have been found and where some late Roman baths can still be seen;[55] and on the other, its abandonment meant that the town was slowly covered by alluvium that came down the adjoining hillsides, which made it an excellent site for excavation.[56] In the Roman period (fig 24), while some Hellenistic houses were merely modified, extensive public buildings were imposed on the remains of others, including a forum, large public baths, and several temples (the peribolus of a pair of these being constructed over what had apparently been the Greek *bouleuterion* – pl 31) and a possible theatre. Traces of a small aqueduct and drains have also been found and the excavations, which are still being extended, have also yielded mosaics, wall-paintings, sculptures and inscriptions; and although, since, as Pliny tells us, the town was granted *ius Latii*,[57] no local magistrates are included, the inscriptions do record the *collegium* of the *dendrophori Glanici*, besides dedications to a number of deities, including the beautiful altar to the ears of Bona Dea (pl 32), several to Hercules and one, set up by M. Agrippa, to *Valetudo*,

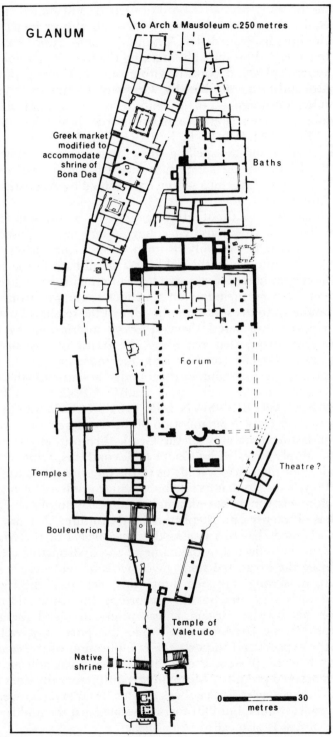

GLANUM

to Arch & Mausoleum c.250 metres

Greek market modified to accommodate shrine of Bona Dea

Baths

Forum

Temples

Theatre?

Bouleuterion

Temple of Valetudo

Native shrine

0 ▬▬▬▬ 30
metres

24 A partial plan of *Glanum* in Roman times (mainly after Rolland) while among the sculptures are a head of Octavia and another possibly of Julia.[58] Still more remarkable is the survival, almost intact, of the two fine monuments (called 'les Antiques') some 250m NW of the excavated remains and presumably marking the town's *pomerium*. One of them, the arch (pl 33), decorated with groups of Gallic prisoners, is dated by Rolland *c* 20 BC but by Gros to AD 10–20,[59] and the other—whether a cenotaph, a mausoleum or merely a memorial—also well-decorated and enclosing two male figures, bears the enigmatic inscription SEX L M IVLIEI C F PARENTIBVS SVEIS (pl 34); though the lettering and the spelling shows that it is early, this cannot be accurately dated, but the suggestion that it is a memorial to Caius and Lucius, the sons of Agrippa who were adopted by Augustus, is not altogether impossible.

Olbia (Almanarre, south of Hyères) presents a different picture. While the extensive excavations by Jacques Coupry have exposed much of the Greek town,[61] the only Roman monument visible in the impressive area now open to the public is a small bath-house cut into the earlier Greek buildings. Extensive Roman remains have, however, been noted in the past, including an aqueduct coming in from the NE and many buildings to the south, on the edge of the seashore, making it clear that a port stood here.[62] Several Greek inscriptions have been found, but apart from that recording the death of a man whose voting-tribe was *Teretina* (so Arlesian), the most interesting one in Latin, discovered in 1909 and written under a statuette (the top of which is unfortunately cut off) reads: GENIO VICINIAE/ CASTELLANAE OL/BIENSIVN L RVPILVS/IACCVS D D C S.[63] This not only reflects the Romanisation of the Greek residents, but also indicates the lasting notability of the Greek fortifications stressed by Strabo[64] and amply revealed by Coupry. Beyond this, while confirming the identity of the place, it leads us to the question of its full name. It is not in Pliny's list (so that its inhabitants may not have been granted *ius Latii* before his time), but although it appears simply as *Olbia* in Strabo, Mela, Ptolemy and Stephanus of Byzantium,[65] it has sometimes been claimed that this is also the *Pomponiana* of the Maritime Itinerary (a theory reflected in the name of the hydropathic establishment adjoining the excavated site). Two pieces of evidence, however, show this to be wrong. For one thing, this section of the Itinerary, evidently of early date and possibly recording the route laid out for Claudius on his way to Britain,[66] was surely designed for a rapid journey from Rome to Arles and while the port may well have flourished for exports and imports the complication of the coast here (especially when the present Presqu'Ile de Giens was still an island) would have delayed progress. More importantly, not only does Strabo tell us that the *Stoechades Insulae* (basically les Iles d'Hyères) were well equipped with harbours, but Pliny actually states that the middle one of the three largest was also called *Pomponiana*.[67]

Moving west along the coast from *Olbia* we come next to *Telo Martius*, certainly Toulon. This appears to have been a purely Roman foundation—at least, it is not mentioned by any Greek author nor, by Latin writers, in a Greek context—but it is already a port, not merely a *positio*, in the Maritime Itinerary and the adjective *Martius* might possibly reflect its use in Caesar's war.[68] Since Toulon has been an important French naval base since the time of Henri IV in the seventeenth century, archaeological research here has been limited, especially on the coast, but several finds have been made over the years, including a number of burial inscriptions that underline the prosperity of the place, while the *Notitia Dignitatum* records a *procurator bafii Telonensis*, indicating the existence of an important official dye-works.[69] Above all, rescue excavations in the 1970s, especially on the north-west of the medieval Vieille Ville, have made some important additions to our knowledge. This particular area, evidently near the edge of the Roman town, was occupied from the first to the fifth century, after which it became the site of a Christian cemetery.[70] The early Christian history of Toulon, however, is a little obscure. A bishop called Augustalis attended the Councils of Orange and Vaison in 441 and 442, but since in both cases his origin, unlike that of the others, is deliberately specified as *loco Telonensi* it is widely believed that Toulon was not his true seat; yet in the sixth century, from 529 onwards, men who clearly were bishops of Toulon did attend other Councils.[71]

Then at some *xii mp* from Toulon is *Taurois* (or *Tauroentum* or *Tauroentium*—different forms appear in different authors).[72] This was for long generally taken to be at la Madrague-de-St-Cyr (where, as at Almanarre, the ancient name is applied to some modern establishments), but the extensive Roman remains still visible at this place (fig 25) are clearly those of a luxurious coastal villa, lasting, as has now been shown, from the first to the third century,[73] and the identification of *Taurois* with le Brusc (first suggested by Vidal in 1895) is now generally accepted. The little harbour here, sheltered by les Iles des Embiez, would clearly have been more suitable for use by the Massaliotes in their sea-battles with Caesar's fleet and not only have a number of Hellenistic houses been uncovered, along with appropriate Greek pottery and Massaliote coins, but also some Roman remains, including traces of an underground aqueduct.[74]

After *Tauroentum* the Maritime Itinerary lists first *Carsicis* and then *Citarista*, but there is little doubt that some scribe (an early one, since the order is the same in both families of the text) idly transcribed the two names. *Carsicis* is certainly Cassis (here dealt with in the section on Marseille, *qv*) and *Citharista* (to turn to Pliny's spelling) was surely la Ciotat.[75] This modern name, however, reflects merely 'the *civitas* (city)' and the title *Citharista* was evidently transferred some 5km inland to a safer place, the modern Ceyreste, probably because of Saracen raids

Arelate (Arles), with *Glanum* (St-Rémy) and *Olbia* (Almanarre)
on this coast in the early middle ages. Relatively little research has been
carried out at la Ciotat, but a few finds, both Greek and Roman, have
been recorded.[76]

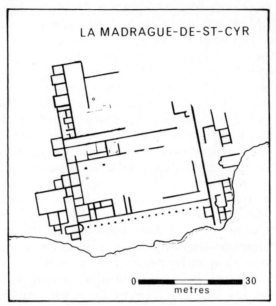

25 The villa of les Baumelles, la Madrague-de-St-Cyr (after Duprat)

To pass over the section of coast retained by Marseille, we come to
Incarus (or *Incarum*) which was presumably Carry since, besides the
evidence of its modern name, it is also just above the *xii mp* from
Massilia recorded in the Itinerary. A lead anchor, apparently Greek, has
been found here and several Roman remains are recorded in the
vicinity.[77] The next place, *Dilis*, is listed as *viii mp* from *Incarus* and *xii
mp* from *Fossae Marianae* (certainly Fos), but while this indicates
somewhere near Cap Couronne (where, confusingly, there is also a
modern village called Carro), recent discoveries at Sénèmes (near
Lauron) seem to confirm the suggestion, first made by the Abbé Papon
in the eighteenth century, that the Itinerary figures should be reversed
and that *Dilis* stood here. Walls near the shore had already been noted in
the nineteenth century and parts of an aqueduct and extensive buildings
were uncovered in the 1950s and 1960s; these were constructed in the
first century, badly damaged, probably by fire, in the third and restored
in the fourth.[78]

Maritima was evidently Martigues. While Ptolemy calls it a *colonia* (an
error repeated in the Ravenna Cosmography), both Mela and Pliny
make it clear that it was merely an *oppidum Avaticorum*, the town of a
tribe, and the latter clarifies its position and omits it from his list of
oppida Latina.[79] A number of finds are recorded here, reflecting its

Romanisation, but the extent of the settlement still requires clarification.[80] *Fossae Marianae* (Fos) was, as its name implies, at the mouth of the canal built by Marius (which is generally believed to be represented, at least in part, by le Bras Mort)[81] but it has suffered in two ways. As Strabo tells us, the shore was so low-lying that when the Massaliotes took over the canal they had to set up towers as beacons (and also built there a temple of Artemis)[82] and when it passed out of use in post-Roman times it was largely submerged; and secondly, the whole area is now covered by the enormous modern port. Nevertheless, several notable finds have been made over the years[83] and the great importance of the place is shown by the fact that on the Peutinger Table it is given a special port symbol—something that is shared only by *Ostia* at the mouth of the Tiber.

Fossae Marianae was linked with *Arelate* not only by the canal and the river, but also by road, and so appears in the land section as well as the maritime section of the Antonine Itinerary.[84] Of the other places on the main roads by far the most notable is *Ernaginum* (St-Gabriel), which, as may be seen from the maps (figs 23, 26), stood at an important road junction. Inevitably, therefore, it appears in all the itineraries,[85] but what is more surprising is the discovery here of the funerary inscription of a man who was not merely a *sevir* of *Aquae Sextiae* and a *navicularius* of *Arelate* but also the patron of the *nautae Druenticae* and of a *corporatio utriclariorum Ernaginensium*. It therefore seems evident that, while the marshy area between la Montaguette and the Petite Crau is now traversed only by small canals, a usable stream did once flow past here to the Rhône (though hardly a branch of the Durance, as has sometimes been suggested).[86] Several remains of the settlement have been found, including some buildings with mosaics, marble columns, an oil press, epitaphs and statues of Dionysus and Cybele.[87]

Much less is known about the places named on the important road running south-east from here. *Tericiae*, which appears only on the Peutinger Table, at *xi mp* from Ernaginum and *xv mp* from *Pisavis*, must have been somewhere near Mouriès but has not been convincingly located[88] and the problem is further complicated by the fact that it is uncertain whether *Pisavis* (also only on the Peutinger Table, at *xviii mp* from *Aquae Sextiae*) was on the left or the right bank of the river Touloubre. As we have already noted above, the evidence of centuriation indicated that it was probably within the territory of Arles and enough has been found, including burials and sculptures, to site it at or near St-Jean-de-Brenasse, though the notable mausoleum was more probably in the territory of Aix.[89]

Following this road eastwards we come, beyond Aix, to another settlement, *Tegulata*, which, although it appears not only on the Peutinger Table but also in the Antonine Itinerary, poses a similar problem. The reason for this is the discovery at Grande-Pugère of one of the boundary-stones referred to above. *Tegulata* itself is usually taken

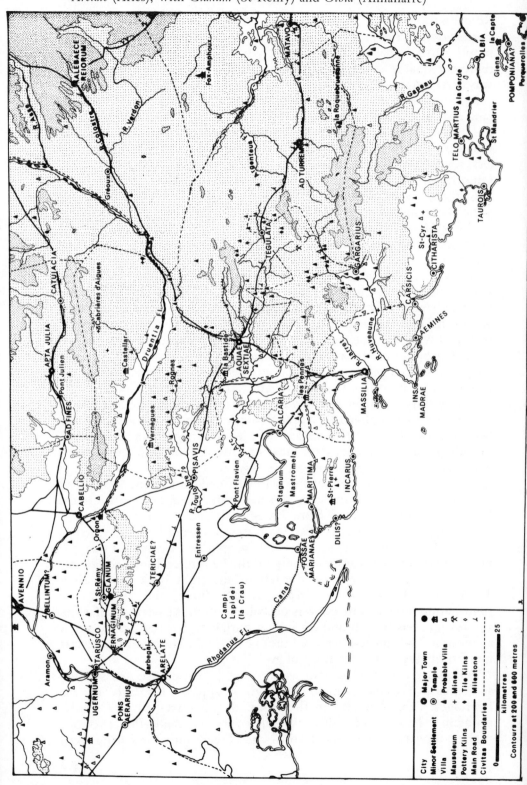

26 The territories of *Arelate, Aquae Sextiae* and *Massilia*

to be at Petite-Pugère, just across the modern boundary between Bouches-du-Rhône and Var, and may well have been administered from Arles, but this also raises the question which *civitas* could claim the most notable monument found in this area, a large mausoleum that was once called the 'arc de Marius'[90]

The more southerly road running from Arles towards Marseille (with a branch to Fos) is especially notable for two things. First, it is likely to have been the only road in the province that has so far yielded a fifth-century milestone[91] and secondly, it crossed the river Touloubre over a very fine bridge. This, the Pont Flavien (pl 35), was restored by Chastel in 1763, but its appearance is largely convincing and besides the lions that sit on top of them both arches retain inscriptions which state that it was built under the instructions of the will of L.Donnius Flavos, a *flamen Romae et Augusti*.[92] Less clear are the settlements along this route. Entressen does not appear in any of the itineraries, but while discoveries here of walls, mosaics, burials and coins may possibly point to a villa, the fact that its medieval name was Transens, along with the absence of any other good evidence for a stopping-place in this area, suggests that it was probably a *mutatio*.[93] The name of *Calcaria*, on the other hand, appears both in the Antonine Itinerary and on the Peutinger Table, but while both put it at *xxxiii mp* from Fos, one puts it at *xiii* and the other at *xxx mp* from Marseille. On our map it is provisionally identified with Vitrolles, where the finds have been increased since the war by the discovery of a Roman factory for treating fish.[94]

One other *vicus* that demands attention is *Gargarius* (St-Jean-de-Gargier). As we have already noticed (p 198 above), this was certainly within the diocese of Arles in the time of Pope Zosimus, but beyond this a large inscription was found here set up by *pagani pagi Lucreti qui sunt finibus Arelatensium* in honour of Q.Cornelius Zosimus, a freedman of Marcellus and a *sevir* of Arles, who had obtained benefits for them from the emperor Antoninus Pius, including, it seems, some baths. Baths have indeed been found near the local church and so have the remains of an aqueduct coming from the SE. Other inscriptions have also been discovered, along with some mosaics and sculptures, and it seems that the place was quite prosperous.[95]

Indeed prosperity is evident in the territory of Arles as a whole, except, of course, in such barren areas as la Crau (*Campi Lapidei*). As may be seen from the map (fig 26), many villas have been identified, including even a few in la Camargue, though not, as is sometimes stated, so far south as Stes-Maries-de-la-Mer.[96] The only one that is usually open to public inspection is that already mentioned at la Madrague-de-St-Cyr (p 201 above), but attention should also be given to some like that recently excavated at St-Michel-à-la-Garde, just outside Toulon. This lasted from the first to the late third century, with some reoccupation in the fourth and fifth, and demonstrated the widespread concentration on the production of olive oil.[97] Besides

Arelate (Arles), with *Glanum* (St-Rémy) and *Olbia* (Almanarre)

wheat, wine and oil, good treatment of fish is also evidenced, not only at Vitrolles but also at such places as Châteauneuf-les-Martigues (on the south side of the Etang de Berre, some 8km east of Martigues itself)[98] and the area is thus typical of the *Provincia* as a whole.

REFERENCES AND NOTES

1 Caesar, *BC* I, 36, II, 5; Avienius, *Ora Maritima* 689–91.
2 *Gallia* VIII(1950), 122, XII(1954), 430, XVIII(1960), 303–05, XXXV(1977), 515.
3 Suetonius, *Tiberius* iv, 1.
4 Mela II, 5, 75, Pliny, *HN* III, 36.
5 *CIL* XII, 654–977, 5490–4, 5804–24; *ILGN* 103–42, 659–60, plus a number that have been found since 1928, recorded in *FOR* v(1936), no 448–9 and *AE passim*.
6 *CIL* XII, 692, 697, 723, 726, 728–31, 733, 738, 5811; *ILGN*, 108, 116. The man, *CIL*, 853.
7 The seven legions are I, II, III, XII, XX, XXII and XXX—no record of VI. The veteran of II is M. Aurelius Difilus (*CIL* XII, 677, no rank given) and those of XX are a *signifer* called Aurelius Valetinus (*sic*, *CIL*, 678) and T.Carsius Curtinus (*CIL*, 678, no rank); the veteran of *Classis Britannica* is . . . ntius Saturninus (*CIL*, 686), who was of African origin.
8 Pliny, *HN* XXXIII, 143 (describing the son as *Arelatis equitis Romani filius paternaque gente pellitum*); Seneca, *De Brevitate Vitae*, 1, 18–19; Tacitus, *Ann* XIII, 53; Syme 1958, 591, 603, 620, 786.
9 *CIL* XII, 671, etc: discussion, with all refs, H-G.Pflaum, 'Une famille arlésienne de la fin du I^{er}siècle et du IIe siècle de notre ère', *Bull de la Soc Nat des Antiquaires de France* 1970, 265–72 (reprinted in Pflaum 1981, 4–11); on Favorinus, W.Schmid, *P-W* VI, 2078–83.
10 For a general survey, Constans 1921, 111–33.
11 Gregory, *Historia Francorum* I, 30; Munier 1963, 9–25; Constans 1921, 105–10. For a review of the sarcophagi, F.Benoit, *Sarcophages paléochrétiens d'Arles et de Marseille, Gallia* Suppl v, 1951.
12 A.Véran, *Congrès archéologique de France* XLIII(1876), 267–97; Constans 1921, 217–29; Wheeler, *JRS* XVI(1926), 174–93; Grenier 1931, 289–95 (with reprint of Wheeler's plan), 1934, 496 (with partial reprint of Véran's plan); Benoit, *FOR* v (1936), 127–8 and plan supplied with map. For more on the Tour des Mourgues, *Gallia* II(1943), 279.
13 Véran, *op cit*, 271; Constans 1921, 224, 309.
14 *Gallia* VI(1948), 209–12; Grenier 1958, 632. Regrettably, this is not shown on the accompanying plan of Arles—fig 36, opposite p 158 of Part I of the same volume—which is in any case not exactly, as it claims, a copy of Benoit's plan from *FOR* v and has a very wrong scale. The 8° change here stated does not appear necessary on the plan included in Constans 1921 (planche XVI, opposite p 274) and is derived from the surely more accurate plan of Benoit, as confirmed by the modern Plan Guide Blay.
15 Constans 1921, 224; *FOR* v, p 127.

16 This appears to be accepted in the plan included in F.Benoit, *Arles*, in the excellent little pocket-book series *La France Illustrée*, Editions Alpina, 1954.

17 *FOR* v, p 128; *Gallia* XVIII(1960), 305.

18 Constans 1921, 229–48; *FOR* v, pp 130–2 (with many sub-references); Grenier 1958, 165–9. R.Amy in Princeton 1976, 87, calls both these arches late Republican, but 'Octavianic' seems probable. The name of the 'Arch of Constantine' is 'debatable' because it had an inscription added in the late Empire (*CIL* XII, 667) which might imply Constantine, either of the Constans, or simply *Constantina*, the title which the *colonia* briefly bore.

19 Eg Véran (reproduced in Grenier 1934, 496), Benoit in *Arles* 1954 (*v* n 15 above) and P.Broise (Plan I, 2, in Chevallier 1982).

20 *FOR* v, p 128, but on the Porte de Laure see also Constans 1921, 227 n 1, suggesting that it was wholly medieval. *Gallia* II(1943) also reveals a blocked postern near the Tour des Mourgues.

21 Constans 1921, 225–6; Wheeler, *op cit*, 187–91.

22 Grenier 1958, 158–68.

23 For a detailed discussion of this, with many sub-references, Grenier 1958, 291–308, 321–2, and, more recently, R.Amy, 'Les cryptoportiques d'Arles', *Actes du Colloque de Rome* 1973.

24 Grenier 1958, 301–04; inscriptions, *AE* 1952, 165–7.

25 Grenier 1958, 297–300; inscription, *CIL* XII, 668 improved by *AE* 1952, 37.

26 *FOR* v, p 141 (no 120 on Benoit's plan); Grenier 1960, 256–63, including photos and Formigé's plan; later excavations, *Gallia* XXX(1972), 514–16, XXXII(1974), 579–81, with revised plan. The tile inscription *CIL* XII, 5701.9 suggests that these baths replaced some earlier ones, but no details are known. For the separate tower, *FOR* v, p 142 (no 125 on Benoit's plan).

27 *FOR* v, p 141, called 'Grands Thermes' (no 99 on Benoit's plan); Grenier 1960, 255–6.

28 *FOR* v, p 132 (no 98 on Benoit's plan); Grenier 1958, 515–17.

29 Constans 1921, 346–50; *FOR* v, pp 137, 148 (nos 53–6 on Benoit's plan). For early Christian churches, *FOR* v, 142–3.

30 Constans 1921, 128–30, 350–1; *FOR* v, pp 138, 145, 148 (no 67 on Benoit's plan); altar, *CIL*, XII, 654.

31 Constans 1921, 123; F.Cumont, *Textes et monuments figurés relatifs aux mystères de Mithra* II, 1899, 403, no 281; Espérandieu 1907, 142; *FOR* v, pp 137–8 (no 157 on Benoit's plan); Grenier 1958, 986.

32 Constans 1921, 351; *FOR* v, pp 138, 183–4 (nos 21 and 56 on Benoit's plan).

33 J.Formigé, 'Remarques diverses sur les théâtres romains à propos de ceux d'Arles et d'Orange', *Mems présentés par divers savants à l'Academie des Inscriptions et Belles-Lettres* XIII(1914), 25–89; Constans 1921, 278–9; *FOR* v, pp 132–5; Grenier 1958, 742–53. Different parts of the statue of Augustus were found from 1750 to 1834; the well-known statue of Venus had been found here in 1651.

34 Constans 1921, 298–324; *FOR* v, pp 135–6; Grenier 1958, 613–39.

35 Constans 1921, 325–31; *FOR* v, pp 136–7; Grenier 1958, 983–7; *Gallia* XXX(1972), 515–17, XXXII(1974), 507, XXXV(1977), 513–15.

36 *CIL* XII, 670; Grenier 1958, 985, *Gallia* XXXV(1977), 515.

37 Sidonius Apollinaris, *Epp* I, xi, 10. Curiously, Stevens 1933, 52, describes the *ludi* as 'games at the amphitheatre', but this is surely wrong.

Arelate (Arles), with *Glanum* (St-Rémy) and *Olbia* (Almanarre)

38 *FOR* v, pp 156–69; Benoit 1954, *passim*.

39 *FOR* v, pp 184–9; Benoit, *op cit*.

40 Ausonius, *Ordo Urbium Nobilium* x:

> *Pande, duplex Arelate, tuos blanda hospita portus,*
> *Gallula Roma Arelas, quam Narbo Martius et quam*
> *Accolit Alpinis opulenta Vienna colonis,*
> *Praecipitis Rhodani sic intercisa fluentis,*
> *Ut mediam facias navali ponte plateam . . .*
> *cf Mosella*, 480–1.

41 *FOR* v, pp 173–84.

42 *Gallia* XXVII(1969), 419–21, XXX(1972), 514–15, XXXII(1974), 505–07, XXXV(1977), 513.

43 Ausonius, *op cit* (n 40 above). Ostia mosaic reproduced in Grenier 1934, 497 and (better) in Chevallier 1975, pl XXVI.

44 Constans 1921, 400; *FOR* v, p 145; Grenier 1960, 84–5.

45 Constans 1921, 394–5; *FOR* v, p 145; Grenier 1958, 160.

46 Constans 1921, 401–04; *FOR* v, pp 144–6; Grenier 1960, 85–8.

47 Constans 1921, 383–99; *FOR* v, p 144 and Plan B opposite p 192, with references to entries; Grenier 1960, 75–85.

48 Benoit, 'L'usine de Barbégal', *RA* 1940, 42–80, summarised in Grenier 1960, 79–82; for earlier odd interpretations, Constans 1921, 387–90.

49 For a good basic discussion, though now subject to some amendments, Constans 1921, 47–78.

50 Ptolemy, *Geog* II, 10, 8; Constans 1921, 63; Jullian VI, 325 n 2; Barruol 1969, 239.

51 Barruol, *loc cit*. Milestone, giving the figure VI (surely from *Cabellio*), CIL XII, 5500, with figure corrected from VII by König no 86.

52 M.Guy, in *Etudes Roussillonnaises* IV(1954), 217 ff, discussed by Benoit in *Acad des Inscriptions et Belles-Lettres* 1964, 156–69, with plan; *cf* Soyer 1974.

53 CIL XII, 531 (+ add p 814); *ILGN* 69; *FOR* v, nos 18, 60, 61, 107, 178, 184, 205, 206, 241; Clerc 1916, 165–78; Constans 1921, 66–74. Not all the stones, of course, were found on their original sites—one was actually discovered in Aix itself.

54 Constans 1921, 71, 74–6. For the letter of Zosimus, Migne, *Patrologia Latina* XX, 642–6. The western boundary of the territory of *Massilia* (*qv*) remains rather doubtful.

55 *FOR* v, no 531.

56 *FOR* v, no 529; Rolland 1946 and 1958; *Gallia* VI(1948), 139–69, VIII(1950), 131–2, XI(1953), 3–18, XII(1954), 448–52, XIV(1956), 241–6, XVI(1958), 95–114, XX(1962), 696–9, XXI(1963), 307–14, XXV(1967), 406–10, XXVII(1969), 435–46, XXX(1972), 530–3, XXXII(1974), 521, XXXV(1977), 527–8. For a good general account up to 1975, C.Goudineau, Princeton 1976, 356–7. On the forum and basilica, P.Gros and P.Varène, *Gallia* XLII(1984), 21–52.

57 Pliny, *HN* III, 37: . . . *Forum Voconi, Glanum, Libii, Lutevani* . . . While most editions omit a comma between *Glanum* and *Libii*, there seems little doubt that this is an error and that the *Libii* are merely one of the several otherwise unknown tribes included in the list—perhaps, as Barruol 1969, 192–3, suggests, people occupying the Camargue.

58 For discussions of these, G.-C. Picard, 'Glanum et les origines de l'art romain provençal', Part I on architecture, Part II on sculpture, in *Gallia* XXI(1963) 111–24, XXII(1964) 1–22, and Barbet 1971.

59 Rolland 1977; Gros 1979.

60 Rolland 1969.

61 *Gallia* VI(1948), 214–15, VIII(1950), 126, XII(1954), 3–33, XIV(1956), 232, XVI(1958), 432, XVIII(1960), 311–13, XX(1962), 699–700, XXII(1964), 594, XXVII(1969), 451–2, XXIX(1971), 457–8, XXXI(1973), 559.

62 *FOR* II, no 43 (with a plan that now needs much revision); *Gallia* XXXV(1977), 501.

63 *Teretina* inscr, *CIL* XII, 388. *Olbia* inscr *ILGN* 44; Espérandieu 1907, IX no 6688; now in Hyères museum.

64 Strabo IV, 1, 5, including Olbia among the ἐπιτειχίσματα founded by *Massalia*.

65 Strabo IV, 1, 5 and 9; Mela 5, 77; Ptolemy, *Geog* II, 10, 5; Stephanus, *sv* (the first in his list of nine cities of this name)

66 *It Marit* 505.7–8. On its date, R. Lugand, 'Note sur l'Itineraire Maritime de Rome à Arles', *Mélanges de l'Ecole Française à Rome* 1926, 124–39, and the present author, *Britannia* I(1970), 37; *cf* Suetonius, *Claudius* 17, 2.

67 Strabo IV, 1, 10; Pliny, *HN* III, 79; *cf* Barruol 1969, 81, suggesting Giens as probable. For a discussion of the *Stoechades*, *v* Marseille p 223.

68 *It Marit* 505.8–506.1. Some writers try to deduce a reference from Silius Italicus, *Punica* xiv, 443 (*et Neptunicolae transverberat ora Telonis*), but this seems no more relevant than the Massaliote helmsman called Telo who appears in Lucan, *Pharsalia* iii, 592.

69 *FOR* II, no 63; *CIL* XII, 392–5, 5757–61 (and, according to Constans 1921, 75, and Benoit, *FOR* II, *CIL* XII, 696, the funerary inscription of an aedile of Arles); *Not Dig Occ* XI, 72.

70 Post-war excavations, *Gallia* XX(1962), 700, XXVII(1969), 456, XXXIII(1975), 565, XXXVIII(1979), 563–4.

71 For Augustalis, Munier 1963, 76–104; curiously, the most notable absentee from these Councils is the bishop of Marseille. For 6th-cent Councils, C. de Clercq, *Concilia Galliae A.511-A.695, passim.*

72 *Eg* Pseudo-Scymnus, Ταυρόεις; Caesar, *BC* II, 4, *Tauroentum*; *It Marit* 506.1–2, *Tauroento*; Strabo IV, 1, 5, and Ptolemy, *Geog* II, 10, 5, Ταυροέντιον. On Stephanus of Byzantium's bizarre theory regarding the origin of Ταυρόεις see p 12 above.

73 *FOR* II, no 138; more recent work, *Gallia* VIII(1950), 127–8, XIV(1956), 231, XXIX(1971), 459–60, XXXI(1973), 561, XXXV(1977), 503, under the titles of les Baumelles and St-Cyr-les-Lecques. The supposed Roman tile kiln has now been shown to be relatively modern.

74 *FOR* II, no 72; *Gallia* VI(1948), 215, XII(1954), 435–6; for a brief summary, Fr Brieu, *Hist Arch* 57 (Oct 1981), 31.

75 *It Marit* 506. 2–4; Mela II, 5, 77; Pliny, *HN* III, 35. Pliny's order, running eastward from Marseille, is *Massilia – promunturium Zao – Citharista*. For a general discussion, Benoit 1965, 103, but in view of Pliny's reliability his identification of *Zao* as Cap Sicié (between le Brusc and Toulon) is difficult to accept and the name has therefore been omitted from our map and so also (for the opposite reason, unreliability) has Ptolemy's ακρον Κιθαριστης (*Geog* II, 10, 5).

Arelate (Arles), with *Glanum* (St-Rémy) and *Olbia* (Almanarre)

76 *FOR* v, no 4; for early medieval forms of the name of Ceyreste (*Cezarista, Cezerista*), *ibid*, no 10.

77 *It Marit* 507. 3–5; *FOR* v, no 149.

78 *It Marit* 507. 5–6; *FOR* v, no 157; *Gallia* xii(1954), 433–4, xx(1962), 687–8, xxvii(1969), 430–2. For a general description, A.Dumoulin, Princeton 1976, 274.

79 Ptolemy, *Geog* ii, 10, 5; Ravennas iv, 28 (244, 8); Mela ii, 5, 78; Pliny, *HN* iii, 34; *ultra fossae ex Rhodano C.Mari opere et nomine insignes, Stagnum Mastromela* (the Etang de Berre), *oppidum Maritima Avaticorum, superque Campi Lapidei* (la Crau) *Herculis proeliorum memoria*. For a useful discussion of the *Avatici* and the geography of this area, Barruol 1969, 194–203.

80 *FOR* v, no 163; *Gallia* xiv(1956), 224, xxx(1972), 524–5, xxxii(1974), 518–19.

81 Constans 1921, 195–205; *FOR* v, no 289.

82 Strabo iv, 1–8.

83 *FOR* v, no 288; *Gallia* viii(1950), 123, xi(1953), 111–12, xii(1954), 432–3, xxv(1967), 403. For a popular account of work by Dr René Beaucaire (originally reported in *Bull de la Soc des Amis du Vieil Istres* 1(1949) and 3(1958)), Eydoux 1963, 201–29 (with illustrations).

84 *It Ant* 299.3; *It Marit* 507.6–7.

85 Vicarello Goblets; *It Ant* 344.1; *It Burd* 533.1. (as *mutatio Arnagine*); Peutinger Table; Ravennas iv, 27 (241, 14)—at least, this seems the most likely identity of his *Augunon*, between *Gabilona* (Cavaillon) and *Ugenon* (Beaucaire); also Ptolemy, *Geog* ii, 10, 8.

86 *CIL* xii, 982. For the Durance theory, Grenier 1934, 507–08 (quoting Ch. Lenthéric); against, Barruol 1969, 238.

87 *FOR* v, no 577; *Gallia* xxvii(1969), 446.

88 *FOR* v, no 393 for finds in this area, but Servane—or at least Servanne Château—is nearly 2 km north of the Roman road.

89 *FOR* v, no 311. For other things in this area, including the mausoleum, *v* p 216, under *Aque Sextiae*.

90 *It Ant* 297. 3–5, with *Tegulata* located at *xvi mp* from *Ad Turrem* (Tours) and *xv mp* from *Aquae Sextiae*, as also on the Peutinger Table; boundary stone, *CIL* xii, 531g; Petite-Pugère, *FOR* ii, no 267; Grande-Pugère, *FOR* v, no 178; mausoleum, Burnand 1975, 102–03.

91 *CIL* xii, 5494, König, no 53, marking *i mp* from Arles and dated AD 435, in the reign of Theodosius II and Valentinian III, set up by the *praefectus praetorio Galliarum* Auxiliaris and found 1573 in Arles but referring to the road from *Arelate* to *Massilia*, It is just possible, of course, that it had been erected on the other road.

92 *CIL* xii, 647; *FOR* v, no 300.

93 *FOR* v, no 299. It is just possible that this might be the otherwise unidentified *ad Vicesimum* of Ravennas iv, 28 (244, 7), since it is just about *xx mp* from Arles.

94 *It Ant* 299.1–3; *FOR* v, no 267; *Gallia* viii(1950), 124. For other suggestions, Benoit 1965, 130, Barruol 1969, 196 (arguing for Calas, but very few finds seem to have been made there).

95 For the letter of pope Zosimus *v* n 54 above; *CIL* xii, 594 (+ 593, 595–8); *FOR* v, no 20, and for aqueduct nos 16, 17.

96 The extent of arrondissements in thinly occupied areas can mislead. For

Arelate (Arles), with *Glanum* (St-Rémy) and *Olbia* (Almanarre)

example, the villa of Stes-Maries cited in Percival 1976, 70, 73, 163, is actually located at Nôtre-Dame-d'Amour, north of the Etang de Vaccares and only about 12 km south of Arles (*FOR* v, no 414; *Gallia* xxii(1964), 588–90). Stes-Maries itself may have been a settlement of some kind (*FOR* v, no 399), but how many of these remains came from wrecks and how many were transported to the place after the remarkable local cult was established? Further, the island *Metina*, sited by Pliny, *HN* iii, 79, *in Rhodani ostio*, may have stood about here.

97 Good summary by J.-P.Brun, M.Gérard, M.Pasqualini, *Hist Arch* no 57 (Oct 1981), 69–70. For other villas, kilns etc shown on the map, *FOR* v *passim*, *Gallia* xviii(1960) – xxxv(1977), *passim*.

98 *Gallia* xxii(1964), 578.

15
Aquae Sextiae (Aix-en-Provence)

Aquae Sextiae owed its name to the fact that C.Sextius Calvinus established a Roman fort there, near some warm springs, in 122 BC after the defeat of the *Salluvii*.[1] The choice of this site was evidently due to the fact that Entremont, only 2½km to the NW of it, had been a stronghold, probably the capital, of the tribe, but for how long a Roman garrison was maintained here is obscure. Plutarch, for example, while confirming that it was near *Aquae Sextiae* that Marius achieved his great victory over the *Teutones*, indicates that it was at a slightly different place that he pitched his army (at a waterless place, to make them thirsty!) and his claim that some Massaliotes fenced their vineyards with the bones of the slaughtered enemy suggests that it was Greeks rather than Romans who for a time controlled this area[2] (*cf* p 42 above). Whatever were the facts, however—and whether or not some of its families with the name Domitii had been granted Roman citizenship by Caesar's opponent L.Domitius rather than his notable grandfather Cn.Domitius[3]—the name of the place survived when it became a *colonia Iulia*.[4]

Its original status, probably granted by Caesar, was that of a *colonia Latina*. Pliny lists it (interestingly, as *Aquae Sextiae Salluviorum*) among his *oppida Latina* and, as several inscriptions show, it was in the voting-tribe *Voltinia* that its citizens were enrolled, and, like *Nemausus* (Nîmes, *qv*) it had at least one *praetor*,[5] but while a *quattuorvir* is duly recorded we also find a *duovir*, which indicates that it was later elevated to a *colonia Romana*.[6] Inscriptions of other officers also appear, as do those of some legionary veterans.[7] On the religious side, there are adequate dedications to Jupiter, Mars, Mercury and Silvanus,[8] but while there is a tradition that Christianity was brought here by a St Maximinus in the first century, the earliest recorded bishop is Remigius, who attended the Council of Nîmes in 394 or 396.[9] In any case, the city flourished greatly, for on the division of the province of *Narbonensis* recorded in the Verona List (*c* AD 312) it became the capital of *Narbonensis Secunda*.

Aix is still a very prosperous city to-day and with virtually no Roman remains to be seen on the surface the reconstruction of its Roman shape is rather difficult. The general belief that the early fort was built on the site of the Bourg St-Sauveur (around the existing cathedral) is fully acceptable, not only because this is the higher piece of land but also because it is towards this that some of the roads that have been identified were originally aligned, but to identify its shape with that of the medieval fortifications is surely wrong: the Roman fort is likely to have been approximately rectangular in form, with walls of timber and earth rather than stone, so that only faint traces of ditches can have interested later builders. While the eastern and southern lines (roughly those of the modern Rue Marie-et-Pierre-Curie and the Rue Paul-Bert) have been tentatively accepted on our plan (fig 27), the others have not, leaving open the question of how far the fort extended towards the west. This general shape is to some extent confirmed by the alignment, recently confirmed,[10] of the supposed *decumanus*, which was presumably laid out as an extension of the fort's street-plan. For the walls enclosing the *colonia* the best evidence is provided by the gate recorded long ago and now under the Palais de Justice, the shape of which, with two round towers and an internal semicircle, is comparable with that of the gates of Arles and Fréjus (*qqv*) and so suggests an Augustan date.[11] A few other stretches of wall have been located, especially in the west,[12] and the apparent size of the enceinte, seemingly offering distinction rather than defence, further strengthens the idea that it was Augustan (*cf Nemausus*).

As for buildings within the walls, for a long time the best known were the baptistry, of late fourth or early fifth century date with eight columns evidently removed from earlier pagan buildings, still to be seen in the cathedral,[13] and the baths underlying the modern 'Thermes Sextius', while other baths were believed to exist in the Place aux Herbes (just south of the Place Richelieu) and a considerable number of mosaics had been located.[14] In more recent times the most notable discoveries have been the early imperial courtyard (modified in the later Empire) which was uncovered during the restoration of the cathedral cloisters in 1976–9,[15] and the group of houses, one with a peristyle, in the Jardin de Grassi,[16] but rescue excavations elsewhere have also yielded results—for example, more buildings and mosaics when the Ecole des Arts was built and another, with a bird mosaic, at the Pasteur car-park.[17]

While some of its hot springs had, according to Strabo,[18] turned cold, *Aquae Sextiae* was ultimately equipped with five aqueducts.[19] The longest, and so perhaps the last, was that from Traconnade, near Peyrolles, some 20km to the NE, considerable stretches of which ran underground. A very much shorter one, also from the NE, came from the Barrage des Pinchinats, and from the east one from Claps (just east of Vauvenargues) and one from St-Antoine-sur-Bayon (just south of

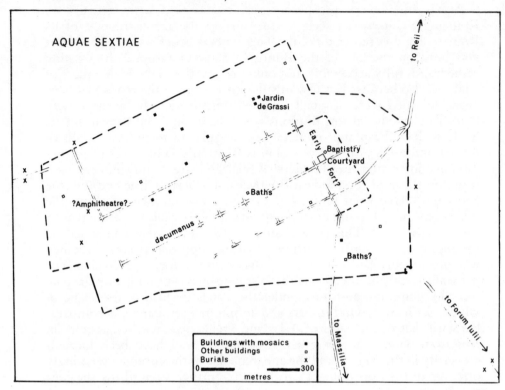

27 A tentative plan of Aix-en-Provence

Mont Ste-Victoire). The precise source of the one coming from the west is a little obscure—it certainly extended as far away as la Bargemone, but the stretches observed north of la Trévaresse were almost certainly separate and related to the estate near Rognes that is referred to below.[20]

The definition of the territory governed from *Aquae Sextiae* raises some problems. To the north, the Montagne du Lubéron, an obvious geographical division of the lands of Aix and *Apta Iulia*, was also the boundary between their ancient dioceses, but elsewhere the boundary between Aix and Arles is far from certain. In the west, although a boundary stone found at or near les Figons offers some help,[21] the milestones along the main road yield little information because, apart from the stone only one mile from Aix itself, their mileage figures are mainly erased.[22] Clerc, using as evidence the appearance on inscriptions of the voting-tribe *Voltinia* (as opposed to *Teretina*, the tribe of Arles)[23] seems to have given Arles too much, and the argument of Constans, bringing the border more into line with that of the diocese,[24] seems preferable, especially since the discovery of the inscriptions of the family of Domitii near Rognes; even he, however, seems to have misused the evidence of one milestone, that from the Plan d'Orgon, which should surely be related to *Cabellio* (Cavaillon, *qv*).[25] South-east of Aix, the matter is complicated by the discovery in this area not of one but of a dozen boundary stones defining the limits with the large amount of Massaliote territory taken over by Arles.[26] Two of them were actually found in Aix itself and it cannot, of course, be certain that none of the others had been moved, but they clearly point to a difference from the extent of the earliest known diocese. Finally, Clerc's suggestion that the *pagus Matavonicus* (around Cabasse) belonged to Aix is not convincing: despite the discovery there of a burial inscription incorporating *Voltinia*, a milestone gives the correct distance (MP xxxiiii) from Fréjus—to which the place belonged when the dioceses were established.[27]

Unfortunately *Matavo* is not the only road-station whose attribution to Aix can be questioned. As the mileages given by the Peutinger Table show, *Pisavis* must have been somewhere near St-Jean-de-Brenasse, but while many finds are recorded in this area there is some doubt as to whether it was on the left or the right bank of the river Touloubre and so whether it was in the territory of Aix or Arles.[28] Then *Tegulata*, to the east, was certainly at either la Grande-Pugère or la Petite-Pugère, where the road crosses the upper waters of the Arc,[29] but the boundary-stones, including one found at la Grande-Pugère itself, seem to suggest that this too may have been controlled from Arles. So the only station that certainly belonged to Aix is *Ad Turrem* which, as its name makes plain, was at Tourves, where discoveries have been slight.[30]

Of the three temples shown on the map (fig 26), little is known about the structure of the one at Castellar (2km east of Cadenet), beyond the fact that it had columns, but the site has yielded many finds, including three dedications to the obscure deity Dexsiva.[31] The temple at la Bastide-Forte, though mainly demolished in 1760 and losing most of its stones in the nineteenth century to help build the canal du Verdon, is somewhat better known because a detailed drawing of it had been made by Peiresc—it was clearly classical in style and, as a statue indicates, was probably dedicated to Mercury.[32] The most impressive remains are those at Château-Bas, Vernègues. Here two, and almost certainly three, classical temples were early erected within a semicircular wall and much of the central one, including some of its columns with Corinthian capitals, can still be seen (pl 36). The inscriptions include one to *Iupiter Tonans* and some have suggested that the buildings were dedicated to the Capitoline Triad, but the sculptures on an altar included Neptune and Mercury as well as Jupiter and Minerva and there was also a dedication to Rome and Augustus.[33]

More numerous than the known temples are the *mausolea* that have been identified in this *civitas*, not only at *Aquae Sextiae* itself but also at *Pisavis* and *Tegulata*,[34] while four more are known in rural areas. Of these the most interesting are at Cabrières-d'Aigues and Rognes, the former because of the splendid bas-relief associated with it (now in the Musée Calvet in Avignon), which shows two men hauling a boat loaded with barrels, clearly indicating that the family here commemorated had some connection with the transport of goods along the river Durance.[35] That just south of Rognes is distinguished not only by the material recovered in its excavation, including statues and inscriptions commemorating three male Domitii (one a *tribunus militum* and *praefectus fabrum*) and one a female Domitia, but above all by the excellent study of it by Yves Burnand, taking all of its implications into consideration.[36]

This study covers not only the wider questions, such as the distribution and character of *mausolea* throughout the province and the origins and significance of the Domitius family, but also includes a careful analysis of Roman remains in the surrounding area. The chief difficulty here, as elsewhere in this part of Narbonensis, is that although a large number of villas have been provisionally located in the past, relatively few have been excavated satisfactorily. This applies to the one at Grand St-Paul, just north-west of the mausoleum, which, from its luxury (including a notable *horologium*) was evidently the centre of the estate of these Domitii and appears to have been occupied from Augustan times to the mid-third century.[37] Some more satisfactory villa excavations have, however, been made since the war, such as that at Peyrolles (where part of the aqueduct has also been re-examined),[38] two near Pélisanne (just north of *Pisavis*) one of them occupied from the first to the fourth century,[39] one at les Milles (sw of Aix), where a temple may also have existed,[40] and finally one at le Grand Loou, Roquebrussanne, in the south-east part of the *civitas*. Here some remains had long been noted, but more recent work has shown that while the site was occupied from the middle of the first century BC a villa was first built (with a well) in the first century AD, but although it was much improved in the second century, with an oil- or wine-press, it now appears to have been abandoned in the third.[41] A pottery kiln is also recorded nearby and, as may be seen from the map, several others have been located elsewhere. Though no mines are known in the territory of Aix, there is no doubt that it was, as now, a prosperous region and the elevation of the city to the capital of a province is not surprising.

REFERENCES AND NOTES

1 Strabo IV, 1, 5: Cassiodorus, *Chronica* puts it in 122 BC: *his consulibus* (C.Domitius and C.Fannius) *Sextius oppidum aedificavit, in quo Aquae Sextiae in Gallis,* which Clerc 1916, 145, takes to mean that Sextius stayed

on a little longer than is sometimes supposed. Livy, *Periocha* lxi, confirms that it was as proconsul that he did this, but his description of the place as a *colonia* is clearly wrong (*cf* Velleius Paterculus I, 15).

2 Plutarch, *Marius* 18 and 21, 3.

3 For a full discussion, Burnand 1975, 222–35. The question is how long it took Caesar to institute the siege of *Massilia*: Caesar, *BC* I, 36, indicates that Domitius had very little time in hand and even the poetical exaggerations of Lucan, *Pharsalia* III, 300 ff do not offer much.

4 *CIL* XII, 705 (rediscovered and confirmed, *Gallia* XVI(1958), 401–02).

5 Pliny, *HN* III, 36: *CIL* XII, 517 (*praetor*), 522, 525, 528, 534.

6 Quattuorvir, *CIL* XII, 524; duovir, 529.

7 Aedile, *CIL* XII, 522; flamines, 408, 519, 521; seviri, 518, 520, 523, 524, 526, 705, 5776 (+ *Gallia* XXXII(1974), 397–8); soldiers, 514–16.

8 *CIL* XII, 498–509.

9 Munier 1963, 49–61.

10 For excavation of the *decumanus* (near its eastern end) *Gallia* XXX(1972), 511, *RAN* V(1971), 31–47: for earlier summary, Grenier 1958, 115–27. As a recently found inscription shows, there was also a corporation of dendrophori: *RAN* XVI (1983), 161–9.

11 Clerc 1916, 362–4, 421–36.

12 Clerc 1916, 459–83; *Gallia* XI(1953), 107.

13 Reconstructed by Formigé in the 1920s: *FOR* V, p 66, with references.

14 *FOR* V, no 241, with general plan.

15 *RAN* XIII(1980), 115–64.

16 First excavations, *Gallia* V(1947), 81–97; later work, *Gallia* XVI(1958), 415–19, XVIII(1960), 296–303; popular account, Eydoux 1961, 361–78.

17 *Gallia* XXXV(1977), 412.

18 Strabo IV, 1, 5.

19 For general refs, Clerc 1916, 503–14 (with plan), *FOR* V, map A (with refs to individual entries).

20 Burnand 1975, 194–5.

21 Clerc 1916, 166, 173; Constans 1921, 69; *FOR* V, no 356.

22 *CIL* XII, 5477 (König no 54) *i mp* fron Aix; the others, *CIL* XII, 5478 (König no 55), *CIL* XII, 312–13 (*ILGN* 648 a–b, König nos 56–7), *FOR* V, no 320 (König no 58).

23 Clerc 1916, 179–84.

24 Constans 1921, pl XIII.

25 Constans 1921, 163: milestone, *CIL* XII, 5500 (König no 86, citing Barruol, *REL* XXVIII(1962), 134, and giving distance from Cavaillon).

26 *CIL* XII, 531 + add, p 814; *ILGN* 69; *FOR* V, nos 18, 60, 61, 107, 178, 184, 205, 206, 241; Clerc 1916, 165–78.

27 Clerc 1916, 183 (based on *CIL* XII, 344); milestone, *CIL* XII, 5470 (König no 46).

28 *FOR* V, no 311. The suggestion that *Pisavis* was at the Val-de-Gon (NW of Pélissanne, *FOR* V, no 323) can surely be dismissed: it is 3½ km from the line of the main road.

29 *FOR* V, no 178, *FOR* II(1932), no 267.

30 *FOR* II, no 216. Tourves is a disappointing place to visit, the earliest recognisable monument being a church tower dated 1674.

31 Clerc 1916, 276–7; *FOR* VI(1939), no 8; *CIL* XII, 1062–4.

Aquae Sextiae (Aix-en-Provence)

32 Clerc 1916, 499; *FOR* v, no 257 (with photo of Peiresc's drawing).
33 *FOR* v, no 370; Grenier 1958, 280–5 (with full refs and plan); inscriptions, *CIL* xii, 501, 513; altar, Espérandieu 1907, no 127; for many buildings in the vicinity, *c* 500m from the temple, observed on air photographs, *Gallia* xxv(1967), 406. Though for some years access to the site was forbidden, visitors are now again made welcome.
34 Aix, *FOR* v, no 241, Burnand 1975, 103–05; St-Jean-de-Brenasse, *FOR* v, no 311, Burnand, 128–9; la Petite-Pugère, *FOR* ii, no 267, Burnand, 128, 129 (*sv* Pourrières).
35 *FOR* vii(1939), no 6 (with photo of bas-relief, Espérandieu 1907, no 6699), Burnand 1975, 117, 146.
36 *FOR* v, no 352, *Gallia* xxvii(1969), 433, Burnand 1975, *passim*. For the other mausolea shown on fig 26, (Lauris and Cucuson), *FOR* vii, nos 13–14, Burnand 1975, 116–17.
37 *FOR* v, no 351; other villas in this area, *FOR* v, nos 347–54; for discussion, Burnand 1975, 149–209.
38 *Gallia* xx(1962), 696.
39 At Nôtre-Dame d'Amour, with mosaics and an oil-press, *Gallia* xvi(1958), 425–6, xxii(1964), 586–7; under the medieval Chapelle St-Laurent, where finds extend to the 4th cent *Gallia* xxx(1972), 525, xxxii(1974), 520, xxxv(1977), 528–9.
40 *Gallia* xxv(1947), 405.
41 *FOR* ii, no 222; *Gallia* xii(1954), 438, xxii(1964), 596, xxxvii(1979), 561–2, xxxix(1981), 538–9; summary, with plan, *Hist Arch* 57(Oct 1981), 78.

16

Massilia (Marseille), with *Nicaea* (Nice), *Athenopolis* (St-Tropez) and *Stoechades Insulae* (Iles d'Hyères)

The earlier relations between Marseille and Rome have been adequately dealt with in the earlier historical chapters,[1] but since Caesar did not impose direct provincial rule on it after its surrender, allowing it to be a *civitas foederata*, its constitution remained intact for some time and so demands some attention here. Our knowledge of its earliest form suffers from the fact that although Aristotle makes two interesting comments on it in his *Politics*,[2] his *Constitution of Massalia* has not survived, but later authors, especially Strabo, tell us a good deal about it in the early imperial period. There was an assembly (a quasi-senate) of 600 *timouchoi*, who held office for life, above them an elected minor council of 15 (the *quindecimviri* that Caesar called out to discuss matters with him before the siege began) and at the top three magistrates— offices that could be held only by men whose family had been citizens of the place for at least three generations.[3] The laws of the city, made fully public, were universally admired for their fairness and the quality of life not only made it an acceptable place for the exile of noble Romans but also led some, including Agricola, to complete their education there.[4] *Massilia* was especially notable for its rhetoricians, not only the Roman exile Volcacius Moschus but also locals such as Agroitas and Pacatus, and for its wealthy doctors such as Charmis (an expert on cold water treatment) and Crinas (who used astrology in connection with medicine).[5] What is not clear is how long the specifically Greek constitution of the city survived and at what date it was replaced by a Roman form. An inscription from Marseille itself records a decurion (Cornelius Cornelianus) and another, from Nice, the appointment of Cn. Memmius Macrinus, a *quaestor* and *duovir* of *Massilia*, as the overseer (*episcopus*) of that subject town, and it seems probable that the change took place in the second half of the second century.[6] Three *equites* are also recorded, Cn. Valerius Pompeius (whose name indicates that his family had long held Roman citizenship and whose voting-tribe was *Quirina*) and Porcius Aelianus and T. Porcius Cornelianus, both with distinguished careers, the latter becoming governor of *Alpes Maritimae* at some time around AD 200.[7] Cn. Valerius was, among other things, patron of the local *centonarii* (firemen) and another man (name unknown, but a *flamen* of Riez) was patron of the Massilian *dendrophori* (woodmen).[8]

As Strabo makes clear, the patron deity of the city was Artemis—a fine statue of her (not, alas a wooden *xoanon*, but of marble and lacking its head) may be seen in the Musée Borély—and temples for her and for Delphinian Apollo certainly stood somewhere on the high ground.[9] Dedications to Athene and to Jupiter Dolichenus have also been found, along with references to and statues of several other deities (Dionysus, Leucothea, Mercury, Ceres, Aesculapius, Hercules, the Matres),[10] but despite recent criticisms Christianity probably reached here fairly early, though the first recorded bishop is Oresius who, along with his *lector* Nazareus, attended the Council of Arles in 314.[11]

In any case, many Christian burials have been found and it is cemeteries, both pagan and Christian, that provide the best indication of the full extent of the city—one in the north in le Lazaret and one in the east in the Plaine St-Michel, the former evidently flanking a road, while another lay south of the port, where also the St-Victor abbey was founded in the early fifth century. These had long been known, as had some parts of the city walls,[12] but much more has come to light since the second world war. Marseille suffered badly in the war, not only being bombed by the Germans and Italians in 1940 and by the allies in 1944 but also, in 1943, having an area just north of the old port rased to the ground on the instructions of Hitler, who called it a nest of spies. When peace was restored, excavations in this barbarously cleared area exposed two interesting features, first the remains of a small theatre and secondly those of part of the ancient port (still called *Lacydon* in Roman times).[13] The theatre (though built in the first century AD, may have overlain an earlier one in timber and was still of Greek type—not surprisingly, since the post of *agonothetes* still continued at least until the second century.[14] The uncovering of parts of the Roman docks (now partly preserved in the Musée des Docks Romains in the Place Vivaux, together with such things as the part of a boat found further east in 1864) confirmed how the harbour had been progressively narrowed since the original Greek settlement.[15]

Even more important excavations were carried out later in the area of the Bourse. Here both an inland extension of the harbour was uncovered and also a stretch of city walls, including a gate. The harbour was bounded by stone quays probably constructed in the first century BC, with upper courses added in the late Empire (pl 37), and to the east of it were a store, in use from the second to the third century, and an impressive square stone basin (pl 38), built in the first but abandoned in the third, to supply fresh water to ships: various other things, including parts of a Hellenistic aqueduct, a Greek cemetery and part of a ship, were also uncovered here. Just north of the inner harbour ran a road that entered the city through a gate with towers of Hellenistic date, as was the wall to the north of it, which had previously been taken to be that built in the first century AD at the expense of the wealthy doctor Crinas, but the best-preserved tower of these defences is the one to the south. Some traces were also found of an earlier Greek wall and also parts of a Roman forewall, evidently built in the late Empire, perhaps when Maximian was besieged here by Constantine. The important excavations were made possible by a delay in modern rebuilding imposed by André Malraux, then Minister of Cultural Affairs, but although several elements have been preserved and kept open to public inspection they are now so hemmed in by large buildings that, as is shown on pl 39, their significance is somewhat obscured.

While the general line of the Greek defences is now reasonably clear (as shown on fig 28), it is still not known where precisely the main Roman attack, described in such detail by Caesar himself (although he was then in Spain) and elaborated not only by the poetical Lucan but also by the technically-minded Vitruvius, actually took place, but since it was surely on the hill of St-Charles that the Roman forces encamped it was presumably in the north-eastern sector.[17]

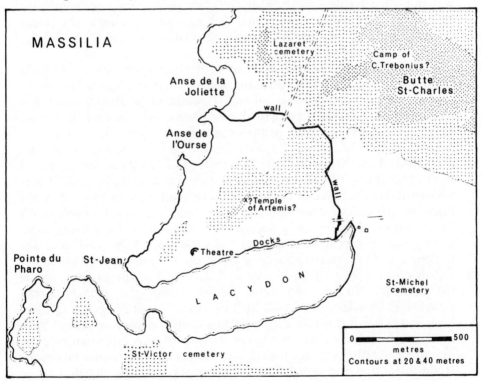

28 A tentative plan of Marseille

As we have seen, Marseille had exercised control over an extensive area during the Republican period, but after her submission to Caesar she lost most of it, especially to *Arelate* (Arles, *qv*) and was left with a very small territory indeed—just about that which had once been occupied by the *Segobrigii*. The only places within it whose names are preserved in ancient sources are *Carsicis*, *Aemines* and the *Insula Madrae*, all in the Maritime Itinerary.[18] That *Carsicis* was Cassis has been proved by the rediscovery in 1930 of an inscription to the *tutela carcitana* which Hirschfeld in *CIL* XII had tended to dismiss as bogus and that the text of the Itinerary here has the names *Carsicis* and *Citarista* out of order is confirmed by the fact that *Citarista* (la Ciotat) was subject to *Arelate*.[19] But although the Itinerary calls *Carsicis* a *portus*, not merely a *positio*, too little has been found here to form a picture of it, and the same is true of *Aemines*, which must have been either in the Calanque de Morgiou or, more probably, the Calanque de Sormiou.[20] *Insula Madrae* appears in the text simply as *Inmadrae positio*, but a correction to *Ins Madrae* seems wholly acceptable, especially since the little Ile Maire has yielded much pottery, ranging in date from the Greek to the Visigothic period, and was clearly often called at by ships.[21] As may be seen from the map (fig 26), a few villas have been identified just north of *Massilia*, but the land was not very fertile—the city derived her prosperity not from local agriculture but from trade and fishing—and perhaps the most interesting thing in it is the temple, probably dedicated to Cybele, located at les Pennes.[22]

Massilia also lost control of most of her daughter cities—*Antipolis* (Antibes, *qv*) deliberately breaking loose, *Agatha* (Agde) becoming subject to *Baeterrae* (Béziers, *qv*) and *Tauroentum* (le Brusc) and *Olbia* (Almanarre) probably subject to *Arelate* (Arles, *qv*). As a result of this, only two towns and one group of islands demand mention here—*Nicaea* (Nice), *Athenopolis* (St-Tropez) and the *Stoechades Insulae* (Iles d'Hyères). That *Nicaea* did remain subject to *Massilia* is demonstrated by the inscription of Cn. Memmius already mentioned, but too little is known about the place in both pre-Roman and Roman times. Several finds are recorded, especially funerary inscriptions of people with Greek names, but the only satisfactory excavations have been those carried out in recent times at the old cathedral of Nôtre-Dame-du-Château, yielding pottery ranging from the second century BC to the fourth century AD.[23] That it was well defended in the early period is indicated by Strabo's inclusion of it among the ἐπιτειχίσματα established by Marseille[24] and, at least after the campaign of Q. Opimius in 154 BC, it must have controlled a fairly extensive area, but both its strength and the amount of land it retained under Roman rule are obscure; the only evidence for the latter is the discovery of a boundary stone (including the word *Massiliensium*) marking the division of its territory from that of *Vintium* (Vence), but this is not very helpful because precisely where it originally stood is not known.[25] Although they seem to have used *Nicaea* for a *cohors nauticorum* (presumably controlled from Frèjus),[26] when the Romans took over *Alpes Maritimae* it was *Cemenelum* (Cimiez, *qv*), a native hill-fort some 2½km inland from *Nicaea*, that they converted first into a military station and then into a prosperous capital city. Nevertheless, since Ti.Claudius Demetrius, *procurator* of the province in the first half of the third century, acted also as *episcopus chorae inferioris* (surely the territory of Nice),[27] the separation of the two evidently continued and this is further confirmed by the fact that Nice (here called *Portus Nicensis*) was represented, though only by a priest and an exorcist, at the Council of Arles in 314 and by 381 had its own bishop, Amantius, who attended the Council of Aquileia.[28]

Athenopolis presents still more problems. Though omitted from the Maritime Itinerary (which does, however, include *plagia* in the *Sinus Sambracitanus* which evidently, from the mileage, is the Golfe de St-Tropez) its importance is reflected by the fact that it is named by Varro, Mela, Pliny and Stephanus of Byzantium, and Pliny, who elsewhere explains the fate of Agde by calling it *Agatha quondam Massiliensium*, calls this town *Athenopolis Massiliensium* (with no *quondam*).[29] But very little has been found here, apart from some notable columns, and its history in both Greek and Roman times still requires a great deal of investigation.[30]

As for the *Stoechades Insulae*, their control by Marseille, at least in the first century AD, is indicated both by Strabo, who says that they are cultivated by the Massilians, and by Tacitus who, when recording the capture there of Valens in AD 69, specifically calls them *Massiliensium insulae*,[31] but some questions regarding them have still to be answered. Ptolemy says that they are five in number and Strabo, who also gives the total as five, says that three of them are notable (presumably in size), but Pliny lists only three and supplies names for them—*tres Stoechades a vicinis Massiliensibus dictae propter ordinem quo sitae sunt. Nomina singulis Prote, Mese quae et Pomponiana vocatur, tertia Hypaea: ab his Iturium, Phoenice, Phila, Lero et Lerina adversum Antipolim*[32]—and this shows that the identification of the *Stoechades* with the present Iles d'Hyères is a little oversimplified. Two former islands in this area are now attached to the mainland, the Presqu'ile de St Mandrier (s of Toulon) and the Presqu'ile de Giens (s of Hyères) and the most likely explanation is that while the five of Strabo and Ptolemy extended from St-Mandrier to the Ile du Levant (omitting the small Ile de Bagaud), Pliny's *Prote* was St Mandrier, his *Mese* Giens and his *Hypaea* Porquerolles, with his *Iturium*, *Phoenice* and *Phila* perhaps being Bagaud, Port-Gros and Levant.[33] If this is correct, *Pomponiana* should be sited on Giens, but since the Maritime Itinerary puts it rather too far—*xviii mp*—from *Telo* (Toulon),[34] Porquerolles remains a slight possibility.

In any case, finds indicating probable ports have been recorded on both these islands[35] and both Giens and Porquerolles have yielded more evidence since the war. On Porquerolles Roman foundations have been located near the Cap des Mèdes[36] and on Giens not only has a square building, possibly a lighthouse, been found near la Tour Fondue but also, near what was then the north shore of the island (on a site rather misleadingly labelled l'Acapte), the impressive Greek shrine of Aristaeus, with much inscribed pottery dating from the second century BC to the first century AD.[37]

REFERENCES AND NOTES

1 For further details of the earlier period, Clerc 1927, I, Salviat 1973, Clavel-Lévêque 1977.

2 Aristotle, *Pol.* 1305b (recording a modification of it), 1321a (admission of foreigners to office).

3 Strabo IV, 1, 5; Caesar, *BC* I, 35

4 For exiles, Sallust, *Catiline* 34 (though Catiline escaped on his way there); Cassius Dio XL, 54 (Milo, who enjoyed eating mullets there); Tacitus, *Ann* IV, 43–4 (Volcacius Moschus and, as a boy, L. Antonius, both under Tiberius), XIII, 47 (Cornelius Sulla, under Nero). For praise, Livy XXXVII, 54, 21–3 (recording a speech of 189 BC); Cicero, *Pro Flacco* 26(63); Valerius Maximus II, 6, 7 (with some very odd details); Tacitus, *Agricola*, 4 (recording his father-in-law's education). For less praise, Athenaeus, *Deipnosophistae* XII, 523c and perhaps Sidonius, *Carmina* xxiii, 155–7, with the possible implication that Encolpius, of the *Satyricon* of Petronius, was supposed to have met the obscene deity Priapus there! (W. B. Anderson, in *Classical Quarterly* XXVIII(1934), 22).

5 For Volcacius Moschus (the exile) and Pacatus, Seneca, *Controversiae* X, *Prol*, 10; for Agroitas, Seneca, *ibid*, II, 6, 12. For Charmis, Pliny, *HN* XXIX, 10, and Galen, *De Antidotis* II, 1, 4; for Crinas (who also financed some town-walling), Pliny, *HN* XXIX, 9.

6 Cornelius, *CIL* XII, 407; Cn Memmius, *CIL* V, 7914.

7 Cn Valerius Pompeius, *CIL* XII, 410 (+ p 812); the Porcii, *CIG* III, 6771, *ILS* 8852.

8 *CIL* XII, 411.

9 Strabo IV, 4, 4; dedication to Apollo, *CIL* XII, 400. The temple of Artemis has been supposed to stand on the highest point (near les Accoules) and that of Apollo on the height above the Fort St-Jean, but while this is likely enough it has still to be proved.

10 Jupiter inscription, with marble statuette, *CIL* XII, 400, now in Stuttgart Museum; other statues etc, *FOR* V, pp 28–9, Espérandieu 1907, *passim*, Euzennat 1973, 46.

11 Oresius, Munier 1963, 9–25. For a useful discussion of early Christianity, Euzennat 1973, 46–7 (with references, p 50); Volusianus and Fortunatus, *CIL* XII, 489.

12 Clerc 1927 II, *passim*; *FOR* V, no 75; Benoit 1951 (on Christian burials); Euzennat 1973, 42; *Gallia* XXII(1974), 516–18.

13 Mela II, 5, 77.

14 *Gallia* I(1942), 199, V(1947), 155–60, XX(1962), 587, XXIV(1966), 1–12; Grenier 1958, 824–7 (with some doubts); Euzennat 1973, 40. For the post of *agonothetes CIL* XII, 410, and *cf CIL* V, 7914 (for Nice).

15 *Gallia* VI(1948), 207–09, VIII(1950), 116–17, XI(1953), 100–02, XII(1954), 426–8, XVIII(1960), 286–90, XX(1962) 687. For a full description of the museum, F.Benoit, *Musée des Docks Romains*, Marseille, 2nd edn, 1965.

16 *Gallia* XXVII(1969), 423–30, XXX(1972), 520–4, XXXII(1974), 512–18, XXXV(1977), 520–4; Salviat 1973, 27–9. For earlier knowledge, including the aqueduct, *FOR* V, no 75.

17 Caesar, *BC* II, 1–5 and 8–16; Lucan, *Pharsalia* III, 453 ff; Vitruvius, *De Architectura* X, xvi, 11–12. The Butte des Carmes, suggested by Jullian I, 208, n 1 and Clerc 1927, II, 190, as the site of the Roman camp is surely inside the Greek fortifications.

18 *It Marit* 506.3–507.1.

19 *CIL* XII, 37, *FOR* V, no 6. That *Citarista* was subject to *Arelate* is shown in a letter of Pope Zosimus (Migne, *Patrologia Latina* XX, 642–6).

20 *FOR* V, no 62 (Morgiou), recording only pottery, and no 63 (Sormiou) recording pottery and some possible buildings.

21 Clerc 1927 II, 308; *FOR* V, no 66. For a preference for Cap Croisette, Barruol 1969, 81.

22 *FOR* V, no 133, with ref to *CIL* XII, 405 (+ p 812).

23 *FOR* I, no 25–7; *Gallia* XII(1954), 441–2; Ducat/Farnoux 1976, 15–19.

24 Strabo IV, 1, 5.

25 *CIL* XII, 7, first recorded as standing in the cathedral of Vence.

26 Laguerre 1975, no 48 (found 1963), improving the interpretation of *CIL* V, 7884, 7887 and 7892 (there taken to be *cohors nautarum*). *Nicaea* must surely have been the only port that *Cemenelum* could reasonably have used.

27 *CIL* V, 7870; Pflaum 1960, 788–90; Laguerre 1975, no 3.

28 Munier 1963, 9–25; Griffe 1964, I, 342.

29 *It Marit* 505.2–4; Varro, *De Lingua Latina* VIII, 35 (*Athenopolitae*); Pliny *HN* III, 35; Stephanus, *sv* Ἀθῆναι πόλεις (κάτα δὲ Φίλωνα ἕξ ...... τετάρτη Λιγυστίων).

30 *FOR* II, no 15; *Gallia* XIV(1956), 232 (Iron Age pottery), XXIX(1971), 460 (columns etc in le Pilon area).

31 Strabo IV, 1, 10; Tacitus, *Hist* III, 43.

32 Ptolemy, *Geog* II, 10, 9; Strabo IV, 1.10; Pliny, *HN* III, 79.

33 For a useful discussion, Benoit 1965, 105, citing J.Mouquet.

34 *It Marit* 505. 7–8; *Alconis*, here said to be *xxx mp* east of *Pomponiana*, was probably near Cavalière, but this is uncertain.

35 Giens, *FOR* II, nos 44–5; Porquerolles, no 47.

36 *Gallia* XXII(1964), 595.

37 Tour-Fondue, *Gallia* XXXIII(1975), 562, XXXVII(1979), 559: l'Acapte (or la Capte) shrine, *Gallia* XXXIII(1975), 562, XXXV(1977), 501, XXXVII(1979), 558–9, XXXIX(1981), 537; *Hist. Arch.* 57 (Oct 1981), 33–4 (with illustrations).

17
Forum Iulii (Fréjus)

Forum Iulii was for long one of the most important cities in *Narbonensis*, but the date of its foundation remains uncertain. As we have seen (p 34), its identification with *Aegitna* can safely be dismissed, though a little evidence has now been found of pre-Roman occupation in the very early Iron Age[1] and since its name first appears in Munatius Plancus's letter to Cicero[2] the *Iulii* in its title evidently goes back to Caesar so that, as also suggested above (p 65), it may well have been on this site that he stationed *Legio VIII* just before he crossed the Rubicon. Whether it was Caesar or Octavian who installed veterans of that legion here, however, is still unclear, but since Plancus does not call it a *colonia* the date either of 35 or 27 BC seems most probable. In any case Tacitus tells us that it was Octavian who brought elements of the fleet here after the battle of Actium in 31 BC[4] and this, combined with the peace achieved by that battle, explains the full title given by Pliny—*Forum Iuli Octavanorum Colonia quae Pacensis appellatur.*[5] Members of both the fleet and *Legio VIII Hispana* are duly recorded in inscriptions,[6] but these are not the only units referred to: for example, one records a soldier of *Legio XIX* (a legion that was lost in the Varian disaster of AD 9 and never re-established),[7] while another, a dedication to Hercules by a *Vexillatio Germanicianorum*, confirms the statement of Tacitus that such a force was posted here for a time in AD 69.[8]

That citizens of *Forum Iulii* were enrolled in the voting-tribe *Aniensis* is confirmed by three inscriptions, but while no less than eight refer to *seviri*,[9] none from Fréjus covers the city's standard magistrates, though a *duovir* who was also a magistrate of neighbouring *Salinae* (Castellane) appears on one found at Cimiez.[10] The city did, however, produce some very notable people at a very early stage. The best-known, of course, is Cn.Iulius Agricola, who was born in AD 40,[11] and his family background is also worthy of note: both his grandfathers had become *procuratores*, his father, L.Iulius Graecinus, became a senator and rose to the rank of *praetor* and his uncle Marcus became at least a *quaestor*.[12] C.Cornelius Gallus, the notable poet and orator who had to commit suicide in 27 BC after boasting too much when prefect of Egypt, presents a problem: Jerome (probably using some lost work of Suetonius as his source) calls him a Foroiuliensis and says that he died in his 43rd year, which puts us back to 70 BC for his birth, certainly before the foundation of the *colonia*, and it seems probable that he was of native origin and so may have come from this area—unless he had simply moved in when the place was first founded.[13] Fréjus was certainly the city of origin of the *procurator* Valerius Paulinus and may also have been the unnamed *colonia* of Cornelius Fuscus which, though he had earlier resigned from the senatorial order, he brought out in support of Galba in AD 68.[14] In later times its distinction declined somewhat, as is demonstrated by the fact that when the separate province of *Narbonensis Secunda* was formed *Aquae Sextiae* (Aix), not *Forum Iulii*, was made its capital. Its first recorded bishop seems to be Ursio, who attended both the Council of Nîmes in 394 or 396 and that of Turin in 398.[15]

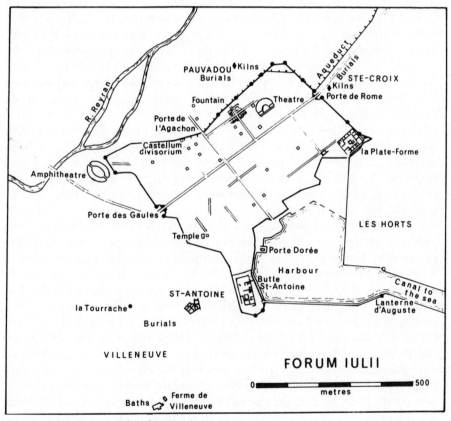

29 Plan of Fréjus (mainly after Février)

Fréjus has several upstanding monuments but, as may be seen from
the plan (fig 29), some important elements are still unlocated. The site
of the *forum* has not yet been identified and although we have
dedications to Jupiter, Apollo, Hercules and the minor deities
Carpantus and Trittia, while Cybele is reflected in the record of a
taurobolium, only one probable temple has so far been found.[16] The
main lay-out of the city has been well established, with a fully
convincing *cardo* and *decumanus* and several other streets parallel to
them, but the short lengths of two roads in the western half, one
running east to west and the other north to south, suggest the
possibility of an earlier pattern[17] and an early reorganisation is also
indicated by discoveries on two of the most fully excavated sites. The
earliest traces of occupation so far found are in the Butte St-Antoine,
not only very early Iron Age pottery but, evidently after a long period
of abandonment, some pre-Augustan structures that were replaced by
imposing buildings of an official kind, probably the base of the
commander of the fleet.[18] Similarly, la Plate-Forme, an area at the east
end of the city carefully levelled out and supported by walls, has also
yielded early structures, including a kiln, that were superseded by still
more sumptuous buildings with their own baths, probably the
residence of the governor of the province when he visited the place.[19]
As for the homes of the upper class in general, while several mosaics
have been noted in the past[20] the most outstanding discoveries inside
the city are the result of work in the 1970s in the Clos de la Tour, west
of the theatre. Here not only have streets been uncovered that confirm
the final lay-out of the *colonia* but a number of houses have been
carefully excavated and planned, some built in the first century and
some in the second, and some remaining in use, after modification
(including, in one case, extension over the north–south road), at least
until the late fourth century.[21]

Of the other main buildings the theatre, while pleasantly situated in a
public park (pl 40), is sadly decayed and although it was carefully
planned by Formigé, whose excavations in 1920 improved on those of
Texier in the early 19th century, further research is still needed to
establish its date.[22] The amphitheatre, smaller than that of Arles but
larger than that of Béziers,[23] has also suffered in different ways. It too
had been studied by Texier, but in December 1959 it was badly affected
by the flooding caused by the collapse of the Malpasset dam further up
the Reyran and has since been restored to make it usable for modern
entertainments—something that conceals much of its original structure. Its *cavea*, large enough to accommodate some 10,000 spectators,
was partly built against the rise of the hill to the east and some evidence
for the existence of a *velum* to cover it has been found, while the *arena*,
surrounded by marble plaques, was sunk some two metres below the
surrounding ground and included a deeper cruciform trench to provide
access for such things as animals to enhance the spectacles there

produced. The date of its construction has not been firmly fixed but appears to be no earlier than the second century AD and whether, as one might suspect, it was preceded by a timber version cannot be established.[24]

The harbour,[25] some 20 hectares in size, was formed from a lagoon slightly inland from the coast, which then ran considerably further north than it does now, and was linked to the sea by a canal, much of whose sides can still be discerned. It is sometimes suggested that the upper channel, bringing water from the Argens, was also originally Roman and that when Adam de Craponne made it in the sixteenth century he was simply restoring it, but since it cuts through Roman drains and a wall this seems improbable and it is not therefore included in fig 29. Though its whole area is now dried out and used for cultivation, three sides of the harbour are still clear and only its northern limit remains a little uncertain. The southern side is nicely defined by a quay and a wall and at the eastern end of it, near the opening to the canal, can still be seen the 'Lanterne d'Auguste' (pl 41): the upper part of this was restored in 1828, but the base is Roman, and on the opposite side of the canal there existed a similar building, the pair of them controlling access to the port. The so-called Port-Dorée, on the NW quay (pl 42), is the surviving part of some baths constructed in the third century.[26]

Considerable stretches of the town walls are preserved, especially in the north-eastern area, and though of early date and so intended to dignify the city rather than actually to defend it, they were provided with towers and a parapet.[27] In the west, the outer side of the Porte des Gaules (pl 43) is fully visible, but the inner part is completely obscured by the later consolidation of the ground behind it. This gate, with a double entrance flanked by a semicircle that ends in two circular towers, bears a considerable resemblance to that of Arles and is probably of Augustan date, but interestingly the base of one round tower immediately to the left of the entrance and evidently never developed, indicates that its plan was changed while it was still being built.[28] The northern gate has not been investigated and the only remaining part of the east gate, the Porte de Rome, is one column of decaying stone now bearing a cross, but the general plan of this, also semicircular, has been recovered by excavation.[29]

Activity was not, of course, confined to the area enclosed by the walls and the overall picture has been substantially improved by recent discoveries. While no burials have ever been found beside the main road leading out from the Porte des Gaules, some had long been recorded in the south-west, not only the well-known and still-standing mausoleum of la Tourrache (pl 44) but also a number in the vicinity of the chapel of St-Pierre[30] and this surely indicates that the baths at the Ferme de Villeneuve, partly excavated by Donnadieu, must have been related less to the naval base than to a suburban complex.[31] Further information on this cemetery was obtained in the late 1970s, when excavations in the Clos-St-Antoine revealed not only more burials but also a remarkable series of buildings beside a hitherto unknown road—a first-century *heroum* commemorating an unidentified notability that was later built over by a normal set of baths which remained in use until the third century, whereafter more burials were inserted.[32] In the north-east a few inhumations had been noted in 1884 beside the main road in the district of Ste-Croix,[33] but a more important cemetery has now been found in Pauvadou, together with not only some buildings beside the road that runs out from the Porte de l'Agachon but also some impressive pottery kilns, two of them enclosed in a carefully built workshop and producing small amphorae in the last quarter of the first century AD.[34] Further pottery kilns have also been found in Ste-Croix and (outside the area covered by the city plan but included in fig 30) at la Madelaine, at Bellevue, at St-Lambert and, in the west, at les Escaravatiers (just south of le Puget), showing that Fréjus was well able to produce much of its own pottery from its especially useful clay.[35]

The most remarkable monument of all is the aqueduct,[36] which began near the source of the river Siagnole (a tributary of the Siagne, not of the Reyran) some 30km due north of Fréjus. Its first section was built along the side of the steep gorge but at one stage it evidently collapsed a little and its course was then improved by the cutting of an astonishing cleft just west of the valley, the so-called Roche Taillée or Roquetaillade (pl 45). It then proceeded south past Callian and having crossed the river Biançon by an underground channel (in an area now confused by the modern creation of the Lac de St-Cassien) it finally ran down the east bank of the river Reyran. Here substantial remains of arches can still be seen wherever it crosses the river's tributaries, from the Avellan southwards, such as those at Bouteillière and those over the Gargalon (pl 46). On its arrival at Fréjus the water was still flowing at a considerable height and because of this it could be conducted along the top of the city walls (pl 47), leaving them only to cut the north-east corner, and ended at a *castellum divisorium* just west of the Porte de l'Agachon. The date of its construction remains uncertain, but while some rebuilding evidently took place, not only at the Roche Taillée but also of the arches over the Avellan and at Sénéquier, it must have been well after that of the walls which it defaced, probably in the second century.

Some of the land allocated to the veterans established in *Forum Iulii* can be presumed from the centuriation that has been deduced from air photographs of the neighbouring plain and it may be that further centuriation, observed near Flayosc (just west of Draguignan), indicates that others were settled much further away.[37] In any case, as is indicated by the extent of the early diocese, coupled with a little evidence from milestones, the *colonia* exercised control over a very large area.[38] In the east, its boundary with *Antipolis* (Antibes) was

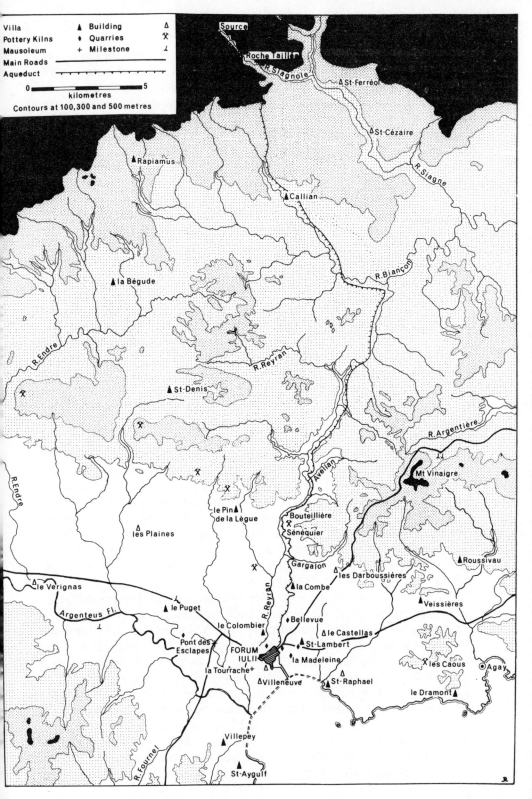

30 The course of the aqueduct of *Forum Iulii* (after Février)

evidently the river Siagne and that with *Salinae* (Castellane) approximately the valley of the Artuby. Although several milestones have been found along the road to *Alebaece Reiorum* (Riez) only two provide mileage figures and these appear to have been measured not from a city but from the road junction near le Muy;[39] the approximate extent of the diocese, however, suggests that the northern boundary partly followed the watershed between the tributaries of the Verdon and the Argens. In the west a milestone of Constantine, found at Cabasse (*Matavo*), gives the figure of XXXIII and this indicates that the *Pagus Matavonicus*, also recorded in an inscription to Caracalla from near here, was controlled not, as Clerc suggested, by *Aquae Sextiae* (Aix) but by *Forum Iulii*[40]—as indeed it was when the dioceses were established. South of this the boundary with the greatly extended territory of *Arelate* is a little obscure, but it seems probable that the industrial area of Collobrières (on which see below) belonged to Fréjus; all the *Stoechades Insulae*, on the other hand, seem to have remained under the control of Marseille.

Of the towns shown on fig 31, our information on those along the coast is derived mainly from geographical sources. *Pergantium*, recorded only by Stephanus of Byzantium, is surely Bréganson, evidently a port in both Hellenic and medieval times, but whether it was of any significant use to the Romans is not certain.[41] Both *Alconis* and *Heraclea Caccabaria*, on the other hand, do appear in the Maritime Itinerary and since the latter is probably Cavalaire, where several minor finds have been made, the former should be at or near Cavalière.[42] *Athenopolis* provides something of a contrast. Omitted from the Itinerary, which refers to the landing here only as the *Sinus Sambracitanus* (evidently the Golfe de St-Tropez), the town itself is named by Varro, Mela, Pliny and, by implication, Stephanus,[43] and the most interesting thing is that while Pliny has just described Agde as *Agatha quondam Massiliensium* he here omits the *quondam* and calls St Tropez simply *Athenopolis Massiliensium*, which should imply that it, like Nice, had remained under Massilian control. Significant finds, however, have been regrettably few and Roman remains are some of the few things still to be laid bare in this well-known town.[44] What little is known of *Portus Agathonis* (not in any Greek or Roman sources, but probably the ancient name of Agay) has already been referred to above (p 13).[45]

Geographical sources, specifically the Antonine Itinerary and the Peutinger Table, also yield most information on the names of the other towns and posting stations. *Ad Horream* is across the border and so is dealt with in the section devoted to *Antipolis* (*qv*), but the two roads linking it with Fréjus require notice. As may be seen from the map (fig 31), both were provided with milestones, but while the group on the northern route range in date from Nero to Valentinian I, the only Augustan stone so far discovered is the single one found on the southern route. This surely indicates that only the northern road was kept in constant repair, but since the original reading of the Neronian stone is said to have included the word RESTITVIT both may originally have been built in the Augustan period.[46] Moving now to the west of Fréjus, *Forum Voconi* was long claimed to be le Muy, where a number of finds had been made,[47] but, as we have seen (p 76), the statement by Munatius Plancus that it was 24 Roman miles from *Forum Iulii* supports the correction of the figures given by the Itinerary (*xii*) and the Peutinger Table (*xvii*) to *xxii*—putting it at les Blaïs, which is also at the right distance from *Matavo*.[48] Some Roman remains had been noted at les Blaïs in the nineteenth century and although nothing is to be seen on the surface several tombs and much pottery have been recovered since the war.[49] As already noted, *Matavo* was somewhere

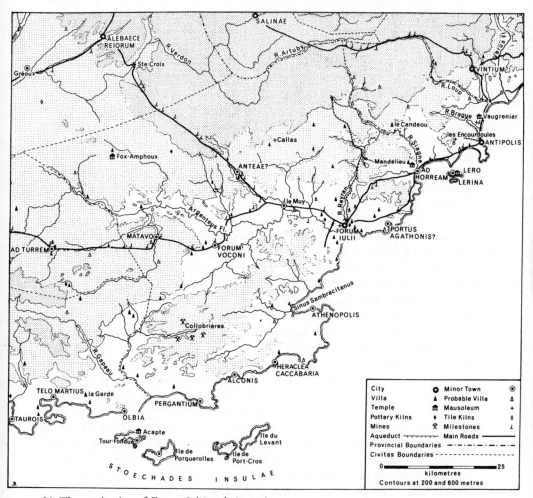

31 The territories of *Forum Iulii* and *Antipolis*

233

near Cabasse and around here considerable finds have been made—several inscriptions, a notable cemetery and, near the chapel of St Loup, the bases of columns.[50] *Anteae* is more difficult to locate. The road to Riez is not covered by the Antonine Itinerary and the only ancient source that includes it is the Peutinger Table, which shows *Anteis* as *xxxii mp* from *Reiis Apollinaris* and *xviiii mp* from *Foro Voconi*. This points to somewhere near Draguignan, but the town itself is hardly a possibility, both because the road passed just to the west of it and because its early medieval name was apparently *Dracenae*, so while several buildings have been recorded in this area, as well as the centuriation referred to above, it cannot yet be sited with accuracy.[51]

The only other road of importance is that which leaves the main route west of Fréjus and runs southwards to join the modern D8, probably leading ultimately to *Athenopolis*. This is most notable for the still surviving Pont des Esclapes (pl 48) and while it now spans only the little stream of le Béal its three arches, with buttresses on the upstream side, lead one to wonder whether some of the main waters of the Argens might once have flowed this way.[52] The Augustan milestone shown south of the Argens at Roquebrune, some 5km west of this bridge, was presumably removed from the main road at some time before its being noted in the church in 1883 and can hardly indicate the existence of another route in this direction.[53]

Both of the temples shown on the map (fig 31) are post-war discoveries. That at Fox-Amphoux, with its neighbouring villa, was located from air-photographs in the 1960s and subsequently excavated and the discovery of a white marble head of Minerva indicates that she was worshipped here: the buildings were erected in the first century AD but after a period of decay the area seems in the fourth century to have been taken over by potters.[54] The shrine at Mandelieu, on the other hand, is a *mithraeum* attached to a first-century villa, to which baths were added in the third century: the whole complex was abandoned near the end of the fourth century and the site was subsequently taken over by a chapel.[55] As for *mausolea*, apart from la Tourrache the only one so far in the territory of Fréjus is that under the villa at Callas, near the ruined chapel of la Trinité.[56]

As may be seen from the maps, a considerable number of other villas have been located. Some of them, such as those at St-Raphael and la Bégude (both named on fig 30), were very large,[57] and the excavation of others, in places such as Roussiveau and Taradeau (just north of *Forum Voconi*) has contributed to our understanding of the oil presses used.[58] While many more surely remain to be found, especially in the valleys of the Argens and its tributaries, agriculture and the cultivation of vines and olives were not the only sources of wealth in this area. Along the coast fishing, of course, took place, and Pliny tells us that a particular kind of fish-sauce—*allex*, a sediment of *garum*—was prepared here.[59] On the industrial side we have already noted the pottery kilns around Fréjus itself and a few others are known in other parts of the territory, while fig 30 shows a number of useful stone quarries, but particular attention must be drawn to the area of Collobrières (fig 31). Here half a dozen mines have been located, producing iron, copper and lead, showing that even the minerals required could mostly be obtained in the land of this prosperous *colonia.*[60]

REFERENCES AND NOTES

1 *Gallia* xxxv(1977), 498 (pottery found in the Butte St-Antoine), Février 1977, 19, 89.
2 Cicero, *Ad Fam* x, 15, 3.
3 Février 1977, 23–4; for 27 BC, *Gallia* xxxviii(1979), 557.
4 Tacitus, *Ann* iv, 5.
5 Pliny, *HN* iii, 35.
6 *Praefectus Classis*, CIL xii, 258, trierarch, 257, veteran of *Coh.1 Classis*, *ILGN*, 26; veterans of *Legio viii*, CIL xii, 260, 261, 263 (inscribed as iix), *ILGN*, 25 (from Ampus).
7 CIL xii, 259; for others, 264 (wife of a centurion of *Leg v Macedonica* and *1 Minervia*) and 265 (corrected on p 808 to *Leg x*).
8 Tacitus, *Hist* ii, 14; CIL xii, 5733.
9 Voting-tribe: CIL xii, 260, 290, 5739—*cf* also AE 1946, 94, of Agricola's father. *Seviri*, CIL xii, 267–72 incl, 3203 (found at Nîmes, funerary inscription of Q.Aurelius Parthenius, *sevir* of Nîmes, Lyon, Narbonne and Orange as well as Fréjus), 5737, *ILGN*, 27.
10 CIL v, 7907.
11 Tacitus, *Agricola* 44, 1; on the date (13 June 40, not 39), R.Syme, *Tacitus* (1958), 20, 262 and R.M.Ogilvie and I.A.Richmond, *Cornelii Taciti de Vita Agricolae* (1967), 301–02.
12 Tacitus, *Agricola* 4, 1, with AE 1946, 94 for Marcus. Where the grandfathers came from is uncertain, but the installation of one of them at Fréjus might help to explain Tacitus's description of the *colonia* as not only *inlustris* but also *vetus*.
13 Jerome, *Chron* 188. For full discussion of this see R.Syme, 'The Origin of Cornelius Gallus', *CQ* xxxii(1938), 39–44 (reprinted in E.Badian (ed), *Ronald Syme: Roman Papers* (Oxford, 1979), 47–54) and J.-P.Boucher: *Caius Cornelius Gallus* (Paris, 1966).
14 For Valerius Paulinus, Tacitus, *Hist* iii, 43. For Cornelius Fuscus, Tacitus, *Hist* ii, 86: several other suggestions have been made but, as Syme has pointed out, a *colonia* on the route from Spain to Italy is most likely, including Narbonne, Béziers, Arles and Fréjus, and this is the one he prefers: R.Syme, 'The colony of Cornelius Fuscus: an episode in the *Bellum Neronis*', *Am Journ of Philology* lviii(1937), 7–18, and *Tacitus* (1958), 683–4.
15 Munier 1963, 49–60; Munier is not convinced of his origin, but see Février 1977, 41, on Ursio and his successors.
16 For a suggested date for the *forum*, A.Donnadieu, *La Pompeii de Provence: Fréjus, Forum Iulii* (Paris, 1927), 111, against which see Grenier 1958, 108–09 and Février 1977, 97. For a temple, Donnadieu, *op cit*, 137, *FOR* ii,

p 6. For dedications, *CIL* XII, 249, 5734 (Jupiter), 247 (Apollo), 5733 (Hercules) 248 (Carpantus), 255 (Trittia), 251 (*taurobolium*); interestingly, another dedication to the obscure Trittia comes from Pierrefeu-du-Var, near the western boundary of the territory of *Forum Iulii* (*CIL* XII, 316).

17 Février 1977, 66–70.

18 *FOR* II, p 3, Février 1977, 86–8, 95–6, *Gallia* XIV(1956), 35–51, XXXIII(1975), 562, XXXV(1977), 498.

19 *FOR* II pp 2–3, Février 1977, 90–6, *Gallia* XX(1962), 171–203, 700–01, XXVII(1969), 450–1, XXXV(1977), 498, XXXVII(1979), 557. As Février points out, one governor, Torquatus Novellius Atticus, did die here while still in office (*CIL* XIV, 3602).

20 *FOR* II, p 14; the placing of these and other building remains shown by squares on fig 29 is derived from Donnadieu's plan of the city as issued with *FOR*.

21 Février 1977, 99–105, *Gallia* XXIX(1971), 449–56, XXXI(1973), 551–8, XXXV(1977), 498–9, XXXIX(1981), 532–3.

22 Grenier 1958, 734–41, Février 1977, 28, 97–9.

23 For the relative sizes, Grenier 1958, 567 n 1, Clavel 1970, 280.

24 Grenier 1958, 606–12, Février 1977, 29, 106–12 (with useful illustrations of it before and after the 1959 catastrophe).

25 *FOR* II, pp 3–4, Février 1977, 80–5. .

26 *FOR* II, p 4, Février 1977, 29, 113–14.

27 *FOR* II, no 4, Février 1977, 71–80. The actual date of the walls is not established, but it must have been considerably earlier than that of the aqueduct which was imposed on stretches in the east and north.

28 Février 1977, 79–80; for comparison with Arles, R.E.M.Wheeler *JRS* XVI(1926), 179–81 n.

29 Février 1977, 71–3.

30 *FOR* II, p 13, Février 1977, 115–16; Burnand 1975, 108–09, 129, dating la Tourrache to the 4th cent.

31 *FOR* II, pp 3, 14(mosaic), Février 1977, 115.

32 *Gallia* XXXVII(1979), 555–7, XXXIX(1981), 535–7; D.Brentchaloff, *Hist. Arch.* no 57(Oct 1981), 45–50 (with illustrations). Interestingly, this site has also yielded many coins of *Antipolis* (*qv*).

33 *FOR* II, p 13.

34 *Gallia* XXXVII(1979), 554–5, XXXIX(1981), 534; Brentchaloff, *op cit*, 40–2 and *RAN* XIII(1980), 73–114.

35 Ste-Croix, *Gallia* XXXIX(1981), 534; la Madelaine, Brentchaloff, *op cit*, 40 (citing Aubenas); Bellevue, *FOR* II no 10H; St-Lambert, *FOR* II, no 101; les Escaravatiers, *Gallia* XXVII(1969), 454.

36 *FOR* II, p 13 and 15 (with a reprint of Donnadieu's somewhat confusing map) also nos 146, 154, 161; Février 1977, 118–24 and 8–9 (partial map). I am especially grateful to M.Février for advice on the course of the aqueduct near Callian.

37 J.Soyer, 'Les centuriations de Provence II', *RAN* VII(1974), 185–7.

38 For a general discussion, Février 1977, 30–2.

39 *CIL* XII, 5446–53, König nos 69–78, with mileages *xxxv* and *xxxvi* on nos 76 and 77. *CIL* suggests a distance from *Salinae*, but there is no known road (nor any administrative probability) to support this; König, sensibly suggesting a distance from le Muy, unfortunately errs in identifying this with *Forum Voconi*.

40 Milestone, *CIL* XII, 5470, König, no 46; *Pagus Matavonicus*, *CIL* XII, 342; from Candumy, 3km south of Cabasse; Clerc 1916, 199.

41 Stephanus, *sv*; Benoit 1965, 102, 106, 184, drawing his main evidence from an early Greek wreck found in the now beached harbour.

42 *It Mar* 505, 4–8; Benoit 1965, 19–20, 107, 129; Barruol 1969, 81; for finds at Cavalaire, *FOR* II, no 16c, and at Cavalière, no 17.

43 Varro, *De Lingua Latina* VIII, 35 (*Athenopolitae*) Mela II, 5(77), Pliny, *HN* III, 35, Stephanus, *sv*, Ἀθῆναι πόλεις (κάτα δὲ Φίλωνα 'ἔξ .... τετάρτη Λιγυστίων).

44 *FOR* II no 15; *Gallia* XIV(1956), 232 (Iron Age pottery), XXIX(1971), 460, (columns etc found at le Pilon, just west of the town).

45 See also Février 1977, 169–70.

46 Milestones on the northern road (largely grouped together and so represented by only two symbols), *CIL* XII, 5456–63, König, nos 27–34; on the southern road, *CIL* XII, 5444, König, no 26.

47 *FOR* II, no 14, recording not only a milestone (*CIL* XII, 5445, König no 68) and an epitaph (*ILGN*, no 31) but also pottery, coins, burials and "substructions sur 6 hectares."

48 Cicero, *Ad Fam* X, 21, 1; *It Ant* 298.1; *REL* XXV(1959), 168–78. See also p 77 for the suggestion that it may have been founded by a Voconius when a legate of Caesar.

49 *FOR* II, no 202, *Gallia* XX(1962), 704, XXII(1964), 591, XXXI(1973), 553; see also *REL* XXXV, *loc cit*.

50 *FOR* II, no 211; G.Bérard, 'La nécropole gallo-romaine de la Calade à Cabasse', *Gallia* XIX(1961), 105–58; *Gallia* XXXI(1973), 552.

51 For finds in this area, *FOR* II, nos 169–74, to which should now be added the villa and cemetery at St-Hermentaire (*Gallia* VII(1950), 126–7, XXIII(1964), 593 and R.Boyer, 'A Draguignan fouilles de Sauvetage de tombes gallo-romaines', *Hist Arch* 57(Oct 1981), 88–89) and the building in sw Draguignan (*Gallia* XXXVII(1979), 553–4). For the selection of the Quartier des Salles as the most likely site, Barruol 1969, 80.

52 *Cf.*Février 1977, 117–18, suggesting that it may have been built over a marshy area.

53 *CIL* XII, 5455, König no 36.

54 For earlier finds here, *FOR* II, no 285; for excavations, *Gallia* XXV(1967), 419, XXVII(1969), 448–50, XXIX(1971), 448–9, XXXI(1973), 555, XXXIII(1975), 560–1, XXXV(1977), 497; for a full discussion, R.Boyer, 'Le site gallo-romaine de Fox-Amphoux', *Hist Arch* 57(Oct 1981), 82–4 (with illustrations). The remains of the temple are left exposed, but when visited in April 1982 were too overgrown for photography.

55 *Gallia* XXXIX(1981), 544–6; L.Aygueparse, M.Fixot, Y.Codou, 'Un temple de Mithra à Mandelieu', *Hist Arch* 57 (Oct 1981), 85–6 (with plan and illustrations).

56 *Gallia* XVI(1958), 437, XVIII(1960), 316–17, XXI(1963), 261–74; Burnand 1975, 108, dating the mausoleum post-Neronian.

57 St-Raphael, *FOR* II, no 1, *Gallia* XVIII(1960), 313–15, XXVII(1969), 454–5; la Begude, *FOR* II, no 150, *Gallia* XVIII(1960), 317–18, XX(1962), 706.

58 Roussivau, *FOR* II, no 10, *Gallia* XXXIII(1975), 565, XXXV(1977), 503; l'Ormeau (near Taradeau), *Gallia* XXXIX(1981), 540–1, J.-P.Brun, M.Pasqualini, 'Les huileries de l'Ormeau à Taradeau', *Hist Arch* 57(Oct 1981), 75–6.

Forum Iulii (Fréjus)

59 Pliny, *HN* xxxi, 95–7, explaining that it could be used for healing bites and ulcers; the *Foroiulienses* called the fish from which they derived it a *lupus* (wolf). For possible places where it was produced (la Gaillarde and the Butte St-Antoine) *v* Février 1977, 38.

60 Grenier 1934, 979, F.Benoit, *REL* xxvi(1960), 229, *Gallia* xxii(1964), 592, claiming that Q.Vibius, whose epitaph was found here, (*CIL* xii, 5756) was a *tabularius* of the mines.

18
Antipolis (Antibes)

As we have already noted (p 12), *Antipolis* was an early Greek foundation in the territory of the *Deciates* and its name, despite the literal meaning of 'a city opposite', was probably merely a graecisation of what the Ligurians called the place. Excavations and discoveries have shown that it was occupied in pre-Greek times, from the tenth century BC onwards,[1] and whether it was founded directly by *Phocaea* or indirectly by *Massalia* it was evidently under Massaliote control before the war of 154 BC (p 32). It seems, however, that it retained a good deal of autonomy. Besides minting some coins of its own, it evidently sided with Caesar, for when he captured *Massalia* it was neither put under direct Roman control, like Agde, nor, like Nice, retained by Marseille, but according to Strabo it became an 'Italiote' city.[2] Pliny, too, lists it as an *oppidum Latinum*[3] and its citizens were enrolled in the voting-tribe *Voltinia*, but its elevation to a full *municipium* is attested by inscriptions of *duoviri* as well as *seviri Augustales* and *flamines*.[4] Inscriptions also record the existence of a *Collegium Antipolitanorum* and a *Collegium Utriculariorum*, though the one for the latter was found not in Antibes but on the Ile St-Honorat.[5] A few early Christian burials have been found, but the earliest known bishop is Armentarius, who attended the Council of Vaison in 442.[6]

Despite a careful study by Février of the maps of the city made through the ages,[7] it is still difficult to reconstruct its whole plan in Roman times. A possible fragment of the pre-Roman Greek wall remains at the side of the Vieux Port (pl 49) and several parts of the late Roman wall, which, as usual, enclosed only a small area, are easy to see, some of them on rocks now almost cut off by the sea, but in the early Empire it was evidently a town of considerable size. One of the most important buildings, probably a temple, with some notable cisterns nearby, has indeed been found very close to the coast, partly under the cathedral and its adjoining Château Grimaldi, but excavations have also revealed some remains of the theatre (destroyed in 1691) under the modern bus station, more than ½km to the west, and there

seems also to have been an amphitheatre in the Rue de Fersen.[8] Baths
and several mosaics are also recorded and the city had two aqueducts,
one drawing water from the Ruisseau Bouillide, some 7km to the
WNW, and the other from the river Brague itself, near Biot, about 5km
to the NNW: parts of the latter were uncovered at Fontvieille in 1963.[9]

Antipolis had a good port, but the coast here was difficult—remains
from a number of local wrecks are well displayed in its museum—and it
may be for this reason that the Maritime Itinerary includes among its
stopping places not only Antibes but also both of the Iles de Lérins.[10]
The early monastery, so influential in the fifth century, was established
on the smaller island, *Lerina* (Ile St-Honorat), but although this has
yielded some notable Roman remains, including a statue of Priapus and
the inscription mentioned above,[11] the more important in Roman times
was *Lero* (Ile Ste-Marguerite, later famous for housing the Man in the
Iron Mask). Strabo records both deliberate settlement here and also an
heroum, Pliny the earlier existence of a town called *Berconum*,[12] and
excavations in the Fort Royal (pl 50) have revealed an impressive series
of structures, including not only buildings with mosaics and wall
paintings, baths, cisterns and a series of cryptoporticoes but also some
fortifications, apparently of the first century BC, with internal
bastions.[13]

On the mainland the area controlled by *Antipolis* presumably
corresponded with that of its early Christian diocese, separated from
the province of *Alpes Maritimae* by the river Loup and from the
territory of Fréjus by the river Siagne. Apart from the city itself, the
only place that is named in our ancient sources is *Ad Horream*, placed by
the Antonine Itinerary *xii mp* from *Antipolis* and *xviii mp* from *Forum
Iulii*,[14] with the latter measurement just reduced to *xvii* on the
Peutinger Table. This indicates somewhere at or very near the crossing
of the Siagne, probably at St-Cassien: cemeteries are recorded here,[15]
but some of the settlement may now be covered by the aerodrome of
Cannes-Mandelieu and the granaries implied by the name have not
been located.

The most notable discovery in recent times has been not a *vicus* but
the temple at Vaugrenier, 4½km north of *Antipolis* itself, parts of which
remain visible in the attractive park (pl 51). It appears to have been built
in the late first century BC but, despite its impressive structure—the
main temple surrounded by a courtyard, three sides of which were
bounded by colonnades, with an additional building on the north (fig
32)—it did not remain in use beyond the reign of Trajan and it is not
known to what deity it was dedicated.[16] A little to the south of this, on
the Plaine de la Brague, stands a remarkable 'pile', formerly decorated
with sculptures of arms, and despite some arguments that it was a
triumphal monument the most likely explanation is that it was the
mausoleum of a distinguished soldier.[17] The remains of another
monument, more widely accepted as a mausoleum since it bore a

funerary inscription to *Balbia Paterna*, are at les Encourdoules, overlooking Vallauris.[18]

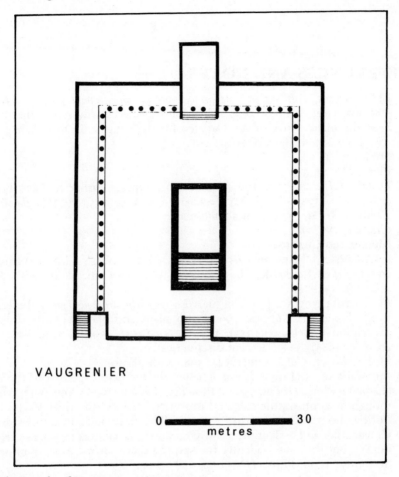

32 The temple of Vaugrenier (after Olivier)

As may be seen from the map (fig 31) a number of villas and probable villas have been located, not only close to the main road but also up the valley of the Siagne, and more doubtless remain to be found. Those near the coast, such as that at la Bocca, Cannes,[19] seem to have been as large and luxurious as one might expect, but perhaps the most interesting is that at le Candeou, just south of Peymenade. This was not at all luxurious, at most a *villa rustica*. The site was already occupied in the late Iron Age and was used as a farm in the early Roman period, but in the second half of the second century AD extensive works were installed here, including both oil presses and oil storage jars: these remained in use until about 270 and after a brief period of simple farming everything was abandoned in the early fourth century.[20] In

241

another field of the economy, *Antipolis* was famous for its fish sauce (*muria*) composed, so Martial tells us, from tunny, not mackerel.[21]

REFERENCES AND NOTES

1 J.H.Clergues, *Antibes: la ville grecque du VIe siècle avant J.-C. et l'habitat protohistorique*, Antibes, 1969. This does not necessarily imply that it had been the main centre of the *Deciates*: for the suggestion that their capital was at Grasse, *v* Barruol 1969, 216.

2 Strabo IV, 1, 10.

3 Pliny, *HN* III, 35.

4 *Duoviri CIL* XII, 175, 176 (a man who appears earlier to have been a *quattuorvir*), 179; *seviri*, 181; *flamines*, 175, 179, 185, 5723 (a *flaminica*). Tacitus, *Hist* II, 15, calls it a *municipium*.

5 *CIL* XII, 189, 187.

6 Munier 1963, 94–104.

7 P.-A.Février, 'Plans anciens de Fréjus et d'Antibes', *Gallia* XVII(1959), 207–13: *cf* A.Rousselle, 'Un nouveau plan moderne d'Antibes', *RAN* IX(1976), 143–54.

8 *FOR* I(1931), no 57: J.H.Clergues: *La recherche archéologique à Antibes: les secrets de son sol*, Antibes, 1966 (with plans and photos of the cathedral excavations): *Gallia* XI(1953), 115–16, XII(1954), 439–40, XVI(1958), 437–40, XLIII(1985), 525–8 (recent discoveries).

9 *FOR* I, no 57: *Gallia* XXII(1964), 598 (with photo).

10 *Itin Marit* 504.5 (*Lero et Lerino insulae*); for the better spelling of the latter (*Lerina*) *v* Pliny, *HN* III, 79 and Ptolemy, *Geog* II, 10, 9 (Ληρώνη ἢ Λῆρος, though he confuses the two and misrelates them to the river Var).

11 *FOR* I, no 72; *Gallia* V(1947), 146–8. The finds include a milestone of Constantine and Valentinian and Gratian (*CIL* XII, 5443 + p 857, König no 25), but this was evidently transported there for use as a column.

12 Strabo IV, 1, 10; Pliny, *HN* III, 79.

13 *FOR* I, no 73: *Gallia* V(1947), 146–55, XXXI(1973), 564–5, XXXV(1977), 505–07, XXXVII(1979), 564–7, XXXIX(1981), 541–3: *Hist Arch* 57 (Oct 1981), 62–6.

14 *It Ant* 297. 2–4.

15 *FOR* I, no 76.

16 *Gallia* XXIX(1971), 466, XXXI(1973), 569–70, XXXIII(1975), 570; *RAN* XI(1978), 143–94; *Hist Arch* 57 (Oct 1981), 79–81.

17 *FOR* I, no 54: Burnand 1975, 109–10, with details of arguments for and against this interpretation.

18 *CIL* XII, 201: *FOR* I, no 68: Burnand 1975, 109.

19 *FOR* I, no 75: *Gallia* XXXIX(1981), 544.

20 *FOR* I, no 163: *Gallia* XXXI(1973), 567–8, XXXIII(1975), 569–70, XXXV(1977), 508–09 (with plan): *Hist Arch* 57 (Oct 1981), 71–4 (with plan and photos).

21 Pliny, *HN* XXXI, 94; Martial XIII, 103.

23 *top left* The course of the aqueduct round the amphitheatre of Arles

24 *top right* Remains of the Constantine II monument in the Place du Forum, Arles

25 *left* The northern side of the Constantinian baths, Arles

26 *right* The interior of the Constantinian baths, Arles

27 *bottom left* A view of the Rhône from the amphitheatre of Arles, showing where it was crossed by the pontoon bridge

28 *bottom right* The aqueduct of Arles entering the city under the gate of la Redoute

29 *top left* The flour mills of Barbégal

30 *top right* A native shrine at *Glanum*

31 *above* The Greek *bouleuterion* of *Glanum*

32 *right* The altar of the Bona Dea, *Glanum*

33 The Arch of *Glanum*

34 The 'Mausoleum' of *Glanum*

35 *top left* The Pont Flavien, near St-Chamas

36 The temple at Château-Bas, Vernègues

37 *top right* Part of the wall of the inner
 harbour, Marseille, incorporating
 reused stones

38 *centre right* The fresh-water tank,
 Marseille, when under
 excavation

39 The fresh-water tank, as now conserved

40 *above* The remains of the theatre of Fréjus 41 The Lanterne d'Auguste, Fréjus

42 *top left* The Porte-Dorée, Fréjus

43 *top right* The Porte des Gaules, Fréjus

44 The mausoleum of la Tourrache, Fréjus

45 *top left* The Roche Taillée (or Roquetaillarde), cut to provide a safer course for the aqueduct of Fréjus when part of it had collapsed along the steep valley of the river Siagnole

46 *top right* The Fréjus aqueduct passing over the Gargalon stream

47 *left* The Fréjus aqueduct built over the north wall of the city

48 The Pont des Esclapes, west of Fréjus

49 *top left* Possible Greek walling underlying more recent work beside the Vieux Port of Antibes

50 *top right* Buildings recently excavated on the Ile Ste-Marguerite

51 *left* Remains of the temple of Vaugrenier

52 Remains of the temple of Riez

53 *top left* The Pierre Ecrite of Cl. Postumus Dardanus. The inscription is cut into the rock immediately left of the parked dormobile

54 *top right* The Pont Julien, 7km west of Apt

55 *left* The tetrapylon of Cavaillon, with the Colline St-Jacques in the background

56 Remains of the Arcades des Fusteries, Avignon

19
Alebaece Reiorum (Riez)

As its name implies, this city was the capital of the Celto-Ligurian tribe of the *Reii* and any connection with the *Albici*, the people who assisted *Massalia* in her struggle with Caesar, has now been satisfactorily disproved.[1] *Alebaece* was probably the name of its antecedent hill-fort on Mont St-Maxime, just to the NE of the town,[2] but in Roman times the settlement developed in the lower area at the confluence of the river Colostre with its tributary the Auvestre. Pliny includes it in his list of *oppida Latina* simply as *Alebaece Reiorum*, but inscriptions show that Augustus made it a *colonia Latina* and it emerges in due course as *Colonia Iulia Augusta Apollinaris Reiorum*[3]. As usual, Roman citizens here were enrolled in the voting tribe *Voltinia*[4] and there are records of several of the normal officials, but it should be noted that most of the relevant inscriptions have been found not in the territory of Riez itself but in that of the more prosperous *civitates* of the lower Rhône: one *pontifex* and *flamen* was honoured by the *dendrophori* of *Massilia*, one *quattuorvir* chose to be buried at *Ernaginum* (St-Gabriel) and two Reian citizens of unrecorded rank died in the land of Nîmes, while a further link with that area is indicated by the fact that the only known *quaestor* and *praetor* acted at some time in the second century as *curator reipublicae Avenniensis* (Avignon).[6] Apart from him (and his name is not known), no notable figures emerge until the fifth century when first the later-canonised bishop Maximus held a Council here to deal with the misbehaviour of the see of *Ebrodunum* (Embrun) in 439 and then bishop Faustus, the ex-abbot of Lérins who was of British origin, not only took part in the Council of Arles in 470 but was also a particular friend of Sidonius Apollinaris.[7]

The most notable monument at Riez is the still-standing row of four monolithic granite pillars, with Corinthian capitals and an impressive architrave (pl 52), and while various reconstructions had long been suggested excavations have now shown that it was indeed a first-century tetrastyle temple, 20–22 m long and 10.75 m broad. Unfortunately most of it had been dismantled in the third or fourth century,

243

probably to provide material for the late Roman town wall, and its dedication is not absolutely certain, but since the only inscription found near the columns is to Aesculapius (son of Apollo), it seems probable that this was the shrine whose importance added *Apollinaris* to the name of the city.[8] As a matter of fact, no inscription to Apollo himself has yet been found in Riez, but, besides an inevitable dedication to the *numina Augustorum*, three to the *Mater Deorum* (Cybele) are preserved, though none actually mentions a *taurobolium*.[9] Nor has any other pagan temple been located and on the religious side the most notable discovery has been the early Christian cathedral, probably of fifth-century date, which stood to the east of, and was aligned with, the still-surviving (though much restored) baptistery (now a museum).[10] This cathedral, south of the Colostre, was built over the remains of early Roman baths and much larger baths have also been found on the Pré de Foire, along with a sufficient number of rich houses and streets to confirm that the city was laid out in a regular fashion: these remains were partly covered by alluvium spread out over the centuries by the changing course of the Colostre, but a bridge built over it in Roman times has also been identified.[11] Minor finds elsewhere suggest that at its height the city covered some 15–20 ha and a reference to walls and gates in the Life of St Maximus suggest that it was walled (along uncertain lines) in the later Empire.[12] A field called les Arènes, near the confluence of the Colostre and the Auvestre, has suggested the possibility of a theatre or amphitheatre, but this has not been confirmed, nor has the existence of an aqueduct, though this is probable enough, bringing water from Laval, near Puimoisson, some 7km NNE of Riez.[13]

As may be seen from the map (fig 33), the central territory of the *Reii* was that of the valleys of the Colostre and its tributaries and the lower reaches of the Verdon, extending as far west as the Durance, but to the north it seems likely that they occupied also the valley of the Asse and even that of the minor river Rancure (the early diocese of Riez stretched even to the Bléone) but on this see the section on *Dinia* (p 248). The eastern limit—which was also the boundary between *Narbonensis* and *Alpes Maritimae*—is well defined by geography but the southern boundary, separating it from the territory of Fréjus, cannot be precisely traced, running largely across a rather barren area. Unfortunately only one of the 11 milestones found along the road past Draguignan has a probable mileage figure on it and even that gives a measurement from neither of the cities.[14] What the stones do show, however, is the importance of this road, and the discovery of another, at St-Jeannet, north of Riez, indicated that it was part of a main route linking Fréjus with Sisteron and other places further north,[15] while a Roman bridge has been identified near Ste-Croix and it, along with part of the road, was satisfactorily examined and photographed before it was submerged in the recently made Lac du Barrage de Ste-Croix.[16] Also of evident importance was the road linking Riez with Aix, which has yielded two milestones, one of Severus and one of Carus.[17] Neither of these roads appears in the Antonine Itinerary, but both are recorded on the Peutinger Table.

Posting stations must surely have existed on these roads, but so far, apart from Riez itself, the only important settlement identified in this area is at Gréoux-les-Bains, where a hot spring still exists, and the origin of its name is provided by a dedication to the *Nymphae Griselicae* made by the wife of the Roman consul T. Vitrasius Pollio.[18] Remains of baths, mosaics and other finds are recorded here and it is evident that it was, in Roman times as now, a spa.[19] The building at Montpezat is less satisfactorily established, but the record of circular foundations and the discovery of two altars suggest that it may have been a temple; the family tomb of a *quattuorvir* of Riez also stood here.[20] Little is known of the economy of the territory and the only rural buildings so far known that can safely be classified as villas, those at Vinon and St-Paul-des-Durance, stood not in the hills but on the lower ground south-west of Gréoux.[21]

REFERENCES AND NOTES

1 G. Barruol, 'Le territoire des Albiques', *REL* xxiv(1958), 228–56, summarised in Barruol 1969, 272–7; for a discussion of their actual territory, see the section on *Apta Iulia*, pp 256–8.

2 G. Barruol, *Archéologia* xxi(1968), 22 and Barruol 1969, 218, citing Février 1964, 84.

3 Pliny, *HN* iii, 36; full title, *CIL* xii, 3291 and 4082 (+ add p 810), abbreviated to *C.I.A.A.* in 358 and 367; for the variation *Colonia Reiorum Apollinarium*, *CIL* xii, 411, 983, 3200; the simpler form *Reii Apollinares* appears not only in the Peutinger Table but also, much earlier, in *CIL* iii, 7397 (recording a centurion who distinguished himself in the Dacian wars).

4 *CIL* xii, 369, 3200, 4082 (+ add p 810) and *CIL* iii, 7397.

5 *CIL* xii, 411 (Marseille), 983 (St-Gabriel), 3200 and 3291 (Nîmes), 3360 (Bouillargues, just SE of Nîmes), 4082 (Bellegarde, 15km SE of Nîmes); for a *quattuorvir* (a former *signifer* of *Leg x Gemina*) who did decide to be buried within Reian territory, *CIL* xii, 367.

6 *CIL* xii, 366 (from Riez); the only inscription recording an aedile (*CIL* xii, 351) comes from Bauduen, just s of Ste-Croix, but even *seviri* appear not only in the territory of Riez (*CIL* xii, 358, 367, 371) but also at Lyon (*AE* 1935, 17).

7 For Maximus, Munier 1963, 61–134; for Faustus, Munier 1963, 159, Sidonius, *Carmina* xvi, 78, *Epp* vi, 9; Sidonius also records the supply of food to Riez by Patiens, archbishop of Lyon (*Epp* vi, 12, 8).

8 Inscription, *CIL* xii 354; early views, *FOR* vi, p 3; excavations, *Gallia* xiv(1956), 55–63, xxii(1964), 554; for full discussion, G. Barruol, *Archéologia* xxi(1968), 23–5.

9 *Numina Augustorum*, *CIL* xii, 360; Cybele, 357, 358, 359.

10 *Gallia* xxv(1967), 393–5, *Archéologia* xxi(1968), 25–7 (with illustrations).

Alebaece Reiorum (Riez)

11 *FOR* VI no 8; *Gallia* XIV(1956), 55–63, XX(1962), 661–3, XXVIII(1970), 448–51, XXX(1972), 533–4 (for the bridge), XXXII(1974), 521–2, XLIII(1985), 519; *Archéologia* XXI(1968), 22, 25.

12 *Archéologia* XXI(1968), 22; *Dynami Patricii Vita Sancti Maximi*, chap 7 (J.-P.Migne: *Patrologia Latina* LXXX, p 36). The rather poor medieval walls, parts of which are still visible, are certainly not of Roman origin.

13 Les Arènes, *FOR* VII, p 3 (citing D.-J.-M.Henry; *Recherches sur la géographie ancienne et les antiquités des Basses-Alpes*, 2nd edn, 1842, 183); aqueduct, *FOR* VI, no 10.

14 One of the three stones listed under *CIL* XII, 5451 is recorded as König no 76 with the figure XXXV, which is the approximate distance from the junction of this road with the main E–W road in the south; the figure of XXXI suggested for König no 73, another stone in this group, is merely derivative.

15 The eleven stones (*CIL* XII, 5445–53, sorted out as König nos 68–78) range in date from Augustus to Hadrian and that at St-Jeannet (*ILGN* 645, König no 79) dates from Aurelian.

16 *Gallia* XXVIII(1970), 452–3.

17 *FOR* VI, nos 8 and 6, König nos 80–1, both now in the museum at Riez.

18 *CIL* XII, 361; T.Vitrasius Pollio was consul for the second time in AD 176.

19 *FOR* VI, no 5.

20 *FOR* VI, no 2; altars, *CIL* XII, 362 (dedicated *Osdiavis*) and 364; tomb, *CIL* XII, 367 (A.Iulius Saturninus, the *quattuorvir* and *ex-signifer* of *Leg* X *Gemina*, provided the epitaph *sibi et suis*).

21 Vinon, *FOR* II, no 294 (recording mosaics etc); St-Paul-lès-Durance, *Gallia* XX(1962) 696, XXX(1972), 528–30 (with plan).

20
Dinia (Digne)

Digne presents problems on both the historical and the archaeological side. Ptolemy, whose account of our area includes several errors, attributes *Dinia* to the *Sentii*,[1] but Pliny makes it clear that the tribe whose capital it became was that of the *Bodiontici*. The full text of his statement, however, needs to be read with some caution. It follows immediately after his list of *oppida Latina* and is worded as follows: *Adiecit formulae Galba imperator ex inalpinis Avanticos atque Bodionticos, quorum oppidum Dinia.*[2] This is usually taken[3] to mean that Galba transferred the two peoples from an Alpine province (whether *Alpes Maritimae* or *Alpes Cottiae*) to *Gallia Narbonensis*, but the meaning of the word *formula* is surely *ius Latii* and the word *inalpinis* can imply the region rather than the province in which the *Avantici* (centred on Gap) and the *Bodiontici* lived. The inclusion of the *Brodionti* on the *tropaeum Augusti* at la Turbie,[4] even if this is merely a variant form of their name, does not disprove this, nor does the fact that some men from here served in a *Cohors Alpinorum* or a *Cohors Ligurum*, but a further question regarding the status of the city does arise. An inscription found at Narbonne, the lettering of which indicates an early date, reveals an aedile, duly enrolled in the voting-tribe *Voltinia*, of COL DINIA LVB . . . (the right-hand part of it has not been found and the meaning of *LVB* . . . is completely obscure);[6] but on the other hand a bronze tablet found at Thoard in 1956,[7] besides giving its precise date (AD 187, the consulship of C.Bruttius Crispinus and L.Roscius Aelianus), records a convocation of decurions in the *curia* of M.A.A.D.B. and whatever A.A. stands for (either *Aelium Aurelianum* or *Aurelium Antoninianum* has been suggested), the letter *M* must mean not *colonia* but *municipium*. The true rank of the city during the early empire and the date at which it acquired it thus remains uncertain. That it was transferred to *Alpes Maritimae* in the late empire, on the other hand, while the *Vappincenses* of Gap and the *Reienses* of Riez remained in *Narbonensis Secunda*, is demonstrated by the *Notitia Galliarum*.[8]

On the archaeological side, though Digne has an attractive museum, with finds gathered from a wide area, little excavation has until recently been carried out here. Local geography imposes some limitations to its extent, but while an altar and part of a granite column are recorded as found in the area of les Sieyes, west of the Bléone, rather more has been discovered east of the river, especially around the romanesque church of Nôtre-Dame du Bourg. Here various things had been noted in the past, including a fourth-century sarcophagus, and excavations in the 1940s revealed not only further burials but also some remains of a Roman building. It is also likely that *Dinia*, like the modern town, had some hot baths and was effectively a spa.[9] A pagan temple may have stood on Mt St-Pancrace, about one km SE of the city, but conversion to Christianity is indicated by the reported building of a church by St Domninus (whose memory is still celebrated here on February 13) and by references to Vincentius and Nectarius, who seem to have been bishops of the place in the late fourth century.[10]

The territory of the *civitas* of *Dinia* was the basin of the river Bléone and its tributary the Bès and, as may be seen from the map (fig 33), its northern and eastern boundaries are nicely defined by mountains, while most of its southern limit can fairly be deduced from that of the early diocese. The western part, however, presents problems, for the lowest reaches of the Bléone formed the boundary between the early dioceses of Riez and Gap, indicating that that of Digne did not reach the Durance. This is of some importance, because it suggests that the Roman settlement at l'Escale belonged to *Vapincum* rather than *Dinia*, but since, as we have just noted, the *Dinienses* were transferred to *Alpes Maritimae* while both the *Vappincenses* and the *Reienses* stayed in *Narbonensis Secunda*, the dioceses may reflect no more than a small transfer of land from one city to another in the late Empire. To which city or tribe it had originally belonged, on the other hand, is still uncertain, since the discovery at l'Escale of an inscription recording the building of a tomb at the expense of the *Vocontii* suggests to some that it was they who held this land on the left bank of the Durance.[11]

In view of this range of possibilities it seems best to deal with l'Escale here. Many finds had long been recorded,[12] but it was not until 1960, when it had been decided to build a barrage across the river, that major excavations took place. These revealed a settlement covering some 5ha with many buildings beside narrow streets along a series of terraces (something that supports the belief that the name of the place was indeed *Scala*) and a square mausoleum on the upper ground. Occupation stretched back at least to the second century BC and although the town suffered destruction in the third century AD it was reoccupied in the fifth.[13] While it was evidently much more than a mere posting station, its development must have derived largely from its relationship to roads—not only the main roads from Digne and Riez to Sisteron, but also because a ford across the Durance probably linked them with the main route from the Alps to the lower Rhône.

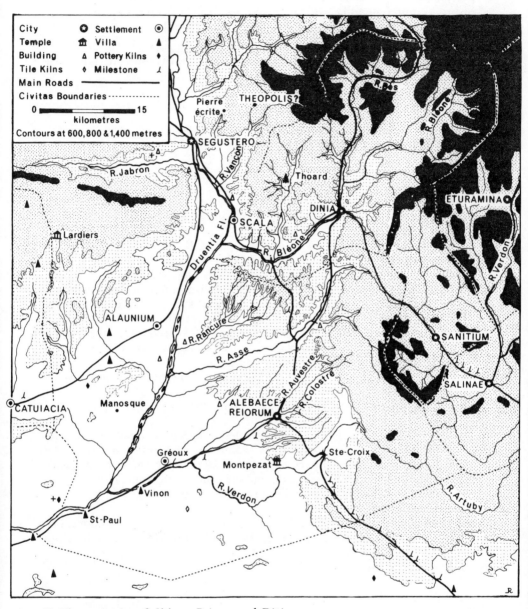

33 The territories of *Alebaece Reiorum* and *Dinia*

Dinia (Digne)

Very little is known about the economy of Digne in the Roman period (it is now called the capital of les Alpes de la lavande) and the only convincing villa so far discovered in its territory is one at Beaucouse, just south-west of Thoard. This had evidently been destroyed by fire, perhaps at the same time as l'Escale suffered, but some coins found with a skeleton in one of its rooms indicate that it was occupied at least in the first century AD.[14]

REFERENCES AND NOTES

1 Ptolemy, *Geog* II, 10, 8.
2 Pliny, *HN* III, 37.
3 *Eg* Barruol 1969, 287, Chevallier 1982, 135.
4 *CIL* v, 7817; the spelling *Brodionti* is repeated in Pliny, *HN* III 137. For discussion, Barruol 1969, 385.
5 For soldiers from here in *Coh III Alpinorum, CIL* III, 8495 and 14321 (both found in Dalmatia); for member of *Coh Ligurum CIL* v, 7885, 7890 and 7902, with *Gallia* IV(1946), 129–35 and *REL* XIII(1947), 21–8.
6 *CIL* XII, 4427, 4461, 4767 and 4903, combined in 6037a. The junction of the fragments makes the first line Q IVLIO C F VOLT BARBARO AEDILI, COL DINIA LVB . . . absolutely certain.
7 *AE* 1961, 156, *Gallia* XVIII(1960), 103–09, *REA* LXIV(1962), 314–25. The plate was not in its original place and had been cut down for the re-use of some of its bronze; now in Digne museum.
8 *Notitia Galliarum* XVII, 2, where it appears as *Civitas Diniensium*; for Riez and Gap, XVI, 3 and 5.
9 *FOR* v, no 16, *Gallia* VI(1948), 215, XLIII(1985), 515–17 (recent improvement).
10 Mont St-Pancrace, *FOR* v, no 16—tiles recorded as found in 1930 (*Rev Archéologique* 1935, II, 104). On St Domninus, Vincentius and Nectarius, R. Aubert and E. van Cauwenbergh (edd): *Dictionnaire d'histoire et géographie ecclésiastique*, Vol XIV(1960), 638, and on Vincentius, Munier 1963, 35–45.
11 *Gallia* xx(1962), 660; C. Goudineau in Princeton 1976, 504.
12 *FOR* VI, no 81.
13 *Gallia* xx(1962), 657–60, XXII(1964), 550–1, XXV(1967), 393, Goudineau *op cit* in n 11; for the mausoleum, Burnand 1975, 117. Finds in Digne museum.
14 *FOR* VI, no 83.

21
Vapincum (Gap)

Vapincum became the city of the *Avantici*, one of the *Inalpini* tribes who, along with the *Bodiontici* (the people of Digne, *qv*), may have been transferred to the province of *Narbonensis* by Galba in AD 69.[1] It probably succeeded a hill-fort on the Colline St-Mens, which rises to 978m just SE of the modern town,[2] but its Roman development evidently owed much to its place on the main routes from the Rhône valley to Italy and its name duly appears on the Vicarello Goblets, in the Antonine and Bordeaux Itineraries, on the Peutinger Table and in the Ravenna Cosmography.[3] It is not, however, mentioned in any of the literary sources and its status remains obscure. Whether or not the *Avantici* had previously been in *Alpes Maritimae* (on which *ius Latii* was conferred by Nero in AD 63)[4] or in *Alpes Cottiae* (taken over as a Roman province by the same emperor on the death of King Cottius),[5] the chapter in which Pliny lists them seems to imply that they already had Latin rights in his time, but no inscriptions have so far recorded any local officials or supplied any indication of their voting-tribe.

Indeed, while Gap has a good museum, most of the inscriptions displayed in it have been collected from a considerable area around and only one from the city itself is really significant: this is a dedication to *Victoria* found in 1867 when the old romanesque cathedral was being demolished and appears to have been attached to a large circular monument.[6] The one thing that is certain is that in Gap, as in so many places in Gaul, a small area (about 2ha) was fortified in the late third century—something that was noted in the nineteenth century and was confirmed in 1971 by the excavation of a round tower and a short stretch of wall in the Place St-Arnoux.[7]

Gap must have become a bishopric in the later Roman Empire—at least, *Civitas Vappincensium* appears in the Notitia Galliarum under *Narbonensis Secunda*[8]—but its earliest known diocese extends much too far for it to be accepted as equivalent to the territory of the Roman *civitas* and other evidence is more helpful.[9] In the first place, *Ad Finem*, which appears in the Bordeaux Itinerary at *xii mp* from *Davianum*

(Veynes) and *xi mp* from *Vappincum* and so must have been near la Roche des Arnauds,[10] clearly indicates the western boundary, while the hamlet with the modern name of le Fein (perhaps reflecting the previous existence of an inscribed boundary-stone?), just 3km south of Chorges (*Caturigomagus*), must similarly mark the eastern limit, and a confirmation of this is provided by the discovery at la Couche (2km SSE of Chorges) of a marble altar dedicated to *Mercurius Finitimus*.[11] To the north, it is just possible that the elusive *Tricorii* (*qv* under Vienne) were governed from Gap, but even if they had no established tribal centre of their own the valley of the Drac could have been as easily administered from Grenoble. To the south, as may be seen from the maps (figs 33, 34), much of the boundary between *Vapincum* and *Dinia* is well determined by hills, but the question remains how far the *Avantici* occupied the left bank of the Durance. The name of the tributary Vançon certainly indicates that they stretched beyond the land immediately opposite *Segustero* (Sisteron), but whether as far as the notable site of *Scala* (l'Escale) is doubtful and that is here dealt with under *Dinia* (Digne, *qv*).

As for the right bank, the discovery at Ventavon of the funerary inscription of Q.Caetronius Tibullus who, having been a *duovir* and *pontifex* of *Ariminum* (Rimini), was also a *flamen* and *curator muneris publici* at *Dea Augusta Vocontiorum* (Die) suggests that the boundary should join the river somewhere near *Alabonte*, whether or not the name of the *pagus Epotius*, of which he was *praefectus*, is really preserved in that of the village Upaix, and this conclusion agrees well with the geography of the area (fig 34).[12]

As the itinerary figures show, *Alabonte* was certainly at Monêtier-Allemont, but while an inscription from here, recording the construction of a *macellum* in memory of someone, also appears to refer to a *pagus*, its name is unfortunately lost.[13] Little is known of the settlement itself, but of the four other local inscriptions two record dedications, one of them to Fortuna and the other to Silvanus.[14] *Ictodurum* is not mentioned in any of the Itineraries and appears only on the Peutinger Table and (as *Idodimus!*) in the Ravenna Cosmography, the former putting it midway between *Vapincum* and *Caturigomagus*, each *vi mp* away. This points to a site just west of la Batie Neuve, but while some parts of the main Roman road have been observed near here this place, too, is largely unknown. Of the two roads shown on the map north of this area, that from *Ictodurum* (roughly corresponding to the modern D14) is accepted as certain on T.I.R. Sheet L32 and is supported by the discovery of a dedication to Apollo by Iustus, a *servus Mercuri et Cereris*, at la Rochette and of another, to Mars, in the Forest-St-Julien,[15] but the course of that running from *Vapincum* is more doubtful. Some reasonably direct link between Gap and Grenoble is certainly to be expected, roughly along the line that had been followed in both directions by Munatius Plancus in 43 BC (p 77 above), but the modern

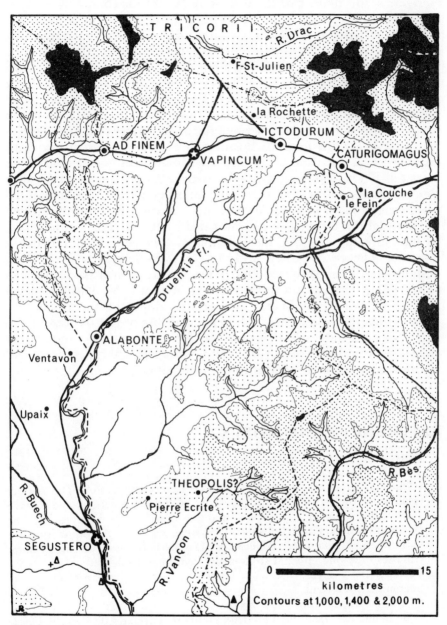

34 The territory of *Vapincum*

N85, through the Col Bayard, involves too many climbs and it therefore seems likely that the Roman road, like the route followed by Napoleon on his return from Elba, passed through the Col de Manse.[16]

Whoever owned estates in an area like this, the emergence of luxurious Roman villas is hardly to be expected; rather, the tenants or peasant farmers would have concentrated on cattle-raising, with transhumance in the appropriate seasons. Nevertheless, it seems that a rich man could choose to retire here and possible evidence for this is provided by the most remarkable of all inscriptions, the so-called Pierre Ecrite.[17] This states that after being praetorian prefect of Gaul (an office he held 409–13), the great Cl.Postumus Dardanus, in association with his wife Nevia Galla and his brother Cl.Lepidus, cut open a road to the place called *Theopolis* and fortified it with walls and gates to provide a general protection for everyone living on his estate. The opening of the road, *caesis utrimque montium lateribus*, in a narrow gorge through which the Riou Jabron flows, is well confirmed by the obvious cutting-back of the cliffs (pl 53), but the position of *Theopolis* itself remains a mystery. The road clearly leads towards St-Geniez, and although nothing significant has been found in that village, a farm 4km to the ENE of it is called Théous, but this is not a fortified site. Similarly, a chapel 2km south-east of St-Geniez and on the slopes of the Rocher de Dromon overlies some early columns, probably of Merovingian date, and it has been suggested that they may have been part of a monument erected over the tomb of Dardanus and Nevia long after their death. All of this, however, still remains to be sorted out.

REFERENCES AND NOTES

1 Pliny, *HN* III, 37; for discussion *v* p 247.
2 Barruol 1969, 290.
3 *It Ant* 342.3, 357.7; *It Burd* 555.6; *Rav Cos* IV, 27(240,9). The correct spelling of the name is a little obscure. Of the Goblets, 1 and 2 have *Vappincum*, 2 and 4 *Vappinquum* and the double *–pp–* reappears in the Bordeaux Itinerary and the *Notitia Galliarum*, while the Antonine Itinerary varies from *Vapincum* to *Vapinquum*; Ravennas' *Bapinco* (variant *Bapnico*) still uses only one *–p–* and so does the Peutinger Table.
4 Tacitus, *Ann* xv, 32.
5 Suetonius, *Nero* xviii.
6 *CIL* XII, 1549; Barruol 1969, 290 n4.
7 G.de Manteyer, 'Le nom et les deux premières enceintes de Gap', *Bull de la Soc d'Etudes des Hautes-Alpes*, 1905, 160–95; *Gallia* xxx(1972), 534–5, xxxII(1974), 523.
8 *Not Gall* xvi, 5. The claim in J.Roman, *Histoire de la Ville de Gap* (Gap, 1892) that Constantinus, who attended the Council of Orange in 441, was bishop of Gap is countered by Munier 1963, 76–93, where he is listed as bishop of Carpentras.

9 For a useful discussion, Barruol 1969, 287–91, and P.-A. Février, '*Gap* et les cités voisines à l'époque romaine', *Bull de la Soc d'Etudes des Hautes-Alpes*, 1975.

10 *It Burd* 555.5–6.

11 *CIL* xii, 75.

12 Ventavon inscription, *CIL* xii, 1529. The place called Les Termes cited by Barruol 1969, 289 n4, is only 3½km s of Gap, so if it had any Roman significance it could only mark the boundary of a *pagus*, not that of the whole *civitas*.

13 *It Ant* 342.3–5, putting it *xviii mp* from *Vapincum* and *xvi mp* from *Segustero*, 388. 1–2, *xvii mp* and *xvi mp*. The inscription, *ILGN*, 226.

14 *CIL* xii, 1525–8.

15 La Rochette, *CIL* xii, 2318; Forest-St-Julien, 1550 (+ p 826)

16 Barruol 1969, 290 n4. A Refuge Napoléon exists at the Col de Manse.

17 *CIL* xii, 1524; *FOR* vi, no 70. For a general discussion, Eydoux 1964, 249–70, with references on p 370, especially to H.-I.Marrou, 'Un lieu-dit "Cité du Dieu"' in *Augustinus Magister* (Paris, 1954), summarised in *Bull Soc Nat des Antiquaires de France*, 1954–5.

22

Apta Iulia (Apt)

This city, situated on the south bank of the river Calavon, controlled a considerable part of the Département de Vaucluse and its background is of particular interest. As Barruol has convincingly argued,[1] this was the land of the *Albici*, the tribe that provided able fighters to assist the Massaliotes in their struggle with Caesar in 49 BC. Caesar himself describes them simply as *barbaros homines, qui in eorum fide antiquitus erant montisque supra Massiliam incolebant,*[2] and while the implied duration of their association with Marseille is notable the identity of their *montes* is not made clear. Fortunately Strabo is more helpful. Having discussed the *Salyes* (*Salluvii*) and noted that their territory included plains as far as *Luerion* and the Rhône (τὴν χώραν . . . μέχρι Λουερίωνος καὶ τοῦ Ῥοδανοῦ πεδιάδα), he then states that 'after the *Salyes* the *Albieis* and *Albioeci* and *Vocontii* occupy the more northerly parts of the mountains'.[3] *Luerion*, which is not mentioned anywhere else, can most reasonably be recognised as the Montagne du Luberon, and since the general location of the *Vocontii* is well known, the land of the others fits into the area around Apt. Whether the *Albieis* and the *Albioeci* (Ἀλβιεῖς καὶ Ἀλβίοικοι) were really two peoples or merely a duplication resulting from Strabo's use of more than one source remains uncertain, but their location is nicely confirmed by several modern place-names (most notably the Plateau d'Albion, some 20km north of Apt) and by an inscription to the deity *Albiorix* or *Albiorica* found at St-Saturnin-d'Apt.[4]

The best known hill-fort in this region is that at Perréal, also in the commune of St-Saturnin but only about 6km NW of Apt,[5] and it is likely enough that this was the main centre of the *Albici* before they incurred the wrath of Caesar. *Apta* itself has produced no evidence of pre-Roman occupation and the choice of the site was clearly dictated by its relation to the great highway leading from the Alpine passes to the Rhône. Pliny includes it in his list of *oppida Latina*, calling it *Apta Iulia Vulgientium.*[6] The *Vulgientes* are not otherwise known and may have been simply the inhabitants of the local *pagus,*[7] but the inclusion of *Iulia* indicates a Latin *colonia*, which is confirmed by five inscriptions,[8] and taking everything into consideration this is one of the strongest pieces of evidence that some at least of these *coloniae Latinae* were indeed founded on the instructions of Caesar (*cf* p 75).

As usual, Roman citizens here were enlisted in the voting tribe *Voltinia* and not only do we have ample evidence for *quattuorviri*, aediles and *flamines*,[9] but it seems that one of them who was buried near Apt, L.Volus Severianus, may also have become a *duovir* of *Colonia Iulia Hadriana Avennio* (Avignon, *qv* p 265) and *sacerdos urbis Romae aeternae*[10]—something that may be related to another inscription which indicates that it was here, at Apt, that Hadrian buried his much-loved horse Borysthenes.[11] *Fabri corporati* of the city are recorded in an inscription of uncertain provenance,[12] but apart from funerary monuments the most numerous finds from the city and its immediate environs are altars inscribed to a variety of deities—five to Jupiter, three each to Minerva and Mercury (who is in one case combined with Mithras), two each to Silvanus, the Matres and the Nymphs and one to Mars.[13] These underline the fully-established Romanity of the place, for only in one case do local deities emerge—an altar found half a league from Apt dedicated *Vogientis et Mercurio* (where *Vogientis* may reflect the *Vulgientes*.)[14] Despite the wealth demonstrated by the many inscriptions and statues however, and although it had a priest as early as AD 314, *Apta* does not reappear in literary sources until a chance mention of it by Sidonius Apollinaris.[16]

Though a large number of burials have been found beside the suburban roads through operations like pipe-laying[17]—and incidentally these have confirmed the existence of secondary Roman roads running towards the north and the south—relatively few excavations have been carried out in the city itself. Some in le Clos (the SE area) in 1902–04 revealed houses with mosaics and painted wall-plaster and also traces of an aqueduct that evidently came from the waters of the Marguerite, while others in 1937–8 exposed traces of large buildings on the site of the Marché aux Truffes (near the centre) and another mosaic in the boulevard Camille-Pelletan.[18] Since the war the most important archaeological work has been on the theatre whose plan, although none of it is visible on the surface, has been well worked out—apparently of Augustan date and with an overall diameter of *c* 90m.[19] Despite these shortcomings, however, a careful study of all recorded finds and of archival documents has enabled Barruol to produce a convincing plan of the main parts of the city, on which fig 35 is based.[20] An important point to note here is that there used to be a southern branch of the river Calavon—now no longer visible—and it was evidently this that dictated the southern line of the fortifications of the late Empire, over which were built the medieval ramparts. Of the other structures shown, apart from those in le Clos, the semicircle just south of the theatre represents that which is visible under the crypt of the cathedral of Ste-Anne, the depth of which, some 4.5km below the present 235m, indicates how far the land level has risen since Roman times; the possible temple to the east of it, under the old church of St-Babylas, may have been dedicated to Mars; the complicated structure north of the presumed *forum* was evidently of great importance, probably the place where, as an inscription tell us, a *flamen* erected his *porticus et arcum cum ostiis*.[21] The 'shrine', on the site of the Reboulin works, was apparently dedicated to the tutelary deity of the *colonia*, as is suggested by the existence here of a *favissa* (an underground reservoir for water and sacred utensils); the baths—surely not the only ones—are under the sous-préfecture and the possible amphitheatre under the bishop's garden. Finds indicate the existence of villas in the immediate neighbourhood and Barruol estimates the population of the city to have been between 5,000 and 10,000.

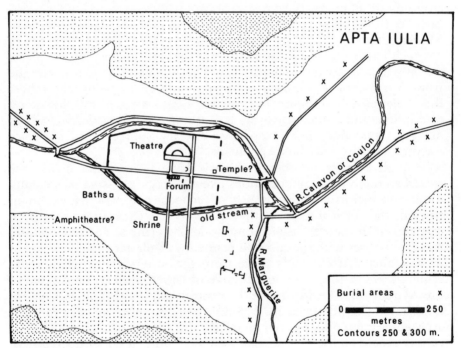

35 Plan of Apt (after Barruol)

To turn now to the territory controlled by Apt, a point on its western boundary is well defined by *Ad Fines*, recorded in itineraries as being *x mp* from *Apta* and *xii mp* from *Cabellio* (Cavaillon).[22] This indicates the existence of a *mutatio* at or near Mariquan (in the commune of Goult, but just south of the confluence of the little river l'Imergue with the Calavon) and although no archaeological evidence for it has yet been obtained its approximate position is not in doubt. Starting from this point, as may be seen from the map (fig 38, p 278), the boundary northwards is well defined by geography, separating off the *civitates* of *Cabellio* and *Carpentorate* (Carpentras) as far as Mont Ventoux, and from there, dividing the *Aptenses* from the *Vocontii* (and taking in the appropriately named Mont d'Albion), it should turn eastwards towards the Montagne de Lure. The southern boundary, for reasons already stated, is certainly the Luberon and only the division of land with the *Sogiontii* to the east, where we have to rely on the limits of the medieval diocese of Apt, remains a little uncertain (for Lardiers, see p 295 under the *Vocontii*).

The only main road through this territory is that from the Alps to the Rhône and this too has been the subject of a fine study by Barruol and Martel, considering not only milestones and bridges and its precise course but also such details as fords.[23] The most notable bridge is the Pont-Julien (pl 54), which owes its remarkable preservation to the fact that while the modern N100 keeps to the north bank of the Calavon the Roman road ran south of it for some miles, so that though still crossable by car it is not subject to heavy traffic. Three inscribed milestones are recorded, but only two of them can be dated—one of Augustus (3 BC) from near Apt and one of Antoninus Pius from Goult[24]—and whether this road had actually been put in proper order in the time of Domitius (or indeed before that of Augustus) remains highly questionable.[25]

Apart from *Apta* and *Ad Fines* the only place in our area that is listed in the itineraries is *Catuiacia, xii mp* east of Apt.[26] This has long been identified with Céreste, but there is good evidence—finds of pottery and burials, and the fact that such *mutationes* were usually placed near river crossings—that it really stood some 2km west of the town, near the present boundary of the départements of Vaucluse and Alpes de Haute-Provence.[27] The *pagus Vordensis*, attested by an inscription from Apt, should have had a centre, presumably at or near Gordes, just north of *Ad Fines*, but this is more likely to have been in the *civitas* of *Cabellio* than in that of *Apta Iulia*.[28] Another most likely place for a settlement is St-Saturnin. Though the hill-fort at Perréal was apparently destroyed in 49 BC, and although Caesar, to judge from his behaviour in northern Gaul,[29] probably balanced his respect for the Greek Massaliotes by reducing his barbarian captives to slavery, some *Albici* surely survived and in this commune, besides the inscription to *Albiorix*, no less than fourteen altars have been found. More than one temple may therefore have existed within this commune, but since the legible dedications vary (three to Jupiter, three to Silvanus, two to the Nymphs and one to the obscure *Obio*),[30] the one site chosen for inclusion on the map is in the hamlet of Croagnes, where statues of Mars, as well as two dedications to him, are recorded.[31]

Though *Apta* was so prosperous, little is evident about the background to its economy. There are no mines here, no pottery kilns have been found and, so far, few villas. Of those shown on the map that at les Crottes, opposite the village of Buoux,[32] was recorded long ago, but the other two have been excavated since the war. That at Banon,[33] near the eastern border, was built in the first century and although it suffered from a fire in the middle of the third continued in occupation until the end of the fourth, while the villa at Redortier,[34] 1km north of Contadour, was also of first-century date and stood at the surprising height of 1164m above sea level—a clear indication of how much yet remains to be discovered at a more normal altitude.

REFERENCES AND NOTES

1 G. Barruol, 'Le territoire des Albiques', *REL* xxiv(1958), 228–56, summarised (and slightly modified) in Barruol 1969, 273–7.

2 Caesar, *BC* I, 34.

3 Strabo IV, 6,3–4.

4 *CIL* XII, 1060.

5 *FOR* VII, no 25; *Gallia* XIV(1956), 251–2, XVI(1958), 402–05, XVIII(1960), 267–8, XX(1962), 676–9.

6 Pliny, *HN* III, 36. Curiously, neither *Apta* nor the *Albici* are listed by Ptolemy, and by the time of the *Notitia Galliarum* (xvi, 3) it has become simply *Civitas Aptensium*.

7 As Barruol 1969, 276–7 points out, –*entes* usually suggests a derivation from the name of a place or area.

8 *CIL* XII, 695 (from Arles) and 1114, 1116, 1118, 1120 (all from Apt).

9 *CIL* XII, 695 and 707 (from Arles), 1114, 1116, 1120 (from Apt) and 1118 (recording a *flaminica*, from Saignon, SE of Apt).

10 *CIL* XII, 1120, with Hirschfeld's comment on it. The main problem that he raises—whether *Avennio* really did become a fully Roman *colonia* under Hadrian—is discussed elsewhere (p 265).

11 *CIL* XII, 1122. For Borysthenes, Cassius Dio LXIX, 10, *SHA, Hadrian* xx, 13.

12 *CIL* XII, 1189. On p 137 Hirschfeld includes two other possible *collegia*, one (no 1082) where the word associated with *soci* is uncertain, the other (no 1110, from Villars) where *soci propoli* appear. Blanchet (*FOR* VII, p 14) translates *propoli* as 'revendeurs', but since πρόπολος in Greek often means simply someone ministering to a deity, and since both these inscriptions are dedications, it may be that neither *propoli* nor *soci* have any significant meaning here.

13 *CIL* XII, pp 139–42, *ILGN*, pp 50–2.

14 *CIL* XII, 1082—that referred to in n12 as dedicated by *soci*; *cf Barruol* 1969, 277 n 1.

15 For reliefs etc, Esperandieu 1907, 239–42, 2556–7; remarkably, one pair of statues, of a woman and her daughter, found in 1721, is now at Chatsworth in Derbyshire.

16 Sidonius, *Epp* IX, ix, i, when Faustus, then bishop of Riez, happened to have visited Apt. The first recorded priest, Romanus, attended the Council

Council of Arles in AD 314 (Munier 1963, 9–25).

17 Eg *Gallia* xiv(1956), 251, xvi(1958), 205–22, 237–41, xviii(1960), 270–3, xx(1962), 663–4, xxii(1964), 87–110, 557–8.

18 For summary accounts of these, *FOR* vii, pp 9–10, but see also n20 below.

19 G.Barruol and A.Dumoulin, 'Le théatre romain d'Apt', *RAN* i(1968), 159–200; later work, *Gallia* xxviii(1970), 439–40. A small part is visible below the museum.

20 G.Barruol, 'Essai sur la topographie d'Apta Iulia', *RAN* i(1968), 101–58.

21 *CIL* xii, 1121, found serving as a basin for a fountain; he also established some *ludi publici*.

22 Vicarello Goblets II and III (though omitted on I and II), *It Ant* 343.4–5, Peutinger Table (with the second figure corrupted to xi).

23 G.Barruol and P.Martel, 'La voie romaine de Cavaillon à Sisteron sous le Haut-Empire', *REL* xxviii(1962), 125–202, with illustrations and a detailed map.

24 Apt milestone, *CIL* xii, 5497, König no 82; Goult stone, *CIL* xii, 5498, König no 84 (with the date of AD 144 suggested); the third stone, from Céreste, *FOR* vi, no 54, König no 83. For other possibilities, Barruol and Martel, *op cit*, 133–5.

25 That Domitius did organise it seems to be assumed by Barruol and Martel (*op cit*, 125) but, as will be observed in other regions, Roman forces were quite capable of using native tracks without wasting time on consolidating them.

26 Vicarello Goblets (iii and iv, *Catuiacia*; i, *Catuiaciam*; ii, *Catulacia*) *It Ant* 343.2 (*Catuiacia*, variants *Catuluca, Cataluca, Catoluca*), Peutinger Table (*Catuiacia*).

27 For Céreste, *FOR* vi, no 54; for correction of this, Barruol and Martel, *op cit*, 167–8 (obs also *ibid*, 141, where the 'Roman' bridge of l'Ecrême, cited by *FOR* as a 'monument historique', is dismissed as merely medieval); *Gallia* xxv(1967), 386–7.

28 *CIL* xii, 1114, in which the *Vordenses pagani* honour their patron C.Allius, a *quattuorvir, flamen* and *augur* of the *colonia*. For the location of the *pagus*, Barruol 1969, 241 and 277 n3.

29 *Cf* Caesar, *BG* vii, 89, 5, where, after the capture of *Alesia*, he claims to have given a slave to each of his soldiers.

30 *CIL* xii, 1060, 1068, 1072, 1090, 1094, 1098, 1099, 1102, 1107, 1177 (misplaced in *CIL*), 1350; *FOR* vii, no 25.

31 *FOR* vii, no 26; *CIL* xii, 1076; *ILGN*, 157.

32 *FOR* vii, no 31.

33 *Gallia* xiv(1956), 240, xvi(1958), 392–9, xviii(1960), 285 (with plan).

34 *Gallia* xxii(1964), 553–4.

23
Cabellio (Cavaillon)

Cabellio was one of the towns of the *Cavares* and excavations of the hill-fort on the Colline St-Jacques, overlooking the modern town, have shown that it flourished in pre-Roman times, with many early imports.[1] Stephanus of Byzantium says that Artemidorus, who wrote towards the end of the second century BC, called it a city of *Massalia*[2] and, as we have seen above (p 42), it was probably after the war with the *Arverni* that it came under Massaliote control and minted coins with Greek inscriptions. Whether it was then that settlement first developed at the foot of the hill, on the site of the Roman city, is not clear, but since it was here that a ferry operated across the broad river Durance,[3] *Cabellio's* prosperity must have developed increasingly as more and more movement took place along the highway from the Alps to the Rhône.

Massalia was surely deprived of the town in 49 BC, but how soon it acquired its full Roman status is a little uncertain. Pliny includes it in his list of *oppida Latina* and Ptolemy calls it a *colonia*, a title that is confirmed by coins inscribed COL CABE, but since some of them are evidently pre-Augustan Caesar may have been responsible for its elevation. We have epigraphic evidence that its Roman citizens were enlisted in the voting tribe *Voltinia* and that *quattuorviri*, *flamines* and *seviri* were appointed,[5] and whatever the validity of the bronze medallion inscribed COLLE VTRI CAB the establishment of a *Collegium Helciariorum* here is probable enough, as demonstrated by the splendid bas-relief of men towing a loaded barge found near Cabrières d'Aygues (in the territory of *Aquae Sextiae*) and now in the Musée Calvet at Avignon.[6] Relatively few inscriptions, however, have been found in the city and apart from its inevitable inclusion in itineraries[7] it is not mentioned in any literary sources. Its first known bishop is Genialis, who attended the Council of Nîmes in AD 394 or 396, and it appears in the *Notitia Galliarum* as *Civitas Cavellicorum*.[8]

A number of burials have been found beside the road leading northwards out of the city, but the only visible monument is the impressive tetrapylon arch (pl 55), which has been dated to the first decade of the first century;[9] It was moved to the Place du Clos in 1880 and before that was incorporated in the bishop's palace. A geometric mosaic has been found near where it now stands and some traces of other buildings, but despite the good collection of small finds in the local museum (many of them from the Colline St-Jacques) no satisfactory plan of the city can yet be produced, though parts of its aqueduct (from the Fontaine-de-Vaucluse) have recently been uncovered.[10]

As is the case with *Avennio* (*qv*), the size of the area controlled by *Cabellio* is questionable. Its boundaries north of the Durance can reasonably be deduced from those of the later diocese (fig 38), but this did not extend south of the river and two milestones found near Plan d'Orgon suggest that the city, with its important ferry, may also have held some land on the south bank. One stone of Augustus, with the mileage figure of vi, is held by some to mark the distance from the boundary between the territories of Arles and Aix along the road linking Orgon with Pélissane,[11] but the other, of Hadrian, appears to have carried the figure iiii, only one mile in excess of the actual distance of its findspot from Cavaillon,[12] and in these circumstances it seems sensible to include here the discoveries made in the environs of Orgon. The existence of a shrine in the hill-fort of Nôtre-Dame-de-Beauregard, overlooking the modern town, had long been supposed and excavations since the war have confirmed it,[13] but rather less is known about the four nearby villas, though that at la Chapelle is said to have had an aqueduct.[14] The two shown north of the Durance, however, owe more to recent discoveries. That near the western boundary, at Caumont, with very large baths, was occupied through-out the Roman period and that in the east, at the hamlet of les Gros, from Augustan times until the middle of the third century.[15] More surely remain to be found.[16]

REFERENCES AND NOTES

1 See especially A.Dumoulin, 'Les puits et fosses de la colline St-Jacques à Cavaillon', *Gallia* xxiii(1965), 1–86, also *Gallia* vi(1948), 224, viii(1950), 138, xiv(1956), 249–50, xx(1962), 670, xxv(1967), 374–5, xlii (1984), 414.
2 Stephanus, *sv Cabellio*.
3 Strabo iv, 1, 11.
4 Pliny, *HN* iii, 36; Ptolemy, *Geog* ii, 10, 8.
5 *Voltinia, CIL* xii, 1050, 1057; *quattuorviri*, 1050, 1051; *seviri*, 1052; for a *flaminica Augusti Cabel* . . . married to a distinguished citizen of *Nemausus*, 3242 (found in Nîmes; for *Cabellienses cf* also 3275, from Nîmes).
6 For the medallion, *FOR* vii, no 62; although of uncertain provenance and rejected by Hirschfeld in *CIL* xii, pp 14, 34 and 131, it is generally

accepted—*cf* Grenier 1934, 538–40 (with illustrations). For the bas-relief, *FOR* vii, no 6 (with photograph), Espérandieu 1907, no 6699.

7 Vicarello Goblets; *It Ant* 343.5 and 388.5; Peutinger Table (as *Cavalline*).

8 Genialis, Munier 1963, 49–51; *Not Gall* xi, 10.

9 *FOR* vii, no 7, P.Gros, 'Pour une chronologie des Arcs de Triomphe de Gaule Narbonnaise', *Gallia* xxxvii(1979), 55–83.

10 *Gallia* viii(1950), 138, xlii(1984), 412–7 (including the aqueduct).

11 *CIL* xii, 5500 (with figure vii), König no 86 (with figure corrected to vi). König accepts this as a displaced stone giving the distance from *Cabellio*, but for the other argument see Constans 1921, 69, 162–3, and Burnand 1975, 43–5.

12 *CIL* xii, 5499 (with figure iiii), König no 85 (with figure omitted in copy but accepted in text.)

13 *FOR* v, no 492; *Gallia* xiv(1956), 222, xvi(1958), 420–3, xviii(1960), 307.

14 La Chapelle, *FOR* v, no 496; the other two are Valdition (no 493), St-Véran (no 494) and St-Andiol (no 497).

15 Caumont (near the chapel of St-Symphorien), *FOR* vii, no 63, *Gallia* vi(1948), 223–4, xiv(1956), 248–9; les Gros (in the commune of Gordes, and more probably in the territory of *Cabellio* than in that of *Apta Iulia*), *Gallia* viii(1950), 138–9, xi(1953), 119–21; on the *pagus Gordensis* Barruol 1969, 241 and 277 n3.

16 It would be especially interesting to know when melons, for which Cavaillon is now justifiably famous, were first grown around here. The Greek μῆλον (apple) becomes *malum* (alternative *pomum*) in Latin and *melones* are not mentioned until Diocletian's Price Edict (vi, 31). *SHA, Carus et Carinus et Numerianus* xvii, 3, alleges that Carinus *inter poma et melones natavit* (which distinguishes them from apples) and Palladius, *De Re Rustica* iv, 9, 6, advises on their cultivation. The Greek πέπων (*pepo* in Pliny, *HN* xix, 65 and xx, 11) seems to be a rather different fruit in the earlier period.

24
Avennio (Avignon)

Occupation of the site of Avignon stretches back to the Neolithic[1] and in the Iron Age a large and important settlement developed here. While it evidently began as a hill-fort on the Rocher des Doms, in the la Tène period it spread well to the south and its prosperity is amply attested by much imported pottery.[2] As is made clear by Mela and Pliny,[3] it belonged to the *Cavares*, but Stephanus of Byzantium calls it a Massaliote city[4] and while he does not here name his source a comparison with *Cabellio*, on which he cites Artemidorus, suggests that it was towards the end of the second century BC that *Massalia* gained control over it. Archaeologically Greek influence is confirmed not only by pottery and coins (including both locally minted coins inscribed in Greek and a vast hoard of Massaliote obols)[5] but also, in early Roman times, by the bilingual burial inscription of Vaalus Gabinius.[6]

Another early inscription, by T.Carisius, *praetor Volcarum*, is taken by some to indicate that in Caesarian times *Avennio* came under the *civitas Volcarum*,[7] but since it simply records a donation by him—something that notabilities often conferred on their neighbours—this seems improbable. In the first century AD Pliny includes it among his *oppida Latina* and inscriptions duly record *quattuorviri* in the voting tribe *Voltinia*,[8] but Ptolemy gives it the title of *colonia* and this seems to be confirmed by an inscription from Apt recording the burial of the senatorial L.Volus . . . Severianus, who is called both a *quattuorvir* of *Colonia Iulia Apta* and a *duovir* of *Colonia Iulia Hadriana Avennio*,[9] which implies that it was already a *colonia Latina* before Hadrian elevated it to a *colonia Romana*. The facts that not only Hadrian but also Claudius did pass this way and that it was the latter that here erected a statue of the deified Drusilla have led some to suppose that the first status was conferred by him,[10] but the title Iulia, if correct, surely points to Augustan times. Colonial status is certainly likely, since Mela puts *Avennio* third in his list of the richest cities in Gaul.[11] Unfortunately, owing to its importance in the Middle Ages, most of Avignon's Roman

265

inscriptions must still be concealed in buildings and apart from those just mentioned the only one that adds a possible officer is that of a *praefectus fabrum*, found not here but at Chateaurenard, south of the river Durance.[12] More surprisingly, apart from the rather obscure St Rufus, the earliest recorded bishop is Nectarius, who attended the Council of Riez in AD 439 and, with his deacon Fontedius, that of Orange in AD 441.[13]

Though it has excellent museums Avignon has only one visible Roman monument still *in situ*, a small part of the Arcades des Fusteries that can be seen at the east end of the Rue St-Etienne (pl 56). The great length of these arcades, two arches high, is well attested not only by occasional discoveries but also by their representation on a picture of 'l'Ancienne Avignon' engraved on a medallion in 1603.[14] Their main function seems to have been to enable the ground to be levelled on which the *forum* was established and in that case they must be of early date. The forum itself, with a number of associated structures including an arch (of which fragments may be seen in the Musée Calvet), lay under the Place de l'Horloge, the Hotel de Ville and the modern theatre and was identified from various excavations in the nineteenth century. Even those carried out in 1853 and 1855, however, raised many problems that are still unsolved and only the buildings that were found in the adjacent area in 1975 and 1977 can be marked with confidence on the plan (fig 36): their dates range from the first to the third century.[15] Whether a theatre existed on the south slopes of the Rocher des Doms, just south of the Palais des Papes, where possible remains are recorded, is still a little uncertain[16] and while several notable statues are preserved very few altars have been found and no temple has yet been identified.[17] On the better side, something that does confirm the wealth of the city is the remarkable number of mosaics, of which splendid examples may be seen in the Musée Calvet, and the grouping of the sites on which they were found must indicate what were the richest areas.[18]

Walls were built around Avignon on several occasions and while those of the fourteenth century, restored by Viollet-le-Duc and still so imposing, are clearly irrelevant to our period, the defences erected in the early thirteenth century (shown on old plans and now identifiable on air photographs) raise an interesting question. These were double fortifications and while the outer ones were certainly newly constructed the inner ones were referred to as 'Roman walls' and this suggests that they, or at least part of them, may have included the remains of some built in the early Roman period; this has not been confirmed archaeologically and their approximate line is therefore shown on fig 36 simply as the probable limits of the early city.[19] Parts of the late Roman walls, however, of the third–fourth century, have been more clearly identified, especially near the *forum* and it was doubtless their construction that accounts for the discovery in this area of some burial inscriptions.[20] All the actual burials so far located have been found

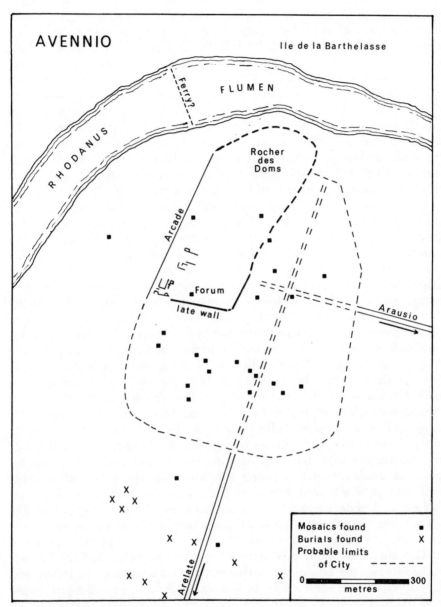

36 A tentative plan of Avignon

much further south, roughly from the area around the modern railway station and beside the Avenue Montclar, whose line has been convincingly identified as that of the main Roman road to the south.[21] None have so far been found to the east, but the road to Orange must have led somewhat in the direction indicated on the plan to avoid the loop of the Rhône east of the Ile de la Barthelasse. What is known of the roads on the other side of the Rhône suggests that the river must have been crossed approximately at the same place as the celebrated Pont St-Bénézet, either by a ferry or possibly by a pontoon bridge similar to that at Arles.[22] Finally, the discovery of several water pipes in the city clearly indicates the existence of an aqueduct. A possible source is the beautiful Fontaine de Vaucluse, 25km to the east, and while this cannot be confirmed some remains recorded near Pontet, just NE of Avignon, and described as several fragments of wall at equal distances apart, or as 'murs de Sarassins', may well have formed part of it.[23]

The extent of the area governed from *Avennio* is somewhat uncertain. Its boundary with *Cabellio* (Cavaillon) can safely be deduced from that of its early diocese, but further to the north matters are complicated by cadastre C of Orange, which seems to have extended well south of the Ouvèze.[24] This may surely have been of temporary significance, however, and, at any rate for the later imperial period, it seems best to include on fig 38 (p 278) the whole of that part of the diocese that lay north of the Durance and east of the Rhône. South of the Durance another question arises. On the one hand Ptolemy,[25] using outdated sources with variable accuracy, attributes *Tarusco* to the *Salyes*, but on the other the diocese of Avignon stretched far to the south, taking in not only Tarascon but also St-Rémy (*Glanum*) and even Eyguières, well to the south-east, and this has led to conflicting conclusions: Jullian[26] made *Tarusco* a *vicus* of *Avennio*, but Constans[27] attributed it to *Arelate*. The course of the Arles aqueduct (fig 23) certainly indicates that *Glanum* was subject to *Arelate*, a fact that limits the conclusions that one can draw from the diocese, but there is another piece of evidence that supports the idea that the *civitas* of *Avennio* extended at least well towards Tarascon—the find near Graveson (which is beside the road junction between the two towns) of the inscription already referred to of a *quattuorvir* whose voting tribe was *Voltinia*.[28] In these circumstances it seems best to accept the suggestion of Barruol[29] that the real boundary between the *Salyes* and the *Cavares* had been not the Durance but the marshy area north of St-Rémy and tentatively to include *Tarusco* with *Avennio*. And one further possibility may be added: if, as we suggested (p 29), it was here that Hannibal crossed the Rhône and if, as Livy stated,[30] some *Volcae* occupied some land east of the river, it could have been precisely this land of the *Volcae* that Pompey handed over to the Massaliotes, who might have controlled it from Avignon rather than from *Glanum*.

The funerary inscription of a man in the voting-tribe *Voltinia* has also been found just north-east of Tarascon itself,[31] but this is of less significance than the one from Graveson, for the town itself has also yielded one of a citizen of *Baeterrae* (Béziers)[32] and this crossing of the Rhône, well established with the building of the *Via Domitia* (p 43) and duly recorded in Strabo,[33] will have attracted travellers from many places. Though its importance declined somewhat after the development of Arles, so that it does not appear in the later itineraries, limited excavations have indicated considerable prosperity[34] and there is the possibility that its people were the *Tarusconienses* that Pliny includes in his list of *oppida Latina*.[35]

Within the territory thus defined two other places demand a brief mention, both of them *mutationes* recorded only in the Bordeaux Itinerary. *Bellintum* is there stated to be *x mp* from *Ernaginum* and *v mp* from *Avennio*, which points clearly to a site at or near les Aubes (2½ km sw of Rognonas), but no finds are recorded here. *Cypresseta*, on the other hand, is listed at *v mp* from *Avennio* and *xv mp* from *Arausio* and these two figures add up to an impossible total (unless the pilgrim deviated from the *Via Agrippina*), so that the location is very uncertain. The most probable identification however, seems to be with Sorgues (5 Roman miles from Avignon), where some possible buildings have been recorded, along with coins and pottery. Les Aubes and Sorgues are, therefore, the places marked under these names on fig 38.[36]

As may be seen from the map, no certain villas have yet been identified north of the Durance, though two buildings, at Vaucroze and Védène, offer some promise.[37] Even south of the river, where several are recorded, the only one to have been investigated in recent times is that at Pui Bouquet, some 7km NE of Tarascon, which was established in the first century BC and where both mosaics and statuary have been found.[38]

As for the milestones shown on the map, that just south of the Durance is undatable but was found near the main Roman road,[39] while that at Tarascon, of Antonine date, may have come from any of the routes that converge here,[40] but the third, placed further east, raises a problem. It was found near the Pont de Courquiou, just east of Maillane, and this has suggested to some that it indicates a fully-maintained road from *Ernaginum* (St-Gabriel) to a river crossing near Noves or one running more directly from *Avennio* to *Glanum*, or that it had come from the known road between *Glanum* and *Ernaginum*.[41] It bears no mileage figure, but the rest of its text, recording repair of the road under Tiberius, is identical with that on a stone found near Agrippa's road further north (marked on the map between *Acunum* and *Novem Craris*)[42] and this surely indicates that this one too originally stood beside the same main road from *Avennio* to *Ernaginum*.

REFERENCES AND NOTES

1 Gagnière 1970, 13–59; *Gallia* XXXV(1977), 532–3. Discoveries include huts in the Chalcolithic period.
2 Gagnière 1970, 62–80.
3 Pomponius Mela II, 5, 75, Pliny *HN* III, 36; *cf* Strabo IV, 1, 11.
4 Stephanus, *sv* Αὐενίων.
5 Gagnière 1970, 66–7, 81 (illn).
6 *CIL* XII, 1038.
7 *CIL* XII, 1028; for an example of accepting the *Volcae*, Gagnière 1970, 67, 85. On the title of *praetor*, *v* Nemausus, p 163.
8 Pliny, *HN* III, 36; *CIL* XII, 1029 (C.OTACILIO.C.F.VOL/ OPPIANO.IIIIVIR, found at Graveson, on which see p 268 below), and 1031 ((I)IIIVIR, unnamed, found at Avignon) *cf* 1039 (not a *quattuorvir* but *tribu Voltinia*).
9 *CIL* XII, 1120 (regarded with some doubt by Hirschfeld, p 130). It may be that it was Hadrian who appointed the unnamed senatorial *curator reipublicae Avenniensis* recorded in a 2nd-cent inscription found in Riez, of which city he was a *patronus* (*CIL* XII, 366).
10 *Eg* Gagnière 1970, 86, Chevallier 1982, 83. Hatt 1962, 92, more probably makes it Augustan.
11 Pomponius Mela II, 5, 75.
12 *CIL* XII, 1027; this anonymous man had also been a *tribunus militum cohortis*.
13 On St Rufus, Gagnière 1970, 166–7; Nectarius, Munier 1963, 61–93.
14 Gagnière 1970, 87–91, with illustrations 92–3, 114–16; more recent discovery, with proof of the upper arches, *Gallia* XXXV(1977), 532.
15 Gagnière 1970, 91, 94–100; *Gallia* XXXV(1977), 533–4.
16 Gagnière 1970, 100, 110–13, with a full discussion of the various views advanced.
17 *Ibid*, illustrations pp 84 (Jupiter Serapis), 102, 109 (?Augustus), 127 (Juno), 130 (Hermes); *FOR* VII, no 64.
18 *FOR* VII, no 64; Gagnière 1970, 113, 117–23 (with illustrations).
19 For the 13th-cent walls, Gagnière 1970, 224, for their possible significance, *ibid*, 154. The eastern line shown on fig 36 differs slightly from Gagnière's suggestion by incorporating the arcade and taking in a little more in the south-east. The reason for this is that early Roman town walls in Gaul, such as those at Arles, Nîmes and Vienne, had no military significance but were honorific, so that the arcade could well have formed part of them and they may have been erected with Hadrian's elevation of the city to a *colonia Romana*.
20 Gagnière 1970, 163–5.
21 Burials (excluding funerary inscriptions that had obviously been moved), *FOR* VII, no 64; Gagnière 1970, 125–6, with a note on the road.
22 Gagnière 1970, 156–7.
23 *Ibid* 154–5.
24 Piganiol 1962, 268–307, modified by P.Gros in Clavel-Lévèque 1984, 275–97.
25 Ptolemy, *Geog* II, 10, 8.
26 Jullian VI, 325.
27 Constans 1921, 63.

28 *CIL* XII, 1029.
29 Barruol 1969, 239.
30 Livy XXI, 26, 6.
31 *CIL* XII, 989; for a better definition of the site, *FOR* v, no 579.
32 *CIL* XII, 985, found 1575, now lost. The appropriate voting-tribe *Pupinia* certainly appeared in the inscription and Hirschfeld emends the recorded text to make P. Caecilius a soldier of the legions *I Minervia* and *VI Victrix*, so he may even have served in Britain.
33 Strabo IV, 1, 3. The Vicarello Goblets do not name it, but one enters *traiectum Rhodani* after *Ugernum* (Beaucaire) and the route indicated in all four of them shows that it was here that the river was crossed.
34 *FOR* v, no 580; *Gallia* VIII(1950), 124 (mosaic), XXV(1967), 405 (marble).
35 Pliny, *HN* III, 37. The order of the names here (*Tolosani Tectosagum Aquitaniae contermini Tasgoduni Tarusconienses Umbranici Vocontiorum civitatis foederatae duo capita* . . . suggests to some that the reference is to Tarascon-sur-Ariège, but since the *Umbranici* have not been located this more important town seems more probable.
36 *It Burd* 553.4–7; the only variation cited by Cuntz is in the Verona MS, which reduces the mileage between *Cypresseta* and *Arausio* to *xiii mp*, but this still makes the total too great. For Sorgues, *FOR* VII, no 67, and P. Broise in *RAN* XVII(1984), 269–70, with other refs and comments on the difficulty of future research.
37 Vaucroze (just south of Bédarrides), *Gallia* XIV(1956), 246–8; Védène, XXV(1967), 383.
38 Pui Bouquet, *FOR* v, no 584, *Gallia* XXII(1964), 590, XXV(1967) 405–06, XXVII(1969), 446, XXX(1972), 533. For the others, *FOR* v nos 541 (s of Noves) 542 (Tarasconnet), 547 (Trou du Loup) 549 (SE of Chateaurenard), 587 (St-Julien).
39 *FOR* v, no 562. Since the fragment of it that was found was uninscribed it is not included in *CIL* or König, and it may have been the one that was removed to St-Gabriel (*FOR* v, no 577).
40 *CIL* XII, 5501, König no 87.
41 *CIL* XII, 5557 (with mention of two possibilities), *FOR* v, no 538 (with references for the possibilities cited), König no 130 (citing the distance of 9 Roman miles from Avignon).
42 *CIL* XII, 5554, König no 127. Both stones are dated by the *trib pot xxxiii* of Tiberius (AD 31–2), by which time Agrippa's road would surely have needed repairs.

25
Arausio (Orange)

The name of *Arausio* is first mentioned in Livy's account of the defeat there by the *Cimbri* and *Teutones* of Cn. Mallius and Q. Servilius Caepio in 105 BC and one of their *bina castra* was surely on the Colline St-Eutrope, now a pleasant park overlooking the modern town and then probably a hill-fort of the *Cavares*.[1] The precise date of the foundation of *Colonia Firma Iulia Arausio Secundanorum* for veterans of *Legio II Gallica* remains a little uncertain, but the statement of Cassius Dio that Octavian, faced with discontented veterans after he had defeated Sex. Pompeius in Sicily, ultimately settled some in Gaul makes 35 BC the most likely.[2] Inscriptions duly record men holding appropriate offices (two *duoviri*, an aedile, a *flamen*, three *seviri*), but none, unfortunately, reveals the voting-tribe in which they were enrolled and no really outstanding local people appear in them with the possible exception of Valerius Bassus.[3] Similarly, relatively few religious inscriptions have been found—just dedications to Jupiter, Mars, Silvanus, Cybele, possibly Isis and one to the traditional local deity *Arausio*; Cybele also appears (as *Mater Deum*) along with *Numen Augusti*, on an altar in honour of Commodus found at Caderousse (4 km sw of Orange) which records a *taurobolium*.[4] Christianity probably developed here relatively early, for Faustinus, a priest of Orange, (though not yet a bishop) attended the Council of Arles in 314.[5]

So far as remains are concerned, Orange is unique in two respects—the remarkably complete survival of two of its monuments and the discovery of numerous marble fragments of inscribed plans of centuriation. Both of the two monuments, the arch and the theatre, owe their survival to their incorporation in fortifications erected in the thirteenth century by Raymond de Baux, Prince of Orange.[6] The arch (pl 57) was restored to its original form partly in the 1820s and then, more successfully, in the 1950s. The modern investigations have shown that it was built over the foundations of an earlier arch or gate, but the inscription on the final version of it has been satisfactorily interpreted to produce a dedication to Tiberius, as *restitutor coloniae*, in AD 26–7. This suggests that it commemorated the suppression of the revolt of Florus and Sacrovir in northern Gaul in AD 21 (indeed, in the reliefs on it the name of Sacrovir appears on one barbarian shield and the capricorn symbol of *Legio 11 Augusta* on a Roman one), but the naval victory also depicted must reflect merely the overall supremacy of Rome.[7]

As for the theatre, the survival of its *cavea* (now nicely restored) is not surprising since it, like the larger one at Vienne and the smaller one at Vaison, was built against a steep hill, and it is the remarkable condition of the stage buildings that is due to their incorporation for a time in medieval structures. These, too, have been largely restored and among the many shattered statues found in this area one, which was reconstructed by Formigé to represent Augustus, has been installed in the central niche. A little doubt, however, surrounds this (especially since the head of the statue was missing) and this needs to be borne in mind when considering the question of when the theatre was built. It is almost identical in size with that of Arles—the overall diameter of this one being 103 m and that of Arles 102 m—but an Augustan date has still to be proved.[8]

This question of date is further complicated by the lack of final certainty on the original nature of what stood immediately west of the theatre. Here another semicircular wall (74m in diameter) was cut into the north side of the hill and since other walls, which became porticos, extended north from it for a considerable distance, it was long taken to be part of a circus or, more recently, a gymnasium, but the possibility also arises that it began as an Augustan theatre that was replaced by the larger one. Its later use is rather more clear: excavations in the 1920s, supplemented by others in the 1950s, revealed the remains of a large temple, probably of second-century date and with vaults beneath it, with the earlier semicircle used as a peribolus. Up the hill to the south of the semicircle, apparently accessible by stairs from it, have been found the remains of a smaller temple and above this again, on another terrace still supported by massive walls (pl 58), a somewhat larger building which has been widely taken to be a capitol.[9]

Evidence for several other buildings has also been noted, including several mosaics, baths in the SW area (near the junction of Rue-St Clément and the appropriately named Avenue des Thermes), parts of an aqueduct approaching the city from the NE and some drains, while an amphitheatre, surely essential for a military colony, probably existed in an area called Les Arènes, out to the west towards Caderousse.[10] While some stretches of the town walls have been recorded (and a few are still visible), some doubts persist regarding both the precise shape of the enclosure and its date.[11] It may be Octavianic or Augustan in origin, though this does not seem to be confirmed by comparison with such evidence as there is for *Baeterrae* (Béziers, *qv*), which is generally taken to be the other military *colonia* founded at the same time, and another question is raised by the geography of the site (fig 37). Besides

273

the great height of the Colline St-Eutrope (which rises to 109m), two small rivers, the Meyne and the Cagnat (both now partly canalised), flowed through the northern, lower, part of the city and it seems possible that the area to the north of the Meyne, now generally taken to be rectangular in shape, may have been either the original fortified area or a late addition to an earlier one that deliberately took in much of the Colline. A good deal of the street system has been established, but while funerary inscriptions have been found in a number of places, including some to the east, near the railway station, the only certain cemetery lies to the south-west.[12]

37 A tentative plan of Orange

That the territory controlled from *Arausio* changed over the years is demonstrated by the centuriation, but much has still to be learned. Some fragments of this famous collection of inscriptions were found in odd places in the nineteenth century, but the main discoveries, beginning in 1949, were made in the Rue de la République—that is, on the north side of the open square that lay immediately north of the theatre—and the find here of several other inscriptions, not relevant to centuriation, indicates that it was near here that the city's *tabularium publicum* stood.[13] A few aspects of Piganiol's brilliant analysis of all the documents require modification—in particular, more actual centuriation has since been observed from air photographs[14]—but his main interpretation is generally accepted. Cadastre A carried a heading that showed that it was erected on the order of Vespasian in AD 77, cadastre B (by far the most complete) probably dates from the reign of Trajan (that is, after the elevation of St-Paul-Trois-Châteaux to *Colonia Flavia Tricastinorum*) and cadastre C probably later still. What is clear is that the centuriation carried out was very extensive and covered virtually all of the territory formerly occupied by the federation of the *Cavares* (not only that of the *Tricastini*), along with a little of the land of the *Helvii* and the *Arecomici* on the other side of the Rhône and some belonging to the *Vocontii* in the east; in the north it overlapped the centuriation (presumably earlier) of the *colonia* of *Valentia* (Valence) and in the east some of the land around *Carpentorate Meminorum* (Carpentras), even though, if Ptolemy is correct in calling it *Forum Neronis*, that town too had been established by Ti.Claudius Nero in 49 BC. This clearly indicates that in founding a military *colonia* every effort was made to ensure that the colonists—and the *colonia* as a city—could take over profitable land, not just whatever lay within a limited area, and this is confirmed by the observation that most of the plots handed back to the *Tricastini* in cadastre B were not really profitable ones.

It does not follow, however, that the situation reflected by cadastre B remained unchanged throughout the Roman period. While the huge area governed from *Arelate* (Arles, *qv*) seems to have stayed under her control at least until the fifth century and much of it is still included in the earliest known Christian diocese, such evidence is lacking here. It may be that rationalisation of the cities' territories was made easier by the *Constitutio Antoniniana* of AD 212 and again by the changes made under Diocletian, but the tentative *civitas* boundaries shown on the map (fig 38) are largely derived from the evidence of early Christian dioceses and so can only be fully accepted in the time of the later Empire. The nearest known settlements of *Ad Letocete* and Beaumes are however, here dealt with under *Augusta Tricastinorum* and *Carpentorate*, while across the Rhône Viviers, Bourg-St-Andéol and Pont-St-Esprit are attributed to *Alba Helviorum* and Chusclan to *Nemausus*, even though all of them may once have been subject to *Arausio*.

REFERENCES AND NOTES

1 Livy, *Periocha* LXVII.
2 Dio XLIX, 34, 4. For a further discussion, *v* p 78 and *Baeterrae* (Béziers), p 150. That it was *Legio II Gallica* is proved by a Vespasianic monumental inscription found 1951 near the Place de la République (Piganiol 1962, 79–89); on the question of whether *Legio II Augusta* was basically a replacement of *II Gallica*, P.-M.Duval in Amy 1962, 156–7.
3 *Duoviri, CIL* XII, 1236 (from Sérignan, 4 km NE of Orange), 1237; aedile, 1235; *flamen*, 1236; *seviri*, 1234, *ILGN*, 185, Piganiol 1962, 18–19; on Valerius Bassus, *ibid* 88–9.
4 Jupiter, *CIL* XII, 1219; Mars, 1221; Silvanus, 1225; Cybele, 1223; Isis(?), Piganiol 1962, 18, 350; *Arausio* (most probably a water deity), *ILGN*, 184. *Taurobolium, CIL* XII, 1222.
5 Munier 1963, 9–25.
6 The arch was converted by Raymond de Baux into a fortified tower outside the town. For an interesting account of its history up to 1824, J.Formigé in Amy 1962, 12–13.
7 For a full discussion, Amy 1962, *passim*; approximate date of arch confirmed by P.Gros, *Gallia* XXXVII(1979), 55–83. For the revolt of AD 21, Tacitus, *Ann* III, 40–7; elements of *Legio II Augusta*, then based in *Germania Superior*, no doubt took part in the suppression of the revolt.
8 For a full discussion, with illustrations and references, Grenier 1958, 754–65 (but note that on p 765, when criticising Caristie for suggesting a later date, he has got the date of the arch wrong).
9 *FOR* VII, pp 104–05; Grenier 1958, 180–8, 398–402; *Gallia* XI(1953), 126–27, XVIII(1960), 268–70; for a useful discussion, C.Goudineau in Princeton 1976, 83–4.
10 *FOR* VII, pp 105–07, 112–13; *Gallia* XX(1962), 676, XLII(1984), 422–6.
11 For varying plans, *FOR* VII; Grenier 1958, 175; Amy 1962, pl I; Chevallier 1982, pl XVI.1. The city was, of course, refortified in the middle ages.
12 *FOR* VII, pp 108–11.
13 Piganiol 1962, 11–16 (history of discoveries); 16–17 (classification of cadastres: note that in this major work he reversed the titles A and B given to the first two centuriations in the earlier article in *Gallia* XIII(1955) 5–39); 325–96 (*tabularium* and its different documents)
14 Soyer 1973–4; Fr,Salviat, 'Orientation, extension et chronologie des plans cadastraux d'Orange', *RAN* X(1977), 107–18; Chevallier 1982, 150–4; G.Chouquer, 'Localisation et extension géographique des cadastres affichés à Orange', in Clavel-Lévêque 1984, 275–95.

26
Augusta Tricastinorum (St-Paul-Trois-Châteaux)

The *Tricastini* are named early in the histories of our area—first in connection with the Celtic invasion of Italy and then with the march of Hannibal (pp 15, 31 above)[1]—and their approximate position is certain, but some doubts persist regarding their extent—whether in pre-Roman times their territory reached as far east as the celebrated hill-fort of le Pègue[2]—and also regarding their early treatment by the Romans. They are not mentioned by Cicero or Caesar, but it is clear that when the *colonia* of *Arausio* (Orange, *qv*) was founded about 35 BC a very large part of their territory was handed over to the colonists. Nevertheless, Pliny includes *Augusta Tricastinorum* in his list of *oppida Latina*[3] and an inscription found at Vaison in 1961 shows that in Flavian times it was elevated to *Colonia Flavia Tricastinorum*.[4] Since it began with *ius Latii* the voting-tribe of its Roman citizens was presumably *Voltinia*, but no inscriptions confirm this and the only known officials are two *seviri* and the *flaminica* recorded at Vaison.[5] Similarly, no notable *Tricastini* are mentioned in literary sources, but the *Civitas Tricastinorum* duly appears in the *Notitia Galliarum* and, whatever the facts regarding the local Christian legends, the first bishop convincingly recorded is Paulus, who attended the Council of Valence in 374; precisely a century later, in 474, Sidonius tells us that this was one of the places assisted by Patiens, bishop of Lyon.[7]

No Roman remains are visible in the city, but its reasonable prosperity is attested by a number of mosaics and a possible theatre has been noted.[8] Similarly, while no temples have been located, a few statues and dedications are known.[9] The size of the town in the earlier empire is to some degree indicated by the location of cemeteries, especially the recently-discovered one that includes a mausoleum,[10] but in view of its relations with *Arausio* an early town wall is unlikely. A later wall, however, is certainly to be expected and it is not unreasonable to suppose that it mostly followed the same general lines as those of the medieval fortifications, much of which survive.[11]

The limits of the *civitas* marked on the map (fig 38) are largely conjectural.[12] The river Roubrion seems the most probable in the

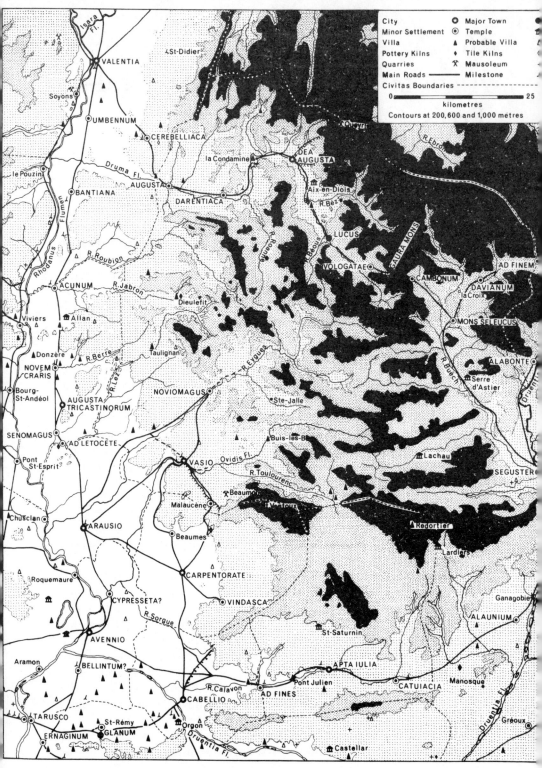

38 The territories of *Apta Iulia, Cabellio, Avennio, Arausio,* the *Tricastini, Carpentorate* and the *Vocontii.* As indicated in the text, many of the boundaries shown on this map are conjectural.

north, since cadastre B of Orange extends to it and the original boundary between the *coloniae* of *Arausio* and *Valentia* must have run about here. Doubts regarding the eastern division between the *Tricastini* and the *Vocontii* have already been noted above, but since in the south some land was restored to our tribe near Suze, just north of the Lez, at least the lower reaches of this river seem likely. At what stage all the land within these limits was taken over—or whether some of it remained permanently under the administration of *Arausio*—is not known, but this is the best place to deal with the settlements named in the area.

Ad Letocete, listed in the Bordeaux Itinerary as a *mutatio xiii mp* north of *Arausio*,[13] was certainly at the point where the *Via Agrippae* crossed the river Lez, just north of Bollène, and its name may possibly be referred to in an inscription found some 7km away at Suze,[14] but although various finds have been made around here, including columns, a mosaic and pottery- and tile-kilns, the precise centre of the settlement has still to be established.[15] Much more is known about *Novem Craris*, *x mp* further north again and so at le Logis de Berre, especially through rescue excavations carried out in the 1960s.[16] This site was occupied throughout the Iron Age and finds of Greek imports indicate that it was an important place on the trade route up the Rhône valley long before the Roman road was built. Roman structures here date from the first century BC and baths and other buildings with hypocausts were developed later, while the limits of the settlement are partly defined by cemeteries. It was destroyed by fire in the third century, but since it is again the fourth-century Bordeaux Itinerary that names it (though only as a *mutatio*) it must have been rebuilt, at least partly, on a neighbouring site, probably under the modern village. *Senomagus*, on the other hand, appears on the Peutinger Table, where it is shown as *xv mp* from *Arausio* and *xviii mp* from *Acunum*, pointing to a site on the road just north of St-Pierre-de-Sénos, which also reflects its name. A number of finds are recorded here, including the remains of some buildings,[17] but the precise site still needs to be established and since so much of the material in the Peutinger Table is of early date it may not have survived as a *mansio* throughout the Empire (though it is probably the 'Bonomago' of the Ravenna Cosmography). *Acunum* is placed *xii mp* south of *Bantiana* (Bances) by both the Bordeaux Itinerary and the Peutinger Table, but while this points to Montélimar all the evidence indicates that the *mansio* was south of the Roubion, at its confluence with the Jabron, not to the north of it like the medieval town. It was here that stood the monastery called Aygunum, in the quarter called Nôtre-Dame d'Aygu, and substantial remains have been found, including several inscriptions—among them one set up by the *utricularii* of Lyon, which suggests that there was a stopping-place here for river traffic as well as travellers by road. Whether the aqueduct of which traces have been found north of Montélimar (and so in the territory of *Valentia*) served this settlement is not clear.[18]

Three other place-names require notice. First, Ptolemy attributes a *Noviomagus* to the *Tricastini*, but in view of his many errors in this field (*eg Alba, Dinia, qqv*) the simplest explanation is that this is Nyons, dealt with by us under the *Vocontii*.[19] Secondly, Strabo puts the lofty place *Aeria* somewhere north of *Arausio* and then describes the hilly land between it and *Durio*, but since he is here citing Artemidorus (a century his predecessor) they were probably native hill-forts, perhaps those at Barry and Géry (the latter on the plateau above *Acunum*).[20]

To turn now to the countryside, while several dedications to and statuettes of various deities have been found, the only convincing temple is that near Allan, with columns, mosaics and *piscinae*, where an inscription to the *Matres Victrices* has been found.[21] As may be seen from the map, however, several villas and probable villas are recorded, especially in the valley of the Berre, and two in particular demand notice. One adjoining the Roman road near Malataverne (just sw of Allan) was uncovered when the autoroute A7 was being constructed.[22] It was apparently built *c* 250 (to judge from a mosaic), temporarily abandoned at the end of the third century and rebuilt in the fourth. Its

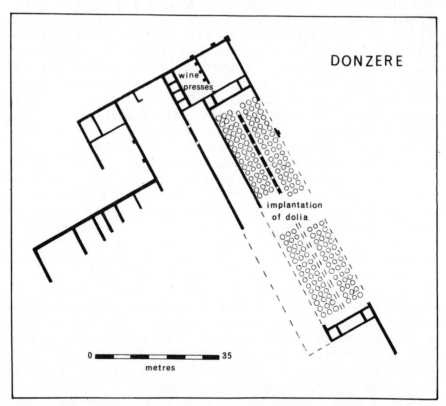

39 The wine-producing villa of Donzère (after Dechandol, Feuillet and Odiot)

large size as well as its location led some to believe that it was a *mansio* rather than a villa, but a most notable element is the evidence for wine storage, and this is carried still further by the villa at Donzère.[23] The residential quarters of this are not yet fully-known, but excavations have revealed both wine presses and the astonishing installation of some 200 *dolia*, suggesting the storage of about 2,500 hectolitres (fig 39). It appears to have been in operation from the late first century AD to the end of the third and is a clear indication that then, as now, the Rhône valley was able to produce first-class wine for widespread sale.

REFERENCES AND NOTES

1 Livy v, 34, xxi, 31—the latter repeated in Silius Italicus, *Punica* iii, 466, and Ammianus Marcellinus xiv, 10, 11.

2 In favour of this extension, which is strongly suggested by the height of the Montagne de la Lance (just s of the upper waters of the river Jabron, fig 38), Barruol 1969, 266–7; against (less convincingly), Boisse 1968, 23–4. For le Pègue, *v* p 22 above.

3 Pliny, *HN* iii, 36.

4 *CRAI* 1961, 359–63; *Gallia* xx(1962), 682, xxvii(1969), 271–3; *AE* 1962, no 143.

5 *Seviri*, *CIL* xii, 5855 (found St-Paul) and *FOR* vii, no 108 (Bollène); Orange, not St-Paul, must surely have been the base of the *duovir* recorded on *CIL* xii, 1236, found near Sérignan. For a full list of relevant (and possibly relevant) inscriptions, Boisse 1968, 182–91.

6 Munier 1963, 35–45 (with some slight doubt that this Paulus might have come from Paris); for general reviews of the Christian traditions, *FOR* xi, pp 15–17, Boisse 1968, 168–71.

7 Sidonius Apollinaris, *Epp* vi, xii, 8.

8 *FOR* xi, no 36; for other discoveries, *Gallia* viii(1950), 136 (mosaic found when school built) and H.Lavagrie, 'Un atélier de mosaïques tardives en Provence', *Gallia* xxxvi(1978), 143–61; Boisse 1968, *passim*.

9 *FOR* xi, *ibid*; the bas-relief of the Matres and altars with busts found at St-Vincent, just w of the city, must surely have come from St-Paul itself: *Gallia* xvi(1958), 384, xxxv(1967), 67–71, with photos.

10 *FOR* xi, *ibid*; recent discovery, 800m to sw, *Hist. Arch.* 78 (Nov 1983), 57–8, with photos.

11 Boisse 1968, 130–1, argues for an early wall, but the plans produced at the end of the book are not wholly convincing. The medieval walls do appear to include some reused Roman stones (observed May 1982).

12 Boisse 1968 follows the diocese line, with the northern boundary just s of Allan and the southern along the lower reaches of the Eygues, but this surely contracts the lasting territory of *Arausio* too much and extends that of *Valentia* unnecessarily far south after *Arausio* had been founded, *cf* Piganiol 1962, 31 and G.Chouquer in Clavel-Lévêque 1984, 275–95. Against the eastern boundary *v* Barruol 1969, 270, and on the general aspect Piganiol 1962, *passim*, and Chouquer, *op cit*.

13 *Itin Burd* 553.8.

281

Augusta Tricastinorum (St-Paul-Trois-Châteaux)

14 *FOR* xi, no 33 *bis* and p 130 (2 *bis* in epigraphic appendix), inscribed ITER PRIMVM A L M. Piganiol, there cited, suggested *inter primum a(d) L(etocete)m*, and for *iter primum a(d) L(etocetem) m(utationem)* v Barruol 1969, 263 n5; but is not the ablative more probable and might not the place (however it was used by the pilgrim) be called a *mansio*?

15 *FOR* vii, no 108; *Gallia* viii(1950), 138, xiv(1956), 258, xxxii(1974), 524; Boisse 1968, 136–7.

16 *Itin Burd* 553.9; *FOR* xi, no 39; *Gallia* xx(1962), 648, xxii(1964), 531–2, xxiv(1966), 518, xxvi(1968), 593–4; Boisse 1968, 134–5, 138. Milestone of Constantine, *CIL* xii, 5555, König no 128. The amendment of the road shown on the map of *FOR* xi by Boisse p 107 is surely correct—one can see it clearly aiming due north.

17 *FOR* vii, no 110; Boisse 1968, 124–5, 133 (with suggestions that the name twice shifted from one site to another).

18 *FOR* xi, no 58; inscription of *utricularii*, *CIL* xii, 1742, improved *FOR* xi, pp 132–3; aqueduct, *Gallia* xviii(1960), 374.

19 Ptolemy, *Geog* ii, 10, 7; for an alternative suggestion, siting it at Pierrelatte, Boisse 1968, 126–7.

20 Strabo iv, 1, 11 (also repeated by Stephanus Byzantinus). The suggestion that the name *Aetea*, included in Pliny's list of *oppida Latina* (*HN* iii, 36), also otherwise unidentified, is a corruption of *Aeria* is a mere guess. For discussions, Boisse 1968, 122–3, Barruol 1969, 243.

21 *FOR* xi, no 59; *ILGN* 257. For religious inscriptions etc from elsewhere, Boisse 1968, 141–6.

22 *Gallia* xxvi(1968), 595, xxix(1971), 435, xxxi(1973), 534. For the nearby milestone of Tiberius, *CIL* xii, 5554, König no 127, and for a note on its actual findspot Boisse 1968, 109–10.

23 *Gallia* xxxviii(1980), 509, xl(1982), 397–8; *Hist Arch* no 78 (Nov 1983), 56–7.

27

Carpentorate (Carpentras)

Carpentorate was the city of the *Memini*, a tribe included in the confederation of the *Cavares* (p 16 above), and its pre-Roman ancestor was presumably the hill-fort of la Lègue, 2km east of Carpentras.[1] While Pliny includes *Carpentoracte Meminorum* in his list of *oppida Latina*, the only city that Ptolemy, using his outdated sources, attributes to the *Memini* is *Forum Neronis*,[2] and this suggests that it may have been founded in 46 BC by Ti. Claudius Nero but, like *Luteva* (Lodève, *qv*), ultimately reverted to its native name. As an inscription found at Orange shows,[3] it also became *Colonia Iulia Meminorum* and this is partly confirmed by one from Carpentras itself, recording a gift to the *Genius Coloniae* by a *sevir Augustalis et Flavianus*.[4] Unfortunately, however, although the city has yielded dedications to Mars, Jupiter and the Nymphs and a number of funerary inscriptions, none of them refers to another official and none makes clear its ultimate status, so that the best, indeed the only evidence for this is provided by one from Beaumes-de-Venise, a funerary inscription of a former *cohortis praetor* whose voting-tribe is *Voltinia*.[5] The city is not mentioned in any other classical sources and, most surprisingly, it does not appear in the original manuscript of the *Notitia Galliarum*, though it is added later—something that suggests that Mommsen may well have been right in regarding the *Notitia* as a purely ecclesiastical document: the first recorded bishop is Constantianus, who attended the Council of Orange in 441.[6]

Though a number of finds have been recorded, including some of foundations and mosaics, it is not yet possible to reconstruct the plan of the Roman city and the one outstanding feature is the commemorative arch.[7] This notable monument, dateable to the first century AD and with a bas-relief showing two chained captives,[8] owes its survival to its having been used as an ecclesiastical porch, and having for long been hemmed in by more recent buildings is now pleasantly exposed to view (pl 59).

The territory controlled by *Carpentorate* can be fairly defined by the ring of hills to the east (fig 38) and in the west, though partly covered for a time by 'cadastre C' of Orange (*qv*), by marshes and the eventual boundary with the diocese of Avignon. The most notable settlement in it, apart from Carpentras itself, was at *Vindasca* (Vénasque). Here again the plan of the town in Roman times cannot be established, but plenty of remains have been noted, including inscriptions and columns built into walls, towers and a baptistery erected when the seat of the bishop was transferred here in the sixth century;[8] and nearby an inscription records the construction of a fountain and a road to it by one C. Veveius Fronto.[9] The other most probable *vicus* is at Beaumes-de-Venise, the successor to the hill-fort of Durban, where again there have been many finds and where a building has been excavated since the war.[10]

No temples have been surely identified in this area, but one must have existed somewhere near St-Didier (3km WNW of Vénasque), since a dozen altars dedicated to Mars were found here dumped in a well (presumably reflecting violent Christianisation).[11] Similarly, no certain villas have been found, though part of a possible one has been excavated at Mazan, but once again, in view of the number of altars found nearby, this too might have been a temple;[12] similar doubts apply to the nature of the building shown on the map at St-Pierre-de-Vassols.[13] Even on the industrial side the only significant discovery has been the third-century pottery kiln at l'Auberle, near Crillon-le-Brave,[14] so a great deal must remain to be uncovered.

REFERENCES AND NOTES

1 *Gallia* xxv(1967), 374; Barruol 1969, 245n.
2 Pliny, *HN* III, 37; Ptolemy, *Geog* II, 10, 8. It is hardly possible that the strange text of Strabo IV, 1, 11—δύο (ποταμοὶ) μὲν ὁι περιρρέοντες πόλιν Καουάρων καὶ Οὐάρων—can be amended to read πόλιν Καουάρων Καρπεντόρατον (or Καρπεντάρωνα), as suggested by Groskurd, since the river Auzon has no notable confluent at this point, though it is joined by several some 15km to the west.
3 *CIL* XII, 1239 a sarcophagus inscribed *COL IVL MEM HERED EX TESTAMENTO.*
4 *CIL* XII, 1159.
5 *CIL* XII, 1187.
6 On this vexed question *v* Rivet 1976 and (against) Harries 1978.
7 *FOR* VII, no 70, Princeton 1976, 199–200; for the arch, Espérandieu 1907, no 243, G.Picard in *REL* XXXVIII(1960), 335 and *CRAI* 1960, 13–16, Gros 1979, *passim*.
8 *FOR* VII, no 49: inscriptions, *CIL* XII, 1175 (a dedication to Mercury) 1179 (a dedication to Silvanus), 1181, 1194–5, 1198; *ILGN* nos 175, 179, 180.
9 *CIL* XII, 1188.
10 Benoit 1965, 112, 166, 169, 176; *FOR* VII, no 77; *Gallia* XVIII(1960), 273–8, XX(1962), 666–9, XXII(1964), 558–9.

11 *FOR* vii, no 51; *CIL* xii, 1161–1172 (one of them, 1170, apparently calling the deity *Mars Nabelcus*).
12 *Gallia* xxviii(1970), 443; altars, *CIL* xii, 1160, *ILGN* no 174, *FOR* vii, no 74.
13 *FOR* vii, no 47b—finds including columns with Tuscan capitals.
14 *Gallia* xxx(1972), 536.

28

The *Vocontii*, including *Vasio* (Vaison-la-Romaine), *Lvcvs* (Luc-en-Diois), *Dea Augusta* (Die) and *Segustero* (Sisteron)

The *Vocontii* occupied a very extensive area and it is likely enough, as has been noted above (p 16), that in early times they controlled a confederation of several tribes—probably the *Vertamocori* (whose name is preserved in the area of Vercors, north of Die), and the *Sogiontii* (based on Sisteron) and perhaps the *Sebaginni* (mentioned only by Cicero and not certainly located) and the *Avantici* (though since in the first half of the first century, before Galba transferred them, they were in an Alpine province and we have dealt with them separately under Gap, *qv*)[1]. Hannibal passed along the borders of the *Vocontii* in his march to Italy, the Romans had to defeat them in 125 BC and even after that they were, apparently, the only people in this province against whom Fonteius had to fight during his term of office. Nevertheless, by the time of Strabo they had become a *civitas foederata*, something that is confirmed by Pliny and gives them a distinction shared in this province only by *Massilia*.[2]

The date of this grant remains uncertain, though Goudineau has argued rather convincingly that it may well have been made by Pomptinus after his suppression of the last revolt of the *Allobroges* in 61 BC,[3] and some other problems are even more difficult to solve. Not surprisingly, Ptolemy names only one town of the tribe, *Vasio*, but Pliny's record of the peoples and places holding *ius Latii* includes the perplexing words *Vocontiorum civitatis foederatae duo capita Vasio et Lucus Augusti oppida vero ignobilia xix sicut xxiv Nemausensibus adtributa* and these raise further questions.[4] The first concerns the *duo capita* and especially the inclusion of *Lucus*, (Luc-en-Diois) rather than *Dea Augusta* (Die), but while Die certainly became the most important town in the northern part of the territory in later times, Tacitus, when recording how Valens threatened *Lucus* on his march towards Italy in AD 69, specifically states *municipium id Vocontiorum est*—something that shows that it still had a distinction of some kind in his time[5]—and the development of Die is a matter to which we must return later. Secondly, while several of the *ignobilia oppida* subject to *Nemausus* (Nîmes, *qv*) have been identified, that city was a *colonia* and it has been argued by some that none could be *adtributa* to a *civitas foederata* and that therefore the other nineteen were not in the territory of the *Vocontii* but just in other parts of the province.[6] Against this, the mere introduction of punctuation will not erase the word *sicut*, 24 cannot be a fraction of 19, and while the fact that *Nicaea* and probably *Athenopolis* remained subject to the *civitas foederata* of *Massilia* (*qv*) does not cover the grant of *ius Latii*, that could easily reflect some of the vagaries of Caesar or even of Pompey before him. Thirdly, the boundary between the territories controlled by the two *capita* remains quite uncertain and since, as we have indicated when dealing with Gap (*qv*), the earliest known dioceses cannot provide satisfactory evidence for the internal division of this *civitas*, even in the late Empire, it seems best to deal with the three most important towns, which we have marked as cities on fig 38, one by one—first *Vasio* (with other known places in the south-western area), then *Dea Augusta* (with the northern area, including *Lucus*) and finally *Segustero* (with the south-eastern area).

Since the Vocontii were a *civitas foederata* and since *Vasio* itself never became a *colonia* of either type, its constitution was quite different from that of most of the cities we have discussed.[7] Neither *duoviri* nor *quattuorviri* appear and while *aediles* and *seviri*, along with *flamines*, *flaminicae* and *pontifices*, are duly recorded, the area is governed by *praetores* and *praefecti*, though remarkably few even of these are mentioned in the very numerous inscriptions that have been found here.[8] The city does, however, appear to have acquired the title of *Vasio Iulia Vocontiorum* and those who acquired Roman citizenship were enrolled in the voting-tribe *Voltinia*. This is so not only in the case of C. Sappius Flavus, a notable military commander who had made a grant of money to the *Respublica Iuliensium* and was himself *praefectus Iuliensium*, but also in that of the best-known citizen of the place, Sex. Afranius Burrus, the praetorian prefect and tutor of Nero, and of L. Duvius Avitus, who became a suffect consul in AD 56.[9] The full name of Burrus clearly suggests that his ancestor had been granted Roman citizenship by L. Afranius as a reward for his service during the Sertorian war in Spain, especially since the historian Pompeius Trogus, also a Vocontian, specifically states that his own grandfather received it from Pompey for that reason.[10] Whether the still greater historian Tacitus also came from here, a possibility persuasively suggested by Sir Ronald Syme, still remains uncertain, but his remarkably benevolent treatment of Burrus in the Annals has to be explained and at least one Tacitus does appear in an inscription from Vaison and a second in one at *Alaunium*.[11] Another notable Vocontian figure is the *eques* Iulius Viator, recorded by Pliny as surviving dropsy, but from which town he came is uncertain.[12] On the humbler side, this was the only *civitas* in the province whose name could be attached to auxiliary army units, the well-known *Alae Vocontiorum*, which served in both the western and the eastern parts of the Empire.[13]

Vasio appears as the very first city in Mela's list of *urbes opulentissimae*, Pliny speaks well of the dessert wine made in this region,[14] there was a local *collegium centonariorum* and *utriclarii* operated on the river Ouvèze (*Ovidis flumen*),[15] so it is not surprising that no less than nine dedications to Mercury have been found here. Many other Roman deities were also honoured, especially Jupiter and Mars, and of the Celtic ones not only a deified Vasio but also the Matres, Belus (partly in Greek), Belisanus (in Greek) and Dullovius.[16] As usual, it remains a little uncertain when Christianity really developed here, but Vaison's bishop Dafenus (?Daphnus), along with the exorcist Victor, attended the Council of Arles in 314.[17]

Very little is known about the pre-Roman history of Vaison, mainly because the Haute Ville, which must surely have been a hill-fort, still has so many attractive remains of the medieval town, but roadworks there have from time to time produced fragments of Iron Age pottery, along with Attic and Campanian imports.[18] In Roman times the town was established on the other side of the river, which, as the presence of *utriclarii* clearly indicates, was then much stronger than it is now, and the splendid Roman bridge across it (pl 60) was evidently built at a relatively early date.[19] So also must much of the town itself have been to justify its great wealth by the time of Mela, but here some difficult problems arise. While it is one of the finest Roman towns to visit, with a magnificent collection of buildings, all too little is known of the history of most of them and in some cases even their precise purpose. The reason for this is that most of them were excavated and reconstructed before modern archaeological techniques had properly developed.

This is especially true of the largest monument, the theatre, the *cavea* of which was cut into the northern slope of the Colline de Puymin. It was excavated by Sautel (with the assistance of a modern M.Burrhus) between 1907 and 1926 and was reconstructed by Formigé in 1932–4, so that, as has justly been remarked, 'Le visiteur aperçoit donc, aujourd'hui, un théâtre du . . . XXe siècle'. Its size, of course, is not in doubt, with a diameter midway between those of Orange and Fréjus, giving accommodation for some 7,000 spectators, but the date of its construction (or enlargement?) is uncertain, though probably some-where in the first century. While its excavation yielded several fine imperial statues, including those of Domitian, Hadrian, Sabina and possibly of Claudius (rather than Tiberius) and some other earlier figures, where—or when—they were originally placed here is not known.[20]

As for the rest of the town so far excavated, it is evident from the direction of the roads, including the colonnaded street of shops (pl 61), that it was not laid out in the formal Roman way, with a *cardo* and *decumanus*, but while a remarkable number of shops and sumptuous buildings have been exposed the date, and indeed the purpose, of most of them remains uncertain.[21] Some recent excavations, however, especially those in the areas of le Thès and la Villasse, have begun to clarify matters. In le Thès, not only the 'Villa du Paon' (so named from the peacock mosaic, one of several revealed there), but still more the little group of shops to the north of it, were evidently in use from the second half of the first century AD to the sixth century, though they suffered from a fire in the late third.[22] In la Villasse, the 'Maison au Dauphin' (named after a dolphin mosaic) has produced still fuller evidence. Here some crude building, constructed in 40–30 BC, was slightly improved in AD 20–30 but it too was not reconstructed in fully Roman style until the Flavian period.[23] So we still need to know where in the town the wealth cited by Mela, who wrote his book about AD 40, was really concentrated.

As may be seen from the plan (fig 40), several public baths have been identified, along with a remarkably preserved set of public latrines (pl 62), and an ample supply of water was needed. Traces of an aqueduct, bringing it from a spring at Nôtre-Dame de Groseau (just east of Malaucène) have been noted, but precisely where it crossed the river is not clear and the most likely site for some sort of *castellum divisorium* is in the building that was formerly called a Nymphaeum.[24] Just to the east of Nôtre-Dame de Groseau and 14km from the town is the great quarry of Beaumont-du-Ventoux, from which much of the stone used in Vaison was evidently brought.[25]

Cemeteries have been found in a number of places,[26] which gives some indication of what the full extent of the city may have been, but the roads to which they were related require further investigation: Vaison was not, of course, on any main route and therefore is not included in any itinerary, nor even on the Peutinger Table. One probable milestone, possibly Trajanic, is said to have been found in the Abbey of St Quentin,[27] but the alleged mileage on it, *lxvi mp*, is too much even for a journey to Luc or Die, though an emended figure of *xlvi* might point to either of those places, and while they must have been connected to Vaison by a road, presumably by way of *Noviomagus* (Nyons) and the upper valley of the river Eygues, its true course is quite unknown and even the other roads shown on our map (fig 38) are largely hypothetical.

Of the *vici* in the south-western part of the Vocontian territory Nyons is in many ways the most interesting. This was surely the *Noviomagus* that Ptolemy attributed to the *Tricastini*, something that is shown not only by its modern name but also by the implications of the inscription found at Tain-l'Hermitage (*Tegna*, in the territory of the *Allobroges*, qv), recording the gratitude to their patron of the *vicani Boxsani et Noiomagenses*.[28] While suitable finds, including mosaics, statues and funerary inscriptions, have been made at Nyons, the plan of the town is not known,[29] but that the *pagus* of which it was the centre was a close neighbour to that of the *Boxsani* (or *Baginenses*) is shown

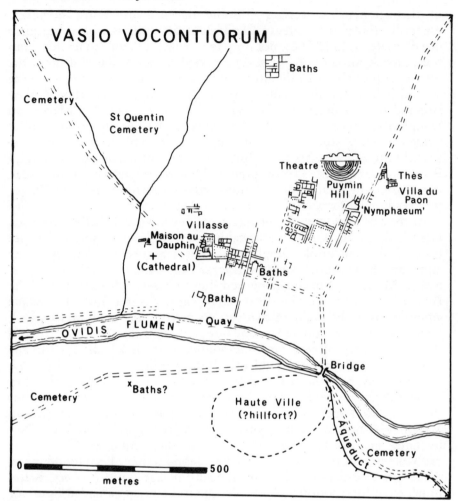

40 A tentative plan of Vaison-la-Romaine

both by the name of Buis-les-Baronnies, where a villa and an
inscription to Minerva have been found, and by the discovery at
St-Jalle, a little to the north of it, of an inscription recording the renewal
of something given to the *pagus Bag . . .* by the aedile L.Veranius
Rusticus.[30] Besides this, an inscription found at Taulignan where there
was also a villa, records L.Voturius Maximus as the aedile of the *pagus
Aletanus*,[31] but the only other convincing *vicus* is that at St-Michel, in
the commune of Malaucène, where a settlement clearly succeeded an
earlier hill-fort.[32] Many finds are recorded elsewhere, for example in
the area of Rasteau, on the right bank of the Ouvèze and 6km
downstream from Vaison, but, while the *praefectus* L.Laelius Fortunatus was buried here and several dedications have been found, no real
centre has been identified, and while Séguret, on the left bank, has also

yielded a great deal, especially dedications to and statues of various deities, this too has not been fully sorted out.[33] As may be seen from the map, the known villas are not very numerous and apart from the two already mentioned the most interesting site is that at Dieulefit, where not only a villa (or at least baths with a mosaic) but also kilns producing the well-known Dieulefit pottery have been located.[34] As the boundaries of the medieval dioceses indicate, however, this must have lain in the northern sector, to which we must now turn.

Lucus (Luc-en-Diois) presents a number of problems. In the first place, while its generally accepted name *Lucus Augusti* suggests a devotional imperial centre, directly analogous to the other *Lucus Augusti* (Lugo), which was founded in Spain at the end of the Cantabrian wars, the only two dedications found here are one to Mercury and the other not to a deified Augustus but to Dea Augusta—surely the Dea Augusta Andarta who is recorded in seven other inscriptions from the valley of the Drôme and was evidently the dominant local deity.[35] Since the genitive *Augusti* appears only in Pliny and is omitted from the place-name in Tacitus, the Itineraries, the Peutinger Table and the Ravenna Cosmography, one is led to wonder whether Pliny, or more probably someone transcribing his text, has made a slight error and that the correct form should be *Lucus (Deae) Augustae*, simply reflecting the translation into Latin of her venerability.[36] Secondly, while one *praefectus Vocontiorum* and one aedile are duly recorded here, very few inscriptions have been found in or near the town and although a few buildings and mosaics have been located (including one of the latter nicely inscribed *Q.Amiteius architectus fecit*), there is no indication that it was ever really prosperous. Nevertheless, although the Bordeaux pilgrim records it only as a *mansio*, it seems certain that it was walled at some time: its northern limit was evidently along the bank of the Ruisseau de Luc and the slope along the general line of the Rue de l'Eglise, extending beyond the end of that street, must have been its western boundary.[37]

Dea Augusta (Die) has yielded much more archaeological evidence, but although it certainly took over control of the northern region from Luc, quite when this happened and whether it really acquired the title of *colonia* (something that is attested only by the inscription on the sarcophagus of a *flaminica designata* of Die that was found not here but in the Champs Elysées of Arles) remains somewhat uncertain.[38] A large number of inscriptions have been found, many of them on stones later used in the town walls, but while the defences were evidently built in the third or fourth century and largely rebuilt in the middle ages (pls 63, 64), the surviving eastern gate, the Porte St-Marcel, clearly incorporated an earlier arch, of which not only parts of one face but also the highly decorated internal vault can still be seen (pls 65, 66).[39] People mentioned in the inscriptions include a *praetor*, three *flamines*, three *seviri* and a *sacerdos* and also an *argentarius*, a *librarius*, a *macellarius* and an *unguentaria*; interestingly, the *sacerdos* and the *unguentaria*, along with six other people, were Pompeii, which suggests that some other *Vocontii*, in this case from the northern region, had, like the grandfather of Pompeius Trogus, served in the Sertorian war.[40] On the religious side, while no temple has yet been discovered, there are dedications not only to the local goddess Andarta Augusta but also to Jupiter, Mars, Silvanus, Isis and Vulcan, while several inscriptions and altars record *taurobolia*, a fact that underlines the suggestion that Andarta may eventually have been identified with Cybele.[41] Some funerary inscriptions are evidently Christian, but quite when Die first became a bishopric is not clear: while it is just possible that Nicasius, who attended the Council of Nicaea in 325, came from here, the first certain bishop is Audentius, who was at the Council of Orange in 441.[42]

As may be seen from the plan (fig 41), a few buildings, some of them with mosaics, have been found both inside and outside the defences and although the supposed theatre or amphitheatre has still not been firmly located, two fragments of a *balteus* were found in the nearby walls in 1961; cemeteries are also recorded.[43] The importance of the city is underlined by the fact that it had two aqueducts, that from Romeyer, some 7km to the NE, leading to an apparent *castellum divisorium* on the Plateau de Beaumes (on the hill overlooking the modern town), and the other from Valcroissant, about 5km to the SSE, which appears to have led directly into the lower area, and several pipes have also been found.[44]

Dea Augusta owed some of its prosperity to its position on a main route between the Rhône valley and Italy, but when this road was fully romanised is not clear: though eight milestones have been found along it—three of them in the present century—none is earlier than the reign of Constantius Chlorus.[45] Since the medieval diocese of Die extended as far west as Crest, Aouste-sur-Sye must evidently be included here, but whether its name also reflects that of Dea Augusta Andarta is uncertain, since while it appears as *Augusta* in both the Antonine and the Bordeaux Itinerary (and is so shown on our map), it is called *Augustum* on the Peutinger Table and *Auguston* in the Ravenna Cosmography.[46] This was a substantial settlement. Several buildings have been located, the medieval maze of streets probably represents the Roman lay-out and it is tempting to believe that the medieval bridge over the Drôme, now reduced to a pile of stones in the river and replaced by a concrete structure, also had a Roman predecessor: part of one of the several Roman inscriptions found here, recovered from a pile of the old bridge in 1952, can still be seen on the south bank.[47]

The next station to the east, *Darentiaca*, is mentioned only as a *mutatio* in the Bordeaux Itinerary and while the mileages there given, *xii mp* from Augusta and *xvi mp* from *civitas Dea Vocontiorum*, add up to an impossible total, the correction of the former to *vii* points to Saillans, the distance of which from Die is confirmed by two milestones, but

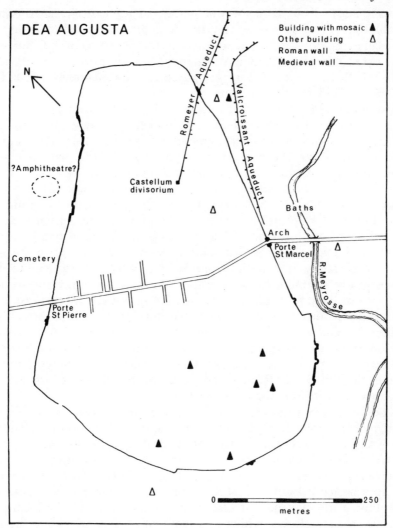

41 A tentative plan of Die

very few other finds have been made.[48] In fact the best-recorded place
on this route is around la Condamine, on the south side of the river and
midway between Pontaix and Ste-Croix: besides the milestones and the
large villa (with an excellent mosaic), this area has yielded several
inscriptions, including dedications to Andarta and Mars (the former by
a *sevir*), one to the *lares* by an *aedile*, the burial of another *sevir* and one
that probably records a *praetor* and *flamen*.[49]

The precise course of the road between Die and Luc is a little
uncertain, depending upon whether one accepts as Roman the Pont de
Quart, across the Drôme just north-west of Aix-en-Diois or that over
the Béz south of that town, but since Luc itself stands east of the river

293

we have adopted the latter on our map.[50] In any case, by far the most notable site in this area is at Aix. A dedication to Bormanus and Bormana and a bronze statue of Pan had long been recorded, but since 1960 extensive excavations have uncovered an important set of sacred baths which were extended in Flavian times and remained in use at least until the end of the third century.[51]

Just beyond Luc one can see a short stretch of the Roman road in the fantastic so-called Chaos of Le Claps, which was caused by a massive collapse in the fifteenth century, and after this most of the named places appear only in the Bordeaux Itinerary. *Vologatae* was evidently at les Bouligons, near Beaurières, but only burials are recorded here.[52] *Gaura Mons*, listed not as a *mutatio* but simply with the words *inde ascenditur Gaura Mons*, is clearly the Col de Cabre, the pass used by the modern road, but the precise site of *Cambonum*, somewhere near Font Vineuse, has still to be established.[53] *Mons Seleucus*, on the other hand, appears not only as a *mansio* in the Bordeaux Itinerary but also in the Antonine and was certainly at la Batie Mont-Saléon. While the settlement itself cannot yet be planned, it was an important religious centre and some 18 inscriptions have been found here, including not only several funerary ones but also dedications to Mars, Mithras, Silvanus and possibly to Jupiter, Isis and an Allobrogian deity. While one to VICT AVG appears to be of second-century date, it was in the fourth century that this place entered history, when Magnentius was defeated here in 353, but the date of the apparently Roman camp seen in the hill-fort of the Serre de la Croix, 6km to the north, is not known.[54]

The Bordeaux Itinerary then lists *mutationes* at *Davianum* (Veynes) and *Ad Finem* (the Roche des Arnaux) and while virtually nothing is known about these places, the latter evidently marks the boundary between *Dea Augusta* and *Vapincum*, the continuation of which southwards we have discussed in dealing with Gap (*qv*)[55] In any case, the appearance at Ventavon of the funerary inscription of Q.Caetronius Tibullus, a notable man of Die who was *praefectus* of the local *pagus Epotius*, clearly shows which city controlled this area, but the only notable building in it is the recently-found small shrine at Serre d'Astier.[56]

A road ran from *Mons Seleucus* to *Segustero* and this brings us into our third and final region, the inclusion of which in the land of the *Vocontii* is confirmed by the discovery at Manosque of the epitaph of an aedile set up by a senator(?) of the tribe.[57] The fortifications still surrounding the splendid hill of Sisteron (pl 67) are only of sixteenth-century date, but this must surely have been a hill-fort and the main part of the Roman town lay at its foot. Set on the main road to Italy, it is duly recorded in itineraries from the Vicarello Goblets onwards, but it appears in no other documents until the *Notitia Galliarum*, where it is included in *Provincia Narbonensis Secunda* (thus fully separated from Vaison and Die, both of which are in *Provincia Viennensis*): it had its own diocese in the early middle ages, but no bishop is recorded here before the late fifth century.[58] For a long time very little was known about it archaeologically—just minor finds, a few burials and two dedications[59]—but in 1946–8 rescue excavations improved matters a little, producing a second-century funerary monument with the statue of a Muse with a lyre, the traces of some buildings and a few fourth-century graves, and further burials and one more building have been located since.[60]

The road south of Sisteron has now been thoroughly investigated, including the Roman bridge over the little river Buès at Ganagobie, and *Alaunium* was certainly at Pied d'Aulun, near Nôtre-Dame-des-Anges: several finds are recorded here, including one inscription of a dedication to the god Alaunius by a Tacitus and another with the word *censor*, part of a marble statue, foundations, columns, water pipes and burials.[61] As the geography suggests, this was probably the most prosperous area, but the villas shown in it, at Dauphin and Mane, together with the building at Villeneuve near the river Durance (which may have been either a villa or a temple), have not been recently investigated, though the pottery works at St-Martin-les-Eaux are a modern discovery.[62]

Some recent research has also been carried out near Sisteron itself, including the minor building at les Bons-Enfants (just south of the city), and at Bevons (to the west) exposing not only another minor building, of first to second-century date, but also a mausoleum.[63] The most important excavations in this region, however, have been concerned with religious sites. While those at le Luminaire, in the commune of Lachau, have produced a vast number of votive objects, including 20 kilograms of lamps, the precise site of the local shrine has still to be established,[64] but that of le Châtelard, near Lardiers, on the border with the *civitas* of *Apta Iulia*, has been fully exposed. The hill-fort here was occupied from the sixth century BC onwards, but in the early imperial period the houses there were levelled and replaced by a large temple approached by a long and well-built sacred way. Besides huge numbers of votive objects, both ceramic and of gold and bronze and ranging in date from the first to the fourth century, several inscriptions have been found: these include at least one to Mars Belado and since he is also recorded on two stones built into medieval houses near Limans, about 10km to the south, it is tempting to conclude that he was the dominant local deity.[65]

REFERENCES AND NOTES

1 For a useful discussion Barruol 1969, 278–94: on the *Avantici* in Roman times, *v* section 14 on *Vapincum* (Gap).

2 On the earlier battles, Chapters 3 and 4 above. On the status of the *Vocontii*, Strabo IV, 6, 4, Pliny, *HN* III, 37.

3 Goudineau 1979, 251–64.

4 Ptolemy, *Geog* II, 10, 8; Pliny, *HN* III, 37.

5 Tacitus, *Hist* I, 66; this does not, however, prove that it had the full legal status of a *municipium*—cf *Ann* XIV, 33, where he applies this word to *Verulamium* in Britain, probably exaggerating its status in AD 60.

6 *Eg* E.Kornemann on *Attributio* in *P.-W.* Suppl VII(1940), 67, followed by Goudineau 1979, 270–2.

7 For a useful discussion of the constitution, Goudineau 1979, 272–303.

8 *Aediles, CIL* XII, 1375, 1514; *seviri*, 1363, 1364, 1367, 1368; *flamines*, 1368, 1372, 1373; *flaminicae*, 1361, 1362, 1363 (=*ILGN*, 206); *pontifices*, 1368, 1371, 1373; *praetores*, 1369, 1371; *praefecti*, 1368, 1375.

9 Sappius, *CIL* XII, 1357 (recording the erection of a portico in front of baths in his honour); Burrus, 1360, 5842; Duvius Avitus, not only *CIL* XII, 1378 (an inscription set up by his wife, improved by *ILGN*, 206), but now also *AE* 1976, 391 (for its discovery, *Gallia* XXXV(1977), 537).

10 The suggestion in Badian 1958, 311, that the name attests the connexion of L.Afranius with this province seems rather an exaggeration; for a better discussion, Syme 1958, 622–3; for Trogus, Justin XLIII, 5, 11–12; several other Pompeii are also recorded in Vaison, *eg CIL* XII, 1438, 1453, 1464.

11 Syme 1958, 611–24; the local Tacitus, making a dedication to Mars, *CIL* XII, 1301, the other, at *Alaunium*, 1517.

12 Pliny, *HN* VII, 78, just two chapters after his account of another Tacitus, possibly a brother of the historian, who evidently died young; the only Iulius Viator recorded on an inscription from our province is one who died at Narbonne (*CIL* XII, 4910).

13 For a collection and discussion of the inscriptions recording the *alae* (including *RIB* 2121 from Newstead) and an argument against the later creation of a *Numerus Vocontiorum*, supporting Mommsen's rejection of the tile stamped D N VOC found in London in 1876 (*EE* IV, 698, VII, 1189a), Goudineau 1979, 303–06.

14 Mela IV, 5, 75; Pliny, *HN* XIV, 83.

15 *Centonarii, CIL* XII, 1282; *utricularii*, 1387, on which see Y.Burnand in *RAN* IV(1971), 149–58, supporting the idea that Ouvèze was the river *Ovidis* mentioned in *CIL* XII, 3316–17 (from the Nîmes amphitheatre) and 4107 (from St-Gilles), as does Goudineau 1979, 184.

16 For dedications, *CIL* XII, 1276–1350, 5841, *ILGN*, 191–204.

17 Munier 1963, 9–25.

18 Goudineau 1979, 184–6; Goudineau/Kisch 1984, 14, with an excellent photograph of the Haute Ville on the opposite page. It is tempting to identify some of the level ringlets in the cleared area as the bases of Iron Age huts, but they could equally well be medieval.

19 *FOR* VII, p 50; Goudineau/Kisch 1984, 76–7. This bridge survived a torrential flood in 1616 and when the retreating German army mined it in 1944 it shuddered but did not collapse!

20 *FOR* VII, p 50 (with earlier Sautel refs), J.Sautel, *Vaison-la-Romaine* (1955) 47–54; Grenier 1958, 766–72; Goudineau/Kisch 1984, 53–5 (including the comment quoted). Statues, Espérandieu 1907 IX, 6772 (alleged Tiberius), 6766(Domitian), 6750(Hadrian), 6768(Sabina) etc.

21 Pre-war excavations, *FOR* VII, no 88 (with full Sautel refs); post-war, *Gallia* VI(1948), 218–22, VIII(1950), 141–5, XI(1953), 123–6, XII(1954), 458–61, XVI(1958), 406–10, XVIII(1960), 278–83, XX(1962), 680–5, XXII(1964), 564–8, XXV(1967), 378–83, XXVIII(1970), 443–7, XXX(1972), 540–1, XXXII(1974), 525–8, XXXV(1977), 535–7. Mosaics, J.Lassus, 'Remarques sur les mosaïques de Vaison-la-Romaine), *Gallia* XXVIII(1970), 35–66, XXIX(1971), 45–72, and H.Lavagne, 'Trois mosaïques inedites de Vaison-la-Romaine et St-Paul-Trois-Châteaux', *RAN* X(1977), 171–88. Summaries, Y.Kisch, *Archéologia* no 152(Mar 1981), 6–21, and Goudineau/Kisch 1984, *passim*.

22 *Gallia* XXV(1967), 378–83, XXVIII(1970), 443–5, XXX(1972), 541, XXXII(1974), 527, XXXV(1977), 536–7, XLII(1984), 429–30; Kisch, *Archéologia* no 152(1981), 14–17 and Goudineau/Kisch 1984, 47–52 (both with plans and photos).

23 For a full and detailed account, Goudineau 1979, 23–80 (excavations), 83–180 (history); *Gallia* XLII(1984), 430; summary, Goudineau/Kisch 1984, 22–4.

24 Baths, *FOR* VII, pp 50–1; recent excavations, *Gallia* XXVII(1970), 443–4, XXXV(1977), 537 (indicating that the north baths were constructed early in the 1st cent, enlarged in the 2nd and abandoned in the 3rd) XLII(1984), 430: *Archéologia* no 152(1981), 18–19; on the identification of the building formerly called 'Basilica' as baths, Goudineau/Kisch 1984, 32–3. Aqueduct, *FOR* VII, p 51; for a map of its course J.Sautel, *Vaison dans l'antiquité* (1926), vol III, pl XCIV. '*Nymphaeum*', *FOR* VII, p 51; correction, Goudineau/Kisch 1984, 46–7. *Nb*: the great arches visible on the south flank of the Haute Ville are not Roman.

25 *Archéologia* no 152 (1981), 19, Goudineau/Kisch 1984, 6–7.

26 *FOR* VII, pp 53–4.

27 *CIL* XII, 5507, König no 89.

28 Ptolemy, *Geog* II, 10, 7: *CIL* XII, 1783.

29 *FOR* XI, no 28; inscriptions, *CIL* XII, 1697, 1698.

30 Buis-les-Baronnies, *FOR* XI, no 13; Minerva inscription, *ILGN*, 1961; reinvestigation of part of villa, *Gallia* XL(1982), 397. Ste-Jalle, *FOR* XI, no 21; *CIL* XII, 1377.

31 *FOR* XI, no 42; inscription, *CIL* XII, 1711.

32 *FOR* VII, no 84; P.Broise in *RAN* XVII(1984), 263–4.

33 Rasteau, *FOR* VII, no 92. Séguret, *FOR* VII, no 93 (with photos of the statues of Jupiter and Silvanus on preceding pages); Broise, *RAN* XVII(1984), 265–6, suggesting St-Joseph as the most likely centre.

34 Baths, *FOR* XI, no 53, *Gallia* XXII(1964), 265–7 (lead pipe inscribed *Lucullus, Mandal f*); potteries, *Gallia* XXXI(1973), 533, XXXVIII(1980), 508–09. For other villas, *FOR* XI, nos 2 (Villette), 31(St-Maurice), 32(Tulette), 56(Eyzahut) and *Gallia* XIV(1956), 258–9 (le Moulin, near Barret-de-Lioure).

35 Mercury, *CIL* XII, 1570, Dea Augusta, *ILGN* 230; for Dea Augusta Andarta, *CIL* XII, 1556–8 (at or near Die), 1555(Ste-Croix, 6km w of Die),

1559(Aurel, 15km sw of Die), 1560(St-Laurent, 3km NW of Die), 1554(3½km N of Luc).

36 Pliny, *HN* III, 37; Tacitus, *Hist* I.66, *It Ant* 357.9, *It Burd* 554.8, *Rav Cos* IV, 27(241,8). For a corruption in the opposite direction, in the name of Aouste, *v* n 46 below.

37 For a general record, *FOR* XI, no 69, with a tentative plan (though wrongly oriented) on p 41; *praefectus*, *CIL* XII, 1578, aedile, 1579, mosaic inscription, *ILGN*, 232; more recent discoveries, *Gallia* XXII(1964), 535 (wall), XXXIII(1975), 229–56 (two new inscriptions).

38 *CIL* XII, 690, on which see the warning advocated by Hirschfeld on pp 161 and 933. Other inscriptions naming the place (*CIL* XII, 1529, 1581, 1587, 1588(?), 3290) all call it simply *Dea Augusta Vocontiorum* and while most of them are probably earlier than the *colonia* one the word *Augusta* (*cf* n36 above) surely refers to the goddess and not to the emperor. Pliny's listing of Luc as the second *caput Vocontiorum* certainly dismisses the description of Die as 'An Augustan colony' (*eg* Princeton 1976, 259), but whether the transfer occurred in the 2nd cent, as used to be believed (*eg* F.Lot, *Recherches* I(1945), 89), or in the 3rd (*eg* Goudineau/Kisch 1984, 12) requires further proof.

39 On the walls, *FOR* XI, p 45, plan (slightly misoriented) pp 48–9, photos pl V; Grenier 1931, 557–60, with older photoes and the suggestion that the arch of the western Porte St-Pierre was also decorated; more recent work, *Gallia* XVI(1958), 383, XXII(1964), 536.

40 *Praetor* and *flamen*, *CIL* XII, 1586 (on which *v Gallia* XXII(1964), 268–9), other *flamines*, 1577, 1586 (the latter also distinguished at Lyon), *seviri*, 1580–2, *sacerdos* (a Pompeius), 1573, *argentarius*, 1597, *librarius*, 1592, *macellarius*, 1593, *unguentaria* (Pompeia), 1594; other Pompeii, 1629, 1638, 1649, 1664, 1670, *ILGN*, 243.

41 For Andarta, n35 above; Jupiter, *CIL* XII, 1563, Mars Masuciacus, 1565 (+ *Gallia* XXVII(1969), 210), Silvanus, 1571, Isis, 1562, Vulcan, 1571, *ILGN* 239 (improved *Gallia* VIII(1950), 135, *AE* 1950, 49), *FOR* XI, pp 133–4); *taurobolia*, *CIL* XII, 1568, 1569, 1576 (for the emperors Philip), *ILGN* 231 (for Septimius Severus and his sons), Espérandieu 1907, I, 315, 317, 318, 320.

42 On Christian inscriptions, A.Blanc, 'Les sarcophages de Die et de Valence', *Gallia* XXXVIII(1980), 215–38; on Nicasius, Griffe 1964, 123 n11, 203; Audentius, Munier 1963, 76–93. Interestingly, Sidonius, who corresponded with Fonteius, the bishop of Vaison, never mentions Die.

43 *FOR* XI, pp 44–7 (including reference to the quarry at Queyrie, NE of the city and shown on the map, fig 38); *Gallia* XVI(1958), 383, XVIII(1960), 370, XXII(1964), 536, XXXI(1973), 533–4, XXXV(1977), 475–6, XL(1982), 397(cemetery).

44 *FOR* XI, pp 45–6; Grenier 1960, 106–11; *Gallia* XXII(1964), 535, XXXV(1975), 475 (parts of the Valcroissant aqueduct).

45 König nos 90–7.

46 *Itin Ant* 358.1, *Itin Burd* 554.5; Rav Cos IV, 27(241,10).

47 *FOR* XI, no 94; *Gallia* VIII(1950), 135, XVI(1958), 383–4, XXXV(1977), 475, XXXVIII(1980), 508; inscriptions, *CIL* XII, 1721–5, *FOR* XI, p 144.

48 *Itin Burd* 554.6–7; milestones, *CIL* XII, 5504 a, b, König nos 95,96; finds, *FOR* XI, no 89.

49 Villa, *FOR* XI, no 80, *Gallia* XXII(1964), 272–4 (with air photo), 272, XXXV(1977), 477–8; Andarta, *CIL* XII, 1555, Mars, 1565, aedile, 1564, *sevir*, 1583, *praetor/flamen* (?), 1584; other finds, *FOR* XI, nos 80, 82.

50 Pont de Quart, *FOR* XI, no 78 bis; bridge across river Béz (on the route preferred by J.-D.Long), no 74 (*sv* Menglon).

51 *CIL* XII, 1561 (and *cf* 494, recording Bormanus at Aix-en-Provence); *FOR* XI, no 78; Grenier 1960, 525; *Gallia* XVIII(1960), 370–1, XXIV(1966), 517, XXVI(1968), 593, XXIX(1971), 429–30, XXXI(1973), 532–3.

52 *Itin Burd* 554.9; *FOR* XI, no 68 and p113.

53 *Itin Burd* 555.2, a *mutatio* placed *viii mp* from *Vologatae* and the same distance from *Mons Seleucus*.

54 *Itin Ant* 537.8, *Itin Burd* 555.3; inscriptions, *CIL* XII, 1531–48 and 5686 (1160, 1188, 1248, 1251), 5696(20) (inscribed vessels); Espérandieu 1907 I, pp 239–40; Barruol 1967, 283 n4 and *Ogam* XV(1963), 362ff. Defeat of Magnentius, here, Socrates, *Hist Eccles* II, 32, Sozomenos IV, 7, 3.

55 *Itin Burd* 555.3–6. The meaning of *Geminas*, a name that appears twice in this area on the Peutinger Table, is very obscure.

56 Caetronius, *CIL* XII, 1529; for a fuller discussion, p 252 above. Shrine, *Gallia* XXXV(1977), 531–2.

57 *CIL* XII, 1514; for other minor finds there, *FOR* VI, no 41.

58 Vicarello Goblets, *Itin Ant* 342.5, 388.2, *Tab Peut*; *Not Gall* XVI, 6. The earliest bishop listed in a Council is Valerius, who attended that of Epaone in 517 (C.de Clerc, *Concilia Gallia 511–695*, Vol CXLVIII A of *Corpus Christianorum: Series Latina*, 35).

59 Inscriptions, *CIL* XII, 1522 (a votive restoration), 1523 (probably a dedication to Numerian); other finds, *FOR* VI, no 68.

60 H.Rolland, 'Premières découvertes à Sisteron, 1946–8', *Gallia* VII(1949), 81–8; later, *Gallia* XII(1954), 447, XX(1962), 663.

61 G.Barruol and P.Martel, 'La voie romaine de Cavaillon à Sisteron sous le Haute-Empire', *REL* XVIII(1962), 125–202 (*Alaunium*, 160–4, bridge, 142–5 and *Gallia* XXI(1963), 314–24); inscriptions, *CIL* XII, 1517, 1518, 1520; other finds, *FOR* VI, no 51 (*sv* Lurs).

62 Dauphin (perhaps two villas), *FOR* VI, no 44, Mane, no 46, Villeneuve, no 45; St-Martin-les-Eaux potteries (with buildings), *Gallia* XXVIII(1970), 453–5, XXXII(1974), 522–3.

63 Les Bons-Enfants, *Gallia* XI(1953), 119; Bevons, XXV(1967), 385–6, Burnand 1975, 117.

64 *FOR* XI, no 10; *Gallia* XXXI(1973), 534–5, XXXIII(1975), 537, XXXV(1977), 476, XXXVIII(1980), 509.

65 *FOR* VI, no 63; Grenier 1960, 527–8; *Gallia* XX(1962), 655–6, XXII(1964), 545–50, XXV(1967), 387–93 (with plan and Belado inscription), XXVIII(1970), 448; Barruol in Princeton 1976, 484. Limans inscriptions, *ILGN* 219, 220, *FOR* VI, no 47; Belado is also recorded at la Tour d'Aigues, 15km s of *Catuiacia* (*CIL* XII, 503).

29
Valentia (Valence)

Though a pleasant and prosperous city, Valence is a major Roman colony of which relatively little is known. To suppose that Ptolemy was correct in placing it in the former territory of the *Segovellauni* is reasonable, provided one accepts the argument that they formed part of the confederation of the *Cavares* (to whom Pliny relates it), and whether or not they originated on the left or the right bank of the Rhône does not much concern us.[1] As we have indicated above (p 62), Valence was probably the '*Ventia*' that, according to Dio,[2] was attacked by Manlius Lentinus during the war with the *Allobroges* in 62 BC and if this is so it confirms the fact that the *colonia* was not founded in pre-Caesarian days: Book 37 of Dio is preserved complete and if the foundation had immediately followed the war he would surely have mentioned it. It follows that, despite its form, *Valentia* is more likely to be the Latinisation of a native name than the imposition of an entirely new one,[3] and since the centuriation of the colony seems to have preceded cadastre B of *Arausio* it appears probable, despite the absence of any inscription calling it *Colonia Iulia* or *Colonia Iulia Paterna*, that it was founded by Caesar—or rather for him, by Ti.Claudius Nero in 46 BC.[4]

The shortage of informative inscriptions raises other problems, including the question of the city's voting-tribe. A *duovir* has long been known, but he was an honorary one who was also a *decurio* of Lyon, the city from which one of the *seviri* also came, and the various tribes of the *quaestores, aediles* and *duoviri* (again all honorary), the records of whom were recovered in 1973, add nothing, nor does the inscription from Die that includes a *pontifex perpetuus* of *Valentia*.[5] This *pontifex* took part in supervising a *taurobolium* there in AD 245 and other inscriptions record *taurobolia*, one found in the city itself and the other, involving the *dendrophori* of *Valentia*, on the north bank of the river at Châteauneuf-d'Isère,[6] which confirms the strength of Cybele here: there is also a dedication to Mercury and evidence for a *mithraeum*.[7] Christianity, however, appears to have been introduced relatively early, perhaps by

Felix and his deacons in the late second century, though the first firmly recorded bishop is Aemilianus, who took part in the Council of Valence (presided over by Florentius of Vienne) in 374.[8]

It is likewise impossible to construct a fully convincing plan of the city. It is generally believed to have covered a rectangle of *c* 700 by 350 m, with the modern boulevards defining its eastern limit, and the line of several modern streets fits well with the centuriation observed on air photographs,[9] but the best evidence has been provided by post-war excavations. While the south gate and one of its towers had been noted in the Rue de la Gendarmerie in 1889, a rescue excavation in 1950 enabled this to be confirmed[10] and parts of the northern defences—here crossed by the sixteenth-century wall—were uncovered in 1973,[11] where it appears that an early republican wall was replaced by another in the early Empire. The extent of the city is also partly defined by burials along the roads to the north and the east (though many of the stones bearing funerary inscriptions had been reused within it) and several buildings are recorded, the best-known being the theatre, apparently just outside the walls to the NW.[12] Aqueducts, of course, also existed, one coming from the north and one from the east, but their precise courses too have still to be established.[13]

The boundaries of the territory shown on the maps (figs 38, 42) are derived mainly from those of the early diocese of Valence and partly from what has been observed on air photographs. The centuriation of *Valentia* appears originally to have extended as far south as the river Jabron, but some land here was evidently taken over by *Arausio* when its cadastre B was established, so that the valley of the Roubion seems the most likely limit that eventually emerged between *Valentia* and *Colonia Flavia Tricastinorum* (St-Paul-Trois-Châteaux, *qv*)[14] In the north, although the *Segovellauni*, and so later the people of the *colonia*, evidently occupied the right bank of the Isère for a short distance before it entered the Rhône, their land probably did not take in *Tegna* (Tain), so that is dealt with under *Vienna* (Vienne, p 313),[15] but because of the position of *Valentia* at the junction of so many roads this still leaves a number of places to be dealt with here whose names are recorded in ancient sources.

Of those on the *Via Agrippae*, *Umbennum* appears only as a *mutatio* in the Bordeaux Itinerary, *xii mp* from *Bantiana*, *viiii mp* from *Valentia*, and was evidently the hamlet of les Battendons, just south of la Paillasse. Several finds have been made here, including two milestones (though the Hadrianic one, giving a mileage of VI, had obviously been moved), but the settlement cannot yet be precisely defined.[16] *Bantiana*, on the other hand, is recorded not only in the Bordeaux Itinerary but also (as *Batiana*) on the Peutinger Table and probably (as *Untiano*) in the Ravenna Cosmography and was obviously at or near Bances (NW of Saulce). Here more remains have been found, not only a milestone of Constantine but also foundations, mosaics, a statuette of Mercury and

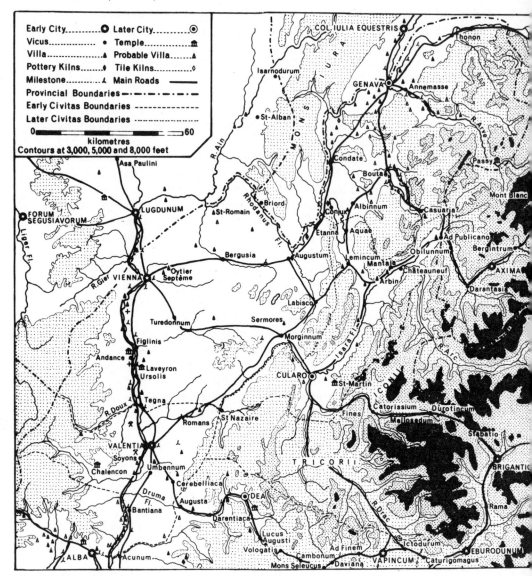

42 The territories of *Valentia* and the *Viennenses*

even traces of an aqueduct.[17] The road from *Valentia* to *Dea Augusta* (Die) is still better covered, by the Antonine Itinerary, the Bordeaux Itinerary, the Peutinger Table and the Ravenna Cosmography, and *Augusta*, (or *Augustum*) certainly at Aouste-sur-Aye,[18] was evidently much more than a mere *mansio*, but the medieval dioceses indicate that this lay in the land of the *Vocontii* (*qv*). The intermediate station on this road, *Cerebelliaca*, is only a *mutatio* in the Bordeaux Itinerary, and since this puts it at *xii mp* from *Valentia* and *x* from *Augusta* it was near the crossing of the stream of Ourches (1 km west of the village of that name), at a place apparently christened Ste-Cerbelle by the Knights Templars. Odd finds are recorded here, but the Constantinian milestone was found off the road, nearer to Upie, and the tile-kilns shown on fig 41 further to the SE.[19] That a substantial settlement stood at Romans-sur-Isère (or at le Bourg-du-Péage, opposite it on the south bank of the river) has yet to be established, but finds have been made and whether or not the early bridge (recorded as a *pons antiquus* in 1189) was Roman, it seems evident that it was here that the road from *Valentia* to *Cularo*, which must have existed, crossed the Isère and it is even possible that the milestone (probably of Claudius II) used in the church at St-Didier was uplifted from it.[20]

Less is known of stations on the west side of the Rhône, since the road is not covered by any itinerary. Soyons may possibly have been the *Solonium* where, according to Dio, Catugnatus was finally defeated but, as we have noted above (p 62), this suggestion is not entirely convincing. There was, however, a very impressive hill-fort here on the Malpas plateau and numerous finds, including several inscriptions, indicate that whenever the north-south road was built (the earliest milestones so far found are of Antonine date) a settlement flourished beside it.[21] Beyond this, traces of iron mining have been noted, both here and further north, near St-Romain-de-Lerps.[22]

As may be seen from the maps, several villas and probable villas have been located in the territory of *Valentia*, on both sides of the river, but the only likely rural temple so far noted is that at Chalencon and even that requires more research.[23]

REFERENCES AND NOTES

1 Ptolemy, *Geog* II, 10, 7; Pliny, *HN* III, 36; Barruol 1969, 267–70.
2 Cassius Dio XXXVII, 47.
3 The Indo-European base *segh-* evidently means something like 'strength', so whatever the precise meaning of *-vellauni* ('good', or 'benevolent'), the centre of the *Segovellauni* could well have become *Valentia*: on these elements see, for example, Holder II, 1444, III, 150; Ellis Evans 254–7, 272–7; Barruol 1969, 373.
4 The overlap of the centuriations observed by Piganiol 1962, 31, and he is surely right (*ibid*) in doubting that the founder for Caesar was L.Nonius Asprenas, even if that was the name of the *propraetor* (a *patronus* of *Valentia*) recorded in the Valence inscription *CIL* XII, 1748; on this see also P.Goessler in *P–W* Supplement 1948, 2154.
5 *CIL* XII, 1750 (honorary *duovir*, tribe *Galeria*), 1751 (*sevir*), 1567 (*sacerdos*); for the 1973 inscriptions (tribes *Tromentina*, *Papiria* and *Sabatina*), *Gallia* XXXIII(1975), 229–39; for another *sevir*, *Gallia* XXII(1964), 276, and for a

Valentia (Valence)

probable *praefectus fabrum* (inscription found at Mauves, just s of Tournon, across the Rhône) *Gallia* XVIII(1960), 199, *AE* 1960, 41.

6 *CIL* XII, 1744, 1745; for the true findspot of the former, *FOR* XI, no 125.

7 *CIL* XII, 1746, *ILGN*, 258 (dedicated to Cautes).

8 For Aemilianus, Munier 1963, 35–45. On Felix and his deacons Fortunatus and Achillaeus, E.Griffe in R.Aubert (ed): *Dict d'Histoire et de Géographie ecclésiastique* XVI(1967), 875; *cf* Blanc 1953, 39, and on the number of Christian sarcophagi in this area, A.Blanc, *Gallia* XXXVIII(1980), 215–28.

9 This centuriation was, in fact, the first to be observed in Gaul: J.S.P.Bradford, *Ancient Landscapes* (1957), 207–10(followed by A.Grenier, *Gallia* XVI(1958), 281–4).

10 *FOR* XI, no 107; Blanc 1953, 11–12, 27; *Gallia* XI(1953), 129.

11 *Gallia* XXXIII(1975), 229–39.

12 Cemeteries and buildings, *FOR* XI, no 107; recent discovery of a building with mosaic in the Place Belle-Image, *Gallia* XXXVIII(1980), 510–11; the theatre, *Gallia* VIII(1950), 135–6, Blanc 1953, 27–36 (with some doubts about a separate amphitheatre).

13 *FOR* XI, no 107 (p 82).

14 For refs *v* nn 4 and 9 above, and Rob, *CR* II(1955), 17–24.

15 Barruol 1969, 295–6, Pelletier 1982, 57, both suggesting that the boundary passed through the place known as les Sept Chemins, 5km SE of Tain.

16 *Itin Burd* 554.2; *FOR* XI, no 108; milestones, *CIL* XII, 5550–1, König nos 123–4.

17 *Itin Burd* 554.1, Rav Cos IV, 26 (239, 1); *FOR* XI, no 100; milestone, *CIL* XII, 5552, König no 125 (correcting *CIL*).

18 *Itin Ant* 358.1, *Itin Burd* 554.5, Tab Peut (*Augustum*), Rav Cos IV, 27 (241, 10, *Auguston*).

19 *Itin Burd* 554.4; *FOR* XI, no 97; milestone, *CIL* XII, 5506, König no 97; kilns, *Gallia* VI(1948), 224.

20 *FOR* XI, nos 124, 126 and p 114 on the 'Voie Meyane' or 'chemin ferrat'; milestone, *ILGN* 651, König no 121.

21 *FOR* XV, no 94; for hill-fort, *Gallia* XIV(1956), 260, XVIII(1960), 376.

22 *FOR* XV, p 18, nos 94, 98.

23 *FOR* XV, no 103.

30

Vienna (Vienne), with *Genava* (Geneva) and *Cularo/ Gratianopolis* (Grenoble)

The *Allobroges* occupied a very large area and even at the time when Hannibal passed through their territory they were, according to Livy, not inferior to any people in Gaul in wealth or reputation.[1] Vienne itself, whether or not it was then their effective capital, owed much of its prosperity to its geographical position, offering an easy crossing of the Rhône just south of the valley of the river Gier, which gave easy access to that of the Loire, and while we must surely dismiss the astonishing claim by Stephanus of Byzantium that it was colonised by Cretans[2], it certainly benefited from Mediterranean trade. The *Allobroges* were, however, very ready to oppose Greek or Roman domination. As we have seen (pp 40–1, above), it was to them that Toutomotoulos of the *Salluvii* fled for shelter and it was they who had to be defeated at the great battle of *Vindalium*. Even after the establishment of the province they tried to maintain some independence, remaining, as Cicero put it, the one tribe in Gaul that really could mount war against the Roman people – something that in his consulship (63 BC) led Catiline to try to persuade them to raise a revolt. Calpurnius Piso had to pacify them in 66 BC and their last rising, led by Catugnatus, had to be suppressed by C. Pomptinus and his legates later in the same decade.

The real change came with the arrival of Caesar in 58 BC. As he himself states, the *Allobroges* were only *nuper pacati* and the *Helvetii* thought that they could be persuaded to let them through because of their antipathy to Rome,[3] yet they supported his action and even agreed to supply food for the peoples he turned back.[4] Thereafter legions were able to winter in their territory and although Vercingetorix, still relying on their past history, tried to bribe their leaders to fight on his side, they opposed him very effectively.[5] Their chief leader in this situation was presumably Adbucillus, whose sons Roucillus and Egus were highly regarded and honoured by Caesar—until his attempt to control their arrogance led them to desert to Pompey just before the battle of Pharsalia.[6]

Vienna (Vienne), with *Genava* (Geneva) and *Cularo/Gratianopolis* (Grenoble)

As with so many cities in this province, the question of when a *colonia* was first established at *Vienna* is still debated, with some suggesting that it was immediately after the defeat of Catugnatus, others at the end of Caesar's Gallic war and others by the Triumvirate. That it was a *colonia Latina* for a time is fully demonstrated by several inscriptions recording *quattuorviri* and that it later became a *colonia Romana* by many more listing *duoviri* (though still enrolled in the voting-tribe *Voltinia*), but the most difficult problem derives from the statement of Cassius Dio[7] that in 43 BC the Roman senate instructed Lepidus (then governor of both *Narbonensis* and *Hispania Citerior*) and Munatius Plancus (governor of *Gallia Comata*) to establish men who had once (ποτέ) been thrown out of *Vienna* by the *Allobroges* at *Lugdunum* (Lyon—a *colonia* that certainly was established at this time). Many have argued that this implies the collapse of a *colonia Romana* founded here either by Caesar or just after the defeat of Catugnatus, but the more attractive idea is one set out by Pelletier, that what Caesar had founded was a *colonia Latina* and that the men expelled (after his assassination in 44 BC) were simply non-Allobrogic Roman citizens (whether or not, as he maintains, they were actually a *conventus civium Romanorum*) and that the *colonia Latina* itself was not then abolished— something that helps to explain the antipathy between Vienne and Lyon that raised its ugly head especially in AD 69.[8] Other dissensions arose here about AD 10–11, when they had to be settled by Tiberius,[9] yet only a few years later (probably in AD 40, when Caligula assumed his consulship, without a colleague, at Lyon), *Vienna* became a *colonia Romana*, with *duoviri* instead of *quattuorviri*, along with other suitable officers, so that in AD 48 in his celebrated speech Claudius could call it *ornatissima colonia valentissimaque Viennensium*.[10]

Its full title became *Colonia Iulia Augusta Florentia Vienna* (or *Viennensium*),[11] and it is rightly included in Mela's list of *urbes opulentissimae*.[12] Although its 500-odd inscriptions are slightly fewer than those from Nîmes, it rapidly overtook that city in distinction and produced the first Roman consul from this province—D. Valerius Asiaticus, the wealthy and greedy man who owned the Gardens of Lucullus in Rome and was first approved of by Claudius but later condemned to death.[13] Other consuls also came from here even in the first century—the brother of Valerius Asiaticus, also L. Pompeius Vopiscus and M. Iulius Vestinus Atticus[14]—and later, in the time of Diocletian, it became the capital of a province. Besides its political distinction, the prosperity of the *civitas* is more widely mentioned than that of any other part of the province, not only by Mela, Pliny and Ausonius, but also by Columella, Martial and Plutarch,[15] and numerous mosaics reflect the wealth of the city itself.[16] On the industrial side, inscriptions duly record *fullonicae, sagarii, dendrophori* and *fabri tignarii*.[17]

Dedications to and statues of many deities have been found here—the

57 The Arch of Orange

58 Walls supporting the possible Capitol of Orange

59 The Arch of Carpentras, now fully exposed to view

60 *top left* The Roman bridge of Vaison

61 *top right* The colonnaded street of shops in Vaison, with the Haute Ville (on the other side of the river Ouvèze) in the background

62 *left* Roman public latrines in Vaison

63 The southern walls of Die

64 *top left* The western walls of Die

65 *top right* The inner side of the Porte St Marcel, Die

66 *left* The internal vault of the Porte St Marcel

67 The town of Sisteron, viewed from the south, across the river Durance

68 A view of Vienne, from the slope of Mont-Salomon: the hill of Pipet, with the theatre built against its face, in the centre, Ste-Blandine on the left and St-Just on the right

69 A surviving stretch of the Augustan walls of Vienne

70 Remains of the Palais du Miroir, opposite Vienne

71 The temple of Augustus and Livia, Vienne

72 Part of the Cybele complex, Vienne.
The flight of steps led up to the shrine of
Cybele and the arch in the rear is part of
the Palais des Canaux

73 The pyramid of the circus, Vienne

74 *above* An inscription built into a chapel, at Grésy-Fontaine

75 *below left* The Roman road running through a gorge, near les Echelles

76 *below right* The mausoleum at la Sarrasinière, south of Andance

77 *top left* A small stretch of the late Roman walls of Geneva

78 *top right* A part of the Diocletianic walls of Grenoble

79 *left* The Arch of Campanus, Aix-les-Bains

80 Partially Roman walls of the Museum of Aix-les-Bains

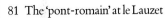

81 The 'pont-romain' at le Lauzet

82 The *frigidarium* of the north baths of Cimiez

83 The early baptistry inserted in the west baths of Cimiez

Celtic *Deae Matres*, Sucellus and Epona, along with the Roman Jupiter, Mars, Mercury, Hercules, Apollo, Bacchus, Minerva, Venus, Tyche, Silvanus and others[18]—and the history of Christianity here is also interesting. While one can certainly dismiss the legend that the pyramid of the circus (on which see below) was the tombstone of Pontius Pilate and also the story that Crescens, a disciple of St Paul, was the first bishop of Vienne, a deacon of this city (even if Sanctus was an adjective rather than his actual name) was certainly one of the martyrs in Lyon in 177 and the bishop Verus (along with an exorcist called Beflas or Beclas) certainly attended the Council of Arles in 314; beyond this, some fourth-century churches have also been identified.[19]

Vienne is surrounded by a number of high hills (pl 68) and in Iron Age times those of Ste-Blandine and Pipet were occupied, together with a lower area, especially near the confluence of the river Gère with the Rhône, no doubt to deal with trade.[20] In the Augustan period the city was soon surrounded by walls, with round towers and some eight gates, that took in not only Ste-Blandine and Pipet but also the hills of Salomon, Arnaud and St-Just (fig 43) and so stretched for about 7.25 km—longer even than those of Nîmes. Much of their course has long been known (some of them are still visible, *eg* pl 69) and the approximate date of their erection was confirmed by the discovery in 1887 of two medieval sarcophagi made out of large stones that are engraved (tribu)NICIA POTE(state) and (m)VROS PORTAS(que). This clearly indicates an inscription very similar to that on the *Porta Augusta* of Nîmes and since they were found near the chapel of St-Georges these stones must have stood over the southern gate of the city, the so-called Porte d'Avignon.[21] Several lengths of the inner walls that were, inevitably, added in the late Empire, have also been observed and it is claimed that a *castrum* replacing an earlier chapel was then constructed on the Pipet hill, while at least one *palatium* was also built in that period—not surprisingly in view of the elevation of the city to a provincial capital.[22]

While the Augustan walls conferred great distinction on the city, however, increasing prosperity did not lead to dense occupation of the hills they enclosed and more convenient sites on the lower ground, extending outside the walls, were soon adopted. On the left bank of the river, this applies especially to the area between the wall and the circus, where luxurious buildings with large baths (the so-called 'Maison d'Orphée'), probably of first–second-century date, were excavated in 1859–60 and 1879–80.[23] Still more significant is the large settlement now recognised across the Rhône. A number of mosaics had been found here over the years and the baths of the 'Palais du Miroir' (partly still upstanding, pl 70) had long been known,[24] but the extensive excavation and admirable conservation of buildings in St-Romain-en-Gal from the 1960s onward, now supplemented by rescue excavations further south in Ste-Colombe, have transformed the situation.[25] Many buildings and mosaics have, of course, also been found within the walls at the lower level, not only to the south but also to the north of the river Gère (especially in the area of St-Martin),[26] but it is quite evident that the city of Vienne extended across the Rhône at an early date, just as did the city of Arles into Trinquetaille. Cemeteries have also been located on both sides of the river, as usual beside the main roads,[27] and there

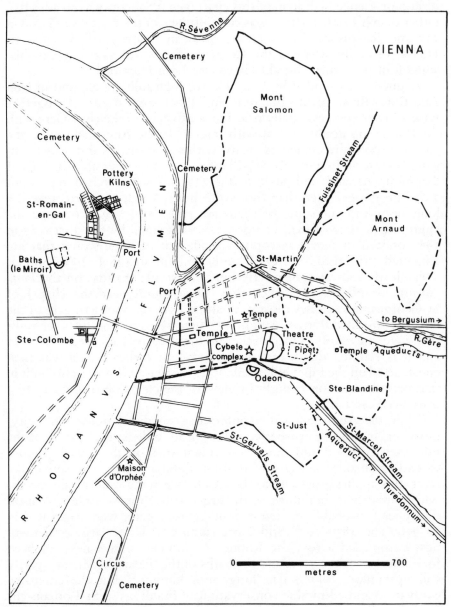

43 A tentative plan of Vienne (after Pelletier)

Vienna (Vienne), with *Genava* (Geneva) and *Cularo/Gratianopolis* (Grenoble)
were ports on both banks; and Vienne, unlike Arles, had a stone
bridge, not just a pontoon one—some have suggested that there were
even two.[28]

To turn now to the major buildings, in the centre of the city is the
Augustan temple (pl 71), standing in what was evidently the forum.[29]
Like the Maison Carrée of Nîmes, which it, though very slightly
smaller, closely resembles, it owes its survival to its use for other
purposes (in this case as the church of Nôtre-Dame-de-la-Vie, then as a
'Temple de Raison' in 1792) and was restored, not perfectly, in the
middle of the nineteenth century. As with the Maison Carrée, the
inscription on it was in bronze letters and the interpretation of the holes
they left has raised problems: though evidently originally built in the
Augustan period, modifications made at later dates have suggested to
some that the inscriptions too were emended, perhaps in the second
century.[30] Several other temples evidently existed and four of them
have been identified with some certainty. That shown on our plan (fig
43) in the area of St-André-le-Haut (NW of the theatre) was partly
uncovered in 1753 and was probably dedicated to Mars,[31] but the one
on St-Blandine (just east of a large modern cemetery) was excavated
more recently, yielding several statues (including one of Juno), and
parts of it were still visible in 1982.[32] Of the other two, one is included
in the upper part of the *cavea* of the theatre and the last is that dedicated
to Cybele.

The theatre, built against the steep slope of the Pipet hill, was first
excavated in 1908 (before which it was widely taken to be an
amphitheatre), with much more work on it in subsequent years and
was opened to the public in 1938. With an overall diameter of 130.4m
and seats for some 13,500 spectators, it is the largest one in the province
and indeed, apart from that at Autun, the largest in the whole of Gaul.
With the *orchestra* and *pulpitum* restored by Formigé, the latter carrying
a frieze with fine animal reliefs, it is most attractive, but the date of its
construction is still disputed, with suggestions ranging from the time of
Augustus to that of Trajan.[33] The post-war excavations of the nearby
Odeon (partly by Canadian archaeologists), on the other hand, have
produced a somewhat clearer chronology. An earlier Julio-Claudian
building was destroyed to make way for its erection and it seems to
have been built in the early second century and to have remained in use
until the fourth, when the site was taken over by potters.[34] The third
theatrical building, the 'Theatre of Mysteries', is much less well
known. It stood between some notable baths (the so-called 'Thermes
du Palais des Canaux') and the little temple of Cybele (15.9 x 10.6m in
size)—too complicated a group to be shown at the scale of fig 43, on
which all three are grouped in what is labelled as the 'Cybele Complex'.
Many remains in this area have now been consolidated and enclosed in
a special public park (pl 72) which demands careful attention by the
visitor. The dedication of the temple to Cybele is proved by, among

309

other things, an inscription to her by the *dendrophori* and a marble statue, but it is surrounded by several Roman houses and shops. It seems to have been built in the first half of the first century AD and to have lasted until the fourth century and both it and the little theatre, which was built a little later than the temple, overlay earlier buildings. The baths also appear to have been built in the late first century.[35]

Rather surprisingly, Vienne had no amphitheatre, but it did have a circus. While the pyramid set in the middle of it (pl 73) had long been known, its true meaning was first realised in 1853 and excavations in 1903–07 established the plan of all of it—455.2m long and 118.4m broad. It was probably built in the early second century and since coins found here included some of Valentinian II it probably lasted at least until the late fourth century.[36] In its stone state it overlaid some earlier structures and it has been suggested that these included the gymnasium where a *gymnicus agon* was, as we learn from the letter of Pliny the Younger to Sempronius Rufus, carried out for some years until suppressed by Pliny's friend, the *duovir* Trebonius Rufus, in the time of Trajan.[37]

Not only numerous houses, but also several baths and many drains have been located in Vienne[38] and the water supply was obviously important. No less than 11 aqueducts have been partly identified—some of them having been restored to use in modern times—and while none is of the spectacular type of those of Nîmes and Fréjus some parts of them are still visible, especially where they were running underground. The majority came from springs near la Gabétière and Jemens, with another in that area from a dam that still exists across the river Suze, but the longest are those from le Puy, near Eyzin-Pinet, which, being designed to serve some of the higher parts of the city, had apparently to follow the contours just above 250m (fig 44). While no *castellum divisorium* has been convincingly exposed, the early date of one of the aqueducts is clearly demonstrated by a series of inscriptions stating that Q.Gellius Capella and D.Sulpicius Censor, both *quattuor-viri*, presented to the city *aquas novas itineraque eorum per suos fundos*, and since these were found in the area near the river Gère it was certainly one of the northern group.[39]

Whether or not they emerged from a federation of several tribes, the *Allobroges* controlled a very large area (fig 42) and most of the boundaries of the *civitas Viennensis* in the early Roman Empire are reasonably certain, but a few minor questions do arise.[40] The western limit, clearly defined by the crest of the Cévennes, raises no problems, but in the north two doubts persist. For one thing, the boundary between *Vienna* and *Lugdunum* on the east side of the Rhône may have run nearer to Lyon than we have defined it and for the other, while it is clear that in Caesar's time the *Allobroges* did own a little land north of the river between Lyon and Geneva, how much of this they retained after the formal organisation of the provinces is not known—probably

Vienna (Vienne), with *Genava* (Geneva) and *Cularo/Gratianopolis* (Grenoble)
no more than the odd bridgehead.[41] In the east, it is not absolutely
certain where the border left the southern shore of the Lake of Geneva
and we have simply followed the most likely ridge, but thereafter two
boundary stones—the one found on the Col de Forclaz, 7km SE of
Passy, and the other on the Col du Jaillet, 3km NW of Megève[42]—give
clear indications, as do the places named *Ad Publicanos* and *Fines*.

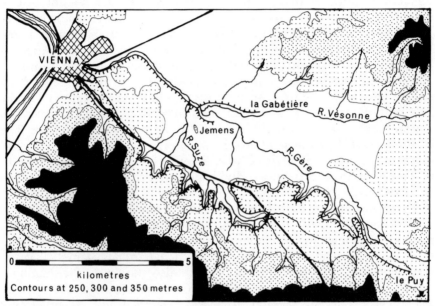

44 The courses of the aqueducts of *Vienna* (after Pelletier)

In the south, the boundaries of *Vapincum*, *Valentia* and the *Vocontii*
have already been discussed in the relevant chapters, but one major
problem remains: under whose supervision were the *Tricorii* and *Iconii*?
As we have already suggested, some more or less direct roads must
have connected *Cularo* with *Dea* and *Vapincum* (the latter approximately on the route taken by Munatius Plancus in 43 BC), but the only one in
this area that is firmly identified is that leading up the Romanche valley
to the Col du Lautaret and so to Italy by way of *Brigantio* (Briançon).
Places along this road are listed both on the Peutinger Table and (in
very garbled form) in the Ravenna Cosmography and although no
finds are recorded four of them can be located with some certainty—
Catorissium near Bourg d'Oisan, *Mellosedum* near Mont-de-Lans,
Durotincum near Villar d'Arène and *Stabatio* near Monêtier-les-Bains—
but unfortunately *Fines* appears only in the Cosmography (inserted
between '*Cantourisa*' and '*Curarone*'!), so no mileage figures are
provided for it.[43] Somewhere between Livet and Gavet, however,
seems to have borne the name Avorand (probably derived from the
Celtic *Icoranda*, meaning boundary), so the place can be marked with

311

confidence on a small-scale map. In any case, as James Elroy Flecker observed, 'High and solemn mountains guard Rioupéroux' (in this area) and it is an ideal place for a frontier.[44] Nevertheless, the administration of the *Iconii* and the *Tricorii* remains a puzzle.

The vast area of the *civitas* proper was not ruled entirely by permanent residents in *Vienna*, as is amply demonstrated by the remarkable number of inscriptions scattered all over it—not just in notable towns like *Genava* (Geneva) and *Cularo* (Grenoble), both of which have produced records of the earlier *quattuorviri* as well as the later *duoviri*, but also in little villages like Grésy-Fontaine (midway between Chambéry and Albertville), where stones recording Taurinus, a *duovir* and *pontifex* as well as one of the *tresviri* in charge of local affairs, now form the basis of the walls of a little chapel (pl 74)[45] In the late Empire, however, it was divided into three, when *Genava* and *Cularo* (later to be renamed *Gratianopolis*) were elevated to cities. The boundaries of their *civitates* (also shown on fig 42) can be derived fairly safely from those of early Christian dioceses and it seems best to consider the three territories individually, first that of Vienne and then those of Geneva and Grenoble.

The Antonine Itinerary lists two routes from *Mediolanum* (Milan) to *Vienna*, one of them terminating there and the other running on through *Lugdunum* to *Gesoriacum* (Boulogne). The first of these includes three stopping-places within the area of the late *civitas*, namely *Labisco*, *Augustum* and *Bergusia*—all three of them also shown on the Peutinger Table, though the first is there named as *Laviscone* and the third as *Bergusium*.[46] *Labisco*, midway between *Lemincum* and *Augustum* and shown as *xiiii mp* from each of them in both sources, is clearly les Echelles, approached from the north-east by one of the most remarkable roads in the province, running through a deep gorge (pl 75).[47] Little has been found here, but of the three local inscriptions one records *vicani* (unfortunately without their full name) and another gives a warning that whoever misused something as a latrine would have to pay a fine to the temple of Jupiter.[48] *Augustum* (Aôste, but evidently extending as far east as St-Génix) is more significant, having yielded more than two dozen inscriptions ranging from the first century to Christian times. Its name was evidently of early origin, since one of them was erected for the *quattuorvir* L.Iulius Fronto (who had also been a *praefectus equitum*) by the *Vicani Augustani*, and besides several dedications to deities some stones record the building of a monument for M.Aurelius Antoninus (perhaps in AD 175).[49] In the early 1960s several minor local finds were made, and investigation into the potteries long ago identified has now been resumed.[50] *Bergusia* (or *Bergusium*) is now Bourgoin-Jallieu: of the two inscriptions recorded one is of sixth-century date, but here too research is developing and some baths have recently been located.[51] The milestone shown between these two towns was found in 1928 and is of Constantinian

Vienna (Vienne), with *Genava* (Geneva) and *Cularo/Gratianopolis* (Grenoble)
date—something that, rather surprisingly, applies to all those marked east of *Vienna*.[52] *Etanna* (Yenne, which was called Eiauna in medieval charters) is not included in the Itinerary, but is shown on the Peutinger Table, and while it, along with *Condate* and even *Genava*, is there sadly mis-sited north of the Rhône, the place is correctly listed as *xii mp* from *Augustum*. Here too relatively few finds have been made, but a useful analysis by Wuilleumier has shown that it, like *Augustum*, was evidently larger than the modern town and existed at least from the second to the sixth century.[53]

The other route that the Antonine Itinerary does record enters our area by way of the *Via Agrippina*, a road that carried milestones ranging in date from the time of Augustus to the fourth century.[54] The only places that it names between *Valentia* and *Lugdunum*, however, are *Ursolis* (var *Ursinis*) and *Vienna* and it is the Peutinger Table that supplies *Tegna* and *Figlinis*. *Tegna* was certainly Tain-l'Hermitage, immediately opposite Tournon, and ample remains have been found here, not only mosaics and burials but also several inscriptions, one of them recording a *taurobolium* at Lyon in AD 184 and another a dedication to a *quaestor* and *duovir* of *Vienna*, who had been appointed a local *tresvir*, set up by *vicani Boxsani et Noiomagenses* (presumably people from Buis and Nyons, in the land of the *Vocontii*)—both reflecting the intensive use of this road.[55] *Ursolis*, placed by the Itinerary *xxii mp* from *Valentia* and *xxvi mp* from *Vienna*, must have been near St-Vallier (the present name of which is derived from that of Valerius, sometime bishop of Viviers, who was also called Valère d'Orsole) and while this too has yielded remains including inscriptions its precise site has now been identified, at le Cappa, not only by masonry but also by a useful air photograph.[56] *Figlinis*, *xvii mp* from *Vienna* on the Peutinger Table, should be near St-Rambert-d'Albon, but some pottery kilns, found long ago about 2.5km south of the present town (that is, near the service station on the modern motorway), while adequately explaining its name, seem so far to have provided the only evidence.[57]

Turedonnum and *Morginnum*, on the most direct road from *Vienna* to *Cularo*, also appear only on the Peutinger Table, and while one of the mileages has evidently been miscopied (between *Turedonno* and *Morginno*, for *xiiii* read *xxiiii*) the rest point clearly to Tourdan and Moirans—something that is largely confirmed by the modern names. Four funerary inscriptions have long been known from Tourdan, but recent excavations, producing finds of the first and second centuries, have now located the true site, just to the NE, at Revel-Tourdan.[58] Moirans, on the other hand, from which three inscriptions are known (again including one of Christian date), requires further investigation and the best modern evidence from this area concerns the large rich villa, of early imperial date, marked just to the north, at Sermores (near Voiron).[59]

The only reference to the road running north to south along the right

313

Vienna (Vienne), with *Genava* (Geneva) and *Cularo/Gratianopolis* (Grenoble)

bank of the Rhône is in the alternative route from *Vienna* to *Lugdunum* included in the Antonine Itinerary—that is, along the route that had been followed, probably before a proper road had been built, by Munatius Plancus in 43 BC.[60] Apart from the extension of the city of *Vienna* across the river, to which we have already referred, by far the most notable place on this road is Andance. About 3km to the south of it, at la Sarrasinière, stand the impressive remains of what was once claimed to be the trophy of Fabius Maximus but is now recognised as an unusually large mausoleum, dating from the first century AD (pl 76): to the north of the village, on the hill of le Châtelet, stood a curious temple (fig 45), apparently of pre-Roman origin, that was later converted to Christian use: and in the area as a whole several buildings and a number of inscriptions, including one mentioning a decurion of *Vienna*, have been found.[61]

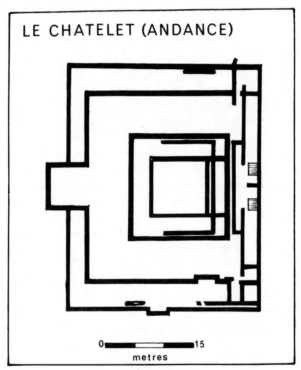

LE CHATELET (ANDANCE)

0 ▬▬▬▬ 15
metres

45 The temple of le Châtelet, Andance (after Morel and Blanc)

As a glance at Sheet L31 of the Tabula Imperii Romani will show, little used to be known of rural sites in the region around Vienne, but since the war substantial improvements have been made. The temple included on our map near Laveyron, which also seems to have had a pre-Roman origin, is not a new discovery and is not absolutely certain,[62] but several villas shown further north, besides that already

314

Vienna (Vienne), with *Genava* (Geneva) and *Cularo/Gratianopolis* (Grenoble)

mentioned at Sermores, illustrate well the agricultural prosperity of the area—for example, the very large one excavated at St-Romain-de-Jalionas[63]—while the less fully known ones at Septème and Oytier (seven and eight Roman miles from *Vienna*) illustrate the fact (already mentioned with regard to Quart and Uchaud, near Nîmes) that many such medieval and modern names must have been derived from milestones rather than posting-stations.[64] Finally, another mausoleum (though it has not survived like that of la Sarrasinière) has been excavated at Clonas-sur-Varèze, midway between *Figlinis* and *Vienna*, with an inscription to P.Licinius Macrinus.[65]

To turn now to the second subdivision of the *civitas*, its capital, the large modern city of Geneva, is somewhat confusing to the visiting archaeologist, not only because of its huge buildings and the roads that are largely redesigned with underpasses, but also because, as shown on fig 46, it now extends over what in Roman times was still part of the *Lacus Lemannus*— a fact immortalised by the name of the Rue de Rive which is now well inland. If one approaches from the north side of the Rhône, however, some things become clear. The bridge that Caesar broke to keep out the *Helvetii* was very near the present one that crosses by way of l'Île[66] and the steep slope up the Rue de la Cité to the Grand' Rue leads one up to what is easily recognised as the pre-Roman hill-fort of the *Allobroges*, refortified in the late Empire with stone walls, some small stretches of which can still be seen in car-parks (pl 77).[67] Many finds made outside this area make it clear that in the prosperous period the city extended a long way south, at least as far as the present Boulevard des Tranchées, and it is just north of this, at le Pin, that the *castellum divisorium* of the necessary aqueduct, bringing water from a spring near Granves, seems to have stood.[68] As shown on the plan, not only private but also several public buildings have been located, as have two ports (now underground), one for the use of the *nautae lacus Lemanni* and the other for the *ratiarii superiores*, two bodies that are both recorded in inscriptions, as also is a *praepositus quadragesimae Galliarum*, which underlines the importance here of trade.[69] Many other inscriptions, now well presented in the museum, also list the other expected officials, not only both *quattuorviri* and *duoviri* (reflecting the change in status of *Vienna*), but also *aediles, pontifices, flamines, seviri* and a *praefectus fabrum*, and while the *vicani Genavenses* were, as usual, supervised by *tresviri*, it is abundantly clear that right from the beginning this was the most important *vicus* in the *civitas*: several legionaries are also recorded, but with regard to some of them, and indeed to other inscriptions, one must remember that the part of Geneva north of the river was then in the territory of *Colonia Iulia Equestris* (Nyon) and even stones found in the medieval buildings in the southern part could have been transported for use.[70]

Many dedications to deities have also been found, not only to the usual ones, such as Jupiter, Mars and Apollo, but also to the Mercury of

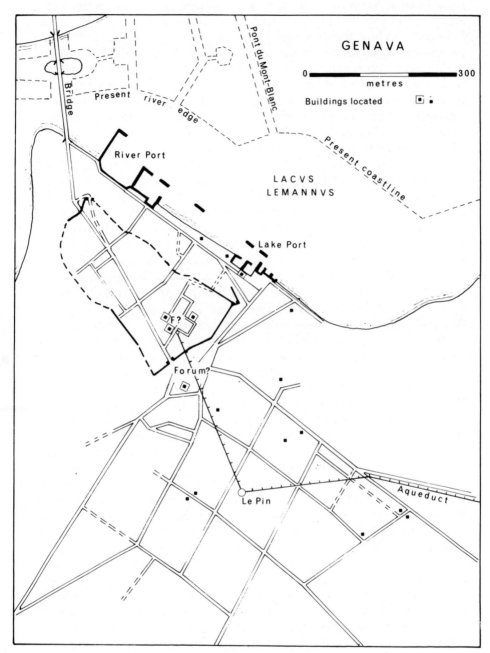

46 A tentative plan of Geneva (after Broise, Maier and Mottier)

merchants and even to the Neptune of sailors.[71] Quite when the city became predominantly Christian is uncertain, but its earliest known bishop, Salonius, a son of Eucherius (the well-known bishop of Lyon), was himself an author and attended the Councils of Orange and Vaison in 441 and 442.[72]

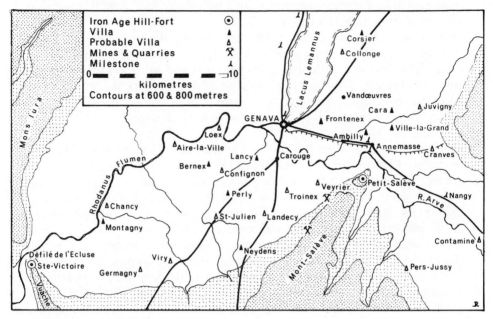

47 The environs of Geneva

As may be seen from the regional map (fig 47), the wealth of the city expanded in the neighbouring area and a considerable number of villas and probable villas have been discovered. Further to the east, both the road along the south shore of the lake and that up the valley of the river Arve present some problems. Neither of them is mentioned in any itinerary, but it seems probable that they had some importance, at least in the period of the late Empire, since milestones have been found near each of them. Those beside the north road are both generally believed to have been transported from the other side of the lake, but while this may well be true of the Severan one at Messery, which gives a figure of *iiii* instead of the 12 Roman miles that separates it from Geneva, it seems much less likely for the other, since this, a Constantian stone found at Hermance, gives the correct figure of *vii*.[73] In any case, more evidence is now emerging and it now seems certain that the pleasant lakeside town of Thonon-les-Bains, where several finds have been made in recent years, was a station along a route that joined the well-known road from *Germania* to Italy somewhere between *Pennelocus* (Villeneuve) and *Acaunum* (St Maurice).[74] The land between the lake

317

Vienna (Vienne), with *Genava* (Geneva) and *Cularo/Gratianopolis* (Grenoble)

and the hills is (and was) a fertile area, with many orchards and vineyards, and the same is true of much of the valley of the river Arve (excluding the gorge of Cluses).

Two milestones, both of early fourth-century date, have been found near Annemasse, which, from the evidence of buildings excavated in it, was evidently a settlement, and a third milestone (undatable) stood near the road at Nangy, to the SE.[75] While a few possible villas have also been noted, however, the most outstanding discovery is the Passy temple. This shrine, apparently dedicated to Mars, stood not in that town itself but up on the hill at les Outards and other odd finds in this area, not only inscriptions but also a possible aqueduct at Servoz (about 7km NE of Passy), suggest that more investigation might reveal a town.[76] Nevertheless, it is difficult to see how this road could ever have crossed the Alps.

The two other roads out of *Genava* are much better known. On the route to *Vienna* the name *Condate*, listed on the Peutinger Table, is generally applied to Seyssel (where an excellent altar to the god Vintius can be seen built into the wall of a church) but its true site, Albigny-Condon, lies south of the town, near the Iron Age hill-fort of Vens and just north of the confluence of the Fier and the Rhône. This fact was already recognised in the nineteenth century and recent excavations have revealed a great deal—streets, buildings, including both baths and shops, and burials—and it is clear that it flourished throughout the Roman period except in the second half of the third century: other finds, including pottery kilns, have been made just across the Rhône, so a crossing of the river here is likely, but quite how a road should run from here to *Boutae* (Annecy) is difficult to understand from the local geography.[77] The town of Conjux (its modern name), shown south of *Condate* and at the north end of the Lac du Bourget, is a recent discovery: kilns at the neighbouring places of Chatière and Portout produced *terra sigillata* pottery and it has now been shown that a substantial Roman town is largely submerged under the lake.[78]

To follow now the other road south from *Genava*, Annecy is listed in the Antonine Itinerary as *Bautas*, but its correct name, *Boutae*, is attested both by an inscription citing the *vicani Bo(utenses)* and by its medieval form *Bouz*.[79] Thanks especially to the work of Pierre Broise, this is the best recorded *vicus* in the whole province, though virtually none of it is now visible. This is due to the fact that while the medieval town of Annecy and, until recently, its modern successor was concentrated beside the little river Thiou (a branch of the Fier, flowing from the lake) and overlooked by the mighty château (now holding a museum well stocked with inscriptions), the Roman town stood further to the north and constant rescue excavations during the development of the northern suburbs have produced an impressive plan (fig 48). As may be seen, it included a basilica and forum, numerous houses, workshops,

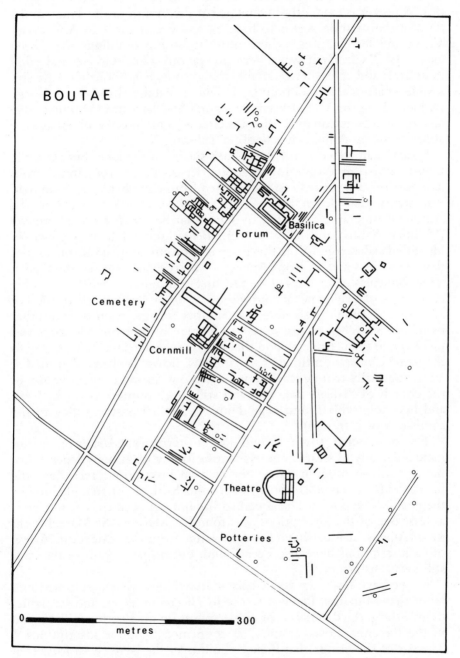

48 A tentative plan of Boutae, north of Annecy (after Broise)

wells and even a small theatre, but the settlement also spread beyond this. A port was evidently maintained at the mouth of the Thiou and a kind of centuriation seems to have extended eastwards to Annecy-le-Vieux and les Barattes, where more imposing buildings have been excavated.[80] Clearly it was a very prosperous *vicus*, with several villas in its area, and at least two notable things in its neighbourhood are still visible—part of the road built by L.Tincius Patalus through the Gorge du Fier (along the V1 between Naves and St-Clair) and the remarkable *horologium* inscription of C.Blaesius Gratus, built into a wall outside the abbey (now an American school) at Talloires.[81]

Roads seem to have run along both shores of the lake, but since the Constantinian milestone found at Veyrier-du-Lac in 1967 must, from its figure of *xxiii*, have been transported from elsewhere, the main road was surely that down the western side.[82] *Casuaria* is listed in the Antonine Itinerary, as edited by Cuntz, at *mp xviiii* from *Darantasia* (Moutiers-Salins) and *mp xxx* from *Boutae* and while it is generally identified as Faverges-Viuz this place is approximately 28 Roman miles from Moutiers and 18 from Annecy. It is true that one MS, the Codex Vindobonensis 181, does give the first mileage as *xxiiii* (a possible corruption of *xxvii*) and of course the *xxx* might be just a corruption of *xx*, but one should also note that another village, with the tempting name of Césarches, is just about 18 Roman miles from Moutiers and just over 30 from Annecy, and that is why we have attached a query to the name *Casuaria* on fig 42.[83] A *vicus* has, however, been identified at Viuz, especially from excavations carried out during the renovation of the church of St-Jean-Baptiste, and still more impressive is the large and luxurious villa found at le Thovey, just across the valley to the south-east of it (fig 49).[84]

The only other town shown in this territory, *Albinnum*, is not included in any itinerary, but its identification with Albens depends not merely on the modern name but on two inscriptions recording the provision by a *praefectus fabrum*, C.Sennius Sabinus, of an aqueduct for the *vicani Albinnienses*. The aqueduct has not yet been traced, but since at least one of the inscriptions was found at Marigny-St-Marcel, 6km NE of Albens, it must have brought water from that direction. A few other inscriptions have also been found, but proper details of the *vicus* still await discovery.[85]

As we have noted (p 76), *Cularo* (Grenoble) is first mentioned in a letter that Munatius Plancus wrote to Cicero in 43 BC and its name, despite the garbled versions of it that appear on the Peutinger Table and in the Ravenna Cosmography, is confirmed by three inscriptions.[86] The site of the bridge that Plancus built over the Isère (with fortlets at each end of it) has not been identified, nor has the place where he stationed his army, but a number of small finds indicate that the *Allobroges* already had a settlement here on the south bank of the river, while no evidence has been found that there was ever a hill-fort on the

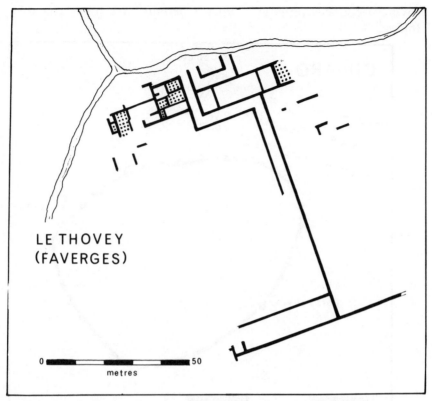

49 The villa of le Thovey, Faverges (after Lesfargues)

great hill overlooking the north bank.[87] That the place was already important in the early imperial period is demonstrated by the appearance among its inscriptions of a *quattuorvir* as well as a *duovir* and most of the other expected officials are duly recorded—*flamines*, an *aedile*, *seviri* and *tresviri*.[88] The epitaphs of three legionary veterans and of D.Decmanius Caper, a wealthy *subpraefectus Equitum Alae Agrippianae*, have been found here, but the most interesting are those of two *librarii* of the *Quadragesima Galliarum*, specifically of the *Statio Cularonensis*, which shows that, despite its distance from the provincial frontier, a customs office existed here.[89] Also of note is the stone erected in honour of Claudius Gothicus—something that demonstrates where the loyalty of this city lay in AD 269, in contrast to the milestones of Tetricus found in the south-west part of the province.[90]

On the religious side, although no temple has been located ample dedications to the normal deities are listed (including one to Isis),[91] but the date of the full transfer to Christianity is a little uncertain. St Domninus, who attended the Council of Aquileia in 381, seems to have been the first bishop, but none is recorded as taking part in the

Vienna (Vienne), with *Genava* (Geneva) and *Cularo/Gratianopolis* (Grenoble)
provincial councils until 441, when Cheretius was present at that of
Orange.[92]

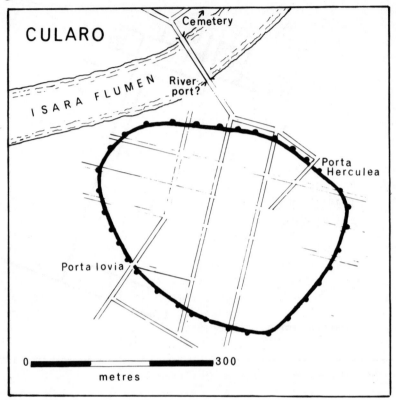

50 A tentative plan of Grenoble

While over 100 inscriptions have been found at Grenoble, from the
archaeological point of view the flourishing city is a little depressing.
Though a fine museum has now been established half way up the hill
north of the river, too little relevant material is displayed in it (or was,
at least in 1983) and when an extensive stretch of the town walls was
exposed in 1962 it was forthwith demolished and only tiny bits of them
can now be seen (*eg* pl 78).[93] Fortunately the course of these defences,
as shown in fig 50, is well established by plans made long ago (they
remained in use for centuries) and the date of their construction is
proved by the two famous inscriptions which not only give the names
of the gates as Porta Iovia and Porta Herculea but also state that the
walls were provided by Diocletian and Maximian.[94] There is no doubt
that the town was considerably more extensive in the early Empire, but
all that is firmly established is the existence of a first-century house and
wells to the south-west of the late enceinte, while various small finds,
including imported material, suggest that the necessary river port was

322

slightly downstream from the probable bridge.[95] Much more satisfactory have been prolonged excavations around the church of St-Laurent, away to the NE on the other side of the Isère, where an extensive cemetery has been uncovered, including a fourth-century mausoleum.[96]

No inscriptions seem to include the name of the town in its later form of *Gratianopolis*, but this was certainly due to a visit here by the Emperor Gratian and it is interesting that it survived his overthrow by Maximus and his murder at *Lugdunum* in 383, so that in the *Notitia Galliarum* this is the *Civitas Gratianopolitana*, from which, of course, its modern name is derived.[97]

Although in recent years some villas have been located near Grenoble, along with the temple and baths at St-Martin-d'Uriage,[98] the more prosperous area was evidently further to the NE and the most important *vicus* was clearly that of *Aquae* (Aix-les-Bains). Whereas *Boutae* has been extensively planned but offers no upstanding remains, the plan of *Aquae* is virtually unknown yet it has three structures still open to inspection. The most notable of these is the Arch of Campanus, set up in the first century for his relations by L.Pompeius Campanus—an unusual monument, 9.15 m high and very well preserved (pl 79).[100] Just to the SW of it is a substantial building, which for long was incorporated in the château of the Marquis of Aix and is now a pleasant museum, holding some fine statues and inscriptions. It is called the Temple of Diana but, as in the case of its namesake at Nîmes (*qv*), this is based on no real evidence and while parts of its structure are certainly Roman (pl 80) it has been so much altered that its original purpose is unknown. Thirdly, impressive remains of the large public baths, apparently served by an aqueduct from Mt Renard (6–7 km to the SE), lie inside the modern Thermes Nationaux and can be inspected during a conducted tour.[101] Unfortunately no certain villas have been located in this vicinity, but the number of inscriptions found not only in Aix itself but also in St-Innocent to the NNW, Grésy-sur-Aix to the NE and Viviers to the S (the last including three of the senator M.Iunius Vestinus Mallo, who had been a legate of *Asia*) clearly indicate its prosperity: a *sevir* also appears, the religious dedications include one recording the building of a temple of Mars and the fact that the place really was, as one would expect, called *Aquae* is confirmed by three inscriptions that include the *Aquenses*.[102]

Aquae is not mentioned in any itinerary, but *Lemincum*, *Mantala* and *Ad Publicanos* are and since there is only one very minor difference between the mileages of the Antonine Itinerary and those of the Peutinger Table[103] their approximate positions can be fixed with some certainty, though all of them demand further investigation. As its name implies, *Lemincum* was not in the centre of modern Chambéry, but in its north-eastern suburb of Lémenc and while the palaeochristian crypt there, with its octagonal baptistry, is well worth a visit, that is the only notable feature: some pottery has been recorded and one inscription, and it also seems possible that an aqueduct, of which a portion was recently noted at St-Alban-Leysse, may have led here.[104] *Mantala* must have been at or near St-Pierre-d'Albigny and here just a little more is recorded, including an inscription describing the dedication of a basilica to Jupiter by C.Licinius Calvinus,[105] but much more has recently been discovered of an extensive settlement, with a shrine of Mercury, on the other side of the river at Châteauneuf-les-Boissons.[106] *Ad Publicanos* was evidently at or near Albertville, probably in the place called Conflans, which reflects the confluence of the Arly with the Isère and is just about 3 Roman miles from *Obilunum* (la Bathie) and 16 from *Mantala*, as stated in the Itinerary. Unfortunately the only inscription from this area that refers to the *Quadragesima Galliarum* is a dedication set up by a *vilicus* at Allandaz, 3 km NW of Albertville, and neither Tournon nor Tours (the two places suggested as the origin of AD TVR . . .) fits the mileages given in our sources.[107]

Another inscription found near here records a *duovir* who was also *praefectus pagi Vale* . . . (presumably covering this area especially since he had acted as fosterfather to the erector) and both dedications to deities and the recent discovery of villas indicate that the valley of the Isère enjoyed prosperity. All three of the villas shown on the map were large and luxurious and each of them stood near a place where notable inscriptions had been found—that at Arbin (Mérande) near the obituary of T.Pompeius Albinus, that at St-Jean-de-la-Porte (next to *Mantala*) near the record of Taurinus, and that at Gilly-sur-Isère (next to *Ad Publicanos*) near a dedication to Apollo and something recording a barrier against floods.[109] It was also near St-Jean-de-la-Porte that was found, built into an old tower, an early inscription set up by the *Ratiarii Voludnienses* and since the name of la Velieude covered an area between the village and the river they were evidently locals, but whether they represented a *vicus* or a *pagus* is unknown and the river port that they must have used has not been identified.[110]

REFERENCES AND NOTES

1 Livy XXI, 31, 5–7: his account indicates that, while they were then a kingdom, there was also a 'senate'. On their eminence, *cf* Stephanus of Byzantium, *sv* Ἀλλόβρυγες citing Apollodorus as calling them ἔθνος δυνατώτατον Γαλατικόν.
2 Stephanus, *sv*.
3 Caesar, *BG* I, 6.
4 Caesar, *BG* I, 11 and 28.
5 Caesar, *BG* III, 6, and VII, 64–5.
6 Caesar, *BC* III, 59–63, with the killing of one of them, *ibid*, 84. The 'senate' into which Caesar had them installed was (like that in Livy, cited

Vienna (Vienne), with *Genava* (Geneva) and *Cularo/Gratianopolis* (Grenoble)

in n1 above) probably that of Vienne, but in view of the implications of Suetonius, *Divus Iulius* lxxvi, 3, the Roman senate is not quite impossible.

7 Dio xLvi, 50.

8 For a full discussion, with notes supplying an ample bibliography, Pelletier 1982, 34–40, 73–80; for an opinion claiming that Caesar founded a *colonia Romana* and that after the Roman citizens had been expelled in 43 BC it was established here, *eg* M.Leglay in Princeton 1976, 980, and for the view that it was Italian traders who fled from Vienne when Catugnatus revolted, *eg* A.Audin, *Essai sur la topographie de Lugdunum*, 1956, quoted by J.F.Drinkwater in *Britannia* vi(1975), 134; *cf* also Jullian iii, 122 n6, and P.Thollard in *RAN* xvii(1984), 116–18.

9 For the dissent, Velleius Paterculus ii, 121; for AD 41, Suetonius, *C.Caligula* xvii, 1 (though he does not mention *Vienna*).

10 *CIL* xiii, 1668 (*ILS* 212) (now preserved at Lyon), inadequately summarised in Tacitus, *Ann* xi, 23.

11 This is recorded in *CIL* xii, 2337, on an inscription to T.Pompeius Albinus (found not at Vienne but at Arbin, 12km se of Chambéry and so within the *civitas*). His epitaph has since been found (*AE* 1935, 5) at Merida in Spain, where he was *subprocurator* of *Lusitania* (as was also stated in the first inscription, and both say that he had been a *tribunus militum* in *Legio vi Victrix*, evidently before its move to Britain). The Merida inscription, while saying that he came from *Vienna*, clearly gives his tribe as *Tromentina*, not *Voltinia*, and while Pelletier (1982, 75) suggests that this means that he was descended from an Italian immigrant, it seems possible that an ancestor might have been enfranchised by Pompey the Great (like the grandfather of Pompeius Trogus) for service in Spain. The only other record of *Tromentina* in this province seems to be that on an amphora of M.Tuccus, found at Uzès (*CIL* xii, 5633, no 296), but another citizen of Vienne was enrolled in it (*CIL* xiv, 296, found at Praeneste) and his complete name (. . . *ttio Cn.filio*) is uncertain.

12 Mela ii, 4, 75; inscriptions, *CIL* xii, 1809–2178, 5864–6, *ILGN* 263–334, plus more recent discoveries.

13 Suffect consul AD 35, *ordinarius* 46; he had also served in Britain. Tacitus, *Ann* xi, 1–3, Seneca, *De Constantia Sapientis* xviii, 2, Dio Lix, 30, Lx, 27, *CIL* xiii, 1668 (*ILS* 212).

14 The other Valerius, *CIL* xiii, 1668; Vopiscus, Tacitus, *Hist* i, 77, *CIL* vi, 2051: Atticus, Tacitus, *Ann* xv, 48, 52, 68–9, *CIL* xiii, 1668 (his Viennese origin is questioned by Pelletier 1982, 290, but supported by Syme 1958, 786). For a general review of senators from here, Pelletier 1982, 286–96.

15 Mela, *v* n12 above; Pliny, *HN* xiv, 26 and 57 (wine), xviii, 85 (white wheat); Columella xii, 23 (pitch used for preserving wine); Martial vii, 88 (his books read in *pulchra Vienna*), xiii, 107 (wine); Plutarch, *Quaestiones Conviviales* v, 3, 1; Ausonius, *Ordo Urbium Nobilium* x, 3 (though curiously this city does not get its own separate entry).

16 J.Lancha, *Recueil général des mosaïques de la Gaule: Vienne, Gallia* Suppl x, Pt iii, fasc 2, 1981.

17 *CIL* xii, 1928, 1930, 1917, 1878, 1911, 1877; for discussion. Pelletier 1982, 330–7.

18 Inscriptions, *CIL* xii, 1809–38; statues, Espérandieu 1907, i, 180 (Epona) etc; full account, Pelletier 1982, 387–413.

Vienna (Vienne), with *Genava* (Geneva) and *Cularo/Gratianopolis* (Grenoble)

19 Eusebius, *Hist Eccles* v, i–ii; Pelletier 1982, 465–8, 1974, 97–119, 169–88. Munier 1963, 9–25; on early churches and monasteries, Pelletier 1974, 65–88. It was, of course, visited by Sidonius (*Epp* v, vi, 1), who also wrote *Epp* VII, i, to its bishop Mamertus.

20 For a useful account, G Chapotat, *Vienne Gauloise: le matériel de la Tène III trouvé sur la colline de Ste-Blandine*, Lyon, 1970; *Gallia* XIV(1956), 263–6, XXII(1964), 511–17, XXXV(1977), 479–81; Pelletier 1982, 42–51.

21 *ILGN* 263 (relating them to the stone inscribed DAT, *CIL* XII, 1843, that has long been known); Grenier 1931, 323–9 (with a drawing of part of the Porte d'Avignon on p 327): *Gallia* XXXIII(1975), 542; Pelletier 1982, 103–09, 491.

22 Walls, Pelletier 1974, 47–53(with plan), *castrum*, *ibid* 62–4, *palatium*, *ibid*, 59–62.

23 Pelletier 1982, 184–8; for other buildings in this area, *ibid* 188–93.

24 Pelletier 1982, 159–64 (preferring the suggestion of Picard in *Gallia* v(1947), 259–70, that the statues of Venus and other pagan deities had been deposited here in Christian times to that of Grenier 1960, 268–76, that they were ornaments installed in the first century). The complete plan of these buildings is still unknown.

25 St-Romain-en-Gal, Pelletier 1982, 122–7, 193–6, 492; H.Stern, 'Mosaïques de la région de Vienne', *Gallia* XXIX(1971), 123–50 (dealing with this area); M.le Glay and S.Tourrenc, *CRAI* 1971, 764–73; *Gallia* XXIV(1966), 500–01, XXIX(1971), 421–5, XXXI(1973), 527–8, XXXIII(1975), 552–4, XXXV(1977), 490, XXXVIII(1980), 525–8 (including pottery kilns); *Hist Arch* no 78 (Nov 1983), 28–31 (with plan and good photographs). Ste-Colombe, *Hist Arch* 78, 34–5.

26 Pelletier 1982, 170–84; *Gallia* XXXV(1977), 479, XXXVIII(1980), 513–16, XL(1982), 403–05 (in the Rue des Colonnes, St-Martin, north of the river Gère).

27 But none, it seems, beside the roads leading E and SE. Pelletier 1982, 476–80; *Gallia* XXIX(1971), 427–8 (the most northerly cemetery). On his plan Pelletier shows the road towards the east running up the hill of Ste-Blandine, but, especially since the recent discoveries in St-Martin, the route on our plan, following that shown by P.Broise in pl XXII.2 of Chevallier 1982, is surely more likely?

28 Ports, Pelletier 1982, 347–8; bridge, *ibid*, 124–5 (with a reproduction between pp 128 and 129 of a drawing made in 1555) and Pelletier 1974, 138–40.

29 On the forum, Pelletier 1982, 118–20. On the temple, Grenier 1958, 393–7, Pelletier 1982, 446–53 and 1974, 59 (on its later conversion to a church).

30 *CIL* XII 1845 (with a plan of the holes but no firm conclusion); *ILGN* 265 (upper line interpreted, after Formigé, as ROMAE ET AUGUSTO CAESARI DIVI F); Grenier 1958, 396–7 (.....ET AUGUSTO CAESARI DIVI F, with .....ET DIVAE AUGUSTAE as the second line); Pelletier 1982, 449–52 (citing many suggestions but preferring HERCULI INVICTO ET DIVO AUGUSTO/ET DIVAE AUGUSTAE to his earlier choice of APOLLINI SANCTO ET etc).

31 *CIL* XII, 1821; Pelletier 1982, 394, 414.

32 A.Pelletier, *Archéologia* 101 (Dec 1976), 53–63; *Gallia* XXV(1977), 479–81; Pelletier 1982, 491.

Vienna (Vienne), with *Genava* (Geneva) and *Cularo/Gratianopolis* (Grenoble)

33 J.Formigé, *Le théâtre romain de Vienne*, 1950 (with foreword by C.Picard); Grenier 1958, 773–80; *Gallia* VI(1948), 224–5; Pelletier 1982, 211–16 (with references to varied suggestions). In the temple included in the upper *cavea*, Pelletier 1982, 415–16, arguing for Bacchus rather than Apollo.

34 *Gallia* VI(1948), 224–5, XVIII(1960), 366–8 (including discovery of ODEV inscription—*AE* 1961, 170), XX(1962), 643–5, XXIX(1971), 425–6, XXXI(1973), 529–30, XXXIII(1975), 539–40, XXXV(1977), 479; for a general account, A.Pelletier, 'Fouilles à l'Odéon de Vienne (1973–6)', *Gallia* XXXIX(1981), 148–69; Pelletier 1982, 217–21.

35 Dedications, *CIL* XII, 1917 etc; statue, Espérandieu 1907, I, 394. Grenier 1958, 780–3; *Gallia* XIV(1956), 266, XVI(1958), 376–7, XVIII(1960), 366, XXII(1964), 511–17, XXIV(1966), 501–08. XXIX(1971), 425–6, XXXIII(1975), 539; C.Picard, 'Le théâtre des Mystères de Cybele-Attis en Vienne', *CRAI* 1955, 229–48; A.Pelletier, 'Construction augustéenne et depotoir tibérien dans la sanctuaire métroaque de Vienne', *RAN* IX(1976), 115–42; Pelletier 1982, 150–5 (baths), 432–8 (theatre and temple), with plan between pp 128 and 129.

36 E.Bizot; *Découverte d'un cirque antique à Vienne*, Lyon, 1910; Grenier 1958, 989–92; Pelletier 1982, 221–2 (with Bizot's plan reproduced between pp 128 and 129).

37 Pliny, *Epp* IV, 22; Pelletier 1982, 222–3 (and for a possible other site for a gymnasium, no 19 on the plan at end of book).

38 For a general review of houses, Pelletier 1982, 169–210 and for baths and drains, 150–67.

39 *CIL* XII, 1882–9; Grenier 1960, 111–17; Pelletier 1982, 131–49 (on whose plan fig 44 is based).

40 For general discussions, Barruol 1969, 295–302; B.Remy, 'Les limites de la cité des Allobroges', *Cahiers d'Histoire* XV, 3 (1970), 195–213; Pelletier 1982, 53–61.

41 Caesar, *BG* I, 11, 5: *Item Allobroges, qui trans Rhodanum vicos possessionesque habebant, fuga se ad Caesarem recipiunt.* The context seems to imply somewhere near the land of the *Ambarri* (subject to the *Aedui*) and it is interesting that the funerary inscription of M.Aucilius, a *decurio* of *Vienna* (*CIL* XIII, 2453), was found at St-Vulbas, on the right bank of the Rhône just 15km above its confluence with the Ain. For the inscription from Briord, claimed to represent a citizen of *Vienna*, *Gallia* XVI(1958), 374, see also *Gallia* XVII(1959), 237, suggesting that it refers merely to a *pagus Viennetonimagensis*, based on Vieu. Pelletier 1982, 59–60 suggests a bridgehead opposite Seyssel, based on *CIL* XII, 2346, though, as we shall see, *Condate* has now been identified 2 km south of the modern town.

42 Forclaz, *CIL* XII, 113, erected on the authority of Vespasian in AD 74 by Cn.Pinarius Cornelius Clemens, commander of the army of *Germania Superior* and specifically defining the boundary between the *Viennenses* and the *Ceutrones*. Jaillet, found 1963 and simply inscribed *fines*, P.Broise, 'Les confins entre Allobroges et Ceutrons, d'après une nouvelle borne', *Congrès des Sociétés Savantes de la Province de Savoie*, 1964, 25–7, *AE* 1966, 243.

43 *Rav Cos* IV, 27 (240–1). The name *Durotincum* is especially interesting since (as pointed out by the present author in *Britannia* XI(1980), 13–14) this is one of the only two examples on the continent that carry *Duro–* as their

Vienna (Vienne), with *Genava* (Geneva) and *Cularo/Gratianopolis* (Grenoble)

prefix (unlike the widely scattered names in the form *–durum*) outside the Belgic area. Was this station, then, first established by Belgic auxiliaries perhaps under the general named in the last note?

44 Barruol 1969, 118, 321–2. While mills still operate in this area, Riopéroux is no longer a 'small untidy village', but the scenery remains.

45 *CIL* xii, 2337, for the fuller text.

46 It Ant 344.3–346.9: in *Rav Cos* iv, 26 (230, 5–7) *Laviscone, Auguston, Birgusia*.

47 That the gorge suffered from falls of stone is demonstrated by the huge inscription on its north flank recording its clearance in 1670 under Carl Emmanuel ii, Duke of Savoy: the tunnel that provides the alternative course now followed by the N6 was built under Napoleon in 1810–13.

48 *CIL* xii, 242 (*vicani*), 243, 244 (*si quis in eo mi(n)xerit spurcit(ia) fecerit* etc).

49 *CIL* xii, 2386–409 (2386–8 to deities, 2389 *Victoriae Augustae*, 2391–2 monument for M.Aurelius); *ILGN* 346–7; six inscribed stones are set in the wall of a church.

50 *Gallia* xxii(1964), 517–19; *Hist Arch* no 78 (Nov 1983), 22, and for several bowls found near here stamped C.Atisius Sabinus, *CIL* xii, 5685, *passim*; C.Laroche, 'Un atelier de potiers à Aôste', *Archéologie en Rhône-Alpes* (1983–4), 38–9.

51 *CIL* xii, 2352, 2353; *Gallia* xl(1982), 399.

52 König no 105, and for the others between here and Geneva 99–104. The roads must have been built in the early Empire, so why have no earlier milestones come to light?

53 P.Wuilleumier, 'Etanna', *Gallia* i(1942), 139–51, with the addition of more inscriptions to *CIL* xii, 2438, including one that probably records a *sevir*.

54 It Ant 356.1–363.2 (this area 358.2–358.5); *CIL* xii, 5509–11, 5541–7, König nos 109–19.

55 *FOR* xi, no 138; *CIL* xii, 1782–4.

56 *FOR* xi, no 143; *CIL* xii, 1786–9 and 5546 (milestone of Claudius); le Cappa, *Gallia* xxxi(1973), 537.

57 *FOR* xi, no 153; stamped products of the kilns, *CIL* xii, 5679 (nos 19–21) and 5680 (no 5).

58 *CIL* xii, 2185–8; recent excavations, *Gallia* xl(1982), 402–03.

59 *CIL* xii, 2304, 2313 (dismissing 180★ in the list of *falsae*). Sermorens villa, *Gallia* xxxi(1973), 532, xxxiii(1975), 542, xl(1982), 405–06. The milestone shown on the map to the west of Morginnum (*CIL* xii, 5508, König no 98) now forms the shaft of a font in a curious little church (combined with the mairie) in the village of St-Paul-d'Izeaux and was first found in a monastery 2km to the ESE, and it is not known to which road it originally belonged.

60 It Ant 358.4–359.1: *Vienna* to *Lugdunum, mp xxiii aut per compendium mp xvi*. Munatius, on his way from Lyon to Grenoble, crossed the river at Vienne (Cicero, *Ad Fam*, x, 9).

61 *FOR* xv, no 123 (covering all the sites mentioned): on the mausoleum, Y.Burnand, 'Le monument gallo-romain dit "La Sarrasinière" à And-ance', *Gallia* xxxvii(1979), 119–40 (with plans and photographs): temple, A.Blanc, 'Le temple du Châtelet à Andance', *CR* vi(1959), 48–51: inscriptions, *CIL* xii, 1799–1802 (as shown by A.Blanc and H.Desaye in

Vienna (Vienne), with *Genava* (Geneva) and *Cularo/Gratianopolis* (Grenoble)

Gallia xxii(1964) 265, the milestone *CIL* xii, 5560 (König no 133) was not found here, but at Roussillon, further upstream on the other side of the Rhône).

62 *FOR* xi, no 147.

63 *Gallia* xxvi(1968), 588–9, xxxiii(1979), 539, xxxv(1977), 478–9, xxxviii(1980), 513.

64 Septème, *Gallia* xi(1953), 130: Oytier, *Gallia* xi(1953), 131, xvi(1958), 380, xxii(1964), 517: *cf* Nîmes, n 64.

65 *Gallia* xxiv(1966), 508–09, *AE* 1967, 289, Burnand 1975, 112–14.

66 L.Blondel, 'Le pont Romain de Genève', *Genava* NS ii(1954), 205–09: the bridge was improved in the 2nd cent.

67 J.-L.Maier and Y.Mottier, 'Les fortifications antiques de Genève', *Genava* NS xxiv(1976), 239–57.

68 For general accounts, L.Blondel, 'Le developpement urbain de Genève à travers les siècles', *Cahiers de Préhistoire et d'Archéologie*, iii(1946), 16–30; P.Broise, 'La cité de Genève dans l'antiquité', *Latomus* 1974; J.-L.Maier, *Genève Romain*, Geneva, 1976; V.von Gonzenbach in Princeton 1976, 347–8. Donor of the aqueduct, *CIL* xii, 2606–7. Recent excavations under Cathedral, *Genava* NS xxviii(1980), 6–15.

69 *Nautae*, *ILGN*, 361; *ratiarii*, *CIL* xii, 2597; *praepositus* xl *Galliarum*, *ILGN*, 363, de Laet 1949, 150, 411–13.

70 *Quattuorviri*, *CIL* xii, 2600, 2617, *ILGN*, 361; *duoviri*, *CIL* 2606–07 (honoured in Nyon, but of Geneva), 2608, 2613, 2614 (a Plinius); *aediles*, *CIL* 2614, *ILGN* 362; *seviri*, *CIL* 2612; *tresviri*, *CIL* 2606–07, 2608, 2618; *praefectus fabrum*, *CIL* 2608; legionaries, *CIL* 2587, 2601–08. For the warning regarding the true origin of inscriptions, Maier, *Genève Romaine*, p 6.

71 Dedications, *CIL* xii, 2585–97, 5878 (Neptune), *ILGN*, 358 (recording the erection of an *aedes* and *porticus* for Maia).

72 Munier 1963, 76–104: the surviving work of Salonius is *Exposita Mystica in Parabolas Salomonis et Ecclesiasten*.

73 Messery, *CIL* xii, 5532, G.Walser, *Itinera Romana i: die römischen strassen in der Schweiz* (Bern, 1967), no 23; Hermance, *CIL* xii, 5535, Walser, *ibid*, no 21.

74 Finds at Thonon include both buildings and pottery kilns: *Gallia* xxiv(1966), 529, xxix(1971), 444, xxxi(1973), 546–7, xxxiii(1975), 557–8, xxxv(1977), 493–4, xxxviii(1980), 534. For the nearby villa at Brenthonne, *Gallia* xxvi(1968), 602–03.

75 Annemasse milestones, *CIL* xii, 5516–7, König nos 100, 99 (the latter, which in 1983 had been moved from the centre of the town to a municipal workshop in the Rue du Parc, now looks illegible); buildings, *Gallia* xxii(1964), 540–1, xxxv(1977), 493; Nangy milestone, *CIL* xii, 5515, König no 101.

76 The temple (not now visible, but just above the Utine, a tributary of the Arve), *Rev Sav* 1920, 21, 1929, 88, 1933, 80, *Gallia* xxxi(1973), 546; inscriptions to Mars, *CIL* xii, 2349, 2350. Servoz aqueduct, *Rev Sav* 1864, 58. One inscription is preserved beside the D902 at les Plagnes (possibly that from the Col de Forclaz, but too darkly concealed to be easily read!).

77 Inscriptions, *CIL* xii, 2561–4 (2 dedications to Vintius, one recording a *praefectus pagi*, one possible milestone): hill-fort, with imports, *Gallia*

Vienna (Vienne), with *Genava* (Geneva) and *Cularo/Gratianopolis* (Grenoble)

xxii(1964), 542–3: Roman town, *Rev Sav* 1863, 15, *Gallia* xxii(1964), 541–43, xxiv(1966), 527–8, xxvi(1968), 601–02, xxxi(1973), 518–19, xxxiii(1975), 557, xxxviii(1980), 533–4, xl(1982), 428; excellent account, with plans and photographs, B.Helly, *Hist Arch* no 78(Nov 1982), 43–6.

78 *Gallia* xxvi(1968), 600, xxxiii(1975), 491, xxxvii(1980), 529–30, xxxviii(1980), 529–30, xl(1982), 425.

79 *It Ant* 347.11; *CIL* xii, 2532. The form Bouz appears in 1315, corrupted to Boeuf by the 16th cent (Broise 1984, 55)

80 Inscriptions, *CIL* xii, 2525–8 (religious: surprisingly no temple has so far been located), 2535 (a *trib Coh* i *Thracum*), 2539 (theatre), 2540–54; excavations, *Gallia* xii(1954), 462, xvi(1958), 392, xviii(1960), 365–6, xx(1962), 641, xxii(1964), 540–1, xxiv(1966), 526, xxvi(1968), 600–01, xxxi(1973), 545, xxxiii(1975), 557, xxxviii(1980), 531–2; Broise 1984, pt I, *passim*.

81 The road, *CIL* xii, 2555, Broise 1984, 224–34; Talloires (though probably originally in *Boutae*), *CIL* xii, 2522, Broise 1984, 285–6. For the whole area, Broise 1984, Pt ii, *passim*.

82 König, no 102, Broise 1984, 291; for the milestone from Letraz, west of the lake, also Constantinian, *CIL* xii, 5513, König no 104, Broise 1984, 272–5.

83 *It Ant* 347.9–11; *cf* Barruol 1969, 79, suggesting somewhere near Ugine (6 km N of Césarches).

84 Viuz, *Gallia* xxiv(1966), 527, xxxi(1973), 545–6, xxxv(1977), 493 (with a statuette of *Mater Dea*), xxxviii(1980), 532–3, xl(1982), 427. Villa at Tovey, *Gallia* xxxiii(1975), 557, xl(1982), 427.

85 Aqueduct inscriptions, *CIL* xii, 2492, 2493, others, mainly epitaphs, 2499–504.

86 Cicero, *Ad Fam* x, 23; Peutinger, *Culabone*, *Rav Cos* iv.27 (241, 5), *Curarore*; *CIL* xii, 2227, 2229, 2252.

87 Laronde-Bligny 1976, 25–6.

88 *CIL* xii, 2235–45, 2249, 2276; *cf* also *ILGN*, 340, recording Clemens, *praefectus pagi Ati*...., but this *pagus* has not been identified.

89 Legionaries, *CIL* xii, 2230, 2233, 2234; D.Decmanius Caper, who also set up dedications to Mars and Saturn and gave 50,000 *sestertii* for statues and other things, 2231, 2218, 2225; *librarii*, 2227, 2252 (illustrated in Lavonde-Brigny 1976, 28), Jullian iv, 305 n4, de Laet 1949, 149, 413–14. *Actor* may perhaps have been the name rather than the title of the man whose obituary appears in *CIL* 2250 (*D.M.Frontonis Actoris huius loci Materna coniugi carissimo* etc, with no erasures); he is not mentioned by de Laet (on *actores*, 414), but is in Laronde-Bligny 1976, 32.

90 *CIL* xii, 2228; Tetricus milestones, *ILGN*, 655, König no 249 (Béziers) and *Gallia* xvii(1959), 420–1, König no 264. (Montgaillard-Lauragais).

91 *CIL* xii, 2215–26, *ILGN*, 337–8.

92 St Domninus, Griffe 1964, i, 342; Cheretius, Munier 1963, 76–93.

93 *Gallia* xxii(1964), 519–26, Laronde-Bligny 1976, 32–4 (both with photographs), *Hist Arch* no 78(Nov 1983), 68.

94 *CIL* xii, 2229, a, b.

95 *Gallia* xxxiii(1975), 538–9 (house under parking site between Rue de la République and Rue Lafayette); Laronde-Bligny 1976, 538–539 (the port).

96 *Gallia* xxiv(1966), 509–11, xxix(1971), 427–8, xxxi(1973), 530–1, xxxiii(1975), 538–9, xxxviii(1980), 511 (funerary inscription found in bed of the Isère), xl(1982), 399–400; Laronde-Bligny 1976, 30–1 (with fine pl ii of the crypt of St-Laurent); Burnand 1975, 119; *Hist Arch* no 78 (Nov 1983), 68–70.

97 *Not Gall* xi, 3.

98 Villas, Veurey (to the NW), *Gallia* xxix(1971), 428, xxxi(1973), 531–2; Gières (to the E), xvi(1958), 377–9; probable villa, Claix (to the SW), xl(1982), 399; temple (St-Martin), xxxviii(1980), 513, xl(1982), 403.

99 For a good general discussion, P.Wuilleumier, *Le passé d'Aix-les-Bains*, Lyon, 1950.

100 *CIL* xii, 2473.

101 Wuilleumier, *op cit*, 4–12, with a full plan of the baths and useful photographs. The Roman baths are included towards the end of the tour, so one can conveniently loiter there to inspect them.

102 *CIL* xii, 2443–87, 5874–6, *ILGN*, 356; Wuilleumier, *op cit*, 2–4.

103 *It Ant* 346.2–6; the only difference is in the mileage between *Lemincum* and *Labisco*, *mp xiiii* in the Itinerary and *xiii* on the Peutinger Table.

104 *CIL* xii, 5873; inscribed pottery, 5686.913, 5695.16; aqueduct, *Gallia* xxix(1971), 443.

105 *Rev Sav* 1867, 39–41; *CIL* xii, 2332; P–W xiv, 1253.

106 *Gallia* xl(1982), 424–5, *Hist Arch* no 78(Nov 1983), 47, with illustrations of two dedications to Mercury and a bronze tortoise.

107 *CIL* xii, 2348; de Laet 1949, 149–50, 159.

108 *CIL* xii, 2346.

109 Arbin (Mérandie, first located 1865–9), *Gallia* xxxii(1974), 63–82 (especially mosaics), xxxviii(1980), 528–9 (aqueduct, baths, *nymphaeum* etc, with reference to a possible military post at Montmélian), xl(1982), 423; *CIL* xii, 2327, discussed in n 11 above): St-Jean-de-la-Porte, *Gallia* xxxv(1977), 492. *CIL* xii, 2337 (already mentioned and shown on pl 74): Gilly-sur-Isère (at Nant les Martins), *Gallia* xxxv(1977), 491, xxxviii(1980), 530 (dating it 2nd–3rd cent), xl(1982), 425; *CIL* xii, 2342, 2343.

110 *CIL* xii, 2331.

PART III

ALPES MARITIMAE

31
Alpes Maritimae

THE PROVINCE

The province of *Alpes Maritimae* owed its origins, though not its final form, to Augustus. In the Republican period the most significant boundary between Italy and Transalpine Gaul had been the river Var and it was, for example, to the Var that Caesar's legate Q.Fufius Calenus conducted the defeated troops of Afranius and Petreius before releasing them.[1] Further to the north, the Alps provided an obvious barrier, but whereas the Ligurian tribes along the coast had already been subdued, those in the interior had been dealt with only when necessity demanded, as when the *Ceutrones*, *Graioceli* and *Caturiges* attempted to prevent Caesar's passage through their territory in 58 BC.[2] In the *Res Gestae* Augustus boasts that he has pacified all the Alps from the Adriatic to the Tuscan Sea,[3] but both the dating of the conquest of this area and the stages by which it was reduced to a true province present problems.

So far as the date of conquest is concerned our best evidence is provided by Cassius Dio's statement that in the consulship of M.Crassus and Cn. Cornelius (14 BC) 'the maritime Alps, occupied even then freely by Ligurians called *Comati*, were reduced to slavery',[4] but this may merely mean that some of the area was still free up to this date and it is most unlikely that everything was achieved in one year. All the tribes involved were, of course, included in the inscription on the *Tropaeum Augusti* at la Turbie, which was erected in 7–6 BC,[5] but the older view, supported by Mommsen and others, that they were there recorded in chronological order of conquest, has now been effectively disposed of,[6] so that one cannot fix dates by reference to the known Alpine campaigns of A.Terentius Varro Murena and P.Silius Nerva, who were operating further to the north and east. Nor can anything of use here be deduced from the fact that six of the tribes listed on the Tropaeum (*Caturiges*, *Medulli*, *Adanates*, *Ecdinii*, *Veaminii*, *Vesubiani*) appear also on the Arch of Susa[7] (erected by Cottius in 9–8 BC), because the date at which Augustus came to terms with Cottius is itself

335

uncertain (especially since, in recording this event, Ammianus refers to him as simply Octavianus, which may put it earlier than is sometimes supposed).[8]

The earliest man known to have been in charge of the area is called not *praefectus Alpium Maritimarum*, but *praefectus civitatium in Alpibus maritimis*.[9] This was C. Baebius Atticus, a former *primus pilus*, who had also been *praefectus civitatium Moesiae et Trebelliae* at a time before *Moesia* became a full province under Tiberius, and a comparison with *Moesia* suggests that he was, as indeed Strabo implies,[10] a military controller rather than a full civilian governor. The headquarters of Baebius, and of other unnamed *praefecti* during this interim period, were no doubt at *Cemenelum* (listed by Pliny, along with *Nicaea* and the river Paillon, under Italy),[11] but which tribes they controlled remains a little uncertain. Some writers have maintained that up to AD 69 they included the *Bodiontici* (centred on Digne, *qv*) and perhaps the *Avantici* (centred on Gap, *qv*), but the evidence for this is not wholly convincing.[12] Another likely suggestion is that the *Vesubiani* and *Ecdinii*, who figure on the Arch of Susa, may have remained under Cottian control until Nero abolished the kingdom.[13] What does seem clear is that the area did not extend quite to the coast, since *Nicaea* remained subject to *Massilia* and both Strabo and Pliny continue to refer to the Var as the boundary between Italy and *Narbonensis*.[14]

Even the date of the conversion of the area into a normal procuratorial province is subject to some doubt. Tacitus[15] tells us that in AD 63 Nero *nationes Alpium Maritimarum in ius Latii transtulit*, but, while this surely provides a *terminus ante quem*, only a supposed connection with Nero's treatment of the Cottian Alps[16] can justify the idea that the province was a Neronian creation. As Pflaum pointed out,[17] the appearance on an inscription of Claudian date from *Carnuntum* of a soldier of *Legio xv Apollinaris*, who came from the little town of *Glanate* (Glandève), and was enrolled in the *Claudia* voting tribe (as were some of the inhabitants of *Cemenelum*) might suggest an earlier development, and to support this Claudius's recognition of the younger Cottius as king[18] might be used (and indeed it would accord better with Claudius's attitude to subject peoples than with Nero's). The overriding difficulty is that the first procuratorial governor known to us is Marius Maturus, who in AD 69 attempted unsuccessfully to resist the advance of Otho's troops.[19]

Records exist of eleven later governors, and although the precise date of only one is known (from the appearance of his name on closely-dated milestones), they may conveniently be listed here in their supposed chronological order:

Date	Name	Title (or description)	Origo
*c*126	L. Valerius Proculus[20]	*Procurator*	*Malaca*
between 117 & 161	C. Junius Flavianus[21]	*Procurator*	Rome?
between 205 & 213	Anon[22]	*Praeses*	?
213	Iulius Honoratus[23]	*Praeses et Procurator*	?
between 193 & 235	T. Porcius Cornelianus[24]	'Επίτροπος καὶ 'Ηγεμών	*Massilia*
*c*233	L. Titius Clodianus[25]	*Praeses et Procurator*	?
between 200 & 250	M. Aurelius Masculus[26]	*Praeses*	?
between 200 & 250	Tib. Claudius Demetrius[27]	*Procurator et Episcopus chorae inferioris*	*Nicomedia*
between 253 & 260 or, acc to Laguerre, 193–235	M. Aurelius Masculus[28]	(*Vir Egregius*)	?
3rd cent	P. Aelius Severinus[29]	*Praeses*	?
*c*300	Annius Rufinus[30]	(*Vir Egregius*) *Procurator et Praeses*	?

The title *praeses*, fairly described by Pflaum as a 'désignation flatteuse pour rehausser le prestige de certains gouverneurs',[31] first came into such use under Septimius Severus. It has no particular administrative significance, but besides here illustrating the progressive rise in status of *equites* it is sometimes useful in helping to establish the date of inscriptions. The implications of the Massilian connections of T. Porcius Cornelianus and of the role of Tib. Clausius Demetrius with regard to *Nicaea* have already been mentioned under *Massilia* (Marseille, *qv*).

From AD 70 onwards the province, while contributing numerous recruits to the army (especially the *cohortes Ligurum*), seems to have remained peaceful and figures very little in history. Whether the schoolmaster Numerianus passed this way or recruited soldiers here to launch the first Severan attack on Albinus in Gaul we do not know,[32] but the anonymous governor cited above was (as the inscription referred to in n22 shows) connected with Fulvius Plautianus, the father of Caracalla's wife and a very close friend of Severus;[33] hence it is not surprising that both Cimiez and Vence have yielded dedications to Severus and Caracalla.[34] Subsequent imperial dedications include those to Elagabalus,[35] Gordian III,[36] Trajan Decius,[37] Valerian[38] and Cornelia Salonina, the wife of Gallienus.[39] This last is of especial interest, since it raises the question of how *Alpes Maritimae* fared during the life of the Gallic Empire of Postumus and his successors, but the limited sources are silent on the matter.

An important change took place in the later period, when the two *civitates* of *Eburodunum* and *Rigomagus* were transferred to the province from *Alpes Cottiae*, and that of *Dinia* (Digne, *qv*) from *Narbonensis* and Embrun replaced Cimiez as its capital. This produced the situation reflected in the *Notitia Galliarum*,[40] and all the evidence suggests that it formed part of Diocletian's general reorganisation of provinces: besides the probable implications of the inscription from Chorges cited in note 30, the Verona List of AD 312–14 already shows *Alpes Maritimae* in the *Dioecesis Viennensis* (and *Alpes Cottiae* in the *Dioecesis Italiciana*)[41] and, most significantly, the Bordeaux Itinerary of AD 333 inserts the words *inde incipiunt Alpes Cottiae* between *mansio Ebreduno* (Embrun) and *mutatio Ramae* (Roche-de-Rame),[42] thus locating the new boundary between the two provinces.

THE INDIVIDUAL CIVITATES

Relatively little is known about most of the *civitates* in this province. To take first the later additions to it, *Dinia* (Digne) has already been dealt with above (p 247) and the other two should really be discussed in a history of *Alpes Cottiae* and can only be summarised here. In the land of the *Caturiges*, *Ebrodunum* (or *Eburodunum*, Embrun) derived its importance not only from its position on the main transalpine road but also from its impressively dominating site and while it evidently controlled *Caturigomagus* (Chorges) that low-lying small town too still retains its medieval fortifications. While neither has been adequately examined archaeologically, both have yielded some important inscriptions.[43] Just to the south, the identification of the middle valley of the Ubaye with the land of the *Savinates* on fig 51 and of Barcelonnette with *Rigomagus* on fig 52 is derived mainly from the convincing arguments of Barruol. While the name of the *Civitas Rigomagensium* appears only in the *Notitia Galliarum*, there is no doubt that a town stood here in Roman times, as indicated by several small finds and inscriptions,[44] and, as any visitor to the modern town will observe, it is much more readily habitable than expected, with its own airfield and several notable houses built by people who had made their fortunes in Mexico when Ferdinand-Joseph Maximilien was its emperor. The lower valley of the Ubaye is very narrow, but a road seems to have been built along it, at least if the so-called pont-romain at le Lauzet (pl 81), avoided by the modern road, was really Roman, and access to Italy was available over the Col de Larche, which is less than 2,000m high, leading to *Pedo* (Borgo San Dalmazzo), where there was an office of the *Quadragesima Galliarum*.[45]

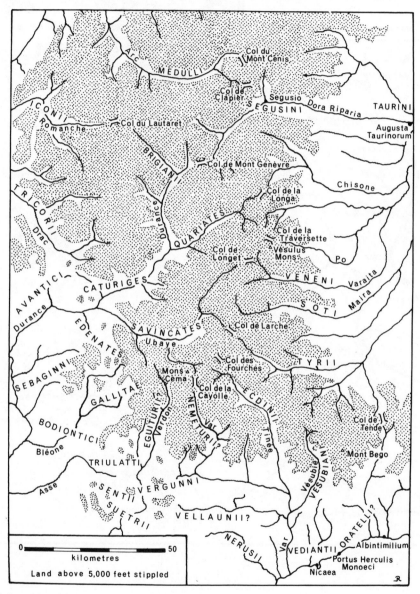

51 Iron Age tribes in the southern Alps (after Barruol)

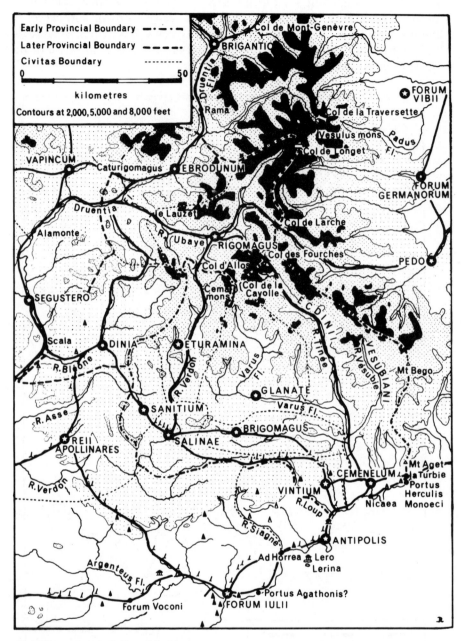

52 The territory of *Alpes Maritimae*

Cemenelum (Cimiez)

Much better known is the original capital, *Cemenelum*, but even here a great deal still needs to be clarified, both historically and archaeologically. The historical sources in which it is mentioned are confined to Pliny, the Antonine Itinerary, the Peutinger Table and the *Concilia Galliarum*,[46] but Pliny mentions it merely as *oppidum Vediantiorum civitatis*, indicating that in his time it had not yet acquired municipal status and the date at which it became a *municipium* is still unknown. That it did, however, is proved by several inscriptions recording *duoviri* (never *quattuorviri*), aediles, *seviri*, *decuriones* and a *flamen*.[47] The inscriptions had also long recorded the existence of *collegia* of *fabri*, *centonarii* and *dendrophori*, but in 1966 there was discovered the dedication of a statue of Mercury by some including *utricularii*—something that suggests that the river Paillon (now largely concealed underground in Nice) was to a certain extent navigable in ancient times.[48] Several dedications to other deities have also been found, not only to Jupiter, Hercules, Mars and Silvanus but also to Abinius, Orevaius, Centondis and the Matres Vediantiae.[49] On the Christian side, while the city revered the martyr Pons, quite when it had its own bishop seems uncertain and the first one recorded is Valerianus, who attended the Council of Reii in 439.[50]

As we have already noted, soldiers were enlisted in cohorts in this area and several were buried here.[51] *The Cohors I Ligurum* evidently served at *Cemenelum* in the early period and the small amphitheatre, at least in the first century, when it accommodated about 500 people, was clearly intended for their use, though its extension in the 3rd century was surely for other purposes.[52] Neither the military base, however, nor the true extent of the pre-Roman *oppidum* and the civil town has yet been established and this leads to the main archaeological problem: while some splendid Roman buildings and streets, along with a museum displaying fine statues, reliefs and inscriptions, are open to the public, they provide a quite inadequate picture of the city as a whole. Though some remains of houses are visible, the three main buildings are all public baths. The survival of so much of the *frigidarium* of the northern ones (pl 82) (once called 'The Temple of Apollo'), which are of early third-century date and overlie some first century structures, was largely due to its incorporation in a farm in the eighteenth century. Of the other two sets, both built in the later third century, the more interesting is the western one, which in the fifth century was converted into a church and had a baptistry built in (pl 83).[53] Work on all these since the war has clarified their date and purpose, but only rescue excavations in more recent years have shown that the town extended well to the south, at least as far as the Avenue Torre de Cimella, where both second-century buildings and burials have been found, while several other buildings and roads have also been identified.[54] Cimiez had two aqueducts, largely of underground type, one bringing water from les Fontaines de Mouraille, about 3km to the north-east, and the other from Tornéo, near Falicon, 4km to the north, and the course of the former, originally traced in the nineteenth century, was largely confirmed when the motorway was being constructed.[55] Just to the SE of Falicon, at l'Aire St-Michel, remains of a mausoleum were located in the early 1960s and while many odd finds have been recorded, that is the only significant discovery made in the area of this *civitas* in the post-war years.[56] Before leaving it, however, we must note that there appear to have been no significant settlements in the lands of the *Ecdinii* and the *Vesubiani*, so that they must have been controlled by *Cemenelum* when they had been detached from the Cottian kingdom.[57]

Vintium (Vence)

Ptolemy places *Vintium* in the territory of the *Nerusii* (*cf* fig 51) and it seems certain that this was indeed correct.[58] No Roman buildings are visible in the attractive little walled town of Vence, but a remarkable number of inscriptions have been found here and in the adjoining territory, some of them built into walls and still visible. They suggest that Vence, like Cimiez, became a full *municipium*—at least, not only *decuriones*, *flamines* and *sacerdotes*, but also *duoviri* are recorded[59]—but the most surprising ones concern the erection of statues and other monuments to a large number of emperors, including Tiberius, Elagabalus, Gordian III, the two Philips, Decius and Valerian.[60] On the religious side, there are two dedications to Mars Vintius and one to Cybele (as Idaea Mater) which also records a *taurobolium*.[61] Some funerary inscriptions are evidently Christian, but while the *Civitas Vintiensium* duly appears in the *Notitia Galliarum* its first recorded bishop is Severus, who attended the Council of Reii in 439.[62]

The question of how far the medieval town walls coincide with Roman ones still requires confirmation, as do the supposed forum and possible amphitheatre, but the existence of an aqueduct is proved by an inscription recording its construction by a M.Claudius Faventinus.[63] In any case, there is no doubt that this was a prosperous *civitas*, producing then, as now, its own wine and olives, and villas are recorded at St-Jeannet to the NE and Courmes to the west of the city.[64]

Salinae (Castellane)

As may be seen from the map (fig 52), a surprising number of milestones have been found along the road (roughly corresponding with the tortuous Route Napoléon, the modern N 85) leading from *Vintium* to *Dinia* by way of *Salinae* and *Sanitium*, but more surprising still is the fact that out of the total of 18 the earliest four, and possibly five, were erected by the proud governor Iulius Honoratus in AD 213[65]—something that suggests that it was then that this route was fully romanised. Nevertheless, the town had acquired its Latin name, which was clearly derived from the local supply of salt, by the time of Ptolemy, who duly places it in the territory of the *Suetrii*. Pliny, however, had mentioned only the tribe as one of those appearing on the *Tropaeum Augusti*, and the place itself is not referred to again until the *Notitia Galliarum*.[66] It certainly acquired its own diocese in the early Christian period, before it was incorporated in that of Senez, and the first recorded bishop is Claudius, who attended the Council of Reii in 439.[67]

It is possible that a small hill-fort once stood on the remarkable peak called le Roc, but in any case minor finds have shown that the Roman town was established just to the west of the modern one, in the area called le Plan. Its full constitution is not known, but among the dozen funerary inscriptions found around here one records two *decuriones*, another a possible *quaestor* and one a *magister fabrorum tignuariorum*, so the place probably enjoyed some prosperity.[68]

Sanitium (Senez)

While Ptolemy includes *Sanitium*, with *Cemenelum*, under the *Vediantii*, there is no doubt that the people really centred here were the *Sentii*, to whom he, with similar carelessness, attributes *Dinia*.[69] The place is not, however, mentioned in any other source until the *Notitia Galliarum*, and while its first recorded bishop is Marcellus, who attended the Council of Agde in 506,[70] the diocese must have existed earlier and at a slightly later date it was extended to take in both Castellane and Thorame. This remained a bishopric until the French Revolution and although the place, lying just off the N 85, is now no more than a hamlet, the attractive church (begun in 1130 and completed in 1242, with later modifications, including some sixteenth- and eighteenth-century tapestries) is still called a 'cathedral'. While this probably incorporates some Roman stone, the only recorded Roman finds consist of coins (including a hoard of 700 bronzes ending with Constantine) and a burial,[71] and elsewhere in the *civitas* Barrème, 6km to the NW, has also yielded coins, burials, and a fragmentary inscription.[72] More significant, however, is the tombstone of L. Velloudius Statutus, found in distant Nîmes, which describes him as a *decurio Sanit(iensum)* as well as a *decurio Col Aug N*—evidently a successful man who moved to richer surroundings.[73]

To judge from the known extent of the diocese, the territory of the *civitas* consisted mainly of the upper basin of the river Asse, the tributaries of which, the Asse de Moriez and the Asse de Blieux (on which Senez itself is situated), converge near Barrème, but the problems surrounding *Eturamina* (*qv*) leave open the question of whether it also took in part of the valley of the Verdon, further to the east and accessible by way of the Col des Robines (now crossed by the N 207). In any case, the economy of the area must have been rather poor, relying mainly on pastoral activity, but the road which we have already mentioned under *Salinae*, which took in Barrème as well as Senez, may have helped trade.

Eturamina (Thorame)

This is the least well-documented component of the province and in fact the belief in its very existence as a separate unit depends solely on ecclesiastical documents. It does not appear in the *Notitia Galliarum*, but the records of the Council of Vaison, held in AD 442, include among the signatories *ex provincia Alpium Maritimarum civit. Eturamine Severianus episcopus*.[74] Presumably this is the same Severianus who had participated in the Council of Reii[75] three years before and the idea that his base was indeed a *civitas* is strengthened by the fact that in the Vaison list the bishops of Uzès and Toulon are described as coming merely from an *oppidum* and a *locus* respectively. Its name identifies it beyond doubt with Thorame, but the main medieval settlement (and so presumably the earlier Roman one) was neither at the present Thorame-Haute nor Thorame-Basse but rather at the little place just west of the latter called Piégut.[76] This stands on a bluff overlooking the river Issole and a glance at the relief on the map and the road D2 joining the two Thorames shows that the northern part of its territory must have comprised the upper valleys of the Issole and the Verdon. How far it stretched to the south remains a matter for speculation, for by the time when the boundaries of dioceses became identifiable it had, like Castellane, been taken over by Senez. In what tribe it had its origin is also uncertain, some suggesting the *Eguiturii*, others the *Vergunni*.[77]

The only recorded finds from the area which may be relevant consist of burials found at Thorame-Haute in 1934 and at Nôtre-Dame-de-Valvert, just south of Allos, further up the valley of the Verdon, in 1933, but the date of these is doubtful.[78]

Brigomagus (Briançonnet)

The identity of *Brigomagus* is confirmed not only by the modern name of the little village of Briançonnet but also by five of the inscriptions found here, four of them dedications to the emperors Severus, Licinius, Valerian and Claudius Gothicus, of which at least two were specifically set up by the *Ordo Brig . . .*, while a funerary monument commemorates a man called Maternus OB HONORES/IIVIRAT ET FLAMONI/BENE GESTOS PATRON COOPTAR BRIG— something that suggests (if he did not come from elsewhere) that this became a full *municipium*.[79] It is not, however, listed in the *Notitia Galliarum* (where, in view of its initial letter, it cannot be confused with *Rigomagus*) and it seems not to have become a bishopric. Even the tribe whose territory it controlled is a little uncertain, but the *Vellaunii*, whose name was included on the *Tropaeum Augusti*, seems the most probable.[80]

The actual site of the city was evidently on the nearby Plaine d'Ouméou, where building foundations have been noted and a bronze statuette and some coins found, but only a few funerary inscriptions and very minor finds are recorded elsewhere in this *civitas* and especially since the two alleged uninscribed milestones (one from Briançonnet, one from Auglun) are highly questionable, it is not possible to show roads around here on the map.[81]

Glanate (Glandève)

While the *Civitas Glanatina* is duly listed in the *Notitia Galliarum* and its bishop Claudius attended the Council of Orléans in 541,[82] virtually nothing is known about the Roman town except its position on the bank of the Var about one km east of Entrevaux. The alluvium of the river has covered its remains and though some foundations and burials were recorded in the early nineteenth century, and some further burials in the 1940s, only slight relics of the post-Roman romanesque cathedral can be seen.[83] Moreover it has yielded no inscriptions and while it had long been known that a centurion of *Legio IV* had set up his own tombstone at Puget-Théniers, about 5km to the east, the really significant discovery was made in 1956 not here but at faraway *Carnuntum*, in *Pannonia*, recording a soldier from *Glanate* who was enrolled in the voting-tribe *Claudia*—suggesting that even this remote city was a *municipium* as early as the first century.[84]

As in so many Alpine *civitates*, little is known about other sites, nor the true course of Roman roads, though one must surely have run up the valley of the Var, and the only important monument is the mausoleum at Fugeret-Argenton, some 16 km WNW of Glandève, known for some time and re-examined in the 1960s.[85]

REFERENCES AND NOTES

1 Caesar, *BC* I, 87.
2 Caesar, *BG* I, 10. So Appian, *Illyrica* 15(iv), expresses surprise that the Romans, having crossed the Alps so often, had never troubled to subject the tribes; even Caesar, he says, had delayed the matter (though Caesar did take steps regarding one transalpine route, stationing Galba at *Octodurus*, *BG* III, 1).
3 *Res Gestae* 26, 3.
4 Dio LIV, 24. The Greek adjective κομήτης presumably translates the Latin *comatus*, but Pliny (*HN* III, 47) specifically states that the *populi inalpini* are referred to as *multis niminibus sed maxime capillatis* and *capillatus* might be what Dio means (*cf* Mommsen, *CIL* v, p 903). But there was also a specific tribe

called the *Capillati*, apparently Cottian (*CIL* XII, 80).

5 *CIL* V, 7817—fortunately, since it is fragmentary, quoted by Pliny, *HN* III, 136–7. For the probable location of the tribes in our area see fig 51.

6 *Eg* Barruol, 1969, 39–40, C.M.Wells, *The German Policy of Augustus*, 1972, 59–60.

7 *CIL* V, 7231.

8 Ammianus XV, 10, 2. The source here used by Ammianus is not known, but elsewhere he only uses the simple Octavianus, as opposed to Octavianus Augustus, when dealing with events prior to 27 BC (XIV, 8, 11, since *Caesarea*, though only reconstructed later, was given to Herod in 30 BC; and XVII, 4, 5, Cornelius Gallus in Egypt, 29 BC); a possible date here might be 32 BC.

9 *CIL* V, 1835. On the career of Baetius Atticus see Pflaum, 1960, 27–8.

10 Strabo IV, 6, 4: ἐπὶ δὲ τοὺς ὀρεινοὺς (*sc* τῶν Λιγύων) πέμπεταί τις ὕπαρχος τῶν ἱππικῶν ἀνδρῶν, καθάπερ καὶ ἐπ᾽ἄλλους τῶν τελέως βαρβάρων.

11 Pliny, *HN* III, 47.

12 *Eg* Barruol, 1969, 287, 385. The evidence consists solely of Pliny *HN* III, 37 where, following a list of places in *Narbonensis* which had already been granted *ius Latii*, he adds; *adiecit formulae Galba imperator ex Inalpinis Avanticos atque Bodionticos quorum oppidum Dinia*; and the idea of a transfer from *Alpes Maritimae* (or *Alpes Cottiae*) depends on the interpretation of *ex Inalpinis*. But this need not mean that they had been part of an Alpine province (just as in *HN* III, 47 Pliny deals with *populi Inalpini* under Italy) and both tribes could fairly be called 'Alpine' in a general sense. In any case, Tacitus, *Ann* XV, 32, tells us that Nero had granted *ius Latii* to *Nationes Alpium Maritimarum*, so that if a transfer were involved it would more probably be from *Alpes Cottiae*.

13 This is the more likely since, at least according to Dio, LX, 24, 4, when Claudius recognised Cottius the younger as king he actually increased his inherited domain. For the location of the *Vesubiani* in the valley of the Vesubie (with adequate communication to the north), see N.Lamboglia, *REL* IX, 1943, 135–45, and Barruol, 1969, 360 (where, in n2, Chilver, *Cisalpine Gaul*, 1941, 26, might be added to the list of those who fell for the illusion of the valley of the Ubaye).

14 Strabo IV, 1, 3; Pliny, *HN* III, 35 and 47.

15 Tacitus, *Ann* XV, 32.

16 Suetonius, *Nero*, 18 (with no date supplied).

17 *AE* 1958, 225; H.-G.Pflaum, *Carnuntum Jahrbüch*, 1961–2, 88 (= *Scripta Varia* II, i), stressing the fact, overlooked by Lamboglia, that the inscription had been shown by Betz to be of Claudian date.

18 Cassius Dio LX, 24, 4.

19 Tacitus, *Hist* II, 12, also mentioned III, 42–3. On his family and career, Pflaum 1960, 95–8.

20 *CIL* II, 1970 Laguerre 1975, p 35, from Malaga; Pflaum, 1960, 274–9.

21 *CIL* VI, 1620, from Rome, and *CIL* XIII, 1812, from Lyon; Laguerre 1975, pp 35–6; Pflaum, 1960, 320–2.

22 *CIL* III, 6075, from Ephesus; Laguerre 1975, p 22; Pflaum 1960, 647–9.

23 *CIL* XII, 7, from Vence, and *CIL* XII, 5430–2 and 5438; Pflaum, 1960, 777–8; the milestones are all securely dated to the fourth consulship of

Caracalla; dedication to *numinibus Augusti*, *Gallia* xxii(1964), 607, Laguerre 1975, pp 30–1.

24 *CIG* iii, 6771 (*ILS*, 8852), from Marseille, where he had become a priest of Leucothea (and his father a *prophetes*); Pflaum 1960, 793–6; Laguerre p 36.

25 *CIL* viii, 8328 and, as restored, *AE* 1911, 100 from Cuicul; Pflaum, 1960, 859–64 (with dating based on E.Birley, *JRS* xl 1950, 59–68).

26 *CIL* v, 7881, (Laguerre, 1975, p 37), from Cimiez; Pflaum, 1960, 855–6.

27 *CIL* v, 7870 (Laguerre, 1975, no 3), from Cimiez; Pflaum, 1960, 788–90.

28 *CIL* v, 7879 (Laguerre, 1975, no 14), from Cimiez, in a dedication to Cornelia Salonina by the *ordo Cemenelensium*.

29 *CIL* v, 7880 (Laguerre, 1975, p 37), from Cimiez.

30 *CIL* xii, 78 (+p 804), from Chorges. The name of the emperor being honoured does not survive, but he is referred to as *restitutor orbis* and a Diocletian date is generally agreed (*eg PLRE* i, 1971, 775); contrast *ILGN* 9, from Barcelonnette, a dedication to Claudius Gothicus, set up by *Proc Ord Brig*, surely the *procurator* of *Brigantio* (and not of *Brigomagus*, as suggested by Espérandieu).

31 H.-G.Pflaum, *Les procurateurs équestres sous le Haut-Empire romain*, 1950, 116.

32 Cassius Dio lxxvi, 5.

33 A homosexual friend according to Herodian iii, 10, 6, but on this and on Plautianus in general see A.R.Birley, *Septimius Severus*, 1971, *passim*, with many references.

34 *CIL* v, 7880 (Cimiez), xii, 5426 (Vence).

35 *CIL* xii, 8 (Vence).

36 *CIL* xii, 9 (Vence).

37 *CIL* xii, 11 (Vence).

38 *CIL* xii, 12 (Vence).

39 *CIL* v, 7879 (Cimiez).

40 *Notitia Galliarum* xvii.

41 *Nomina Provinciarum Omnium*, in A.Riese (ed), *Geographi Latini Minores*, 1878.

42 *It Burd* 556.9.

43 For a general discussion of the *Caturiges* and their settlements, Barruol 1969, 341–4. Inscriptions, Embrun, *CIL* xii, 77, 81, 84, 85, 87, 89, *ILGN* 8; Chorges, *CIL* xii, 75, 78, 5707. For the place-names, Strabo iv, 1, 3, Vicarello Goblets, *It Ant* 342.1–2, 357.5–6, *It Burd* 555.7–8.

44 Inscriptions from this area, Barcelonnette, *CIL* xii, 82, 90, *ILGN*, 9; Faucon (just ne of the town), *CIL* xii, 86, 88, 92; Condamine-Chatelard (10km ne), *CIL* xii, 76, (a dedication to Victoria). Finds, *FOR* vi, nos 94–9. General discussion, Barruol 1969, 347–57.

45 De Laet 1949, 146–7; *CIL* v, 7852.

46 Pliny, *HN* iii, 47, Ptolemy, *Geog* iii, 39, *It Ant* 296.5, Peutinger Table (as *Gemenello*), *Not Gall* xvii, 7.

47 *Duoviri*, *CIL* v, 7905, 7907 (also a *duovir* of Fréjus), 7912, 7913, 7915; aedile, 7919; *seviri*, 7905, 7907, 7909, 7916, 7920; *flamen*, 7913; *decurio* (also an *eques*), 7903; for all inscriptions, Laguerre 1979, *passim*.

48 *CIL* v, 7881, 7904, 7905, 7906, 7920, 7921; *utricularii*, *AE* 1965, no 194, Laguerre 1975, no 66; general discussion, Benoit 1977, 45–50.

49 Jupiter, *CIL* v, 7870, Hercules, 7869, Mercury, 7874, Mars Cemenelus.

7871, Silvanus, 7875, Abinius, 7865, Orevaius, 7866, Centondis, 7867, Matres, 7872, 7873; Benoit 1977, 37–45.

50 Griffe 1964, 162; Munier 1963, 61–75; Benoit 1977, 125–62.

51 Men of *Cohors I Ligurum*, *CIL* v, 7885, 7889–91, 7898–9; *II Ligurum*, 7900; *Cohors Gaetulorum*, *AE* 1964, 243–5. Several other inscriptions—*CIL* v, 7884, 7887, 7888, 7892, *AE* 1964, no 249 (Laguerre 1975, no 48)—also record *nautici*, but they must surely have operated from Fréjus and perhaps occasionally Nice.

52 *FOR* I, p 10; P.-M.Duval in *Gallia* IV(1946), 77–136; Grenier 1958, 599–606; Benoit 1977, 27–30.

53 *FOR* I, no 32, and no 36, for finds in the St Pons area; *Gallia* IV(1946), 77–136, VIII(1950), 130, XIV(1956), 234–8, XVI(1958), 440–7, XVIII(1960), 322–4, XX(1962), 709–13, XXII(1964), 607–08, XXVII(1969), 456–8, XXIX(1971), 462–3; Grenier 1960, 463–4; Benoit 1977, 55–94.

54 *Gallia* XXII(1964), 608, XXIX(1971), 463–4, XXXIII(1975), 508, XXXV(1977), 508, XXXVII(1979), 568; for a general account, with illustrations, D.Mouchot, 'Les fouilles de Cimiez', *Hist Arch* no 57 (Oct 1981), 55–60.

55 *FOR* I, pp 10–12 (with 19th-cent plan); Grenier 1960, 55–60; *Gallia* XXIX(1971), 463, XXXI(1973), 567; *Hist Arch* no 57 (Oct 1981), 61 (with photographs).

56 *Gallia* XXII(1964), 607, Burnand 1975, 127.

57 For a discussion of these tribes, Barruol 1969, 359–60.

58 Ptolemy, *Geog* III, 1, 37; for their territory, Barruol 1969, 368–9 and for the supposed boundary stones with Nice, *CIL* XII, 7.

59 *Duoviri*, *CIL* XII, 17, 18, *ILGN*, 1; other titles, *CIL* XII, 17–20, *ILGN*, 1, 3.

60 *CIL* XII, 5, 7–12, + 13 (unnamed).

61 Mars, *CIL* XII, 2, 3 (the latter set up by M.Rufinius Felix, who was a *sevir* of *Salinae* and an inhabitant of *Cemenelum*); Idaea Mater, *CIL* XII, 1.

62 *Not Gall* XVII, 8; Munier 1963, 61–75.

63 On all earlier finds, *FOR* I, no 114; aqueduct, *CIL* XII, 6 (improved on p 803).

64 *FOR* I, no 124 (St-Jeannet), no 148 (Courmes).

65 *CIL* XII, 5427–39 (König nos 2–18); elaborate Iulius Honoratus ones, citing the 17th *trib pot* of Caracalla, 5430–2, 5438, ?5439 (nos 6–8, 13a, 17).

66 Ptolemy, *Geog* III, 1.38; Pliny, *HN* III, 137 (citing the *Tropaeum*); *Not Gall* XVII, 5. On the tribe, Barruol 1969, 376–9, citing N.Lamboglia in *REL* VIII(1942), 132–6.

67 Munier 1963, 61–75.

68 Odd finds, *FOR* VI, no 35; inscriptions, *CIL* XII, 65 (epitaph of a *miles Cohortis* XIIII *Urbanae*), 66 (two *decuriones* of *civitas Sal*), 67 (?*quaestor* of *civitas Sal*), 68 (*magister fabrorum tignuariorum*), 69–74, *ILGN*, 10, 11, 16.

69 Ptolemy, *Geog* II, 10, 8 (*Sentii*), III, 1, 39 (*Sanitium*); for a discussion, Barruol 1969, 382–5, suggesting that the *Triulatti* were also included in this *civitas* and citing N.Lamboglia in *REL* X(1944), 21–4.

70 *Not Gall* XVII, 5; Munier 1963, 162–88 (*Marcellus de Santio*).

71 *FOR* VI, no 26.

72 *FOR* VI, no 24; *CIL* XII, 71.

73 *CIL* XII, 3288.

74 Munier 1963, 102.

75 Munier 1963, 71.

76 Barruol 1969, 380–1. Piégut has the chapel of Nôtre-Dame-de-Thorame and the remains of a medieval tower.

77 For the *Eguiturii*, N.Lamboglia, *REL* x(1964), 16–17; for the *Vergunni*, Barruol 1969, 379–81.

78 *FOR* vi, nos 20, 84. One of the tiles used in the burials at Thorame-Haute, now in the museum of St-Germain-en-Laye, carries the inscription *supposuit furno iii Idus Iulias/die solis/abuit tegulas/inbrices*, but this could surely be post-Roman.

79 Severus, *CIL* xii, 56 (+p 804), Licinus, 57, Aurelian, 58, Claudius, *ILGN*, 9; . . . RIGOMA . . . on *CIL* xii, 60.

80 Barruol 1969, 369–73.

81 Briançonnet, *FOR* i, nos 229–30; Auglun, no 225; other inscriptions from this *civitas*, *CIL* xii, 19, 63, 5704.

82 *Not Gall* xvii, 6; *Concilia Galliarum 511–695* (Vol cxlviiiA of *Corpus Christianorum: Series Latina*), 131–46.

83 *FOR* vi, no 32; *Gallia* i(1942), 282–3; Barruol 1969, 373–6. Glandève is the only Roman city whose name does not appear on Michelin 1:200,000 maps.

84 Puget-Théniers, *CIL* v, 7983; for the *Carnuntum* inscription *v* n17 above.

85 *FOR* vi, no 21, *Gallia* xxii(1964), 551–3, Burnand 1975, 117–18. One other inscription from this *civitas*, dedication to Mars at la Penne, *CIL* xii, 2.

Select Bibliography

The form of this bibliography is designed primarily to identify the works indicated by abbreviations in the References and Notes and in the Appendix to Chapter 1. For further sources the reader should consult the relevant volumes of *FOR*, the extensive bibliography in pp 779–814 of Chevallier 1975 and, for Greek and Latin authors, Duval 1971.

Allen 1980 D.F.Allen (ed D.Nash): *The Coins of the Ancient Celts*

Amy 1962 R.Amy, P.-M.Duval, J.Formigé, J.J.Hatt, A.Piganiol, C.Picard & G.-C.Picard: *L'Arc d'Orange* (Suppl xxvii to *Gallia*)

Amy 1979 R.Amy & P.Gros: *La Maison Carrée de Nîmes* (Suppl xxvii to *Gallia*)

ANRW H.Temporini & W.Haase (edd): *Aufstieg und Niedergang der Römischen Welt* (still in progress)

Arch Archéologia (a periodical now supplemented by *Hist Arch*, qv)

A Rh -A 1983–4 *Archéologie en Rhône-Alpes: protohistoire et monde gallo-romain: dix ans de recherches* (issued by Musée de la civilisation gallo-romaine de Lyon)

Baccrabère 1977 G.Baccrabère: *Etude de Toulouse romaine* (Chronique no 3, Institut Catholique de Toulouse)

Badian 1958 E.Badian: *Foreign Clientelae (264–70 BC)*

Badian 1964 E.Badian: *Studies in Greek and Roman History*

Badian 1966 E.Badian, 'Notes on Provincia Gallia in the Late Republic', in Chevallier 1966, pp 901–18

Badian 1967 E.Badian: *Roman Imperialism in the Late Republic*

Badian 1972 E.Badian: *Publicans and Sinners*

Barbet 1971 A.Barbet: *Recueil des peintures murales de la Gaule i: Province de la Narbonnaise i, Glanum* (Suppl xxvii to *Gallia*)

Barruol 1963 G.Barruol, 'Le pont romain de Ganagobie', *Gallia* xxi, 314–24

Barruol 1968 G.Barruol, 'Essai sur la topographie d'Apta Iulia', *RAN* i, 101–58, and (with A.Dumoulin) 'Le théâtre romain d'Apt', *ibid*, 159–200

Barruol 1969 G.Barruol: *Les peuples préromains du sud-est de la Gaule* (Suppl i to *RAN*)

Barruol 1976[1] G.Barruol (ed), *Ruscino i* (Suppl vii to *RAN*)

Barruol 1976[2] G.Barruol, 'La résistance des substrats préromains en Gaule méridionale', in D.M.Pippidi (ed), *Assimilation et résistance à la culture gréco-romaine dans le monde ancien*, pp 389–405

Barruol/Martel 1962 G.Barruol & P.Martel, 'La voie romaine de Cavaillon à Sisteron sous le Haut-Empire', *REL* XXVIII, 125–202

Barruol/Py G.Barruol & M.Py, 'Recherches récentes sur la ville antique d'Espeyran à St-Gilles-du-Gard' (as *Heraclea*), *RAN* XI, 19–104

Benoit 1954 F.Benoit, *Sarcophages paléochrétiens d'Arles et de Marseille* (Suppl v to *Gallia*)

Benoit 1958–62 F.Benoit, 'Nouvelles épaves de Provence', *Gallia* XVI, 5–39, XVIII, 41–56, XX, 148–76

Benoit 1961 F.Benoit, *Fouilles sous-marines: l'épave du Grand Congloué à Marseille* (Suppl XIV to *Gallia*)

Benoit 1965 F.Benoit, *Recherches sur l'hellénisation du Midi de la Gaule* (reprinted 1980)

Benoit 1966 F.Benoit, 'La romanisation de la Narbonnaise à la fin de l'époque républicaine', *REL* XXXIII, 287–303

Benoit 1977 F.Benoit: *Fouilles de Cemenelum 1: Cimiez, la ville antique*

Blanc 1953 A.Blanc *Valence romaine*

Blanc/Desaye 1964–75 A.Blanc & H.Desaye, 'Inscriptions nouvelles de la Drôme, de l'Ardèche et des Hautes-Alpes', *Gallia* XXII, 265–80, XXVII, 206–24, XXXIII, 229–56

Bligny *v* Lavonde/Bligny

Boisse 1968 C.Boisse, *Le Tricastin des origines à la chute de l'Empire Romain*

Broise 1969 P.Broise, 'Eléments d'un ordre toscan provincial en Haute-Savoie', *Gallia* XXVII, 15–22

Broise 1973 P.Broise, 'La civilisation romaine en Savoie', Ch III in P.Guichonnet (ed), *Histoire de la Savoie*

Broise 1984 P.Broise, *Le vicus gallo-romain de Boutae et ses terroirs*, nos 24 and 25 of *Annesci* (Société des Amis du Vieil Annecy)

Broughton T.R.S.Broughton, *The Magistrates of the Roman Republic* I (509–100 BC), 1951, and II (99–31 BC), 1952

Burnand 1971 Y.Burnand, 'Un aspect de la géographie des transports dans la Narbonnaise rhodanienne: les nautes d'Ardèche et de l'Ouvèze', *RAN* IV, 149–58

Burnand 1975 Y.Burnand, *Domitii Aquenses: une famille de chevaliers romains d'Aix-en-Provence: mausolée et domaine* (Suppl v to *RAN*)

Bury 1923 J.B.Bury, *History of the Later Roman Empire*

Chapotat 1970 G.Chapotat, *Vienne gauloise*

Chevallier 1966 R.Chevallier (ed), *Mélanges d'archéologie et d'histoire offerts à Andrè Piganiol*

Chevallier 1975 R.Chevallier, 'Gallia Narbonensis: bilan de 25 ans de recherches historiques et archéologiques', *ANRW* II, 3, 686–828

Chevallier 1976 R.Chevallier, *Roman Roads* (translation of *Les voies romaines*, 1972)

Chevallier 1982 R.Chevallier, *Provincia*

CIL *Corpus Inscriptionum Latinarum*, Vol v (ed Mommsen, 1872) including part of *Alpes Maritimae*, Vol XII (ed Hirschfeld, 1888) *Gallia Narbonensis* and part of *Alpes Maritimae*

Clavel 1970 M.Clavel, *Béziers et son territoire dans l'antiquité* (Vol 112 of *Annales littéraires de l'Université de Besançon*)

Clavel-Lévêque 1977 M.Clavel-Lévêque, *Marseille grecque*

Clavel-Lévêque 1984 M.Clavel-Lévêque (ed), *Cadastres et espace rural: approches et réalités antiques* (Table Ronde de Besançon, Mai 1980)

Select Bibliography

Clemente 1974 G.Clemente, *I Romani nella Gallia meridionale (II–I sec a C)*

Clerc 1916 M.Clerc, *Aquae Sextiae*

Clerc 1927–9 M.Clerc, *Massalia*

Clergues 1966 J.Clergues, *La recherche archéologique à Antibes*

Colbert de Beaulieu 1973 J.-B.Colbert de Beaulieu, *Traité de numismatique celtique*

Constans 1921 L.-A.Constans, *Arles antique*

CR Cahiers Rhodaniens (1953 onwards)

CRAI Comptes rendus de l'Académie des Inscriptions et Belles-lettres

Degrassi A.Degrassi, *Fasti Capitolini*

de Laet 1949 S.J.de Laet, *Portorium: étude sur l'organisation douanière chez les Romains surtout à l'époque du Haut-Empire*

Desaye *v* Blanc/Desaye

Ducat/Farnoux 1976 J.Ducat & B.C.Farnoux, 'Origines grecques et romaines', Ch II in M.Bordes (ed), *Histoire de Nice et du pays niçois*

Duval 1957 P.-M.Duval, *Les dieux de la Gaule*

Duval 1962 *v* Amy 1962

Duval 1968 P.-M.Duval, 'Le milliaire de Domitien et l'organisation de la Narbonnaise', *RAN* I, 3–6

Duval 1971 P.-M.Duval, *La Gaule jusqu'au milieu du Ve siecle* (Vol I of *Sources de l'histoire de France*)

Ebel 1976 C.Ebel, *Transalpine Gaul: the Emergence of a Roman Province*

EE Ephemeris Epigraphica

Ellis Evans D.Ellis Evans, *Gaulish Personal Names*, 1967

Espérandieu 1907–28 E.Espérandieu, *Recueil général des bas-reliefs de la Gaule Romaine*

Espérandieu 1929 *v ILGN*

Espérandieu 1936 E.Espérandieu, *Répertoire archéologique du Département des Pyrenées-Orientales: période gallo-romaine*

Euzennat 1973 M.Euzennat, 'L'époque romaine', Ch II in E.Baratier (ed), *Histoire de Marseille*

Eydoux 1961 H.-P.Eydoux, *Résurrection de la Gaule*

Eydoux 1963 H.-P.Eydoux, *Hommes et dieux de la Gaule*

Eydoux 1964 H.-P.Eydoux, *Réalités et énigmes de l'archéologie*, 2nd edn

Février 1964 P.-A.Février, *Le développement urbain en Provence de l'époque remaine à la fin du XIVe siècle* (partly summarised and revised in *JRS* LXIII(1973), 1–28)

Février 1977 P.-A.Février: *Fréjus (Forum Iulii) et la basse vallée de l'Argens*, 2nd edn

FOR Forma Orbis Romani: Carte archéologique de la Gaule romaine. The relevant volumes are: I *Alpes-Maritimes*, 1931; II *Var*, 1932; V *Bouches-du-Rhône*, 1936; VI *Basses-Alpes* (now Alpes de Haute-Provence), 1937; VII *Vaucluse*, 1939; VIII *Gard*, 1941; IX *Aveyron* (including a very small area of our province), 1944; X *Hérault*, 1946; XI *Drôme* (J.Sautel, edd A.Grenier & P.-M.Duval), 1957; XII *Aude* (A.Grenier, C.Boyer & P.Héléna), 1959; *Ardèche* (A.Blanc, ed P.-M.Duval), 1975. The maps of Vols I–X spread over various départements, but from Vol XI onwards each has its own map

Formigé 1949 J.Formigé, *Le Trophée des Alpes (La Turbie)* (Suppl II to *Gallia*)

Gagnière 1970 S.Gagnière & J.Granier, *Avignon, de la préhistoire à la papauté*

Gallet de Santerre 1980 H.Gallet de Santerre, *Ensérune: les silos de la terrasse est* (Suppl XXIX to *Gallia*)

Gallia Gallia, the most important journal, 1942 onwards

Gascou 1983 J.Gascou, 'Les dendrophores d'Aix-en-Provence d'après une inscription trouvée récemment', *RAN* XVI, 161–9

Gayraud 1981 M.Gayraud, *Narbonne antique, des origines à la fin du IIIme siècle* (Suppl VIII to *RAN*)

Genava Genava, a journal covering Geneva and the surrounding area

Goudineau 1976 C.Goudineau, 'Le statut de Nîmes et des Volques Arécomiques', *RAN* IX, 105–14

Goudineau 1978 C.Goudineau, 'La Gaule transalpine', Ch V (pp 679–99) in C.Nicolet (ed): *Rome et la conquête du monde mediterranéen*, Vol II

Goudineau 1979 C.Goudineau, *Les fouilles de la Maison du Dauphin à Vaison-la-Romaine* (Suppl XXXVII to *Gallia*)

Goudineau/Kisch 1984 C.Goudineau & Y.de Kisch, *Vaison-la-Romaine*

Grenier 1931 A.Grenier, *Manuel d'archéologie gallo-romaine I* (Généralités, travaux militaires)

Grenier 1934 A.Grenier, *Manuel d'archeologie . . . II* (Les routes, navigation, occupation du sol)

Grenier 1937 A.Grenier, 'La Gaule Romaine', in Tenney Frank (ed) *An Economic Survey of Ancient Rome*, Vol III, 379–644

Grenier 1958 A.Grenier, *Manuel d'archéologie . . . III* (Capitole – forum – temple – basilique – théâtres – amphithéâtres – cirques)

Grenier 1960 A.Grenier, *Manuel d'archéologie . . . IV* (Aqueducs – thermes – villes d'eau – sanctuaires d'eau)

Griffe 1964–6 E.Griffe, *La Gaule chrétienne à l'époque romaine*, Vols I & II

Gros 1979 P.Gros, 'Pour une chronologie des Arcs de Triomphe de Gaule Narbonnaise', *Gallia* XXXVII, 55–83

Gros 1981 P.Gros, 'Les temples géminés de Glanum: étude préliminaire', *RAN* XIV, 125–58

Gros 1984 P.Gros, 'L'Augusteum de Nîmes', *RAN* XVII, 123–34 (*v* also Amy 1979)

Guilaine 1976 J.Guilaine (ed), *La préhistoire française*

Harries 1978 J.Harries, 'Church and State in the *Notitia Galliarum*', *JRS* LXVIII, 26–43

Hatt 1966 J.J.Hatt, *Histoire de la Gaule Romaine* (2nd edn)

Hatt 1976–7 J.J.Hatt, 'Les fouilles du Pègue (Drôme)', *Gallia* XXXIV, 31–56, XXXV, 39–58 (*v* also Amy 1962)

Hist Arch Histoire et Archéologie (les Dossiers) (a periodical supplementing *Archéologia*)

Holder A.Holder, *Alt-Celtischer Sprachschatz*, 1896–1907 (reprinted 1962)

ILGN E.Espérandieu, *Inscriptions latines de Gaule (Narbonnaise)*

ILS H.Dessau, *Inscriptiones Latinae Selectae*, 1882–1916 (since *ILGN* includes all the relevant additions to *CIL* V & XII up to the 1920s, references to this work are not included in the notes, but it does include a *CIL* index)

Jannoray 1965 J.Jannoray, *Ensérune, contribution à l'étude des civilisations préromaines de Gaule méridionale*

Jones 1964 A.H.M.Jones, *The Later Roman Empire, 284–602*

Joulin 1901 L.Joulin, 'Les établissements gallo-romaines de la plaine de Martres-Tolosanes', *Mémoires présentés par divers savants à l'Académie des Inscriptions et Belles-Lettres* XI, i

Joulin 1907 L.Joulin, 'Les établissements antiques du bassin superieur de la Garonne', RA^4 XI, 94–118, 226–42

JRS Journal of Roman Studies

Jullian C.Jullian, *Histoire de la Gaule*, Vols I–VIII (1908–26)

König I.König, *Itinera Romana III: Die Meilensteine der Gallia Narbonensis*, 1970

Labrousse 1968 M.Labrousse, *Toulouse antique des origines à l'établissement des Wisigoths*

Lafaye/Blanchet 1909 C.Lafaye & A.Blanchet, *Inventaire des mosaïques de la Gaule I*

Laguerre 1969 G.Laguerre, 'L'occupation militaire de *Cemenelum* (Cimiez–Nice)', *RAN* II, 165–84

Laguerre 1975 G.Laguerre, *Fouilles de Cemenelum II: Inscriptions antiques de Nice–Cimiez (Cemenelum, Ager Cemenelensis)*

Lancha 1981 J.Lancha, *Recueil général des mosaïques de la Gaule: Vienne* (Suppl X, Pt iii, fasc 2, to *Gallia*)

Laronde–Bligny A.Laronde, 'Naissance d'une ville', Ch II, and B.Bligny, 'Neuf siècles de recueillement', Ch III, in V.Chomel (ed), *Histoire de Grenoble*

Lauxerois 1983 R.Lauxerois, *Le Bas Vivarais à l'époque romaine: recherches sur la cité d'Alba* (Suppl IX to *RAN*)

Lavagne 1979 J.Lavagne, *Recueil général des mosaïques de la Gaule: Province de Narbonnaise: partie centrale* (Suppl X, Pt iii, fasc 1, to *Gallia*)

Liou 1973–75 B.Liou, 'Directions de recherches archéologiques sous-marines', *Gallia* XXXI, 571–608, XXXIII, 571–605

Manière 1971 G.Manière, 'Une officine de tuilier gallo-romain à Couladère, par Cazères (Haute-Garonne)', *Gallia* XXIX, 191–9

Martel 1962 *v* Barruol–Martel 1962

Munier 1963 C.Munier, *Concilia Galliae A 314–A 506: Corpus Christianorum, Series Latina* CXLVIII

Nickels/Marchand 1976 A.Nickels & G.Marchand, 'Recherches stratigraphiques et ponctuelles à proximité des remparts antiques d'Agde', *RAN* IX, 45–62

Octobon 1962 F.C.E.Octobon, *Castellaras et camps: enceintes celto-ligures du Departement des Alpes-Maritimes*

Olivier/Rogers 1978 A.Olivier & G.Rogers, 'Le monument romain de Vaugrenier', *RAN* XI, 143–94

Passelac 1970 M.Passelac, 'Le *vicus* Eburomagus: éléments de topographie, documents archéologiques', *RAN* II, 71–101

Pelletier 1974 A.Pelletier, *Vienne gallo-romaine au Bas-Empire, 275–468 apres J–C* (continuous page numbers at the *foot* of each page)

Pelletier 1982 A.Pelletier, *Vienne antique de la conquête romaine aux invasions alamanniques (IIᵉ siècle avant – IIIᵉ siècle après J–C)* (originally 1972, but with brief references to discoveries 1972–81)

Percival 1976 J.Percival, *The Roman Villa*

Pflaum 1960 H.-G.Pflaum, *Les carrières procuratoriennes équestres sous le Haut-Empire romain*

Pflaum 1978 H.-G.Pflaum, *Les fastes de la Province de Narbonnaise* (Suppl XXX to *Gallia*)

Pflaum 1981 H.-G.Pflaum, *La Gaule et l'Empire romain: Scripta varia II*

Picard *v* Amy 1962

Piganiol 1962 A.Piganiol, *Les documents cadastraux de la colonie romaine d'Orange* (Suppl XVI to *Gallia*) (*v* also Amy 1962)

PLRE A.H.M.Jones, J.M.Martindale & J.Morris, *The Prosopography of the Later Roman Empire, AD 260–395* Vol I, 1971; J.R.Martindale: *AD 395–527* Vol II, 1980

Princeton 1976 R.Stillwell (ed), *The Princeton Encyclopedia of Classical Sites*

P–W A.Pauly, G.Wissowa & W.Kroll (edd), *Real-Encyklopädie der Klassischen Altertumswissenschaft*, 1893 onwards

Py 1978 M.Py, *L'oppidum des Castels à Nages* (Suppl xxxv to *Gallia*)

Py 1981 M.Py, *Recherches sur Nîmes préromaine* (Suppl xli to *Gallia*)

RA Revue archéologique

RAN Revue archéologique de Narbonnaise, the most important journal for our area, 1968 onwards

REA Revue d'études archéologiques

REL Revue d'études ligures

Rev Sav Revue savoisienne

Richard 1975–76 J.-C.M.Richard, 'Notes de numismatique narbonnaise', I, *RAN* VIII, 259–73, II (with P.Soyris), *RAN* IX, 219–46

Rivet 1976 A.L.F.Rivet, 'The *Notitia Galliarum*: Some Questions', in R.Goodburn & P.Bartholomew (edd), *Aspects of the Notitia Dignitatum*

Rolland 1946 H.Rolland, *Fouilles de Glanum* (Suppl I to *Gallia*)

Rolland 1951 H.Rolland, *Fouilles de St-Blaise* (Suppl II to *Gallia*)

Rolland 1956 H.Rolland, *Fouilles de St-Blaise 1951–6* (Suppl VII to *Gallia*)

Rolland 1958 H.Rolland, *Fouilles de Glanum 1947–56* (Suppl XI to *Gallia*)

Rolland 1965 H.Rolland, *Bronzes antiques de Haute-Provence* Suppl XVIII to *Gallia*

Rolland 1969 H.Rolland, *Le Mausolée de Glanum* (Suppl XXI to *Gallia*)

Rolland 1977 H.Rolland, *L'Arc de Glanum* (Suppl XXXI to *Gallia*)

Salviat 1973 F.Salviat, 'Marseille grecque', Ch I in E.Baratier (ed), *Histoire de Marseille*

Salviat 1977 F.Salviat, 'Orientation, extension et chronologie des plans cadastraux d'Orange', *RAN* X, 107–18

Seeck 1876 O.Seeck, *Notitia Dignitatum: accedunt Notitia Urbis Constantinopolitanae et Latercula Provinciarum* (reprinted 1962)

Sherwin White 1973 A.N.Sherwin White, *The Roman Citizenship*, 2nd edn

Soyer 1973–4 J.Soyer, 'Les centuriations de Provence', Pt I, *RAN* VI, 197–232; Pt II, *RAN* VII, 179–99

Stern 1957–63 H.Stern, *Recueil général des mosaïques de la Gaule*, I

Stevens 1933 C.E.Stevens, *Sidonius Apollinaris and his Age*

Syme 1958 R.Syme, *Tacitus*

TIR Tabula Imperii Romani: relevant sheets, L31 (*Lugdunum*), 1934 and 1938, L32 (*Mediolanum*), 1966

Tchernia 1978 A.Tchernia, P.Pomey *et al*, *L'épave romaine de la Madrague de Giens (Var)* (Suppl XXXIV to *Gallia*)

Villard 1960 F.Villard, *La céramique grecque de Marseille*

Walbank 1970 & 1979 F.W.Walbank, *A Historical Commentary on Polybius*, Vol I (revised edn), 1970, III, 1979

Vittinghof 1942 F.Vittinghof, *Römische Kolonisation und Bürgerrechtspolitik unter Caesar und Augustus*

Ward-Perkins 1981 J.B.Ward-Perkins, *Roman Imperial Architecture*

Index

2. GEOGRAPHICAL

3. PEOPLES AND TRIBES

4. INDIVIDUALS

The names in capitals are those of Roman emperors

5. GENERAL